a guide to
EASTERN LITERATURES

Also by David M. Lang

THE GEORGIANS (*Praeger Ancient Peoples and Places Series*)
A MODERN HISTORY OF SOVIET GEORGIA (*Praeger Asia-Africa Series*)
LIVES AND LEGENDS OF THE GEORGIAN SAINTS
THE WISDOM OF BALAHVAR
ARMENIA: Cradle of Civilization

a guide to EASTERN LITERATURES

Edited by

David M. Lang

PRAEGER PUBLISHERS
New York · Washington

BOOKS THAT MATTER

Published in the United States of America in 1971
by Praeger Publishers, Inc., 111 Fourth Avenue,
New York, N.Y. 10003

Library of Congress Catalog Card Number: 79-157114

Printed in Great Britain

CONTENTS

LIST OF CONTRIBUTORS

J. DEREK LATHAM is Senior Lecturer in Arabic at the University of Manchester and the author of *Saracen Archery* (London, 1970).

ELIZABETH EPPLER is Senior Research Officer at the Institute of Jewish Affairs in London. She has contributed to the *Penguin Guide to Literature* (vols. 1 and 2) and the Jewish Book Annual (New York.

MARY BOYCE is Professor of Iranian Studies in the University of London. She is the author of a number of articles on pre-Islamic Iranian Literature and a translation of *The Letter of Tansar* (Rome, 1968).

A. A. HAIDARI is Lecturer in Persian at the University of London. He has written articles on Persian Literature and has published collections of his own stories and essays in Persian.

JOHN RICHARD WALSH is Head of the Department of Turkish Studies in the University of Edinburgh.

DAVID MARSHALL LANG is Professor of Caucasian Studies at the School of Oriental and African Studies, University of London. Among his publications are *The Georgians* and *Armenia: Cradle of Civilisation.*

A. K. IRVINE is Lecturer in Semitic Languages at the School of Oriental and African Studies, University of London.

I. M. P. RAESIDE is Lecturer in Gujarati and Marathi at the School of Oriental and African Studies, University of London. He has published translations of short stories and a novel from Marathi.

RALPH RUSSELL is Reader in Urdu at the School of Oriental and African Studies, University of London, and co-author (with Khurshidul Islam) of *Three Mughal Poets* and *Ghalib: Life and Letters.*

CHRISTOPHER H. B. RYENOLDS is Lecturer in Sinhalese at the School of Oriental and African Studies, University of London, and author of *Anthology of Sinhalese Literature* (1970).

E. C. G. BARRETT was Lecturer in the Language and Literature of Malay from 1957 until his retirement in 1971.

List of Contributors

YIN C. LIU is Lecturer in Chinese at the School of Oriental and African Studies, University of London, and author of *Fifty Chinese Stories.*

TAO TAO SANDERS is a Junior Research Fellow in Chinese at Wolfson College, Oxford.

DAVID L. SNELLGROVE is Reader in Tibetan in the University of London. His publications include: *Buddhist Himalaya* (1957), *Himalayan Pilgrimage* (1961), *Four Llamas of Dolpo* (2 vols, 1967 and 1968), *The Hevajra-Tantra* (2 vols, 1959) and *Nine Ways of Bon* (1967).

CHARLES R. BAWDEN is Professor of Mongolian in the University of London. He is the author of a number of books and articles on the literature and history of Mongolia, including *A Modern History of Mongolia* (1968).

W. E. SKILLEND is Lecturer in Korean, School of Oriental and African Studies, University of London. He is the author of *Kodae Sosol: A Survey of Korean Traditional Style Popular Novels* (1968).

ANNA ALLOTT is Lecturer in Burmese at the School of Oriental and African Studies, University of London.

C. J. DUNN is Professor of Japanese in the University of London and has made a special study of the *Kabuki* and puppet drama of Japan.

KENNETH STRONG is Lecturer in Japanese at the School of Oriental and African Studies, University of London. He is the author of *The Buddha Tree* (1966) and *Footprints in the Snow* (1970), both translations of Japanese novels.

GENERAL EDITOR'S PREFACE

There are many developments in modern world history which justify only too well the gloomy adage that 'East is East and West is West and never the twain shall meet'. Certainly there has seldom been so great a need as exists today for men of goodwill everywhere to exert themselves in all sincerity to further the cause of East-West harmony.

Only too often we trace the causes of strife to conflicting interests in the political, military or economic sphere. It seems that East-West understanding could be most fruitfully pursued on the basis of mutual respect and appreciation in the artistic, cultural and literary fields. Political, social and cultural attitudes are often subtly connected. We need to fight continually against any delusion that the nations of Asia and Africa are bearers of civilisations inferior to our own.

The modern European and American citizen should surely reflect on what he owes to the Eternal East, in the realms of art, religion and philosophy. 'Ex Oriente Lux' is a motto which deserves the respect of all educated men.

Fortunately there is ample evidence of spontaneous public interest in the treasure house of Eastern literature, philosophy and learning. Every year UNESCO brings out fresh volumes in its series of representative works of Oriental literature in Western translations. Publishers in England and America are continually sponsoring new translations from Chinese and Japanese, Persian and Arabic, and the languages of India and Pakistan. Classic renderings by such giants as Edward Fitzgerald, Sir Richard Burton and Arthur Waley are reprinted in ever larger editions, sometimes in paperback form.

There is, of course, no shortage of information on the countries and the literatures of Asia. But this data is for the most part scattered through the pages of general reference books, or else contained in weighty specialist tomes not easily available to the general reader. The plan of the present work permits the reader to find in one volume the salient facts about most of the main literatures and individual authors of Asia, discussed in close relationship with the history and social backgrounds of the lands where these writers lived.

This volume is designed for a wide public, including especially school and university students. The General Editor, the individual contributors, and the publishers hope that it may also serve as a small contribution to East-West understanding.

It remains for the General Editor to thank those colleagues who have generously given of their expert knowledge to the writing and compiling of this Guide. They deserve credit for the patience and forbearance with which they have compressed a wealth of information into the narrow compass which this work demands. It has been a pleasure to work with such a team; it is my hope that the response of the reading public will match the enthusiasm of the contributors themselves.

DAVID MARSHALL LANG
School of Oriental and African Studies,
University of London
18 May 1970

ARABIC LITERATURE

J. Derek Latham

HISTORICAL BACKGROUND

The history of northern and central Arabia, the birthplace and cradle of Arabic literature, is little known before the second century BC. In any case, it need not detain us; it is only necessary to mention the period immediately prior to the rise of Islam, which is taken to date from AD 622. The general picture is of pastoral nomads, or Bedouin, roaming the desert in search of pasture or plunder as they struggle to survive in a land of scant and uncertain rainfall. The basic pattern of their society has survived until now and presents certain well-defined characteristics. Since there is no security for the individual in the desert, the tribe is the basis of society and duty to the tribe is an overriding loyalty. This sense of duty, which is but rarely subordinated to personal feelings, is sustained by ties of blood relationship, and the tribe in its divisions and sub-divisions is held together by a belief in common descent.

The government of the pre-Islamic tribe was vested, not in a hereditary ruler, but in a general assembly of all members who elected a leader by acclamation. The latter had no authority to impose duties or sanctions, but was essentially a first among equals. Two aspects of Bedouin society calling for comment are the status of women and the role of poets. As regards the first, let us say only that in the nomadic tribe women enjoyed greater freedom than in the urban civilisation of later Islam. However few their rights, they were at least not subject to seclusion and the veil. As for poets, it is worth noting a recent observation that in their society they probably enjoyed greater power than does the modern press in ours. Certainly a poet was highly esteemed as the spokesman and archive of his tribe, and to him it fell to boost its morale by recalling and recording its glories and to undermine the spirit of its enemies by publicly exposing them to scorn, ridicule, and contempt.

A tribe's main assets lay in livestock. Camels, the most vital possession, supplied most of life's basic needs and provided an indispensable mode of transport in the desert. Horses were prized but were less hardy in hot, sandy wastes and therefore used with discrimination. To augment the meagre means of sustenance, Bedouin would frequently resort to raids. These were mostly aimed at the seizure of camels or other booty for, when men were slain, the duty of exacting a life for a life (or, less commonly, the payment of blood-money) devolved upon kin. Such conditions were apt to lead to intertribal wars and feuds, thus adding to the natural hazards of the environment. By way of respite there were four sacred months during which all fighting was forbidden.

As regards religion, there was a general belief in shadowy supernatural beings known as *jinn*, and magical powers were thought to inhere in, and emanate from, places, objects (notably stones), animals, and even soothsayers, sorcerers and poets. Cults centred on a tribal god and its shrine, or, in some cases, supratribal gods, but there was no formal priesthood, and by the seventh century AD the importance of the cults was probably more social and economic than religious. Allusions to the action of 'time' both in pre- and post-Islamic poetry are frequent, but, for the nomad, time was neither a deity nor a religious force, but a personalised entity determining man's destiny.

The values of the nomad were essentially determined by the challenge of desert life. Unwavering devotion to the group impelled him to defend, maintain, and enhance the prestige of tribe and self, and to this end he worshipped the ideals of physical courage in war, endurance in hardship, perseverance in adversity, tenacity in pursuit of vengeance, defence of the weak and of those entitled to protection, hospitality and generosity to guests, and the exercise of wisdom and experience within the bounds of tribal standards. His outlook on all such matters is clearly mirrored in his poetry.

The inhabitants of central and northern Arabia were not all Bedouin. Here and there small sedentary communities could be found in oases such as Yathrib (later called Medina) where people cultivated palms and practised simple forms of agriculture, a calling which the Bedouin despised. Furthermore, in the century before Islam the northern frontier scene was dominated by two semi-nomadic Christian principalities founded by tribes of southern Arabian origin: the Monophysite Ghassānids of the Syrian desert in the west and the Nestorian Lakhmids of Ḥīra on the Euphrates in the east, the former subsidised by Byzantium, the latter supported by Sasānid Persia. It was the function of both to serve the interests of their respective superiors by supplying troops and protecting frontiers and trade against Bedouin attack. The courts of both states attracted and generously patronised the poets of Arabia, among them some of the finest known to Arabdom. To Ḥīra, indeed, the very language of literature may well owe much of its development and standardisation. The decline and fall, first of the Lakhmids, then of the Ghassānids, precede the rise of Islam, and it is as much with their disintegration and final dispersal as with the success of Muḥammad's mission that the pre-Islamic, or 'pagan' era (*jāhiliyya*), may be said to end. By the close of this epoch the Arabs were already in full possession of a common poetic language which seems to have originated in Najd, matured in the north, and spread throughout the peninsula on the tongues of professional reciters. At the same time, a language suitable for literary prose was beginning to take shape in artistically phrased apophthegms and in the rhythmical, rhymed articulations of orators and soothsayers.

Between AD 570 and 580 Muḥammad, the Prophet of Islam, was born in Mecca, an important emporium and centre of transit trade in the Hejaz which owed much of its prosperity to a pagan Arab practice. At certain periods of the year it was customary for tribes to make a pilgrimage to the repository of some sacred stone or other, and at the same time to profit from the opportunities for trade. Since the sanctuaries in and around Mecca drew tribesmen from all parts of the peninsula, the economic interests of the town were well served, and wealth and prestige accrued to the mercantile community. Leadership of the latter was concentrated in the hands of Quraysh, a recently sedentarised tribe remarkable for its business acumen and powers of organisation. To this tribe Muḥammad's own family belonged, though it was not of the dominant elite. When, after his Call around the age of forty, Muḥammad began to advocate monotheism, denounce idolatry and preach the doctrine of Judgement, his words not unnaturally fell on poor soil. At first he met with little real opposition, but as his denunciations of Mecca's religious and cultural traditions gained strength, so also did the antagonism of the Meccans against him. After ten years or so in Mecca, his progress was so indifferent and his position so precarious that as soon as a favourable opportunity to leave presented itself, he took it. Being invited to intervene as arbitrator in the internal affairs of Yathrib, at that time rent by Arab tribal feuds, Muḥammad decided to accept and, having assembled his followers, emigrated to the town thereafter to be styled City (*madīna*) of the Prophet, i.e. Medina. The year of the emigration (hijra, or Hegira) was 622, subsequently the first year of the Muslim calendar.

In spite of initial difficulties, notably with the Jews who rejected his claim to prophethood, Muḥammad finally established himself at Medina as the head of a politico-religious community which he led, not by consent as a kind of tribal chief, but as an absolute ruler with a mandate from God (*Allāh*) who had sent him to proclaim *islām*, 'submission' to His will. Within the new community faith, not blood, was the bond. In practical terms, greater unity was achieved by suppression of blood feuds among brothers in Islam; all disputes were to be settled by arbitration, and, as long as Muḥammad lived, it was he who was arbiter. The next eight years he spent in Holy War (*jihād*) against the idolatrous Meccans and in the political manipulation of the Bedouin tribes of north-west Arabia. To put an economic blockade on Mecca and at the same time increase the wealth and prestige of his own community, he adopted the legitimate and profitable expedient of raiding Meccan caravans. Once begun, the struggle continued and in spite of reverses Muḥammad prosecuted his campaign with courage, skill and diplomacy until he brought it to its logical conclusion with the conquest of Mecca (630). In 632 he died, leaving behind him a powerful and influential monotheistic community, guided not only by his personal example, but also – and primarily – by the sum of revealed, but as yet uncompiled, pronouncements which we know as the Koran (*al-Qur'ān*) and which Muslims accept as the literal word of God.

Muḥammad was succeeded as head of the community by Abū Bakr who assumed the title of *Khalīfa* (whence the English 'caliph'), 'vice-gerent', i.e. the Prophet's deputy on earth. On Abū Bakr's death the office passed successively to 'Umar ibn al-Khaṭṭāb, 'Uthmān and 'Alī, son-in-law of the Prophet. With the death of 'Alī in 661 the Orthodox Caliphate, as the period spanned by these four rulers is called, ended amid the turbulence of civil strife, and power passed to Mu'āwiya, governor of Syria, a member of the prominent Meccan family of Umayya and founder of the Umayyad dynasty. By this time the Arabs had already swept out of the peninsula, occupied Iraq and destroyed the Persian Empire, and wrested Syria and Egypt from the Byzantine Empire. Now they stood on the threshold of new conquests that within a century were to carry Islam across North Africa to Spain, north-eastwards across central Asia, and south-eastwards to the Indus valley.

The transfer of power to the Umayyads was accompanied by the removal of the seat of government to Damascus, where the old theocratic concept of government was abandoned. Henceforth, until the accession of the Abbasids in 750, we are concerned with an Arab kingdom based on the supremacy of an Arab warrior class. The emergence of such a class outside Arabia originated in the conditions of the early conquests. To control the conquered provinces, it had become the practice to install Arab governors and troops in garrison towns and bases. Under the Caliph 'Umar a register of these Arabs and their families had been instituted and those included were entitled to pay, rations and other benefits from the state. Henceforth the Arabs were a military caste subsidised from imperial revenue and the spoils of conquest. A non-productive class combined with the question of conversion presented problems which ultimately destroyed the Arab kingdom. The Arabs, it should be realised, did not always offer the sword as the only alternative to Islam, nor did they confiscate all land within the conquered territories. On the contrary, since Christians and Jews were tolerated and protected by Islamic law in return for the payment of dues and the acceptance of certain disabilities, the Arabs, being motivated less by religious zeal than is commonly supposed, had no ambition to convert their protected subjects and thereby deprive them of their status as first-class taxpayers with second-class citizenship. The advantages of conversion did not, however, escape the conquered peoples and vast numbers hastened to embrace Islam. The reality belied the hope and theory. To the early Arab way of thinking, Islam and Arabism were one, and membership of the Muslim community entailed membership of an Arab tribe which, unless inherited by birth, could only be attained by accepting the status of client (*mawlā, pl mawālī*). To their dismay, the Mawali Muslims found themselves not only socially inferior, but also unable, in the main, to achieve economic equality with the Arab Muslims who refused, after a certain date, to allow them a Muslim rate of taxation. The Mawalis' bitter resentment at Umayyad disregard for their rights finally found expression in support for the defeated Arab party, or *shī'a* (whence Shī'ites), which had sided with 'Alī in his dispute with Mu'āwiya. Defeated politically, the Shī'ites sought victory by religious means and, in so doing, laid the foundations of that basic religious schism which has since persisted between Sunnites (orthodox Muslims) and Shī'ites (the schismatics). Disseminating a claim of legitimate succession in Muḥammad's line (the Hāshimite family), they found ready listeners among the Persian Mawali. At the same time a totally contrary view with wide appeal among the nomadic and semi-nomadic elements of Iraq was being pressed by another dangerous offshoot of the 'Alī-Mu'āwiya conflict. This was the troublesome Khārijite party, whose religious outlook was as militant as it was fanatic. Proportionately as the foundations of Umayyad power were weakened, opposition to their regime hardened, and from Kūfa and Khurāsān, respectively the major areas of Hāshimite and Mawali strength in Iraq and Iranian Asia, it gained in intensity until it crystallised in the Abbasid revolution which terminated ninety-two years of Umayyad rule.

The Umayyad period is an age of transition characterised by disruption of the old Arabian social structure. The trend is towards sedentarisation and urban life materially enriched by the spoils of conquest. Yet tribalism with all its divisive forces persists, and the prevailing mood is one of tribal passions and nostalgia for the traditional values of desert Arabia. It is therefore an age of poets and anthologists. Fear lest the meaning of the Koran be lost gives birth to the sciences of philology and lexicography, and the rules of Arabic grammar begin to be formulated in Kūfa and Baṣra, whose importance in the history of Arabic letters cannot be overestimated. The diffusion of Arabic outside Arabia follows in the wake of political and administrative expansion, and for some of the provinces, such as Egypt and Syria, the use of Arabic both in literature and common speech has come to stay. The study of Prophetic Tradition (*ḥadīth*), recounting what Muḥammad said or did, commences and the foundations of Islamic law are laid. Finally, the seeds of a court literature are sown and a chancery style is born.

The accession of the Abbasids – so named after al-'Abbās an uncle of the Prophet – was a turning point in the history of the Empire. With the establishment in Spain of an independent Umayyad dynasty (756–1031) political unity of the Empire vanished for ever and there began a process of fragmentation that was to continue while Islam was still expanding. In the east the seat of government was moved eastwards from Syria to Iraq where, in 762, the second Abbasid caliph founded a new capital, Baghdad. The change of dynasty was accompanied by a change in the concept of government: the highest office of the state was henceforth an autocratic caliphate enjoying the authority of religion, enforcing its will by means of a non-Arab imperial army, and governing through a complex bureaucracy administered by a hierarchy whose recruitment depended on the grace and favour of the sovereign. Not the least important consequence of the revolution was a change in the status of the Arab military aristocracy. Its wars of conquest over, it had nothing to contribute to an expanding peacetime society whose economy owed nothing to its presence. The Mawali, on the other hand, were not merely an economic mainstay of the community; they were also a pillar of the revolution strong enough to command attention from a regime that was, in any case, committed to redressal of their grievances. In the new structure, therefore, the exclusive right of Arabs to preferment and privilege was doomed. Gradual erosion of their political power was the natural concomitant of non-Arab penetration – notably Persian – into Abbasid administration. What the Arabs lost politically they gained in letters. Arabic was not alone the language of religion and the medium of intercourse; it was the language of the social class to which the Mawali sought access and, as such, was to enjoy greater facilities for its development than ever before in the sense that it was to be used to introduce fresh ideas and images and to enrich the old culture with new concepts and standards of eloquence. For nearly three centuries more the literature of the Islamic Empire, as it is now appropriate to describe it, was to be written exclusively in Arabic, much of it by Muslims of non-Arab, or mixed, descent with unsurpassed mastery of the lore and literary idiom of the Arabs. Not that the supremacy of Arabic and its cultural tradition went unchallenged; on the contrary, that same supremacy owed its very survival to a reaction against the threat of anti-Arab polemic at a time when the dynasty was committed to the patronage of theological sciences based on the study of Arabic. The threat, which came to a head during the first half of the ninth century, sprang from the literary activities of the Persianising *Shu'ūbiyya* movement and represented the aspirations of a powerful secretarial class bent on promoting not only the Sasanid tradition in administration, but also the old Persian spirit in literature. From its failure positive gain accrued to the Arabic humanities.

If the nascent Arab-Muslim culture thrived on the versatility and liveliness of the Persian mind and experienced even the stimulus of Indian influences, it derived its vital spirit from the substratum of eastern Hellenism, encountered first in Syria, then in Egypt, Mesopotamia, and Jundayshapur, a centre of Byzantine immigration in Persia. In the ninth and tenth centuries the rendering of Greek scientific and philosophical thought, which had begun under the Umayyads with the sporadic efforts of individual translators, was officially organised and continued on a grand scale under the Abbasids. Largely for want of direct contact with Greek letters, which most often reached the Arabs (meaning hereafter the people of the Muslim-Arab culture) through the medium of Syriac, the poetry, drama, and belles-lettres of the Greeks remained a closed book. In philosophy and the sciences, on the other hand, the market boomed, and by the tenth and eleventh centuries the output of Hellenistic transmissions had assumed significant proportions and been enriched by the original contributions of native scholars whose stature is most apparent in such fields as algebra, geometry, trigonometry, and optics. Of all branches of Greek learning, philosophy and logic were the most significant for the future of Muslim-Arab society in that they supplied the means of averting a danger which, if allowed to go unchecked, must surely have undermined the essential system of Islam. The danger lay mostly in the revival of dualism among the old Perso-Aramaean population of Iraq which tended to rise to the surface with the resurgence of Persian national aspirations. To meet the challenge, the Muʻtazilites, or 'seceders' – in the first century of Islam, a wholly orthodox movement opposed to doctrinal and practical extremism – took up the whole armoury of Aristotelian logic in defence of the faith. Success bred intolerance; once recognised by the Caliph Ma'mūn (813–33) as the official mouthpiece of Islam, the movement imposed its dogma on traditional orthodoxy by inquisition and itself sank into heresy as it slowly, but surely, exalted reason above the Koran and, in an effort to vindicate God's absolute unity, stripped Him of His attributes, while at the same time infringing that very concept by making Him the servant of His own justice. With the accession of Mutawakkil (847–61) the pressure was eased and the tables turned as waning Abbasid power yielded to traditional Islam. But there could be no return to the old position; orthodoxy had to compromise with reason and in the event Muʻtazilism was hoist with its own petard. Koran and Prophetic Tradition were reconciled with the demands of Greek reason, and a new scholastic theology associated with Ashʻarī (*d* 935) – himself a former Muʻtazilite – gradually established itself as orthodox, overcoming both the Muʻtazilites and, in due course, the more intractable fundamentalists. Nor were these the only problems confronting Islam in these formative centuries. At one end of the scale all manner of heterodox beliefs stemming from the older Asiatic religions took upon themselves the Shīʻite label, while at the other asceticism, evolving under the influence of primitive mysticism from fear of God to love of God, assumed a wide range of esoteric attitudes classified as Sufism and embraced at the farthest limit sheer pantheism and antinomianism. This is not the place to analyse the 'two-and-seventy jarring sects' and their place in the religious and social history of the medieval Muslim world. It must, on the other hand, be clearly understood that Arabic literature, of which by far the greater part is religious, is scarcely intelligible if torn from its theological setting.

The star of Abbasid power, which never shone more brilliantly than in the days of the fabled Hārūn ar-Rashīd (786–809), reached and passed its zenith during this caliph's reign. After his death visible decline set in, hastened by a protracted civil war between his sons Ma'mūn and Amīn, whose strength lay, respectively, in Khorasan and Iraq. Though the final victory was Ma'mūn's, his idea of transferring the capital definitively to Merv was prudently discarded and Baghdad was retained. But the door was now open to political disintegration, for in 820 Ṭāhir, one of Ma'mūn's Persian generals, created the fatal precedent of making himself a *de facto* independent ruler in eastern Iran. The hereditary local principality or governorship was henceforth to be an increasingly familiar means of satisfying the various aspirations not only of the Persians but also, in due course, of other peoples of the Muslim world. As for the caliphate itself, from the time of Mu'taṣim (833–42) it gradually fell under the domination of Turkish slave troops to which it had initially been obliged to turn for support. Finally reduced to impotence by the power of his Turkish army chiefs, the caliph became little more than a puppet presiding over an empire of breakaway provinces whose rulers used the caliphate only to secure *de jure* recognition for *de facto* authority. Finally, in 945 whatever claim to independence the caliphate may still have had vanished with the occupation of Baghdad by the Būyids, or Buwayhids, a local dynasty from western Persia. Although of Shī'ite persuasion and therefore theoretically opposed to the Sunnite caliphate, the Būyids took no steps to extinguish the latter but wisely allowed the titulars to reign. Already in the west a counter-caliphate had been declared in Spain (929), and the whole of north-west Africa lay well beyond the reach of Baghdad. In Egypt the Turkish Ṭūlūnids (868–905), the first autonomous rulers of the country, had come and gone and the Ikhshīdids (935–60), also of Turkish origin, held sway. Between Syria and Iraq Bedouin tribes had seized power where and when, and for however long they could. However ephemeral their rule one of their dynasties at least, the Ḥamdānids of Aleppo (945–1004), won immortal fame by its patronage of Mutanabbī, a glorious name in Arabic literature. In 1258 the Iraqi caliphate was swept away for ever by the Mongol conquest of Baghdad. For most of the time since the advent of the Būyids all effective power had lain with Persian and Turkish commanders, princes or majordomos, and in spite of attempts by certain caliphs to regain control – notably after the fall of the Seljuq sultanate (1055–1194), it was all to no avail.

The caliphate of Baghdad fathered the golden age of Arabic civilisation, and until the tenth century Baghdad remained the undisputed metropolis of Islamic culture, even when Mu'taṣim ruled from Samarra (from 836). During the first century of Abbasid rule the prominence of the old Persian gentry is the salient feature of the new order. Thriving on ceremonial, it forms the backbone of a complex administration comprising a series of *dīwans*, or ministries, controlled by a vizier (*wazīr*), or principal minister. Its educational needs are supplied by the diffusion of professional knowledge through a didactic and ceremonial literature which, once implanted, expands to embrace an encyclopaedic range of knowledge. Concurrently, the philologists of Baṣra and Kūfa – and later Baghdad – labour successfully to avert the threat to Arabic and meet the demands on the language created by secretarial and scholastic needs. Poets and writers focus their eyes on the lucrative patronage of the caliph, his court and his dignitaries. A monetary and mercantile economy flourishes, business booms, and in the ninth century we see the emergence of a prosperous bourgeoisie whose members, aspiring to the life and cultural ideals of the ruling class, often become prominent both in offices of state and religious scholarship. An international population throngs a capital rich in the amenities of urban life. Scholars – at no loss for paper since its introduction *c* 800 – converge on bookshops, libraries and mosques. Physicians are registered and hospitals flourish. Such is Baghdad in its heyday. For the provinces standards are set by the capital and, in letters at least, its example is followed as local rulers seek fame and glory through the patronage of poets and literati.

Egypt and Syria escaped the fate that befell Iraq. After destroying the Fāṭimid counter-caliphate (Shī'ite, 967–1171) Saladin, the Kurdish founder of the Ayyūbid dynasty, had welded the two countries into a powerful military state capable of combating the Crusades. This regime the last Ayyūbid's Turkish troops in Egypt had transformed into their own Mamlūk ('[White] Slave') sultanate whose forces were to check the Mongol advance in Syria (1260). Establishing a purely nominal Abbasid caliphate in Cairo (1261), the Mamlūks ruled Egypt and Syria on a non-hereditary basis, first as a Kipchak, then as a Circassian sultanate until subjected in 1517 to the new and mighty power of the Osmanli, or Ottoman, Turks. After the capture of Baghdad in 1534 almost the whole of the Arabic-speaking world formed part of the Ottoman Empire until its defeat in the 1914–18 war. In the west only Morocco escaped the long arm of the Ottomans, but Spain, of course, had already been completely regained by Christianity with the capitulation of Granada in 1492.

Although some of the best-known works of Arabic literature appeared between AD 1000 and 1400 the progressive subjection of the Arabs to Turkish rulers precipitated an irreversible decline in their culture. Iraq was absorbed into an eastern Islamic empire in which the Persians supplied Turkish administrative and cultural needs. Thus the vitality that might have invigorated the Arabic humanities was diverted into the creation of Muslim literatures first in Persian, then in Turkish. Political turbulence and the rise of a military feudal society at home, as well as economic setback abroad, sapped the prosperity on which Arabic letters had flourished. Patronage declined and, in any event, Persian and Turkish patrons preferred poetry and literary artistry in the tongues they understood. The triumph of religious orthodoxy and an expanding body of illiberal ulema accelerated the degenerative process. After 1258 Arabic culture found its centre of gravity in Egypt and it remained there until the nineteenth century. Arabic, however, was not the tongue of the dominant class and inevitably linguistic standards plunged and the literary horizon, for all that it was illumined by the occasional blaze of light, grew dark.

The first light of a new dawn broke with Napoleon's invasion of Egypt in 1798. With it came a glimpse of the printing press and a slight knowledge of European civilisation. It also brought to Egypt, among the Ottoman troops sent to expel the French, the man soon to be its ruler: Muḥammad 'Alī (1769–1849), an able Balkan soldier. Impressed by European administrative and technical efficiency, he aimed to reproduce the pattern by importing European instructors, sending pupils to Italy and France, and creating new educational institutions. To provide textbooks he founded the Būlāq Press in 1822, and in 1828 journalism made its debut with the publication of an official gazette, *al-Waqā'i' al-Miṣriyya* (Events in Egypt). Translations into Turkish and Arabic were the keystone of his programme, and a School of Languages was created under the directorship of Rifā'a Rāfi' aṭ-Ṭaḥṭāwī (1801–73). These early efforts made relatively little impact on Arabic letters until the reign of Ismā'īl (1863–79) and even then their influence was in no way comparable to that exerted from another quarter. In Beirut and Lebanon Arab Christians had long been in touch with European Christianity and so, in the first half of the nineteenth century, they welcomed the opening of American and French mission schools. In 1864 the American Protestants founded what is now the American University of Beirut, and in 1875 came the Jesuit Université St Joseph. The role of these centres in transmitting western ideas and simultaneously reviving Arabic language and culture was vital to the *Nahḍa*, or Arab Renaissance. Equally important was the British occupation of Egypt (1882), for it gave opportunity for political and economic stability as well as relative freedom of speech and a refuge to the new generation of Syrians stifling under Ottoman repression. With them also came European ideas of nationality out of which sprang the beginnings of Arab nationalism. In Muslim religious circles modernism was associated with Christians and therefore suspect, but in due course the spirit of revival, gaining impetus from the Afghan Pan-Islamist reformer, Jamāl ad-Dīn al-Afghānī (1839–97), found a ready adherent in the Egyptian Muḥammad 'Abduh (1849–1905) who sought to rejuvenate Islam by the reformulation of doctrine in the light of modern thought. The conservatives rejected his view, and the modernists never wholly understood it, but at least he succeeded in dividing religion from politics and inspiring lay followers such as Qāsim Amīn (*d* 1908) and Sa'd Zaghlūl (*d* 1927) to seek social and political reform.

The end of the 1914–18 war saw the start of a long and bitter struggle with the West. The Great Powers, notably Britain and France, fixed or confirmed the political frontiers of the Arab states – many of them new – much as we know them today. Self-determination has been won only by degrees and under pressure. Since 1945 Arab efforts have been directed not only towards the eradication of western political footholds, but also towards the dislodgement of the old ruling class, often identified with foreign interests. The Jewish presence in Palestine arouses the deepest resentment, with international repercussions.

MAIN TRENDS IN LITERATURE

THE MEDIEVAL PERIOD

(i) Poetry

The first achievement of decisive importance in the literary history of the Arabs was the creation of the *qaṣīda*, a formal ode *sui generis*, which attained structural and technical maturity in the sixth century AD and set certain standards which subsequently became the only acceptable criteria for classical poetry. Usually a composition of 50–100 lines cast in one of a wide range of quantitative metres, the *qaṣīda* is of relatively simple structure. The unit of composition is the line (*bayt*) consisting of two sharply defined halves. Perfection demands that each line be grammatically intelligible without reference to a following line. It is the rule that the hemistichs of the first line should rhyme. In succeeding lines the same rhyme and metre are sustained throughout the poem, but beyond the opening line the rhyme occurs only in the second hemistich. The consonant of a poem's rhyming syllable, often in conjunction with the name of its metre, is a usual means of identification. Thus, a *lāmiyya* is a poem whose rhyming consonant is 'l' (*lām*).

The aim of the earliest *qaṣīda* was glorification of the poet's tribe. Hence, praise of self, family or tribal group (or distinguished representatives thereof) or patron, with or without satirical denunciation of enemies or rivals, is central to the classical ode. The standard *qaṣīd*-scheme is tripartite, comprising (i) the *nasīb*, an amatory elegiac prelude in which the poet, in melancholy vein, evokes the memory of some past love; in a typical situation, particularly dear to the old poets and not unlike that portrayed in Tennyson's 'Locksley Hall', he will halt at the site of a former encampment, address the site or companions, and recall the happiness of days when a girl whom he loved and courted dwelt with her tribe nearby and departed when camp was struck; the purpose of the *nasīb* is to secure the attention of the audience; (ii) the *waṣf* 'description' which is often a *raḥīl*, i.e. a description of a perilous and uncomfortable journey through the desert made by the poet on a fast camel or a horse, which he regularly likens to fleet-footed beasts of the chase; from this often follows a graphic description of wild life, the hunt, natural phenomena, and so forth; (iii) *madīḥ*, a panegyric or boasting, and/or *hijā'*, commonly styled satire, but best described as imprecatory stigmatisation or abusive polemic. From the end of the sixth century of the hijra the poet often rounds off his ode with an 'envoi' consisting of *ḥikam*, i.e. general reflexions on life.

Side by side with the tripartite scheme the classical tradition recognized the threnode (*marthiyya*, *rithā'*) as a separate entity in two parts: (i) a prelude consisting of the poet's reflexions on life, death, and time or fate, and (ii) a record of the qualities of the deceased and consolation of the bereaved.

The origins of the *qaṣīda* are uncertain, but the view that it was a studied arrangement of short pieces (*qiṭ'as*) is convincing.* Many *qiṭ'as* as old as the earliest *qaṣīdas* survive and are traditionally regarded as fragments of other such poems, though there is no reason why a fair proportion of them should not stand in their own right as boasts, satires, battle-songs, and so forth. Martial courage and fortitude (*ḥamāsa*) is the predominant theme of occasional poems, short or long, and in this category may be classified some superb songs of vengeance or rebellion by outlaws and brigands. The foremost representative of this sub-group is the smouldering and irascible Shanfarā.

The standards set by the old Arabian *qaṣīd*-poets demanded the concentration of ideas and images in small verbal compass. If visual images of high fidelity were to be achieved – and this was the aim – concision entailed peculiarly sensitive discrimination in the choice of words. The successful poet therefore had to be one who could make a restricted selection of emotive words from the luxuriant thesaurus of the Arabic language and then harness their latent energy to the projection of realistic pictures alive with movement and colour. The technique of occasional verse calls for no special comment. The fact that *qiṭ'as* could be viewed as fragments of *qaṣīdas* speaks for itself.

Since the transmission of early Arabic poetry was oral and written collections of poets' works (*dīwāns*) only appeared well after the rise of Islam, the distinction between what is genuine and what is not has challenged modern scholarship. Here is not the place to discuss the problem: rather let us focus attention on what are taken to be the finest products of the time. These are the seven *qaṣīdas* which have come down to us in a collection constituted by Ḥammād ar-Rāwiya ('the Rhapsode'; *d c* 772) and known for some still uncertain reason as the *Mu'allaqāt* (Suspended (Odes)). Regarding their authenticity it is enough to echo Arberry's impression, conveyed in the epilogue to his engaging study, *The Seven Odes*, that they do in fact belong to the period assigned them by Arab tradition and seem, as claimed, to be the work of seven distinct poets, each with his own style and personality. Whatever their distant roots and evolutionary history, the *Mu'allaqāt* blossomed in and about the north Arabian frontier provinces. A striking feature is their diversity

*R. B. Serjeant, *Prose and Poetry from Ḥaḍramawt*, pp. 56-7.

of theme and content within a structurally limited framework. Imru' al-Qays, the oldest and most venerated, combines unashamed licentiousness with a rare skill for depicting natural phenomena, exemplified in an unforgettable storm-scene. Ṭarafa excels in an arresting, if – to western taste – curious, portrayal of his camel; Zuhayr, an unaffected stylist, moralises in pacific tones; Labīd finds his true vocation in highly picturesque descriptions of the wild; 'Antara is a master of grandiloquent and belligerent vainglory; a worthy emulator in the boast is 'Amr, a defiant fire-breathing warrior who opens his ode with a call for wine and, in the exaltation of his tribe, sings the martial courage of its womenfolk in battle; Ḥārith is the eloquent defender of his tribe's honour in boast and satire. The odes of three other poets – Nābigha, A'shā, and 'Abīd b. al-Abraṣ – are often included among the *Mu'allaqāt*. Nābigha as panegyrist, first of the rulers of Ḥīra, then of the Ghassānids, is the archetypal court poet.

Because of its central role in the pagan social order and its embodiment of pagan values, poetry found no great patron in the Prophet, and although at Medina he found it expedient to utilise the influence of poets in his own cause, his lifetime and the period of his immediate successors form no glittering chapter in the annals of poetry. The recovery of poetry during the remainder of the first century of Islam is associated with a marked trend towards occasional verse; this change of emphasis met the new needs in a changing society involved in historically momentous events. The political and religious discord in which the Orthodox Caliphate ended supplied the very stuff of which poetical invective (*hijā'*) and battle-songs were made, and in this field none could harness the old technique to a new cause more eloquently than the Khārijite religious fanatics. The *hijā'* of the Umayyad courts was somewhat different in kind and function inasmuch as it served as a weapon of pre-emptive attack in defence of the ruler's prestige. In form and substance, however, it presented no real difference.

More interesting from our point of view is the emergence of love-poetry (*ghazal*). This development which began *c* AD 670 is associated first with Mecca, then with Medina. Now politically peripheral to Damascus and militarily *hors de combat*, yet rich from the spoils of conquest, the Holy Cities had become the home of singing, dancing and amorous adventures. The new style was marked by the use of lighter metres corresponding to homonymous musical modes and there was less aversion to enjambment. The trend towards greater self-expression favoured simpler and more natural diction. The main themes were much the same as those of the *nasīb* in the formal ode, but the desert setting was usually discarded, and instead of a girl from a neighbouring tribe, a town lady of another household became the object of the amorous quest. The nocturnal visit was to become a common theme, and the appearance of the 'malicious slanderer' and 'prying censor' ushered in a conventional fiction commonly encountered in Arabic love-poetry, namely that of the ever-present threat of the kill-joy bent on the undoing of lovers. The Meccan phase of the *ghazal* is linked with the name of 'Umar b. Abī Rabī'a; the Medinese, or so-called *'udhrī* (from the tribe 'Udhra), with that of Jamīl. For the one love is joyously realisable, the goal natural fulfilment, the tone sensual – though not improperly so; for the other, it is despairingly transcendent, the end unattainable, the spirit *courtois*. In the second century of Islam the *'udhrī* manner flourished in Iraq, the putative source of the influences that shaped its growth. In Syria the Meccan manner, accentuated to the point of libertinism, found a daring continuator in the hedonistic caliph Walīd II (*d* 743) who also took up the wine theme abortively attempted by Abū Mihjān (*d c* 637) during the Orthodox Caliphate. Inspired by the bacchic verses of 'Adī b. Zayd,* a pre-Islamic Christian poet of Ḥīra, he is the precursor of Abū Nuwās, of whom more will be said later. An invigorating revival of the *qaṣīda* at the end of the seventh and beginning of the eighth centuries was achieved by three of the finest representatives of the art: Farazdaq, Jarīr, and Akhṭal. Adapted to the political needs of Damascus and the tastes of Umayyad Arab society, notably the erstwhile Bedouin of Baṣra and Kūfa, their poetry breathes the old tribal spirit. All three of them were panegyrists and satirists, and are best known for a measure-for-measure vituperative affray which raged for many a year between Jarīr, on the one hand, and Farazdaq and Akhṭal, on the other. A much admired *qaṣīd*-poet of the same generation, but of a different kind, was Dhū 'r-Rumma, the greatest of an archaising school harking back to Bedouin sonority and verbal exuberance. But there could be no true reversion to type, for the function of the *qaṣīda* was no longer what it was. In an atmosphere increasingly remote from the desert, the exploitation of the ode as a means of livelihood, as well as its involvement with the philological schools, had made stylisation inevitable.

The advent of the Abbasids brought no rapid or dramatic developments in poetry. Late Umayyad tendencies were confirmed and accentuated, and evolution consisted in 'physiological' rather than 'anatomical' change. Strict metrical conformism persisted, but diction and themes were brought into closer harmony with life at court and in the more cultured urban centres of Iraq. A certain accommodation of Persian spirit to Arabic form and language made for greater variety and lightness of theme as well as polish and spontaneity of invention. The *qaṣīda*, now the stock-in-trade of panegyrising laureates, was not unaffected, but it was in thematic verse that the new spirit was most obvious. In nothing was it more apparent and consistent than in the *ghazal*. Popularised at Baṣra by Bashshār b. Burd, this genre established itself as a form of entertainment in the court of Hārūn ar-Rashīd and was developed in its chivalrous form by 'Abbās b. al-Aḥnaf. In its sensual form it was transported to new heights – and moral depths – by the profligate Abū Nuwās, a versatile poet of consummate skill with little time for the monotonous desert

*'b.' between two names stands for 'ibn' – 'son of'.

ode and its outmoded grandiloquence, strange words, and incongruous conventions. By the Arabs Abū Nuwās came to be regarded as leader of the 'modernists' whose work is characterised by simplicity and charm and a refreshing inclination towards new themes, images and metaphors. In themes and treatment the golden-age poets struck out in different directions, even if their example was not always followed. Thus, while Abū Nuwās handled the themes of wine and love with subtle ease and cultivated the hunting-poem as an independent genre, Abān b. 'Abd al-Ḥamīd (*d c* 816) treated material of Indian and Persian provenance in iambic-like couplets and wrote didactic poems on cosmology, logic and fasting. Abū 'l-'Atāhiya made himself master of simple religious and moral poetry.

Yet, even while the modernists were contriving to breathe more freely beneath the yoke of metrical unity and monorhyme, the tyranny of poetic convention was already finding an ally in the developing art of rhetorical figures (*badī'*). Enlisted in the cause of diversification, the new art thrived on the morphological peculiarities of Arabic and drew strength from the numinous value which the Arabs attribute to words. Though rarely pleasing to western taste, conditioned as that is to different stylistic ideals, *badī'* could be highly effective and appealing in the hands of a great poet: that it was an abomination in the hands of pedantic hacks is axiomatic. The formal recognition of *badī'* is usually associated with its appearance in the *qaṣīdas* of one of Hārūn's court-poets, Muslim b. al-Walīd (*d* 823). By the end of the ninth century it was well established, and from the tenth its use in the highest forms of poetry was virtually mandatory. Once oriented upon the criteria of verbal form, the concept of poetry inspired by *badī'* induced a tendency to subordinate ideas to locutions, and poetry, relegated from the ninth century onwards to a position of importance secondary to that of prose, entered upon a period of decline. The effects were not immediate nor can we begin to speak of an age of decadence before the eleventh century. The great anthologies of Abū Tammām (*qv*) and Buḥturī revived the appeal of classicism which now took on a new and lasting importance. A complex blend of the old classical tradition with *badī'* resulted in neo-classicism, of which prominent features were certain modifications of thematic structure and shifts of emphasis such as may be observed in the extension of panegyric in the *qaṣīda* with corresponding reduction of the *nasīb* and *waṣf* to relatively brief formalities. In important poets, whether they be neo-classicists such as Abū Tammām, or the incomparable Mutanabbī, or modernists such as Ibn al-Mu'tazz, there is no lack of individuality and inventiveness within acceptable structural limits. From the end of the tenth century departure from established patterns becomes rare, and great names are few. Among these are the Syrian Abū 'l-'Alā' al-Ma'arrī (*d* 1057) and the Egyptian Ibn al-Fāriḍ (*d* 1235). The first is remarkable for his epigrammatic and double-rhymed poems, *al-Luzūmiyyāt* (Poems of Necessity), in which, with unaccustomed candour and disregard for convention, he gave voice to a rationalism and cynical pessimism that were to win admirers in the nineteenth and twentieth centuries. The second ranks as the greatest of Arab mystical poets and is chiefly renowned for the inimitable manner in which he succeeded in imparting an inward and wholly spiritual meaning to the formal love-poem.

All the poetical forms, themes, techniques, and conventions of the eastern classical tradition were known to Muslim Spain. For a number of reasons, however, the flowering of Spanish-Arabic poetry came comparatively late, running from the end of the tenth century throughout the eleventh. In so far as it has a physiognomy of its own, the work of the Andalusian poets is characterised by a predilection for natural description and an imagery moulded by refined hedonists to landscapes and seasons. At its best in a happy blend of lyrical charm and gentle mood, it touches its tenderest note in the poems of the lovelorn Ibn Zaydūn (*d* 1071). The full scale of its sounds is explored to the point of sensuous fascination by Ibn Khafāja (*d* 1139), a poet with a passion for gardens. A notable break with tradition was the Andalusian recognition of strophic verse. The first form to win acceptance was the *muwashshaḥ*, commonly consisting of between five and seven stanzas. In most cases the poem opens with a couplet whose rhyme scheme recurs at regular intervals separated by three or more independently rhymed lines. A simple scheme is AA bbbAA, cccAA, etc. A colloquial 'catch-line' – not infrequently in the indigenous Romance dialect – usually rounds off the poem. Elaborate schemes occur, but only four or five seem to have been common. As regards metrics some authorities postulate an original syllabic, or accentual, system, but others hold that even the most unfamiliar metres can be explained as modifications (inversion included) of the classical. The themes are mostly amatory or panegyrical, nature providing the setting. Simplicity of diction and construction is characteristic and, in certain positions, loss of case-endings in rhyming words permits a freedom of expression otherwise impossible. A highly popular strophic form in the vernacular was the *zajal* whose great exponent was Ibn Quzmān (*d* 1160). Both genres were carried to the East, but neither ever seriously competed with the conventional ode, even in Spain.

(*ii*) *Prose*

Apart from poetry and above the level of everyday speech, there also existed in pre-Islamic Arabia aphorism, formal orations (*khuṭbas*), and oracular utterances by soothsayers cast in rhymed prose. In the realm of narrative certain legends and stories of intertribal wars also circulated. The sum of such elements may have amounted to an oral tradition containing the seeds of literary developments in prose, but it did not amount to literature. The first, greatest and most enduring monument of prose composition was the Koran, the undoubtedly authentic record of Muḥammad's formal pronouncements which Islam regards as divine revelations and the inimitable word of God. In its arrangement, which was not attempted until after the Prophet's death, the Koran is unsystematic. It consists of one hundred and fourteen chapters (*sūras*) subdivided into verses and arranged, except for the first, roughly in order of length. Since the longer and generally later *sūras* precede the shorter and earlier, we have a work whose arrangement is chronologically back to front. For this and other good reasons the Koran is, for the untutored, something of an enigma. As it was delivered over a period of twenty years during which Muḥammad's position radically altered, it also varies in style and content. Apart from religious and moral teaching, it includes not only social and legal rulings, but also such matters as arguments against Muḥammad's opponents and comment on major events. The vehicle of expression is rhymed prose (*saj'*) in which the rhyme, unlike that of poetry, is neither constant nor strict. Stylistically, the *sūras* of the Meccan (and therefore earlier) phase of the Prophet's mission differ vastly from those of the Medinese period. In his earliest utterances the style is concise and oracular, consisting of cryptic oaths and rhymed phrases. By contrast, the late pronouncements are of much greater length and couched in loosely rhymed rhetorical prose more suited to legislation. The literary appeal of the Koran rests almost entirely on its unequalled aesthetic qualities inherent in its untranslatable lyricism and rhetoric, its emotive rhyme patterns, rhythms and refrains, and the sublime tones of its music and diction.

The place of the Koran in Arabic literature is central. For although its divine character precluded direct imitation (and that to the extent that *saj'* as a regular ornament of secular prose literature appeared only relatively late), it brought into life disciplines considered vital to exegesis (e.g. philology and lexicography based on the study of the desert poets) and the application of its commandments and principles (e.g. theology and jurisprudence). Not only did it thus set the course to be followed by the Arabic humanities, but it also demonstrated that the scope of supratribal Arabic could be extended beyond the bounds of poetry.

The period spanning the years between Muḥammad's death and the fall of the Umayyads saw the birth of functional prose, notably in the sphere of narrative and politico-religious rhetoric, but we are almost on the threshold of the Abbasid era before we encounter prose with a conscious literary purpose. This begins its history with the epistles (*rasā'il*) of 'Abd al-Ḥamīd, principal secretary to the last Umayyad caliph, Marwān II. Their appearance marks the beginning of belles-lettres (*adab*), and the scene is set for the development of a court literature created independently of the philologists of Baṣra and Kūfa, by and for the secretarial class. Marrying the Persian spirit with the imagery, sonority and parallelism of Arabic rhetoric, 'Abd al-Ḥamīd made the epistle an instrument wherewith to expound royal and court ethics, administrative practice and ceremonial. In the new Abbasid caliphate the doyen of the nascent secretarial school was his pupil, Ibn al-Muqaffa‘, creator of a simpler but more gracious and polished prose style, whose manuals of protocol and free adaptations of Middle-Persian court-literature set a trend in discreet and entertaining didacticism. While Ibn al-Muqaffa‘ and his school were thus occupied, the more conservative but wide-ranging philologists, in their zeal to preserve the excellence of the Arabic language, ran it to ground at source, amassing and classifying whatever they encountered in the way of tribal tradition and historical information. Foremost among them was Abū ‘Ubayda (728–824) whose labours took in the whole of the north Arabian tradition. Since the death of Muḥammad the collection and transmission of *ḥadīth* (accounts of what the Prophet said or did) had been a perennial preoccupation of the Medinese, and now in the eighth century the special interest which some had shown in the life and military expeditions (*maghāzī*) of Muḥammad inspired an arrangement and expansion of *ḥadīth* into the first monumental biography of the Prophet. Its author was Muḥammad b. Isḥāq (*d* 768) whose work made use of the Arabian narrative style and owed little, if anything, to outside influence. By the end of the century a mature legal literature was already in existence and in the sphere of philology important technical treatises had been produced. In both fields the literary significance of these developments lies in their prose style which was shaped for the specific ends of exposition and argument under the background influence of Greek logic.

The ninth century was the age of high Abbasid culture during which the wide humanistic concept of letters developed by Ibn al-Muqaffa‘ and progressively reduced by less able and imaginative successors to a straitened secretarial canon was brought to perfection in the works of an incomparable master of Arabic prose. This was the prolific and encyclopaedic scholar and essayist, Jāḥiẓ, at once a Saint-Simon and an Addison, whose entertaining portrayals of contemporary society exemplify the manner in which he sought to enlarge the scope of belles-lettres. Uniting the old, but as yet unexploited, Arabic philological tradition with the finer elements of secretarial literature, he gave a new but unmistakably Arabic tone to letters and checked the primacy of old Persian themes and values in chancery *adab* whose repetitious fustian he scorned. His aim was to combine instruction with diversion, and to this end he presents and comments on a vast range of such widely divergent topics as theology, science, metaphysics, rhetoric, the qualities and characteristics of social and racial groups, and so on. The rich store of Greek learning opened by the school of translators stimulated both Jāḥiẓ and his contemporaries and reinforced them in their stand against Sasanid tradition and the derisory anti-Arab polemic of the Shu‘ūbiyya. The final triumph of the counter-offensive launched by Jāḥiẓ was achieved some years later by the critic and philologist, Ibn Qutayba, who confined the old Iranian influence to the realm of administration and protocol and assembled from the Arabic humanities the literary bases both of general culture and secretarial education. Like poetry, *adab* was to undergo a gradual change characterised by an ever-growing emphasis on style. The process was helped along by the appearance of formal analyses of literary technique, beginning with a basic treatise on *badī'* in poetry from the pen of Ibn al-Mu'tazz (*d* 908). With the general acceptance of a formal canon the application of conceptual and psychological criteria as advocated by Jurjānī in his *Asrār al-Balāgha* (Secrets of Eloquence) stood little chance. With the tenth century came a rage for epistles and occasional prose pieces (*fuṣūl*). The prose art of chancery correspondence (*inshā'*) soon followed and with it an allusive and highly mannered style replete with *badī'* and adorned with *saj'*. Of this kind of literary virtuosity, the epistles of the Būyid secretary Ibn 'Abbād provide a classic example. *Saj'*, which had begun during the ninth century to creep into polite literature via pulpit oratory and the like, was henceforth *de rigueur* in artistic prose.

In the second half of the tenth century belles-lettres took a new and refreshing turn: Hamadhānī brought in the *maqāma*, a quaint kind of anecdotal sketch in *saj'*, animated and coloured by the spirit of contemporary Islamic life and intended to amuse, interest and instruct. The invariable hero of the piece is a wandering scholar-rascal with an astonishing talent for extracting money from his public by witty displays of erudition, rhetorical ingenuity and supposedly impromptu versification. The tale, woven around these basic ingredients, is told by a narrator – equally invariable – who is represented as an eye-witness of the scenes depicted. Standardisation of the genre followed a century or so later when Ḥarīrī, modelling himself directly on Hamadhānī, surpassed him in verbal elaboration, inventiveness, breadth and depth of allusion without, however, sacrificing the spirit of his predecessor. To those for whom subordination of subject to style and sound to sense have no literary appeal Ḥarīrī is artificial and recondite, and his work evokes a blend of Lyly's *Euphues* with Joyce's *Finnegan's Wake*; to the Arabs, his *maqāmas* are the ultimate in a species of composition in which simplicity is no merit.

In the course of the ninth century the science of *ḥadīth*, hitherto subservient to jurisprudence, achieved the status of an independent discipline with a literature of its own. Precipitated by orthodox reaction to Hellenism and the rationalist stand of the Mu'tazilites, the literary activity of the movement aimed at a re-appraisal and subject classification of the Traditions then in circulation, the essential criterion of authenticity residing in the *isnād*, or chain of transmitters prefacing the text of each *ḥadīth*. Of six highly esteemed collections resulting from this activity, two were deemed the most authoritative, and of these two that of Bukhārī soon took precedence, ultimately ranking second only to the Koran. The literary interest of *ḥādīth* collections lies both in style and a multifarious subject-matter which takes in all kinds of situations relevant to faith and works and serves as a guide to the kind of public and private behaviour expected of good Muslims.

From *isnād*-criticism and the collection and organisation of material on the life and activities of the Prophet historical writing received a new impetus. As we have seen, Ibn Isḥāq had made a significant start, and after him came Wāqidī (*d* 823), author of a work on the expeditions of the Prophet. Moving in another direction, Wāqidī's secretary, Muḥammad b. Sa'd (*d* 845) compiled an enormous biographical dictionary of the Prophet, his Companions and their associates. In another work Wāqidī extended his interest to the first two centuries of Islam, and later Balādhurī (*d* 892) applied himself in continuous annalistic narrative to the history of the early conquests and the provinces. The first and foremost universal history was penned by Ṭabarī (*d* 923), a traditionist whose background is clearly discernible in his vast and indispensable *Tārīkh ar-Rusul wa-l-Mulūk* (History of Prophets and Kings). After treating the history of mankind from creation until his own time, he presents the events of each year not as a straightforward narrative, but in the manner of the *ḥadīth*, in a series of disconnected accounts offered by different authorities. By the end of the ninth century, however, history had begun to cut itself loose from religion and establish itself as a discipline in its own right. Developing in two main forms, the chronicle and the biography (the latter mainly in the 'Who's Who' style), it was to branch out into a multiplicity of subdivisions from compendia of regional and local traditions and provincial and urban chronicles to historico-geographical encyclopaedias, biographies of scholars, judges, saints, and eminent men in all significant walks of life. The first great historian of the 'secular' school was a Būyid official, Ibn Miskawayh (*d* 1030) whose *K. Tajārib al-Umam* (Experiences of Nations) recounts in lively detail and with relative impartiality the course of history right down to his own day. Not all who followed aspired to his standards. The fashion for contemporary annals, chronicled by the secretarial class and largely restricted to the doings of the ruler, his court and officials, opened the door to marked political bias and the suppression of truth. Moreover, the intrusion of courtiers and officials into the domain of annalistic history ushered in a dynastic and ethical concept of history quite foreign to the broader and more factually concrete view of the old religious scholars and ultimately tended to transform what should have been a science, or at least a record in simple narrative, into dynastic panegyric more admired for its style than for its veracity. Fortunately the trend had no appeal in Syria and Egypt and therefore scarcely survived the fall of Baghdad. From the eleventh century a good deal of literary effort went into biographical collections, historical encyclopaedias and voluminous compilations of all branches of knowledge. In each class variety was achieved largely by differences of aim, scope or arrangement. Thus the biographer for instance, might confine himself to the notabilities connected with a specific town or city, as does al-Khaṭīb al-Baghdādī (*d* 1071) in his fourteen volumed *History of*

Baghdad or to a certain social or professional class, as does Yāqūt (*d* 1229) in his dictionary of men of letters. At the other end of the scale we find the celebrated universal biographer Ibn Khallikān (*d* 1282) who, beyond excluding the first two generations of Muslims, set himself no limits to the range of illustrious personalities listed in his *Wafāyāt al-A'yān* (Obituaries of the Eminent). In historiography great popularity began to attach to a method of exposition initiated by Ibn al-Jawzī (*d* 1200), a famous polymath of Baghdad: after a prefatory abridgment of early Islamic history summaries of the events of each year were followed by obituary notices of the personages deceased in the same year.

In many Western minds Arabic literature is identified with the *Arabian Nights*, or *Alf Layla wa-Layla* (Thousand and One Nights), which is widely imagined to be a typical product. The truth is otherwise: perhaps no English epithet can convey the cultured Arab's view of that work more aptly than the colloquial term 'pop.'. The history of the *Nights*, which had their origin in a translation of a Persian collection of tales, goes back as far as the eighth century and extends, in its first oriental phase, as far as the sixteenth. In the process of evolution, characterised by wearing down and replacement of the old substance, the work acquired a markedly Arab stamp. Yet the fact is that into a frame-story of Indian origin there was woven a mass of non-Arabian material, mainly from India, Persia, Syria, Mesopotamia and Egypt. Given the nature of the work and its circulation in a number of recensions, it is hardly surprising that the *Nights*, barely squeezed into the framework of classical literature, do not reach the highest standards of literary quality and style. High Arab taste for *adab*, spurning tales of sheer fantasy and superstition, required literary entertainment to be edifying and purposive and finely balanced between erudition and aesthetic creation. A good example of anecdotal literature conforming to such criteria is the *Nishwār al-Muḥāḍara* (rendered freely, but not inappropriately, by an English translator as 'The Table-Talk of a Mesopotamian Judge') of Tanūkhī (*d* 994).

A vast work comparable to the *Nights* in length of evolutionary process is *Sīrat 'Antar*, a romance of Arab chivalry spanning five hundred years and revolving around the exploits of 'Antar, an Islamised epic hero. A similar collection of story-cycles, *Sīrat Banī Hilāl* (Saga of the B. Hilāl), grew up around the great migration of the Bedouin tribe of Hilāl which, after erupting from the Arabian Peninsula, spent several centuries in a westward movement across Egypt and North Africa. Neither the *Nights* nor the historical romances referred to are held to represent a high form of Arabic literature. Their emergence into any kind of prominence is in fact a phenomenon of the age of cultural decline which begins in the twelfth century.

It is neither intended nor is it practicable to consider here the extensive writings of geographers, cosmographers, philosophers, mystics, theologians and lawyers, much less to penetrate the technical and scientific sectors of literary production. But it is obligatory to make the reader aware of their existence and very real importance in the Arabic corpus. Nor need we pursue the course of Arabic literature through the long years of decline leading to centuries of stagnation. In the main, the enthusiasm for summaries and compilations was maintained and, under the constricting pressures of scholasticism, accompanied by a shift of interest in the direction of theology and mysticism, the latter often at the popular level of hagiography. In Syria and Egypt the growth of the new military states and the conflict with Christendom stimulated the production and proliferation of theoretical and practical treatises on war and weapons. Between the fourteenth and fifteenth centuries a passion for historiography reached its peak in the Mamlūk state, bequeathing a legacy of some of the most interesting works in the field.

In its broad outlines the prose literature of Muslim Spain conformed to patterns received – for the most part belatedly – from the East. The spirit of freshness and individuality which it unmistakably bears are a matter for detailed analysis of a kind which cannot be undertaken here. Something of its importance and interest, however, may be gleaned from the biographies of such authors as Ibn Ḥazm, Ibn Ṭufayl, and Ibn al-Khaṭīb. In North Africa the fourteenth century brought forth the most remarkable writer of the western Arab world – Ibn Khaldūn. He was neither a poet nor a belletrist, but a historian and thinker whose attempt to explain the pattern of history and human society places him in the first rank not merely of Arab, but also of world thinkers.

SINCE 1800

A stir of literary activity in Syria and Egypt, stimulated by nineteenth-century contacts with the West, heralded a new era in Arabic literature. To what endeavours writers should put their talents and in what form they should express themselves were issues on which they were soon divided. The problem of literature was inseparable from, and complicated by, language. Literary Arabic, even in its least exalted forms, was, as indeed it remained up to the advent of radio (which is, albeit slowly, accustoming the ears of all classes to the standard language), intelligible only to the educated and is almost as far from the vernacular as Latin from Italian. For some – the minority – the resources of expression were to be found only in the works of great medieval masters, and inevitably their creations suffered from the limitations imposed by the material in which they worked. Based upon classical models, these were in every sense anachronistic. The leader of the school was Nāṣīf al-Yāzijī (*d* 1871), a Lebanese Christian whose *Majma' al-Baḥrayn* (Confluence of the Two Seas) was a scholarly attempt to revive the *maqāma* in the style of Ḥarīrī. To literary innovation Yāzijī and his followers had nothing to contribute; the classical tradition to which they were committed was governed by peculiarly Islamic canons of thought, taste and style at a time when Arabic writers educated in the West were trying their hand at rendering and adapting European fiction. To convey the essential concepts of contemporary western thought, new norms were required, and fluency and directness of expression were needed to replace the ornamental, esoteric devices of classical belles-lettres.

Despite memorable regenerative efforts by Taḥṭāwī, translator of *Télémaque* and author of a well-known work on Paris, the awakening of Egyptian letters prior to the British occupation was more apparent than real. From the middle of the nineteenth century the scene was dominated by the Syrian-Lebanese, who on the whole were Christians in contact with the missions. To this Syrian-Lebanese element was owed, *inter alia*, the birth of non-official journalism which, although soon forced from its native soil by political pressures, rapidly took root in Egypt under predominantly Christian management. From the outset the free press afforded literary innovation the opportunities it sought and needed. The division between the journalist and the creative prose-writer was slight and the two were almost invariably combined in the same person. Without daily papers, magazines and periodicals the acceptance of fiction as an Arabic literary genre is difficult to conceive. Their pages carried serials and short stories to the literate public and as journalism evolved so also did public taste. Its evolution moreover was accompanied by the development of a narrative style suited to the needs of fiction.

Nineteenth-century translations of western literature, chiefly French, introduced the Arab world to drama, the novel and the short story. Drama, pioneered by the Syrian Mārūn an-Naqqāsh with a verse translation of Molière's *L'Avare* (1848), constituted a truly new departure from accepted genres. The most remarkable figure in the field was the Egyptian 'Uthmān Jalāl who wrestled boldly with Molière, Racine, and Corneille. With Najīb al-Ḥaddād's renderings of works by the same three authors as well as others by Voltaire and Hugo, adaptation gave way to modified translation and paved the way for the literalism expected of today's translators for what has become the classical theatre.

The novel had much the same antecedents as dramatic literature. Translation and adaptation preceded imitation of western models, but progression from the one stage to the other was relatively slow. Scope for imitation in a society for which European concepts of social behaviour were as yet meaningless, if not outrageous, was limited. Moreover, the contempt in which the lettered classes held the vulgar art of story-telling was as discouraging as the problem of dialogue which, as in drama, posed the perennial question: how could literary Arabic, awkward and even absurd in the mouths of modern characters, be replaced by the more natural colloquial for which there were neither literary precedents nor prospects? When the Arabic novel came at last it was, not surprisingly, historical, heroic and focused on the past glories of the Arabs and Islam. Foremost, if not first in the field, was Jirjī Zaydān whose twenty-two historical romances in the tradition of Scott and Dumas appeared between 1891 and 1914. In 1905 Ya'qub Ṣarrūf, a Lebanese expatriate, introduced the socio-historical novel with his *Fatāt Miṣr* (Egypt's Heroine) and in 1907 social criticism entered fiction with Muḥammad al-Muwayliḥī's *Ḥadīth 'Isā b. Hishām* (Narrative of 'Isā b. Hishām). This imaginative revitalisation of the old *maqāma*, simplified and suitably adapted, created a trend in Egyptian letters which continued until 1914.

Since the periodical press was the great Maecenas, episodic and short fictional forms had a natural advantage over the novel inasmuch as they were better suited in length, plan and structure to the media of publication. The first short stories appeared between 1870 and 1886 in *Al-Jinān*, a Lebanese periodical edited by Buṭrus al-Bustānī, a prominent encyclopaedist and man of letters whose son, Salīm, was the most notable contributor of original, as well as translated, fiction of this type. From 1886 until the close of the century no one else tried seriously to establish himself as a short-story writer. The early years of the new century saw some progress towards originality, this time in Egypt, although translations (mainly of English authors) tended to predominate. What is more, original writers by no means distinguished themselves. The short story, when not more of a homily or embellished essay, was regularly marred by virtual absence of plot and action, stunted characterisation, sentimentality and gross technical faults.

Of all forms of literary expression, that most in vogue was that which proved most convenient – the essay. In this domain the leading light was the Egyptian Muṣṭafā Luṭfī al-Manfalūṭī, a conservative whose best work in the genre is characterised by an elegant style and manner of presentation of which cultured Arab taste is peculiarly appreciative. His collection of essays *an-Naẓarāt* (Reflexions, 1910) is a classic of its kind.

By 1914 an important and imaginative school of Syrian-Lebanese writers and poets, eager to break with the past, had taken firm root in America and gradually assumed leadership of the modernist movement which their compatriots – and, for the most part, co-religionists – had started in Syria and continued in Egypt. An effective challenge came from a group of young Egyptian Muslims dedicated to the ideal of a slow, but realistic, change without rejection of their own heritage. Within the limits of the periodical press to which they were very much tied, they sought and achieved higher standards of style and content. French and English influence still held and the new writers, according to background, were to tread the path of authors such as Rousseau, Vigny, Musset, France, Zola and, in particular, Maupassant, or to a lesser degree, Carlyle, Dickens, Jerome and Shaw. At the same time they moved towards the creation of a distinctive Egyptian literature. Their leading representative was the 'French-wing' Muḥammad Ḥusayn Haykal whose

Zaynab (published anonymously, 1914) can be considered the first Arabic novel of manners. For all his technical failings, the author of this fictional biography of a Delta village girl makes a real attempt at psychological analysis, and the use of the colloquial in dialogue gives his characters life and movement.

Between the wars important novels were few, mostly Egyptian, and written by realists in search of their country's psyche. The measure of their success varied. In Maḥmūd Taymūr, a true Maupassant, European characters often lurk behind Egyptian masks; Ibrāhīm al-Māzinī in his novel of manners *Ibrāhīm al-Kātib* (1931) even forgets the mask. The autobiographical novel – the genre of self-made men of pure Egyptian descent – goes deeper. Into this class we may squeeze Ṭāhā Ḥusayn's *al-Ayyām* (The Days), justly acclaimed for its style and depth of emotion, though to some the former is diffuse and the latter sentimental. The art of the novel proper however gained more from the originality and tautness of style of Tawfīq al-Ḥakim, displayed first in his *Return of the Spirit* and later in his *Diary of a Rural Prosecutor*, a true product of the native soil.

Between 1914 and 1921 the short story passed from embryo to infancy in the hands of Mīkhā'īl Nu'ayma (Na'īma) in America and Muḥammad Taymūr in Egypt. In Maḥmūd, the latter's younger brother, the art found a gifted exponent who was to achieve unity of style and presentation and to probe, with brevity and realism, the rural and urban soul of Egypt. Where Maḥmūd Taymūr succeeded many failed, but at least by 1939 technical competence and local colour were more in evidence, and writers no longer sermonised or pandered to the moralists.

Since the war the Arabic novel and short story have steadily improved and with the spread of education serious fiction enjoys a wider public. As in the past, the same name is often linked with both genres. The general mood is nationalist and socialist and scepticism combines with angry pity for the poor. Egypt is not alone in the field; Lebanon and Iraq are there, and, in North Africa, Tunisia has made her début. Regional differences are now strongly marked. For Egypt, Najīb Maḥfūẓ unfolds the social evolution of a small trader's family through the period 1917–44 in a skilful Cairene trilogy; Yūsuf as-Sibā'ī poignantly portrays the plight of Cairo's poor and heaven's blind cruelty in his *as-Saqqā' Māt* (The Water-Carrier Died, 1952); 'Abd ar-Raḥman ash-Sharqāwī successfully makes the problem of Egypt's landlords the theme of his crisply written *al-Arḍ* (The Earth, 1954); tender and unembittered, Muḥammad 'Abd al-Ḥalīm tells touching human stories of the Delta; uniquely and with perfect mastery, Kāmil Ḥusayn projects the trial of Jesus through the eyes of Jew, Roman and Apostle in his *Qarya Ẓālima* (Sinful City, 1954); Yūsuf Idrīs, currently unsurpassed in the art of the short story, is an unregimented social realist with a talent for moving but unsentimental sketches of Egypt and, like others of his stature, does not shun the colloquial in dialogue. In the able Idrīs Suhayl the Lebanon has an influential Sartre and in the highly talented Laylā Ba'labakkī a Françoise Sagan whose unconventional style and ideas first blossomed in a daring confessional novel, *Anā Aḥyā* (I Live, 1958). Iraq's authors, of whom the most outstanding are Dhū'n-Nūn Ayyūb, 'Abd al-Malik Nūrī and Fu'ād Tekerli, tend to be morose and violent and incline towards rebellion, godlessness and materialism.

The evolution of original dramatic literature since the end of the last century is inseparable from the names of three Egyptians, two of whom are already known to us: Aḥmad Shawqī (*d* 1927), Tawfīq al-Ḥakīm and Maḥmūd Taymūr. The first, a lyric poet with six historical plays to his credit, is a transitional figure bridging the gap between the two centuries to which he belonged equally; the second, a polished and subtle prose writer with a large and varied dramatic output, is seen at his best in dramas with modern social themes; the third, a keen observer with a gift for depicting the natural, excels at comedy. Symbolism in its most sophisticated form is associated with the French-influenced Egyptian Bishr Fāris (*d* 1963) and the Lebanese Aḥmad Makkī. Their work, like many plays of the classical theatre, is more suitable for reading by the intellectual than for presentation on the stage to a wider public. In recent years hostility to the West and Israel has inspired a crop of political plays whose popularity is assured.

In Muslim poetry the nineteenth century witnessed no drastic break with the past in favour of wholesale imitation of western genres. The sanctity of the *qaṣīda* as the supreme form of poetic expression remained inviolable and Egyptian and Syrian poets were generally content to pour indifferent wine into old bottles. Offended by the staleness, sensitive palates contrived to improve the vintage, making a return to Golden Age standards a vital part of the process. At the same time a desire for change found satisfaction in the modernisation of themes, notably in the direction of patriotism and social comment and the creation of new images based on nineteenth-century discoveries. The first great representative of the modern neo-classical school was Maḥmūd Sāmī al-Bārūdī (1840–1904), a robust and grandiloquent master of the classical repertoire whose leadership and example bore fruit in the elegant and powerful lyricism of Shawqī and the moving eloquence of a great and sympathetic advocate of his native Egypt and her people, Ḥāfiẓ Ibrāhīm (*c* 1869–72 – 1932). Among the Christians of Syria and Lebanon new religious forces precipitated a trend away from the *qaṣīda*. Treading the path of the Maronites who had used the *muwashshaḥ* and *zajal* in their hymns for almost four centuries, the western Protestant missionaries with the expert aid of men like the Yāzijīs turned the popular *zajal* to the same purpose as they strove to reproduce the rhyme schemes and accentual metres of English quatrains. In 1852 they published their hymnal, *Tarnīmāt li-l-'Ibāda* (Songs of Worship) which provided the necessary models and impetus for original composition. The new form accompanied the Syrian-Lebanese emigrants to Egypt and America, and in Syro-American, or *mahjar* poetry, in which traditional forms and themes were abandoned in favour of self-expression in relatively simple language, the genre was to predominate. Of the *mahjar* poets, the most outstanding were Khalīl Jibrān (Gibran) and Amīn ar-Rayḥānī (Riḥānī) neither of whom was daunted by innovation. In 1904 Rayḥānī, influenced by Whitman, introduced the prose-poem (*shi'r manthūr*) of which Jibrān subsequently became master.

In the Arab countries progress was slower, but during the first decade of our century gradual acceptance of strophic forms gave rise to a 'non-denominational' romantic movement represented in Egypt by Abū Shādī and by other poets in Syria, Lebanon and Tunisia. Acquaintance with western epic and dramatic poetry, combined with a desire to translate and imitate, created the need for a vehicle that was at once more suitable than strophic verse and less repugnant to conventional taste than prose-poetry. For many Egyptian poets the solution lay in blank verse (*shi'r mursal*) based on accepted Arabic metres which they modified as and when necessary. Traditional metres were also made the basis of an experiment in *vers libre* (*shi'r ḥurr*) by Abū Shādī, in a style reminiscent of Swinburne's, but his lead was not widely followed. With the end of the Second World War there came a reversal of attitude towards the idea of free verse and despite periodic assaults on it, it has found favour in varying degrees throughout the Arab world, particularly with the younger generation of left-wing poets. The focal point of the new trend was Iraq where the poetic inspiration of Badr Shākir as-Sayyāb (*d* 1964) and Nāzik al-Malā'ika found expression in two different forms of verse. Of these, that employed by the latter to cast a monostrophic ode proved less popular than Sayyāb's technique which allowed structural irregularity with extensive use of enjambment. Generally speaking the freedom exercised by free-verse poets has never been absolute, for notwithstanding the invention of new feet, the subordination of form to content, greater simplicity in subject, style and diction, and a tendency to realism and self-expression, the preservation of metrical rhythms familiar to the Arab ear is a discernible pre-requisite of success in the genre. It is important to note, moreover, that despite the challenge of the new poetic forms the traditional *qaṣīda* is by no means dead. Still vigorous, it retains a firm hold on certain sections of the literary public.

Without some reference, however brief, to the nature and importance of western literary figures as influences, not merely in the field of poetry but in that of literature generally, our sketch of recent years would be incomplete. It is therefore fitting to conclude by noting that for those eager to blaze new trails in the fifties the works of Sartre, Camus and T. S. Eliot (notably *The Wasteland*) became major sources of inspiration in Beirut, Cairo and Baghdad. A name which is neither French nor British, but which should nevertheless be associated with later post-war trends is that of the great Spanish poet of the thirties, Federico García Lorca.

INDIVIDUAL WRITERS

–**'Abbās b. al-Aḥnaf** (*d* after 808). Arab poet with Persian connexions and background. A favourite of Hārūn ar-Rashīd, he introduced the *ghazal* at court. He apparently cultivated only the one genre, and that chiefly in the *'udhrī* manner (see p. 16). Though linguistically simple and direct, his poetry is stereotyped, sentimental and less impressive than that of Jamīl (*qv*). It was nevertheless enjoyed in its day and seems to have been much appreciated in Spain. (*EI*², I, 9–10)

'Abd al-Ḥamīd, called **al-Kātib** 'the secretary' (*d* 750). A Persian Mawla from Iraq, he was principal secretary to the last Umayyad, Marwān II. He is the putative creator of the epistolary genre in Arabic and father of artistic prose. His most important extant works are six epistles, of which the best known is that dealing with the dignity and office of secretary. Another, dedicated to Marwān's son and heir, aims to instruct the prince in royal ethics, protocol and other matters pertaining to the correct execution of his duties. Both treaties prefigure later and more elaborate works on similar themes. 'Abd al-Ḥamīd exploits to the full the lexical stock of Arabic synonyms, but his mastery of the genre ensures that his reiterations, unlike those of later writers of lesser stature, do not pall. His style is varied, ranging from the simple and direct to the more elaborate and complex. His themes and spirit bear a Sāsānid stamp, but his language, imagery and cadences are those of Arabic poetry and rhetoric. One epistle bears signs of Greek stylistic influences. (*EI*², I, 65–6).

Abū 'l-'Alā' al-Ma'arrī (973–1057). A free-thinking Arab poet from Ma'arra, near Aleppo. Loss of sight in early life accentuated a natural pessimism which wide travel, including a disappointing visit to Baghdad in 1007, did nothing to alleviate. Returning home in 1009, he spent the rest of his highly ascetic and misogynous life in his native country as a teacher and lecturer. His earliest poems, collected under the title of *Saqṭ az-Zand* (Tinder Spark), are markedly influenced by Mutanabbī, whom he greatly admired. A later collection, *Luzūm Mā Lā Yalzam* (Necessity of the Unnecessary), or, more briefly, *al-Luzūmiyyāt* – the title refers to the rhyme system – is remarkable for the provocative candour with which the poet, a sceptic and cynic, dares to view religion and society. An imaginary journey through Heaven and Hell is the subject of his main prose work *Risālat al-Ghufrān* (Epistle of Pardon). In this poets and writers are encountered in unexpected destinations in the next world and give the author an opportunity to develop literary and philosophical themes. The tone is ironical and the style elaborate. Abū 'l-'Alā' is also the author of an epistolary miscellany and a collection of literary discourses on Koranic maxims (viewed by the orthodox as imitative blasphemy). Both are in an elaborate and often obscure style.

Abū 'l-'Atāhiya ('crackbrained') (748–826). The father of religious poetry. Born in Kūfa of a lowly Arab family with Mawali antecedents, he grew up in circumstances which permanently affected his outlook and character. A panegyric of the Abbasid caliph Mahdī (775–85) gave him the entrée to court circles. In spite of disgrace early in the reign of Hārūn ar-Rashīd, his talent for love poetry on which he had thrived during a dissolute youth restored him to favour. In middle age he suddenly turned to ascetic, contemplative poetry in pessimistic vein, in which he preached, with evident antagonism towards the great and wealthy, the transience of the world and its vanities and the virtues of piety. The sincerity of his repentance has been doubted. The directness of his poetry both in content and diction is unconventional and his metres are short and simple. His spontaneity is partly attributable to a limited formal education. The popularity of his work which is less inspired and technically inferior to that of his great contemporary, Abū Nuwās, may be ascribed, partly at least, to the fact that some of it was set to music by his friend, Ibrāhīm al-Mawṣilī, a well-known musician. (*EI*², I, 107–8)

Abū Firās al-Ḥamdānī (932–68). Warrior-poet, Syrian Arab born of a Byzantine slave mother. Orphaned as a child he was reared by his cousin, Sayf ad-Dawla, the Ḥamdānid ruler. Appointed governor of Manbij in 947, he fought with distinction against rebel Arab tribes and, from 950, against the Byzantines. After capture by the latter at Manbij (962) he was taken to Constantinople from his prison in Kharshana and remained there until 966. (The view that he was captured twice, the first time in 951, is untenable.) Upon release he was made governor of Ḥimṣ, only to die in 968 in a rising against his nephew, Abū 'l-Ma'ālī, Sayf's successor. His pre-captivity odes record the events of war and extol the feats and valour of Sayf and himself. Much of their appeal lay in their embodiment of traditional Arab ideals projected by a heroic warrior with first-hand experience of his subject-matter. His *Rūmiyyāt* (Byzantine Poems) are essentially a record of the captive's nostalgia, emotional stress and irritated confusion at Sayf's delay in ransoming him. Because of a closeness of tone and feeling they have often been compared to Ovid's *Tristia.* Their real greatness probably lies in the immediate emotional impact evoked by their sincerity and lyricism. (*EI*², I, 119–20)

Abū Nuwās (*c* 747–813). Exceptionally gifted poet, doyen of the 'modernists'. Born in Persia to a father of south Arabian descent and a Persian mother, he was much averse to the north Arabian tradition and scorned the rugged sonority and conventions of the old desert-encampment ode. After education at Baṣra, then Kūfa, he moved to Baghdad. After the fall of the Barmakids

(803), his Persian protectors at the court of Hārūn ar-Rashīd, he fled to Egypt. Upon return he found great favour with Hārūn's son and successor, Amīn (809–13). The circumstances of his death are obscure. An inveterate wine-bibber and homosexual, Abū Nuwās devoted much of his talent to the service of his passions. Although at his best in his drinking-songs in which he thrills the senses with artistically ingenious tributes to wine and the paraphernalia of the bacchic banquet, or in his love-lyrics, notable for their gaiety and wit as well as frank indecencies, his flair for poetry is unqualified. His satire is cynical, acrimonious, immoderate and obscene, his elegy tender and touching. The hunting-scene of the old *qaṣīda* he treats with superb artistry as an independent genre. He even attempted religious poetry, only to be warned off by Abū 'l-'Atāhiya. Because of Persian influences in his work, he has been wrongly accounted a Shu'ūbī. (*EI*², I, 143–4)

Abū Tammām (*c* 805–45). Neo-classical poet, son of a Damascene Christian wine-merchant. He studied in Egypt and later rose to fame as leading panegyrist of the reign of Mu'taṣim (833–42). His poetical merits have always been controversial. A predilection for conceits and allusions blended with archaising sonority often burdens his verse with ponderous and tortuous artificiality. Yet he can strike brilliant notes – hence the controversy surrounding him. Gnomic musings often introduce his panegyrics, and historical events figure prominently in his odes. His famous *Ḥamāsa* (Martial Courage) is an anthology of ancient Arabic verse on many themes. Together with Buḥturī's anthology of the same name it played a central role in the revival of classicism. (*EI*², I, 153–5)

-Akhṭal (*c* 640–710). Christian Arab poet in the pre-Islamic tradition. Born into the tribe of Taghlib, he became in manhood a staunch supporter and panegyrist of the Umayyads. Along with Farazdaq he engaged in a long and celebrated war of satire against Jarīr (*qv*). The formal perfection of his odes won him the acclaim of the philologists of Baṣra and Kūfa. (*EI*², I, 331)

Bashshār b. Burd (*c* 714–84). Famous Iraqi poet of the late Umayyad/early Abbasid period and first major Arab poet of non-Arab extraction. The son of a Transoxianan freedman, he was born in Baṣra where he formed important connexions amongst the philologists. After its foundation he resided at Baghdad. Blind from birth, he depended on rhapsodes to transmit his poetry. Hence not all verses ascribed to him are genuine. His disability and background, combined with artistic sensitivity, made for a non-conformist character given to political expediency and intellectual vacillation. His Central Asian descent is reflected in his association with the Shu'ūbiyya and in his heretical tendencies redolent of Zoroastrianism. Religious ambivalence brought a dramatic end to an unruly and licentious life. He was a mordant satirist, powerful panegyrist and above all a master of love-lyrics in which he created new trends and popularised certain themes. His work is spontaneous and uncomplicated, but it marks the beginning of conscious use of rhetorical devices in poetry. (*EI*[2], I, 1080–82)

–**Bukhārī** (810–70). Author of the most venerated collection of Prophetic Traditions (*ḥadīth*). The descendant of a Persian Mawla, he was endowed with a prodigious memory and keen eye for detail. After the pilgrimage to Mecca (826) and a stay in the Hejaz, he travelled widely in search of traditions. He ended his days in a small village near Samarqand. His collection, called *aṣ-Ṣaḥīḥ* (The Authentic), is said to have taken sixteen years' labour. It contains more than seven thousand entries selected from six hundred thousand traditions known to Bukhārī and arranged according to subject matter. Since many are quoted under more than one head, the traditions included number less than three thousand. In orthodox Islam the work ranks second to the Koran. Another collection of the same name by Muslim (*d* 875) is regarded with almost equal esteem, and the two works together are known as the 'Two *Ṣaḥīḥs*'. Bukhārī also wrote the biographies of transmitters in his *isnāds*. (*EI*[2], I, 1296–7)

–**Farazdaq** (*d* 728–30). Famous Umayyad satirist and panegyrist. Born in Yamāma in central Arabia, he was of Tamīm, the same tribe as that of his rival Jarīr (*qv*), but of a different branch. Tribal politics provided the background to a perennial verbal war with Jarīr, in which Farazdaq had Akhṭal's support. Despite an Islamic veneer the spirit of his poetry is Bedouin. Glorification of tribe and self are prominent, and his invective, couched in base and indecent language reflects the urbanised Bedouin culture of Baṣra and Kūfa. Although in general conforming to the old *qaṣīda* pattern, he frequently shortens or omits the *nasīb*. (*EI*[2], II, 788–9)

–**Ghazzālī** (Muḥammad) (1059–1111). Important religious thinker and writer who reconciled orthodox formalism with mystical idealism. After study at Ṭūs (his native town), Jurjān, and Nishapur, he became professor of religious sciences at Baghdad in 1091. Breaking under the strain of scepticism he left his post in 1095, withdrew to Damascus for a time, and turned to mysticism. In 1106 he returned from his travels to Nishapur and later to Ṭūs. His *magnum opus*, *Iḥyā' 'Ulūm ad-Dīn* (Revitalisation of Religious Sciences), is an exposition in four parts of his concept of religion as a faith rooted, not in casuistry and systems, but in spiritual experience. His *Tahāfut al-Falāsifa* (Incoherence of the Philosophers) is a studied criticism of Arabic Neoplatonism. Among his other works we may single out *al-Munqidh min aḍ-Ḍalāl* (Deliverer from Error), his religious autobiography. (*EI*[2], II, 1038–41)

–**Hamadhānī,** dubbed **Badī' az-Zamān** 'Wonder of the Age', (968–1008). Belletrist and creator of the *maqāma* genre. Of Persian origin, he was born, as his name indicates, in Hamadhān in Central Iran. In an odyssey across Persia he lived on his wits as he searched for patrons, becoming, in turn, the protégé of Ibn 'Abbād, the Būyid vizier, and the sultan Maḥmūd of Ghazna. He finally settled in Herat where he died. Endowed with a prodigious memory, a command of language, ingenuity and wit, he was a master of improvisation and burlesque. His *maqāmas*, of which the recurrent hero is Abū 'l-Fatḥ al-Iskandarī and the narrator 'Īsā b. Hishām, are important mirrors of Islamic urban life. His style is less elaborate and allusive than that of Ḥarīrī. He also wrote poetry and epistles in rhymed prose. (*EI*², III, 106–7)

–**Ḥarīrī** (1054–1122). Arab philologist and belletrist of Baṣra, noted for his perfecting of the *maqāma*. His *maqāmas* (*c* 1100) conform strictly to the structural pattern set by Hamadhānī, the names of the narrator and hero being changed to al-Ḥārith b. Hammām and Abū Zayd of Sarūj, respectively. His work in the genre has been known – partly at least – to Europe since the seventeenth century. Incomparable by Arab standards, it is apt to leave the uninitiated with an impression of unedifying linguistic virtuosity characterised by recondite allusions and untranslatable sequences of word-play, rhyming syllables and consonantal jugglery. It must, however, be recognised as the product of a master of Arabic language and learning with a vitality of its own. Ḥarīrī is also the author of a philological work on solecisms entitled *Durrat al-Ghawwāṣ* (Pearl of the Diver). (*EI*², III, 222)

Ibn 'Abbād, styled **aṣ-Ṣāḥib** (938–95). Scholar and man of letters, probably the most splendid personage of the Būyid period. Of Persian origin, he was much admired by the vizier Ibn al-'Amīd through whose patronage he rose to high office. After the death of the prince Mu'ayyad ad-Dawla, he became vizier of his successor, Fakhr ad-Dawla, and remained such until his death. A true Maecenas, he did much to promote literary culture at the Būyid court. In addition to theological, philological and other works, he produced a seven-volumed dictionary, *al-Muḥīṭ* (The Ocean), and a collection of ornate secretarial epistles. His style is moulded to the requisites of *saj*'. (*EI*², III, 671–3)

Ibn al-Fāriḍ (1182–1235). Cairene mystic poet of great renown. As a young man he was attracted to a contemplative life in the Muqaṭṭam Hills overlooking Cairo. After spending fifteen years in Mecca he returned to Cairo where he lived out his life in simplicity and humility. Although venerated as a saint, he rejected earthly acclaim. His poetic output was relatively small, but taken as a whole it has a beauty, delicacy, emotion and religious depth that are unsurpassed in Arabic mystical poetry. His medium is the formal ode. Amorous union is his recurrent theme, and his vocabulary and symbolism are erotic. His mannered style does not pall, because of a felicitous sensitivity to harmony, melody and rhythm. Though reading like ecstatic love lyrics, his poems radiate a spirituality consistent with their esoteric meaning. His two most famous poems are his *Khamriyya* (Wine Poem), which treats of the intoxication of divine love, and his *Naẓm as-Sulūk* (Mystic's Progress) – also called the 'Great Poem in Ṭ'. (*EI*², III, 763–4)

Ibn Ḥazm ('Abenhazam') (994–1064). Outstanding Andalusian author, scholar and thinker. A native of Cordova (of indigenous stock despite his claims to Persian ancestry), he began his career in politics. As Umayyad power in Spain collapsed, he see-sawed between office and prison before abandoning his profession (post 1027–31) to devote himself entirely to scholarship. He died in Montija, Huelva. His first prose work, *Ṭawq al-Ḥamāma* (Dove's Neckring), written in Játiva *c* 1023, is a classic of high *adab*. In polished prose interspersed with poetry he develops the theme of chivalrous love and the psychology of lovers. In spirit the *Ṭawq* is truly Andalusian, owing much to Ibn Ḥazm's own observations. Its universal appeal is witnessed by translations into several European languages. His *magnum opus* is a huge and erudite, if polemical, study of comparative religion, *K. al-Milal wa-n-Niḥal* (On Religious and Philosophical Sects), generally considered the first systematic and critical treatise on the topic. A literalist position in theology and law – Ẓāhirism – embroiled him with influential theologians, and his works were publicly burned in Seville. Some four hundred books are attributed to him, but of these (many of which were probably short tracts) comparatively few have survived. (*EI*², III, 790–99)

Ibn Jubayr (1145–1217). Andalusian man of letters, famed for an important travel-book (*riḥla*) which was the first and among the best of its kind. Born in Valencia, he studied in Játiva and later became secretary to the governor of Granada. From there he started on his first pilgrimage to Mecca (1183–5) to atone for the sin of having drunk wine. Embarking for Alexandria at Ceuta in Morocco, he reached Egypt by way of Sicily and Sardinia and then set out for Mecca via Cairo and the Red Sea. On his way back he passed through Iraq and Syria and at Acre took a ship for Sicily whence he made for Spain. His literary reputation rests on his day-by-day account of this eventful pilgrimage. To the modern reader those parts of his journal which have the greatest stylistic appeal are certain simple but graphic narratives remarkable for an unaccustomed animation. For the historian and geographer the work is valued for its wealth of information. As regards sequence and structure, the *riḥla* provided a model for the great Moroccan traveller, Ibn Baṭṭūṭa (1304–69 or 1377), whose book also incorporates material from his Andalusian predecessor. After a second trip to the East (1189–91) of which he left no record Ibn Jubayr undertook a third. He died, however, during his stay in Alexandria. (*EI*², III, 755)

Ibn Khaldūn ('Abd ar-Raḥmān) (1332–1406). Brilliant historian and political theorist. Born in Tunis into an Andalusian immigrant family, he took up a political and administrative career and during the first phase of his life served various rulers in Barbary and Spain. In 1375 he withdrew from the turbulence of political life to a quiet spot near Oran (Algeria). There he spent four years writing his universal history, *Kitāb al-'Ibar* (Instructive Examples) which he prefaced with an introduction entitled *al-Muqaddima* (Prolegomena). After another four years in Tunis he left for Egypt and in 1387 performed the Pilgrimage to Mecca. In 1400 he was taken to Damascus where he played a leading part in negotiations with the Tatar conqueror Tamerlane. He died and was buried in Cairo. The *K. al-'Ibar* proper is important mainly as a source of North African political history. The *Muqaddima*, however, is of universal interest and has been hailed in modern times as a work of genius. Toynbee even goes so far as to describe it as 'the greatest work of its kind that has ever yet been created by any mind in any time or place'. It is a theory of history in which the author anticipates many modern concepts of history and sociology. Careful scrutiny of past records and current events lead him to conclude that political, social and economic phenomena present patterns sufficiently constant to permit the formulation of general principles underlying the genesis of political units, the evolution of states, etc. He recognises that due allowance must be made for environmental influences. His other works include an autobiography. (*EI*², III, 825–31)

Ibn al-Khaṭīb, styled **Lisān ad-Dīn** (1313–74). Andalusian belletrist, poet, biographer and historian. Born in Loja, he spent his youth in Granada and began his career in the Naṣrid chancellery. From 1354 to 1359 he was right-hand man of Riḍwān, vizier of Muḥammad V. Upon the latter's deposition he fled to Morocco and settled for a time in Salé. In 1362 Muḥammad V, now restored, persuaded him with some difficulty to return to Granada as vizier. His position and temperament made him many enemies and in 1370 he stole away to Morocco where his foes succeeded in having him assassinated while in prison on a charge of heresy. He was a prolific author with a gift for artistic prose. His historical writings, which include a monograph on Granada (*al-Iḥāṭa*) and a history of the Naṣrids (*al-Lamḥa al-Badriyya*) as well as a diary of his travels in Morocco (*Nufāḍat al-Jirāb*) and a poetic history of the Muslim west, have unique value as historical source material for his period. He was also the last great *muwashshaḥ* poet in Spain. He also wrote a work on the plague in which he detects what we now know as infection. (*EI*², III, 835–7)

Ibn al-Muqaffa' (*c* 721–57). Pioneer of the secretarial school of artistic prose writers, often spoken of as the creator of Arabic prose. A Persian noble by birth (originally named Rūzbeh), he spent most of his life as a Zoroastrian, but finally embraced Islam. After a sound education in Arabic at Baṣra and additional training under Bedouin mentors, he began his career as an Umayyad official, subsequently passing into Abbasid service. At thirty-six he was put to death for alleged heresy, although intellectual arrogance towards the Arab aristocracy was probably the true cause of his fate. His name is primarily linked with *Kalīla wa-Dimna,* an Arabic translation of the Pahlavi version of the Sanskrit *Panchatantra.* Around two jackals, K. and D., a series of fables are developed in which birds and animals utter maxims on sound government, good conduct, etc. Adapting his material to the tastes of his readers, the translator added material of his own. The end-product is a masterpiece of Arabic prose literature in its own right. Apart from translating the *Khudāy-Nāmeh*, a Pehlevi history of Iranian kings, Ibn al-Muqaffa' also wrote original works which include *al-Adab al-Kabīr*, an ethical and didactic tract for men of state, and an epistle entitled *K. aṣ-Ṣaḥāba* and addressed to the Caliph Manṣūr on the organisation of the state with suggestions for reforms, notably in the army.

Ibn al-Mu'tazz (861–908). Neo-classical poet, son of an Abbasid caliph through a slave mother. On the death of his cousin Mu'taḍid, he was proclaimed caliph but after one day's reign he was assassinated. Until his proclamation he seems only to have been a scholar and man of letters. As a poet he turned conventional metres and classical diction to new uses (*eg* in epistolary and descriptive verse). The virtues and martial successes of Mu'taḍid he lauded not only in a series of panegyrics, but also, unconventionally, in an epic-type poem in more than four hundred verses covering the caliph's whole life. His *dīwan* also includes an apology for the Abbasid dynasty. Anthologist and critic as well as poet, he wrote the first treatise on literary figures in poetry (*K. al-Badī'*). In prose he seems to have popularised descriptive pieces and literary epistles on a range of themes. (*EI*[2], III, 892–3)

Ibn Qutayba (828–89). Essayist, literary critic, philologist, lexicographer and historian. The son of a Persian father, he was born either in Baghdad or Kūfa. After several years as cadi of Dīnawār, he taught in Baghdad where he subsequently died. In philology he was an eclectic of the so-called Baghdad school. Despite his origins, he was anti-Shu'ūbiyya and staunchly defended the Arabic humanities which, as a devout Muslim, he greatly respected. He set out to stem the flowing tide of Perso-Aramaean thought, Greek philosophy and scepticism and to provide the secretarial class with a comprehensive education in Arabic culture. Limiting the influence of the Persian tradition, he sought to produce the *homo islamicus*. To him, Arabic language was all-important, and in his *Adab al-Kātib* (Culture of the Secretary) he teaches correct usage. His greatest work was the 10-volumed *'Uyūn al-Akhbār* (Sources of Information) in which he takes subject after subject (government, war, eloquence, etc.) and treats them anecdotally with adapted references to Tradition, Arabic poetry, wisdom of Persian kings, etc. His *K. al-Ma'ārif* (Subjects of Knowledge) is perhaps the oldest general history in Arabic and takes in Biblical legends and the history of the southern Arabian kings. In his *K. ash-Shi'r wa-sh-Shu'arā'* (Poetry and Poets) he applies aesthetic as well as philological criteria to selected Arabic verses. The title of his *Tafḍīl al-'Arab* (Superiority of the Arabs) speaks for itself. (*EI*[2], III, 844–7)

Ibn Quzmān ('Aben Guzmán') (*c* 1078/80 – 1160). A Cordovan of excellent family, but of dissolute ways, he was the principal literary exponent of the Andalusian *zajal* (popular ballad). Despite a sound education in the Arabic humanities, he chose to be a wandering minstrel singing popular lyrics in the vernacular. His themes are often taken from formal poetry and parodied or modified to his taste. To his one hundred and fifty-nine *zajals* contained in Nykl's *Cancionero* (1933) additions may now be made on the basis of another manuscript. His poems are one of the few surviving sources for the study of Hispano-Arab dialect. (*EI*[2], III, 849–52)

Ibn ar-Rūmī (836–96). Poet of Byzantine extraction, native of Baghdad. Lampoonist as well as panegyrist, he was poisoned by a vizier who feared his satire. His failure to win recognition in high places caused him bitter disappointment and a sense of grievance which found its way into his poetry. His work is highly individual, its originality lying in the treatment of single themes – often in philosophical vein the subjective development of his ideas, and the concreteness of his observations. His satires are sharp, but not coarse. In diction he is simple and pleasing. (*EI*², III, 907–9)

Ibn Ṭufayl (Abū Bakr, whence Lat. 'Abubacer'), (*c* 1100–10 – 1185). Andalusian philosopher with mystical leanings and literary talent, born in Guadix. Versed in medicine and science, he became physician to the Almohad Abū Ya'qūb Yūsuf (1163–84) in Marrakesh where he subsequently died. He was a friend of the young Ibn Rushd (Averroes) whom he recommended to the Almohad. His fame rests on a philosophical romance, *Ḥayy b. Yaqẓān* (Alive, son of Awake), known to Europe in Pococke's Latin translation *Philosophus Autodidactus* (1671). The narrative develops around the growth and mental progress of a new-born child, Ḥayy b. Yaqẓān, who is reared by a gazelle on a desert island and evolves until he attains the maturity of the perfect philosopher. Ḥayy's meeting with an unexpected newcomer whose views coincide with his own ends in their agreeing to go to the island from which the stranger hails in order to convert the inhabitants to their philosophical religion. The confusion they cause convinces them of their error in interfering with traditional beliefs. Philosophical religion, they learn, can only bring happiness to the few, and then only if they withdraw from the world. Philosophy is not the supreme goal, but mystical contemplation. Based on an earlier work by Ibn Sīnā (Avicenna), the story poses the problem of the relationship between religion and philosophy. (*EI*², III, 330–34)

Ibn Zaydūn (1003–71). Celebrated Andalusian poet in the classical tradition, born in Cordova where he saw Umayyad power collapse and pass to an Arab oligarchy led by Abū 'l-Ḥazm b. Jahwar. The inspiration of his masterpieces was the beautiful Umayyad princess, Wallāda, a socially unconventional poetess, who, having fired and responded to his love, forsook him for Abū 'l-Ḥazm's vizier. When all persuasion, poetic and otherwise, had failed to regain her, he lampooned his rival in an epistle of great literary merit and erudition. Imprisonment followed, and, while in gaol, he wrote some of his tenderest poems. Having escaped, he wrote another, now famous, epistle appealing for clemency. He was successful and restored to favour. Not long after the death of Abū 'l-Ḥazm he again fell into disfavour and, after wandering from court to court, entered the service of the 'Abbādids of Seville. He was with Mu'tamid at the conquest of Cordova. Sent on a mission to Seville, he died there. Though not original in form or style, Ibn Zaydūn's poetry has an appealing freshness and charm. Using his metres to the best advantage, he captures highly individual moods and experiences. Transitions in the sequence of his images, emotions and ideas are smooth and natural. His feeling for natural beauty is characteristic. (*EI*², III, 973–4)

Imru' al-Qays (*d c* 540). Pre-Islamic poet whose famous *mu'allaqa* is perhaps the most esteemed of all Arabic poems. His life story is shrouded in so much legend that fact can barely be distinguished from fiction. The son of one Ḥujr whose father had established the ephemeral desert kingdom of Kinda in central Arabia, he is said to have been banished by his father because of an incurable passion for poetry which the latter despised. Wandering among the tribes, he kept bad company and soon became a notorious womaniser. Nevertheless it was upon him that the eventual duty of avenging his father's assassination devolved. His own death is attributed to the treachery of Justinian with whom he had allied himself. His poetry is graphic, passionate and highly individual in treatment. Somewhat fancifully he has been credited by various Arab writers with the invention of certain features of the old *qaṣīda*, notably the deserted encampment theme.

–Jāḥiẓ (776?–869). Belletrist of rare intelligence (but of repulsive appearance), unique prose-writer and greatest essayist in Arabic literature. An Arab of humble origins with black African ancestry, he was born in Baṣra where he acquired an excellent all-round education. Temperamentally neither a courtier nor a bureaucrat, he was quick to abandon a career in the service of the caliph Ma'mūn. This did not prevent his remaining in Baghdad, however, where he spent much of his life. Although a Mu'tazilite, he was spared Mutawakkil's inquisition and, having achieved widespread fame, finally died of old age in Baṣra. A man of catholic tastes and insatiable curiosity, he was familiar as well with the speech and lore of the Bedouin in the markets as with the refinements of Persian culture and the discipline of Greek learning. His encyclopaedic knowledge of gnomic and technical literature he harnessed to the study of mankind, to which end he cultivated all disciplines and all elements of society. His writings, therefore, leave a revealing picture of all aspects of contemporary life and widen the scope of Arabic literature. His work is the most perfect example of *adab* as conceived by the literati of high Abbasid culture. He is credited with almost two hundred works, of which thirty survive in whole and fifty in part. The best known is his seven-volume *K. al-Ḥayawān* (On Animals), an amorphous, but picturesque, treatise of greater literary than zoological interest, demonstrating animal evolution and the unity of creation and touching on human geography, climatology and animal psychology. His *K. al-Bayān* (On Clarity of Expression) is an anecdotal treatise intended to illustrate the Arabs' gift for poetry and the resources of their language. The *K. al-Bukhalā'* (On Misers) is an incisive analysis of avarice directed primarily at the stingy Persian bourgeoisie of Iraq. Deliberately discursive, Jāḥiẓ usually aims to teach by entertainment and contrives to hold one's interest by random changes of topic and shifts from jest to earnest and vice versa. He is gay, witty and loquacious, is a keen observer with a sense of humour which makes him a good caricaturist, and he has an independence of spirit which leaves him free to shock and scandalise his fellows, particularly the ponderous Persian secretaries whom he dislikes. His style is balanced, harmonious, vigorous and so individual as to be immediately identified. (*EI*², II, 385–7)

Jamīl (*c* 660–701). Poet of the Arab tribe 'Udhra whose name is linked with the Medinese, or '*udhrī*, love-lyric. The Hejaz and Nejd were his homelands, but he travelled as far as Egypt. After falling hopelessly in love with Buthayna, whose parents married her to another, he forever lamented his loss poetically in tender, passionate tones. His verses, of which not more than eight hundred survive, constitute a poetry of sublimation exalting self-discipline and the nobility and purity of love. (*EI*², II, 427–8)

Jarīr (*d c* 730). Umayyad poet of central Arabian origin, living mostly in Iraq, particularly famed for his verbal battles with Farazdaq and Akhṭal (*qqv*). His unblemished life, lived according to comparatively high Islamic standards, contrasted with Farazdaq's scandalous ways. Koranic and religious touches are a feature of his poetry, but his piety does not deny him the use of cutting and unseemly language in satire. His *dīwān* also includes panegyric and, to a lesser extent, finely executed elegies. His style is natural and his diction fluent. Akhṭal admired his treatment of the *nasīb* and his skill in the use of simile. (*EI*², II, 479–80)

–Jurjānī ('Abd al-Qāhir) (*d* 1078). Philologist and author of works on literary criticism of whose life we know very little more than that he hailed from Jurjān in north-east Persia. Apart from a number of grammatical works he wrote two treaties on poetics and rhetoric: firstly, *Dalā'il al-I'jāz* (Proofs of Inimitability), in which he aimed to demonstrate the inimitability of the Koran on the basis of syntactic stylistics, and secondly, *Asrār al-Balāgha* (Secrets of Eloquence), a penetrating analysis of literary figures according to logical, psychological and aesthetic criteria. Because he is presenting new and original ideas, his periods are apt to be prolix. He is, however, a lively and sensitive writer, and his best work is literature in its own right.

–Mutanabbī ('Would-be Prophet') (916–65). Outstanding Arab poet, son of a Kūfan water-carrier, educated at Kūfa, Damascus, and in the desert. Involved at an early age in politico-religious movements, he was imprisoned in 933 after leading an abortive revolt in which he claimed prophethood (whence his name). From 948 he enjoyed the patronage of the Ḥamdānid Sayf ad-Dawla, who, as champion of Islam against the Byzantines, afforded scope for true panegyric. After nine poetically glorious years, he fell under a cloud and took refuge in Egypt. Much disillusioned there with the patronage of the Ikhshīdid 'regent', a negro and former slave, he finally fled to Baghdad in 960. In 965 he was murdered by bandits while returning to Baghdad from a visit to the Būyids in Shīrāz. Mutanabbī's arrogance made him many enemies, and his poetry was much criticised for alleged plagiarism and infelicitous imagery. For all the controversy that long raged around him, he has proved to be the most-quoted of all Arab poets and his very real merits have earned him due recognition. In his *qaṣīda* construction he tends – exceptionally for an Arab poet – to aim at interconnexion and coherence of the verses so that the poem presents itself as a whole rather than as a series of independent lines. His spirit, ideals and virtues are purely Arab.

–Shanfarā, fl. end of fifth century AD (*d* 510(?)). Desert poet. Captured as a child and reared by the tribe of Salamān, he later learned, through an offence, the truth of his origin. Severing all tribal connexions, he roamed the desert as an outlaw. His poetry, a record of defiance, bitterness, ferocity and pride, projects a sharply defined picture of the hardship, hunger and privation of a life shared only with the creatures of the wild. It makes an immediate and lasting impression and must be accounted among the finest verse in the Arabic language.

–Tanūkhī (–Muḥassin) (938–94). Arab belletrist, son of a cadi of Baṣra. Some time before 965 he was appointed Hanafite cadi of a town near Ahwāz, but in 970 he was in disgrace in Baghdad. In 977 he won the friendship of the Būyid ʻAḍud ad-Dawla, but from 980 their relationship deteriorated and by 983 he was in utter and final disgrace. The remainder of his life – spent in Baghdad – was uneventful. His three major works are *K. Nishwār al-Muḥādara* (Table-talk), *K. al-Mustajād min Faʻalāt al-Ajwād* (On the Best Traits of the Generous), and *al-Faraj baʻd ash-shidda* (Relief after Distress). The first is an unmethodical miscellany of anecdotes, each suitable for recounting in different situations. The second is an anecdotal collection centred on the theme of generosity and magnanimity. Both works, particularly the first, in which his father is a prominent informant, draw on oral sources. The third is a collection of illustrations of deliverance from impending disaster at the eleventh hour. Its aim is to inspire men of culture with confidence and fortitude. The work is one of a genre initiated 150 years earlier by Madā'inī and continued after Tanūkhī. By their very nature Tanūkhī's writings present an uneven style. They are revealing social documents whose author is best described as an optimistic moralist with a gift for light entertainment.

–Tawḥīdī (Abū Ḥayyān) (*c* 922/32–1023). Essayist, philosopher and exceptionally talented prose-writer and stylist. Born either in Iraq or in Persia, he studied in Baghdad and earned his living as a scribe. He then sought, in Rayy, the patronage of the renowned Būyid viziers, Ibn al-ʻAmīd and Ibn al-ʻAbbād, but being of a difficult and misanthropic nature, he got on with neither and in due course peevishly caricatured them in *K. al-Wazīrayn* (The Two Viziers). During the period 983–6 his fortunes improved under the patronage, in Baghdad, of Ibn Saʻdān, vizier of the Būyid prince Ṣamṣām ad-Dawla. There he was greatly influenced by a Neoplatonist, Abū Sulaymān al-Manṭiqī, around whom he developed a series of conversational pieces entitled *al-Muqābasāt*. Apart from a ten-volumed anthology of *adab* and a work on Jāḥiẓ (*qv*) whom he admired, he wrote *K. al-Imtāʻ wa-l-Mu'ānasa* (On Gratification and Good Company), a touched-up record of miscellaneous conversations with Ibn Sa'dān. His works also include a treatise on friendship. After Ibn Sa'dān's death he never seems to have prospered materially. He is said to have been buried in Shīrāz. His work is remarkable for incisive characterisation and for the light it sheds on contemporary society and culture. (*EI*², I, 126–7)

'Umar b. Abī Rabī'a (644–712). To the best of our knowledge, the first Arab love poet. The son of a rich Meccan of the tribe of Quraysh, he seems to have spent his youth in Medina and his adult life in Mecca. Because he is an archetype, the facts of his biography, obscured as they are by fiction, are difficult to establish. Even such of his poetry as can be regarded as genuine – imitations have been fathered on him – shows signs of retouching and 'improvement'. The impression he leaves is that of a boastful philanderer and irresistible heart-breaker. His verse, unlike that of the Bedouin poets, is urban and reflects the life of a pleasure-loving man-about-town. His love is sensual and human, real and realistic without at the same time sinking to indecent or depraved levels. He is the antithesis of Jamīl (*qv*) who idealises and sublimates love into a hopeless and unrequited form.

BIBLIOGRAPHY

EI². – *Encyclopaedia of Islām*, new ed. by H. A. R. Gibb and others, in course of publication, Leiden, 1954 to date; A–I so far published. (Replaces a now largely outdated work, 4 vols. and suppl., 1913–34; detailed bibliographies with entries.)

PEARSON, J. D. *Index Islamicus* Cambridge 1958; 2 supplements, 1962 and 1967. (Indispensable classified list of periodical articles covering, so far, the period 1906–65. Contains details of periodicals mentioned below.)

SECTION 1

BROCKELMANN, C. *History of the Islamic Peoples* English version, London, 1949; New York, 1960.

GABRIELI, F. *The Arabs: a Compact History* English version, New York, 1963. *Muhammad and the Conquests of Islam* London, 1968. (Excellent paperback.)

GIBB, H. A. R. *Mohammedanism: an Historical Survey* 2nd edn., London, 1961.

GRUNEBAUM, G. E. von *Medieval Islam* Chicago, 1953.

HOLT, P. M. and others *The Cambridge History of Islam*, 2 vols., Cambridge, 1970.

LÉVI-PROVENÇAL, E. *Histoire de l'Espagne musulmane* (2nd edn., 3 vols., Paris, 1950–53. (Standard work on Muslim Spain up to AD 1031.)

LEWIS, B. *The Arabs in History*, 4th edn., New York and London, 1966. (Excellent up-to-date summary with bibliography. Paperback edn. See same author on Abbasids in EI², s.v.)

SAUVAGET, J. *Introduction to the History of the Muslim East: a Bibliographical Guide* Berkeley and Los Angeles, 1965. (Based on C. Cahen's 2nd edn. of Sauvaget's *Introduction à l'histoire, etc* (Paris, 1961). Standard critical bibliography.)

WATT, W. M. *A History of Islamic Spain*, New York and Edinburgh, 1965.

SECTION 2

A. *The Medieval Period*

ABD-EL-JALIL, J.-M. *Brève histoire de la littérature arabe* 8th edn., Paris, 1963.

ARBERRY, A. J. *Arabic Poetry: a Primer for Students* Cambridge, 1967. (Arabic text with facing literal translation and notes, preceded by a very useful introduction covering such points as metres, imagery, *etc*. Available in paperback.)

The Holy Koran: an Introduction with Selections London, 1953.

The Koran Interpreted World's Classics, London, 1964. (Best literary translation.)

Moorish Poetry: a Translation of The Pennants, an Anthology Compiled in 1248 by the Andalusian Ibn Sa'īd Cambridge, 1953.

The Seven Odes [Mu'allaqāt] London, 1957 (Studies and translations.)

BLACHÈRE, R. *Le Coran* Paris, 1957. (Annotated translation of the Koran with index.)

Histoire de la littérature arabe des origines à la fin du XVe siècle de J-C. in course of publication, vol. I, 1–3, Paris, 1952–66. (A major work.)

BROCKELMANN, C. *Geschichte der arabischen Literatur* (2nd edn., 2 vols., Leiden, 1943–9. Supplements to 1st edn., 3 vols., 1937–42).

EI², ARTICLES 'Ghazal', 'Ḥadīth', 'Ḥamāsa', 'Hidjā' '[*Hijā*]; on metrics, see 'Arūḍ'; on stylistics, rhetoric, *etc*, see 'Badī'', 'Balāgha', 'Bayān'; on legends, story cycles, *etc*, see 'Alf Layla wa-Layla', 'Sīrat 'Antar' (*sv* 'Antar), 'Ayyām al-'Arab', 'Hilāl'.

GABRIELI, F. *Le più belle pagine della letteratura araba* Milan, 1957.

La storia della letteratura araba Milan, 1951.

GARCÍA GÓMEZ, E. *Poesía arabigoandaluza: breve síntesis histórica* Madrid, 1952.

GERHARDT, M. I. *The Art of Story-Telling: a Literary Study of the Thousand and One Nights* Leiden, 1963.

GIBB, H. A. R. *Arabic Literature* 2nd rev. edn., Oxford, 1963.

GONZÁLEZ PALENCIA, A. *Historia de la literatura arabigo-española* 2nd edn., Barcelona, 1945.

GRAF, G. *Geschichte der christlichen arabischen Literatur* 5 vols., Rome, 1953–60.

GRUNEBAUM, G. E. von 'Islamic Literature: Arabic' *Near Eastern Culture and Society* ed. T. Cuyler Young, Princeton, 1951.

A Tenth Century Document of Arab Literary Theory and Criticism Chicago, 1950.

'The Aesthetic Foundation of Arabic Literature', *Comparative Literature*, 4, 1952.

'Aspects of Arabic Urban Literature', *Al-Andalus* 20, 1955.

KRITZECK, J. ed. *Anthology of Islamic Literature* London, 1964.

LATHAM, J. D. 'Classical Arabic Literature' in *A Bibliographical Introduction to Islamic and Middle Eastern Studies*, ed. Hopwood and Grimwood-Jones, Leiden, 1971.

LYALL, Sir Charles *Translations of Ancient Arabian Poetry* repr. London, 1930.

MORLAND, H. *Arabic-Andalusian Casidas* London, 1949.

MUBARAK, Z. *La prose arabe au IVe siècle de l'Hégire* Paris, 1931.

NICHOLSON, R. A. *A Literary History of the Arabs* 3rd edn., Cambridge, 1953. (Standard work.)

NYKL, A. R. *Hispano-Arabic Poetry and its Relations with the Old Provençal Troubadours* Baltimore, 1946.

PÉRÈS, H. *La poésie andalouse en arabe classique au XIe siècle* 2nd edn., Paris, 1953.

ROSENTHAL, F. *A History of Muslim Historiography* 2nd edn., New York and London, 1968.

THAʿĀLIBĪ *Laṭā'if al-maʿārif* (The Book of Curious and Entertaining Information), trans. and ed. C. E. Bosworth, Edinburgh, 1968.

TRABULSI, A. *La critique poétique des arabes* Damascus, 1956.

VERNET, J. *Literatura árabe*, Barcelona, n.d. [*c* 1966.]

WIET, G. *Introduction à la littérature arabe* Paris, 1966.

B. *From 1800*

Many general works mentioned in the preceding section contain material on this period.

ABDEL-MEGUID, A. *The Modern Arabic Short Story* Cairo, n.d. [*c* 1955].

ABUSHADY, A. Z. 'Contemporary Egyptian Literature', *Middle Eastern Affairs*, 2, 1951.

ARBERRY, A. J. *Modern Arabic Poetry: an Anthology with English Verse Translations* repr. Cambridge, 1967.

BLACHÈRE, R. 'La poésie arabe au ʿIraq et à Baġdād jusqu'à Maʿrūf al-Ruṣāfī', *Arabica*, 9, 1962.

CACHIA, P. J. E. 'Modern Arabic Literature', *The Islamic Near East* ed. D. Grant, Toronto, 1960.

GABRIELI, F. (i) 'Correnti e figure della letteratura araba contemporanea', *Oriente Moderno* 19, 1939; (ii) 'Contemporary Arabic Fiction', *Middle East Studies* 2, 1963.

GERMANUS, A K. J. 'Trends of Contemporary Arabic Literature', *Islamic Quarterly* 3 and 4, 1956 and 1957.

GIBB, H. A. R. 'Studies in Contemporary Arabic Literature', *Studies on the Civilization of Islam*, London, 1962. (Articles reprinted from the *Bulletin of the School of Oriental and African Studies* (*BSOAS*) between 1928–9 and 1933.)

HUSSEIN, M. K. (i) 'Modern Egyptian Literature'; (ii) 'Modern Egyptian Story Writers', *Indo-Asian Culture*, 6, 1957.

JARGY, S. 'Poètes arabes d'avant-garde', *Orient* 18, 1961.

KHAWAM, R. *Nouvelles arabes* Paris, 1964.

KHULUSI, S. A. (i) 'Modern Arabic Fiction with Special Reference to Iraq' *Islamic Culture* 30, 1956; (ii) 'Modern Arabic Poetry', *ibid.* 32, 1958; (iii) 'Trends of Short-Story Writing in Iraq', *Proceedings of the 24th International Congress of Orientalists, 1957*.

KRACHKOVSKY, I. Y. (i) 'Der historische Roman in der neueren arabischen Literatur' in *Welt des Islams* 12, 1930–1; (ii) 'Die Literatur der arabischen Emigranten in Amerika, 1895–1915', *Monde Oriental*, 21, 1927.

LANDAU, J. M. *Studies in the Arab Theater and Cinema* Philadelphia, 1958. (Contains biographies of Shawqī, Tawfīq al-Hakīm and Maḥmūd Taymūr as well as the fullest list of Arabic plays and translations from 1848 to 1956.)

MAKARIUS, R. and L. *Anthologie de la littérature arabe contemporaine* Paris, 1964.

MINGANTI, P. 'Il movimento iracheno di poesia libera', *Levante* 8 i 1961.

MOREH, S. 'The Iraqi Poet Nāzik al-Malā'ika and Free Verse, *etc*', *Hamizrah Hehadash* xvi, 1966.

PELLAT, CH. 'La prose arabe à Baghdad', *Arabica* 9, 1962.

PÉRÈS, H. *La littérature arabe et l'Islam par les textes: les XIXe et XXe siècles*, 6th edn., Algiers, 1955. (Useful introduction in French (texts in Arabic) and full bibliography with details of works, *etc* in European languages.)

'Le roman, le conte, et la nouvelle dans la littérature arabe moderne' *AIEO*, 3, 1937.

ROSSI, P. 'Impressions sur la poésie d'Irak, etc.', *Orient* 12, 1959.

SAÏD, K. 'Origines et tendances de la poésie arabe moderne', *Orient* 18, 1961.

SCHOONOVER, K. 'A survey of the Best Modern Arabic Books', *Muslim World* 42, 1952.

VECCIA VAGLIERI, L. 'Notizie bio-bibliographiche su autori arabi moderni', *Annali dell' Istituto Universitario Orientale di Napoli*, N.S.1, 1940.

The bulk of material on modern – and especially contemporary – authors is to be found in periodicals. The reader should therefore consult the sections on modern Arabic literature in Pearson's *Index Islamicus* and supplements (see above). Among translations and studies of individual authors in book form the following are worthy of note:

Kāmil ḤUSAYN

Qarya ẓālima – City of Wrong, trans. K. Cragg, Amsterdam, 1959.

Ṭāhā ḤUSAYN

(i) *An Egyptian Childhood* [*al-Ayyām*], trans. E. H. Paxton, London, 1932; (ii) *The Stream of Days* [*al-Ayyām*], trans. H. Wayment, 2nd rev. edn., London, 1948; (iii) CACHIA, P. *Ṭāhā Ḥusayn, etc*, London, 1956.

Tawfīq al-ḤAKĪM

(i) *Maze of Justice*, trans. A. S. Eban London/Dublin, 1947; (ii) *Diario de un fiscal rural*, trans. E. García Gómez, Madrid, 1955.

Khalīl JIBRĀN

(i) *The Voice of the Master*, trans. A. R. Ferris, London, 1960; (ii) *The Procession*, trans. G. Kheirallah, New York, 1958; contains biographical sketch.

MARTÍNEZ MÓNTAVEZ, P.

Siete cuentistas egípcios contemporáneos Madrid, 1964.

Mīkhā'īl NU'AYMA

El rumor de los párpados, trans. L. Martínez Martín, Madrid, 1958.

SECTION 3

In the case of authors for whom we indicate entries in EI² the reader should consult that source. Additional bibliographical data will be found in Pearson's *Index Islamicus* and supplements.

Abū 'l-Alā' Al-Ma'arrī

(i) NICHOLSON, R. A. *Studies in Islamic Poetry*, Cambridge, 1921; especially important for the *Luzūmiyyāt*; (ii) *The Luzūmiyāt*, trans. A. Rihani, New York, 1918; (iii) *The Letters of Abu 'l-'Alā'*, trans. D. S. Margoliouth, Oxford, 1898.

Ibn Al-Fāriḍ

(i) *The Mystical Poems, etc*, trans. A. J. Arberry, Dublin, 1956; (ii) *The Poem of the Way*, trans. A. J. Arberry, London, 1952.

Ibn Ḥazm

(i) *El collar de la paloma*, trans. E. García Gómez, Madrid, 1952; with important introduction; (ii) *The Ring of the Dove*, trans. A. J. Arberry, London, 1953; (iii) *Epître morale*, trans. N. Tomiche, Beirut, 1961; (iv) Asín Palacios, M., *Abenházam de Cordoba*, 5 vols., Madrid, 1927–32.

Ibn Khaldūn

The Muqaddimah, trans. F. Rosenthal, 3 vols., London, 1958; the translation in no way reflects the style of the original; (ii) MAHDI, M., *Ibn Khaldun's Philosophy of History, etc*, London, 1957.

Ibn Al-Khaṭīb

ANTUÑA, M. *El polígrafo granadino Abenaljatib*, Escorial, 1926.

Ibn Al-Muqaffa'

(i) *Le livre de Kalila et Dimna*, trans. A. Miquel, Paris, 1957; (ii) Gabrieli, F., 'L'opera di Ibn al-Muqaffa'', *Rivista degli Studi Orientali*, 13, 1932.

Ibn Qutayba

HUSEINI, I. M. *The Life and Works of Ibn Qutayba* Beirut, 1950.

Ibn Quzmān

(i) *El cancionero de Aben Guzmán* Madrid, 1933; text in Latin alphabet, partial transl. by A. R. Nykl; (ii) HOENERBACH, W. and RITTER, H., 'Neue materialien zum *Zacal* I: Ibn Quzmān', *Oriens* 3, 1950.

Ibn Zaydūn

COUR, A. *Un poète arabe d'Andalousie*, Constantine, 1920.

–Jurjānī

Die Geheimnisse der Wortkunst, etc, trans. H. Ritter, Wiesbaden, 1959.

–Mutanabbī

Poems of al-Mutanabbī; a Selection with Introduction, Translations, and Notes by A. J. Arberry, Cambridge, 1967.

–Shanfarā

The L-Poem of the Arabs, trans. J. W. Redhouse, London, 1881.

–Tanūkhī

(i) *The Table-Talk of a Mesopotamian Judge*, trans. D. S. Margoliouth, London, 1922; (ii) FAKKAR, R. *At-Tanûẖî et son livre la Délivrance après l'angoisse* Cairo, 1955.

JEWISH LITERATURE

Elizabeth E. Eppler

HISTORICAL AND CULTURAL BACKGROUND

National literatures usually reflect the history of a people and land throughout the ages, and the influence which neighbouring or immigrant cultures had upon the cultural development of the national literature. This rule applies only partly to Jewish literature embracing three millennia and stretching over five continents.

Literary historians have made several attempts to divide Jewish literature into convenient periods, but these are invidious and often confusing. Neither is it really expedient to make geographical divisions, for these break down hopelessly as soon as the Jewish diaspora stretches over the globe. Moreover Hebrew literary creativity has once again, after three thousand years, returned to the Middle East where it originated. It has come to a new life imbued by the ancient spirit, enriched by the vicissitudes of three thousand years of dispersion, and inspired by the experience of a new homeland; the very language in which this literature is written is, perforce, a unique phenomenon. The ancient tongue of the Old Testament has given way to Aramaic, Greek, Arabic, to all the languages of the dispersion, to that peculiar bastard language, Yiddish, only to be revived, refurbished and once again made into the living, vital, elastic instrument that is the language of a reborn nation in Israel.

THE OLD TESTAMENT

According to Jewish tradition, the *Massoretic* text of the twenty-four Books of the Old Testament was laid down around 250 BC. Bible critics of the last century held that the oldest part of the written Bible was the Song of Deborah (Judges V) dated about 1200 BC, and the most recent Psalms dated around AD 70; furthermore, that some Books were not included in the Canon until the first century AD.

New light has been shed upon the whole problem since the discovery of the Dead Sea Scrolls. While some of the Scrolls raise serious doubts as to the origin of Christianity, the Biblical texts among them proved the existence of an unbroken tradition from the second century BC to the present day. Archaeological excavations carried out in recent years revealed other scrolls and fragments, all demonstrating this unbroken continuity in Jewish traditional literature.

This Biblical text has remained a live instrument in the hands of later Jewish writers and, by using its language and moulding it to the needs of the hour, writers and poets have kept it alive for three millennia. Jewish post-Biblical literature begins with the Apocryphal and Apocalyptic Books which form a connecting link between Bible and Talmudic and Aggadic literature of about the middle of the second century AD. This literature also provides a link for Christians between the Old and New Testaments. The Apocrypha were intended to be a continuation of the Bible. Indeed, they follow the same lines – history, prophecy, poetry and didactic writings. The only part of Biblical writing which is scantily represented is law. As time progressed, these books remained in the hands of the privileged few. Hence, the name Apocrypha (hidden), for which a new Hebrew name, *Geniza*, was found. Another reason for this name was that some of these were attributed to authors of various of the Biblical books, such as the Epistle of Jeremiah, the Book of Baruch and the Wisdom of Solomon. Their distant origin was explained by the fact that they had been hidden away until revealed at the appointed time.

The Apocalyptic books are really not very different from the Apocrypha, except that the former are chiefly of a prophetic nature. The main difference between these and the Biblical prophetic books is that the latter were divinely inspired. There are other characteristics, *eg* those of style and the fact that the authors of the Apocalyptic books are not revealed.

The books have to be seen against the background of the period in which they were written, a period of tribulation, beginning with the fall of the First Temple, Graeco-Syrian rule, and ending with the fall of the Second Temple and dispersion. These three hundred years of vicissitudes were interrupted only by the Hasmonean rebellion and the eighty years of peace under the rule of the Hasmoneans. The second Commonwealth was rather a poor period in Jewish history and did not produce all the glories foretold by the Biblical prophets. The discrepancy between Prophetic promises and reality resulted in the special Messianic tone of this literature, always pointing to a better future. Coupled with this, there is great enthusiasm for the Law of God. Ever since Ezra, the Law, the *Torah* became the centre of Jewish life, and this religious zeal found its expression in both Apocryphal and Apocalyptic literature, since the Apocrypha exhorted the reader to a way of life through Law, and the Apocalyptic books promised consolation to the sufferers of the present, if they adhered to the Law. Moreover, these books, just like the Biblical ones, promised reward to the righteous and punishment to the wicked. Finally, this literature has two more important features, namely, the Last Judgement and the Kingdom of God. Both ideas are well founded in the Prophets, but the atmosphere surrounding the Apocryphal and Apocalyptic books was conducive to the expression of Messianic hope for a better future. The growth of belief in the Kingdom of God was to lead to the eventual rejection, by the Jewish authorities, of the entire literature. A contributing factor to this was also the manifest Hellenic, *ie* alien, influence upon this literature.

THE MISHNAH

The destruction of the Second Temple in AD 70 did not end Jewish settlement in Judea. The Sanhedrin left Jerusalem for Jabneh, already a seat of learning, and this city was, until AD 135, the centre of Jewish culture, with R. Yochanan Ben Zakkai, its founder, in the middle. Around him gathered scholars and pupils and, from their discussions, grew the Rabbinical literature. From the exposition and discussion of the Law as set down in the Pentateuch, grew *Mishnah* (the Oral Law), evolved by the *Tannaim*, the scholars associated with the Jabneh school. The *Tannaim*, beginning with Yochanan Ben Zakkai about AD 70, are divided into four generations. After Yochanan, among whose contemporaries were Hillel and Shammai, representing two opposite schools of interpretation and exegesis, came the generation of R. Akiba (AD 100–130), who was executed by the Romans during the Bar Kochba Revolt. It was at Akiba's school that the first literal Greek translation of the Old Testament was prepared by Aquila, a proselyte pupil of Akiba. The style of Aquila's translation is inferior in style to the Septuagint but is more accurate. To Aquila was also ascribed the Aramaic translation of the Pentateuch, *Targum Onkelos*, of about the fifth century.

The first two generations of *Tannaim* regarded literature as part of life, a means to teach the correct way of living, and sought to systematise both the already written and the oral tradition in an endeavour to propagate their didactic qualities. The third generation, that of Rabbi Meir, attempted to resort to the methods of secular knowledge and science, in order to achieve a better and fuller understanding of the *Torah*. Thus, Jewish literature ceased to be a purely religious exercise. Centuries later when, as a reaction to emancipation and enlightenment, orthodox Jewry retreated behind the high walls of a spiritual ghetto, scorning and even prohibiting the study of secular culture, the enlightened, in their own defence, held up the example of Meir and other *Tannaim* who claimed the right to delve into the secular sciences. The last generation of *Tannaim* was overshadowed by R. Yehuda Ha-Nassi (150–210), the great Patriarch who eventually codified the *Mishnah*. His teaching was so popular and, at the same time, so authoritative that many traditions which survived and were eventually set down were called *Baraitha* (outside) or *Tosephta* (addition) because they were not included in the canon of R. Yehuda. A man of great culture and exquisite manners, R. Yehuda regarded life in its totality, computed from larger and smaller incidents forming part of a great divine scheme. The *Mishnah*, therefore, is an expression of this doctrine. It employs a new language, a mixture of Hebrew and Aramaic, no longer containing the majestic images of Biblical mythology, the powerful phrases of the prophets or the poetry of the Psalms. The form of expression was not the spoken language but a sort of scholarly, staccato idiom. It deals with every aspect of human life, law and morality, matters of the mind, body and soul. Thus, literature was not an independent force but became the written expression of that sometimes intangible concept, the Jewish way of life. In the *Mishnaic* sense this means that man's mind and conscience are inseparable and, therefore, their expressions in religious, ethnical, intellectual or aesthetic literature are equally indivisible. Written by Rabbis who were at the same time artisans whose life and not livelihood was the Law, the *Mishnah* is scholarly and popular at the same time, it is a book about matters sacred written by laymen, since its authors were Rabbis (Teachers) and not priests. The *Mishnah* is divided into six *Sedarim* (Orders). These divide into sixty-three *Massechtot* (Tractates) which, in turn, are divided into *Perakim* (Chapters), and each *Perek* into paragraphs which are the actual *Mishnah*. The six Orders are: *Zeraim* (Seeds), the laws of agriculture; *Moed* (Festivals); *Nashim* (Women), the laws of marriage and divorce; *Nezikin* (Damages, civil and criminal law); *Kodashim* (Holy things), sacrifices; *Tohorot* (Purification), personal and ritual purity.

THE TALMUD

Between AD 220–500, five generations of *Amoraim* developed the *Talmud* (Teaching or Doctrine) as a natural continuation of the *Mishnah*, the text of which is always printed with the *Talmud*. The Talmudic text is called *Gemarah* (supplement, completion, teaching), and often includes, in addition to the *Mishnah* text, elements even older than the latter. By contrast to the *Mishnah*, most of it is written in Aramaic, the vernacular spoken at the time; where Tannaic or other traditional material is used, the Hebrew language is employed. Two distinct works are called *Talmud*, the Palestinian, *Talmud Jerushalmi*, completed about AD 370, and *Talmud Bavli*, the Babylonian, completed a hundred years later. The language of the first is Western Aramaic, that of the second, Eastern Aramaic, akin to Mandaean. Political and religious persecution in Palestine accounted for a Jewish exodus to more hospitable and tolerant lands such as Persia and Babylonia and, while the great seats of learning in Palestine declined and ceased to exist by AD 350, new important scholastic centres were established in Sura, Pumbedhita and Nehardea. The Palestinian and Babylonian *Talmud* each bear the clear imprint of the environment from which they originate. The Palestinian, more terse in style, contains less of the elaborate casuistry of the Babylonian. The former is the result rather of *ad hoc* debates, the latter of systematic discussion of points made in the *Mishnah*, with an eye to posterity. An *Amora* was an orator who chose a Mishnaic passage in which a *Tanna* briefly formulated his view. He then went on to expand, elaborate, clarify and freshly develop his original idea. Being independent thinkers of authority, the *Amoraim* made original contributions to Rabbinic literature. Like the *Tannaim*, they made their living as artisans, agriculturists, physicians, tradesmen. Some of them, the 'Princes of the Captivity in Babylonia' or the patriarchs of Palestine, were aristocrats, but their social standing did not afford them higher authority in the world of learning.

Talmudic material consists of two integral elements, *Halachah* and *Aggadah*; the first, the Law and discussion of the Law which forms by far the major part, and the second, a form of teaching, fable, entertainment, explanation. Built upon the foundation of the *Mishnah*, the *Talmud*, although divided into the same six Orders, often departs from the main subject under discussion and introduces new explanations, debates, sometimes with only a very tenuous relationship to the debated subject. This creates both a tremendous richness of material and a difficulty in obtaining an overall view of the entire work. The method applied is that of debate. A legal thesis of the *Torah* is taken and explained, commented upon, debated, illustrated by means of exemplary fables and didactic anecdotes, until agreement is reached on its application or validity. While the *Mishnah* is a Code of Law, the *Talmud* is like an encyclopaedia which gives direct or indirect information on every aspect of human life as approached by Jewish teaching. This code of behaviour is based on the Pentateuchal concept that life is regulated by the Divinity, and man's reward is determined by two factors, his relation and attitude to God and to his fellow men.

The *Talmud* is thus a complex work of legal, ethical, moral and literary value. It forms the most important link in the chain of Jewish literary tradition. Jewish literature, beginning with the Bible, developed through the *Talmud* and later exegesis and commentary and, although changing through the influence of fresh internal and external stresses, kept the basic national heritage at its focal centre.

THE MIDRASH

The ever-growing fables, didactic anecdotes and stories which went into explaining some point of law or tradition are known under the collective name of *Midrash*, meaning 'study' or 'enquiry'. At first, the *Midrash* was an explanation of the Scriptures but, by contrast to the Talmudic exegesis, in applying poetic material, it gives the Biblical story and characters a colourful setting. The Rabbis, in an endeavour perhaps to popularise a character or underline the importance of an event, surrounded these characters or events with legendary additions, thereby inspiring their audience to deeper thinking, or simply to emphasise a moral teaching. The *Midrash*, though appearing in the *Talmud* in the form of *Aggadah*, has developed as a specific literary genre into two main forms, *Halachic* and *Aggadic*. The former illustrated the practical rules of life and ritual, the latter, more homiletic, explained Scripture itself.

While the Talmud is a commentary on the *Halachah*, taking the laws one by one and seeking the Biblical foundation of each, the *Halachic Midrash* is a commentary on the legal sections of the Pentateuch and derives the *Halachah* from each verse of the text. The *Halachic Midrash* consists of three parts: *Mechilta* (Rule or Measure) on Exodus from Chapter XII to the end; *Sifra* (the Book) on Leviticus, and *Sifre* (Books) on Numbers and Deuteronomy. On the other hand, the *Pesiktah* (Sections) contains chiefly *Aggadic* discourses on sections of the Bible. These *Midrashim* contain a great deal of *Tannaic* material, *ie Aggadah* already included in the Talmud. Later *Midrashim*, like the 4th century *Tanchuma* (named for its supposed author), contain commentary to the whole Pentateuch, while the *Midrash Rabba* explains the whole Pentateuch and the Five Scrolls (Esther, Ruth, Lamentations, Ecclesiastes and Proverbs). This is a highly complex work, dating from different periods, the oldest being *Genesis Rabbah*. The *Midrash Hagadol* (Great Midrash), although similar in name and extent, is different in style and content. There are, in addition, a number of smaller *Midrashim* and anthologies.

While the *Midrash* forms an integral part of Jewish religious tradition, as a literary genre it influenced the development of modern Hebrew and Yiddish literature. The fables, proverbs, folk tales, anecdotes, parables, puns and jokes survived because Bible, *Talmud*, *Mishnah*, *Gemarah* and *Midrash* remained living instruments of Jewish national and spiritual survival. Study and intimate knowledge of this unique national heritage has been the supreme goal towards which generations of Jews strove. Though they were considered sacred, they were never allowed to become the property of the intellectual elite – there is no division of clergy and laity in Judaism. On the contrary, rich and poor alike, from early childhood to their last days, studied, repeated and enlarged upon this vast complex of law and legend. While the *Midrash* contains elements of the folk-lore of other cultures (*eg* the Beast Fables of *Talmud* and *Midrash* were borrowed directly or indirectly from India), and while, in later periods, more foreign elements were added to the fund of stories, the dispersion resulted in distinctly *Midrashic* elements being detectable in the folk-lore of host nations.

Although at the time of the conclusion of the *Talmud*, the Jewish diaspora extended over large sections of the Roman Empire and the Caliphates, the main centres of learning remained in Babylonia and Persia where, until the ninth century, Jews were granted a measure of autonomy under the leadership of the Exilarch. Heading the schools of Sura and Pumbedhita stood the *Geonim* of whose extensive work, however, only fragments survive. They were responsible, at least in part, for arranging the liturgy. They wrote prayers and hymns, fixed the order of service and established the system of *Minhag* (custom) which determines much of the social, religious and commercial practice in Judaism. The early *Geonim* used Hebrew, superseded by Aramaic, and eventually Arabic. The most important of Geonic writings are the *Teshuvot* (Answers or Letters). These originated from the fact that, while the Exilarch (*Resh Geluta*), Jewish Viceroy of the Khalif, acted as a secular head of the Community, the *Geonim* of Sura and Pumpedhita were regarded as the judicial and religious heads of the autonomous community. Their authority and influence extended over all the Mohammedan countries of North Africa and the Iberian Peninsula, and probably other parts of Europe. Their opinion and guidance were sought from many far-flung places and, in response to such enquiries, the *Geonim* sent letters which were eventually collected and edited in great anthologies, such as *Halachot Gedolot*, by Shimon Kayyara in the ninth century. The majority, however, remained as loose letters, many were lost, a great many rediscovered (*Geniza*), chiefly in Egypt. The literary importance of the *Geonic* letters lies not so much in their own stylistic value as in the fact that they were the first examples of a still surviving Hebrew literary mode, *She'elot u-Teshuvot* (Questions and Answers), opinion or guidance on contentious ritual, moral or social problems. These are, traditionally, opinions expressed not *ex cathedra*, but in a persuasive form, and often reflect the social mores of the time.

At the height of *Geonic* influence, in the eighth century, there suddenly appeared a reaction against Rabbinism, taking the form of Karaism. The real reasons for this revolutionary movement were, the unsuccessful bid for the Exilarchy by its founder, Anan Ben David, and the parallel struggle in Islam between Sunnites and Shiites. Just as the Shiites in Islam relied exclusively on the Koran, the Karaites claimed that Judaism has no need or even use for anything but the *Kera* or *Mikra*, the Biblical Text. In addition to Anan Ben David's *Books of Laws*, several other Karaite books survive, most of them in Arabic, but the Sect produced also some Hebrew literary works, such as Shlomo Ben Yerucham's *Milhamot Elohim* (Wars of the Lord), a poetical treatise violently attacking Rabbinism. We also are indebted to the Karaites for the first Hebrew Grammar, *Sefer Ha-Dikduk*, and a large Hebrew dictionary, *Iqqaron.* One of the most outstanding literary products of the period is Yehuda Hadassi's (1075–1160) *Eshkol ha-Kopher* (A Cluster of Cyprus Flowers), an encyclopaedic work written in rhymed acrostics, in which the author criticises not only Judaism but also Christianity and Islam. Although Karaism faded by about the end of the twelfth century, it survived sporadically late into the sixteenth century, when the Lithuanian Isaac Troki wrote *Hizzuk Emunah* (The Strengthening of the Faith), a defence of Judaism and an attack on Christianity. Karaism, now almost completely extinct, had, nevertheless, a positive, though indirect, effect on Rabbinic literature. The need to fight the Karaites with their own weapons produced some of the highlights of Rabbinic thinking and writing, as shown in the work of Saadya Gaon.

Born in Upper Egypt in 882, Saadya Ben Yoseph at the age of twenty settled in Sura where he became *Gaon*, and died there in 942. He was the first of a long line of enlightened Jewish scholars, believing that Judaism was a special culture expressing the religious, philosophical, national and cultural aspirations of a people, capable of absorbing and assimilating the literary and scientific tendencies of the day.

Saadya was a true polyhistor, grammarian, philosopher, liturgical poet, exegete and apologist. He had won world fame early in life and his Arabic translation of the Bible, which began to take the place of the Aramaic *Targum*, marked a turning point in the cultural and literary history of Judaism. Saadya created the bridge across which Jewish and Arab cultures met and cross-fertilised each other, a process culminating in the Golden Age of Sephardic Jewry, when Jew and Arab lived peacefully together on the Iberian Peninsula and along the southern shores of the Mediterranean. Because Saadya's Arabic translation of Scriptures played this very important role, it has been compared both with the Septuagint and with Moses Mendelssohn's German translation of the Bible, although these did not result in the same happy relationship between Jewish and other cultures. It would seem that totally alien cultures cannot be assimilated by translation alone.

Saadya's conflict with the Karaites was responsible for his exile from Sura, and these years of exile produced his most important works. He arranged a prayer book, wrote Talmudic essays, compiled rules for the Calendar and wrote his memorable *Sefer Yetsirah* (Commentary on the Book of Creation). In 933, he completed his masterpiece, *Emunot Ve-Deoth* (Faiths and Knowledge). This work was the first systematic attempt to harmonise the concepts of a revealed religion with those of Greek philosophy. Saadya held that reason was identical with faith; no Jew should discard the Bible and form opinions of his own reasoning, but he should endeavour to prove the revealed truths.

JEWISH CULTURE IN SPAIN

The origins of Jewish settlement in Spain are lost in legend, but written evidence exists of a Jewish presence in Spain as early as 418 when the Bishop of Majorca wrote of the forced conversion to Christianity of Jews on the island of Minorca. The Visigothic rulers of Spain did not show more kindness to Jews than did their predecessors, the Romans. But neither Rome, nor the

Church, nor the Visigoths succeeded in converting all the Jews. When, in 711, the Arabs invaded Spain, they allowed Jews to settle in Cordoba, Granada, Elvira and Toledo. While this led to violent attacks on the Jews by Christian writers, it also resulted in Spain becoming a refuge for Jews, gave them economic ascendancy and a situation conducive to cultural development. In these relatively propitious conditions, Hebrew literature had its first revival. The first Jewish personality whose life and work are known to us is Hasdai Ibn Shaprut (915–70), a courtier of the Caliph Abd-al-Rahman III, in Cordoba. Hasdai was a physician by profession, but his greatest merit was that of a patron of scholarship and the arts. Although he wrote some poetry, he was not renowned for his Hebrew or grammar. But he set the pattern of Jewish statesmanship and stately living in Spain which was to follow for the next four hundred years. In his letter to the King of the Khazars, he describes his duties at the Court of the Caliph; from contemporary sources we know that he was regarded by Babylonian scholars as the head of the Cordoba Academy and that he brought there the two outstanding Hebrew grammarians of the day, Menachem Ben Zaruk from Tortosa, and his critic, Dunash Ibn Labrat from Fez, the originator of Hebrew metric verse.

During the rule of the next two Caliphs, Cordoba remained the centre of Jewish literary life, but other centres began to develop, and, half a century after Hasdai's death, there already existed a great cultural and political centre in Granada at whose head stood Shmuel Ha-Nagid (Ibn Nagdela) (993–1055). First Minister to the ruler of Granada, Shmuel started life as a pharmacist, was also a Talmudic scholar and acted as Rabbi to the community. His great scholarship is demonstrated in his *Mevo Ha-Talmud* (Introduction to the Talmud), still regarded as a standard work. But he was, in addition, a poet of great sensitivity and originality. His poems reflect the vicissitudes of his life, triumph and tragedy, but in a curiously impersonal style, akin to that of the Psalms. At least thirty of these are included in the liturgy. The comparative economic and political security of Jews contributed to their absorption of much of their environment, and to the increasingly worldly aspect of their literature. The earliest poets were inspired by the Bible, *Talmud* and *Midrash* alone, and their works were modelled largely on the Biblical style. It was in Spain that Hebrew poets for the first time sang of love, of nature and human emotions. Their poetry was on two levels, the devotional and the secular, just as Jewish life in the diaspora was lived on two levels. Among the outstanding figures of this period were Shlomo Ibn Gabirol (1021–58 or 1070), who was born in Malaga and had an unhappy youth, indicated by his melancholy verse in which he seeks comfort in God. In this vein, he wrote the series of poems, *Keter Malchut* (Royal Crown). Ibn Gabirol, though an outstanding poet, survived chiefly through the Latin translation of his major philosophical treatise, *Mekor Chayim* (*Fons Vitae*), attributed to 'Avicebron' until, in the nineteenth century, Salomon Munk identified him with Ibn Gabirol.

Moses Ibn Ezra (1060–1139) was born in Granada and wrote in both Hebrew and Arabic. His rather gloomy poetry earned him the name 'poet of penitence'. But his hymns, some of which are included in the liturgy, far from being sad, are expressions of hope. His most important secular book, *Tarshis* (The Topaz), speaks of love, wine, song, the beauties of nature and the vicissitudes of life. It is written in metric prose, each verse ending with the same word but having a different meaning, showing Arabic influence. Abraham Ibn Ezra (1092–1167) was born in Tudela. He had a hard life, travelled greatly, and achieved renown as mathematician, Bible commentator, wit and poet. In his commentary to the Bible, he applied the critical methods of free research. He was the first to maintain the now universally accepted view that the Book of Isaiah contains the work of two prophets, but he never doubted the divine origin of the Bible. It was probably Ibn Ezra's highest merit that, writing in Hebrew, he brought to the Jews of France and elsewhere in Europe this new scientific method of exegesis, hitherto written only in Arabic.

This work was helped by the grammarian and exegete David Kimchi (1160–1235), a native of Southern Spain who settled in Provence and was later much admired also by the Christian scholars of the Reformation period.

Concurrently with the emergence of the early Spanish school of poets and scholars, another great centre of Jewish learning grew up in France, mainly in Troyes. Just as Spain afforded an environment conducive to poetry as well as learning, so did medieval France inspire a more profound and concentrated study of scripture and *Talmud*. Jewish schools emerged along the Rhine, and important centres were based in Mainz, Worms and Speyer. Having studied at all these schools, Shelomo Iẓḥaki (1040–1105) known from his initials as *Rashi*, settled in Troyes where he wrote his great commentary to the Bible and *Talmud*. In the former, he relied much on the *Midrash*. By contrast to Ibn Ezra's exegesis, Rashi's is popular and even contains a great many French words which he used so that his readers should more easily understand. Rashi was followed by other notable commentators, among them Rabbi Shmuel Ben Meir (Rashbam), but France and the Rhineland were not the home of great poets.

The Crusades brought destruction and despair to the Jews of Europe, and the only place where they were able to continue life in comparative freedom remained Spain. Yehuda Halevi, the most outstanding Hebrew poet of this 'Golden Age', was born in Toledo in 1085, when the city was the cultural centre of Spain, in which Arabs, Christians and Jews lived side by side, and where the cross-fertilisation of eastern and western cultures reached its peak.

This peaceful atmosphere is reflected in Halevi's poetry which is almost entirely worldly and consists of love poems, serenades, wedding odes, epigrams in easily rhyming verse, and is only occasionally wrought with deep passion. In later life when he earned his living as a physician, Yehuda Halevi wrote his now famous philosophical dialogue, *Kuzari*, through which he intended to establish a purely Jewish school of thinking in which no trace of Greek or Arabic influence might be found. His passionate attachment to the Jewish people and its tradition, his yearning for the restoration of ancient glory, are shown clearly in his *Songs of Zion*, written about 1140 in Damascus on his way to his beloved Jerusalem. The date of his death has never been established, for legend has it that, soon after his arrival in the Holy Land, he was trampled to death by a Bedouin rider.

With Yehuda Halevi, Spanish-Jewish secular poetry reached its highest peak. Persecution, migration, restrictions, all forced Jews to turn inward and away from the host cultures. There were few exceptions. An example of the lighter vein of prose and poetry was, however, the *Tachkemoni* of Yehuda Ben Schlomoh Al-Harizi, written between 1214 and 1220, a series of stories written around the central figure of Tachkemoni, in rhythmic prose, in a witty and racy style, and with great mastery of the Hebrew language. Indeed, Al-Harisi is often considered the father of Jewish humorists and satirists.

The invasion of Andalusia by the Almohades put an end to the flourishing Jewish communities, and many Jews fled from the Caliphate of Cordoba rather than forcibly convert to Islam. Among them was Moses Maimonides, then thirteen years old. The family settled first in Fez but, pursued by the Almohades, went on to Palestine in 1165. Moses Maimonides settled finally in Egypt where, gaining great fame as a physician, he completed in 1168 an Arabic commentary to the *Mishnah*. Maimonides' supreme achievement, which won universal recognition for him and his philosophical school, were his two major works, *Yad Ha-Hazakah* (The Strong Hand) and *Moreh Nevuchim* (Guide of the Perplexed). The first, also called *Mishneh Torah*, is a fourteen-part, systematically arranged summary of Rabbinical Law in which Maimonides gave clear decisions as to which Talmudic opinions were to be accepted or rejected, thus laying himself open to attack. The lucidity of his thinking, the manner in which he simplified the intricate and often involved Talmudic argument, rendered his work an indispensable tool in the hands of future students. The great Code having been completed, Maimonides began to write his *Guide for the Perplexed*. This was written in Arabic and became the focal point of a major controversy among Jewish scholars. Fundamentally differing from his predecessors, Maimonides, for the first time in Jewish thinking, applied the Aristotelian method of reasoning to demonstrate that absolute truth is based upon faith and reason in equal measure. He chose Aristotle on the one hand, the doctrines of Moses and the Rabbis on the other, summarised both and, by selecting the points of agreement, reconciled two schools of thought hitherto believed to be diametrically opposite. The *Guide* is not an abstruse philosophical work, although its study requires profound knowledge of both Aristotle and Jewish literature. It was translated into Hebrew during Maimonides' lifetime, and studied by Mohammedans and Christians alike.

After his death in 1204, the controversy continued. Among his commentators were such eminent scholars as Gersonides (Levi Ben Gershon) who, in his *Milhamot Elohim* (Wars of the Lord), propounded the ideas of Maimonides, and Chasdai Crescas who, in his *Or Adonai* (Light of God) opposed him, and was later to influence Spinoza. Although Aristotelian philosophy has lost ground in modern European thinking, Maimonides' reasoning remained an exemplar long after it had become acceptable to the faithful.

THE MIDDLE AGES

The Middle Ages brought many changes in the life of European Jews. Mass migration and pressure by the Crusades caused a dispersion of Jewish settlements eastwards to Poland and Russia, Bohemia, Moravia, Hungary and Rumania. The ensuing years, probably as a result of these tribulations, were almost barren so far as belles-lettres were concerned. Ghetto life, partly self-imposed for reasons of defence, partly enforced, produced an inward-looking, scientific literature and a vast number of translations. Among these, the Hebrew translations from Arabic were the most important and had the greatest impact not only upon Jewish, but also on Christian, scholarship. Judah Ibn Tibbon and his son Samuel were amongst the most prominent translators. But original scholarship ran parallel with these translations.

Moses Ben Nachman (Nachmanides) (1195–1270) was perhaps the most outstanding Jewish scholar of this period. Of Spanish birth and training, he embraced the French school's devotion to the *Talmud*, and reconciled the differences between the two schools of Jewish literature. Throughout the eleventh to the fourteenth centuries, French scholars made additions, *Tossafot*, to Rashi's *Talmud* commentary. Whereas the Spanish scholars aimed at simplification, Tossafists sought close casuistical analysis. Nachmanides, though admiring this method of elucidation, saw its faults and, by vigorously defending Maimonides against his French critics, achieved a golden mean between the two extremes. His poetry, now included in the liturgy for the Day of Atonement, testifies of great gentleness in which his emotions often overtook reason. His commentary on the Pentateuch, of lasting value, appealed to the intellectual, the theologian and the mystic simultaneously. Nachmanides played a considerable part in the development of *Kabbalah* (mysticism), more by the imprint of his personality upon his contemporaries than by formally subscribing to it. He did not share the Kabbalist belief in the eternity of the world and, unlike them, believed that God's attributes could be defined.

The earliest forms of mysticism had few literary expressions, although, in the thirteenth century, possibly as a protest against Maimonidan rationalism and intellectualism, writers began to extol a 'religion of the heart'. By the end of the thirteenth century, the movement took firm hold of masses of Jews whose imagination was fired by stories of miracles and the appearance of a new Messiah. At this point, Moses of Leon wrote the most famous Kabbalistic work of the Middle Ages, the *Zohar* (Splendour). This did not appear under the name of its author, but was attributed to Shimon Bar Yochai, a second century Palestinian Rabbi whose name has been linked with several miraculous events. The *Zohar* was an immediate success, although of no great literary merit, for it is written in an involved and difficult Aramaic idiom. Despite this, it is a book of much spiritual beauty and depth of emotion. The basic tenet of *Kabbalah* was that the *Torah*, the divine revelation, had the sole objective of uniting man's soul with that of his creator. But *Kabbalah*, a mixture of supreme devotion and absurdity, was to forge the strongest literary bonds between Judaism and Christianity. It inspired Christian defenders of Judaism, such as Pico di Mirandola and Reuchlin in the fifteenth and sixteenth centuries, and led twentieth century Christian thinkers to become admirers of Martin Buber. *Kabbalah* influenced Jewish ritual, created great centres such as Safed and Salonika, produced the pseudo-Messiahs, Solomon Molcho and Shabbetai Zevi, and was the originator of the eighteenth century Chassidic movement led by Baal Shem Tov. The literary yield of *Kabbalah* was meagre, even though Hebrew printing presses existed at this time and produced the *Zohar* in many copies. A few outstanding works, such as *Ha-Pardes* (Garden) by Moses Cordovero (1522–70) and *Shnei Luchot Ha-B'rith* (Two Tables of the Covenant) by Isaac Hurwitz, are worth mentioning. The most notable writers active at this time were Israel Nadjara (1550–1628) and Moses Hayim Luzzatto (1707–47). Nadjara was possibly the greatest of mystic poets in Safed. He borrowed the language of the Song of Songs and, in his *Zemirot Yisrael* (Songs of Israel), applies the boldest, most sensuous imagery to express the bond existing between God and Israel. One of his Aramaic songs, *Yah Ribbon Olam* (God, Master of the Universe) is still one of the most popular hymns in the liturgy. M. H. Luzzatto was born in Padua and died in Akko. He was barred from his native land for his Sabbatanian beliefs. In addition to devotional works, he wrote the first Hebrew drama, *La-Yesharim Tehillah* (Praise be to the Righteous), an allegorical play, and some literary historians assert that modern Hebrew literature began with him.

JEWISH LITERATURE IN ITALY

Persecuted both in Spain and by the Crusaders, Jews found refuge in most parts of Italy, including Rome, again causing cultural inter-action and cross fertilisation, this time between Judaism and Christianity. Just as in Spain Jewish writers adopted the Moorish style, so the classical revival in Renaissance Italy left a deep imprint upon the Hebrew poets. Immanuel Ben Shlomo (Manuello) (1270–1330), the Rome poet and scientist, was a versatile writer on a variety of subjects. Imitating the style of Al-Harisi, Manuello adopted the form of sonnet and wrote satirical, witty and easily rhyming verse. His frivolity led to trouble since the main subject of his poems was woman and love. His secular prose also speaks of love, and some of his stories are reminiscent of Boccaccio, both having used the same source material, the thirteenth century *Cento Novella Antichi*. In later years, this frivolous vein disappears from Manuello's poetry and, like the Italian poets of his time, he too adopted the *dolce stil nuovo*, the sweet new style, singing of heavenly, not earthly, love. The concluding chapter of Manuello's *Divan* is a description of Heaven and Hell, *Ha-Tofet ve Ha-Eden*, clearly written under the influence of Dante whom he met in Rome and with whom he formed a close friendship. It is believed that Dante's complimentary remarks about the Jewish people (*Paradiso* 80–81) and his use of Hebrew and Jewish expressions can be attributed to his friendship with Manuello.

Kalonymos Ben Kalonymos, a contemporary of Manuello, was born in Arles, but it is known that he lived in Rome at about 1321, from which city he wrote his major poetic works. *Even Bohan* (The Touchstone) and *Massehet Purim* (The Treatise of Purim). Kalonymos was a Latin scholar of note who, at the request of Robert of Anjou, translated into Latin many of the Arabic and Hebrew classics. The influence of the Roman poets is obvious in his writing. His *Even Bohan* written in rhymed prose is a satire on contemporary mores, while his *Massehet Purim* is a parody of Talmudic casuistry and a humorous travesty of the laws and customs of Passover. The most important follower of Manuello was Isaac da Rieti (1338–*c* 1451) of Rome, physician to Pope Pius II. His *Mikdash Me'at* (The Lesser Sanctuary) is yet another imitation of Dante, written in the metre of the Italian stanzas.

During the fifteenth and sixteenth centuries, Jewish writers and scholars were dispersed chiefly in Italy, the Low Countries, France, Germany and the Hapsburg Empire. While poetry and secular literature in general declined in the last generation of pre-expulsion Spain, the influence of the French and German philosophical schools became increasingly apparent.

In the secular field, the travellers appear, such as Benjamin of Tudela, a twelfth century merchant who, in his *Massaot Binyamin* (The Travels of Benjamin), describes his journeys to many lands including England. Several Jewish travellers explored the Holy Land, and Jews participated in the discoveries of Columbus and Vasco da Gama. Some of these voyagers sought and even claimed to have unearthed descendants of the Ten Tribes. Antonio de Montasinos even persuaded Manasseh Ben Israel into believing that the Ten Tribes lived in what is now Brazil. Manasseh based his 'Hope of Israel' on this account, and used it to induce Cromwell to allow Jews to resettle in England.

Historical literature of the Jews also flourished in this period. Medieval persecutions, the martyrdom of individuals and entire communities are lamented in the *Selihot* (supplications). Most of them are written in verse by the more outstanding of the poets. Several thousand of these special supplications are included in the liturgy, recited chiefly during the days preceding the New Year, on the Festival of the New Year itself, the Ten Days of Repentance, the Day of Atonement, Fast Days and the anniversaries of national disasters.

Above all others, two figures stand out among the writers and scholars of the late fifteenth and early sixteenth centuries. The first, Isaac Abarbanel (or Abravanel) (Lisbon, 1437–Venice, 1508) is renowned for his leadership at the time of the expulsion of Jews from Spain in 1492 and afterwards. A scholar and mystic philosopher, Abarbanel was a great statesman, at one period treasurer of King Alonzo of Portugal, after whose death he fled to Castile and settled in Toledo where he began writing his commentary to the Books of Samuel, Judges and Joshua. He became involved in managing the finances of Queen Isabella of Castile and his close association with the Catholic Kings enabled him to try to alleviate the horrors of the Inquisition. Had not Torquemada thwarted his efforts, the Catholic Kings would have accepted his offer of several thousand pieces of gold to prevent the expulsion. Although he and his family were exempted from the expulsion order, he left Spain and settled first in Naples where he was drafted into the service of King Ferdinand. When the latter was defeated by the French, Abarbanel went with him to Messina, but he eventually became domiciled in Venice where, once again, he was engaged by the government. Amidst all these political and financial activities, he completed his commentary, employing a new method which takes into account the historical factor of the Biblical narrative. At the same time, he maintained his firm belief in the divine revelation, and went further than any of his contemporaries in his implicit belief in the coming of the Messiah whose advent he predicted for the year 1513. Despite many shortcomings as a writer, Abarbanel made a deep impression on his generation, including the Christian scholars of his time.

The second major figure of this epoch was Joseph Caro (Spain, 1488–Safed, 1575). After the expulsion, he first went to Turkey but, in 1535, continued to Palestine where he joined the already existing circle of mystics. His early works include *Bet Josef*, in which he codified the leading authorities of the *Talmud*. But his main achievement was the *Shulhan Aruch*, written in the later years of his life and printed first, in 1564, in Venice. Although of no literary worth, it became a most popular book as the code of Jewish life which set forth the precepts and practices of Judaism.

THE EUROPEAN ENLIGHTENMENT

The beginning, during the Reformation, of a new era in European letters generally was reflected in Jewish contemporary writing. French encyclopaedists and German Protestant authors influenced Jewish thinkers of that time, the sharp controversy shaking the foundations of Christianity, upsetting for ever the hegemony of the Catholic Church in Europe and resulting in similar upheavals in Jewry. At the centre of this maelstrom was Baruch Spinoza (1632–77).

Spinoza may be considered the watershed dividing the Jewish Middle Ages and the Renaissance from the new, enlightened era. At the core of his philosophy were two beliefs, that God and the Universe were one, and that the law of cause and effect ruled the cosmos and so robbed man of his own free will. These concepts were to make a deep impression on future generations of Jewish and non-Jewish thinkers. Spinoza's followers and detractors consciously and subconsciously introduced a new aspect to thinking and writing, which resulted in a completely different style of literature no longer addressing only the initiated but appealing to the masses, and employing the vernacular and Yiddish as well as Hebrew, culminating in ever-growing sophistication.

As has been stated already, modern Hebrew literature is dated conventionally from Moshe Hayim Luzzatto, *ie* the middle of the eighteenth century. This is no coincidence. The rationalist movement of the eighteenth century which originated in France and Germany, affected their Jewish population despite the fact that Jews had little intellectual contact with the surrounding cultures since their dealings with non-Jews were confined to commerce, and their children were educated in Jewish schools where secular subjects were almost completely ignored. From the great desire to break away from both the physical and spiritual confines of the ghetto sprang a reaction, in the form of a national renewal, to the indignities suffered by Jews in most European countries. The *Haskalah* (enlightenment) heralded a real renaissance of Jewish cultural and spiritual endeavour, and found expression in both Hebrew and Yiddish. Although the true *Maskilim* advocated the exclusive use of Hebrew, the first real breakthrough was the early Judeo-German translation of the Bible by Moses Mendelssohn (1729–86), and the commentary of Naphtali Hirsch Wessely (1725–1805) which presented, in a new, contemporary manner, the Bible to the young generation, at the same time emphasising the beauty of the ancient Hebrew language. The movement spread from Germany to Russo-Poland and Galicia thus reaching fruition in the new great centres of Eastern Europe.

It might be appropriate to pinpoint the beginning of the new era at the moment of Moses Mendelssohn's arrival through the gates of Berlin. The social and economic conditions in Europe which preceded the French Revolution, together with the development of industrial society on the one hand, and the restrictions of ghetto life on the other, inevitably led to the expression of liberalising movements within Jewry. Necessarily history was to determine the course of literary and spiritual life, and there began a revolutionary change which soon gathered momentum.

The two hundred years which ensued witnessed the emancipation of Jews in most European countries, particularly in west and central Europe, and resulted in unprecedented literary activity. The remarkable transition from Ghetto Jew to free citizen, the emergence from a self-contained existence, the normalisation of life in all its aspects, were interpreted in prose, poetry and drama. New, inner tensions were created between traditionalists and moderns; Hebraists and Yiddishists; those seeking a specifically Jewish expression of these new ideas; and those advocating total assimilation.

Hebrew as a vehicle of expression, however, remains paramount and survives as the cohesive factor. Throughout the ages, Hebrew has steadfastly remained the language of literary and spiritual communication. It has continued a live instrument in the hands of its users, has become a constant in a changing pattern of Jewish life, and has never become the tongue of the chosen few, although it was no longer the language of daily social intercourse. But it retained an aura of 'sacredness' and was referred to as *Lashon Hakodesh* (the sacred tongue), a reminder that Hebrew was the carrier of hallowed tradition, as well as the expression of more pedestrian thoughts. Just as the Jewish religion was the Jews' portable fatherland, the Hebrew language remained their mother tongue, whether spoken or only written, and this is clearly demonstrated in literary trends. Emancipation of the Jews in each country led to their writing in the language of that country, and seeking to express, in its vernacular, specific Jewish values. Jewish literature no longer meant literature written for Jews only. But the Jewish philosophical and ethical writings which emerged in Russian, German, French and Italian interpreted to the Jews the new modern values of the society which surrounded them and aimed at their total absorption. This trend led to a dangerous development; the emancipated western Jew began to lose interest in world Jewry, his concern with the historical past became academic. Jewish learning in the West, for instance, applied methods of abstract research to matters Jewish, developing the new school of *Wissenschaft des Judentums*, while the social, economic and political disabilities under which the Jews in Eastern Europe laboured, evoked a purely philanthropic interest among western Jews.

By contrast, modern Hebrew literature became the expression of belief in the existence of a Jewish people, of an historical awareness of the continuity of Jewry. It made a successful attempt to evaluate the changes in emancipated Jewish life in terms of the Jewish people as a whole, and not merely as applicable to one country or another. It became permeated by the need for Jewish spiritual survival and the preservation of a Jewish historical identity. But increasing emancipation, and especially the growth of free and democratic societies in the West in which Jews found progressively firm footing, carried the danger of acculturation of which the *Maskilim* became more and more conscious. This great dilemma manifested itself in the literature of the last two centuries which witnessed, first, the liberation of Jews from the Ghettoes, second, the most calamitous tragedy ever to befall a people when a third of its sons and daughters were brutally annihilated and, last, the realisation, in the establishment of the State of Israel, of the hopes of two thousand years.

During the time which elapsed between Moses Mendelssohn and the flourishing of an indigenous Hebrew literature in the new state of Israel, Jewry underwent not only the greatest cataclysm and national revival, but a fundamental internal change. In numbers alone, this was, until the advent of Hitler, a time of development. It is estimated that there were no more than one and a half million Jews at the end of the seventeenth century; at the outbreak of World War II, they numbered about sixteen and a half million. Their social stratification had altered radically; from the artisans, peddlers, shop-keepers, money-lenders grew the Jewish communities whose emancipated members gradually entered all the professions, industry and commerce. The quest for survival as Jews, together with the Messianic idea of the return to Zion and the awakening class consciousness of the proletariat – of which large numbers of Jews were a part – resulted in the realisation that diaspora Jewish society was doomed to dissolution because its unhealthy structure rendered it especially vulnerable. In contrast, those who assimilated the culture of other nations, who abandoned the use of Hebrew and, in many instances, even Yiddish, were in the forefront of the movement of complete secularisation and fought against the idea of national revival. In this, Yiddish played an interesting and even tragic role. As the language of the Jewish masses, mainly in Eastern Europe, it developed in two directions. Just as Hebrew, it was the bearer of enlightened ideas mostly among the poorer classes and, probably for this very reason, it became the expression of the idea that the socialist revolution would resolve all diaspora problems. Tsarist oppression in Russo-Poland brought the inevitable reaction of a desire for political freedom and social equality. The Marxist doctrine that religion was the opiate of the people seeped through to Jewish protagonists of the socialist cause, and the proclamation of internationalism and abolition of the nation-states concept were diametrically opposed to the idea of unity of the Jewish people with its roots in history and religion. The rise of the pietist, *Hassidic* movement with its anti-intellectual, sensualist, nihilistic tenets added to the ferment.

THE HASKALAH

While, historically, the hundred years between 1780 and 1881 can be defined as the era of *Haskalah*, with its three distinct periods of rationalism, romanticism and realism, its literary expressions do not fall into these sharply specified categories, as all three or a combination of them appear throughout.

The one all-embracing concept of the *Haskalah* is best expressed in Yehuda Leib Gordon's (1830–92) famous stanza:

Awake my people! How long will you sleep?
Night has taken flight, the sun shines bright.
Awake, lift up your eyes and look about –
Become aware of time and place.

The writers of the *Haskalah* gathered round their own periodical, *Ha-Meassef* (The Ingatherer), founded in 1785 by the members of the Society for the Cultivation of the Hebrew Language, whose contributors included Mendelssohn, Wessely and other philosophical and educational writers. But there were others, such as the playwright David Franco-Mendez (1713–92) who was influenced by Racine and Metastasio. From Germany, the movement spread eastward to Galicia, where the new rationalistic approach to ancient sources was initiated by Salomon Judah Rapoport (1791–1867) considered the founder of the 'science of Judaism' (*Wissenschaft des Judentums*), the scientific study of Hebrew philosophy, Jewish history and the philosophy of Judaism.

This school no longer studied the Bible, *Talmud* and *Midrash* as part of religious knowledge, but introduced a large measure of scholarly criticism into a field which was hitherto regarded as sacred. A contemporary of Rapoport, Nachman Krochmal (1780–1840) wrote a fundamental philosophic work, *Moreh Nevuchei Ha-Zeman* (Guide to the Perplexed of To-day), which was published in 1851 by Leopold Zunz, a notable follower of the early *Maskilim* in the science of Judaism. Krochmal borrowed not only the title from Maimonides, but also his method of applying an alien philosophy to the examination of the Jewish values. Krochmal adopted Hegel's interpretation of the evolution of universal history in which thesis, antithesis and synthesis follow logically. Examining Jewish history by this method, Krochmal concluded that a recurring pattern was ever present in the development of the Jewish people which, expressed in the 'spiritual absolute', was the motive force behind Israel's destiny, ensuring its permanence and survival. The Galician school also produced the first Hebrew satirist, Yitzhak Erter (1792–1851), criticising and even mocking the *Hassidim*, protesting against hypocrisy, deriding ignorance and superstition. In collaboration with his younger, like-minded friend, Joshua Heshel Schorr (1814–95), Erter founded *He-Halutz*, a literary annual in whose columns appeared Abraham Krochmal (1823–88), son of Nachman, and the first poet of note, Meir Halevi Letteris (1800–71), both leaders of the *Haskalah*. Letteris was memorable for his Hebrew Faust, *Ben Abuya*, the translation into Hebrew of Racine's plays and Byron's *Hebrew Melodies*. *He-Halutz* was followed by a series of other annuals, *Bikkurei Ha-Ittim* (Contemporary Selections (1821–32)), founded by Shalom Hakohen; *Kerem Hemed* (1833–1856), edited by S. L. Goldenberg and S. Sachs, and *Otzar Nehmad*, edited by Blumenfeld. *Bikkurei Ha-Ittim* carried contributions by the greatest Jewish polyhistor of the time, Shmuel David Luzzatto (1800–65), a fervent opponent of the rationalist interpretation of traditional sources, who, in his criticism of Maimonides, expounded the absurdity of trying to reconcile faith and reason.

HEBREW WRITING IN RUSSIA

It was not until the 1830s that Hebrew became a living literary language in Russia and, when it appeared, it did so with a hitherto unequalled vigour. Referred to as the 'treble cord' are the first three amongst Russian *Maksilim*, Isaac Dov Levinsohn (1788–1860), the scholar and essayist, Mordehai Aaron Gunzburg (1795–1846), the journalist and satirist, and Abraham Dov Hakohen Lebensohn (Adam Ha-Kohen) (1794–1878), the poet. Levinsohn, steeped in both traditional Jewish and secular knowledge, set out to break down the prejudices against all forms of secular learning and the study of Hebrew as a living tongue. His success and popularity were due to his subtlety. Instead of attacking religion, he defended the new ideas by quoting examples of earlier scholars who extolled the need to introduce, into the study of Jewish sources, modern scholarly methods. Another reason for his popularity was the stringent manner in which he dealt with scurrilous attacks on the Jewish religion, a form of antisemitism in the reign of Nicholas I. Gunzburg, whose influence was equally great, was the leader of the Vilna group of intellectuals, a versatile scholar who wrote a History of Russia in Hebrew, advocated the need for comprehensive education in Hebrew, translated Philo, and began a universal history, the only completed volume of which was widely read. Another native of Vilna was Lebensohn, the *Haskalah's* first poet of note. Lebensohn lacked the intellectual equipment of his fellows, never knew a foreign language well enough to savour the beauty of European poetry, but was endowed with an instinctive poetic sense and turbulence of feeling which his poetry revealed. The Hebrew language, of which he was a master, was in his hands, a pliable instrument. Once again, there come to life the powerful images of the Prophets and the poetic metaphors of the Psalms. This reversion to the language of the Bible makes Lebensohn's poetry somewhat antiquated, but he has to be read against the background of his own time. His son and pupil Micah Joseph Lebensohn (1828–52), who died young, had a more profound effect on the whole movement. Educated in Berlin, he had the advantage of knowing German well and was deeply inspired by the '*Sturm und Drang*' movement, especially by Schiller. His German education included attendance at lectures by L. Zunz under whom he studied Jewish history. This influenced his choice of Jewish historical subjects in his volumes of poetry, *Shirei Bath Zion* (Songs of the Daughter of Zion), six long poems on themes from ancient and medieval Jewish history. His *Kinnor Bath Zion* (The Harp of the Daughter of Zion), contains shorter poems and translations from Horace, Virgil, Schiller, Mickiewicz and Alfieri. His third volume is a translation of part of Schiller's version of the *Aeneid*.

The greatest of all the romantic poets was Yehuda Leib Gordon (1830–92), whose artistry may lack the touch of genius, but whose emotional power and perfect command of the language set him far above his contemporaries. This is especially apparent in his handling of philosophical problems. Schiller's influence is obvious in Gordon's historical cycle of poems, *Love of David and Michal* (1857) on the life and adventures of King David.

The eighteen-fifties saw the emergence of the first Hebrew novel, *Ahavat Zion* (The Love of Zion), by Abraham Mapu (1808–67). This takes place at the time of King Hezekiah and is written in the language of that period. The artificial, complicated plot adds to the difficulty of enjoyment, but the very introduction of this literary genre into Hebrew letters is an important event which was appreciated also by its contemporary readers, since it was an extremely popular book. Mapu's second novel, *Ashmat Shomron* (The Sin of Samaria) (1865) was set in the same epoch, but is better constructed. Its underlying theme of false prophets and allusion to the contemporary world emerges with much vigour. Mapu's attack on the hypocrisy of his time and his call for a change, speak most clearly in his *'Ayit Tzabua* (The Painted Hawk) (1857–64), whose characters are drawn from reality and are the prototypes of small-town Jewish life. This call for a change in Jewish life by depicting the pitiful inhabitants of the small town, the *Luftmenschen*, and the hypocrites, the bloated rich and exploited poor, was the motif best expressed by Shalom Joseph Abramovitz, more widely known by his pen-name, Mendele Mocher Sepharim or Seforim (1835–1917). (See biographical section p. 87.)

Among Mapu's contemporaries, Peretz Smolenskin (1842–85) became not only the most popular writer of his generation, but an important forerunner of the Zionist Movement. While at *Yeshiva*, he acquired a Russian education and, on his expulsion from the Rabbinical Academy, went to Odessa where he developed into the most important contributor of *Ha-Melitz*. He travelled in Germany and Bohemia, but eventually settled in Vienna where he perfected his knowledge of literary Hebrew. His nationalist views are expounded in *Am Olam* (Eternal People), while his estrangement from orthodox bigotry and path to the Zionist Movement are depicted in his biographical work, *Ha-Toeh Be-Darkei Ha-Hayyim* (The Wanderer on the Roads of Life). For a time, he served on the staff of the Alliance Israélite Universelle in Rumania but when, in 1880, the Alliance sponsored emigration of East European Jews to the West, he bitterly opposed the organisation and, together with Laurence Oliphant, an Englishman, attempted to found a Palestine Colonisation Association.

THE ZIONIST MOVEMENT

The Russian and Rumanian pogroms in the 'eighties put an end to the *Haskalah*. Its place was swiftly taken by the Zionist Movement, born out of a combination of historical, political, economic, social and cultural factors in both Eastern and Western Europe. But the aims, although not the means of achieving them, were common ground between its various protagonists – the establishment of a new, free, healthy Jewish society in the ancient Homeland where conditions for the development of a Jewish cultural life using the Hebrew language would prevail. Theodor Herzl, an assimilated Viennese journalist, published in *Der Judenstaat* (1896) the political formula for the solution of the Jewish problem. Unbeknown to him, however, the same longings inspired a group of East European Jewish writers and thinkers in whose hands the idea merged into a living reality. East and West met on the political platform of the Zionist Congress, but literary expression of the idea came almost exclusively from the East, as did the first pioneers who returned to Palestine to fulfil the ideals of their mentors.

This was the generation, the *Chovevei Zion* (Lovers of Zion), of Menahem Dolitzky (1856–1931), a poet in both Hebrew and Yiddish; Asher Shapira (1840–1900), author of a visionary ballad on the advent of the Messiah who would lead his people back to Zion; Naftali Herz Imber (1852–1902), an early settler in Palestine, author of *Hatikvah* (The Hope), which became the anthem first of the Zionist Movement and, later, of the reborn State of Israel; David Frishman (1862–1922), the Hebraist, editor of *Ha-Yom* (The Day) and *Ha-Dor* (The Generation), two important journals in which he made notable contributions to the evolution of Hebrew as a modern language; Nahum Sokolow (1859–1936), the first European Jew to write in Hebrew, editor of *Ha-Tzefirah* after the death of Slonimski, author of the *History of Zionism* (1917–20), and one of the great Zionist political leaders who, with Chaim Weizmann, participated in the negotiations which led to the Balfour Declaration of 1917.

By this process of evolution Hebrew literature became not only an expression, but an instrument of Jewish cultural and spiritual rebirth and survival. Indeed, at the turn of the century, Hebrew literature boasted such giants as Asher Ginsberg (known by his pen-name, Ahad Ha-am), Hayyim Nahman Bialik, Mordecai Zvi Feirberg, Micah Joseph Berdichewski, Isaac Leib Peretz, Shoffman, Joseph Chaim Brenner, Bershadsky, A. N. Gnessin, Joshua Steinberg, Yaakov Fichman, Zalman Shneur, Yaakov Steinberg, David Shimonowitz, Shaul Tchernichowski, Avigdor Hameiri and many others.

This epoch marked a veritable rebirth of Hebrew culture which, for the first time, appeared as a happy blend of the secular and traditional, reflecting the experience of a long historical and literary past while adopting the ideas of a new modern world. The passionate belief in the spiritual values of Judaism and the necessity for them to permeate the political movement, was propagated by Ahad Ha-Am and found its counterpoint in the burning desire for Jewish spiritual liberation as expressed in the poetry of Bialik. The influence of foreign cultures no longer gave rise to controversy; the modern media of expression served as a vehicle to emphasise the ancient values. These poets, writers and thinkers were equally influenced by Nietzsche and Dostoevsky, the ancient Greeks and the masters of the *Midrash*.

Many of them, such as Mendele, Sholem Aleichem, Brainin, Peretz, Frug and others, wrote in Yiddish as well as in Hebrew (see biographical section, pp. 81–90). Indeed, Yiddish, the language spoken by millions of Jews in the small towns (*Shtetl*) and larger centres, became the tongue of the diaspora, a kind of Jewish Esperanto.

The word *Yiddish* is derived from the modern German *Jüdisch Deutsch* or Jewish German. It is the language spoken chiefly by the Polish and Russian Jews whose forbears, early in the Middle Ages, were invited to Poland from the Rhineland, to form a trading class intermediary between the nobles and the serfs. They kept their Middle High German tongue, writing and printing it in Hebrew characters to this day. Though based on Middle High German vocabulary and construction, Yiddish was cut off from living German, hence its irregularities of grammar and spelling. It continued to absorb Hebrew and Aramaic words and expressions, together with Slav ones, Polish and Russian, and has a few of older, Romance origin.

Yiddish reached its peak in the early years of this century and, until the end of World War II, remained a much-used language. It has declined considerably since, due chiefly to the increased use of Hebrew after the establishment of the Jewish State, but of course also, because of the extermination of Eastern European Jewish masses.

The most renowned Yiddish writer of all time is Sholem Aleichem (Sholem Rabinovich) (see pp. 89–90), whose works have been translated into most European languages and have added considerably to the knowledge of a now extinct Jewish way of life. Another great figure is Sholem Asch (see biographical section, p. 78) whose novels, again translated, convey not only the atmosphere of the *Shtetl* but, for the first time, introduce into Jewish literature the controversial subject of Judaism's encounter with Christianity.

Yiddish as a literary expression also flourished, until the outbreak of World War II, in the United States, the Soviet Union and Poland. The United States opened its doors to the persecuted Jews at the turn of the century, and became the home of many important Yiddish writers, including Sholem Aleichem, Asch, Glatstein, Leivick, Brainin, Gordon, Goldfaden and others (see biographical section, pp. 78–90). The holocaust swallowed the flower of Yiddish and Hebrew poets and writers who remained in Europe.

Mention must be made here of those Yiddish writers and poets left in Russia after the 1917 Revolution. Many of them stood in the forefront of the revolutionary struggle, and hoped and believed that the victory of Bolshevism would liberate the oppressed Jewish masses along with the workers and peasants of Tsarist Russia. They made a tragic error. At first, during the lifetime of Lenin, Yiddish and even some Hebrew cultural life expanded but, after Lenin's death and with the advent of Stalinist terror, all these aspirations were stifled. A few managed to escape, but the best of them fell victim to the Stalinist purges. During the liberalisation since Stalin's death, a number of Yiddish classics have been published in Russia: a volume each of Sholem Aleichem, Peretz and Mendele, two or three anthologies of poetry and prose, and a Yiddish monthly, *Sovietish Heimland*. Although the last-named is written in excellent literary Yiddish, it has little Jewish content, and the poetry published is strongly reminiscent of Soviet socialist realism.

The birth of political Zionism and its consequence, the resettlement of Jews in Palestine, offered a natural and most fertile background to the development of new Hebrew letters. It is true that the older generation of poets and writers still had their roots in the diaspora and, in addition to those mentioned above, the doyens of Hebrew literature, such as the Nobel Laureate, S. Y. Agnon, A. Shlonsky, Alterman, Shimoni, Greenberg and others (see biographical section, pp. 77–89) still reach back to the sources of Jewish existence, thereby creating a synthesis of old and new, and continuing, as it were, the thread of Jewish tradition. But the prospect of a new life, a society created by Jews for Jews, an abiding love for the very soil of Palestine, bred a new type of poet. First came the settlers, children of the *Shtetl* freed from the fetters of ghetto life, such as Rahel Bluvstein (see p. 81), who personified the idea of *Halutziut* pioneering), and never recalled diaspora life in her poetry. This *Halutzic* spirit also produced a series of important philosophers, both religious and secular, such as Rabbi Avraham Hakohen Kook, the most tolerant of modern orthodox philosophers, A. D. Gordon, the exponent of *Halutziut* as the ideal Jewish way of life in which the spiritual and social needs of a Jew can find fulfilment, and many others.

The Holocaust also produced its poetry and prose, though chiefly in Yiddish or the vernacular of the lands in which millions of Jews perished.

THE STATE OF ISRAEL

From the depths of despair, Jews were raised to the heights of elation when, in 1948, the State of Israel was proclaimed. The trauma of the Holocaust, the fight for independence, self-determination, and free immigration, the War of Independence following the establishment of Israel, and the wars and vicissitudes surrounding her, are themes all of which find expression in the work of the first generation of *Sabra* writers. *Sabra* is the fruit of the prickly pear and is the name given to Israelis born in Palestine, for this new, brash, proud, independent, self-sufficient type of Jew has a golden heart just like the fruit of the cactus which is prickly outside, but sweet in taste.

Their mother tongue is Hebrew, they speak, think and write it, and each of them contributes to its ever-increasing vocabulary. For them, Hebrew is a living language, not the sacred tongue of the Bible. They grew out of the landscape of Israel, not the narrow streets of the *Shtetl.* Their imagery is that of the Biblical landscape invested with a new life – the tree-clad hills of Galilee and the rich meadows of the Valley of Jezreel. The previous generation, with one foot still in the diaspora, translated for them the poetry and prose of other literatures, but the *Sabras*, whose second language is usually English, learned first-hand from Hemingway, Steinberg and Faulkner. Representative of this generation is Moshe Shamir whose first novel was inspired by *Kibbutz* life and pinpointed the conflict between the immigrant and native generations. One of his other novels has as its hero a *Sabra* and portrays his life in school, youth movement and *Palmach* (the Commandos of the Underground Army under the Mandate). Shamir's best work is the *King of Flesh and Blood* (translated by David Patterson, London, 1965), an historical novel of epic dimensions, set in the period of the Second Temple. The short stories of Nathan Shaham expose the complex human relationships of the *Kibbutz.* The first authentic Yemenite novels were written by Mordechai Taviv, whose heroes, members of this exotic tribe, now live in the cities and villages of Israel. Benjamin Tammuz explores the confrontation between Jew and Arab. Hanoch Bartov, in his novels and other works, analyses the complexities of Israeli society when, as a result of Independence, hosts of immigrants arrived in Israel, each wave consisting of Jews of all colours and backgrounds, each of them to be absorbed and welded into a new, free society. Aharon Megged, novelist and playwright, chooses his own contemporaries as heroes, and introduces the fresh humour of Israel onto the stage. But the most forceful interpreter of the psychology of the Israeli, his attitude to the Jewish people and his environment, is S. Izhar. In poetry, too, there is a new vein as represented by Hayim Guri, one of the most popular of contemporary poets, who emerged from the atmosphere of the fight for independence and who, perhaps, expresses best the yearning of Israeli youth for a peaceful, normal life. A son of the *Kibbutz* and veteran fighter, A. Hillel, reverts to the language and imagery of the Bible, even the archaic language. Aba Kovner, a survivor of the Holocaust, a veteran resistance fighter in the woods of Lithuania, arrived in Israel on the eve of the Declaration of Independence. He, more than any other, interprets the tragedy and heroism of the Holocaust to a generation most of whom, at best, are bewildered by the massacre of Jews.

Contemporary Hebrew literature in Israel is a phenomenon akin to other national literatures, yet different, just as the Jewish people is somehow different from other peoples. Having survived two thousand years of dispersion almost solely through the abiding value of their cultural heritage, Jews did not have to create a new literature in a vacuum. It grew naturally, as a continuation of the long chain which had its first beginnings in the very same place. When the poets of Israel gaze upon the rugged, eroded desert of the Negev, they behold the same landscape as did the poets and prophets of the Bible. For the new generation who did not experience the vicissitudes of diaspora life, confrontation with its realities is often painful. Their reality is the present, and many of them wish that Jewish history had begun only in 1948. The presence of the older generation, the survivors of the concentration camps, of Jews who brought with them the heritage of five Continents, the ever-increasing sense of unity with Jews who live in the continuing diaspora, free in some countries, oppressed in others, all contribute to the cultural ferment of Israel. Political tension, religious controversy, the continued threat of war on the one hand and national pride and a sense of fulfilment on the other, are all factors which find literary expression in a variety of forms, novels, short stories, satire, drama, poetry, criticism and philosophical writing.

In 1967, the Israelis underwent the trauma of yet another major conflict during the Six Day War. The most recent Israeli writing for the first time shows a deep searching into the inner consciousness of the present generation. A collection of transcripts of recorded conversations with over a hundred young men interviewed by writers and journalists was published under the title *Siach Lohamim* (Soldiers Speak). Because of the free rein these young men – all born after 1948 – give to their emotions, the sense of relief instead of the euphoria of victory, it is a poignant document, at times beautifully written. Another very successful book published 10 months after the 1967 war was *Hasufim Batzariah* (Exposed in the Turret), by Shabtai Tevet. The main message of this book, according to its author, is that it exposes the sharp contrast between life in Israel and that in the Diaspora. 'For generations', he says, 'the Jew was characterised by his belief that faith was more important than existence. In Israel, existence is more important than faith.'

But, while a new, indigenous literature is born every day in the ancient land, it also forms part of world Jewish literature, for many eminent Hebrew and Yiddish writers live and work in the far-flung countries of the dispersion, chiefly the United States and Latin America. The most important are mentioned in the biographical section.

In conclusion, mention must be made of the renaissance of Jewish consciousness in the Soviet Union since 1967. It is expressed chiefly in Russian in the form of protest literature, but there are clear indications of a re-awakening of Hebrew and Yiddish as well.

INDIVIDUAL WRITERS

Abravanel (Abarbanel), Isaac (Lisbon 1437–Venice 1508). Hebrew philosophic writer, one of the most influential Jews in Spain before the expulsion. Treasurer to the Kings of Portugal, Spain and Naples. He was well versed in Latin, in addition to Jewish literature, and wrote a commentary to the Bible which was, in parts, translated into Latin and used by Christian scholars. He was of the philosophical school of Maimonides.

Abravanel (Abarbanel) Judah (Leone Ebreus, Leo Judeus) (Lisbon *c* 1460–Naples before 1535). Son of Don I.A., left Spain in 1492 and lived as a physician in Genoa and Naples. Influenced by Pico de la Mirandola the elder, became a neo-platonist and wrote his *Dialoghi dell' Amore* (in Spanish or Hebrew) in which he expounded the view that love was the governing force of the world. His son was forcibly converted, and on this theme he wrote the elegy *Telunah al ha-Zeman* (1503).

Agnon, Shmuel Yosef (formerly **Tschatsky)** (Poland 1888–Jerusalem 1970). Hebrew novelist and short story writer who settled in Palestine in 1908 and became the doyen of Hebrew literature. He chose as his subject the life of the East European Jewish diaspora. His *Hachnasat Kallah* (1922), meaning literally 'The Dowry of the Bride' but translated into English under the title *The Bridal Canopy*, is not a narrative in the usual manner, but rather a series of stories woven together from tales, parables, fables, proverbs and other folklore material. He wrote many short stories and a novel, *Tmol Shilshom* (2nd ed. 1947) (Days of Yore), describing life in Jaffa and Jerusalem before the First World War. His *Oreach Nata Lalun* (A Guest to Stay), 1945, is his final summing up of his own life. Was awarded Nobel Prize for literature in 1966.
Collected Works: 6 vols., Tel Aviv, 1935.
In Engligh: *In the Heart of the Seas*, New York, 1948, *Days of Yore*, New York, 1948, *The Bridal Canopy*, *A Guest for the Night*, New York, 1968.

Ahad Ha-Am, pseud. of Asher Ginzberg (Russia 1856–Tel Aviv 1927). Hebrew philosopher and essayist. Transformed Zionism, hitherto a purely political movement, into a spiritual one. He was influenced by English and French positivist thinkers and sociological and psychological theories of the time. Like John Stuart Mill and Renan asserted that nations, like individuals, had a distinct ego. Saw Palestine as a spiritual centre which would extend its influence upon world Jewry. He founded the famous monthly *Hashiloach* (1897–

1926) which has become a most important source of modern Jewish knowledge. *Al Parashat Derachim* (The Parting of the Ways), 4 vols., Odessa, 1895–1913; 2nd ed. in 4 vols., Berlin, 1920, with new introduction; *Igrot Ahad Haam* (Letters) 6 vols., Berlin, Jerusalem, 1923–6. *Selected essays*, trans. L. Simon, Philadelphia, 1912; *Essays, Letters, Memoirs*, Oxford, 1916.

Al-Harizi (Alcharisi) Yehuda Ben Schlomoh (*c* 1165–1235). Hebrew poet in pre-expulsion Spain who spent some time in Provence and even further north where he earned a living as translator of scholarly works. His masterpiece is a translation into Hebrew of the Arab poet Al-Hariri's *Magamas* under the title *Machberoth Ithiel*, short stories in rhymed prose which, in translation, faithfully reproduce the original style. His *Tachkemoni* is a similar work in Hebrew, consisting of fifty stories, both humorous and serious thoughts on Hebrew literature; his liturgical poems also survive.

Alfasi, Isaac Ben Jacob, known as **Rif** (nr. Fez 1013–Lucena 1103). Hebrew poet and religious writer, Rabbi in Fez until he had to escape to Spain in 1088. Although his poetry is lost, his *responsa* and *halachot* (compendium to the Babylonian Talmud) form a most important part of Jewish traditional literature.

An-Ski (originally **Solomon Samuel Rappaport)** (Vitebsk 1863–Warsaw 1920). Yiddish author and dramatist. Social revolutionary, member of the Bund, the Jewish Socialist movement in Poland, author of its anthem (The Oath). Lived in France and Switzerland, but returned to Russia in 1905. Best remembered for his play *The Dybbuk* (Trans. H. G. Alsberg and W. Katzin, 1917), first performed by the Habima Theatre in Russia in 1920.

Gesamelte Shriftn, 15 vols., Warsaw, 1925; *Ashmodai* (Poems) 1904; *Der Dybbuk*, Odessa, 1916.

Asch, Sholem (Kutno 1880–London 1957). The most prolific of the last generation of Yiddish writers of short stories and novels, who tried his hand even at drama. He had a wide experience of Jewish life in Eastern and Western Europe and America, and treats the past and present with equal skill and understanding. Wrote in Hebrew and Yiddish simultaneously and portrayed, with sympathy, life in the small Jewish communities. He caused a great stir in Jewish literary circles by his 'Christian' novels of Jesus and Mary, but he treated them as a series of Biblical stories. Most of his work has been published in English. *Mother*, 1930; *Sabbatai Zevi*, 1920; *In the Beginning*, 1935; *Motke the thief*, 1935; *Salvation*, 1951; *Three Cities*, 1933; *The War Goes on* (also under the title *The Calf of Paper*), 1936; *Children of Abraham*, 1942; *My Personal Faith*, 1942; *The Nazarene*, 1939; *Song of the Valley*, 1939; *Three Novels: Uncle Moses, Chaim Lederer's Return, Judge Not*, 1938; *What I Believe*, 1941; *The Apostle*, 1943; *East River*, 1946; *One Destiny, An Epistle to the Christians*, 1948; *Tales of my People*, 1948; *Mary*, 1949; *Moses*, 1951; *The Prophet*, 1956; *A Passage in the Night*, 1952; *From many countries: the collected short stories*, London, 1958.

Barash, Asher (Poland 1889–Israel 1952). Hebrew novelist and short story writer. As a young man went to Palestine and settled in Tel Aviv. Depicts the life of Jews in Galicia chiefly in his novels *Tmunot Mibet Mivshal-Haschechar* (Pictures from the Brewery) 1928; and *Ahava Zara* (Strange Love) 1938. His later novels and short stories describe the new life in Israel in a simple realistic style. He also edited an anthology of modern Hebrew Poetry under the title *Mivchar Ha-shirah Ha-ivrit Hahadasha* (1938).

Ben Yehuda, Eliezer (Perelman) (Vilna 1858–Jerusalem 1922). Hebrew scholar, essayist and editor whose chief merit was the development of the Hebrew language as a spoken tongue. He founded his own periodical *Hazevi* in 1885 in Jerusalem, but was denounced to the Turkish authorities; the periodical was suspended and he himself imprisoned. After his release, he continued the struggle. His historical achievement in the field of linguistics is his dictionary of the Hebrew language, *Millon ha-lashon ha-ivrit*, Jerusalem, Berlin, 1908, now newly edited by the Hebrew Academy in Israel.

Collected essays; 2 vols., Jerusalem, 1929; *In Memoriam*, essays, ed. J. Klausner, Jerusalem, 1924.

Berdichewski Micah Joseph (pseud. Micha Yoseph Bin Gorion) (Podolia 1865–Berlin 1921). Hebrew novelist, essayist and philosopher, a colourful and controversial figure in modern Hebrew literature, and one of the most prolific writers of his day. From the town which was the cradle of *Hassidism*, for some years he represented extreme secularism in Jewish life. He chose as his motto the 'transvaluation of values', a concept borrowed from Nietzsche. Jews were more important to him than Judaism, and the renewal of the Jewish nation meant for him that Israel should be like any other people. He then came into conflict with Ahad Ha'am's spiritual Zionism. The characters of Berdichewski's short stories are men of flesh and blood with a deep attachment to the soil, and disillusioned young men who have abandoned Jewish traditional life but have not managed completely to absorb European culture. This dichotomy is characteristic of Berdichewski who wrote revolutionary essays in a language borrowed from the Bible, the *Talmud* and even the *Zohar*. His essays in literary criticism took the form of subtle portraits of writers of his time, published in the volume *Baerev* (In the Evening) (Warsaw, 1910). Under the pseudonym of Bin Gorion he collected and adapted two volumes of legends from the close of the Bible down to his time (*Me-Ozar ha-Aggada*). They were also published in German.

Collected works (20 vols., Warsaw-Leipzig, 1921–5). Short stories: *Me-heavar ha-karov* (From the Recent Past, 1909); *Batim* (Houses, 1920); *Garei Rehov* (Strangers in the Street, 1921).

Bergelson, David (Uman 1884–1952). Yiddish writer, author of short stories and novels. His career is divided by the Russian Revolution into two distinct periods: the pre-revolutionary period, when he took his subjects from the small Jewish towns; and in the latter phase when he portrayed episodes of the

hectic post-revolution years and became an ardent follower of the Soviet regime. He fell victim to the Stalinist purges. His novel *After All* is considered one of the best in Yiddish literature.
Collected works: 6 vols., Berlin, 1922. *Penek*, Moscow, 1937; *Birobidjaner*, Moscow, 1935.
Bialik, Hayyim Nahman (Ukraine 1873–Tel Aviv 1934). Considered as the greatest modern Hebrew poet both in content and in form. Primarily a lyricist, his poetry has great force, impulsiveness, and passion. Having broken away from the traditional upbringing of the Talmudic High School, he came under the influence of the *Haskalah*. He moved to Odessa where he met Ahad Ha-am and other leading thinkers, and wrote his first poems, but was too shy to have them published; made his debut with an article in the Hebrew literary daily *Ha-Melitz*. Encouraged by his contemporaries, he published his poetry. His financial situation forced him to leave Odessa for Zhitomir in 1892, where he married the daughter of a wealthy timber merchant. During the four years he spent in the forests, he continued writing poetry, but eventually turned to teaching. Whilst teaching, his reputation as the leading Hebrew poet was established by the publication of his first epic poem *Ha-Matmid* (The Talmud Student) in *Ha-Shiloach*, Ahad Ha-am's monthly. In 1900 he was able to return to Odessa where, through the aid of his friend and patron, Ravnicki, he became a teacher at the recently established Hebrew school. This was the turning point in his life. His fame began to travel all over Europe, for his poems were translated into Russian and German. With Ravnicki, he established the publishing houses *Moriah*, and later *Dvir* which for twenty years issued many books in all fields of literary endeavour.

Bialik himself wrote stories and essays, and tried his hand at translation (*Don Quixote* and Schiller's *Wilhelm Tell*) with great success. He remained in Russia during the First World War and even the first years of the Soviet regime, which did not molest him. But he soon left for Berlin and, in 1923, settled in Palestine where he reorganised the publishing house *Dvir* and, for the rest of his life, played the role of leader in the cultural revival in the Jewish national home. But his poetic muse fell silent, and he wrote chiefly stories, fairy tales and essays. In collaboration with Ravnicki, he collected and edited the legends of the *Talmud* and *Midrash* in *Sefer Ha'agada*. Bialik's poetry underwent a great change from the time he wrote *El ha-Zippor* (1893) to his last poem, *Yatmut*, which rates as his best, and which he wrote shortly before his death. The poems of his first ten years are imbued by unbounded love for the ancient Judaism of the Bible and *Talmud*. But this love soon becomes a tragic, a nostalgic love for something that is doomed to extinction. Tormented by the dilemma of how a nation, dispersed as the Jews are, will live on, he wrote his classic poem, *The Dead of the Desert*, in which, as in his essays published at about that time, he becomes the rebuking and sternly reproving prophet. His admonishment of the people reaches a polished climax in the

poem, *This too is God's Chastisement* (1905) and *In the City of Slaughter* (1905), written after the Kishinev pogrom, which he describes in a manner moving the reader to impotent rage as well as to tears. The revolt against Israel's oppressors suddenly turns into a revolt against Heaven, and the denunciation of cowardice and weakness becomes a summons to self-help and self-reliance. All his motifs, a longing for a full life on earth, the craving for love, the revolt against oppression and persecution, the vision of vengeance, the struggle between Judaism and other civilisations and the awesome vision of the End concentrated in his most profound allegoric work, *The Scroll of Fire*. In lamenting the destruction of his people, Bialik also foreshadows a new beginning of a more complete life, in that not all which is old will be cast aside for the sake of the new, but only that part which has become obsolete; in place of it, a new Jewish life would absorb all that is best in the new age.
Collected works: Tel Aviv, 1954.
In English: *Far over the Sea*, Cincinnati, 1929; *Knight of Onions and Knight of Garlic*, New York, 1939; *Poems*, ed. L. V. Snowman, 1929.

Bluvstein, Rahel (Poltava 1890–Jerusalem 1931), outstanding Hebrew woman poet who went to Palestine from the Ukraine as a pioneer, in 1908. Her poetry has no trace of diaspora life but is pervaded by a love for the land of Israel and its people.
Collected poems: Tel Aviv, 1954.

Boraischa, Menahem (formerly **Goldberg**) (Poland 1888–New York 1949). Yiddish poet, began to write devotional poetry but Polish antisemitism evoked his anger against his environment. His chief work is the two-volume poem *Der Geyer* (The Wayfarer) 1943, a spiritual Odyssey. The *leitmotif* in his latter work is the Jew in a Gentile environment. *Durkh Doires* (Through Generations) is a posthumous volume.

Brainin, Reuben (Lodz 1862–New York 1939). Belonged to Ben-Avigdor's circle of 'new writing', the first in modern Hebrew literature to write biographies of Hebrew writers. He also contributed short stories to the *Sifre Agorah* (Penny Books) series started by Ben Avigdor, like his *Mi-Gibbore Yisroel* (One of the Heroes of Israel) whose hero, Moses the bricklayer, bears with equanimity but undying hope all the mishaps of life.
Avraham Mapu (Warsaw, 1900); *Peretz Smolenskin* (Warsaw, 1896); *Collected Essays:* 2 vols. (New York, 1923–37); *Chayye Herzl* (New York, 1919).

Brenner, Joseph Hayyim (Novi Malini 1881–Jaffa 1921). Came from the Ghetto, studied in Yeshiva and privately in high school, enlisted and served in the Russian army but, at the outbreak of the Russo-Japanese war in 1904, escaped to London where he lived in abject poverty, editing the Hebrew periodical, *Hameorer* (The Awakener). Like most of his contemporaries, he was attracted to Socialism and for a time became an adherent of the *Bund* (the Jewish Socialist Movement). Soon, however, he found that he could not reconcile his deep-rooted Jewishness and love for the Hebrew language with the

extreme tendencies of the movement, and became a Zionist. In 1908 Brenner settled in Palestine where he became leader of the pioneer groups and a founder of the *Histadruth ha-Avodah* (General Confederation of Labour). Having seen the beginning of the realisation of Zionist dreams he was killed in the Arab riots of 1921. The stormy life he led is reflected in his writing which is chaotic, turbulent, yet full of compassion for his heroes. His novels are full of often irrelevant detail, rather a series of episodes than a coherent narrative; still, they show a deep understanding of the varied situations of life. The novels portray life as he saw it in Russia, and the London Ghetto, and later the struggles of early Jewish settlement in Palestine. His short stories (collected edn. 1898) are rooted in the poverty, misery and darkness of the Ghetto.
Novels: Ba-Choref (Winter); *Mi-Saviv le-nekudah* (Around the Point); *Me-ever li-Gevulin* (Beyond the Frontier); *Mi-kan Umikan* (From here and there); *Ben Mayim la-Mayim* (Between the Waters); *Shekel ve-Kisholon* (Loss and Tumbling). Short stories: *Min ha-Metzar* (From the Depths).

Feffer, Itzik (Kiev 1900–? 1948), Yiddish writer and poet, from a working-class family, started his career as a compositor. His main subject was the Bolshevik Revolution, and he was highly regarded by the new regime in USSR. Fought in the Red Army in both wars. During World War II was a member of the Jewish Anti-Fascist Committee in which capacity he toured England and the USA. He was executed during the Stalinist purges.
Vegn Sich (About Himself) 1924; *A Shteyn oif a Shteyn* (Stone upon Stone) 1926; *Roitarmeyish* (As in the Red Army) 1942; *Di Shotns fun Warshawer Geto* (The Damage of the Warsaw Ghetto) 1944.

Frishman, David (Poland 1862–Berlin 1922). Born into a well-to-do enlightened family in Lodz where Jews no longer lived in the narrow confines of the Ghetto, his command of several European languages, especially German, afforded an opportunity of intimate knowledge of European literature which was to lead to a synthesis of the Jewish and the European tradition. He had an equally good grounding in traditional Hebrew sources and a deep love for the Hebrew language. Published his first short story at eighteen in Smolenskin's monthly, *ha-Shachar* (The Dawn). His versatility made him sought after and he became a collaborator of Nahum Sokolov on the journal, *He-Assif* (The Gatherer) then became assistant editor of *Ha-Yom* (The Day), the first Hebrew daily which Dr Kantor started in 1884. When the latter ceased publication in 1888, he went to Breslau University whence he returned to Warsaw in the early nineties. Here he translated into Hebrew from German, French and English the works of Goethe, Heine, Anatole France, Byron, Shakespeare, Nietzsche, Tagore and several historical works. During the First World War, he lived in Odessa and Moscow, and finally in Berlin, where he died. His chief contribution to Hebrew literature was as a short story writer, although he was an eminent critic, poet and feuilletonist. As an observer of human nature, he introduced psychological emphasis and analysis of the mental state of his

subject. Frishman's short stories fall into two main groups: the first, *Yom ha-kippurim* (Day of Atonement), *Hazkarat Neshamot* (Memorial Service) and *Tikkun Shel Shavuot* (The Shavuot Night Recitation) describe the tragedies resulting from the apostasy of children abandoning narrow ghetto-life. The second, exemplified by *Mitzvah*, *Tithadesh*, *Le-Erez Yisrael*, etc., contains sketches on the theme of Jewry's struggles and unfulfilled passions. With love for his characters, a great deal of understanding and fine humour, Frishman sketches the conflict between the narrow confines of Ghetto life and the wider life outside, intruding and luring away the inhabitants of the Ghetto. His best stories are *Bamidbar* (In the Desert, Berlin, 1923), a series of biblical stories using some episode or precept of the Pentateuch.
Collected works: ed. Frishman (20 vols., Warsaw, 1923–7).

Gabirol or **Ibn Gabirol, Solomon Ben Judah** (Malaga *c* 1021–Valencia *c* 1058). Hebrew poet and Arabic philosopher, a protégé of Samuel ha-Nagid, began writing poetry at sixteen and, at nineteen, composed a Hebrew grammar in verse. He was a prolific and deeply religious liturgical poet, but his secular poetry was mainly concerned with his own cruel fate. His chief philosophical work, *Fons Vitae*, written in Arabic, is extant only in Latin translation. Written in dialogue, it is a neo-platonic work with elements from Aristotle and Philo. He influenced Duns Scotus, Spinoza and Schopenhauer. The Hebrew translation, *Mekor Chayim*, influenced the Kabbala. The work was not considered that of a Jewish author, and the true identity of 'Avicebron' was discovered by S. Munk. His *Royal Crown*, in Hebrew, explains his philosophy.
Selected religious poems: ed. I. Davidson, trans. I. Zangwill, 1923; *Fons Vitae*, ed. C. Baeumler, 2 vols., 1945.

Glatstein, Yaacov (1896–   ). Born in Lublin, now lives in the United States, an intellectual poet. In his early youth, came under the influence of Leyeles, who was only a few years older but already an acknowledged poet and leader of the introspective school. Soon, however, Glatstein emancipated himself from this influence and became, what he still is, a law unto himself. He gave his own name as the title of his first volume of published verse, a daring proposition; more discreetly, he titled his second *Credos* (1929). While in his critical essays he advocated logic, his poetry is outlandish, expressionist. His chief motifs are Jews, God and Lublin. In addition to several volumes of fine poetry, Glatstein writes elegant prose and is a discerning literary critic.

Goldfaden, Avraham (Ukraine 1840–New York 1908). Father of the Yiddish theatre, playwright and poet. Began writing light comedy in the early seventies, but was unable to produce his plays in Russia and, therefore, went to Jassy, Rumania, where, in 1876, he founded the first professional Yiddish theatre. His success prompted others to form Yiddish troupes, but he himself returned to Russia in 1880. Besides plays, he also wrote some Hebrew poetry, and started a satirical weekly in Lemberg and another in Czernowitz. The Russian authorities eventually banned his theatre and, after a first successful visit to New

York in 1887, he finally settled there in 1903. His plays are still performed in Hebrew in Israel.
Dos Yidele (collected Yiddish poems) 1866.
Plays: *Di Yidene* 1869; *Di Rekruten; Di Bobe mit'm ainikl; Shmendrik; Di Shtume Kalle; Kabtsanson & Hungerman; Bar Kochbah; Shulamith; Doktor Almosado; Ben Ami; Di Kishef-Macherin.*
Gordon, Yehuda Leib (Vilna 1830–St Petersburg 1892). Hebrew novelist, poet and essayist; most important poet of the *Haskalah*, the first to employ not only the Hebrew of Biblical style, but the most exact impressions of post-biblical literature, thus founder of a new style of Hebrew poetry. Imprisoned in 1879 by the Russian authorities for political conspiracy, contracted an incurable disease in prison. After his release, became editor of the journal, *Ha-Melitz*. His first romantic poems with a Biblical setting were *The love of King David and Michal* (1857); later, he dedicated another long, but no longer romantic, poem to King David. In 1860, he published a collection of fables, *Mishle Yehuda*, a mixture of Talmudic legends and European fables. His poetic work, first published in Russia and later in Israel, had a lasting influence on Hebrew poetry.
Halevi, Yehuda Ben Samuel (Tudela *c* 1080–Palestine, after 1143). Hebrew poet, Arabic philosopher, physician. Lived in Granada, Cordoba and Toledo, where he took an active part in the literary life of his time. His early poetry was light and brilliant, but became increasingly serious and nationalistic, culminating in his *Songs of Zion*. They followed his essay *Kuzari* (before 1140), an essay of national revival. In 1141, he set out on his longed-for journey to Palestine, but stopped on the way to Egypt. His religious and liturgical poems still survive in some Jewish liturgies. Little is known of his life in Palestine, and many legends surround his death there.
Selected poems: trans. N. Salaman, 1924; *Kitab-al-Khuzari*, Eng. trans. H. Hirschfeld, 2nd edn., 1931; *Selections*, trans. I. Heinemann, 1948.
Hameiri, Avigdor (Pen name of Emil Feuerstein) (Hungary 1886–1970). Hebrew poet, raised in a traditional Jewish atmosphere but deeply influenced by the Hungarian poet Endre Ady. In 1910, founded the short-lived Hebrew periodical *Hayehudi*. Translated many Hungarian poets into Hebrew, among them *Tragedy of Man* by Madách, a sort of Hungarian *Faust*. During the First World War served in the Austro-Hungarian Army and fell prisoner to the Russians. His war-time novel *Hashigaon Hagadol* (The Great Madness) left a deep impression on modern Hebrew writers. After the war, settled in Palestine and, on the establishment of the State of Israel, became first editor of the Israeli equivalent of Hansard. Was awarded the Israel Prize, 1968.
Ibn Ezra, Abraham Ben Me'ir (Tudela 1092–Calahora 1167). Hebrew poet, grammarian, scientific and religious author. Left Spain before 1140 and wandered in Italy and Provence; visited London in 1158 where he wrote two short works. In his secular poems maintains a light, even jocular vein; his

liturgical verse is philosophical; his prose is erratic. One of the most gifted Jewish personalities who had not only a deep knowledge of, but also a great affection for, the Hebrew language.

Ibn Ezra, Moses (Granada 1060–N. Spain 1139). Hebrew poet and literary critic, a high court official in Granada; as a patron of poetry, encouraged the young Judah Halevi. Although he wrote a large number of important and secular poems, his most important work is *Kitāb al-mumhādarah wal-mudhākarah* in Arabic: a study and our chief source on the Spanish Hebrew poetic school.

Katznelson, Jehuda Loeb (Tchernigov 1847–Petrograd 1917) (pseud. Bukki ben Yogli) Hebrew writer and scholar. One of the most forceful exponents of the idea that the physical and spiritual survival of Judaism is bound up with the land of Palestine. A physician by training, Katznelson wrote a penetrating study of the origin of hygiene among ancient Jews, *Yesodeh Tumah ve-Taharah*, 1902. But in his poetry and prose he wrote beautiful legends and fantastic tales. One of his best known stories is the 'Song of the Nightingale', *Shviat ha-Zamir*, 1903. Other works include *Kevurot Neshamot*, 1907, *Remach Avarim*, 1908.

Leivick, Halpern (Minsk 1888–New York 1962). Yiddish poet. Arrested and imprisoned for revolutionary activities in Russia 1906; sentenced to life imprisonment in 1912, he escaped while being transported to Siberia and settled in New York. This background, coupled with a deep resentment towards a stern father, and months spent in a TB sanatorium, are reflected in his poetry. His style is visionary, bordering on the mystical, but he had the largest following among contemporary Yiddish poets. Published twenty prose dramas, ten volumes of poetry, hundreds of essays and newspaper articles.

Geklibene Verk (Selected works), 5 vols., Vilno, 1925–8; *Liedel fun Gan Eden* (Song of the Garden of Eden) Chicago, 1937; *In Treblinka bin ich nit Gewen* (I haven't been to Treblinka) New York, 1945; *Mit der Sheris Hapleyta* (With the Survivors) New York, 1947; *Di chassene fun Fernwald* (Wedding in Foehrenwald) New York, 1949.

Levinski, Elchanan Leib (pseud. **Rabbi Karov**) (nr. Vilna 1857–Odessa 1910). Hebrew publicist and novelist, one of the leaders of the *Chovevei Zion* Movement. Wrote an Utopian work: *Mass'a l'Eretz Israel be-Shnat Tat* (Journey to Israel in the year 2040) Odessa, 1892. He also wrote travel sketches of Russia.

Luzzatto, Moses Hayim (Padua 1707–Acre 1747). Hebrew poet, mystic and scholar, son of a wealthy merchant. At the age of seventeen wrote his first drama, *Maasei Shimshon* (ed. A. M. Haberman, 1950). This was followed by a number of studies on Hebrew versification, *Leshon Limudim* which contrasted the Italian neo-classic style with the earlier, Arabic style of Hebrew poetry. In 1727 he wrote an allegorical play, *Migdal Oz* (Tower of Strength) which marks the beginnings of modern Hebrew drama. As a result of persecution and excommunication, Luzzatto went to Amsterdam, where he continued his literary work and wrote *La-Yesharim Tehillah* (a morality play based on Guarini's *Pastor Fido*, a gem of modern poetry), and his most popular ethical work, *Mesillat Yesharim* (1740) (The Path of the Upright), crit. ed. with trans. M. M. Kaplan, 1936.

Luzzatto, Shmuel David (Known as **Shadal**) (Trieste 1800–Padua 1865). Hebrew writer, a master of Hebrew style, also wrote in Italian. Of a noble but poor family, in early youth dedicated his life to regenerate his nation. From 1829 taught at the Padua Collegio Rabbinico which was eventually ruined due to political events. The emotional, yet scientific, attitude to Jewish religion and history, pervades also his poetry, much of which is on national themes.

Kinnor Na'im (Pleasant Harp) Verse. 2 vols., 2nd edn., 1913; *Collected Essays in Mechkere Ha-Yahadut* (Sources of Judaism) 2 vols., 1913, *Autobiografia del S.D.L.*, 1882.

Maimonides (Moses Ben Maimon) known as **Rambam** (Cordoba 1135–Fostat, Old Cairo 1204). Hebrew religious writer and Arabic philosopher. As a result of Almohade persecution of the Jews, his family left Spain in 1160 and lived in Fez; he then went for a short while to Palestine and eventually to Cairo where he was Rabbi, and physician to the Sultan. He wrote important works on Jewish law: *The 613 Commandments*; A Commentary in Arabic on the whole *Mishnah* (1168) and the greatest of all expositions of Jewish Law: *Mishne Torah* or *Yad Ha-Hazakah* (1180). His chief philosophical work, *Guide of the Perplexed* (*Dalālat al-Ha'irin*, Heb. *Moreh Nevuchim*; Heb. trans. Samuel ibn Tibbon and Judah al-Harizi) was completed in 1190. He also wrote *responsa* and medical works.

The Guide of the Perplexed, trans. M. Friedländer, 3 vols., 1881–5; *M: The Guide of the Perplexed*, select. with intro. and comm. by J. Guttmann, 1952.

Manger, Itzig (Jassy 1900–1969). Yiddish poet. Son of a tailor, his literary talent was discovered while still at school in Czernowitz. From Jassy, he moved to Warsaw in 1929 and left there only at the outbreak of World War II. From 1941–51 he lived in London and, since then, in New York. Writing both poetry and prose, he uses some traditional motifs presented in a tuneful and artistic manner.

Shtern Oifn Dach (Star on the Roof) Bucharest, 1929; *Chumesh-lider* (Songs of the Bible) 2nd edn., 1936; *Noente Geshtaltn* (Figures) 1938; *Volkens ibern dach* (Clouds over the Roof) London, 1947; *Hotsmach Spil* (poetic drama) London, 1947; *Jubilee edition of his works*, Geneva, Paris, 1951.

Mapu, Abraham (Slobodka-Kovno 1808–Konigsberg 1967). Hebrew novelist. Known at an early age for his great erudition in Jewish studies, he studied also the Latin and European languages. His first novel *Ahavat Zion* (The Love of Zion), Vilna, 1853, marked a turning point in Hebrew literature. Set in the time of the prophet Isaiah, it describes life and events of the time as recounted by a contemporary. It displays a noticeable influence by the eighteenth-century French novelists. His second novel, *Ashmat Shomron* (The Sin of

Samaria) is set in the same period, has an even more complex plot and uses the same kind of imagery.

Ahavat Zion (Ammon, Prince and Peasant) trans. F. Jaffe, 1887; *In the Days of Isaiah*, trans. Shapiro, 1902.

Markisch, Peretz (Polonoya 1895–?1948). Yiddish poet and playwright. Wrote originally in Russian but, in 1917, turned to Yiddish. From 1924 was one of the leading figures of the Kiev group of Soviet-Yiddish writers. With a large number of other Jewish writers was arrested during the Stalinist purges and, at his trial, denounced the methods by which 'confessions' had been extorted from them. His best works are the epic accounts of Jewish martyrdom and heroism during the Nazi period, especially *Milchomeh* (War) 1948 and *Der Oifshtand in Geto* (The Rising in the Ghetto) 1947, a tribute to the Jewish heroes of the Warsaw Ghetto.

Mendele Mocher Seforim (Shalom Yaakov Abramovitch) (Minsk 1835–Odessa 1917). Alternatively known as the grandfather of Hebrew and of Yiddish literature, Mendele had three phases in his literary career. After the publication of his novel, *Ha-avot ve-habanim* (Fathers and Sons), in 1867 in Hebrew, he wrote only in Yiddish until 1886 when, partly with translations into Hebrew of his own writings, partly by writing new works, he reverted to Hebrew. But his greatest achievement was the transformation of Yiddish, hitherto the colloquial idiom of masses of Jews, into a highly sophisticated literary language. His short stories and novels, full of colour, satire and gentle criticism, were a new feature in Jewish life in Eastern Europe. No one before him wrote about the beauty of the countryside in which his heroes and his readers lived. Unlike his predecessors among the *Maskilim* (enlightened), who wrote largely under the influence of German thinkers, Mendele was deeply influenced by Russian literature, though he was familiar with German literature as well. By chosing the pseudonym Mocher Seforim (the bookseller), Mendele sought to assume the traditional role of the travelling Jewish bookseller of his time, that of carrier or disseminator of knowledge, both religious and secular, who, at the same time, was the link between the Jewish communities, dispersed all over Russia and Poland. Mendele travelled all over Russia until 1881, when he settled down as director of the Hebrew school in Odessa and where, except for a few short visits abroad, he spent the last thirty years of his life. During this time, Odessa had become the centre of Jewish cultural and national activity, and Jewish life and letters began to mirror the intensity of Jewish national aspirations largely as a reaction to increasing persecution and pressure. But Mendele, in daily touch with the leaders of the Zionist Movement, never abandoned his belief in the permanence of the Jewish Diaspora. He therefore advocated the necessity of cultural, educational and social autonomy for the Jewish minority in the Diaspora.

Works: In Hebrew: *Michtav al devar ha-Hinuch* (Letter on the Matter of Education, 1856); *Mishpat shalom* (The Case of Peace, 1860); *Toldot ha-Teva*

(3 vols., 1862–72, Natural History); *Ha-avot ve-habanim* (Fathers and Sons, novel, 1867); *Sippurei Maasiot* (1881, Short Stories); *Ba-yamim ha-hem* (In Those Days, autobiographical novel, 1889); *Massaot Binyamin Ha-Shlishi* (The Travels of Benjamin The Third, novel, 1878); In Yiddish: *Fishke der Krummer*, 1869 (trans. into English 1929 and 1960); *Die Takse* (The Meat Tax, a play, 1869); *Die Klatshe* (The Mare, 1873); *Der Prisiv* (The Call-up, [drama], 1884); *Dos Wunsh-fingerl* (The Wishing-Ring, 1889). Recent English versions: *Fishke the lame*, trans. G. Stillman, 1960; *The Parasite*, trans. G. Stillman, 1956; *The Nag*, 1955. *Collected works in Yiddish* (17 vols., Cracow, 1911–12); in Hebrew, Berlin, 1922.

Niger, Shmuel (pseud. of Shmuel Charney) (Dukor Minsk 1884–1956). Yiddish literary critic and essayist, champion of Yiddish language and literature which he considers as the chief instrument of Jewish spiritual survival. Started his literary life in Vienna. Having settled in the United States in 1919, wrote in Hebrew and Russian. His analytical studies of Yiddish writers are of great literary and historic value.

Yiddische shreiber, Warsaw, 1912; *Sholem Aleichem*, New York, 1928; *Mendele Moicher Sforim*, Chicago, 1936; *In Kampf far a nayer dersteeung*, New York, 1940; *H. Leivick*, Toronto, 1950; *Y. L. Perez*, Buenos Aires, 1952.

Peretz, Isaac Leib (Zamosc 1851–Warsaw 1915). Came from a traditional Jewish background but, in early youth, became an adherent of *Haskalah* and made his literary debut in *Ha-Shachar* in 1875 with some Hebrew poems attacking Hassidism. Unhappy in his personal life, he moved to Warsaw where he studied law, but returned to practise as a lawyer in Zamosc, where he divorced his first wife, married for a second time and turned his attention to Yiddish, publishing his first story in 1888. From then on, he became a central figure of Yiddish literature, guiding young writers. Influenced by major trends in European, chiefly Russian and German, literature, he founded a new school. His stories and plays combined social outlook with national content, blending the best traditions of Jewish writing and philosophy with modern trends. When barred from practising as a lawyer, he became an official of the Warsaw Jewish community and spent the last twenty-five years of his life in that great centre of Jewish life and letters.

Collected works: 18 vols., Vilna, 1912; 12 vols., New York, 1920. In English: *Stories and Pictures*, trans. Helena Frank, Philadelphia, 1936; M. Samuel, *Prince of the Ghetto*, 1948; *The Book of Fire*, trans. J. Leftwich, 1961; *Stories from P.*, trans. S. Liptzin, 1964; *In this world and the next*, trans. M. Spiegel, 1958; *The Three Canopies*, New York, 1948.

Rosenfeld, Morris (pseud. of Moshe Jacob Alter) (Boksa 1862–New York 1923). Noted as the poet of the Jewish working class. Left Russia at the age of twenty, lived for a while in London's East End working as a tailor, spent some years in Amsterdam as a diamond cutter and finally settled in New York in 1886. He sings primarily of the 'sweatshops' and the abject poverty of the

Jewish proletariat. He also wrote two operettas and biographies of Yehudah Halevi and Heinrich Heine.
The works of Morris Rosenfeld, 6 vols., 1908–10. *Songs from the Ghetto*, trans. in prose with Latin transcription of original, Leo Wiener, Boston, 1898.
Samuel Ha-Nagid (Samuel Ben Yoseph Ibn Nagdela or **Nagrela** (Cordoba 993–Granada 1055), Hebrew poet of the 'Golden Age', successful business man, Arabic scholar. His mainly didactic poetry is noted for elegance rather than poetic depth, and follows Arab models. He also wrote an introduction to the *Talmud* and grammatical works. *Diwan*, ed. D. S. Sassoon, 1934; *Kol shire Samuel Ha-N.*, ed. A. M. Haberman and M. Abramson, 2 vols., 1947.
Shapiro, Lamed (Ukraine 1875–New York 1948). Yiddish novelist and essayist, stylistic reformer, who described the Tsarist pogroms and with his sea stories introduced a new theme into Yiddish literature. Translated into Yiddish the works of Victor Hugo, Sir Walter Scott, Dickens and Kipling.
Shlonsky, Avraham (Russia 1900–). Went to Palestine in 1921 and, although he became one of the most virile poets of the new Jewish National Home, whose lightness of form and magical rhythm grips the reader, he clearly shows the influence of Soviet Russian poets. In 1925, with Steinmann, edited a literary periodical which marked the first revolt in Hebrew literature. Translated Pushkin, Shakespeare, Romain Rolland and modern Russian poets. Founded the *Sifriat Poalim* (Worker's Library).
Shneur, Zalman (White Russia 1887–New York 1959). Son of the mystic S.Z. of Ladi, had both traditional and secular education. In his youth, went to Odessa, at that time a centre of the Jewish literary revival; subsequently lived in Warsaw, Vilna, Switzerland and, after the war, in Paris. Like many who came from the narrow confines of the Pale of Settlement, he revolted against traditional Judaism, but at the same time he felt a great empathy with his suffering people and the grave injustices against them. While a rebellious spirit pervades all his lyric works, he wrote a number of mature poems, chiefly on the Alps and the Harz mountains. Into most of these, he injected a Jewish note. Eventually, he turned to Zionism in which he, too, saw the solution of the Jewish problem. His best-known poem is the great ode *Vilna*, depicting life in the ancient Jewish community known as Jerusalem in Lithuania.
Noah Pandre, 1936; *Noah Pandre's Village*, 1938.
Sholem Aleichem, pseud. of Sholem **Rabinovitch** (nr. Poltava 1859–New York 1916). With Mendele Mocher Seforim and Peretz forms the triumvirate of the most important Yiddish writers, but distinguished by his very original style and wry humour, with which he describes his characters. Indeed, it is this capacity to laugh at himself which always helps the Jew to meet and overcome the many vicissitudes of life. The inhabitants of the township of Woronka where he spent his childhood and early youth left an indelible impression on him, and the citizens of his fictitious town of *Kasrilivke* are all modelled on them. His childhood was marred by the death of his mother and the financial

difficulties of his father. From the age of twenty-one to twenty-four, he became a Government Rabbi in Luben. During this time, he wrote his first articles in Hebrew for *Ha-Melitz*. Having married his childhood sweetheart, he moved to Kiev where he devoted all his time to writing and spent the fortune inherited from his father-in-law on financial transactions, publishing and sponsoring young writers. The misfortunes experienced in the world of finance are described in the adversities of his hero, Menahem Mendel. From 1883, he wrote almost exclusively in Yiddish, and adopted his pen-name which is, in fact, the common form of Jewish greeting 'Peace be unto you'. From 1888, he edited and published the first Yiddish literary annual ever to pay contributors, *Di Yiddishe Folksbibliotek*, designed to raise the standard of Yiddish. Although financially unlucky, he became extremely popular as a story teller, and his name soon became a household word in thousands of Jewish homes. From 1905 on, he travelled extensively in England, the United States, Germany, Italy and Switzerland until, on the outbreak of World War I, he settled in the United States. Immensely prolific, his writings fill many volumes and range from novels to short stories, comedies, essays, sketches and an autobiography. His works are frequently translated into most European languages, and are widely read and often performed on stage and screen. He is most certainly the best internationally known Yiddish author of his time.

Collected works: 14 vols., New York, 1908–14; *Chayey-Adam* – autobiog., New York, 1920.

Works in English: *Stories and Satires*, trans. C. Leviant, 1959, *Adventures of Mottel the Cantor's Son*, trans. H. & T. Kahana; *Selected Stories*, 1956; *The Great Fair*, 1955; *Inside Kasrilivke*, New York, 1948; *Jewish Children*, New York, 1929; *The Old Country*, New York, 1946; *Tevye's Daughters*, New York, 1949.

Singer, Isaac Bashevis (Poland 1904–). The youngest surviving member of the Singer family, carries on the tradition begun by his brother, I. J. Singer, and his sister, Esther Keitman. Originating from Poland and from an ultra-orthodox family (he lives in the United States), his novels and short stories reflect life in Eastern Europe. In many of his works one encounters some of the themes and characters of his older brother. *Satan in Goren* is set in a seventeenth century small town where Jews eke out a listless existence until Satan intervenes and turns this dull backwater into a hotbed of vice, bringing to the surface all the wickedness which is embedded in these poor, dejected people. *The Family Moscat* is Singer's most important novel, dedicated 'to I. J. Singer, who was not only the older brother but a spiritual father and master'. It is a saga involving three generations, mostly the descendants of pious rabbis who become involved in complex love affairs. As the story develops, Singer's impressionism becomes more and more apparent. A deep empathy with his characters is depicted by his wry humour. *In My Father's Court* is a vast collection of memories of a rabbinical court in Eastern Europe, of which he is the best surviving witness. *Short Friday* is a collection of short stories. His other works include *The Magician of Lublin, The Slave, The Spinoza of Market Street.*

Smolenskin, Peretz (Russia 1842–Merano 1885). Hebrew author, leader of the National Progressive Movement. Attracted by the *Haskala,* went to Vienna at the age of twenty-five, but soon discovered that enlightenment led to assimilation. He found his own answer and, in his monthly periodical, *Ha-shachar* (The Dawn), founded in 1869, proclaimed his beliefs that a great people cannot live on the past alone, it must have faith in its own future. He wrote a series of essays and books to prove this idea. At the same time, he was one of the best protagonists of the new Hebrew novel. His great novel, a veiled biography, *Ha-toe Be Darkei Ha Hayyim* (The Wanderer on the Paths of Life, 3 vols.) was serialised in *Ha-schachar,* where he also published his two fundamental treatises: *Am Olam* (The Eternal People) (1872), and *Et Lataat* (Time to Sow). His last novel, *Kevurat Chamor* (The Burial of an Ass) is considered his best. *Sifre Peretz ben Moshe Smolenskin* ed. L. Rosenthal, 1887.

Sutskever, Abraham (*b* Lithuania 1913). Yiddish poet, editor of the Yiddish quarterly, *Di Goldene Keyt* (Tel Aviv). Was a leader of the 'Young Vilna' group before the war, survived Nazi occupation by escaping to Siberia. After the war, returned to Poland from where he emigrated to Israel. His poetic style is truly modern.

Di Geheime Shtot, Tel Aviv, 1948; *Di Festung,* New York, 1947; *Lider fun Ghetto,* New York, 1947; *Fun Vilnoer Ghetto,* Moscow, 1944; *Sibir,* 1950.

Tchernichowski, Shaul (Russia 1873–Tel Aviv 1943). Hebrew poet. His chief characteristic is that he brought a new quality to Hebrew poetry: a secular tendency emphasising the will of Jews to be like all other nations, an emancipation from the Ghetto, and sometimes even from Jewish tradition. There is a degree almost of paganism in his poetry. He does not perceive a conflict between his Judaism and the world at large. Born in the Crimea, *ie* outside the Pale of Settlement; and, although his parents were observant Jews, his early years were spent with his gentile contemporaries. He first became acquainted with Hebrew at the age of seven, and indeed it was his first teacher who implanted in him his deep love of the language. At fifteen, he composed his first long Hebrew Biblical poem; went to Odessa to attend a commercial high school, and after graduation prepared for university entrance examinations in order to study medicine. Having failed these, he left Russia in 1899 and entered the University of Heidelberg. Already in Odessa he came into contact with the *Chovevei Zion* movement and the many writers and thinkers around it, among them the young essayist, Josef Klausner, who induced him never to write in any language but Hebrew. He stayed four years in Heidelberg, and studied for another three years in Lausanne.

As a young man of fine physique and vivacity, he led a gay life and was continuously entangled with women, all of which is mirrored in his poetry.

He returned to Russia in 1907 and was employed as an itinerant doctor. When war broke out, he was drafted as an army doctor. After the war, he settled in Berlin and went to Palestine in 1930.

His poetry differs greatly from that of his predecessors, indeed, he is unique in Hebrew poetry for the sensuous beauty of his love lyrics and nature poems. His songs are of a fleeting love that knows no disappointment and is ever ready for new adventures. After the love lyrics, came the pantheistic songs to heathen deities. He was even nicknamed 'Hellene' and 'Heathen', but he also sang of Biblical heroes, and wrote 'Idylls', describing the life of the Jews in his native Crimea. In his prose he never achieved the stature of his poetry. He was an unrivalled translator, especially in the accomplished, metrically true, translations of the *Gilgamesh* and *Kalevala*, the *Iliad* and *Odyssey*.

Collected Poems, 1951.

BIBLIOGRAPHY

ABRAHAMS, Israel *Jewish Life in the Middle Ages* New York, 1969; London, 1932.

BAER, Yitzhak *History of the Jews in Christian Spain* 2 vols., Philadelphia, 1961; 1966.

BARON, Salo W. *Social and Religious History of the Jews* 11 vols., New York, 1952– .

BERMAN, Leon *Histoire des Juifs de France* Paris, 1937.

COHEN, A. *Everyman's Talmud* new edn., New York and London, 1949.

DANBY, H. *The Mishnah* new edn., New York and London, 1954.

DUBNOW, Simon M. *Die Geschichte des Chassidismus* 2 vols., Berlin, 1931; 1932.

DUBNOW, Simon M. *History of the Jews in Russia and Poland* 3 vols., Philadelphia, 1946.

DUBNOW, Simon M. *Weltgeschichte des jüdischen Volkes* 3 vols., Jerusalem, 1938.

ELBOGEN, Ismar *A Century of Jewish Life* Philadelphia, 1944.

ELBOGEN, Ismar *Geschichte der Juden in Deutschland* Berlin, 1935.

FINKELSTEIN, Louis (Ed.) *The Jews: Their History, Culture and Religion* 4 vols., Philadelphia, 1949.

FRIEDMAN, Philip *Martyrs and Fighters* New York, 1954.

GILBOA, Y. A. 'Hebrew Literature in the U.S.S.R.' in *The Jews in Soviet Russia since 1917*, ed. L. Kochan, London, 1970.

GREENBERG, Louis *The Jews in Russia* 2 vols., New Haven, 1944.

GUTTMANN, Julius *Philosophies of Judaism* London, 1964.

HALKIN, Simon *Modern Hebrew Literature* New York, 1950.

HUSIK, Isaac *A History of Mediaeval Jewish Philosophy* new edn., New York, 1950.

KLAUSNER, Josef *Historia shel ha-safrut ha-ivrit ha-hadashah* (History of Modern Hebrew Literature) 2 edn. 6 vols., Jerusalem, 1958.

KLAUSNER, Josef *A History of Modern Hebrew Literature* New York and London, 1932.

MADISON, Charles A. *Yiddish Literature, its Scope and Major Writers* New York, 1968.

MEYER, Peter 'The Jewish Purge in the Satellite Countries', *Commentary*, September 1952.

PATTERSON, David *The Hebrew Novel in Tzarist Russia* New York and Edinburgh, 1964.

RAISIN, Jacob S. *The Haskalah Movement in Russia* Philadelphia, 1913.

RABINOVICH, Isaiah *Major Trends in Modern Hebrew Fiction* Chicago and London, 1968.

RIBALOW, Menachem *The Flowering of Modern Hebrew Literature* New York and London, 1959.

ROBACK, A. A. *The Story of Yiddish Literature* New York, 1940.

ROTH, Cecil *History of the Jews in England* Oxford, 1941.

ROTH, Cecil *History of the Jews in Italy* Philadelphia, 1946.

SACHAR, Howard M. *The Course of Modern Jewish History* New York, 1958.

SCHWARZ, Solomon M. *The Jews in the Soviet Union* Syracuse (New York), 1951.

SHMERUK, CH. *Jewish Literature in the Soviet Union During and Following the Holocaust Period* Jerusalem, 1960. (Yad Vashem Studies 4.)

'Yiddish Literature in the U.S.S.R.' in *The Jews in Soviet Russia since 1917*, ed. L. Kochan, London, 1970.

SHOLEM, Gershom *Major Trends in Jewish Mysticism* 3rd edn., New York, 1946.

SOKOLOW, Nahum *History of Zionism* 2 vols., London, 1919; rev. ed. New York, 1969.

SPIEGEL, Shalom *Hebrew Reborn* New York, 1930.

STEINSCHNEIDER, Moritz *Jewish Literature from the Eighth to the Eighteenth Centuries with an Introduction on Talmud and Midrash* New York, 1965.

WALLENROD, Reuben *The Literature of Modern Israel* New York, 1956.

WAXMAN, Mayer *A History of Jewish Literature*, new edn. 4 vols., New York, 1960.

PERSIAN LITERATURE

Old Iranian Literature

Mary Boyce

HISTORICAL BACKGROUND

Old Iranian is used here to comprise Old and Middle Iranian literature, composed *c* 700 BC to AD 1000. This literature has a striking homogeneity, although it was produced, not only over a long period of time, but also by diverse peoples, speaking distinct, though related, Iranian languages. Their ancestors had formed originally one branch of the Aryans, an Indo-European group of tribes, some of whom, *c* 1800 BC, entered upper India and there evolved the language and literature of the Rig-veda. Others invaded the land called after them, Iran. The first of these Iranian peoples to be known to history, from the ninth century BC, are the Medes, who established, in north-western Iran, a hegemony over other Iranian tribes. In the sixth century they were overthrown by the Persians, another Iranian people living in south-western Iran (still called after them Pars or Fars). Under the Achaemenian dynasty the Persians ruled a vast empire, stretching in its heyday from Egypt and Asia Minor in the west to the borders of India. The Persians were famed, not only for their fighting qualities, but also for their wealth, culture and admirable administration. In the north-east, however, their subjects included Iranian peoples of less advanced civilisation; and beyond this frontier were other nomad Iranians, still living in the era of heroic barbarism, who frequently vexed the imperial peace.

It was in this north-east region that the state-religion of the Persians, Zoroastrianism, had its birth. It was preached by Zarathushtra, priest and prophet, probably in the late seventh century BC, before these lands were conquered by the Achaemenians. His teachings were a reform of the existing Iranian religion, which had much in common with that of the Vedas; and many ancient beliefs and observances survive in Zoroastrianism.

In 331 BC Persia was conquered by Alexander. After his death its lands were divided among his generals, but in the third century BC a new Iranian empire was established by the Parthians (whose homelands were in the north-east), led by the Arsacid dynasty. Their empire was long-lived, but less extensive and less centralised than the Achaemenian. In the third century AD it was overthrown by the Persians once more, whose second empire, the Sasanian, enjoyed power and splendour almost equal to the first. It succumbed in the seventh century to the desert Arabs, who established Islam by the sword in place of Zoroastrianism, which had remained the dominant religion of Iran throughout the rise and fall of dynasties. The Arab conquest caused a break in the continuity of Iranian culture, for it brought not only a new religion, but also the impact of a foreign literature and a foreign language, whose influence in the course of the next three centuries changed the chief language of Iran from Middle Persian to the modern speech.

The Arabs also introduced their own script. The Iranians, like other Indo-European peoples, had no system of writing of their own; and although Darius the Great adapted Babylonian cuneiform to record Old Persian in his rock-inscriptions, in general under the Achaemenians writing remained associated with the foreign languages used on Iranian soil. Aramaic was the language of administration and commerce; but slowly successive generations of scribes introduced into it more and more Iranian words, until by the beginning of the Christian era a number of Iranian languages (notably Middle Persian or Pahlavi, Parthian, and Sogdian, a language of the far north-east) were being written in varieties of the Aramaic script, in which a quantity of Aramaic words remained fossilised, as ideograms representing Iranian equivalents. This rather cumbersome form of writing was not used for literature, but only for practical needs. There seem to be two main reasons for this. Firstly, the old Iranian literature was in the main poetic, and closely associated with the music to which it was sung. Secondly, it was cultivated orally by minstrels, who were wholly divorced by profession and training from the scribes. The minstrel-poet had to master versification and music, fixed epithets and techniques of extempore composition, as well as learning an immense amount by heart; whereas the scribe was concerned with scripts and ideograms, weights and measures, accounting, laws and the conventions of correspondence.

In between these two groups were, in a sense, the Zoroastrian priests. From their ranks came judges and administrators, who worked with scribes; and there were also priestly scholars, who, in Sasanian times, studied medicine, astronomy and other sciences with the aid of foreign books. But there were also serving priests, who worshipped the gods with hymns and liturgies composed by their forefathers in the oral tradition, which they learnt by heart, together with a vast quantity of non-liturgical texts, committed to memory, word for word, without recourse to books. During the Sasanian period the Zoroastrian church took the great step of writing down these sacred works. (In this it may have been influenced a little by Manichaeism, a rival religion whose prophet Mani, in the third century AD, adapted a Syriac script for writing the Iranian versions of his scriptures.) At first the Pahlavi script must have been used; but probably in the sixth century the Zoroastrians evolved from it the more precise Avestan alphabet, solely to record their holy texts.

Much of this written Zoroastrian scripture was lost under Islam; but it is largely due to what survives, supplemented by a few Persian or Arabic renderings of individual works, that we know anything of the old Iranian literature. It is the fact that this literature remained oral until a late date which gives it its unity over a long period; for oral literature is immensely conservative, and one finds individual works existing for centuries, recreated in Parthian and Middle Persian from Avestan originals. This conservatism, together with anonymity and a common style, makes it impossible to establish individual authorship; and it is not until the very end of the period that the names of one or two court-poets and priestly writers are known and handed down.

THE LITERATURE

Old Iranian verse was unrhymed, with accentual metres, in which the stresses were fixed, but the number of syllables fluctuated within certain set limits. Secular poetry appears always to have been sung, usually to an instrument; and the loss of the accompanying music makes it impossible to estimate its quality truly. Poetry was very widely cultivated, by professional and amateur; but it was almost all lost after the Arab conquest, when the introduction of rhymed, quantitative verse put the old poems out of fashion. We know of it now mostly through allusions, and through homilies against its charm and sweetness. Only two groups of verse survive to any extent, namely the epic poetry of the minstrels, indirectly, and the hymns of the priests.

Three main cycles can be traced in the surviving epic: the Kayanian, devoted to the exploits, probably in the eighth to seventh centuries BC, of the ancestors of Vishtasp, Zoroaster's princely patron; a cycle celebrating the deeds of Rustam, a hero of the Saka people who invaded eastern Iran in the second century BC; and the Arsacid cycle, praising the kings of the Parthian empire. It is probable that, because of intermarriages, all three cycles were sung at the same princely courts in the north-east, and that after centuries of oral transmission they became mingled together in long heroic poems. The Sasanians, as upholders of the Zoroastrian faith, claimed descent from the Kayanians, and so these poems were recited at their court also, with added exploits of their own, still told in the heroic manner despite the sophistications of this later age. This minstrel epic was drawn on by learned priests for a written prose history of the world from the Iranian Adam down to Sasanian times, called the *Khwaday-Namag* (Book of Kings). This great work survives in two forms: Arabic prose translations (which in turn provided the basis for Islamic historical writing), and the noble Persian verse-epic, the *Shāh-nāme* written by Firdausi in the tenth century. For his work Firdausi used a rendering into classical Persian of the *Khwaday-Namag*, made by Zoroastrian scholars for a Muslim prince; but it is evident that oral epic was still alive in north-east Iran in his own day, and that he recast the prose stories under its inspiration, but with the new enrichments of quantitative metre and rhyme. The result is a great poem, which still preserves something of the fire and warlike splendours of Iran's heroic age.

Only two small fragments of the epic survive in Middle Iranian: a scrap from a Sogdian version of the Rustam cycle, preserved by the Manichaeans, and a Middle Persian redaction of Parthian verses recounting the deeds of Zarer, son of Vishtasp. This, the *Ayadgar i Zareran*, suffers from a longer oral transmission than the *Khwaday-Namag* version (probably down to the ninth century), and from the obscurities of the Pahlavi script; but the old verse-pattern is discernible, together with poetic conventions found again in the *Shāh-nāme*. Something moreover of the nobility of the old epic survives, handed down by men orally for some fifteen-hundred years.

There exists also a Middle Persian prose-work, the *Karnamag i Ardashir*, which is probably the last remnant of an old Persian epic tradition. This celebrates the deeds of the founder of the Sasanian dynasty, in much the same form as in the *Khwaday-Namag*. These have little historical authenticity, and are cast partly in the same mould as deeds attributed to Cyrus the Great, according to Herodotus. Probably therefore the old epic stories of Achaemenian Persia lived on orally in Pars down to Sasanian times, and were adapted to later kings; but in the main Sasanian literature derives its themes from the north-east, adopting them from there with the Zoroastrian religion.

Among the Iranian Ossetes of the Caucasus there survives a remarkable series of prose tales about a group of heroes called the Narts. These, handed down orally till the beginning of the nineteenth century, are thought to represent an ancient heroic cycle, possibly originally in verse, current among the Sarmatian-Alanic tribes, the ancestors of the Ossetes. They cannot be dated, but presumably go back well into the pre-Christian era.

Post-heroic narrative poetry is represented by the long Parthian work *Vis u Ramin*. This, more romance than epic proper, tells, with a wealth of warlike and romantic detail, the loves of the two persons from whom it is named. It belongs probably to the first century AD, and was written down in Pahlavi script, in a version compiled by 'six wise men' some time after the Arab conquest. In the eleventh century a Persian poem was made from it by Gurgānī. This alone survives, together with a Georgian version.

There was also a less-regarded prose literature of entertainment, in the form of short stories, also unwritten. A story-teller was kept at the Sasanian court, who was forbidden to repeat himself except at royal command. In the sixth century there became popular a number of written works deriving from Indian originals, which consisted of a frame-story linking a series of such shorter tales. Of these *Kalila u Dimna* survives in an Arabic version, and there are later renderings also of the *Book of Sindbad*, the *Tuti Name*, and *Balauhar and Budasaf*. The *Thousand and One Nights* is said to have its origin in a similar Sasanian work, the *Hazar Afsan* or 'Thousand Tales'.

The world of the priest was naturally remote from that of the professional entertainer, but the basic conventions of religious and secular poetry appear to have been the same. There are two main groups of sacred verse composed in Avestan, the otherwise unknown language of the Zoroastrian scriptures once spoken in north east Iran. One consists of the seventeen Gathas (hymns) attributed to Zoroaster himself, which are composed in an archaic dialect. These are in an ancient Indo-Iranian priestly convention in so far as stylistic devices are concerned, and the fact that they are addressed by a priest to his God; but they are deeply original in intensity of feeling and loftiness of thought, which can only be partly apprehended today, since to its own complexity is added the obscurity of the language. These hymns, like those of the 'Younger Avesta', are chanted, but never to an instrumental accompaniment. Five different strophic patterns occur within them.

The other group of sacred verse comprises the *Yashts*, hymns to lesser divine beings, some of them 'old' gods of the Indo-Iranian pantheon. Five or six, which are known as the 'great *Yashts*', plainly contain very ancient matter, some of it pre-dating Zoroaster; but only the prophet's own words were sacred enough to be preserved in the speech of his own day. The other hymns were, in the usual manner of oral transmission, recreated by successive generations of priests, so that we have them in the later form in which Avestan became fixed as the sacred language. There is unevenness even in the great *Yashts*, several of which are very long (the *Mihr Yasht* has one hundred and forty-five verses); but they contain some fine poetic passages, vivid with the emotions of worship and awe, or enriched by similes, or allusions to old myth and legend, imaginatively conveyed. All the *Yashts*, whether ancient, or rather colourless later compositions, appear to have three stresses to the line, and an average line-length of eight syllables. Similar versification, though with rather greater metric variety, is to be found in the Iranian hymns of the Manichaean church, which also contain some striking passages. In them there is to be seen, however, some influence from Semitic models, especially in the free use of abecedarian devices, which belong to a written convention.

The main liturgies of the Zoroastrian church are of ritual rather than literary significance; and it is only the liturgical parts of the Avesta which survive. In former times this work was a vast compilation of twenty-one books, which included works 'on cosmogony and eschatology, astronomy and natural history, law and medicine, the life of the prophet and the history of man, extracts from ancient myth and collections of gnomic lore'. These books gradually disappeared under Islam; but during the Sasanian period they had all been translated into Middle Persian, with commentaries, and although this translation, called the *Zand*, is itself largely lost, the learning embodied in it was adopted and used by scholars of Muslim Iran.

One interesting work, the *Bundahishn* or 'Creation', surviving in a ninth-century redaction, consists of a compilation of passages taken from the *Zand*. Its style is plain and often awkward, because of an Avestan syntax underlying the Middle Persian; but its interest lies in the antiquity of the material. 'Here is preserved an ancient, in part pre-Zoroastrian picture of the world, conceived as saucer-shaped, with its rim one great mountain-range, a central peak thrust up, star-encircled, to cut off the light of the sun by night; a world girdled by two great rivers, from which all other waters flow; in which yearly the gods fight against demons to end drought and famine, and to bring protection to man . . . Not only is the matter ancient and often poetic, but the manner of presentation, although arid, is of great antiquarian interest; for after the distinctively Zoroastrian account of creation, the speculative learning and legendary history is set out in traditional oral fashion, that is to say, in schematised mnemonic lists: so many types of animals, so many kinds of liquid, so many names of mountains, so many great battles. This is the learning of ancient Iran, as it must have been evolved and transmitted by generations in the priestly schools.'

Other types of oral composition are also represented in the secondary religious writings (which are themselves too numerous to name in detail here, and which are moreover mainly of greater theological than literary interest). Among these are various branches of 'wisdom' literature, including a considerable number of mantic works. One category, 'visions of the homes of the dead', is represented by the *Arday Viraz Namag*, which tells how the just Viraz saw in a trance visions of heaven and hell. This work existed evidently in Avestan, but survives in a Middle Persian redaction. It is one of the most popular Zoroastrian works, and is thought to have influenced the Islamic *mi'raj*, and so, indirectly, Dante. A literature of prophecy, looking before and after over the whole sweep of man's existence, is represented by the *Zand* of the lost Avestan *Bahman Yasht*, and by the Middle Persian verse *Jamasp Namag*, with its prose elaboration. This Iranian prophetic literature exerted influence on Greco-Egyptian prophetic writings from at least the second century BC.

More mundane types of wisdom-literature are represented by the riddle-poem *Drakht i asurig* (The Babylonian Tree), about a contest for precedence between date-palm and goat. Such works were meant both to entertain and instruct, by sharpening the wits. There is also a prose-work, deriving from an Avestan original, about a riddle-contest between a sorcerer Akht and a Zoroastrian Joisht, who triumphs over his foe.

Middle Persian is rich in collections of *andarz* or gnomes, represented also in the lost Avestan *Barish Nask*. These embody, not the mantic wisdom of vision and prophecy, but that of observation and prudence. Many are trite, stating the obvious; but some are imaginative, and a few embody moral utterances of a high order. In course of time many of the old *andarz* were incorporated in the Islamic *adab* literature, and so lived on in more sophisticated elegance.

There is a longer treatise, the *Menog i Khrad* (Book of the Spirit of Wisdom) attributed in its present form to the sixth century AD, which has something in common with the *andarz* in both style and content; but this work has not only a consecutive thread, but also a stylistically elaborate preamble. Intricate introductions are to be found to other sixth-century works, and it is probable that by this time prose, being written down, was developing elegant complexities of its own. Two political treatises, the *Testament of Ardashir* and the *Letter of Tansar*, both originating in the first Sasanian reign, were elaborated at this time, and both survive in Arabic or Persian versions. They are interesting works, for their historical content, style, and Machiavellian treatment.

Tansar, the writer of the original letter, was a well-known Zoroastrian priest; and it is to the priests of Iran that we owe, not only the preservation, directly and indirectly, of such of the ancient literature as we possess, but also the literary experiments which gradually led to a more general use of writing, even for bardic works. Through their labours we can apprehend something of Iranian literature as it stretches back into a remote past, and can also follow the slow process of an oral literature becoming a written one. The Islamic conquest occurred when this process was going on, and diverted the course of Iranian letters into new channels.

BIBLIOGRAPHY

BOYCE, M. 'Middle Iranian Literature' in *Handbuch der Orientalistik*, ed. B. Spuler (Leiden, 1968), 1ste Abteilung, Band IV 2.

FRYE, R. N. *The Heritage of Persia* (London, 1962), with bibliographies covering history and culture.

GERSHEVITCH I. 'Iranian Literature' in *Literatures of the East*, ed. E. B. Ceadel (London, 1953).

'Old Iranian Literature' in *Handbuch der Orientalistik*, ed. B. Spuler (Leiden, 1968), 1ste Abteilung, Band IV 2.

GHIRSHMAN, R. *Iran*, New York and Harmondsworth, 1954.

PERSIAN LITERATURE

Classical and Modern Literature

A. A. Haidari

HISTORICAL BACKGROUND

In spite of its apparent continuity, there have been many breaks in the political history of Persia. The Achaemenid empire founded by Cyrus in 559 BC had been eventually overthrown by Alexander the Great in 331 BC. This marked the opening of a period of Hellenistic influence under the Seleucids. They were followed by the Parthians, who in turn were succeeded by the Sasanians (AD 224–642). Their rule was brought to an end by the Islamic invasion. This event had profound consequences and opened a new period in the history of Persian civilisation. Yet the Islamic conquest did not involve a complete break with the past. So far as Islam was identified with the Arabs, Persia resisted assimilation. But in due course Arab Islam gave way to a wider conception and took over the idea of universal empire from the Eastern Roman empire on the one hand and Sasanian Persia on the other.

The new empire of which Persia formed part was ruled first by the Umayyad Caliphs from Damascus and then by the ʻAbbasid Caliphs from Baghdad.

A new brilliant civilisation based on Islam developed, to which Persians made important contributions. Under the Sasanian and earlier dynasties literary activity in Persia appears to have been limited. What survives is chiefly court literature, religious and legal documents, and legendary stories of the ancient kings of Persia, such as the *Kar Namak of Ardashir*, written in Pahlavi. Under the stimulus of Islam there was a flowering of Persian talents; and the artistic temperament and natural genius and power of assimilation of the Persian people, as Sir Hamilton Gibb has pointed out, found their finest expression. With the fragmentation of the Caliphate in the ninth century semi-independent dynasties were founded in Persia and elsewhere. The rulers of these dynasties, on the whole, were orthodox Muslims and the movements they led do not represent, as is sometimes claimed, anti-Muslim Persian nationalist movements. In the eleventh century the invasion of Persia by Turkoman tribes under the Saljuqs brought about a radical change in the ethnic composition of the population of the country: henceforth, alongside the Persian element there was an important Turkish element. The Mongol invasion of the thirteenth century, which brought to an end the ʻAbbasid Caliphate, was later followed by the conquest of Timur. In the succeeding period some of the Turkoman tribes which had passed through Persia in Saljuq and post-Saljuq times began to turn back eastwards, this movement culminating in the establishment of the Safavid empire. The most important feature of this was the adoption by Persia of the Shīʿī sect of Islam as the official religion of the country. The resulting separation of Persia from the rest of the Islamic world prepared the way for the eventual emergence of a national territorial state, though under the Safavids nationalism and patriotism were still largely religious sentiments.

Political unity in Islamic times was repeatedly disrupted; but underlying the fragmentation of political authority there was a striking continuity in the traditions of civilisation. The memory of the old Persian empire never entirely died and there lived on a pride in old Persian traditions; but the cohesive force of civilisation was Islam. The function of the state was to create conditions in which the good life could be lived. The religious classes, the *ʿulamā*, played an immensely important part in the transmission of learning. As the guardians of Islamic tradition and knowledge they were a stabilising force of great importance. Alongside the *ʿulamā* were the 'men of letters', the *udabā*, who were the guardians of literary, as opposed to Islamic, tradition. They had a less specialised training than the *ʿulamā*, who were rigorously trained in the religious sciences; but the distinction between them became less sharp with the growth of the religious schools, or *madrasas*, under the great Saljuq dynasty (AD 1037–1157), since both were trained in these institutions. The mystics, the *ʿurafā*, too, often studied in the *madrasa*, which thus had great influence in forming the cultural and literary climate of the day.

The royal courts also played an important part in the spread of literary activity. Many of the rulers and their ministers were patrons of learned men and poets; literary men were highly esteemed and sought after. Sometimes for reasons of prestige and sometimes because of a genuine desire for learning, rulers would seek to attract to their courts distinguished scholars. Ministers and courtiers were expected to be familiar with all fields of knowledge; and the royal court was not infrequently a circle of learned men. Maḥmūd b. Sebuktakin, the Ghaznavid (reigned 998–1030), Sanjar (reigned 1117–57), the last of the great Saljuqs and Ḥusain b. Manṣūr b. Bāyqarā (reigned 1488–1506), the Timurid ruler of Herat, to mention but three examples, had brilliant courts at which they assembled poets, writers and scholars. Among the other arts that flourished under the Timurids were miniature painting, carpet-weaving, pottery, and metal work.

Under the Safavids, although literature suffered a decline, the period is regarded as the golden age of arts and crafts and in particular architecture. Shah ʿAbbās I (1586–1628), the greatest ruler of the dynasty, moved the seat of government from Qazvin to Isfahan, where he constructed a splendid capital with magnificent mosques and palaces. He also built numerous caravanserais, some of which are still to be seen today along the high-roads of Persia as monuments to his enterprise.

The Safavids were overthrown in 1722 by the Afghans, who in their turn were defeated by Nāder Shah, who founded the Afshar dynasty in 1736. He made Meshed his capital and favoured his Sunnī subjects at the expense of the Shī'as. Nāder was a brilliant soldier and is chiefly famous for his campaigning in India. His assassination in 1747 was followed by a period of unrest and tribal strife until Karīm Khān established his supremacy. He ruled from Shiraz (1759–79), but although he exerted effective control over much of Persia, he never assumed the title of Shah. With his death a struggle for the throne broke out, and lasted for fifteen years until 1794 when Āghā Moḥammad Khān, the Qajar leader, established himself as the ruler of Persia.

The Qajar dynasty lasted throughout the nineteenth century into the twentieth century. As a result of the revolution of 1905–6, a constitution was granted in 1906 and a consultative assembly was established. The Qajar dynasty was finally succeeded by the Pahlavi, whose founder Reza Shah assumed the throne in 1924. Under Reza Shah's son, the present reigning monarch, Iran has developed into one of the most prosperous and stable countries of the Middle East.

MAIN TRENDS IN LITERATURE

Literary activity in Persia in the period immediately following the Muslim conquest in the seventh century AD was largely confined to those who wrote in Arabic. The generally spoken language of the Sasanian court was called *darī*, which was written in the Pahlavi alphabet. The language of the people meanwhile underwent profound changes; and gradually new Persian emerged as a literary language. The most striking difference between Pahlavi and new Persian is the introduction of an immense Arabic vocabulary into the latter. New Persian spread over a wide area and became the medium for a rich literature, which had not been the case with Pahlavi. In freeing Islam from an exclusive attachment to the Arabic language and an Arab background, Persian did much to universalise Islam and thus to expand and preserve it. It is not until the tenth century AD, when we find a new Persian literature, written in the Arabic script, that a fresh literary era begins and the ancient traditions of Persia are incorporated into the culture of Islam. New Persian literature is not only Persian but, more strikingly, it is also Islamic. New Persian was fashioned and polished by Muslim Persians who were well versed in Arabic, and had, at the same time, a love for their own spoken language.

New Persian in the Arabic script was first written in the ninth century in eastern Persia and came to flower in Bukhara, the capital of the Samanid dynasty (AD 874–999). In the succeeding centuries there was in literature, perhaps more in poetry than prose, a growing tendency towards elaboration and subtlety in language and formal perfection rather than originality of thought; and towards a preoccupation with mystical and philosophical themes. In prose, in spite of the considerable change in vocabulary, the use of grammatical forms, and the structure of the sentence, there is a striking stability in language and literary form for something like a thousand years. The Persian of the earliest period is closer to contemporary Persian than, for example, the English of Chaucer to the English language of today. The area in which Persian was used was not confined to the geographical limits of Persia; it spread to both Turkey, where it had a great influence on Ottoman Turkish literature, and India, where an important school of Persian literature developed.

POETRY

Persian poetry, which adopted the Arabic system of prosody (*'arūz*), began sporadically in east Persia in the ninth century. The earliest extant Persian verse belongs to the Samanid period (AD 874–999). In the scattered works of some early poets such as Vaṣif and Shahīd-e Balkhī a mixture of Arabic and Persian is found. With few exceptions the earliest Persian poems are lacking in literary merit in comparison with the poetry of later ages. Their significance lies only in their antiquity. The longest poem belonging to this period is the *Dāneshnāme* of a certain physician called Maysarī, a unique copy of which is preserved in the Bibliothèque Nationale in Paris. The best author of the late ninth century was Shahīd-e Balkhī, who is looked upon as a poet and a philosopher. Later poets had a high opinion of his work.

By the tenth century AD Persian had become a polished and melodious medium. Proof of this statement is to be found in the extant poems of Rūdakī (*d* 940). He is known as the 'father of Persian poetry'. Islamic Persian literature began in the age of Rūdakī. He was a versatile and apparently prolific poet. He is said to have written poems in the form of the *qaṣida* (purpose poem), *qit'a* (fragment), *maṣnavī* (long narrative poem), and *ghazal* (lyric). He was the first known poet to have used the latter form. Some seven thousand couplets only, comprising eulogies, wine songs, and love poems are extant. In his eulogies Rūdakī, unlike later poets, seldom indulges in exaggeration, but when he does, his poetical conceits are not lacking in beauty. His wine songs are simple, and contain some attractive similes. The following is an example in praise of wine:

Be pākī gū'ī andar jām mānand-e golābastī;
Be khushi gū'ī andar dīde-ye bī-khāb khābastī.
Agar may nīstī yeksar hameh 'ālam kharābastī;
Agar dar kālbad jān tā nadidastī sharābastī.

With regard to purity one would say that it is like rose water in the goblet,
With regard to happiness one would say that it is like sleep to the sleepless eye.
If there is no wine, all hearts are utterly broken;
If thou hast not seen the soul in the body (behold) it is wine.

In his love poems Rūdakī reflects on the shortness of life and the deceitful nature of the world;

In jehān pāk khāb kerdār ast;
Ān shenāsad ke delsh bīdār ast.

This world is entirely dream-like;
He whose heart is awake knows this.

Rūdakī's major work was a *masnavī* version of the *Kalila u Dimna*, of which only a few fragments remain. The chief characteristics of Rūdakī's poetry are its lucidity and clarity; and more than a thousand years after his death, he is still read and appreciated.

Epic

In the latter half of the tenth century a few years after Rūdakī's death, the age of the Persian epic began. The origin of the epic tradition in Persia goes back much further and is intimately connected with mythology. The main sources for the Persian epic are the Avesta and Pahlavi books and recensions of these in new Persian and Arabic works. The first poet to compose an epic was Mas'ūdī-e-Marvazī, who lived in the latter part of the tenth century. Little is known about him. It is alleged that he composed a *Shāh-nāme* (Book of Kings), completing it about AD 910. Judging from a few scattered verses in early texts, Marvazī's poems seem immature in substance and form, and suggest that the Arabic metres had not yet been fully assimilated. Another early poet of great importance who began to write a *Shāh-nāme* was Daqīqī; but an untimely death, probably in 975, cut short his work. The theme of Daqīqī's *Shāh-nāme* is the story of Gushtāsp and the advent of Zoroaster. It consists of a thousand couplets and was subsequently incorporated into the *Shāh-nāme* of Firdausī. In his epic as well as in a few other forms of poetry attributed to him, a strong inclination to Zoroastrianism can be detected. Indeed, in one couplet Daqīqī exclaims:

> By God, he will never see Heaven;
> Who does not follow the path of Zoroaster.

The Zoroastrian elements in Daqīqī's poetry show that there was still nostalgia for the past, especially among poets. Daqīqī's poems show a degree of maturity comparable to the works of Rūdakī.

As well as the poetic versions of Marvazī and Daqīqī, there were others who attempted prose versions of the *Shāh-nāme*. The most important of these is known as the *Shāh-nāme* of Abū Manṣūrī. This was a collection of Persian stories and traditions made by a number of bibliophiles under the supervision of Abū Manṣūr Moḥammad b. 'Abd al-Razzāq Ṭūsī, who was *sipahsālār* (army commander) of Khorāsān in 960–1.

But the *Shāh-nāme par excellence* is the *Shāh-nāme* of Firdausī which is undoubtedly the greatest epic in Persian literature. The Samanid dynasty had already passed its zenith when Firdausī wrote; but it was the Samanid period which had created the language Firdausī used and perfected; and it was eastern Persia, then the refuge of the old traditions, which provided the background for Firdausī and his *Shāh-nāme*.

From incidental references in the *Shāh-nāme* it appears that Firdausī was about forty years old when he began to write his monumental work. The first version of the *Shāh-nāme* was completed in 994 and the second in 1009. It was the latter version which was presented to Sultān Maḥmūd, whose court at Ghazna Firdausī had joined a few years earlier. When he did not receive what he considered due recognition he left Ghazna. He spent a few more years completing his third and final version. This great poem consists of sixty-thousand couplets, including a satire on Sulṭān Maḥmūd, the authenticity of which is open to question. The *Shāh-nāme* is a history of the Persian kings from the earliest times to the death of the last Sasanian king, Yazdegerd III, in AD 651. The early part deals with the legendary history of Persia and concerns the struggle between Turān and Irān, which has been interpreted by some as the struggle between the nomad element of the population and the settled element. Firdausī depicts the rise and fall of a variety of dynasties and there is a certain uniformity in his treatment of the episodes he selects; and underlying his descriptions there are certain constant, or fairly constant, themes. His comments are broadly confined to observations on the inevitability of change and the uncertainties of life. As literature the *Shāh-nāme* bears witness to its author's gifts as a superb story-teller and its literary worth is beyond dispute. Firdausī not only depicts the battle scene with vividness but also tells romantic tales with sensitivity. He excites, moves, and surprises the reader in turn. His characters are heroes and giants, but his language is comparatively free from hyperbole. In a well-known scene when Rustam the mightiest of all Persian heroes, who dominates the book, encounters Esfandiār and after a fight is about to kill his formidable foe, he says laconically:

> Even now your head will roll in the dust;
> (And) the heart of your kind mother will grieve.

In the famous episode when Rustam realises he had unwittingly killed his son Sohrāb, the poet illustrates the state of the wretched father with this simple statement:

> He was dripping with blood and tearing his hair;
> His head covered with dust and his face with tears.

Even in his rhetorical verses Firdausī's fluency is apparent. As an example the following often quoted couplet may be mentioned:

> Borīd-o darīd-o shekast-o bebast;
> Yalān rā sar-o sīneh-o pāy-o dast.

He (Rustam) cut off the heads, tore open the breasts, smashed the feet and bound the hands of the warriors.

Firdausī, like his predecessor Daqīqī, selected for his *Shāh-nāme* the *mutaqārib* metre which in orthodox Persian prosodic terminology is:

Fa'ūlon, fa'ūlon, fa'ūlon, fa'ūl.

Although the language of Firdausī is of the utmost simplicity, contrary to common but mistaken belief in Persia, a great number of Arabic words can be found in the *Shāh-nāme*. It is merely the uncommon Arabic words which the poet avoids. This restraint was probably not deliberate; Firdausī was simply writing in the language current in his native Khorāsān. His style is vigorous and compelling; and it is largely through his epic that the heroes of the past and their stories have remained alive in the minds of the Persian people down to the present day.

The Qaṣida

Very different from the epic was the *qaṣida* or 'purpose poem' first written by Rūdakī. The majority of *qaṣidas* are panegyrics, but sometimes they are elegies and lamentations, and occasionally they also deal with philosophical or biographical matters. The opening verse or *maṭla'* of the *qaṣida*, the two halves of which rhyme, sets both the metre and the rhyme. The minimum length of a *qaṣida* is fifteen to twenty couplets. Persian *qaṣidas* for the most part consist of between thirty to fifty couplets; but *qaṣidas* of over a hundred couplets are not infrequent, and the longest Persian *qaṣida*, said to be one by Qā'ānī, has three hundred and thirty seven couplets. The *qaṣidas* and *ghazals* of a poet, together with any short fragments (*qit'a'āt*) and quatrains, were collected in a volume, the *qaṣidas* and *ghazals* in alphabetical order according to the last letter of the last word of each couplet, and this collection was known as the poet's *dīvān*.

The early exponents of the *qaṣida* were mostly contemporaries of Firdausī, namely Unṣurī, Farrukhī, and 'Asjadī. Unṣurī (*d* 1040), was regarded as the doyen of the poets at the court of Sultān Mahmūd. He was not only the favourite of the Sultān but was acclaimed by his fellow poets also. The *Dīvān* of Unṣurī is alleged to have contained thirty thousand couplets, of which only some two thousand are extant. These are mostly panegyrics, in the Turkistanī or Khorāsānī style of which the following verse is an example:

Shāh-e gīty khosrov-e lashkar kash-e lashkar shekān;
Sāye-ye yazdān shah-e keshvar deh-e keshvar setān.

The king of the world, the monarch who leads his army and defeats (other) armies
The shadow of God who bestows and seizes kingdoms.

Among the lost works of Unṣurī is the romance of *Vamiq-o 'Azrā* based on a Sasanid fable; only a few disconnected verses have been preserved. He also apparently wrote *ghazals* in imitation of Rūdakī; but these too have been lost.

Although Farrukhī (*d* 1037) ranked below Unṣurī in the court circle he was regarded by some critics as his superior in literary merit. The opening verse of a famous *qaṣida* by Farrukhī consisting of one hundred and seventy five couplets begins as follows:

Fesāne gasht-o kohan shod hadīs̈-e Eskandar;
Sokhan now ār ke now rā halāvatīst degar.

The story of Alexander has become an outworn fable,
Bring forth something new because what is new has a different sweetness.

Farrukhī's poems are more graceful and easy than those of Unṣurī. Tradition relates that Farrukhī like Rūdakī as well as being an able poet was also skilled in the playing of the lute. That is why, perhaps, the melody of his poetry, in general, stands out. The following is an example:

Bar āmad nilgūn abrī ze rūy-e nīlgūn daryā;
Cho ra'y-e 'āsheqān gardān cho tab'-e bīdelān sheydā.

A blue cloud rose from the blue sea;
Changeable like the mood of lovers, frenzied like the nature of those who have lost their hearts in love.

The third of this trio, 'Asjadī (*d* 1025) is more given to artificial devices in his poetry than the other two, and is inferior to them. His most famous and most frequently quoted *qaṣida* is one written on the conquest of an idol temple.

Following in the steps of the early masters, there have been a great number of panegyrists in the long history of Persian literature; among them Manūchehrī, Anvarī and Khāqānī were outstanding, and had a great influence on later poets. The theme, vocabulary and style of the poems of Manūchehrī (*d* 1041) show a strong Arabic influence; and he uses many unfamiliar Arabic words. Some of his poems, however, are among the best descriptive poems in the Persian language and are marked by joy and gaiety. He was a skilled exponent of the *mosammaṭ*, a form of multiple poetry.

Anvarī (*d* 1169), one of the court poets of Sanjar, is regarded by many writers as the greatest of all Persian panegyrists. His most famous *qaṣida* in praise of his patron opens with the following verse:

Gar del-o dast bahr-o kān bāshad;
Del-o dast-e khodāygān bāshad.
If heart and hands are sea and treasure,
They are the heart and hands of my lord.

In Anvarī the *qaṣida* achieves its full maturity. His style is graceful and confident and his language polished. He also wrote satirical verses as well as *ghazals* of high quality. The latter influenced, in particular, Sa'dī.

Khāqānī (*d* 1199) is also considered as one of the masters of the *qaṣida*, but in contradistinction to Anvarī his *qaṣidas* are written in a somewhat heavy style. His allusions and metaphors are often far-fetched, but some of his elegiac poems, *ghazals* and fragments are easy and moving.

Another *qaṣida* writer of some originality and much esteemed by writers is Nāṣer-e Khosrou (*d* 1072). His *qaṣidas*, although mainly dealing with weighty matters, including Ismā'ilism to which he was a convert and of which he was an ardent propagandist, have nevertheless an underlying spirit of joy. Among panegyrists perhaps Nāṣer-e Khosrou stands almost alone in that he does not seek the favour of a particular patron. Indeed he rebukes his fellow poets in harsh words, for their praise of kings and courts. Thus:

> Man ānam ke dar pāy-e khūkān narīzam;
> Mar in qeymatī dorr-e lafẓ-e darī rā.
>
> I am the one who does not cast before swine
> This precious pearl, the *darī* word.

The list of panegyrist poets is a long one and only a few of the most outstanding have been mentioned.

The Ruba'ī

Almost contemporary with Nāṣer-e Khosrou is the greatest writer of the *ruba'ī* (the quatrain), 'Omar Khayyām (*d* 1129), who was made famous in Europe by Fitzgerald's translation. Khayyām is a poet of singular originality, who conveyed his philosophy of life through the medium of the simplest form of Persian verse, the *ruba'ī*, which consists of four *meṣra'* hemistichs (whence called *ruba'ī*) and like the epigram, it is always complete in itself.

The Ghazal

Although *ghazals* (lyrics) were written in the early period, as mentioned above, this form of verse was comparatively neglected until the thirteenth century. Like the *qaṣida* it is composed on a single rhyme and may be written in one or other of a great variety of metres. It consists of a succession of couplets, usually not less than five or more than fifteen. The two lines of the first couplet rhyme with one another and with the second line of the following couplets. The individual couplets are often complete in themselves and independent of each other. In spite, however, of an apparent lack of unity, the *ghazal* is commonly held together by a subtle and underlying harmony. The theme of the *ghazal* is largely love – sacred or profane, in all its manifestations.

The second half of the thirteenth century and the first half of the fourteenth are often regarded as the golden age of Persian poetry. It was in this period – a period when Persia suffered the terrible Mongol invasion – that the three greatest poets of Persia lived, namely Sa'dī, Rūmī and Ḥāfeẓ, and it was they, above all, who excelled in the *ghazal*. Sa'dī was born in Shīrāz in AD 1292 and died there after a long and eventful life. He is both versatile and prolific, writing poems of all types; but it is his *ghazals* for which he is most praised. The secret of his popularity may be attributed to, firstly, his understanding of human nature and his ability to depict profane love; secondly, the simplicity of his language and the lucidity of his style; and thirdly, the unity of meaning running through each *ghazal*, which more than any other characteristic distinguishes his *ghazals* from those of other poets. Some of Sa'dī's *ghazals* are mystical, as for example the *ghazal* beginning:

I am happy through the world because the world is happy through Him;
I love the whole world because the whole world is His.

The majority, however, deal with profane love. Sa'dī is basically a moralist, not only in his *qaṣidas*, but also even in his love poems, in which also he sometimes indulges in admonition. Although as a preacher Sa'dī is at times severe, nevertheless a tone of joy and cheerfulness runs through his poetry giving it charm and grace. He lacks the vitality and profundity of his contemporary, Rūmī, and the subtlety and sensitivity of Ḥāfeẓ; but it was Sa'dī's success in establishing the *ghazal* that paved the way for Ḥāfeẓ, who, although the most consummate master of the *ghazal*, recognised the authority of Sa'dī.

Rūmī, a native of Balkh, died in Konya in 1273, and is certainly the greatest mystical poet of Persia (see also below p. 121). He became a mystic under the influence of Shams-e Tabrīz, the mysterious dervish under whose name Rūmī composed his *dīvān* known as the *Kulliyāt-e-Shams-e Tabrīz*, consisting of over forty thousand couplets. 'Rūmī's lyrics,' states the late Professor Nicholson, the leading authority on Rūmī, 'reach the utmost heights of which a poetry inspired by vision and rapture is capable, and these alone would have made him the unchallenged laureate of mysticism.' The theme of Rūmī's *ghazals*, some of which throb with passion and life, is sacred love; and in some of them he reflects on metaphysical problems; in spite of this one of the characteristics of Rūmī's *ghazals* is their genuine joy and vitality. For example, a long lyric begins with these lines:

I was all tears, I became all laughter,
I was dead, I became alive;
The grace of love came,
And I became perpetual happiness.

They are also distinguished by a melodious quality and almost every *ghazal* of his *dīvān* has a music of its own. Rūmī does not restrict himself to the accepted and well established tradition of Persian lyrics. The majority of *ghazals* seldom exceed ten couplets, but in Rūmī's case a lyric often reached fifteen couplets, or even more. Not only in length, in form also, Rūmī is a non-conformist in his *ghazals*, some of which resemble panegyrical odes or *qaṣidas* more than lyrics. Unlike many of the versifiers of earlier centuries, Rūmī seldom sacrifices meaning for rhyme. He has a poor opinion of rhyme for its own sake, as he says:

> When I am thinking of rhyme, my beloved tells me:
> Do not think of anything except of seeing me!

But sometimes Rūmī's concentration on ideas and meaning and his neglect for words and forms led him to extremes.

It is reported by more than one biographer that Rūmī composed his lyrics while in a state of ecstasy and that these were written down by his disciples, and it seems probable that Rūmī wrote, or to be more exact, recited his *ghazals* when in a state of exaltation.

Ḥāfeẓ, like Sa'dī, was born in Shiraz and died there in 1389. He is by common consent the greatest of the lyric poets of Persia. His greatness lies in the fact that he maintains a harmonious balance between words and meaning. In Ḥāfeẓ the *ghazal* reached its perfection both in form and diction. Sa'dī and Rūmī, though masters in their own right, lacked the perfect sense of balance of Ḥāfeẓ. His vocabulary is rich and varied, maintaining here again a balance between common speech and the literary language. He avoids those rare and tiresome expressions which filled the verses of the professional panegyrists of earlier centuries. His choice of the right word and attractive compounds adds to the beauty of his poetry. While using literary artifices, to which the Persian language so readily lends itself, he is careful not to use them to excess so that what he writes may be understood by ordinary people. It is not surprising then, if a copy of the *dīvān* of Ḥāfeẓ is to be found in almost every Persian household. Fitzgerald understood this well when he wrote that 'Ḥāfeẓ is the most Persian of the Persians'. That is why Persians unreservedly trust the word of Ḥāfeẓ whether they understand it or not. In fact, too much is made by critics of allegorical tendencies, which may or may not exist, in Ḥāfeẓ lyrics. Gertrude Bell, the best translator of Ḥāfeẓ so far, in her introduction to the *dīvān* perhaps rightly states: 'The tendency in dealing with a mystical poet is to read into him so-called deeper meaning, even when the simple meaning is clear enough and sufficient in itself.' Ḥāfeẓ is one of those who has suffered from this process. When he cries: 'The beloved is gone without bidding farewell to lovers' it would seem that he means what he says; the line gains nothing from a mystical interpretation. In reading Ḥāfeẓ, nevertheless, one is often perplexed as to whether the love depicted is sacred (*haqīqī*) or profane (*majāzī*). The problem is to distinguish between the two, and it may well be, as it has been suggested, that profane leads to sacred love. Whatever the truth, the fact remains that Ḥāfeẓ was a mystic, and it cannot be denied that an undercurrent of mysticism runs through his love poems.

To discuss the nature of Ṣūfism or Islamic mysticism is too wide a subject for this essay, but it should be mentioned briefly that Ṣūfism in essence is concerned with the separation of man from God, the longing of the mystic lover for the beloved and their ultimate reunion. As Ḥāfeẓ says:

Mojd-ye vaṣl-e to kū kaz sar-e jān bar khīzam;
Ṭāyer-e qodsam-o az dām-e jahān bar khīzam . . .
Where are the glad tidings of union with thee
That I may abandon all desire of life.
I am the bird of holiness, and would escape from the net of this world.

In Persian poetry the *ṣūfī* is often contrasted with the *zāhed* or 'ascetic' and formally pious man who knows nothing of love. Ḥāfeẓ goes further; he condemns both the asceticism of the *ṣūfī* and orthodoxy. This he does without malice and with a subtle irony combined with a mild and sympathetic humour, as reflected in this verse:

Be kūy-e mey forūshānash be jāmī bar nemīgīrand;
Zehī sajjādeye taqvā ke yek sāghar nemīarzad.

In the quarter of the wine-sellers they will not exchange (the prayer mat of piety) for a glass of wine,
What a splendid prayer mat of piety that is not worth a goblet of wine!

The Dīvān of Ḥāfeẓ consists of some six hundred lyrics of which at least half may truly be called great. Many of them defy translation.

The Maṡnavī

The *maṡnavī* is a longish narrative poem in rhymed couplets, and is a suitable vehicle for epic and romantic stories and subjects dealing with mysticism, ethics, or philosophy. Unlike the *qaṣida* and the *ghazal*, each of which reached its height in a particular period, the *maṡnavī* does not belong to any specific epoch. Rūdakī was the first poet to write a *maṡnavī*; and there was a long succession after him. The best known *maṡnavīs* are those written by mystics. The first purported mystic *maṡnavī* was the *Hadīqat al Haqīqa* (The Garden of Truth) by Sanā'ī (*d* 1140). He was followed by 'Aṭṭār (*d* 1230) and Rūmī, whose *maṡnavī* is the greatest of all and is known as 'The *Maṡnavī*'. It consists of six books, making in all twenty-five thousand couplets. The basic theme of the *Maṡnavī* is love; and Rūmī is chiefly concerned with problems and speculations bearing on the conduct, meaning and purpose of life. Contrary to the view held by some, Rūmī is not a pantheist. He believes in a personal God, whose glory and splendour are to be observed in the universe. Like Sanā'ī and 'Aṭṭār, Rūmī uses allegories and tales, sometimes to drive his point home and sometimes in order to comment upon some spiritual truth. Rūmī's style is often almost colloquial and from time to time he introduces passages of lively dialogue. He is a master of satire; and his descriptions of human nature show a deep understanding and are often humorous. His comments on life, like those of Shakespeare and Goethe, are of universal application. Rūmī in his *maṣ̤navī*, even more than his *dīvān*, is concerned with meaning and sometimes is careless of the form. On the other hand he can rise to great heights of eloquence, and no other poet makes his point with such compelling force. Taking the *maṣ̤navī* as a whole, however, one tends to agree with Nicholson's judgement that 'Great poet as he (Rūmī) is, he loves Truth more than Art'. Nevertheless, the *maṣ̤navī* is the most profound and the greatest work of Persian, and perhaps Islamic, literature.

Neẓāmī wrote five *maṣ̤navīs* known, therefore, as the *Khamseh* (quintet). They differ from Rūmī's *maṣ̤navī* and are romantic *maṣ̤navīs*. They are highly esteemed and found many imitators. The first of these five is didactic; three are historical romances, based upon ancient Persian and Arabic tales, and the last is a reworking of the Alexander romance. The most famous of the five is *Khosrou o Shīrīn*, and it is regarded as the greatest poetic romance in the Persian language.

The Indian School

The period of decline begins as early as the fourteenth century. The last great classical poet was Jāmī (*d* 1492), who was remarkable for the quality and the quantity of his literary work in both poetry and prose. Persian poetry had been cultivated in India for some time, and the romantic *maṣ̤navīs* of Amīr Khosrou (*d* 1306), written after the model of Neẓāmī, were of high quality. In the fifteenth and particularly the sixteenth century many Persian poets were attracted to the court of the great Moghuls. The style of the Indian School which reached the height of its glory during the sixteenth century found its way back to Persia and became the dominant style under the Safavids (1500–1736) and was known as the Indic style (*sabk-e Hindī*). Its greatest exponent was Ṣā'eb (*d* 1677), whose poems are distinguished by fine imagery. The Indian style at its worst is marred by verbal intricacies, but at its best it has originality and a peculiar subtlety of its own. Another poet belonging to the late Safavid period who made a special contribution is Hātef, who became well-known thanks to his famous *Tarjī' band* or stanzaic poem. Its theme is the essential unity of all concepts of divinity and the poem is of lasting merit both as regards its form and diction.

PROSE

Persian prose, although it has attracted less attention than Persian poetry, is not negligible. In its early development it was subject to certain limitations.

Arabic as the language of the Qur'ān enjoyed enormous prestige; the medium of intellectual disciplines, since they were concerned chiefly with the religious sciences, was Arabic. Partly for this reason Persian scholars, in the early centuries after the Muslim conquest, for the most part wrote their learned works in Arabic, which has largely remained the language of theology down to the present day. One of the oldest extant pieces of Persian prose is the introduction, finished in 975 or 978, to the prose *Shāh-nāme* of Abū Manṣūr Moḥammad b. ʻAbd al-Razzaq Ṭūsī (see above, p. 114). Other early works include a philosophical essay and a treatise on the astrolabe by Abū Jaʻfar Moḥammad b. Ayyūb Ṭabarī, written apparently in 965, a translation into extremely simple Persian of Ṭabarī's commentary on the Qur'ān made between 960 and 977, and Balʻamī's abbreviated translation of Ṭabarī's history, the *Ta'rīkh al-Umam wa'l Mulūk*, made in 963.

Under the great Saljuq dynasty (1037–1157) there was a significant increase in the writing of Persian prose; and with the decline in Islamic learning which took place after the Mongol invasion of the lands of the eastern caliphate in the thirteenth century, Arabic was superseded by Persian as a literary medium except in theology. The main vehicle for imaginative works, however, continued to be verse. Broadly speaking Persian prose from its beginnings to the first half of the eleventh century had a relatively simple vocabulary and was somewhat limited in subject matter. During the following century there was an increase in vocabulary, especially in the Arabic element, and a tightening up of syntax. Conciseness and eloquence, and sometimes vividness, mark much of the work of this period. In the first half of the thirteenth century there was a tendency towards greater artifice and ornateness, and in the Mongol and post-Mongol period the dominant tendency was towards florid and ornate prose until the latter part of the nineteenth century, when a reaction began and the foundations of a modern school of prose were laid.

It is only possible in this essay to touch briefly upon the main types of Persian prose writing. The central theme of Persian culture was Islam. Knowledge was sought primarily so far as it served the purposes of the 'ideal' community; and scholars tended to limit their interests to subjects having a direct relation to the achievement of salvation. Even literary art was to some extent pursued so that through it religious truth might be better expounded. There was not, of course, a complete synthesis and there were contradictory elements, which do not fit into the general pattern.

Theological works

Serious theological works of an orthodox nature tended to be written in Arabic and only popular literature in Persian. Al-Ghazzālī (*d* 1111) wrote a Persian summary of his celebrated *Revivification of the Religious Sciences* under the title *The Alchemy of Happiness* (*Kīmīyā ye Sa'ādat*). A later example is the *Jami'-e 'Abbāsī*, a popular version of the Shī'ī faith, by Bahā al-Dīn Amulī (*d* 1620–1). There are several theological works in Persian belonging to the extreme Shī'ī sects, notably those of Nāṣer-e Khosrou, *Ṣūfī* treatises, such as the *Mirṣād al-'Ibād min al-mabda' Ilā'l ma'ād* by Najm al-Dīn Rāzī (*d* 1256), which in a lucid prose outlines for the believer what he needs to know to achieve salvation, and many hagiographical and biographical works.

Belles-lettres

This class of literature is concerned with humanistic, as opposed to religious, knowledge, with the traditions of civility as opposed to pure scholarship. It constitutes a varied literature of pleasing erudition, which touches upon Greek philosophy, ethics, history, and Iranian, Arab, Indian and Hellenistic literature. A central position is held by the 'Mirrors for Princes' in the evolution of which Ibn al-Moqaffa' played an important part. They were incidentally concerned with the art of government and represent the ethics of the official classes. Their purpose was edification. Among the early Persian mirrors are the *Qābūs-nāme* of Kay Kavūs (written in 1082) and the *Naṣihat al Mulūk* of Al-Ghazzālī. A later mirror, which achieved considerable popularity, especially in India, is the *Akhlāq-e Mohsenī* of Kashefī (composed in 1494–5). 'Mirrors' in the medieval style were still being written at the beginning of the present century.

Of somewhat similar character are the administrative handbooks, of which an outstanding example is the *Sīyāsat-name* of Nezām ul-Mulk (*d* 1092), who sets out for the Sultan the lines on which he should administer his kingdom. The book, which contains numerous anecdotes and examples from history illustrating the points which the author makes, is written in economical prose which is at times extremely vivid. Nezām ul-Mulk's dominant care is for the stability of the kingdom, which, in his view, depended on justice and right religion; heresy, since it threatened stability, is strongly attacked.

Diverging from the 'Mirror', but having to some extent the same purpose, namely edification – though the emphasis upon diversion is much stronger – are the various collections of tales, such as the numerous versions of *Kalila u Dimna*, and the *Gulestān* of Sa'dī, in whom prose of a somewhat stylistic type found its greatest master.

Belonging also to this general class of literature are various collections of documents. Some of these consist of genuine documents of historical interest; others are composed as models of style and form the material for 'the science of writing' (*'Ilm al-inshā'*), as applied specifically to the art or style ideally used by the state secretary. One of the earliest masters of this art was Rashīd al-Dīn Vaṭvāṭ (*d* 1182–3).

Historical works

Most Persian histories are chronicles; and many are universal histories. The function of the state, as the Muslim conceived it, was to create conditions in which the good life could be lived, and histories were partly composed to illustrate this view. The function of the historian also was thus mainly one of edification. His disposition, like that of the mediaeval English historian, was to record rather than to explain. He did not pretend to recreate the past and ignored, for the most part, the development of human character and personality. The great period of Persian historiography was the Īlkhān period (1256–1335), during which Jovaynī, Rashīd al-Dīn, Vaṣṣāf and Hamdullāh Mustawfī wrote.

Not all historians conformed to the general pattern: one who deserves special mention is Bayḥaqī (*d* 1077), who was employed in the chancellery of the Ghaznavid ruler, Mas'ūd. His work, variously known as the *Tarīkh-e Bayḥaqī* and the *Tarīkh-e Mas'ūdī*, which has only come down to us in part, is an intimate account of contemporary events.

Another type of history which flourished in Persia was the local history. Although the chief interest of the Muslim was centred on the Islamic community, his loyalty was also accorded to his local town or province. Many of the local histories consist largely of biographical material and almost always contain some geographical matter. Typical examples are the *Tārīkh-e Bayhaq* of Ibn Funduq (written in 1667–87), the *Jāmi'-e Mufīdī* of Moḥammad Mufīd (completed in 1679), and the *Tārīkh-e Tabrīz* of Nāder Mīrzā (written *c* 1884–5).

Biographical literature

This consists mostly of biographical dictionaries, biographies of individuals, families, tribes and biographical material in histories. Biographical dictionaries are seldom universal and are usually confined to a particular group, a tendency which reflects the corporate nature of medieval Persian society. The classes most frequently forming the subject of these works are Shī'ī divines, Sayyeds, and Ṣūfīs, as in the *Nafakhāt al-Uns* of Jāmī (written in 1476), and poets as in the *Tazkerat al-Sho'arā* of Dowlatshāh (completed in 1487). Many of the lives of saints and Ṣūfīs belong to hagiographical rather than biographical literature. The biographical dictionaries, like their Arabic prototypes, are concerned primarily with the contribution of the individual to the building up and transmission of Islamic and Persian culture. The biographer, like the historian, was concerned to record rather than to interpret. He is preoccupied with stock Islamic virtues and qualities, such as piety, learning, beneficence and justice, and seldom gives details of 'private' life.

Geographical literature

The impulse to the production of geographical works was largely practical: they were required for administrative purposes. Some are adaptions of the Arabic route books, others are original. Among the latter are the *Nuzhat al Qulūb* of Hamdullāh Mustawfi, which includes a graphic picture of Persia in the time of the Īlkhāns, written in clear and lucid Persian; and a geography of Ḥāfeẓ-e Abrū (*d* 1430). Those geographies which are not route books tend to combine the geographical knowledge handed down by past generations with personal observations, and show a certain liking for the wonderful and the supernatural. Historical works, as stated above, often contain valuable geographical sections. The *Ḥudūd al-ʻĀlam*, written in 982–3 by an anonymous author, is the earliest extant Persian geography.* Another early work, dealing *inter alia* with cosmography, geography and astronomy, is the *Tafhīm*, which the author, al-Bīrūnī, wrote in two versions, one in Persian and the other in Arabic. It is of considerable scientific and literary merit. Nāṣer-e Khosrou (see also above, p. 118), among numerous works, wrote a *Safar-nāme*, describing a hard and difficult journey he made from Khorasan to Egypt. It is written in a simple, yet elegant, style typical of the eleventh century.

Philosophy

In the field of philosophy and abstract thought Persian writers tended to be epitomists and compilers. Perhaps the best known work on philosophy is the *Akhlāq-e Nāṣerī* of Naṣīr al-Dīn Ṭūsī (*d* 1274), who had great influence on later Persian and Ottoman thought. His debt to al-Fārābī, the first Muslim thinker to seek to harmonise the political philosophy of Plato with Islam, is considerable; and also to Ibn Sinā, and directly and indirectly to Plato and Aristotle. He quotes freely from them all and from the Qur'ān, the Traditions and other sources.

Modern trends

The nineteenth century was a period of change in many fields of Persian life. In literature already towards the end of the eighteenth century, although the old forms of composition were still being followed, various influences, including contact with the west, were bringing about change. It is noteworthy that the founder of the Qajar dynasty, Aghā Moḥammad Khān (*d* 1797), took the lead in encouraging a new method of writing. It was during the long reign of his successor, Fath ʻAlī Shah (1797–1834) that a literary movement began to take

* Critical trans. by V. Minorsky, London, 1937.

form. Some modern Persian critics tend to over-emphasise the importance of this movement by presenting it as a great turning point in Persian literature. In fact the ideal of those who belonged to this movement was the simple style of the early classical period, and under their influence the bombastic writing which had become current in the later Middle Ages gave way to a more natural and simple style.

The prevailing prose style of the early Qajar period came to be known as *Naṣr-e Dīvānī*. This was the style of the court circle; and it was used, broadly speaking, in all the official writings of the age. Compared to the style of the thirteenth and fourteenth centuries it is simple, but compared with the prose of a half century later it is artificial and ponderous. The greatest writer of this period is Qā'em Maqām, whose well-known *Monshā'āt* (collection of writings) is regarded as the best prose of its age, and representing a new approach to the delicate art of letter writing. Apart from Qā'em Maqām, Garrūsī, Veṣāl and Neshāṭ, who constituted a small literary circle, were responsible for creating an enhanced interest in prose writing.

In the second half of the nineteenth century, prose literature began to undergo a transformation in style and subject matter – political tracts and works drawing attention to social and political evils in Persia began to be written. Among the writers of this period were Malkam Khān (*d* 1908) and Zayn ul-'Abedīn Maraghe'ī, the author of the well-known *Sīyāhat-name*. This book is a severe criticism of the country's social ills; it also criticises the florid writings of the past. The purpose of the writer was to awaken people's minds.

Journalism

The first Persian newspaper was an official organ founded in 1848; but it was not till the turn of the century that a vigorous and lively press developed in Persia, although there had been earlier a number of papers published among Persian communities living abroad. The most famous of them was *Qānūn* which was founded in 1890 in London by the above-mentioned Malkam Khān who was one of the most striking figures in the Persian awakening, and who was also regarded as one of the most influential exponents of modern Persian prose. In his writing Malkam is admired above all for the lucidity and directness of his style which is combined with a distinctive grace and freshness.

In discussing the modern Persian press special mention should be made of a series of satirical articles entitled *Charand parand* (balderdash) which appeared in the newspaper *Ṣūr-e-Esrāfīl* during the constitutional movement. 'Alī Akbar Dehkhodā, writer of these articles, paved the way for writers in plain writing (*sādehnevīsī*) who followed him.

In the field of drama also some pioneering works were produced, one of the earliest of which is a play entitled *Vazīr-e Lankarān.* Translation from European sources received an impetus with the introduction of the printing press to Persia in 1816–17. Besides the translation of Morier's *Hājjī Bābā* by Mīrzā Habīb, other popular translations appeared before the constitutional movement began in 1905 and played a significant part in the literary movement of the period.

The constitution of 1905 which was granted by Moẓaffar ud-Dīn Shah was followed after his death in 1907 by two years of unrest and counter revolution. The popular hope that all would be well after the despotism had been overthrown and the constitution established was not fulfilled. Foreign intervention continued and during the World War of 1914–18 Russian, Turkish, German and British troops were active in the country. A group of nationalists who supported the central powers emigrated to Berlin and founded there the newspaper *Kāveh,* which was undoubtedly the standard bearer of a new literary movement, characterised by patriotic and modernist tendencies. The editor of the paper was Taqizadeh, who had played a prominent part in the constitutional revolution and throughout his long life was ever a prominent figure in the political and literary world of Persia. The contributors to *Kāveh* were a small group of Persian writers and scholars, among whom Jamālzādeh and Mohammad Qazvini were outstanding. It was through the efforts of this group, in particular the last named, that western methods of scholarship spread, and many classical texts were edited. The first short story of Jamālzādeh, who was to become famous as a short story writer, appeared in *Kāveh* in 1921. It was entitled 'Persian is as sweet as sugar' and on the one hand it attacked, in an amusing way, the use of pompous language and europeanised Persian diction, and on the other enthusiastically supported the Persian spoken by the common man. This lively and witty short story, full of telling idioms and expressions, was later included with five other short stories in the collection known by the title *Yekī būd yekī nabūd* (Once upon a time). The book was a great success, and opened a new phase in Persian prose.

Modern Prose

Jamālzādeh is indeed rightly regarded by Persian writers as the founder of contemporary prose. It was he who laid the foundation of a new genre of story-telling, rich in local colour and vivid idioms. Another writer of outstanding importance is Ṣadeq Hedāyat who founded a school of writing of his own. He is generally regarded by the educated public as the leading author since the Second World War and by his admirers as unrivalled. Although Hedāyat began to write during the reign of Reza Shah (1924–41) and had already written some of his principal works before the abdication, his main works were written after this event. It is true that *Bufe kūr* (The Blind Owl), by common consent Hedāyat's masterpiece, was written when the dictatorship was still at its height, but it was not until 1941 that it was printed in Tehran. The first edition was published in Bombay where Hedāyat went in 1937. *Bufe kūr*, unlike Hedāyat's earlier works, which deal with social ills, is morbid and dreary, yet the book contains descriptive passages of striking originality and even poetical beauty. Jamālzādeh, as stated above, introduced current idioms into his writings; Hedāyat went further and made the introduction of slang into literature fashionable. His readers, however, are predominantly the intellectuals and educated classes and not those people whose language he so painstakingly collected.

Among the followers of Hedāyat, Ṣādeq Chūbak comes closest to him. Chūbak is also basically a short story writer and uses slang as much as or more than Hedāyat. This is not to say that Chūbak is merely an imitator of Hedāyat. He has great originality and his prose is often more eloquent and his choice of words more apt than that of Hedāyat. In contrast to Hedāyat, Chūbak is not a prolific writer. Since his first book *Khayme Shab bāzī* (The Puppet Show), which was published in 1945, he has only published five other books; but all are to a varying degree of high quality. Another well-established writer, who also belongs to the post-war period, is Jalāl Āl-e Aḥmad. He first became known as a writer in 1945 with the publication of *Dīdo Bāzdīd* (The Exchange Visit). This is a collection of twelve short stories, directed mainly against superstition and religious hypocrisy, and showing a wide sympathy for the oppressed. Subsequently he wrote several fictional and non-fictional books, the last of which *Khasī dar mīqāt* (A Straw in Time) was published in 1966. The theme of this book which is the record of the author's pilgrimage to Mecca is modelled on Nāṣer-e Khosrou's famous *Safar-nāme* (see above, p. 126) and contains passages of moving beauty.

Bozorg 'Alavī is another leading contemporary writer. He printed his first book *Chamadān* (Suitcase) in 1934. He is the author of several collections of short stories and other works in all of which his leftist political views are reflected. He has a genuine sympathy for the under-dog and the oppressed and writes with conviction. His best known book is *Cheshmhāyash* (Her Eyes) which is a novel. Moḥammad Hejāzī is a writer of a very different stamp from 'Alavī. Though he has waned somewhat in popularity in recent times he is a writer of considerable skill and influence. Hejāzī appeared on the literary scene at the beginning of the twenties and soon became one of the most popular novelists and essayists during the reign of Reza Shah and after his abdication. His fame as a novelist rests mainly on his third novel *Zībā* (The Beautiful One) printed in 1931. Among his short stories *Bābā Kūhī* is the most widely read. As an essayist Hejāzī has few rivals among contemporary writers. He has published several collections of essays, among which *A'īne* (The Mirror) is the best known.

'Alī Dashtī, like Hejāzī, is another public figure who is also a celebrated writer. He avoids colloquial language and deliberately uses foreign, especially French, words and arabicised terms, which give to his writing a touch of affectation. Dashtī began his career as a journalist, founding *Shafaq-e Sorkh* in 1921. Among his various short stories *Sāyeh* (Shadow) printed in 1946 and *Fetneh* (Sedition) are well-known. In the last few years Dashtī has turned his attention to literary criticism and has written five books on five different classical poets, which are interesting as personal appreciations of great masters.

Apart from the seven major writers discussed above, who have made their mark on contemporary Persian literature, there are a number of minor writers such as Moḥammad Mas'ūd and 'Abbās Khalīlī, who had some influence both through their newspapers and their books. It is in the short story, rather than the novel, that modern writers such as Hedāyat, Chūbak and 'Alavī, excel. But in recent years among the younger rising writers, 'Alī Moḥammad Afghānī by his first long novel *Shouhare Āhū Khānum* (Mrs Āhū's Husband), has, perhaps opened a new phase. Its publication in 1961 placed Afghānī in the forefront of fiction writers. The book, written in a literary style, is, however, uneven and at times prolix.

In the field of research and scholarship since the pioneering work of the late Moḥammad Qazvīnī, much work has been done. Literary periodicals such as *Yadegār*, *Sokhan* and *Yaghmā* have exercised a marked influence in university circles and beyond. Forūzānfar, Homā'ī, Ṣafā, Ṣadīqī, and above all, Minovī are men of great scholarship and learning and in their books and articles they have made valuable contributions.

As regards poetry in the modern age there was in the first half of the nineteenth century still a backward-looking tendency. This can be easily seen in works of two major poets of the period, Ṣabā (*d* 1822), and Qā'ānī (*d* 1853).

It was only in the latter part of the nineteenth and early twentieth century that modern trends in literature began. Poets such as 'Āref and 'Eshqī, to name only two, wrote on national and patriotic themes. Another was Īraj (*d* 1925), whose easy and pleasing style made him very popular. A new form of poetry, the *taṣnīf*, a kind of popular ballad, was also introduced. Among the poets who wrote on classical lines, Sādiq Amīrī, known as Adib-al Mamālek (*d* 1917), and Bahār, are outstanding. The latter is held by some of his admirers to be the greatest poet of the last few centuries. However this may be his *qaṣidas*, which are written in the Turkistani style of the classical masters, deserve attention. Another writer of interest is the poetess Parvin (*d* 1941), who appears to have modelled herself on Nāṣer-e Khosrou, and used classical forms to express modern themes.

Since the Second World War, poetry has gained a new vitality. It may be roughly divided into three categories: 1 Poems on classical lines; 2 Poems in blank verse; and 3 Poems on modern themes in traditional forms. Among modern poets Shāhriyār, Ra'dī and Nīmā Yūshij are worthy of mention. The last of these experimented in blank verse and has great influence on young poets. Among his followers Shāmlū is counted as one of the most successful. The poetess Farrokhzād also is regarded by some of her admirers as an outstanding figure in modern Persian poetry.

To sum up: it can be affirmed that certain of the more regularly cultivated literary forms express enduring elements in the motivations of society and its intellectual and spiritual attitudes. In poetry the discreetness of the Persian mind is apparent. Islamic Persia through Khayyām, Sa'dī, Ḥāfeẓ, Rūmī and others has enriched world literature. These poets in their search for truth and perfection in their delicately balanced verses, richly charged with evocative power and hinting at hidden depth, have, perhaps, been inspired by the Persian landscape with its exquisitely delicate and beautiful flowers and refreshing streams set against a background of magnificent mountains and grim deserts. In prose the most striking fact is the continuity in the cultivation of Mirrors for Princes, which hold up the just ruler and implicitly protest against the failure to achieve that ideal. It is this heritage which today modern writers are transmuting into a new expression of the hopes and aspirations of their own age.

INDIVIDUAL WRITERS

'Alavī (*b* 1907). Bozorg 'Ạlavī was born of a merchant family in Tehran. He was educated in Germany and on returning to Persia he became a member of an underground Marxist group. In 1937 'Alavī, with fifty-two other persons, was arrested and remained in prison until the allied invasion of Persia in August 1941. After his release from prison 'Alavī became one of the founders of the Tudeh Party. A few years after the end of the war 'Alavī left for Europe, and he is now a visiting professor at Humboldt University in East Germany. He is well-known for his novels and short stories.

Āl-e Aḥmad (*b* 1920). Jalāl Āl-e Aḥmad was born in a village near Tehran. His family belonged to the religious classes. By the end of World War II, like most intellectuals of the time, he had affiliations with Tudeh party and later became a schoolmaster. After a few years he resigned from his post and became a full-time writer. In his later writings, Āl-e Aḥmad devoted his energies to a defence of traditionalism against the increasing encroachment of the west. He is also interested in folklore, dialects and rural customs, on which subjects he has written three books, the first of which, *Aurāzān*, was published in 1953.

Anvarī (1126–91). Auḥad al-Dīn 'Alī Anvarī was born in Abivard at a village in the Khavarān Steppe and hence at first wrote under the pseudonym of Khavarī. Later he changed this to Anvarī. He is said to have studied at the Mansuryia Madrase of Ṭūs. He later joined the court of Sultan Sanjar (*d* 1157) who took him to Merv; and eventually he became the most celebrated poet of that court. Besides poetry Anvarī was interested in astrology and philosophy, and was a great admirer of Avicenna. Although Anvarī survived Sanjar some thirty or forty years, his main reputation derives from that monarch's reign.

'Aṭṭār (*d* 1230). Shaykh Farīd al Dīn 'Aṭṭār was born in the city of Nishapur, probably about 1130; he spent thirteen years of his childhood in Ṭūs, and then after travelling extensively he finally settled once more in his native town, where he is alleged as a very old man to have met his death at the hands of the Mongols during the sack of Nishapur in 1229–30. As his pseudonym suggests, 'Aṭṭār was by profession a druggist or physician. He flourished as a poet in the post-Sanjar period, *ie* after 1157. A vast literary output is attributed to him, but only about thirty volumes are extant. The most famous of them is the *Manteq al-Ṭayr* (The Language of the Birds), a mystical allegory in verse.

Bahār (1886–1951). Moḥammad Taqī Bahār, who succeeded his father as the Persian Malek'ush-sho'rā (poet laureate), was born in Meshed in 1886. He had a traditional education. He began to compose poetry in his early youth. He moved to Tehran, where he joined the progressive front in the fight against the despotism of the Qajar monarchy. He founded the newspaper *Nou Bahār*, and became a deputy in the national consultative assembly. He fell out of favour with Reza Shah and was exiled to Isfahan, but was then recalled to the capital and made Professor of Literature at Tehran University. During the Second World War Bahār became Minister of Education for a short period. He died in 1951. Among the best known of Bahār's early *qaṣidas* is *Demāvand*. Among his later ones, a *qaṣida* entitled *The Owl of War* is outstanding.

Chūbak (*b* 1916). The noted short story writer. Ṣādeq Chūbak was born in Būshire. He received his early education in Shiraz and then attended the American College in Tehran where he completed his course in 1937. At present he is working at the central office of the National Iranian Oil Company in Tehran.

Daqīqī (*d* 975). Abū Manṣūr Moḥammad b. Aḥmad Daqīqī was born in Balkh and met an untimely death at the hand of a slave when still a young man. Some of Daqīqī's poems bear witness of a strong inclination towards Zoroastrianism. Daqīqī owes his fame to the fact that Firdausī incorporated many of his verses into the *Shāh-nāme*.

Dashtī (*b* 1895). 'Alī Dashtī was born in southern Persia into a strict religious family. In his early youth he moved to Tehran where he founded the newspaper *Shafaq-e Sorkh* in 1921, which became the leading paper of the time. Because of his anti-government articles, Dashtī was imprisoned in the early years of Reza Shah's reign, but later he was elected to the national consultative assembly and played an active part. In the post-war period he was appointed Ambassador to Egypt and the Lebanon respectively. He is now in his seventies, and a member of the Senate.

Dehkhodā (1879–1956). 'Alī Akbar Dehkhodā, the son of a landowner from Qazvīn, was born in Tehran and educated in Persia and Europe. He became the co-editor of the celebrated newspaper, *Sur-e Esrāfīl*, which was founded in 1907 at the outset of the Persian constitutional movement. With a group of other democrats, Dehkhodā went into exile in Europe at the beginning of the war. He then went to Istanbul and published a newspaper called *Sorush*. While still abroad, Dehkhodā was elected to the National Consultative Assembly. After the First World War he held several important academic positions, and the later part of his life was devoted entirely to scholarship.

E'teṣāmī, Parvīn (1906–41). Parvīn E'teṣāmī, the poetess who died prematurely in 1941, is recognised as a literary personage of special distinction. She was the only daughter of E'teṣām al-Molk, the well-known translator of European books and sometime editor of the journal *Bahār*. Parvīn in her poetry is primarily concerned to illustrate moral principles. Her style is graceful. Although she wrote in the traditional forms the theme of her poems is new, insofar as she deals with the everyday life of women.

Farrukhī (*d* 1037). Abol Ḥasan 'Alī b. Jūlūq Farrukhī of Sīstān was one of the four prominent poets at the court of Sultān Maḥmūd of Ghazna. Among his prose works, the *Tarjomān al Balāqa* (Interpreter of Eloquence) on prosody is now attributed rather to al-Radūyānī.

Farzād (*b* 1910). Mas'ūd Farzād was born in Isfahan early this century and educated at the American College in Tehran. He writes prose and poetry, and first became known in 1933 when he wrote a satirical book in collaboration with Hedāyat. He is best-known as a translator of Shakespeare. During the Second World War he joined the Persian section of the BBC in London as a broadcaster and later became Cultural Attaché at the Persian Embassy in London. He now holds the post of Professor of English Literature in the Pahlavi University in Shiraz.

Firdausī (941–1019). Abolqāsem Hasan b. 'Alī Firdausī was born at Ṭūs about AD 941 to a family of *dehqāns* or small landowners, a class which the Arab conquest had not effectively displaced. From incidental hints in the *Shāh-nāme* it appears that Firdausī was about forty years old when he began his monumental work at the court of Sultān Maḥmūd of Ghazna. Little is known of Firdausī's early education, but he must have been from his childhood well-versed in traditional Persian learning. During the latter part of his life Firdausī fell out of favour with the Sultan, and died at the age of nearly eighty and was buried at Ṭūs.

Forūghī (*d* 1943). Moḥammad 'Alī Forūghī was born in Isfahan. He attended the Dārol Fonūn in Tehran as a medical student, but abandoned the practice of medicine in the interest of literature and philosophy. He occupied several prominent public positions, including that of the Head of the Persian Academy, founded during the reign of Reza Shah. He was the first Prime Minister of Moḥammad Reza Shah, the present reigning sovereign.

Ghazzālī (1059–1111). Abū Ḥamid Moḥammad Ghazzālī was born at Ṭūs in 1059, about the time of Alp Arslān's accession to the Saljuq throne. Together with his brother Aḥmad, he was educated first by a *ṣūfi* friend of his father, and afterwards at one of the *madrasas* of his native city. He also studied for a while in Gorgan and then went to Nishapur where he continued his studies and began to attract attention by his writings. This brought him to the notice of the great minister, Neẓāmu'l Molk, who in 1091 appointed him a professor in the Neẓāmiyya Academy which he had founded and endowed twenty-five years before at Baghdad. After Ghazzālī had held this post with great distinction for four years he resigned in order to follow a life of meditation and writing. Ghazzālī is regarded as one of the greatest theologians and mystics Islam has ever produced. He was a prolific writer. The most famous of his works is the

Ihyā ul-ulūm addīn, which is a compendium of his metaphysical system. He died in his native town Ṭūs in AD 1111.

Ḥāfeẓ (1324–89). Moḥammad Shams-ud Dīn Ḥāfeẓ was born in Shiraz. The word Ḥāfeẓ, which means 'keeper' or 'preserver', was chosen by the poet as his pseudonym because he knew the whole of the Qur'ān by heart. Regarding his childhood, early youth, and education, not much is known. This has given rise to a great body of legend concerning his life. The relatively long reign of Shah Shojā' in Fars (1365–84) saw the full blossoming of the flower of Ḥāfeẓ's genius. Apart from a short sojourn in Yazd, Isfahan and Hormoz, Ḥāfeẓ never left Shiraz, where he died and was buried.

Hātef (*d* 1783). Sayyed Aḥmad Hātef, who flourished towards the end of the eighteenth century, famous for his *tarji' band* and regarded as the most important poet of this period. Hātef was born and brought up in Isfahan. He was a learned man and well versed in Arabic. He spent some time in Kashan and Qum, where he died.

Hedāyat (1903–51). Ṣādeq Hedāyat was born in 1903 in Tehran. He belonged to a cultured and wealthy family, who for generations had produced prominent public figures. In the late twenties Hedāyat went to Europe on a government scholarship. He never took a degree but contact with the literary and intellectual life of France stimulated him and when he returned to Persia in 1930 he devoted his time to writing. In the course of twenty years, he wrote some thirty books, many of which were collections of short stories, and he became recognised as Persia's foremost modern writer. In 1951, after an absence of twenty years, he returned to France and in April of that year committed suicide in Paris.

Ḥejāzī (*b* 1899). Moḥammad Ḥejāzī was educated at the French Roman Catholic school, St Louis, in Tehran. He then travelled to Europe for higher education, becoming an expert in telegraphic communications. Returning to Persia, he occupied several governmental positions in the Ministry of Posts and Telegraphs and was for some years the editor of the Ministry's monthly magazine. In 1937 he was appointed head of the press section of the newly established governmental institution, the Sāzmān-e Parvaresh-e-Afkār (The Bureau for the Orientation of Public Opinion). In his new capacity, Ḥejāzī was to become the editor of the journal *Irān-e Emrūz*, the mouthpiece of the Bureau. After the abdication of Reza Shah in 1941, Ḥejāzī occupied several high positions, including the directorship of the state-controlled Radio and the Propaganda Department. He has been a Senator for several years.

Jamālzādeh (*b c* 1895). Sayyed Moḥammad 'Alī Jamālzādeh was born in Isfahan towards the end of the last century. His father was Sayyed Jamāl al-Dīn, one of the leading preachers of the constitutional period. After having completed his elementary education Jamālzādeh went to Beirut in 1908 for higher education. From Beirut after a short stay in Egypt he went to France (1910), to study law in the University of Dijon, where he took a degree. During the First World War he travelled to Berlin to join a group of Persian nationalists who had gone there in protest against foreign intervention in Persia. In 1916 this group founded the famous journal *Kāveh*, to which Jamālzādeh was a regular contributor and his first short story, which laid the foundation of his fame appeared in it. After World War I Jamālzādeh went to Switzerland and held a post in the International Labour Office in Geneva, where he now lives in retirement.

Īraj (1841–1925). Īraj Mīrzā, the Jalalu'l Mamālek, was born at Tabrīz in 1841. He was a grandson of Fath 'Alī Shah. He began his education at home under a tutor employed by his father, who was himself a poet of average talent. Later Īraj went to the Dārol Fonūn of Tabrīz for higher education and to study French, in which he became well-versed. He began to write poetry when he was only fourteen. He held a succession of appointments; he first became private secretary to the Amīr Nezām, and the Chief Minister of Nāṣir al-Dīn, and later head of the Education Office of Tabrīz and finally Chief Inspector of the Revenue Office in Khorasan. Īraj visited Europe and Russia. He spent the last years of his life in Tehran, where he died in 1925. Īraj is regarded as one of the founders of modern Persian poetry. His *Dīvān* has gone through several editions and is still read with interest.

Jāmī (1414–92). Nūrod Dīn 'Abdur Raḥmān Jāmī, who was born in the small town of Jām in Khorasan, is regarded as the last in the line of literary geniuses whom Persia has produced. As Professor E. G. Browne states, he was at once a great poet and a great mystic as well as a great scholar. It is reported that even as a boy Jāmī showed remarkable quickness and ability and as he grew and pursued his studies he began to write. Sām Mīrzā in the *Toḥfa-i Sāmī* mentions that he wrote forty-six volumes. One pleasing characteristic of Jāmī was his refusal to flatter or humble himself before the rich and powerful, a rare virtue among the poets of that day. Jāmī visited Baghdad in 1472 when he was returning from the pilgrimage to Mecca. He died at Herāt in 1492.

Kasravī (*d* 1946). Sayyed Aḥmad Kasravī was born at Tabrīz into a family belonging to the religious classes. In his early youth when a student of theology, he supported the constitutional movement of 1905 and later joined the American Memorial College of Tabrīz as a pupil teacher. He then became a member of the Democrat party of Tabrīz, was exiled to Tehran and later was appointed head of the Department of Justice in Khūzistān. Because of his open criticism of the military régime during Reza Shah's reign he was dismissed from his post. He then practised as a lawyer. Kasravī was a fearless and prolific writer, who wrote both scholarly and popular books. Among his scholarly works *Shahryārān-e gomnām* is well-known. He also edited a periodical called *Paymān* and a newspaper entitled *Parcham*, in both of which he attacked superstitions and proclaimed a self-made religion which he called *Dīn-e Pāk*. Kasravī was an outspoken and ardent propagandist for his new religion and an uncompromising opponent of those who did not share his views. He was assassinated in the Ministry of Justice in the winter of 1946.

Khāqānī (*c* 1126–99). Afzal al-Din Badīl b. 'Alī Khāqānī was born in Shīrvān. His mother was a Nestorian Christian and this perhaps accounts for traces of Christian metaphors in some of his poetry. Although Khāqānī wrote poetry of various kinds it is in *qaṣida* that he excels, and he is ranked with the classical masters such as Anvarī. His well known *qaṣida* on *Madā'en* is a fine example of his poetry. Besides travelling within Persia, he also visited Baghdad and went on the pilgrimage to Mecca. He died and was buried in Tabrīz.

Khayyām (*d* 1129). Abo'l Fatḥ 'Omar b. Ebrāhīm Khayyām was born in Nishapur. He was primarily a philosopher, astronomer and mathematician. Some hold him to be a mystic as well, though others such as the Ṣufī Najm al-Dīn Rāzī, who regards Khayyām as the arch free thinker of his time, refute this. He was held in esteem at the court of the great Saljuq ruler, Malek Shah, and was a contemporary of Ghazzālī, with whom, it is reported, he discussed philosophical and religious topics. Thanks to the genius of Fitzgerald, Khayyām is known throughout the western world as the writer of the famous *Rubaīyyāt*. Khayyam died and was buried near his birthplace, Nishapur.

Manūchehrī (*d* 1041). Abū al Najm Aḥmad Manūchehrī was born in Damghān. He took his pseudonym from the name of his patron Manūchehr b. Qābūs, the fifth ruler of the Ziārīd dynasty. Manūchehrī's poems in description of nature are enchanting. In some of his other poems, however, he employs so many Arabic words and phrases that they are almost incomprehensible to a Persian reader.

Malkam Khān (*d* 1908). Mīrzā Malkam Khān was born of Armenian parentage in New Julfa adjoining Isfahan. He achieved prominence at the court of Nāṣer-al Dīn Shah. He was a man of liberal views and strongly advocated reform. He became envoy at the Court of St James but eventually fell from favour. He remained in London and founded the journal *Qānūn* in 1890. Through this and his other publications he exercised great influence on the intellectuals and those who supported the movement for constitutional reform.

Mīnovī (*b* 1902). Mojtabā Mīnovī was born at Tehran and after his graduation from the higher teachers' training college he became a schoolteacher. In 1929 he was sent to Europe as an official in the office having charge of Persian students in Paris and London. After returning to Persia he came back to London and stayed there fourteen years. He was then appointed to a Professorship at Tehran University. He is an excellent scholar of classical Persian and Arabic and while in Europe he spent much time in research, especially on manuscript collections.

Nāṣer-e Khosrou (1003–86). Abū Mo'īn Nāṣer-e Khosrou, the poet, traveller and Ismā'īlī propagandist was born at Qobādīyān, a small town near Balkh.

In his youth he joined the court of Mas'ūd at Ghazna and then that of the Saljuqs as a scribe (dabīr). Later he left the court to travel widely as he recounts in his well-known *Safar-nāme*. His travels, which lasted seven years, took him to Egypt, then under the Fatimids. He became an ardent convert to Ismailism. In some of his *qaṣidas* he eulogises the Fatimid caliphs and strongly attacks the Caliph of Baghdad. This lead to his being persecuted when he returned to Persia and the last years of his life were spent in moving about until he finally settled in Yomgān, a small village near Badakhshān, where he died in 1086.

Neẓāmī (1140–1205). Abū Moḥammad Eliās b. Yūsof Neẓāmī was born at Ganja. His father died when he was still young and his mother, who was of a noble Kurdish family, seems not long to have survived her husband. Neẓāmī as a writer of poetical romances, such as *Khosrou o Shīrīn* and *Leylī o Majnūn*, has no rival in Persian literature. Neẓāmī was a pious man, yet singularly devoid of fanaticism and intolerance. He was held in esteem at the court of the Shervānshah, but was not a court poet in the ordinary sense. He seldom left his native town, Ganja, where he lived a life of retirement and died there in 1205.

Nīmā (*d* 1958). Nīmā, who was born at Yūshīj in Māzandarān, is one of the modern school of 'free verse' (*shi'r-e āzād*). As a result of his pioneer work, a large number of modern poets began to write 'free verse'. Nīmā's best-known poem is entitled *Afsāneh*. Although his admirers have over-emphasised its greatness, it nevertheless laid the foundation of a new genre of poetry in Persian literature. Nīmā died in Tehran in 1958.

Qā'em Maqām (1779–1835). Mīrzā Abol Qāsem Qā'em Maqām was born at Farāhān in 1779. His father was Mīrzā Isā, known as Mīrzā Bozorg, who held an eminent position at the court of Fath 'Alī Shah. Qā'em Maqām himself became the first minister of Moḥammad Shah (Fath 'Alī Shah's successor) but his career was abruptly cut short by death in 1835, inflicted upon him by order of the master whom he had served. He was the first statesman to abandon the florid style of official correspondence. His well-known *Monsha'āt* shows him to be a prose stylist of no mean order.

Ra'dī (*b c* 1905). Gholām 'Alī Ra'dī Āẕarakhshī was born in Tabrīz, where he received his primary and secondary education. He then graduated from the Faculty of Law in Tehran. After this he went to France, where he obtained a doctorate of Law. Ra'dī has held several eminent positions, including that of Persia's representative at UNESCO, which post he occupied for several years. He is now a Senator. Ra'dī began to write poetry early in life. He is a master of both the *ghazal* and the *qaṣida* and his famous *Negāh* (The Look) is considered to be one of the greatest of all Persian odes.

Rūdakī (*d* 940). Abū 'Abd Allāh Ja'far b. Moḥammad Rūdakī was born at Rūdak near Samarqand. He is regarded as the first great poet in the long history of Persian literature. Rūdakī was held in great esteem at the court of Amīr Naṣr-e Sāmānī, who was a patron of the new Persian literary movement which was then beginning. It is reported that Rūdakī was also skilled in playing the lute, and that he accompanied the recitation of his own poems on this instrument. Several of Rūdakī's contemporaries and many later Persian poets have referred to the blindness which affected Rūdakī but no existing poems of his indicate that he was blind. His own poems, however, are completely free from any trace of self-pity and he nowhere mentions his blindness.

Rūmī (1207–73). Jalālo'd-Dīn Moḥammad, better known as Rūmī (*ie* 'of Rūm' or Asia Minor, where the greater part of his life was spent) was born at Balkh in the autumn of AD 1207. Soon after that date, the jealousy of Moḥammad Khārazam Shah compelled his father, who was known as Bahā'-ud-Dīn Valad, to leave his homeland and migrate westwards. He passed through Nishapur where according to the well-known story, Shaykh 'Aṭṭār met him in AD 1212 and predicted his greatness. From Nishapur the exiles went to Baghdad and Mecca, and after a further eleven years of wandering finally settled in Konya, then the capital of 'Alā'od-Dīn Kayqobād, the Saljuq ruler of Rūm. Rūmī seems to have studied the esoteric sciences, chiefly with his father until the death of the latter in AD 1231, when he went for a time to Aleppo and Damascus to seek further instruction. About this time he came under the influence of the celebrated saint Borhano'd Dīn of Termeẕ and later under the even greater influence of Shams-e Tabriz, under whose name he composed his *Dīvān*. Rūmī is without doubt the greatest *ṣufī* poet whom Persia has produced and his mystical *Maṣnavī* deserves to rank amongst the great poems of all times. Rūmī died in Konya where he was buried, and his disciples regard his tomb as sacred.

Sadīqī (*b c* 1905). Gholām Ḥosein Ṣadīqī was born in Tehran, and educated there and at the Sorbonne, at which he took his degree. Upon his return to Persia he was appointed Lecturer in Sociology and Philosophy in the University of Tehran. He later became Minister of Posts and Telegraphs in December 1951 and shortly afterwards in July 1952 was appointed the Minister of the Interior. He is now a Professor in the University of Tehran and Head of the Faculty of Sociology. His chief work is the treatise, *Les Mouvements religieux iraniens au IIe et au IIIe siècle de l'Héjire* (Paris, 1938).

Ṣā'eb (1603–77). Moḥammad 'Alī Ṣā'eb was born in Isfahan, son of a wealthy Tabrīzī merchant who had migrated to the Safavid capital. Ṣā'eb travelled widely and besides a pilgrimage to Mecca went to Kabul and Herāt and finally to India, where he stayed six years. At the court of Shāh Jahān, Ṣā'eb enjoyed favour and fame, so much so that Shah 'Abbās II invited him to return to Persia and made him his poet laureate. Ṣā'eb spent the remainder of his life in his birthplace, Isfahan, where he died.

Sanā'ī (*d* 1140). Abu'l Majd Majdūd b. Ādam of Ghazna is the first of the three great mystical *maṣnavī* writers of Persia; the other two being 'Aṭṭār and Rūmī. Of Sanā'ī's life little is known save that he was attached during his youth to the court of Bahrām Shah. After he became a mystic he left the court and instead of writing court poetry began to compose *maṣnavīs*. His best known work is the *Hadīqat al-Haqīqa*, which he completed shortly before his death.

Shahrīyār (*b c* 1905). Moḥammad Hosein Shahrīyār was born at a village near Tabrīz. After his early education in Tabrīz he entered the *Dar al-funūn* in Tehran and then studied medicine but did not complete his course. He was given a minor post in the Ministry of Agriculture and devoted his spare time to writing poetry. A collection of his early poems appeared in 1932 and had considerable success. Since then he has published four volumes of poetry. These contain verse of all kinds, but he is best known for his *ghazals*, in which he imitates Ḥāfeẓ. Shahrīyār also writes Turkish poetry, and his *Heydar Bābā* is regarded by his fellow Azarbayjanis as a masterpiece.

Zākānī (*d* 1371). 'Obayd-e Zākānī, who was born at Zākān, a village near Qazvin, is the most remarkable parodist and satirist Persia has produced. From his writings it appears that he had little affection for his native town. He left this to go and live in Shiraz, to which he was much attached and where he died. Zākānī wrote both prose and poetry. Among his prose writing the *Akhlāq ul-Ashrāf* (Morals of the Nobles) and amongst his poems, the satire *Mūsh-o gorbeh* (The Mouse and the Cat), are best known. Although some of his other poems are also of high quality, they have not enjoyed the popularity they deserve.

BIBLIOGRAPHY

ARBERRY, A. J., trans. *Fifty Poems of Ḥāfiẓ* Cambridge, 1947.
ARBERRY, A. J. 'Persian Literature', in *Legacy of Persia* Oxford, 1943.
BELL, G. L. *Poems from the Divan of Ḥafiẓ* London, 1897.
BROWNE, E. G. *A Literary History of Persia* 4 vols., Cambridge, 1928.
FARZAD, M. *The Main Currents in Persian Literature* London, 1965.
GRUNEBAUM, G. E. von, *Islam* New York, 1961; London, 1955.
JACKSON, A. V. W. *Early Persian Poetry* New York, 1920.
KAMSHAD, H. *Modern Persian Prose Literature* Cambridge, 1966.
LAZARD, G. *Les Premiers Poètes Persans* Paris, 1964.
MO'TAMEN, Z. 'A. *Tahāvvol-e She'r-e Fārsī* Tehran, 1959.
ROGERS, A., trans. *Persian Plays* London, 1890.
RYPKA, J. *History of Iranian literature* Dordrecht, 1968.
SAFĀ, Z. *Tārīkh-e Adabiyāt dar Īrān* 2 vols., Tehran, 1957.
SHAFAQ, R. Z. *Tārīkh-e Adabiyāt-e Īrān* Tehran, 1942.
STOREY, C. A. *Persian Literature* 5 parts, London, 1927–53 *etc.*

TURKISH LITERATURE

J. R. Walsh

HISTORICAL BACKGROUND

The Ottoman Empire, from which the modern Republic of Turkey derives, was the most important and enduring of all the political creations of Islam. Apart from its heartland in Asia Minor (Anatolia), its territories included most of what is today called the Arab World – Morocco being the exception – Greece and the Balkans, and much of Armenia and Georgia. Within these frontiers there was developed an ethnic amalgam which nearly a century and a half of assertive nationalisms has not yet wholly dissolved. It survived for over six centuries under the same dynasty, providing conditions of permanence and stability never previously achieved by any Islamic state, and assuring the security within which Muslim civilisation was allowed to cultivate its own characteristic human types and institutions.

The Turks originate in the steppes of Central Asia, where their traditional economic and social organisation was based on a life of pastoral nomadism. Their language, although somewhat similar to Hungarian and Finnish in that it has an agglutinative structure and observes vowel harmony, has no other European representative, and even in Central Asia it is markedly distinct from Mongolian and Tunguz, along with which it is commonly associated in a so-called Altaic family.* The earliest written document of the language dates from the first quarter of the eighth century AD in a bi-lingual (Turkish and Chinese) stele discovered near the confluence of the Orhon and Selenga Rivers in Northern Mongolia. Here was located the capital of the Göktürk Empire which had been founded about the middle of the sixth century AD and exerted its control over the whole of the Central Asiatic steppe. It was the western branch of this nomadic state that the Arabs came into contact with in the course of their expansion beyond the Oxus early in the eighth century, and in

* Ottoman Turkish was originally written in the Arabic character, but in 1928 this was officially replaced by a modified form of the Latin alphabet. The spellings of proper names, titles and technical terms in the present article are according to the modern system. The characters not found in English, or differing in their pronunciation are:
a as in *art* e as in *bed* i as in *hit* ı as in *fir-tree* ö and ü as in German c as j in *jar* ç as ch in *church* g as in *gore* ğ as y (of *yes*) after front vowels; after back vowels it is not pronounced; as in French ş as sh in *shed*.

ever increasing numbers these Turks were brought into the Caliph's domains to serve as slave troops in his armies, until by the middle of the ninth century they held virtually all political power in their hands. Dynasties such as the Tulunids in Egypt (868–905) and the Gaznevids in Afghanistan and Persia (962–1183) were of Turkish origin, but the decisive grip of the steppe peoples on the destinies of Islam came with the foundation of the Selcuk Empire in Persia in 1037. Within a quarter of a century the whole of the Middle East as far as the frontiers of Egypt was under its sway, and in 1071 at the battle of Manzikert (to the north of Lake Van) the defences of Byzantium were breached and Anatolia was for the first time opened to massive migration from the East.

A branch of the dynasty, the Selcuks of Rum, established themselves there in 1077, ultimately locating their capital at Konya (classical Iconium). The sultans of the line exercised a hegemony of sorts over the Turkish tribal groups distributed throughout Anatolia, and having survived the onslaught of the First Crusade in 1097, the state achieved a relative stability and prospered from the increase in commercial activity which this encouraged. Anatolia, in fact, was the one region of the vast Selcuk territories that did not experience the general collapse of the dynasty at the beginning of the twelfth century which led to the fragmentation of the Empire into a number of mutually hostile military principalities. The Sultanate of Rum was to enjoy this peace for about a century, until 1204 when the Byzantines, driven out of Constantinople by the opportunist adventurers of the Fourth Crusade, re-established themselves in strength in Western Anatolia and for over half a century mustered their resources for the recovery of their lands from the Franks. The Turkish tribes who had formerly occupied these regions were now displaced, and the balance that had been achieved by the Selcuk sultans was upset. The tribes fought for territory among themselves, and the security of the caravan routes was jeopardised; but the ultimate blow was to come from the Mongols who, in 1243 at Kösedağ (near Sivas), defeated the armies of the Sultan and reduced him to the status of a puppet ruler.

In 1261 the Byzantines recaptured Constantinople and withdrew their forces from Anatolia, leaving a power vacuum that was immediately filled by the surrounding Turkish tribes. By now central government no longer existed, and the whole of Anatolia was divided into twenty or more petty tribal states (*emirates*), covetous of each other's lands and frustrated by lack of resources. It was the good fortune of the Osman-Oğlu (known in Europe as the Ottomans) to have occupied the regions evacuated by the Byzantines; for as the attention of the latter was ever increasingly occupied with their affairs in Europe, neither the will nor the power to protect their Asian possessions remained to them, and the Ottomans were steadily able to expand their territories against the dwindling opposition. Their successes here attracted to their ranks the manpower of the neighbouring *emirates*, depleting their strength until they, too, fell as easy conquests to the Ottomans. Osman, the founder of the new dynasty, died in 1326, and in the same year the important Greek city of Bursa fell to his son and successor, Orhan. With the capture of İznik (Nicea) in 1330 and İzmit (Nicomedia) in 1337, Byzantine power disappeared from Western Anatolia, and one by one the Turkish *emirates* were being absorbed until by the time of Orhan's death in 1362 Ottoman territories extended as far east as Ankara.

Since 1346 the Byzantine Emperor had been dependent on Ottoman military assistance both in his struggle for the throne against rivals and in his wars against the Bulgarians and Serbians, and in 1353 Orhan was granted a base on the European side of the Gallipoli peninsula in recognition of these services. It was from here that the Turks pressed north into the Balkans under Murad I (1362–89), taking the important cities of Edirne (Adrianopolis) and Filibe (Plovdiv) and crushing the resistance of the Slavs, Hungarians and Wallachians (the battle of the Maritza, 1365). It was in his reign that the renowned Janissary corps was founded, a standing army of foot-soldiers all of whom had been collected in their adolescence from the subject Christian population, converted to Islam and trained in the service of the Sultan. In 1387 Murad defeated the Karaman-Oğlu, the last great rival to Ottoman dominance in Anatolia, and in 1389 on the plain of Kosovo (to the west of Priština) the final effort of the South Slavs against the Ottoman tide also ended in defeat.

The invincibility of the Ottomans came to an end in 1402 on the plain of Ankara where Bayezid I, the redoubtable son of Murad, was defeated and taken captive by Timur (Tamerlane), and for a while Anatolia lapsed into its former anarchy. But a century of unbroken success had assured to the descendants of Osman a prestige that could survive even this calamity, and after a confused decade of wars among the sons of Bayezid, in 1413 Mehmed I was able to restore the dynasty and re-establish its former frontiers. With his son, Murad II (1421–51), the expansions began once again, though in fact they were really a consolidation of the Ottoman position against challenges from the outside. The most serious of these was the Balkan alliance led by the Hungarian John Hunyadi and the Albanian George Castriot, but at the battle of Varna in 1444 and again on the plain of Kosovo in 1448 this menace was overcome, and the Ottomans emerged as the unassailable power that was to dominate the Danube for the next four centuries.

THE OTTOMAN EMPIRE

What Murad achieved in the military sphere his son, Mehmed II, known as the Conqueror (1451–81), was to parallel in the organisation of the Empire. In 1453 Constantinople (henceforth to be known as Istanbul), the last remnant of the Byzantine Empire, was captured and made the new capital of what in many respects was an Islamic Byzantium. A centralised administration served by men trained since childhood in the Palace, an army that had at its core the highly professional regiments of the Janissaries, and, above all, a judicial class that brought the laws and ideals of Islam to the furthest corners of the Empire gave an organic unity to the patchwork of territories that Mehmed had inherited. It was a century before his innovations reached full development, but it was owing to him that the state found a purpose other than the annual campaign and that it could survive when the campaigns yielded nothing but disaster. Territorially he added little to the Empire, but he drove the Genoese and the Venetians from the shores and islands of the Black Sea and the Aegean, and he asserted his domination over the Eastern Mediterranean.

Bayezid II (1481–1512) was confronted with the problems which the new order had created, and in particular with the disaffection of the Turkish military element which sensed that it was being forced out of the direction of affairs. Revolts in Anatolia, usually expressed as religious insurrections, threatened to separate the region from the Empire and ally it with a new state which had arisen in Northern Persia, the Safevids. The situation was finally resolved by Bayezid's son, Selim I (1512–20), who on the Plain of Çaldıran in 1514 inflicted a crushing defeat on the armies of the Safevid ruler, Şah İsmail I, and neutralised the attraction exerted on Anatolia from this quarter. In 1516–17, Syria and Egypt were wrested from the Mamlûks, bringing not only the wealth of the Nile Valley into the Ottoman economy, but also gaining for the dynasty the custodianship of the Holy Cities of Arabia and a semi-legitimate right to the title of Caliph.

Ottoman power reached its zenith in the reign of Selim's son, Süleyman I (1520–66), who within two years of his accession had taken Belgrade and the island of Rhodes. In 1528 siege was laid to Vienna. The Ottomans had ravaged Pest in 1526, and finally occupied Buda in 1541.

In the Mediterranean the Turkish fleet under the command of the formidable Barbarossa, operating out of Algiers, was all-powerful; Tunisia was incorporated into the Empire in 1534 and only the island of Malta proved able to hold out against the determined efforts made against it in 1565. Naval activity was even extended to the Persian Gulf, though with little success; but on land in the East, Baghdad was taken in 1534 and Ottoman domination was imposed on the Tigris-Euphrates valleys. In Europe, too, Ottoman might made itself felt beyond its own natural frontiers, and in 1525, after his defeat by the Hapsburgs at Pavia, Francis I effected an alliance with the Turks despite the disapproval of Christendom, opening thereby a new era in continental diplomacy. In this reign the state conceived by Mehmed II achieved its final realisation, and it was in every respect the Golden Age of Ottoman history.

Unfortunately, the glamour of this period was to inhibit initiatives to change and growth for about three centuries. Adherence to its ideals and practices was so stubbornly maintained in a world of rapid technological advancement that the state soon became an archaism among the nations. The military sciences which developed in Europe after the Thirty Years' War were ignored. The Janissaries degenerated into a self-perpetuating menace to internal peace, becoming all the more intractable at home, as they were proven increasingly ineffectual on the battlefield. Each century, of course, had a few military successes to restore hope and confidence, but the balance showed clearly the accumulating bankruptcy of Ottoman arms. The economy of the Empire, too, stagnated as progress in oceanic navigation reduced the importance of the Mediterranean as a commercial highway; and in an ignorant attempt to maintain its revenues the state imposed burdens on agriculture that were to become unbearable. There was a steady depopulation of the countryside, and the more distant provinces were ridden by bandits who, when they could not be suppressed, were acknowledged as the agents of the Sultan.

Convinced that it possessed all the final truths in the elaboration that had been given to Islam, Ottoman learning was impervious to influences from the outside; rarely stimulated to thought, the intellect atrophied; and creative energies were conditioned by society's limited capacity for understanding and appreciation. Ottoman man was more concerned with saving his soul than solving the problems of this transitory life; art, at the best, was but adventitious, and under no circumstances could it be allowed to disturb or provoke.

The still centre of this inertia was the Sultan himself who, even when not the plaything of palace intrigue or coerced by his ministers, rarely had the imagination to conceive or the will to initiate improvement in the order of things. To his subjects he held his position by divine selection, and let him be the most outrageous imbecile, he was still entitled to reverence and obedience. He presided over the debris of a once magnificent edifice, which still seemed marvellous because the illusions it had created were so powerful. And it is here, probably, that we touch upon the charm of Ottoman civilisation. For though the material world was crumbling about him, his unshakable faith and his sense of noble heritage gave the Ottoman an assurance and a dignity that decade after tedious decade of failure merely enhanced. Where we might expect a despairing, sullen surrender to misfortune, he remains, instead, cheerful and optimistic, sure that he is capable of great enterprises still and never hesitating in their attempt. He was the bravest of soldiers, the kindest of masters, the most pious of God's slaves, and an irritating puzzle to Europe where these virtues were being sacrificed to material progress.

Since the beginning of the seventeenth century the political decline of the Ottoman Empire is marked by treaties, each of which makes further inroads into her prestige and her territories: Sitvatörök (1606), Carlowitz (1699), Passarowitz (1718), Küçük Kaynarci (1774) and Jassy (1792) ushered the Empire into the nineteenth century as a cadaver for the dissection table of European and Russian imperialism. Efforts to arrest the decay were made by reforming sultans like Selim III (1789–1807) and Mahmud II (1808–39), and the latter did actually succeed in shaking off the incubus of the Janissaries, replacing it with a modern army on the European model (1826), and in restoring some of the central authority of the government by crushing the provincial despots (*derebeyis*). But the time had passed when the Ottoman Empire could control its own destinies; she was the centre of the vexing Eastern Question to which the cabinets of Europe were proposing answers that rarely took her own true interests into account. Nationalism, too, was spreading among the subject minorities: in 1816 Serbia gained home rule, and the rebellion that broke out in Greece in 1821 led to the total loss of the province in 1830. Egypt, though not in any nationalist sense, became virtually independent under its rebellious governor, Muhammad Ali, in 1839. In all these events the Great Powers were busily engaged with their own rivalries, and none more so than England who was determined to deny Russia access to the Mediterranean. It suited her purpose, therefore, to have a Turkey strong enough to resist Russian pressure, and to this end she instigated a programme of internal reforms which were intended to guarantee security of life, property and honour to all the subjects of the Sultan, to make taxation more equitable, and to assure to Muslim and non-Muslim alike equality before the law. This is the period known in Ottoman history as the Tanzimat, and its two key documents are the *Hatt-ı Hümayun of Gülhane* (November 1839) and its re-affirmation in a decree of 18 February 1856. Reforms of the kind envisaged in these documents were impossible in any Islamic state, for Islam is not a state religion but the state itself, and such measures implied a secularisation of religion. Failure to live up to them only afforded Europe further pretexts for interference in the Sultan's affairs, and encouraged other minorities to feel that they could rely on outside help in their bids for independence.

The Tanzimat gave new impetus to the westernisation of the Ottoman state: statesmen had to be trained in the languages and usages of Europe, so education underwent a drastic revision, creating a young generation more sympathetic to the ways and fashions of Europe than to their own oriental heritage. The reaction against this took place in the reign of Abdülhamid II (1876–1909), a Sultan who sought to regulate the pace of the innovations to the capacity of the country to absorb them; his interventions were seen as a repression of God-granted liberties, and many of the young intellectuals fled into exile where, known as the Young Turks, they spread propaganda against their government. Their ideas found a welcome reception in the officer class of the army, whose education, too, had been on the western model, and in 1908–9 they led a revolution which deposed the Sultan and re-established constitutional government.

The military figures who now assumed the direction of affairs proved quite as despotic and infinitely more inept than Abdülhamid, and they immediately involved the country in a series of disastrous wars in the Balkans and North Africa, bringing the economy into bankruptcy. Their supreme folly, however, was to ally their exhausted nation to Germany in World War I, compelling the wretched Turkish soldiers to face armies superior to them in everything but courage on all the far-flung frontiers of the Empire. With the exception of the Dardanelles, and the victory at Kut in 1916, the Turks experienced little but defeat, and when an armistice was signed in October 1918 Turkey was a nation that no longer had the will to survive. The new Sultan Mehmed VI was prepared to do whatever the Allies bid him to, and in the Treaty of Sèvres (August 1920) signed away the self-respect of his people along with most of their territories.

But the treaty was to be still-born. The Allies found themselves unable to occupy all the territories they had conquered, so they allowed the Greeks to invade Anatolia. This was the final humiliation which proved to be insupportable: the hatred of the Greek for the Turk that had been frustrated for nearly a century was now unleashed on what was thought to be a defenceless people. However, the Armies of the East, which had had no engagements since the Bolshevik Revolution of March 1917 took Russia out of the war, were still intact, and under the leadership of Mustafa Kemal (later to be known as Atatürk), the only Turkish general to emerge from the war with a record of victory, these forces were used to resist the Greek advance and eventually to drive them back into the sea (October 1922).

While the military activities were going on, Kemal, in April 1920, had formed a new government in Ankara which claimed to be more representative of the will of the people than that of the Sultan in Istanbul. In 1923 the Allies concluded a new peace treaty with this government, and in the same year Turkey was declared to be a Republic. The Sultan was banished into exile in November 1922 and in March 1924 the last representative of the Ottoman dynasty, who had lingered on with the semi-religious title of Caliph, was also expelled from the country.

THE REPUBLIC

Until his death in November 1938, Kemal ruled the Republic of his creation as a dictator, determined to deliver it from the torpor which he believed Islam had imposed upon it and to convert it into a dynamic western nation. He closed the theological schools, abolished the religious courts, disbanded the dervish orders, replaced the Holy Law with the Swiss Civil Code, and even replaced the Arabic script with one in Latin characters. He prevented the wearing of the fez so that the country should not even retain an oriental appearance, and in 1934 women were accorded full legal and political status, a reform that penetrated to the very heart of Islamic society.

Turkey of today is still in the course of achieving the goals which Atatürk set for it. Though a neutral in World War II, the necessity of maintaining a large military establishment then and ever since has been a great burden to an economy the balance of which is every year being further upset by a relentlessly increasing birth-rate. Politically she is the most stable of all the countries in the Middle East – even the military coup which overthrew the Democratic Party's government in May 1960 was bloodless – and as a member of the United Nations and the North Atlantic Treaty Organisation she has always shown herself responsible and co-operative. Although the life of the big cities might give the impression that the aims of Atatürk have been largely achieved, and while the generations produced by the new education which he instituted may seem reasonably faithful facsimiles of western models, Turkey is still at heart an Islamic nation.

MAIN TRENDS IN LITERATURE

The collapse of the Selcuk sultanate of Rum under the Mongol invasion of 1243, leading to the partitioning of Anatolia among the tribal leaders into over twenty independent principalities, created the conditions favourable to the development of a written Turkish literature in this region. Since its foundation in 1077, the cultural orientation of the dynasty had always been towards Persia, and throughout the twelfth century, as the East became ever more strife-ridden, scholars, artists and craftsmen fled west to the security and prosperity of Konya, overpowering by their presence and prestige any attempt at self-assertion by Turkish culture. Indeed, these Turkish tribal groups had little contact with the life of the capital, or with the indigenous Christian culture of the provinces they dominated; in general, they followed their traditional nomadic occupation of sheep-husbandry, preferring the atmosphere of the camp to that of the city, and their chiefs were more attached to the conventions of the steppe than to Islam. What they knew of Islam came through the preaching of itinerant dervishes, men themselves of rudimentary culture who, largely by the devotion and abnegation they exhibited in their personal lives, were able to win the respect of these simple people and influence their thought and behaviour.

Once they had become sovereigns in their own right, however, these tribal chiefs patterned their attitudes on the Selcuk example, the only Muslim royalty of which they had experience. They set up residence in cities, built mosques and other pious edifices, assembled courts about their persons and projected themselves as the defenders of Islam and the patrons of the culture associated with the faith, including literature. As Turkish was their only language, the books written in their names had to be in the vernacular; but at the same time had, also, to reflect their new pretensions. Thus, in the works of the thirteenth and fourteenth centuries which have survived to us, we find no allusion to the popular oral literature of the tribes nor to its legendary hero-figures such as Dede Korkut, Seyyid Battâl and Emîr Dânişmend; neither does the lyrical poetry draw its vocabulary or its imagery from nomadic life. Instead, we have translations or imitations of the long Persian narrative poem (*eg* the *Yûsuf ve Züleyhâ* of Şeyyâd Hamza; the *Süheyl ü Nevbahâr* of Mes'ûd ebn-i Ahmed), versified lessons and sermons (*eg* the *Garîbnâme* of Âşık Paşa; the *İskendernâme* of Ahmedî), and a lyrical poetry of mystical religious fervour (especially the work of Yunus Emre and his imitators).

Mysticism, it should be remarked, was not in conflict with orthodoxy at this period in Anatolia as in other parts of the Islamic world. The dervish order which grew up around Mevlâna and his successors in Konya was the only feasible religious organisation for a region such as Anatolia where there had not as yet developed a uniform system of theological and judicial education that could supply the teachers, spiritual leaders and magistrates necessary for the survival of an Islamic state. Dervishes of this order or of similar communities dispersed throughout the hinterlands, and as their teaching had to be entertaining if they were to hold the attention of their audiences, they became perforce poets and musicians. This intimate association between poetry and religion was to persist down the centuries in Ottoman literature; and since a poem could always be taken to mean more than it actually said, true literary criticism was often to be inhibited by piety.

The lack of a common education, as well as the absence of a common literary dialect, prevented any of these early productions from exerting an influence outside their own confined environment; writers of talent continued to look to Persia for their models and were assiduous in their imitation. Although Turkish has no long vowels and its traditional poetry was quantitative and accentual in metre, the entire apparatus of Persian prosody, based on a qualitative metrical system, was followed, and it became conventional that any Turkish vowel could be treated as long or short depending on the requirements of the foot. As this would have destroyed the morphology of the metre if carried to excess, Persian and Arabic words had to be introduced to establish and maintain the rhythmic character of the line, and out of this practice was to develop the macaronic Ottoman literary language.

POETIC LITERATURE

In all three Islamic literatures the unit of the poem is the *beyt*, a line consisting of two hemistichs (*mısra'*). Each *beyt* is self-contained both in thought and in syntax, and even in a narrative poem it must be capable of isolation in both these respects. Working under this limitation, the poet was forced into a conciseness of utterance that is often epigrammatic in impact; and to achieve effect he had to resort to word-play and rhetorical tropes which create an impression of contrivance and artificiality.

The verse forms of Persian poetry, too, were accepted without modification. The most common of these were: (*a*) the *gazel*, a short poem usually of from five to ten *beyts*, each ending in the same rhyme, in the last of which the poet mentions his own pen-name (*mahlas*). The theme of the *gazel* was love or wine, and the images associated with these are manipulated as are the notes of a musical scale to achieve novelty and freshness. (*b*) the *kaside*, a long mono-rhymed poem of up to a hundred or more *beyts*, generally written in praise of some individual from whom the poet expected a reward. The opening section of the *kaside*, known as the *nesib*, is separable from the remainder and can be concerned with virtually any topic that can later be made pertinent to the individual to whom the poem is addressed. When written in glorification of God the form is known as *tevhid*, and when in praise of the Prophet, *na't*. (*c*) the *mesnevi*, usually a long narrative poem of unspecified length, the rhyme being confined to the hemistichs of each *beyt*, rather like couplets. This is the vehicle for much of the story-telling in Islamic literature, in which familiar themes are re-worked in a formalised manner and only the felicity of language conveys an air of originality. The form is also used for didactic poems, or any versified subject of a length which would preclude mono-rhyming. (*d*) the *rübâ'î*, a short poem of four hemistichs, the first, second and fourth of which must rhyme together. The form is suitable for the epigram, and is used to give succinct expression to a single idea. Each of these forms is written in one of the various metres, which must be maintained throughout the entire poem. The collected *kasides*, *gazels* and *rübâ'îs* of a poet are known as a *divan*; *mesnevis* are treated as single books, or else collected in fives and given the name *hamse*.

But the imitation did not rest with the merely formal aspects; the entire aesthetic of Persian poetry, too, was absorbed into Turkish and the same artistic ideals pursued. It was the way in which these ideals were understood that determined the course in which Ottoman poetry was to develop. To some it was the extension of prayer, or else the pulpit for parsonical exhortation; others treated it as the medium for philosophical musing; and by many the imagery was taken literally, making it secular and anacreontic. Yet even the latter could be translated to transcendental terms by the sufistic expedient of holding the beloved and all the details of his beauty to represent God and His qualities, love itself as the yearning after God, wine as the divine essence, etc. Thus, a typical *gazel* may be set in a tavern where the poet, in the company of his convivial friends, listens to the musicians and singers and calls repeatedly for wine from the cup-bearer until finally he becomes drunk and insensible; this, we are to assume, is an allegory of the human spirit rising above the vanities of the world. And if he expresses a wish to end the evening in the embraces of the cup-bearer or some other comely youth, we are to understand the chaste aspiration to total involvement with God. But, of course, it was the apparent meaning that was most often intended and understood; and yet, in this vast corpus of love poetry it is surprising how seldom erotic lubricity and salaciousness are to be encountered.

Islamic society was everywhere masculine, women being confined to the house and the circle of the family, and veiled against the glances of strangers when they ventured out-of-doors. The young Ottoman, therefore, had no experience of females outside his own immediate family until he married, and as a consequence his sexual urges had to be satisfied in acts of sodomy. This is particularly true of the classes from which the poets arose: the students of the theological colleges who could not marry until they had completed their long education, living for years with one another in dormitories; or the palace servants, slaves of the Sultan, who would have had to leave their privileged lives in the court if their master gave them permission to marry. In most of these homosexuality was not the neurotic malady common today; it was no reflection on a man's virility, nor did society express too great a disapproval. The male prostitute was part of the entertainment industry; he was the dancing-boy, the singer, the tavern servant, and it was the physical adornments and the artificial manners of these epicene creatures that provided the imagery for the poet. Yet, it is true that no young boy who had left the protection of his family, to become, say, an apprentice to a tradesman, was safe from the prevalent paederasty. Not until the eighteenth century were poems addressed to women, and on their first appearance they seemed rather daring and indecent.

It was not until the reign of Mehmed II (1451–81) that the conditions requisite for coherent literary activity first obtained in Ottoman society. Institutions of higher education (the *medreses*) were founded, producing literate men of common culture and outlook. The language of the capital became the standard and its intelligibility could be assumed throughout the Empire. There was the wealth to be expended on patronage, and the leisure that needed diversion and amusement. The Sultan himself set the example for the cultivation of letters; he was a poet of modest abilities, the author of a small *divan*, and he rewarded other poets whose works he admired, even fixing a stipend on the Persian poet Câmî in Herat. Men of talent from every quarter of the Islamic world were attracted by the opportunities and rewards of Istanbul, and as the fashions of the capital became increasingly those of the provinces, there came into existence a cultural infrastructure which assured a constant supply of recruits to the mainstream of artistic life.

BELLES-LETTRES AND HISTORY

There was, also, a constant demand for secretaries to feed the bureaucracy through which the centralised administration operated. Such employment was beyond the abilities of those trained in the palace establishment and beneath the dignity of the *medrese* graduates, so men who had been privately educated and possessed a gift of phrase were assured of positions that could often lead to high office. The elaborate epistolary style that was used in state correspondence called for literary talents of special quality seldom recognised today;

the tedious verbosity that seems designed to conceal meaning was in its time but the normal observance of a carefully regulated protocol.

It was not this style, however, that was used in the prose works of Ottoman literature. Although every author tried to achieve elegance in his writing, it was realised that to be too ornate would interfere with the flow of ideas and irritate the reader. So, with the exception of those works of deliberate prose artistry, the general style was periodic and rhythmic, the meaningful units being fairly short and linked together with punctuating rhymes. When handled by a competent and inventive writer, the effect is pleasantly musical; but it can be unspeakably dull when it is, as so often, perfunctory imitation.

History is the chief form of prose composition. The earliest histories of the Ottomans – *eg* those of Âşıkpaşazâde (*d* 1502+) and Neşrî (*d* 1512+) – were written in the crude, simple style of folk-narrative, and although their information was used by later historians the esteem in which they were held was low. The first great histories of literary merit were in Persian – the *Heşt Bihişt* (The Eight Paradises) of İdris Bitlisî (*d* 1520) and the *Mirâtü 'l-Edvar* (The Mirror of the Ages) of Lârî (*d* 1571) – and it was after having translated the latter that Sâdeddin Efendi (*d* 1599) composed his own famous history of the Ottoman dynasty, the *Tacü 't-Tevarih* (The Crown of Histories). Similar in style and organisation was the general history of the world by his contemporary Âlî (*d* 1600) entitled *Künhü 'l-Ahbar*. Works of more ambitious stylistic aims appear in every period, especially those devoted to individual reigns – *eg*, the *Tabakâtu 'l-Memâlik* (The Stages of the Regions) on that of Sultan Süleyman I by Celâl-zâde Mustafa Çelebi (*d* 1567) – or to particular events, like the *Üss-i Zafer* (The Basis of Victory) on the destruction of the Janissaries in 1826, written by Es'ad Efendi. But, in general, the styles of Sâdeddin and Âlî set the standard for this type of writing. From the year 1709 down to the end of the dynasty, official historiographers were appointed to chronicle year by year the events of the Empire. The first of these was Naima (*d* 1716), and his successors included such famous names as Râşid (*d* 1735), Vâsif (*d* 1806) and Cevdet Paşa (*d* 1895).

BIOGRAPHY

The same urge to extend to the present day works on subjects having a historical continuity also influenced biographical writing. The lives of the learned men (*ulema*) and the dervishes, classified according to the reigns in which they died, were recorded in Arabic by Taşköprüzâde (*d* 1561) and translated into Turkish by Mecdî (*d* 1591). The work was continued on the same plan by Atâ'î (*d* 1635) and Şeyhî (*d* 1732), but after the middle of the eighteenth century the *ulema* had become too numerous to make any further continuation practicable.

More important for the history of Ottoman literature was the class of works known as the *tezkerâtü 'ş-şüara*, or biographies of the poets. The earliest of these, the *Heşt Bihişt* (The Eight Paradises) of Sehî (*d* 1548), was done in imitation of the *Mecalis ün-Nefa'is* (The Assemblies of the Exquisites) by the Çagatay poet, Ali Şir Nevâî, and it found continuators in Latifî (*d* 1582), Âşık Çelebi (*d* 1572), Kınalı-zâde (*d* 1604), Ahdî (*d* 1594), *etc*, in an unbroken sequence down to modern times, culminating in the *Son Asır Türk Şairleri* (Turkish Poets of Recent Times) of İbnü 'l-Emin Mahmud Kemal, which was completed in 1942. Many of these works have a literary value all of their own, and indeed Âşık Çelebi is to be regarded as one of the masters of Ottoman prose. But, in addition, they are the equivalent of literary criticism, reflecting the tastes and standards of the various periods. Josef von Hammer-Purgstall's *Geschichte der Osmanischen Dichtkunst* (Pest, 1836–8), which was based on these works, lists over two thousand names in its index; and even if many of them may be discounted as amateur dabblers, we are still left with an impressive quantity, showing the important position occupied by poetry in the aesthetic life of the Ottoman.

Other classes of biographical writing take for their subjects the calligraphers, musicians, architects, mystics, Grand Vezirs, Foreign Secretaries, and the occupants of the office of *şeyhülislâm*, and there are some devoted to the *ulema* and poets of particular cities, such as Bursa, Edirne, Amid, etc. Learned works dealing with the Islamic sciences continued to be written in Arabic, but there were, also, numerous books in Turkish ranging from the exegesis of the Kurân to Arabic grammar; and many of the classical monuments of Islamic learning were either translated or provided with interpretive commentaries.

GEOGRAPHY, *etc.*

Geography (*eg* the *Cihannümâ* (World-Mirror), of Kâtib Çelebi, *d* 1657), travel (*eg* the *Seyahatnâme* (Travels), of Evliya Çelebi, *d* 1682), politics (*eg* the *Risale* (Monograph), of Koçi Bey, *d* 1640+), ethics (*eg* the *Ahlâk-ı Âlâ'î*, (The Alâian Ethics), of Kınalızâde Ali Çelebi, *d* 1572), philosophy, the physical sciences, mathematics, etc. are all represented by works produced in each period. What is most astonishing is that this great volume of writing was done before printing had been introduced into the Ottoman Empire, when books had to bear the high cost of being written individually by calligraphers. In Istanbul and the big cities the latter were highly respected, and many of them were men of deep learning to whom we owe careful copies of important works.

EARLY PRINTING

The first press to print Ottoman works was set up in 1729 by a Hungarian convert to Islam, İbrahim Müteferrika, but because of the opposition of the conservative *ulema* and the general low level of literacy in the country, it had brought out only seventeen books by the time of his death in 1745. Printing was carried on sporadically after this until 1831 when an official government press was established to publish the court gazette (the *Takvim-i Vekayi*), and in 1840 the use of these facilities was made available for private ventures. Gradually commercial printing houses were opened to keep pace with the demand for text-books required for the new system of education which the Tanzimat had introduced, and for the needs of the widening literacy which resulted from it.

JOURNALISM AND FICTION

The first privately-owned newspaper – the *Ceride-i Havadis* (The Journal of Events) – began to appear regularly in 1840, and as the appeal of this form of informative writing on current events slowly spread, it found competitors in the *Tercüman-ı Ahval* (The Interpreter of Affairs, 1860) and the famous paper edited by the pioneer of literary reform, Şinasi Efendi, known as the *Tasvir-i Efkâr* (The Illustration of Ideas, 1862). Weekly and monthly journals, many of them literary, were to follow, completing the literary spectrum in which new conceptions of literature could be displayed. The old literature had been the product of dilettantism, sustained by the caprices of patronage, and the profession of letters, as such, did not exist. But there was now a viable economic basis for a literary career, and not only in pedestrian journalism. Due to the poor communications of the period there was always a dearth of news to fill the columns of the papers, and they had consequently to rely on feature writers and columnists, a characteristic which they retain down to the present. These writings were didactic, polemical and, above all, humorous; and when from the pen of such masters of the short essay as Ahmed Midhat (*d* 1912) and Ahmed Rasim (*d* 1932) they have the directness, balance and unity of true art, lifting them above the usually ephemeral nature of their themes. The form is today represented by Falih Rıfkı Atay (*b* 1894) and Burhan Felek, though the general trend in others is towards the political and the controversial.

Another way of assuring reader loyalty to a newspaper was the serialisation of novels, and this, too, has remained one of the constants of Turkish journalism. For long after the Tanzimat, literacy was so limited that an author could not rely on an adequate income from direct publication of his novels, but serialisation in a newspaper guaranteed an initial return and stimulated interest for the purchase of the work when it later appeared in book form. Beneficial as this was as an incentive to novel-writing, the necessity of maintaining the interest of the reader from day to day meant that the early original novels consisted of contrived episodes, thus debarring the authors from the opportunity for descriptive or interpretative passages. Characterisation, too, was impossible within these confines, so the novel became peopled with stereotypes and caricatures, and the formula has persisted even into modern works. As the number of newspapers increased, native creative talent was not able to keep pace with the demand for this type of story-telling, and there was an ever growing dependence upon translations and adaptations (frequently unacknowledged) from foreign languages, particularly French. Under this influence many Turkish novels took on an alien air: they are given their settings in the cosmopolitan society of Istanbul where imported values and attitudes would not seem too outlandish, and their conflicts and crises are those of Europe rather than Turkey. It was not until after the Second World War that novels of an elemental Turkish quality begin to be written by authors of village backgrounds. The short-story, unsuitable for newspaper serialisation and too long for most of the literary journals, did not find the same markets as the novel, and apart from Ömer Seyfettin (*d* 1920) and Sabahattin Ali (*d* 1948), the form has found few distinguished exponents in modern Turkish literature.

At the centre of all these innovations there was the problem of the language, and in one way or another it continues to bedevil creative effort even at present. The educational reforms of the Tanzimat produced a generation wholly different in intellectual background to their *medrese* forbears; the study of Arabic and Persian steadily gave way to French, and with the publication in 1850 of Cevdet Paşa's *Kavaid-i Osmaniye* (The Principles of Ottoman), Turkish was for the very first time given academic status. Journalism required a normative idiom of immediate intelligibility, denuded of all that the old Ottoman writers regarded as stylistic essentials; and yet, men of education could not bring themselves to descend wholly to the colloquial. The compromise was in many respects very satisfactory: abstract ideas and the new concepts of European origin were normally expressed in Arabic words, but the dynamic syntactical structure became increasingly Turkish. The two towering literary figures of the period, Namık Kemal (*d* 1888) and Ziya Paşa (*d* 1880), fashioned it into an expository style that was both simple and dignified. In the novels of this and the succeeding generation, and especially in those of Hüseyin Rahmi Gürpınar (*d* 1944), the dialogues are frequently given in Istanbul colloquial; and, of course, even the earliest dramatists realised that it would be absurd to have characters of low social status speak anything but the vernacular.

Many of the poets, however, and notably those associated with the journal *Servet-i Fünun* (The Treasure of the Arts) which was founded in 1891, tried to reproduce the involuted subjectivity of French Romanticism by ferreting among the lexical resources of Arabic for exact or suggestive equivalents for their nebulous conceptions, making the language, if anything, even more obscure than the old Ottoman. The practice, also, passed into the prose-writing of this school, and the inevitable reaction came in 1911 with the *Genç*

Kalemler (Young Authors) movement which fled to the realist extreme of demanding that only the language of the people be used in literature. Each of these groups contained writers of enduring merit – Cenab Şahabettin (*d* 1934), a poet and essayist of the *Servet* movement, has an established importance in the history of Turkish prose-writing, and the *Genç Kalemler* short-storyist, Ömer Seyfettin (*d* 1920) is already of classic stature.

The latest, current movement in Turkish letters is headed by the writers of 'purified Turkish', to whom literary considerations are distantly secondary to the overriding nationalistic aim of eliminating from the language all words of foreign origin and replacing them with resurrections from historical dictionaries or neologisms of their own ill-informed contrivance. Unfortunately, these writers are abetted by the official Turkish Linguistic Society, which is able to control the teaching of the language in the schools, and is, thereby, gradually depriving the young generation of the enjoyment of their proper literary heritage. By far the more authentically Turkish are the authors who have created the current fashion for the primitive novel; men of provincial or village origins, innocent alike of dogma and sophistication. The success of writers like Yaşar Kemal (*b* 1922) and Orhan Kemal (*b* 1914) is probably as much due to the way in which their descriptions of the hardships of Anatolian life have pricked the conscience of the reading public of Istanbul and Ankara as to any artistic merit; it is only in this manner that one can explain the toleration shown to their poor construction, fairy-tale characterisation and naive sentimentality.

Islamic Ottoman society had no experience of theatre apart from the childish Karagöz shadow-plays and a vulgar type of popular entertainment known as the *ortaoyunu*. There was, therefore, no precedent upon which native dramatists could build, and when the first theatres were opened in Istanbul around the 1860s they had to rely on translations or adaptations from European languages. Indeed, French plays were the staple repertoire: Ahmed Vefik Paşa (*d* 1890) made versions of almost the whole corpus of Molière; Racine, Corneille, Dumas père et fils also found translators. Yet efforts at original composition were not lacking: the great innovator Şinasi printed a one-act play in 1860, and Namık Kemal, who thought the theatre the highest form of creative writing, wrote no less than six full-length plays. The name most identified with the form, however, is Abdülhak Hâmit Tarhan, whose dramas in verse and in prose are regarded as monuments of post-Tanzimat literature. It was probably the importance attached to dramatic writing by Kemal and Hâmit that inspired so many later writers of reputation to try their hands in this type of composition, but almost without exception their works give the impression of having been written to be read rather than acted. Istanbul and Ankara today support a large number of theatres and the companies associated with them, but among the modern Turkish dramatists there is hardly one whose work would bear translation to the stages of Europe or America. The commercial Turkish cinema has wholly abandoned itself to the lowest common denominator of box-office appeal, and is only to be spoken of as a national disgrace.

FOLK POETRY

Alongside the classical literature, there has always existed a folk-poetry created by a class of wandering singers (*saz şairleri*), known generally as the *âşık* or *ozan*. These composed their songs in the traditional qualitative metres of the Turks, in a simple four line stanzaic form to which the name *koşma*, *türkü* or *şarki* is variously applied. The unschooled simplicity and the patent sincerity of this poetry constitute its chief appeal and place it in marked contrast with that of the educated classes; but century after century the same sentiments recur in the same forms, unrelieved by inventiveness in language or change of personality on the part of the poet, so that the simplicity and sincerity themselves seem to become contrived and formalised. It is probably improper to judge this poetry as written literature, for it was always accompanied by music and intended for singing rather than reading. On a somewhat higher level, but still to be regarded as folk-literature, were the hymns (*ilâhî*) composed by the dervishes for use in the services held in the monasteries. These use the same popular metres and verse-forms, but they share the same religious outlook as the more sophisticated productions of the classical writers, adding a passionate fervour that is frequently concealed in the latter by their very artistry.

INDIVIDUAL WRITERS

Bakî (1526–1600). Mahmud Abdülbakî Efendi, the foremost poet of the sixteenth century, in whose work the classical style of *divan* poetry finds its most perfect expression. He was born into a poor Istanbul family, and as a child he served an apprenticeship as a saddler, but his innate abilities won him access to a *medrese* education, while his qualities as a poet afforded him entry into the literary circles of the capital. After a short career as a *medrese* teacher, he entered the judicial branch of the learned profession and between the years 1576–82 held the post of *kadi* in such important cities as Edirne, Mecca and Medina. In 1584 he became *kadi* of Istanbul, and in 1585 was appointed supreme judge (*kazasker*) of Anatolia. He further approached the pinnacle of the learned career in 1591, when he was designated *kazasker* of Rumili, and he was now in line for the office of *şeyhülislâm*, the chief judicial dignitary of the Empire. However, he died without having obtained this ultimate ambition.

The static world of the *divan* poet is presented to us in all its crystalline symmetry in the *divan* of Bakî. Unlike his contemporary Fuzulî and the other mystics, he is untroubled by the exhausting pursuit of the infinite; and he is too intellectually fastidious to descend to the frivolities of the *vers de société* that was beginning to find favour at this time. Though he was capable of writing movingly, as in his famous elegy on Sultan Süleyman, his normal tone is one of withdrawn serenity, and his imagination stimulates but does not precipitate him into utterance. All his themes and his attitudes are those of his predecessors, but his language is the realisation of what they so strove after and so seldom attained. Bakî is the totally uncommitted artist, with no lesson or message to impart other than that art creates its own reality. No other Ottoman poet has matched his sustained excellence in the writing of *gazels*, but the standard he set assured the high quality of the work of all subsequent generations.

Ekrem, Recâi-Zade Mahmud (1847–1914). One of the most influential figures in the literary reforms of the late nineteenth century, Ekrem was born in Istanbul in 1847 into a wealthy and prominent family – his father, Recâi Efendi, was director of the state publishing house. Poor health interfered with his formal education, but at the age of fifteen he entered government employment in the secretariat of the Foreign Office where he came under the influence of other young writers to whom the occupational study of the French language had opened new literary horizons. His life was spent in public service, advancing to such high offices as Minister of Charitable Endowments and of Education, and when he died in 1914 he was a distinguished member of the Senate.

Ekrem's works include poetry, drama, the novel and literary criticism, but it is in the latter field that he retains his importance in the history of Turkish literature. Between the years 1880 and 1887 he was teacher of literature at the Mülkiye *lycée* in Istanbul, and the substance of his lectures was published in 1879 under the title *Tâlim-i Edebiyat* (The Teaching of Literature). The work is a theoretical analysis of literature, throughout which there is an implicit rejection of all that was characteristic of the old poetry and prose, and it provided the new generation of writers with a rationalised aesthetic for their innovations. Although today its assumptions often seem arbitrary and its reasoning naive, its appearance delivered a devastating blow to the traditional conception of literature which had never been formulated into such a coherent system. His poetry is patently based on French models – when not fashionably melancholic and pessimistic, saturated with an embarrassing sentimentality – and it is ironical that the old *divan* poetry, which for all its artificiality was authentic to its own environment, is today more attractive and pleasurable than his imported attitudes. Of his three novels only *Araba Sevdası* (Love in a Landau) which appeared in 1896 deserves mention because of the new realism which it introduced into this form. As a critical commentary on the manners of certain sections of contemporary Istanbul society, it is still very amusing and can be read for more than its merely historical interest.

Fikret, Tevfik (1867–1915). The most important poet of the *Servet-i Fünun* school, Fikret was born in Istanbul in 1867, the son of a minor government official. After he had completed his education at the famous Galatasaray *lycée* in 1888, he was employed for a while in the Foreign Office, but in 1890 he returned to his old school as a teacher. He left there in 1896 to take up another teaching post at the American endowed school, Robert College. In 1909 he was appointed Director of Galatasaray *lycée*, but he resigned the following year and returned to Robert College where he remained until his death in 1915. Between the years 1895 and 1901 he was the editor of the weekly journal *Servet-i Fünun* which, under his direction, became the focus of the modern literary movement in Turkey.

The uneven quality of Fikret's poetry has driven critical evaluation to extremes of admiration or condemnation. Subjective and sentimental, many of his early poems are on the level of greeting-card verses, and some are so ridden with poeticism as to seem a travesty of the literary innovations they were intended to represent. But in middle life he underwent a profound psychological change which completely altered his personality, enshrouding him in an impenetrable melancholy, and estranging him from his religion, his environment and his friends. His most important collection of poems appeared in 1900 under the title *Rübab-ı Şikeste* (The Broken Lute), and in this we find a concern and a compassion for the human condition such as had never before been expressed with such moving sincerity in Turkish poetry. Many of the poems are *tableaux* of daily life, and although he never abandons the classical metres and his vocabulary is still that of Ottoman, his technical ability is such that he can adapt both to a simple conversational style and an effortless lyrical flow. For all the disdain he showed for his society in his personal life, he is Turkey's greatest humanist and his memory is still revered even by the present-day generation which usually has to read him in translation.

Fuzulî (*d* 1556). Unanimously recognised as the greatest lyric poet of the Turkish language, Mehmed Fuzulî was born in Hille (in Iraq) towards the end of the fifteenth century. The Tigris-Euphrates region was at this time the border between Persian and Arabo-Turkish culture, and consequently his education was tri-lingual. His proficiency in these languages was to a degree that allowed him to compose works of merit in all three, and he shows evidence of having, also, received a thorough education in all the usual branches of Islamic learning. For a long time he lived in Baghdad, both under the Safevid Persians and the Ottomans, and his reputation was sufficiently established by 1534, when the city fell to Sultan Süleyman, for him to be granted a stipend out of public funds in recognition of his merits. He died of the plague in 1556 and was buried in the holy city of Kerbala.

The fame of Fuzulî among the Turks is based chiefly on three of his numerous works:

(1) The Turkish *Divan.* Written in the Azeri dialect – slightly different from that of Istanbul, but easily intelligible to all Western Turks – the poems in this work are at the same time the most sublime and the most passionate expression of mystical love in the whole of the literature. The dominant mood of melancholy is born of a yearning that can never know satisfaction, that would, indeed, be frustrated did it ever attain its object. For agony is the avenue down which the soul must proceed to maintain awareness of the evanescent divine reality to which all life is oriented. He speaks as a spirit doomed to humanity, but with a directness and a simplicity that make even the artificialities of the traditional verse forms which he is compelled to employ seem uniquely designed for this utterance. What Hafiz is to Persian poetry, so is Fuzulî to Turkish. He, also, composed a large Persian *divan* of very much the same character.

(2) *Leylâ ve Mecnun.* A long narrative poem dealing with the ill-starred love of the Romeo and Juliet of Islamic legend. Although it had provided the theme for many such similar poems both in Persian and Turkish long before Fuzulî, he treats the story as an allegory of the human spirit in quest of God. It is this underlying concept that invests the various incidents of the narrative with portentous significance, illustrating the stages of spiritual development in terms of self-immolation in love. It can not be denied that the responsive-

ness of the Ottoman imagination to any work of mystical implication has contributed to the esteem in which this poem is held, but that it is a masterpiece is evident at once when it is compared with other versions of the same theme.

(3) *Hadikat üs-Suadâ.* This is a prose work, interspersed with verses, describing the martyrdom of Huseyn, the son of the Caliph Ali, at Kerbala in AD 680. The event has been elaborated into a passion-play by the Shī'a sect of Islam, and it was this sect that was to become the state religion of Persia in the time of Fuzulî. It shows the curious ambivalence of Ottoman orthodoxy that a work of this nature could be accepted without demur and even be regarded as a holy book. It is written in the ornate, rhymed prose characteristic of works of artistic intention, and although it does not achieve the technical standards of the Istanbul style, it has a freshness and vigour which contribute to the poignancy of the moving incidents of the narrative.

Hâmit, Abdülhak Tarhan (1852–1937). Poet and dramatist, and probably the most celebrated personality of modern Turkish literature. He was born in Istanbul in 1852, the son of the historian and physician, Hayrullah Efendi. His early education was received from private tutors and for a year or so he attended school in Paris (1863). In 1865 he went to Persia with his father who had been appointed ambassador, and after the latter's sudden death he returned to Istanbul (1868), where he received employment in various government offices. In 1876 he was sent to Paris as Second Secretary to the Embassy, and from here was transferred to several other cities, becoming First Consul in Bombay in 1883. His wife died in Beyrut when returning from this last appointment (1885). The following year he was sent as First Secretary to the London Embassy, and he was to remain here on and off in various important posts until 1908. In this year he was appointed ambassador to Brussels, where his second wife, an Englishwoman he had married in 1890, died. He returned to Istanbul from Brussels in 1912, and received an appointment to the Senate. After the proclamation of the Republic he was elected to the new Parliament as one of the members from Istanbul. He died in 1937, and was given a state funeral, mourned by the whole nation.

Hâmit is of a genius so rare that it is impossible to capture the nature of its variety in a single label. Clearly he belongs to the school of Namık Kemal and Recaî-zade Ekrem, but whereas they are the earnest journeymen of the new culture, Hâmit is its compulsive singer, spontaneously reacting to its every manifestation in a poetry that creates its own forms and lives by its own laws. He is by turns romantic, realist, lyrical and heroic, and at times he is all these at once. His biographers present us with a sophisticated man-of-the-world possessing elegant manners polished by a lifetime of diplomatic restraint, but tell us very little of the poetic possession that restlessly drove him to the heights and the depths of emotion.

Hâmit wrote more than forty works, half of them dramatic in form, but dramas intended to be read rather than acted. He has no sense of theatrical construction, and character development exists not at all; in fact, as in the old *mesnevis*, the story is but the setting for the thoughts and feelings of the author, and even in the prose plays these are expressed with the passion and urgency of poetry. The plays are usually on semi-historical themes in foreign settings: *Duhter-i Hindû* (The Indian Maiden, 1875), a prose play with occasional verse passages, concerns the love of an Indian girl for a heartless English colonial officer. *Târık* (1879), in prose also, deals with the conquest of Spain by the Muslims, giving a highly idealised picture of Islamic chivalry. The fame this work achieved in the Near East led him to write a sequel, *İbn-i Musa*, which though completed in 1881 was not published until 1919. In the meanwhile he had written another play in the classical metres with a Spanish setting: *Tezer* (1880), dealing with the love of the ruler 'Abdurrahman III for a Christian girl. Two of his plays took their themes from Corneille: *Nesteren* (1877), written in the syllabic metres was adapted from *Le Cid*; while *Eşber* (1880), in the classical metres, is based on *Horace*. The work which he himself liked best was *Finten* (written in 1887 but not published until 1918), in prose and verse, a melodrama, set for the most part in London, with echos of *Othello* and *Macbeth*.

The most famous of his poems is *Makber* (The Tomb) published in 1885 after the death of his first wife, and its sequel *Ölü* (The Dead) which also was brought out in the same year. *Garam* (Desire), which though not published in book form until 1923, was written *c* 1877; it is a long, romantic narrative, and one of the most successful efforts at the verse story in the new literature.

Nabi, Yusuf (1642–1712), the pre-eminent literary figure of the late seventeenth century. He was born and educated in Urfa, and at the age of twenty-four went to Istanbul where he became secretary to Musahib Mustafa Paşa, one of the most prominent political men of the period and a close confidant of Sultan Mehmed IV. He enjoyed the patronage of Mustafa Paşa for about twenty years, accompanying him on his campaigns and provincial appointments, a position which placed him at the heart of state affairs and afforded opportunity to become acquainted with all the leading personalities of the capital. When Mustafa Paşa died in 1686, Nabi, probably to escape from the anarchy which was all but destroying public life, retired to Aleppo where he enjoyed the revenues of certain concessions. Here he remained for nearly twenty-five years, until 1710 when the governor of the province, Baltacı Mehmed Paşa, was appointed Grand Vezir and brought him back to Istanbul with his entourage. He died two years later, having acquired in his life-time a reputation in virtually every known aspect of literary production which was to make its influence felt down to the middle of the nineteenth century.

It is as a poet that Nabi is best remembered, and in particular as a writer of *gazels*. In these, lyricism and sententiousness are interwoven in an imagery so disciplined that some critics have found them mundane and uninspired. His *divan* was collected in his old age when his youthful exuberance had passed, and the poems reflect the mature reaction of the cultured, pious Muslim to a world in which neither life nor possessions were secure; a dignity found in resignation to the will of God and an indifference towards the rewards and disappointments of life. Without the ecstatic raptures of the mystics or the frivolity of the secular poets, it is the simple, practical tone in which this attitude is expressed that has made his *divan* so popular, and many of his verses have become proverbial.

In a long poem of advice to his son, the *Hayriye*, he prescribes that conduct of life that fulfills the Muslim ideal of dignity with piety, making shrewd incidental comments on the evils of the age. His long narrative poem, the *Hayrabad*, is an adaptation from a Persian work by Ferîdüddin Attâr, but with many additions. Its highly Persianised language gives it quite a unique character in Ottoman *mesnevi* literature, a merit that has generally been lost sight of in modern criticism which condemns this excessive use of a foreign vocabulary.

In prose he wrote an account of the campaign which led to the capture of the Polish city of Kamieniec in 1672; a description of his pilgrimage to Mecca and Medina in the year 1678; a continuation of the life of the Prophet begun by Veysî Efendi but left incomplete at his death in 1628. As a writer of ornate prose he does not achieve the stature of Nergisî or Veysî, mainly because his imagination is too much restricted by the limitations of poetry and he is unable to take advantage of the freedom allowed by this form for the expansion of imagery. However, after his death his personal letters were collected and, for generations, they were used as a model of polite correspondence.

Namık Kemal (1840–88). Poet, dramatist and chief architect of the literary reforms of the *Tanzimat*. He was born in Tekirdağ (on the shores of the Marmara) on 21 December 1840, the son of a minor government official who had married into a wealthy and influential family. His mother having died when he was very young, he was raised and privately educated by her parents. He accompanied his grandfather, Abdüllâtif Paşa, during his official appointments to Kars and Sofia, and in 1857 he came to Istanbul, already enjoying a modest reputation as a poet. In 1863 he received employment in the Government Translation Bureau where he became acquainted with the modernists of the period. He wrote articles for the *Tasvir-i Efkâr*, the newspaper edited by the reformer, Şinasi Efendi, and when the latter went to Europe in 1865 he became its editor. He was an active supporter of the Young Turk movement, and in 1867 he fled to Paris to escape exile to a distant quarter of the Empire. While in Europe he was closely involved with the other Young Turks in exile, and in June 1868, while in London, he began to publish a revolutionary newspaper, *Hürriyet* (Freedom). In 1870 he was allowed to return to Istanbul, where for a few months in 1872 he was associated with the radical newspaper *İbret* (The Example). His political writings were embarrassing to the government, so the newspaper was banned for a while and he was sent away from

Istanbul as administrator (*mutasarrıf*) of Gallipoli. At the end of 1872 he was discharged from this office, and he returned to Istanbul and resumed his articles in *İbret*. In 1873 his play *Vatan* (The Fatherland) was produced, but the popular excitement caused by its patriotic sentiments worried the government, which once again closed down the newspaper and exiled him to Cyprus. He returned to Istanbul in May 1877, but before long his presence in the capital was to prove unwelcome to the government, leading to another exile. The remainder of his life was spent in official appointments at a distance from Istanbul: Lesbos (1879), Rhodes (1884) and Chios (1887), in which latter post he died on 2 December 1888. He is buried in Bolayır, on the Gallipoli Peninsula.

Kemal was a man intoxicated by ideas, and it is his misfortune that as the passage of time has made these ideas commonplace, so too have his writings lost their original impact. As a poet, he remained faithful to the classical metres and forms, but the themes of patriotism and freedom which recur mark the first efforts at political verse in the literature. Journalism was his true métier and, more than any of his contemporaries, it is he who can be credited with the creation of the simple expository prose style from which all modern styles derive. Although the political, social and literary battles which he waged in the columns of over a dozen publications have long since been won, and his high-minded earnestness now seems rather immature, he still emerges as a man of lucid mind and heroic courage.

His two novels – *İntibah* (The Awakening, 1876) and *Cezmi* (1880) – are perfunctory ventures into a form for which he had no real talent. He was, in fact, not really interested in people as individuals, but rather as symbols of ideas and mouthpieces of his journalism. Thus, hardly one of his six plays is actable today: *Gülnihal* (1875), a tale of a virtuous young lover's triumph over the tyranny of a wicked Paşa who seeks to deprive him of his beloved, is less tedious than the rest, but it, too, is more proper to the chamber than the stage. His historical writings are mainly devoted to the glories of the Ottoman past and the heroes of Islam, showing the curious dichotomy of a nature that longs for the west while it cherishes the east. As a literary critic, he laid the foundations on which the modernist movement grew, and no voice was more persuasive than his in the dialogue between innovation and tradition. Kemal himself was not really a creative writer, but without his pamphleteering the creative writing of modern Turkey might not have developed as it has.

Necatî (*d* 1509). İsa Çelebi, the foremost exponent of the *gazel* form in the fifteenth century. Of his early origins we have little definite information, but it is reported that he was the slave of a wealthy woman of Edirne who provided for his education, and that sometime afterwards he settled in Kastamonu. He came to Istanbul to enter the secretarial service of the Council of State during the reign of Mehmed II (1451–81), and when Bayezid II came to the throne in 1481 he also appears to have enjoyed the royal favour. He was appointed secretary to Prince Abdullah when he was sent to the province of Karaman as governor, and after the death of this prince in 1483 he returned to Istanbul where he received the patronage of both the palace and certain leading statesmen. In 1504 he was appointed to one of the highest secretarial offices (*nişcancı*) in the suite of Prince Mahmud, the governor of Manisa, and he remained in this post until the death of the prince in 1507. He returned to Istanbul where he died in 1509.

Necatî is the first authentically Turkish voice in classical Ottoman literature, and it was he who introduced into the *gazel* those features which were to characterise it throughout the centuries. Although he adhered closely to the Persian structure and confined himself to the traditional themes of love and wine, his fund of imagery was drawn from the commonplace experiences of daily life, giving a homely reality to the transcendental notions all poetry was presumed to imply. He is characteristically Turkish, too, in his fondness for practical wisdom; proverbs abound in his verses, and even his own style tends towards the trenchancy of the proverbial phrase. He is witty, especially given to the play of words; and he observes with sympathy the pathos of life. It was in these ways that Necatî made this exotic importation familiar to its new environment; and all that is later to make the Turkish *gazel* distinctive has its origins in his work.

Nef'î (*d* 1635). Ömer Nef'î Efendi, the acknowledged master of the *kaside* form in Ottoman literature, was born near Erzurum, probably about the year 1572. His family must have been of some consequence, for his father, Mehmed Bey, was a confidant of the Han of the Crimea, and he himself shows the benefits of having received a good education. He came to Istanbul during the reign of Sultan Ahmed I (1603–17) and found employment in certain government offices. The *kasides* which he wrote in praise of Ahmed and the sultans who succeeded him (and especially Murad IV, 1623–40) won him great fame in the capital, and similar poems dedicated to the leading statesmen of the age were rewarded handsomely. But along with these poems of fulsome praise he also composed some of the most scurrilous satirical verses in the whole of Ottoman literature, aiming his shafts fearlessly even at those in positions of power and authority. Murad IV actually ordered him to stop making these attacks, and when Nef'î did not comply, the Sultan turned him over to one of his victims who promptly had him strangled and his body thrown into the sea (27 January 1635).

Nef'î is probably the most paradoxical figure in Turkish literature. The *kasides* in his Turkish *divan* are of an astonishing artistry; whether the theme be spring, fate, love or war, his imagination develops it through an imagery that is vividly pictorial in its effect. And his language, both in sound and sense, accommodates itself to the theme, varying from majestic sonority to caressing delicacy. His *gazels*, too, though they have not attracted so much praise, are clearly the work of a superb artist. His Persian *divan*, also, is in no respect inferior; to the Ottoman man of culture the transition from one language to the other required but the minimum of effort. Yet it was this artist of the written word who composed the coarse obscenities which are collected in his satirical *divan* entitled *Siham-ı Kaza* (The Arrows of Fate); redeemed by neither wit nor imagination, the torrent of abuse which he spews forth on rival poets and virtually anyone, great or small, who incurred his displeasure – not excluding his own father – exposes one of the serious defects of Ottoman society. There was simply no middle ground between the upper and lower classes where an average of decorum could prevail; if one abandoned the standards of the élite, the only alternative was the vulgarity of the masses. The abuse of others always finds a ready audience, and it is to be suspected that the popularity of Nef'î in his own time was due as much to his audacity as to his artistry.

Nergisî (*d* 1635). The greatest of all Ottoman writers of artistic prose, Mehmed Nergisî was born in Bosnia towards the end of the sixteenth century, the son of the *kadi* Nergis Ahmed Efendi. He, too, entered the learned profession, and after a short period as a *medrese* teacher, passed on to a judicial career, holding appointments as *kadi* of various cities in the European provinces of the Empire. When Sultan Murad IV set out on his Persian campaign in 1635, Nergisî was taken along to write the official history of the expedition. However, shortly after the army left Istanbul he suffered a fall from his horse from which he died.

Unlike poetry, Ottoman prose was not wholly committed to Persian models; and because of the greater flexibility given it by the numerous gerundial constructions possible in Turkish and the scope allowed by a vocabulary drawn from three languages, it was capable of syntactical complexities and rhythmic subtleties unparallelled in Arabic or Persian. Masters of this ornate prose style such as Ali b. Sâlih (*d* 1544), the author of the *Hümâyunnâme*, a translation of the Persian version of the tales of Bidpai, Âşık Çelebi (*d* 1572), the biographer of the poets, and Veysî (*d* 1628), who wrote a life of the Prophet, had made something distinctly Ottoman of this synthetic idiom, and in Nergisî the tradition which they developed finds its perfection. He wrote seven works in this style, five of which are collected under the title *Hamse*. Two of these, the *Nihalistan* and the *Meşakk ul-'Uşşâk*, are collections of moral tales, many of which recount the author's own experiences; they are charming in the simplicity of their subject matter, just as their language and style is startling in its invention and ingenuity.

Nevaî, Ali Şîr (1441–1501). The greatest figure in Eastern Turkish (Çagatay) literature, he was born in Herat (in present-day north-west Afghanistan) in 1441, the son of an official at the court of the descendants of Timur. From his childhood he had been a friend of the Timurid prince, Hüseyn Baykara, and when the latter seized Herat in 1469, restoring order to the region which had been in a state of anarchy since the death of the great Şahruh in 1447, Nevaî was appointed his seal-bearer. In 1472 he was elevated to one of the highest positions in the Council of State, second only in authority to the Sultan. He died in 1501, and the public mourning which followed in Herat is said to have been without precedent. Not only was he one of the most productive writers of the period, but he used his wealth and position to patronise other writers, artists and musicians, and made Herat in his lifetime one of the most brilliant cultural centres of the Islamic World.

Çagatay arose as a kind of common idiom out of the variety of Turkish dialects which were intermingled with one another in northern Persia and Central Asia in the period of political and social turmoil created by Timur, and as a literary language it was virtually the creation of Nevaî. Though he admired Persian literature and actually composed a *divan* in this language, he maintained that Turkish was in many respects a superior medium of literary expression and, by his own example, sought to propagate its use. He wrote four *divans* in Çagatay, containing the poems of his adolescence, young manhood, middle age and old age; each of these *divans* is given a particular title and the whole collected under the name, *Haza'in ül-Ma'ânî* (The Treasures of Ideas). In emulation of Nizamî he composed a Turkish *Hamse*, five long narrative poems, the themes of which are taken from his model but treated with such independence in re-arranging incidents and shifting emphasis that each has an air of originality. His *Mecalis ün-Nefa'is* (The Assemblies of the Exquisites) is a biographical work on the poets of the Timurid period, the first of its kind to be written in Turkish. In all, he composed about thirty works in verse and in prose, dealing with subjects as diverse as music, prosody, philology, morals, history, etc., and the contemporary manuscripts of these which have survived to us are in themselves monuments of Persian art and calligraphy as they had developed under his patronage in Herat.

The influence of Nevaî on early Ottoman literature is more subtle than that of the Persian masters. The latter were to be imitated, and the degree to which the imitation approximated the model was the measure of its success. Nevaî not only showed that Persian poetry could be written in Turkish, but his own prestige, both as an author and as the patron of the most renowned literary figures of the age in Persia, gave the Ottoman poets confidence in what they were doing and the assurance that it had a worth entirely its own. That Persian did not become the language of culture among the Ottomans as it had in the Selcuk state is in no small measure to be attributed to the achievements of Nevaî.

Refik Halit Karay (1888–1965). Novelist and satirist, and the most brilliant prose stylist of modern Turkish. He was born and educated in Istanbul, and after completing his studies in the Galatasaray *lycée*, he held a minor appointment in the Treasury for a short while. He left there in 1909 to become a full-time journalist, contributing in the meanwhile satirical articles to the humorous magazine *Kalem*. His writings offended the Committee of Union and

Progress which had been ruling Turkey since the deposition of Sultan Abdülhamîd; in 1913 he was exiled to Sinop, from where he travelled to other parts of Anatolia during the war years. He did not return to Istanbul until 1918, by which time the Committee had fled the country; his opposition to the latter put him into favour with the new administration and he received the appointment of Postmaster General. He was hostile to the nationalist movement led by Atatürk, who actually had his name placed on a proscription list; so when the nationalists came to power he was obliged to flee for safety to Syria and the Lebanon (1922). He remained in exile for fifteen years, until pardoned in 1938, when he returned to Istanbul and resumed his career in journalism, editing the satirical magazine *Aydede*.

The first work to win him fame was a collection of short stories based on his observations in Anatolia, published under the title *Memleket Hikâyeleri* (Tales of the Country, 1919), and this announces, too, the character of all the numerous stories and novels which were to follow. He is an amused observer of life, with an unfailing perception of weaknesses and follies, all to be recorded without compassion or tenderness. This abrasiveness might be found unsympathetic were it not that it is never malicious, and he is usually as unsparing of himself as he is of others. Self-mockery is a long established feature of Turkish humour, and the modern satirical writers are following in a well-worn track. Refik Halit's distinction lies in the elevation of this kind of humour from the anecdotal, giving it a literary form. In most of his seventeen novels he singles out some aspect or other of society which he finds vulnerable to his humour, and around this he weaves a simple story. However, it is probably the books in which his articles and personal memoirs are collected that will prove most interesting to future generations, providing as they do many entertaining sidelights on one of the most dramatic periods of Turkish history.

Şeyhî (*d* 1431). The author of the first long narrative poem of artistic merit in Ottoman Turkish. He was born in Kütahya, probably in the last quarter of the fourteenth century when this was still the capital city of the Germiyan emirate. We have no definite information about his life, beyond that at some time he travelled in Persia to complete his education and returned with qualification in the medical sciences which enabled him to earn his livelihood as a doctor, specialising in diseases of the eye. His contacts with the Ottomans are said to have begun in 1415 when he treated Prince Süleyman who had been taken ill in Ankara while on campaign in the East; and later we have certain poems written in praise of Sultan Murad II (1421–51), to whom, also, his *Husrev ü Şîrin* is dedicated. He died about 1431 and is buried in Dumlupınar, not far from Kütahya.

For about a century and a half Şeyhî's *Husrev ü Şîrin* was regarded as the model Turkish *mesnevi* by Ottoman critics, despite the fact that it was a conscious attempt at translating the Persian work of the same title by the great Nizâmi, and, moreover, that it was never completed. In their eyes the theme was but the thread upon which the true matter of poetry was to be strung; fresh imagery, choice language, quotable observations and a general air of effortlessness were what they looked for above all in poetry. Earlier attempts to adapt this form to Turkish, even when based on Persian originals as in the case of Gülşehrî's *Mantık ut-Tayr* (1317) and Mustafa Darîr's *Yusuf ve Züleyhâ* (1366), seemed barbarous in language and clumsy in technique, while semi-popular religious and didactic works like Âşik Paşa's *Garib-nâme* (1329) and Ahmedî's *İskender-nâme* (1390) were hardly regarded as literature by the mandarins of the sixteenth century. It was Şeyhî who first showed that Turkish was capable of achieving some of the grace of Persian in narrative poetry, and the tradition of the form in Ottoman literature must be reckoned as beginning with him.

Yahya Kemal Bayalti (1884–1958). Regarded by many as the greatest Turkish poet of modern times, Yahya Kemal was born into a wealthy and important family in Üsküp (Skopje, in Yugoslavia) in 1884, where his father, İbrahim Naci Bey, had for a time been mayor. He received his early education there and in Salonika. In 1902 he went to Paris to join the Young Turks in exile, and while there studied at the École Libre des Sciences Politiques. In 1908 he returned to Istanbul where he edited a literary journal, and between the years 1915–23 he taught history and literature at the University. After the defeat of Turkey in World War I, he became active in politics and entered Parliament. He was ambassador to Poland (1926) and Spain (1929), and from 1935 to 1946 he again sat as a member of Parliament. In 1948 he was appointed ambassador to Pakistan, but retiring after one year, he returned to Istanbul where he died in 1958.

Yahya Kemal is a paradox in the modern literature of Turkey: for the most part his poems are written in the classical metres, and their themes are nostalgic of a past glory and the quality of life it had bred in his people. Unimpeachably nationalist, as is attested by the high honours accorded him by the Republic, he still insists on the Ottoman values, expressing a sentimental continuity between the old and the new, markedly in contrast with the strident, inconoclastic patriotism of his contemporaries. Like his beloved *divan* poets, his fame was achieved in his life-time without ever having collected his poems into a book, and it is only in recent years that these are being published by a society organised for this purpose. Nor do these poems amount to more than a slender volume; yet each is a masterpiece of harmony between sound and meaning, a gem polished by tireless revision and unique among the undisciplined dross of self-commiseration that constitutes the bulk of modern Turkish poetry. In Yahya Kemal we experience the trauma that westernisation has inflicted upon Turkey, and the civilised restraint of the statement makes the predicament felt all the more poignantly.

Yazicioğlu Mehmed (*d* 1452). The author of the *Muhammediyye*, a long work in a variety of verse forms on Islamic cosmology, the lives of the earlier prophets, the biographies of Muhammed and the first four Caliphs, and on the aspects of heaven and hell. The details of his own life are obscure, but it is generally accepted that he was born in Malgara (in Thrace) about the end of the fourteenth century, the son of a certain Yazıcı Salâhaddin, himself the author of the first work in Turkish on astrology, the *Şemsiyye*. Mehmed apparently received a good education, but at some time in his career he became a disciple of the holy-man, Haci Bayram Veli, after which he retired to Gallipoli where he remained as a pious recluse until his death in 1452. Numerous legends have grown up about his sanctity, further concealing the historical personality.

Originally written in Arabic, the *Muhammediyye* was translated by him into Turkish in 1449 so that his countrymen might have the benefit of it. Based on the writings of the most eminent doctors of the faith, unlike most works of popular piety its language is not simplified and the quotations from the Kur'an and the Traditions of the Prophet with which it is liberally interspersed are given in the original Arabic. Though most of the people who venerated it as a holy book could understand it but imperfectly, it at least afforded them access of a sort to areas of religion which were otherwise the exclusive preserve of the learned classes. And almost as important, it expressed a wholly straightforward orthodox attitude instead of the suspect sufistic extravagances usually met with in poetry. His brother, Ahmed Bîcân, made the work further accessible in a simply written prose version entitled the *Envar ul-Âşıkîn* (The Lights of the Lovers).

BIBLIOGRAPHY

I. HISTORICAL

BABINGER, Franz *Die Geschichtsschreiber der Osmanen und Ihre Werke* Leipzig, 1927.
Mehmed der Eroberer und Seine Zeit Munich, 1953.
BIRGE, John K. *A Guide to Turkish Area Study* Washington, 1949.
COLES, Paul *The Ottoman Impact on Europe* New York, 1968.
GIBB, H. A. R. and BOWEN, Harold *Islamic Society and the West* vol. I, parts 1 and 2, Oxford, 1950–57.
HAMMER-PURGSTALL, Josef von *Geschichte des osmanischen Reiches* 10 vols., Budapest, 1827–35.
LEWIS, Bernard *The Emergence of Modern Turkey* Oxford, 1961.
VAUGHAN, Dorothy M. *Europe and the Turk* Liverpool, 1954.
ZINKEISEN, J. W. *Geschichte des osmanischen Reiches in Europa.* 7 vols., Hamburg-Gotha, 1840–63.

II. CULTURAL AND LITERARY

BOMBACI, Alessio *Storia della letteratura turca* Milan, 1956.
GIBB, E. J. W. *A History of Ottoman Poetry* 6 vols., London, 1900–09; New York, 1958–63.
HAMMER-PURGSTALL, Josef von *Geschichte der osmanischen Dichtkunst* 4 vols., Pest, 1838.
LYBYER, Albert H. *The Government of the Ottoman Empire in the Time of Suleiman the Magnificent* Harvard, 1913.
MANTRAN, Robert *La Vie quotidienne à Constantinople au temps de Soliman le Magnifique et de ses successeurs* Paris, 1965.
SPIES, Otto 'Die türkische Prosaliteratur der Gegenwart', *Die Welt des Islams* Band 25, Heft 1/3, 1943.
WHITE, Charles *Three Years in Constantinople* 3 vols., London, 1845.

III. WORKS IN TRANSLATION

Ottoman poetry was so particular to its own society that it cannot be translated without appearing grotesque or ridiculous. The specimens included in the works by Gibb and von Hammer mentioned in Section II above give very little indication of the genuine literary quality of this poetry, and could hardly excite interest, much less admiration. Prose, too, when it ventures beyond pedestrian factuality, is poorly accommodated by the European languages. Modern Turkish does not present the same difficulties, and several novels and short stories have been successfully translated into English, French and German. The following list, apart from the two anthologies, is restricted to the authors mentioned in the text of the article.

Anthologie des Ecrivains Turcs d'Aujourd'hui. Publiée par la Direction Générale de la Presse au Ministère de l'Intérieur. Istanbul, 1935.

BAYATLI, Yahya Kemal

Selected Poems of Yahya Kemal Bayatli, trans. S. Behlül Toygar. Istanbul, 1965.

CELÂLEDDIN RUMÎ

The Mathnawí of Jalálu'ddín Rúmí. 3 vols., trans. Reynold A. Nicholson. London, 1926–34.

Selected Poems from the Dīvāni Shamsi Tabrīz trans. R. A. Nicholson, Cambridge, 1898.

FUZULÎ

Leyla and Mecnun, trans. by Sofi Huri, London, 1970.

NABİ, Yusuf

Les Conseils de Nabi Efendi, trans. Pavet de Courteille, Paris, 1857.

ALİ ŞÎR NEVAÎ

Muḥākamat al-Lughatain, trans. Robert Devereux, Leiden, 1966.

OERLEY, W. A., ed.

Die Pforte des Glücks. Die Türkei in Erzählungen der besten zeitgenössischen Autoren. Stuttgart, 1963.

ARMENIAN AND GEORGIAN LITERATURE

D. M. Lang

HISTORICAL BACKGROUND

The Armenians and Georgians, both Christian peoples of long standing, are the creators of two ancient and important cultures in the region of the Caucasus.

The Caucasian isthmus is situated between the Caspian and the Black Sea. To the north, its foothills merge into the great plains which extend into Southern Russia and the Central Asian steppe lands. To the south, the Caucasus gives access to the rich country of Mesopotamia. Invaders from the north have always had to fight their way over or round the colossal peaks of the Great Caucasus range, and then skirt the massif of Mount Ararat in Armenia, before fanning out into Iran to the south-east, or Asia Minor to the south-west.

Armenia and Georgia have been inhabited by primitive man since the Old Stone Age. Both countries played a prominent part in the invention and diffusion of copper and bronze-working. From the migrations of the Indo-Europeans, around 2000 BC, onwards, the rugged contours of the Caucasian range and the Van region have provided a refuge for displaced tribes, so that the whole area is a veritable museum of ethnic types and anthropological lore.

During the Middle Bronze Age, around 1500 BC, magnificent local cultures grew up in Armenia and Georgia, as confirmed by archaeological finds in the Araxes basin, also around Lake Sevan, and on the Trialeti hills. The pastoral tribes of Transcaucasia came under the cultural aegis of the Hittites to the west of them, as well as of the Hurrians and the Mitanni people to the south.

The origins of the Armenian and Georgian nations are ancient, and only partially known to history. The Armenians are sometimes said to have immigrated from the direction of the Balkans, along with the Phrygians with whose language Armenian has affinities. However, the bulk of the Armenian population is certainly autochthonous, although the Armenian language belongs to the Indo-European family. The Georgians represent a fusion of ancient Anatolian tribes with local populations living along the Kura valley. Their language is quite distinct from that of the Armenians: Georgian forms, together with Svan and Mingrelo-Laz, a distinct group of Ibero-Caucasian languages within the framework of the Caucasian language family as a whole.

State organisation in Armenia and Georgia has a long and interesting tradition. The renown of the semi-mythical Colchian kingdom of King Aietes and the enchantress Medea is enshrined in the story of Jason and the Argonauts. On the territory of Armenia, there existed from 850 to 590 BC the mighty kingdom of Urartu, centred on Lake Van. The Urartians were fully-fledged rivals of the Assyrian empire, and at one time fought their way to the Mediterranean coast. They have left behind a legacy of buildings, inscriptions, metal work and fresco-painting.

Armenia and parts of Georgia feature prominently in the writings of Herodotus and Xenophon. They were both under the suzerainty of the Great Kings of Iran of the Achaemenid dynasty. Following the conquests of Alexander the Great, two important kingdoms grew up: that of the Orontids, then of the Artaxiads in Armenia, and that of the Iberian monarchs at Mtskheta-Armazi in Georgia. The most famous of all these dynasts was Tigranes the Great of Armenia (95–55 BC), whose might was shattered by the Roman generals Lucullus and Pompey. After the death of Tigranes, the region became a bone of contention between Rome and Parthia for many years.

A key event in the life of Armenia and Georgia was the conversion of these lands to Christianity early in the fourth century AD: Armenia was converted in 301 by St Gregory the Illuminator; Georgia by St Nino thirty years later. The Armenians refused to subscribe to the theological dictates of the Council of Chalcedon (451); this later led to a schism with the Georgian Church, which became an autocephalous Church within the Eastern Orthodox communion. Both countries have offered up many heroic martyrs to the Christian faith; in 451, the Armenians withstood the onslaught of a Persian army two hundred thousand strong, intent on rooting out the Christian religion completely.

The Sasanian kings of Persia failed in their attempts to impose state Zoroastrianism on Armenia and Georgia, though many Iranian cultural influences remain to this day. Early Christian architecture reached magnificent heights in both countries, and contributed a number of elements to Byzantine and to Western Gothic and Romanesque architecture.

The Arab caliphs conquered Armenia and Georgia about AD 650, and *amirs* or viceroys sat in Dvin and Tbilisi (Tiflis). After two centuries of Arab rule, the local dynasts forgot their feuds, and grouped together to withstand alien oppression. This led to the emergence of a powerful dynasty, that of the Bagratids, who ruled at Ani in Armenia until 1045, and in Georgia at Kutaisi, then Tbilisi, right up to the Russian annexation in 1801.

The Armenian kingdom of Ani, and also that of the Ardsrunis around Lake Van, were both annexed by the Byzantines in the eleventh century, and then overrun by the Seljuq Turks, who defeated the Greeks at Manzikert in 1071. The Armenians then formed a separate kingdom in Cilicia, on the Mediterranean, with a capital at Sis; the Cilician kingdom included Tarsus, birthplace of St Paul. This lasted until 1375, when the region was overrun by the

Egyptian Mamluks. In Georgia, however, a series of battling monarchs managed to maintain national independence. King David the Builder (1089–1125) co-operated with the Crusaders against the Saracens. Queen Tamar (1184–1213) ruled over a mighty realm stretching from the Caspian Sea to Trebizond, and including large portions of Armenia as well.

The invasions of the Mongols from 1220 onwards brought Georgia's golden age to an end, and also imposed terrible sufferings on the local Armenian population. Many monasteries and libraries were sacked and burnt. Eastern Georgia was reduced to vassalage under the Mongol Il-Khans of the line of Hulagu, while Imereti, the land west of the Suram range, remained independent under a separate line of Bagratid rulers. There was a partial resurgence during the reign of King Giorgi V of Georgia (1314–46), known as the Brilliant, but the onslaughts of Timur Leng between 1386 and 1403 dealt blows to the economic and cultural life of Georgia and Armenia from which the land never fully recovered. The last king of united Georgia was Alexander I (1412–43), under whose sons Georgia was divided into squabbling princedoms. At this period, Greater Armenia was under the domination of the Turcomans of the Black Sheep, and those of the White Sheep (as the rival hordes were named).

The fall of Constantinople to the Ottoman Turks in 1453 isolated Georgia and Greater Armenia from Western Christendom. During the next three centuries, the country was a battleground on the frontiers of the two great empires of the Ottoman Turks and the Safavis of Iran. However, the establishment of the Armenian patriarchate of Constantinople under Ottoman patronage led to a concentration of Armenian commercial and intellectual talent in the Turkish capital. In Greater Armenia, the torch of national sentiment was kept alight right up to 1828 by the plucky Armenian meliks or clan chiefs of Karabagh, and also by the mountaineers of Sassoun, near Lake Van, who fought on until 1894. Valuable work in maintaining Armenian cultural traditions was and is done by the Armenian Catholicos-Patriarchs, resident to this day at Echmiadzin, in the shadow of Mount Ararat.

The approach of Tsarist Russia introduced a new element into the situation of Armenia and Georgia. Peter the Great's expedition to the Caspian provinces of Persia was greeted with enthusiasm by the Georgian King Vakhtang VI (1711–24), as well as by the Armenians living in Persia and elsewhere. Although Peter was obliged to retreat, a revival of Georgian sovereignty took place under King Erekle II (1744–98). Raids by Lezgian mountaineers from Dagestan, economic stringency and other difficulties compelled Erekle to adopt a pro-Russian orientation, leading to the signature of the Treaty of Georgievsk in 1783. Russia thereby guaranteed Georgia's independence, in exchange for her acceptance of Russian suzerainty. In spite of this, Tbilisi was sacked by the Persian eunuch Agha Muhammad Khan Qajar in 1795, in the course of which catastrophe the prince of Armenian ministrels, Sayat-Nova, was cruelly put to death.

Complete annexation of Georgia by Russia followed in 1801, though the king of Imereti in Western Georgia held out until 1810. Large sections of Eastern Armenia were captured by the Russians in the Russo-Persian war of 1826–8, Erevan being taken by storm by General Prince Paskevich-Erivansky. Further stretches of Armenian territory were annexed by Russia following the victorious war of 1877 against Turkey.

The latter part of the nineteenth century was marked by an increase of nationalism among the Georgians and Armenians. The Georgians formed a powerful Social-Democratic organisation, to the left wing of which Stalin belonged at one time. The Armenians founded the nationalist society of the Dashnaks, which came into conflict with the Tsarist as well as with the Ottoman Turkish authorities. Terrible massacres of Armenians took place under Sultan Abdul Hamid in 1895–6, while a genocide campaign planned by the Young Turk junta under Talaat and Enver Pashas wiped out the majority of the surviving Turkish Armenians in 1915.

The fall of the Tsarist empire in 1917, and the collapse of the Ottoman empire, favoured the creation of independent Transcaucasian republics in 1918. However, the withdrawal of British and White Russian interventionist forces enabled the Soviet Union to impose its writ in the area during 1920–21.

Since that time, both Armenia and Georgia have been constituent republics of the USSR. Tremendous strides have been made in industrialisation, and in collectivisation of agriculture. Academies of Sciences and Universities have been set up in both Erevan and Tbilisi, and instruction in the Armenian and Georgian vernacular languages introduced in schools and institutions of learning throughout the two lands. Georgia has become a tourist showplace, and Soviet Armenia a national home to which dispersed Armenians throughout the world look with affection and regard.

MAIN TRENDS IN LITERATURE

Neither Armenian nor Georgian were written languages prior to the early fifth century AD. However, both countries already had a long tradition of oral literature, as well as of writing in other idioms (Urartian, Middle Iranian, Greek, Latin) prior to the invention of alphabets for Armenian and Georgian.

Thus, hundreds of Urartian inscriptions from the Van region, and from that of Erevan, have been collected and published, the best collection being that of the Soviet scholar Giorgi Melikishvili. Boundary stones with Iranian inscriptions in Aramaic characters have been recovered from the Sevan region, while the bilingual epitaph of Princess Serapita (Greek and Middle Iranian) from Mtskheta-Armazi dates from about AD 150. Ancient sources refer to centres of higher education in Colchis, while King Artavazd II of Armenia composed plays and other works in Greek. The priestesses of Anahit intoned odes and hymns to the patron goddess of Armenia, some of which have been recorded by the chronicler Moses of Khorene. Pious Georgian writers of the Middle Ages stress that a holocaust of Zoroastrian books took place when Georgia was converted by St Nino in the fourth century.

The Armenian and Georgian alphabets were composed by Christian missionaries early in the fifth century, largely to further the propagation of the Gospels in the vernacular, and to make possible the celebration of the divine liturgy. The invention of the Armenian alphabet is attributed to St Mesrop Mashtotz, who completed his task about AD 404, and also helped to provide an alphabet for Georgia. These two alphabets have many points of resemblance; they retain in essentials the order of the Greek alphabet, though new characters were devised for the many sounds which are peculiar to Armenian and Georgian. Both these alphabets are written from left to right, unlike the Semitic alphabets, which run from right to left.

The disciples and followers of St Mesrop form a brilliant pleiad, and are often known as 'the Interpreters', since they set themselves to adapt in Armenian the principal classics of early Christian literature. Several of these writers of the early period were also brilliant original thinkers, such as the philosophers Eznik of Kolb and David the Invincible. Armenian historiography also begins in the fifth century, with Agathangelos and Faustus of

Buzanda. The best known of Armenian historians, Moses of Khorene, is now assigned to the eighth century. The seventh century brought forth a kind of Armenian Newton in the person of Ananias of Shirak, renowned as a geographer and astronomer. Devotional literature is represented by Gregory of Narek (945–1010), and then by the two great Cilician doctors, Nerses Shnorhali, or 'the Gracious' (1102–73) and Nerses of Lampron (1153–98).

Original Georgian literature begins with lives of saints, the first surviving one being that of St Shushanik (composed about 480). Other early works include an account of the conversion of Georgia by St Nino, and semi-legendary stories of the exploits of King Vakhtang Gorgaslani, a hero of the fifth century. Much of this material was subsequently woven into the Georgian Annals. The Georgians were the first to give a Christian colouring to the Buddhist legend of Barlaam and Josaphat, which is known in Georgia as the *Balavariani.* The beginnings of a philosophical school in Georgia were laid by the Neoplatonist Ioane Petridsi (*d* 1125), who strove to impart to Georgian Orthodoxy a deeper metaphysical content.

During the Middle Ages, Armenian and Georgian ecclesiastical literature followed different paths. The Armenians were intent on avoiding assimilation by the Greeks, with their ambitious emperors and Cesaro-Papist pretensions. The Georgians, however, were keen to adapt their liturgy and theological literature to that of the Greeks, and avoid all suspicion of heresy. Georgian monasteries were established on Mount Athos, Mount Sinai and at Jerusalem, and important manuscript libraries grew up there.

However, both Armenians and Georgians devoted much loving care to illuminating Church manuscripts. The finest examples are the Gospel manuscripts, particularly those decorated by the Cilician school headed by Thoros Roslin and Sargis Pitzak.

The Armenians lost their political independence relatively early in the Middle Ages, so that cultural life centred increasingly on the Church. This gave the Church a dominance in the field of literature, and meant that relatively few works of Armenian secular literature were written down prior to the nineteenth century Renaissance. The Armenians made up for this by their wonderful troubadours, who were both poets and minstrels, and enjoyed wide popularity in Turkey and Persia, as well as in the Caucasus. The Armenians also handed down by word of mouth the remarkable cycle of heroic tales which is known as *David of Sassoun*, or *Daredevils of Sassoun.*

The more devil-may-care Georgians, on the other hand, threw off from time to time the dead hand of the monks, and produced some highly sophisticated epics and romances. The finest of these is the national epic by Shota Rustaveli, a contemporary of Queen Tamar, called *Vephkhis-tqaosani* (The Man in the Panther's Skin). Imitations of the Persian *Book of Kings* by Firdausi circulated widely in Georgian adaptation, as did a version of the ancient love story of Vis and Ramin, who were a kind of Persian Tristan and Isolde.

After the Mongol invasions, and the ravages of the Ottoman Turks and the Persian Shahs, belles-lettres revived in Georgia during the eighteenth century with the lexicographer Sulkhan-Saba Orbeliani; his kinsman King Vakhtang VI (1675–1737), who founded a printing press in Tbilisi and had the Georgian annals edited and completed; and Vakhtang's son Vakhushti (1695–1772), the historian and geographer. The main poets of the period were David Guramishvili and Besarion Gabashvili, also the illustrious Armenian bard Sayat-Nova, who was court poet to the Georgian King Erekle II, and composed his verse in Armenian, Georgian, and Turkish.

The first Armenian printed book was published at Venice as early as 1512. It was in Venice too that a remarkable Armenian cultural revival took place from the early eighteenth century onwards, with the establishment of the Catholic Armenian Order of the Mekhitarists on San Lazzaro island, which remains today an academy of Armenian culture and learning. There is also a Mekhitarist monastery in Vienna, where important works of scholarship are written and published.

Within Greater Armenia, Echmiadzin assumed prominence during the second half of the eighteenth century, when Catholicos Simeon established a press (1774) and a paper factory through the financial assistance of the Armenian merchants in India. The Lazarev Institute in Moscow, founded in 1815, soon became an important centre of Armenian studies. In Turkey, Armenian theatres, journals and clubs flourished in Istanbul right up to the massacres of 1895 and 1915.

The annexation of Georgia and Eastern Armenia by Tsarist Russia early in the nineteenth century naturally had important repercussions in the field of literature. Though Erevan remained a small provincial town until the Soviet era, Tbilisi rapidly developed and flourished as the headquarters of the Russian viceroyalty of the Caucasus. The Georgian and Armenian theatres revived there under the initiative of Giorgi Eristavi and Gabriel Sundukian respectively.

Romantic poetry flourished in Georgia under the lead of such brilliant talents as Nikoloz Baratashvili and Alexander Chavchavadze, and later the bard Akaki Tsereteli. A universal genius appeared in the person of Prince Ilia Chavchavadze (1837–1907), who was also a prominent politician and man of affairs. The Armenians excelled in the historical and realistic novel, with such writers as Raffi and Shirvanzadeh. Hovhannes Tumanian and Avetik Issahakian were the leading Armenian poets, both of them surviving into the Soviet era.

The advent of the Soviet regime in Armenia and Georgia greatly contributed to the growth of a large reading public. Writers' Unions were set up, ensuring authors a regular income so long as they did not openly oppose the regime. However, many leading literary figures in both Armenia and Georgia were liquidated by Stalin and Beria during the nineteen-thirties. Among the victims were the Georgian novelist Mikheil Javakhishvili, and the poets Paolo Iashvili and Titsian Tabidze; in Armenia, the holocaust claimed the poet Eghishe Charentz, who was acclaimed as the Armenian Mayakovsky. However, both poetry and prose writing flourish in Armenia and Georgia today; amid a mass of hackwork and second-rate social realism, there are several figures in both countries who maintain a high level of creative originality. The national theatres are in a flourishing condition.

Several Georgian and Armenian writers have carved out a successful career for themselves in America, where they write in English. Such are the Papashvilis, the irrepressible authors of *Anything Can Happen*, and also the novelist William Saroyan.

INDIVIDUAL WRITERS

Abovian, Khachatur (1805–48). Father of the modern Armenian intelligentsia. Born at Karaker, Erevan district. Climbed Mount Ararat with Professor Parrot of Dorpat University, and was educated at Dorpat. Famous for his epic novel, *The Wounds of Armenia*, published after his death. Worked as a teacher and school inspector, and was dismissed by Russian authorities for his patriotic advocacy of Armenian culture. Died at Erevan in mysterious circumstances, possibly suicide.

Akopian, Akop (1866–1937). Born at Ganja (Kirovabad): the father of Armenian proletarian poetry. The son of a poor swineherd, Akopian was expelled from the local Gymnasium in 1886 for writing poems attacking the repressive policy of Tsar Alexander III. Took an active part in the revolutionary movement in Caucasia, and was sent abroad on Bolshevik party business in 1911. His poems in praise of the 1917 Revolution were translated into French and German, and admired by Romain Rolland.

Artavazd II, King of Armenia, reigned 55–34 BC. A noted patron of the Greek theatre in Armenia. According to Plutarch's *Life of Crassus*, Artavazd was so expert in Greek language and literature that he himself wrote tragedies, orations and histories. Some of these were still extant in Plutarch's time, *c* AD 100, but they have now perished. Artavazd was deposed by Mark Antony and Cleopatra, and murdered by them, together with his family.

Baratashvili, Prince Nikoloz (1817–45). Born in Tbilisi: leading Georgian Romantic poet, a kind of Georgian Byron. Famous for his unhappy love affairs and spirited, turbulent nature. Served as Deputy Governor of Ganja, and died there of exhaustion and overwork. Though none of his verses were published during his lifetime, such masterpieces as *Merani, my Steed* and the epic, *Georgia's Destiny*, were recited all over the country.

Charentz, Eghishe (1897–1938). Born in Kars: leading young bard of the Armenian revolutionary movement: murdered in prison. Bold experimenter with modernistic forms and striking imagery; known as the Armenian Mayakovsky.

Chavchavadze, Prince Ilia (1837–1907). Born at Qvareli, in Kakheti: noted writer, thinker and poet, 'ruler of thoughts' of the Georgian people in the nineteenth century. Studied law at St Petersburg University, and founded popular newspaper *Iveria* (1867). Represented Georgia in the Upper House of the Russian Duma following the 1905 Revolution. Assassinated at Saguramo near Tbilisi, 1907. His realistic novels, such as *Katsia adamiani?* (Do you call this a man?), pilloried the backwardness of the Georgian countryside, and his influence may be traced in every sphere of Georgian social and intellectual life.

Gamsakhurdia, Konstantine (*b* 1891). Born in Western Georgia: educated in Germany, and began his literary career with novels of a 'decadent' flavour. Later celebrated the development of Soviet society in Georgia with several impressive works. Excels also in the historical novel, notably *The Hand of Great Master Constantine* (English version by Eristavi, Moscow, 1959), set in eleventh century Georgia, and relating the saga of the building of the Cathedral of the Life-Giving Pillar at Mtskheta. Member of the Georgian Academy of Sciences, and a sparkling, witty conversationalist.

Issahakian, Avetik (1875–1957). Armenian poet. Born in Alexandropol (Leninakan): studied in Germany and lived many years in France. Returned to the Soviet Union in 1928, and awarded Order of Lenin, 1945. Died at Erevan. A friend of the composer Komitas, Issahakian could claim to be a spiritual descendant of such great troubadours as Sayat-Nova. His philosophical poem *Abulala al-Maarri* (1909) has been translated into many languages.

Kldiashvili, David (1862–1931). Born at Simoneti, near Kutaisi: outstanding writer of stories and short novels, particularly vivid in their portrayal of the life and ways of the peasantry and simple folk of Western Georgia. Served as an army officer under the Tsarist regime, and was several times disgraced for his Georgian patriotic views. Also wrote several comedies. Died at Simoneti.

Leonidze, Giorgi (1899–1966). Born at Patardzeuli, Kakheti: began his poetic career as a member of the symbolist group called the Company of the Blue Drinking Horn, but later rehabilitated himself by writing verse eulogy of Stalin. Died at Tbilisi, 1966. A poet of great lyric pathos and genuine feeling. Also a literary historian, member of the Georgian Academy of Sciences and director of the Institute of History of Georgian Literature. A flamboyant, genial personality, known to all as 'Gogla', unselfish, kindly and approachable to the peasant and student alike.

Ninoshvili (Ingoroqva), Egnate (1859–94). Born at Chirgveti, Guria province: remarkable prose writer, author of many powerful stories, including a novel about the Gurian uprising of 1841. The first Georgian working-class author, comparable in some respects to Maksim Gorky. Toiled on the Batumi seafront, and contracted tuberculosis in the Zestafoni manganese works. Played a prominent part in launching the Georgian Social-Democratic movement in 1892. Died at Chirgveti.

Orbeliani, Sulkhan-Saba (1658–1725). Born in Kartli: Georgian lexicographer and fabulist, author of the *Book of Wisdom and Lies*, (English trans. by J. O. Wardrop, London, 1894) which contains many witty tales and wise maxims.

Composed the first systematic Georgian dictionary. Became a monk in 1698, and was later converted to the Roman Catholic Church. Undertook a diplomatic mission to Louis XIV and to the Vatican in 1713–16, and died in Moscow after following his master King Vakhtang VI into exile in Russia.

Qazbegi, Alexander (1848–93). Georgian novelist. Born at Stepandsminda, Caucasus: scion of the hereditary princes who guarded the Darial Pass which joins Russia to Georgia. Studied at the Agricultural Academy in Moscow, but fell into bad company and ruined his finances and his health. Returned home and worked as a shepherd, then as a professional writer and actor. Later, Qazbegi went out of his mind, and died in an asylum in Tbilisi. Qazbegi wrote stories and novels about the life and heroic past of his native mountains, including *Elguja* and *Khevisberi Gocha*; also several fine dramas. With his descriptions of wild and grandiose scenes in his native Caucasus, Qazbegi evoked with masterly power the inner conflicts of the human soul.

Raffi, pen-name of *Akop Melik-Akopian* (1835–88). Born in Salmas, Persia: most talented and popular of all Armenian novelists, author of a large number of brilliant stories and historical novels. Worked as a teacher in Tabriz, Persia, and travelled extensively in Turkish Armenia. Died in Tbilisi. His historical novel *Samuel* is an evocation of life in pagan Armenia. Revered as a prophet of Armenia's national revival, his works are constantly reprinted, and several have been translated into Russian, French, English and German.

Rustaveli, Shota, flourished about 1200. National bard of Georgia, author of the romantic epic *Vepkhis-tqaosani* (The Man in the Panther's Skin). Traditionally, Rustaveli was a native of Rustavi in Meskheti, and a courtier of Queen Tamar (1184–1213). He is said to have studied in Athens and at Iqalto in Kakheti province, to have fallen in love with his sovereign Tamar, and to have died a pilgrim in Jerusalem, where his full-length portrait has been discovered on a fresco. Copies of his epic poem are traditionally included in every Georgian bride's dowry; the work has been translated into English, French, German, Russian, Czech, Hungarian and Japanese.

Shirvanzadeh, pen-name for *Alexander Movsessian* (1858–1935). Born in Shamakhi, Soviet Azerbaijan: founder of Eastern Armenian realistic school in the novel and drama. Played an active part in political life of the Armenian community in Azerbaijan – his pen-name means 'son of Shirvan', *ie* of modern Soviet Azerbaijan. One of his most popular novels, *Chaos*, contains an unforgettable picture of early days in the Baku oil industry. Died in Soviet Armenia.

Siamanto, pen-name for *Atom Yarjarian* (1878–1915). Born in Akn, Asia Minor: a poet of highly original technique, Siamanto's verses are pessimistic, even cataclysmic in tone. His ode, *Agony and Torch of Hope*, commemorates the massacre of Armenians at Adana in 1909. Siamanto also chanted the exploits of Armenian freedom fighters, such as Andranik. Once dismissed as 'decadent', his poems are now universally appreciated, even by Soviet critics. Murdered by Young Turk government, 1915.

Tabidze, Galaktion (1892–1959). Born at Chkviisi, near Kutaisi. Galaktion Tabidze is generally regarded as the greatest Georgian poet of the twentieth century. His highly musical verse is based on inner melody, replete with fresh imagery. His vivid imagination and infectious emotion always find a ready response among the general public. He was a member of the Georgian Academy of Sciences.

Tumanian, Hovhannes (1869–1923). Born in Dsel, Lori district: one of the most popular of Armenian poets. His poem *Anush* was made into an opera by Armen Tigranian, and *Almast* likewise adapted for the operatic stage, by Alexander Spendiarian. His house-museum is one of the sights of Erevan. Died in Moscow.

Vazha-Pshavela, pen-name for *Luka Razikashvili* (1861–1915). Born in Pshaveti, mountain Georgia: outstanding original poet of the Georgian mountaineers. Worked as a teacher among his fellow highlanders, and was deeply imbued with their rich folklore and ancient traditions, which found expression in his superb mythological and nature poems. He also excelled as author of nature stories, many of which have become children's classics. Died at Tbilisi.

BIBLIOGRAPHY

HISTORICAL BACKGROUND

ALLEN, W. E. D. *A History of the Georgian People* London, 1932.

DER NERSESSIAN, Sirarpie *Armenia and the Byzantine Empire* Harvard, 1945.
The Armenians London and New York, 1969.

HOVANNISIAN, Richard G. *Armenia on the Road to Independence, 1918* University of California Press, 1967.

LANG, David M. *The Georgians* London and New York, 1966.
A Modern History of Georgia London and New York, 1962.

LYNCH, H. F. B. *Armenia. Travels and Studies* 2 vols., London, 1901.

ORMANIAN, Patriarch Malachia *The Church of Armenia* new edn., London, 1955.

LITERATURE

BALAVARIANI, The *A Tale from the Christian East* trans. D. M. Lang, London, Berkeley and Los Angeles, 1966.

BOYAJIAN, Zabelle C. *Armenian Legends and Poems* 2nd edn., London and New York, 1958.

CHAVCHAVADZE, Ilia *The Hermit* trans. Marjory Wardrop, London, 1895.

ETMEKJIAN, James *The French influence on the Western Armenian Renaissance* New York, 1964.

GAMSAKHURDIA, Konstantine, and others *Mindia, the Son of Hogay, and Other Stories by Georgian writers* Moscow, 1960.

KORIUN *The Life of Mashtots*, trans. B. Norehad, New York, 1964.

LANG, David M. *Landmarks in Georgian Literature* London, 1966.
Lives and Legends of the Georgian Saints London and New York, 1956.

MOSES, of Khoni *Amiran-Darejaniani.* A cycle of medieval Georgian tales, trans. by R. H. Stevenson, Oxford, 1958.

RUSTAVELI, Shota *The Man in the Panther's Skin*, trans. Marjory Wardrop, London, 1912.

SARKISSIAN, Karekin *A Brief Introduction to Armenian Christian Literature* London, 1960.

TOTOVENTS, Vahan *Scenes from an Armenian Childhood*, trans. M. Kudian, London, 1962.

URUSHADZE, Venera *Anthology of Georgian Poetry* (trans.) 2nd edn., Tbilisi, 1958.

VISRAMIANI *The Story of the Loves of Vis and Ramin*, trans. J. O. Wardrop, London, 1914.

ETHIOPIC LITERATURE

A. K. Irvine

HISTORICAL BACKGROUND

Despite her geographical situation in Africa, Ethiopia's national outlook and cultural aspirations were formerly expressed in terms of her place in the Eastern Christian oecumene. As a Christian monarchy ante-dating Islam, her principal contacts had led overland to the Coptic Patriarchate of Alexandria, whence traditionally she received her Abunas, or Metropolitans, while her position on the Red Sea trade route to India and close proximity to pro-Persian South Arabia had forged ties of respect and friendship with Byzantium during the earlier centuries of the Aksumite Empire. Although her basic population was Cushitic – negroid elements had been driven to the western extremities of the land in antiquity and were of slight significance – the culture which she displayed to the outside world was markedly Semitic with a strong Judaic flavour. This situation arose because at various times during the first millennium BC waves of emigrants from the relatively advanced Arabia Felix had crossed over into Eritrea and gradually infiltrated the highland regions of northern Ethiopia, where their superiority in material culture gave them an advantage over the original population. It would be misleading, however, to think of a mass invasion or total subjugation. Rather it was a peaceful process of colonisation which led to the absorption of a few Semites by native tribes who thereby received advances not only in agriculture and technology but also in social and political organisation and religion. South Arabian language and writing also were to become indigenised as Classical Ethiopic (Ge'ez). The Judaic elements too are undoubtedly to be ascribed to South Arabia, where the presence of Jews is attested from Biblical times. The seizure of the Red Sea trade by the Ptolemies gave this inland culture a fruitful period of gestation so that by the second century AD we find the first mention of the city of Aksum under a Hellenised king, Zoscales. Aksum was probably much older than this but only now did external factors, notably the weakness of Meroe, permit an unknown Aksumite ruler to create an empire out of the tribal elements of the Horn of Africa. This was extended and consolidated by a series of able kings who have left fragmentary accounts of their conquests in various inscriptions of the third and early fourth centuries, and Meroe itself fell to one of them. The last and most illustrious was Ēzānā, but his greatest achievement was to accord state recognition to Christianity, which had been introduced by the Tyrian Frumentius around AD 330. How deeply the new faith was embedded in the people is uncertain but it was strongly enough maintained for Aksum to become recognised in the west as a protector of the faith and to be subjected to the full onslaught of Christian influences from Egypt and Syria. Obscure as later history is, at no time does the status of Christianity appear to be in any internal danger. The event associated above all with Aksum at this time was the intervention of the Negus Kālēb or Hellestheaeus at the behest of Justin I to overthrow the Jewish ruler of Ḥimyar in AD 523–5, though he was not able to maintain his hold there for long.

The subsequent seven centuries are a period of deep obscurity. Initially Aksum was physically and spiritually isolated from her Christian contacts by the spread of Islam, which gradually overran all the coastal regions of her empire and spread from Egypt into the Sudan. For Ethiopia the main effect was a reassertion of the Cushitic strata of society and a cultural reorientation southwards towards Lāstā and Shoa. The seventh and eighth centuries also saw the northern provinces overrun by Beja tribes from the Sudan. Occasional shafts of light are thrown by contemporary Arabic records, for Ethiopia still managed occasionally to obtain her Metropolitans from Alexandria and the Muslim rulers of Egypt clearly felt it advantageous to tolerate this link. In fact, after a period of dissolution and decadence, Ethiopia seems to have recovered some of her power and cohesion by the tenth century, despite at least one serious revolt by Judaised Agaw tribes. Then, around 1137, an Agaw dynasty, the Zāgwē from Lāstā, usurped the throne and remained in effective control till 1270. It is remarkable indeed that Ethiopia should have maintained her independence during this period despite such internal confusion and there is little doubt that it was only her impregnable terrain which saved her from being overwhelmed by Islam.

The Zāgwē dynasty, though despised by Ethiopians, seems to have done much good for the country through building churches and missionary activities, while one king, Lālibalā, is regarded as a saint. Nevertheless, age-old tensions between north and south culminated in the 'restoration' of a line of kings claiming descent from Solomon and the Queen of Sheba in 1270. Traditionally, the change was engineered by the Metropolitan Takla Haymānot in return for various suspiciously generous concessions to the Church, but in fact it was probably attended with violence. The ruling centre now lay in Amḥarā and from here on documentation is abundant. The first problem facing the Solomonids was the hostile Muslim presence in the south and by his conquest of Ifāt and Adal, 'Amda Ṣeyon (1314–44) secured the internal peace of his kingdom while the Church was strengthened by many conversions and the founding of monasteries. The next ninety years were of slight significance but from 1434 to 1468 Ethiopia had one of her ablest rulers in Zar'a Yā'qob. He too achieved substantial successes against the Muslims but his chief claim to fame was his internal reforms in the Church and the state administration, both ruthlessly carried out but with the effect of definitively establishing the character of the Ethiopian Monophysite Church by suppressing its pagan and Judaic elements, and of consolidating the central rule of the Negus by removing power from the provincial Rāses.

His successors were unable to maintain his conquests and the Negus Lebna Dengel (1508–40) succeeded only in temporarily halting the aggression of Adal by some resounding victories in 1516. However, he left a legacy of hatred amongst the Muslims who regrouped themselves and, under the notorious Imām Aḥmad Grāñ, attacked Ethiopia in 1529. His major offensive was finally launched in 1531 and the Negus was compelled to live the life of a fugitive till his death, his kingdom attacked on every quarter, while immense destruction was inflicted on the land. Salvation was to come from outside. In the preceding century increasing numbers of Europeans had penetrated to the Court and this had led to prolonged negotiations with Rome and Portugal for material and military aid and co-operation between the two Churches. A Portuguese mission which stayed in the country from 1520 to 1526 achieved little, but eventually, early in the reign of Claudius (1540–59), four hundred Portuguese mercenaries arrived and with their help the Muslim threat was averted.

Although this was decisive in preserving Christianity in Ethiopia, it was not before the Muslims had overrun and pillaged almost the entire land. The state, however, survived only to witness the start of three centuries of Gāllā infiltration from the south. Until their eventual assimilation they were to prove a constant negative danger to Ethiopian culture. Nevertheless, Claudius now entered into cordial relations with Portugal and Rome, and no obstacle was laid in the path of the entry of Jesuit missionaries who made supreme efforts to convert the people to Roman Catholicism. The degree of their success can be gathered from the exacerbated academic disputes which ensued, though little official counteraction was taken until the Negus Susenyos (1607–32) himself succumbed and embraced Catholicism, promising the submission of his people also. This proved too much to bear and a civil upheaval compelled him to abdicate. The Jesuits were cruelly expelled and the land plunged into a xenophobic mood.

Although external threats were now largely removed, for more than two centuries confusion reigned and the country became increasingly feudalised. The Gāllā encroachment continued but they began to be absorbed. Forces of regionalism are evidenced in the northwards shift of the Capital to Gondar under Fāsiladas (1632–67). Europe was to know little of the country until James Bruce made his epic journey there in the seventeen-seventies. It was now in what is known as the Era of the Judges when 'there was no king in Ethiopia; every man did that which was right in his own eyes'. The Rāses assumed greater powers and regional kings set themselves up. The Church alone served as a unifying force and the situation was saved only by the emergence of a northern prince who, proclaiming himself King of Kings with the prophetic name of Theodore in 1855, managed to reunite the country and suppress feudalism. Although he reinspired the tired people, his senseless cruelty and incipient madness eventually alienated them and led to his defeat at the hands of the British in 1868. The task of consolidating the nation was brought to fruition by his successors, particularly Menelik (1889–1913), and this, together with the disruptive effects of European imperialism on the Near East and Africa, definitively established Ethiopia as an African state when she entered the world arena under her present Emperor.

MAIN TRENDS IN LITERATURE

The most striking features of Ethiopic writing are its exclusively Christian flavour and its apparent dependence on foreign inspiration. There is virtually nothing of purely profane intention, unless in the field of oral literature, which really reflects its African surroundings, and even secular topics, such as Court annals, are infused with Christian morality and idealism. Ethiopia took its full share of the standard works which circulated in the Christian Near-East and thereby preserved much of theological interest, but one might be forgiven the impression that her literature is not worth studying from any other aspect. However, this would be unfair. In fact, there exists a sizeable corpus of original compositions which, though mainly of local relevance, do contain much deserving of attention. Even works of pure translation may command respect in that the translators have often produced more than a mere literal rendering of the original but have rather adapted it to the spirit of the milieu for which it was intended.

The reasons for this bias are to be sought in the dichotomy between the Church and Court with their dependence on formality and tradition, and the people, the true carriers of the native culture. The clergy alone possessed education so that literature became entirely a prerogative of the Church. The only centres of learning were the monasteries, some of which achieved great power and influence, and within the structure of the state all their creative strivings were directed towards the greater glory of God and the Negus. Writing on a secular topic would have been unthinkable. For this reason too the personal element is hardly apparent in Ethiopic writing. The names and lives of few authors or translators are memorable and many works are anonymous, for a book is estimated for its practical use rather than for its originality or ideas. Even today in Ethiopia the word *maṣḥaf* (book), will suggest to most a work which is moral and improving, while the *maṣḥaf, par excellence*, is the Bible.

Ethiopic literature has its roots in the Aksumite period. A few short inscriptions of South Arabian inspiration and type survive from an earlier date but are only marginally literary. Later it is known that Zoscales was 'acquainted with Greek literature' but how thoroughly is not stated. Certainly, the monumental inscriptions in Greek and, later, Ge'ez of AD 200–350 suggest Hellenistic inspiration stylistically but the drafters could actually have been Greeks. The first book certainly known to Aksum was the Bible. No doubt Greek texts of this work already circulated for the benefit of foreign residents when Aksum first embraced Christianity, but as more of the people adopted the new faith, the need for a native text must have been felt, and around AD 450 the task of translation was started, probably with the Gospels. Although tradition attests to a Court Scribe at the time of Ēzānā, it is likely that the translation was rather made by exiled Syrian monks since the text employed is the Lucianic recension of Antioch, which Frumentius would not have used. Moreover, several stylistic features suggest Greek and Aramaic influences and these languages have also bequeathed many loan-words to Ge'ez. The entire work was completed, except for Maccabees, in 676. In addition to the canonical books of the Bible, a number of apocrypha were included, notably Enoch and Jubilees, and works of this class were always held in particular regard. Only a handful of other works, all translations from Greek, have survived from this period. The monastic *Rules of Pachomius* have a particular relevance to the structure of Ethiopian society and are highly esteemed, as indeed is the collection of early Christian writings known as *Qērellos*. An interesting curiosity is the *Fisālgos* (Physiologus), a collection of instructive stories from natural history of Syrian origin, which finds a reflection in the Ethiopians' love for such tales in oral literature.

Apart from a very few inscriptions and a couple of land charters, no written documents have survived from the Dark Ages. Nevertheless, the facility with which writing was resumed around 1300 strongly suggests that it cannot have been dormant and it is tempting to suppose that the inevitable self-justification of the new Solomonid dynasty resulted in the suppression of much historical material. For religious works the uncertain links with Alexandria would make transmission difficult and it is probably no chance that the literary renascence associated with the Solomonids coincides with a similar revival in Alexandria itself.

After the restoration the output of literature remains constant till the eighteenth century. Now Ge'ez was solely a language of the Church, understood only by the clergy. Indeed, some writers of outstanding ability were monks of Egyptian origin. For translations the medium was probably always Christian Arabic, though occasionally the indirect influence of Coptic can be detected. Cases are actually known where an original Ge'ez work required to be conceived in Arabic first. The various genres had been established within the first two centuries and three periods of particular attainment may be distinguished.

The first is above all associated with the reign of 'Amda Ṣeyon, whose conquests had brought Ethiopia a measure of stability and peace, and with the Abuna Salāmā (*d* 1390). The needs of the re-established Church first demanded a revision of the old text of the Bible on the basis of the Arabic 'Vulgate' of Alexandria. Theological writing generally was encouraged since the Church also required basic works of ritual, and various anaphoras, liturgies, homilies and the like were translated from Arabic. Amongst the earliest we find the *Horologium*, a work on the conduct of monks ascribed to and named after Philoxenus of Mabug, and the *Maṣḥafa Genzat* (Book of Burial) which prescribes funerary rites. Mention should also be made of the *Sēnodos* and *Didascalia*, both vital in determining the religious life of Ethiopia. While much of this activity merely made standard materials available to the clergy, works such as the *Fekkārē Iyasus* and the *Book of the Mysteries of Heaven and the Earth* from later in the century are remarkable specimens of original writing.

A genre of particular significance to Ethiopia is hagiography. Amongst the earliest examples is a translation of the apocryphal *Acts of the Apostles* (*Gadla Ḥawāryāt*), and somewhat later the *Acts of the Martyrs* (*Gadla Samā'tāt*) and the *Synaxarium* (*Senkessār*) were translated, the latter expanded to include lives of native saints. A vast corpus of such literature grew up in the succeeding centuries as the lives of Aksumite, Zāgwē, and later kings and saints were elaborated, and their importance to the historian cannot be overstated since, despite their fantastical accretions, valuable information can be gleaned from them on early ecclesiastical and political history.

Secular writing is represented at this time by historiography. A translation of Joseph Ben Gorion's *History of the Jews* may perhaps be seen as reflecting the Israelite pretensions of the State. Although Court annals did not become a norm till much later, an eye-witness account of 'Amda Ṣeyon's campaigns of 1332 has survived which displays great vitality and literary merit. Later chronicles, however, which exist either as parts of larger works or as records of individual reigns, are purely factual and objective, piously and uncritically glorifying the Negus. Midway between history and theology stands the renowned *Kebra Nagast* (Glory of the Kings), which embodies many stories and legends of Ethiopia's past. It was written in justification of the new dynasty early in the century and, despite its naivety and lack of connection, stands at once as a major work of literature and as the national saga of the Ethiopian people.

Singing and recitation are central to the service of the Church and from this date stem the earliest examples of religious poetry. In the hagiographies are found specimens of the very popular type known as *malke'* (image). The *Weddāsē Māryām*, a volume of hymns of Coptic origin in praise of the Virgin Mary, reflects the veneration in which she was held. Although superior to products of later centuries, they do not compare for directness and originality with the Amharic *Royal Songs* which are preserved in the chronicle of 'Amda Ṣeyon and are the work of unsophisticated soldiers.

The reign of Zar'a Yā'qob, himself a writer of no mean merit, marks the next high point of literary endeavour. Hagiography was intensified with the addition of national lives, notably of the Zāgwē kings. The widespread reforms he initiated in the Church led to his personally writing several political and religious tracts in furtherance of his policies, the greatest being the *Maṣḥafa Berhān*. Religious poetry was also actively encouraged by him and to his reign belong collections such as the *Argānona Māryām Dengel*, the *Egzi'abḥēr Nagsa*, and, above all, the *Deggwā*. Although these now contain original compositions, the restrictive atmosphere of the age is mirrored in their lack of vitality and freshness.

The outstanding development of this time, however, is miracle literature, a genre to prove of intense appeal to the people so that it came to pervade other branches of literature, such as hagiography. The *Ta'āmra Māryām* (Miracles of Mary), provided the initial spur. These take us right out of Ethiopia into a literature whose origins may be traced back to medieval Europe, though Ethiopia made a substantial contribution of its own to the canon. The genre was extended to cover other holy persons, notably Christ and St George.

The troubled period of the Muslim invasions and the subsequent Jesuit interlude form the third peak in Ge'ez literature. Directly responsible for this revival was the Arab convert 'Enbāqom, a profound scholar who translated several works from Arabic, notably the story of Baralām and Yewāsef. He also played a major role in initiating a polemical literature directed against Islam, and side by side with this were composed tracts dealing with the problems of renegade Christians. To this period also is attributed a version of the Alexander Book, though it may actually be much earlier.

The polemical character of sixteenth-century writing was intensified by Jesuit attacks on the Monophysite faith which provoked a flood of apologetic writings, the most famous of which is the *Confession of Claudius*, the work of the Negus himself. Of the innumerable tracts of this type may be mentioned the *Ṣawana Nafs* and the *Fekkārē Malakot*. To the same religious climate belongs the translation from Arabic of the *Haymānota Abaw*, a collection of Patristic homilies, letters and exegetic works. Even after the expulsion of the Jesuits similar apologetic writings, some very vitriolic, continued to be produced, but they now centred on internal disputes.

The sixteenth century witnessed important advances in historiography. The so-called '*Abbreviated Chronicle*' was founded on the basis of an account of Grāñ's invasions and was continually added to into the nineteenth century. Official Court annals also were begun under Sarṣa Dengel (1563–97) and continue for the next two hundred years, while in 1602 there appeared a work of paramount value to Byzantinists, a translation from a lost Arabic original of the *Chronicle* of John, Bishop of Nikiu. But perhaps the most remarkable work is Bāḥrey's *History of the Gāllā* (1595) which betrays a historical sensitivity unique for its time. Law is not a genre otherwise associated with Ge'ez but the social confusion of this period led to the translation from

Arabic of a major legal treatise, the *Fetḥa Nagast*, which was to become the basis of civil and ecclesiastical law in Ethiopia.

The seventeenth and eighteenth centuries were a period of relative decadence in literature. The last major translation from Arabic is the *Faws Manfasāwi* in the late seventeenth century. Important annals were still composed in Ge'ez but by the nineteenth century active encouragement was being given to the use of Amharic for this purpose and Ge'ez was relegated to the status of a liturgical language. The last hundred years have seen the virtual extinction of active writing in Ge'ez and the emergence of a new literature which employs the vernaculars and owes its inspiration to Europe and Africa.

INDIVIDUAL WRITERS AND WORKS

Apocrypha. Of the apocryphal and deuterocanonical books accepted into the canon of the Ethiopian Church, Enoch, which exists complete only in Ge'ez, and Jubilees are particularly important. The 'Shepherd' of Hermas and Baruch also deserve attention. Post-Classical literature too contains many such works, some original and many translated from Arabic. The Book of Maccabees exists only in a poetical version written some time before 1450. For such works see R. Basset, *Les apocryphes éthiopiens*, Paris, 1882–1909. R. H. Charles has translated Enoch (Oxford, 1912) and Jubilees (London, 1902).

Argānona Māryām Dengel (Organ of the Virgin Mary). A collection of hymns in praise of the Virgin Mary composed or inspired by Zar'a Yā'qob, who is also accredited with the collection *Egzi'abḥēr Nagsa* (God has reigned). Zar'a Yā'qob had ordained many festivals in honour of the Virgin, which probably accounts for the numerous such collections made in his reign. Generally uninspired, they lack the vitality and dramatic feeling of earlier poetry, perhaps because of the religious climate. The genre is studied by A. Grohmann, *Äthiopische Marienhymnen*, Leipzig, 1919.

Bāḥrey. A monk at the court of Sarṣa Dengel (1563–97) who wrote a remarkable *History of the Gāllā* in 1595. Probably an eye-witness to their incursions, he was free and unprejudiced in his outlook and his penetrating study of Gāllā sociology, history and religion is not typical of Ethiopic historiography. He shows no fatalism about their successes, attributing them to their freer ethnic constitution as compared to the categorised social structure of the Ethiopians. See I. Guidi, *Corpus Scriptorum Christianorum Orientalium, series aethiopica*, 3.

Baralām and Yewāsef. The Ethiopic version of Barlaam and Josaphat, translated from Arabic in 1553 by 'Enbāqom. This Indian Buddhist legend is widespread throughout the medieval East and West and the Arabic version used by 'Enbāqom is not later than the thirteenth century. In Ethiopic it is given a strongly Christian veneer. Trans. E. A. W. Budge, Cambridge, 1923.

Deggwā. The most important collection of hymns in the Ethiopian Church. Traditionally the work of the sixth-century Metropolitan Yārēd, the reputed inventor of Ethiopian music, the original version is not later than the fifteenth century. As yet unedited and unstudied, it is a primary source for the elucidation of musical notation. Various redactions of later date are known but the manuscripts in Europe mostly represent an abridgement made under Sarṣa Dengel (1563–97).

Didascalia. A collection of canons and commandments ascribed to Jesus Christ, the Apostles and St Clement, translated from Arabic at the instigation of Abuna Salāmā in the fourteenth century. It contains the canons of the earlier Church Councils, including Nicaea, and apocryphal Arab canons. The religious and ecclesiastical rules showed the need for reform in the Ethiopian Church and may have motivated Zar'a Yā'qob's measures in the next century. Trans. T. P. Platt, London, 1834.

'Enbāqom (Habakkuk). An Arab merchant from Iraq or the Yemen by name of Ṣāliḥ who embraced Christianity in Ethiopia in the early sixteenth century and ultimately became a monk. Knowledgeable and pious, he became Abbot of Dabra Libānos and thus leader of the monks of Ethiopia. After 1526 he devoted himself entirely to study. His *Anqaṣa Amin* (Gate of the Faith) written under Claudius, is an apologetic tract against Islam which uses the Qur'ān itself in refutation. The work is remarkable in recognising the universality of Christianity as against the nationalism of Islam. Several translations by him from Arabic exist, notably *Baralām and Yewāsef.*

Falāshās. An Agaw remnant living scattered through several provinces of Ethiopia who claim to be Jewish but probably perpetuate some of the Judaic elements in the Aksumite Empire. They have a literature of their own in Ge'ez, some of which is shared with the Christians. The *Te'zāza Sanbat* (Commandments of the Sabbath), translated by J. Halévy, Paris, 1902, is particularly important. Otherwise Falāshā literature contains much hagiographical material and many prayers. See W. Leslau, *Falasha Anthology*, New Haven, 1951.

Faws Manfasāwi (Spiritual medicine). A penitential manual translated after 1680 from the Arabic of Michael, Bishop of Atrib and Mabig in Egypt. Of some theological significance, it is the last major work of translation from Arabic into Ge'ez.

Fekkārē Iyasus (Interpretation of Jesus). A notable example of the apocalyptic literature so favoured by the Ethiopians. It is an eschatological tract on the tribulations at the end of time and predicting that a King Theodore will come from the East as a saviour. The purpose was probably to favour Theodore I (1411–14), then involved in a civil war, and the name was actually adopted by Lij Kāsā when he became Emperor in 1855. Translated into Russian by N. Weinberg, St Petersburg, 1907.

Fekkārē Malakot (Interpretation of the Divinity). A sixteenth-century apologetic tract directed against the Jesuits. Of Michaelite origin it argues for the incomprehensibility of God by the human intellect and that only the elect can approach his Divinity. It opposes the doctrine that man is made in the image of God. Contorted and obscure, it is regarded as a classic statement of the Monophysite view. Trans. E. Cerulli, *Scritti teologici etiopici dei secoli XVI–XVII*, Città del Vaticano, 1958.

Fetḥa Nagast (Legislation of the Kings). The fundamental codification of ecclesiastical, civil and penal law in Ethiopia. It was translated from the Arabic *Nomocanon* of Ibn al-'Assāl, a work written in the eleventh century for the benefit of Christians living in Egypt under Muslim jurisdiction, and as such is not entirely relevant to the needs of Ethiopia. In translation much was misunderstood and it is so difficult and obscure as to have become proverbial. Trans. I. Guidi, *La legislazione dei Re*, Rome, 1899.

Gadla Ḥawāryāt (Acts of the Apostles). A translation of the apocryphal 'Acts' made from Arabic not later than 1379. It contains the life and martyrdom of each Apostle and is based on the version current in Alexandria in the thirteenth century. Portions with Gnostic leanings are omitted as being meaningless in Ethiopia. Trans. E. A. W. Budge, *The Contendings of the Apostles*, London, 1901.

Haymānota Abaw (Faith of the Fathers). An anthology of excerpts from the homilies of the Church Fathers and of tracts on the mystery of the Trinity and the Incarnation, etc., assembled in defence of the Monophysite faith and translated from the Arabic of Ibn Rajā during the reign of Claudius. Several redactions exist, differing according to religious trends of the time. Greatly favoured in Ethiopia now, it ranks beside the *Qērellos* as the principal source for the knowledge of Patristic writing in Ethiopia.

Inscriptions. Of the earliest inscriptions in South Arabian script those in pure South Arabian language were probably the work of colonists around 500 BC. Others differ slightly in language and nomenclature and may stem from the indigenised earlier waves of Semites. By the beginning of the present era the script and language are evolving well on the way towards Ge'ez. In Aksum Greek was used in several lengthy monumental texts, notably in an anonymous one quoted by Cosmas Indicopleustes from Adulis, and in those of Ēzānā. During the latter's reign Ge'ez began to be employed in the inscriptions and Greek disappeared. It is probable, nevertheless, that Greeks influenced early Aksumite epigraphy and style. Examples of all types are published in E. Littmann's *Deutsche Aksum-Expedition, IV*, Berlin, 1913, and also in Budge's *History of Ethiopia*. The most penetrating analysis of the earlier types is by A. J. Drewes, *Inscriptions de l'Éthiopie antique*, Leiden, 1962.

Kebra Nagast (Glory of the Kings). Written during the reign of 'Amda Ṣeyon, it contains a medley of legends and mythical interpretations relative to the Israelite origins of the legitimate ruling family, the Solomonids, and is clearly in justification of their restoration in 1270. The central narrative of the book is the Queen of Sheba's visit to Solomon, the birth of her son, Menelik, and his journey to Jerusalem to see his father and bring the Ark of Zion to Aksum. Innumerable sources, probably including native legends, have been assembled and elaborated to create this national epic. It has been translated into English by E. A. W. Budge, *The Queen of Sheba and her only Son Menyelek*, London, 1922.

Malke' (Image). A type of verse composition of Coptic origin which celebrates the praises of a saint in an indeterminate number of verses, each metaphorically describing part of his body, starting with the head and proceeding to the soles of the feet. It was very popular in the seventeenth and eighteenth centuries and several collections exist. It early became almost obligatory to insert one at the end of the life of a saint.

Maṣḥafa Berhān (Book of Light). The most significant work of Zar'a Yā'qob, epitomising his political and religious reforms. Oratorical and tortuous in style, it reveals his ruthless and uncompromising nature before the internal and external dangers threatening his realm. His purpose was to defend the faith of Christ and to assert the supremacy of the Negus over Church and State. The book includes exhortations against civil strife, refutations of the Stephanite and Michaelite heresies, and attacks on magical and pagan practices. Trans. C. Conti Rossini, *Corpus Scriptorum Christianorum Orientalium, scriptores aethiopici*, 48 and 52.

Maṣḥafa Mesṭir Za-Samāy Wa-Medr (Book of the Mysteries of Heaven and Earth). An original composition of the mid-fourteenth century which contains the author's interpretations of esoteric revelations delivered to him by an angel. It has four sections dealing with the secrets of creation and the angels' rebellion; an interpretation of the Apocalypse of St John; an interpretation of the mysteries of the Divinity and its symbols; and cabbalistic interpretations of scriptural cyphers. Trans. E. A. W. Budge, London, 1935.

Philosophy. A genre conspicuously absent in Ethiopia since the theistic *Ḥatatā Zar'a Yā'qob* was shown to be a nineteenth-century forgery by an Italian missionary. Otherwise, collections of aphorisms and wise sayings appeal very much to the Ethiopian mentality. The most popular is the *Maṣḥafa Falāsfā Ṭabibān* (Book of the Wise Philosophers), a sixteenth-century translation from Arabic, which contains material from various Greek, Latin, and Oriental philosophers. Trans. G. H. Cornhill, *Das Buch der weisen Philosophen*, Leipzig, 1875.

Qenē (=*λειτουργία*). A poetic genre especially used to accompany the recitation of the Psalms and Canticles. The oldest examples go back to the late fifteenth century and by the seventeenth it had become the commonest type of poetic composition. Initially simple, it latterly became very elaborate with obscure imagery derived from the Bible. A mode reserved for initiates, *qenē* is a major item in the training of a priest and is most appreciated when improvised. There is one stanza with uniform rhyme and various types are recognised with from two to eleven lines. The metrical rules, which are very strict, are not yet properly understood. See A. Schall, *Zur äthiopischen Verskunst*, Wiesbaden, 1961.

Qērellos (Cyrillus). An assemblage of Christological writings by St Cyril of Alexandria and others, translated from Greek in the Aksumite period. The writings are anti-Nestorian, referring mostly to the Council of Ephesus (431), and insist on the unity of Christ incarnate. Parts are translated by S. Grébaut in *Revue de l'Orient Chrétien*, 1910 and 1911, and F. Altheim, *Die Araber in der alten Welt, IV*, Berlin, 1967.

Salāmā, Abuna. An Egyptian monk who became Metropolitan in Ethiopia in the mid-fourteenth century and died about 1390. Closer ties with Alexandria and the literary revival there induced him to strive to raise the standards of Ge'ez writing also, though perhaps not so much to instruct the native clergy as to combat dissident elements amongst them. He composed liturgies and homilies and hagiographical works, and with his name are linked the *Sēnodos* and the *Didascalia.* He was also associated with the revision of the Aksumite text of the Bible when he probably used the revised Arabic text of Alexandria.

Ṣawana Nafs (Refuge of the Soul). An apologetic tract in the form of a letter directed to the King (Claudius) in the mid-sixteenth century, enunciating Ethiopia's adherence to the Monophysite faith in its native form. It is directed against the Jesuits. Trans. E. Cerulli, *Scritti teologici etiopici dei secoli XVI–XVII, II,* Città del Vaticano, 1960.

Senkessār (Synaxarium). Translated from Arabic in the late fourteenth century. It contains short lives of the saints arranged for reading in Church on their name days throughout the year. The translation is rather weak but in time native saints were added so that the work has a local interest. Trans. E. A. W. Budge, *The Book of the Saints of the Ethiopian Church*, 4 vol., Cambridge, 1928.

Ta'āmra Māryām (Miracles of Mary). The most renowned work in Ethiopic miracle literature. The genre originated in France in the twelfth century and spread rapidly all over Europe with local additions. The Crusades took them to the Near East and between 1237 and 1289 they had been translated into Arabic. From Palestine they moved into Egypt where further native elaboration occurred. Under Dāwit I (1382–1411) the Arabic corpus found its way into Ge'ez. There again it was adapted and augmented until various collections existed of widely differing size. Under Zar'a Yā'qob they were used for liturgical purposes and so in the sixteenth century an accepted canon of thirty-three miracles was established, additional material customarily being placed at the end. Only this canon is used for illuminations in manuscripts. The Ethiopic collection incorporates stories originating in France, Spain and Italy. A monumental study of the legends and their sources is E. Cerulli's *Il libro etiopico dei miracoli di Maria*, Rome, 1953, and several collections have been translated by Budge.

Weddāsē Māryām (Praises of Mary). A collection of hymns and laudations to the Virgin Mary, arranged according to the days of the week, and associated with Abuna Salāmā. It enjoys great respect in Ethiopia and is frequently appended to the Psalter. One of the earliest examples of Ge'ez religious poetry, it is probably of Coptic origin through an Arabic intermediary. Published by K. Fries, Uppsala, 1892.

Zar'a Yā'qob. Emperor of Ethiopia (1434–68). When he became Negus after a youth spent in confinement he found the state in political and religious disorder. The Church was split by heresies, particularly the Stephanites who denied the cult of the Cross and the Virgin Mary, and the Michaelites who denied human comprehension of God. His own and his predecessors' conquests had brought many Muslims and pagans into the empire. He was unyielding and bitter in his struggle to consolidate his realm and Christianity as an indivisible unity and thereby alienated many of the clergy. Part of his programme involved the composition of propaganda works towards this end (*cf Maṣḥafa Berhān*) and a major flowering of writing in all genres ensued.

Zēnā Eskender (History of Alexander). Translated from Arabic reputedly in the mid-sixteenth century but probably much earlier, to judge by its style. The Alexander legends, deriving from the version of Pseudo-Callisthenes, are widespread throughout the Old World but the Ethiopic text has developed radically away from the accepted canon. The hero is described as a Christian saint and his legendary and historical deeds are set in a suitably Christian context. The Alexander Book with several associated Ethiopic texts is translated by E. A. W. Budge, London, 1896 and 1933.

BIBLIOGRAPHY

HISTORICAL BACKGROUND

WALLIS BUDGE, E. A. *A History of Ethiopia* 2 vols., London, 1928.

JONES, A. H. M. and MONROE, E. *A History of Ethiopia* Oxford, 1955.

ULLENDORFF, E. *The Ethiopians* 2nd edn., Oxford, 1965.

LITERATURE

CERULLI, E. *Storia della letteratura etiopica* Milan, 1956.

GUIDI, I. *Storia della letteratura etiopica* Rome, 1932.

LITTMANN, E. 'Geschichte der äthiopischen Litteratur', *Geschichte der christlichen Litteraturen des Orients* ed. C. Brockelmann, Leipzig, 1907.

There is a rich selection of Ethiopic works of all types in the series *Corpus Scriptorum Christianorum Orientalium* and *Patrologia Orientalis*.

INDIAN AND PAKISTANI LITERATURE

I. M. P. Raeside and R. Russell

HISTORICAL BACKGROUND

ANCIENT TIMES

Archaeological evidence of the stone-age cultures of India has been obtained from almost every part of the sub-continent and shows a development of technological skill that is roughly comparable to that of Palaeolithic Europe. The Neolithic revolution came late and the first dateable signs of metal-using cultures are found from about 3000 BC in the form of settled village sites in Baluchistan and Sind which are patently outliers of the Middle Eastern cultures to the west. These persisted even when a much more elaborate civilisation had grown up in the Indus valley about 2500 BC. This was the Harappan culture which takes its name from one of the two major sites in the Indus basin, Harappa and Mohenjo Daro, which were systematically excavated from 1924 onwards and revealed an advanced and hitherto entirely unsuspected civilisation which built large brick houses and public buildings, had excellent sewers, a still undeciphered writing system and a pantheon that included a mother-goddess fertility figure and a 'horned god' who is temptingly easy to equate with the god Śiva of later Hinduism. Of course all the places mentioned so far lie within the borders of modern West Pakistan, but it is meaningless to distinguish between the history of India and Pakistan at this stage or any other before 1947.

The end of the Harappan civilisation came fairly suddenly early in the second millennium BC and coincides closely with the arrival of Aryan invaders from beyond the north-western passes, so that it is hard not to imagine some connection between the two events. However there is continuing controversy among Indian scholars – controversy in which local patriotism plays a large part – as to whether the Harappans were in fact the direct ancestors of the modern Dravidians, the dark-skinned peoples of South India, who would in this case have been driven to the tip of the continent rather as the Celts were driven to the fringes of Europe by later invaders. It is perhaps safer to say only that the Harappans were already a mixed race, as is shown by their skeletal remains, and that their cult of the mother goddess was disseminated all over India among the non-Aryan peoples.

The Aryans, a race of nomadic horsemen and cattle breeders, speaking a language directly related to the main languages of Europe, came down into India in a series of waves or marauding bands and brought with them their masculine pantheon of sky and sun gods, their priests, their practice of exuberant animal sacrifices and the hymns that celebrate them. These hymns, dating from between 1500 and 1000 BC, make up the *Ṛg-veda*, the oldest monument of Indian literature. For a thousand years these people developed in a way that we can only guess at from fragmentary evidence – gradually turning from a nomadic life to agriculture in settled villages, spreading continually eastward in the north Indian plain, evolving from tribes to tribal groups and thence to minor kingdoms ruled by hereditary or elective monarchs. It must have been a period of continual petty warfare as this enterprising people spread out over northern India, and probably it was the cattle raids and inter-tribal feuding of these shadowy years which eventually gave rise to the epic battles of the *Mahābhārata*.

The Aryans evolved socially as well. They had always had priests to perform their sacrifices, but now these came to form a priestly caste which mediated with the elemental gods through the king on behalf of the people, and thus the basic divisions of Indian society, popularly known as castes, became first fixed. The original wild tribesmen became stratified into social layers: kings and noblemen (*kṣatriyas*), priests (*brāhmaṇs*) and the common herd (*vaiśyas*). All these were and still are *dvija* – twice born – that is born again when they are initiated to full adult membership of their caste. The fourth caste of labourer (*śudras*) was almost certainly added during the years of Aryan expansion to accommodate the conquered and the children produced by intermarriage with the previous occupiers of the land. It must be significant that the correct term for the fourfold division of caste is *varṇa* which means 'colour', for the Aryan invaders were a fair-skinned people by comparison with the darker aborigines.

By 600 BC we find that a series of kingdoms or semi-republican nation-states have grown up in north India along the course of the Ganges. Among these the kingdom of Māgadha (roughly modern Bihar) was pre-eminent. In the north-west the confusion of pre-Aryan peoples and laggards in the Aryan advance was overrun by Cyrus of Persia about 530 BC and the area became part of the Persian Empire. Here Gandhāra with its capital Taxila was the chief state, and it was this corner of India only that fell to Alexander in 327 BC. More important than political history, it was this period that produced a religious revival that appealed to the growing class of prosperous merchants by offering them more personal involvement than did the somewhat arid sacrificing ceremonies of Vedic practice. In the middle of the sixth century BC Mahāvir and Buddha both emerged from the aristocracy of small kingdoms lying along the Ganges. Both preached a doctrine that is essentially atheistic and encourages man to a deliberate and personal purification of his soul from the dross of the material world. In both cases the religions produced by their teaching, now called Jainism and Buddhism respectively, achieved positions of great power and influence in later times although their final states are very different.

During this time also the literary languages of north India first appear. Classical Sanskrit evolves from Vedic (the language in which the *Vedas* were recited – for they were never written down) as the tool of orthodox religion and of the *brāhmaṇ* caste. But alongside Sanskrit we also find the popular speech of the more important centres turning into acceptable literary languages known as Prakrits. The early Buddhist and Jain works were in Māgadhi Prakrit.

In 321 BC Candragupta Maurya seized the throne of Māgadha and founded the first Indian Empire. He conquered the north-west as far as Afghanistan from the Indo-Greek successors of Alexander. His son conquered the Deccan, that is peninsular India, as far as Mysore; and his grandson, the great Aśoka, in 260 BC defeated the last major kingdom to hold out against him – Kalinga in modern Orissa. Aśoka became a convert to Buddhism, organised his empire with great efficiency and adopted the useful policy of causing his edicts and instructions to be carved on rocks and specially erected pillars where they can be read to this day. His empire had close connexions with Ceylon and sent Buddhist missionaries there. It was on friendly terms with the kingdoms of the extreme south, the Tamil-speaking country, and in Aśokan inscriptions we find for the first time the names of southern 'kings' (Cera, Cola, Pāṇḍya), but it is hard to say exactly what stage of civilisation had been reached in the Dravidian south at that time.

The Mauryan empire declined from Aśoka's death in 232 BC and virtually disappeared in 180 BC when the Bactrian Greeks overran the north-west. The India of the next five hundred years is a confusing jumble of evanescent kingdoms. Waves of invaders from central Asia supplanted each other in north-west India with monotonous regularity. From these kings one might single out Kaniṣka who is chiefly remarkable for the bitterness with which scholars argue about his dates notwithstanding the fact that the Śaka era, a dating system still widely used in India, starts from AD 78, the supposed year of his accession. In the Deccan the Sātavāhanas flourished in their capital at Pratiṣṭhāna (modern Paiṭhan) on the Godavari and for a short time at the end of the second century claimed to control an area that stretched from Kāthiā-wāḍ in the West to the Krishna delta. In the far south Ceras, Colas and Pāṇḍyas still ruled, the Ceras in modern Kerala on the west coast. In the first century AD the Colas came out on top and established a trading route across the peninsula entirely under their own control. At one end of it was Arika-medu, where Wheeler's excavations found numerous signs of contact with Rome: it was during these centuries that the scale of trading grew enormously, in spite of political vicissitudes. Continual contact with central Asia was assured by the repeated passage of conquering armies through the north-western passes. Roman ships came for spices and Indian (Cola) fleets sailed to the East Indies to get them. Craft guilds flourished in the cities. Broach was the main port for trade with the West, but on the whole Indians were not much inclined to sea-faring themselves and left transport across the Indian Ocean to Arab sailors. Increased trade brought greater wealth and power to the merchants, the third layer of society among whom were the main adherents of the break-away religions Buddhism and Jainism, and their patronage produced the Buddhist *stupas* and cave temples which begin to appear from the second century BC. The Aryan religion, usually called Brahmanism at this particular time, produced no extant buildings. It was still predominantly an affair of sacrificing, for which only temporary sites and specially built fires and altars were needed, though there is no doubt that about this period it began increasingly to absorb the local cults and godlings of the indigenous peoples and evolve its new classic trinity of Brahma, Śiva and Viṣṇu, moving towards a more personal relationship between the individual and god. Buddhism and Jainism both suffered schisms, the former spreading abroad through China and South-east Asia as far as Japan, while the Jains moved south to the Deccan, to their present places of concentration – Gujarat and Mysore.

MEDIEVAL INDIA

The next thousand years of Indian history, from *c* AD 300 to 1300, continues with a confusing welter of kingdoms, some large, many small and scarcely worthy of note except that often all we know of them is that they are recorded by a few laudatory inscriptions or produced a great writer whose work recalls the name of his patron. The major kingdoms of the north were those of the Gupta dynasty – which was almost an empire, based on the old capital of Pāṭaliputra in Magadha in the fourth and fifth centuries and breaking up at last under the impact of fresh invasions. This time it was the Huns, a branch of the same central Asian tribe that overthrew the Roman empire. From 606 to 647 Harṣa ruled from Kanauj in western UP – a king who looms large in Indian tradition because of the Sanskrit biography of him by Bāṇa, but who in fact never ruled more than the northern plains. Later came the rule of the Pālas in the east (modern Bihar and Bengal), who between the eighth and the tenth centuries strove against the Pratihāras of the Delhi region for control of Harṣa's old capital, Kanauj. Around the periphery the hill kingdoms arose. Kashmir appears as an entity from the seventh century; Nepal became independent of Tibet in 878 and the Rajputs of mysterious origin arrive during the ninth and tenth centuries to found numerous petty kingdoms in the hills of Rajasthan.

In the south between the sixth and eighth centuries the growing power of the Pallava kings who ruled from Kancipuram south-west of Madras gave a firm regional basis for the growth of Tamil culture. They were at war continually with the Pāṇḍyas of Madurai further south, and on the north with the Cālukyas of Bādāmi who had succeeded the Sātavāhanas. During this time more of India's fascinating minority groups arrived. On the coast of Kerala Arab traders settled – the ancestors of the Malabar Muslims – and in the eighth century Zoroastrians driven out of Persia by the Arab conquest fled to the coast north of Bombay to found the flourishing Parsi community. In the ninth century the Cālukyas of the northern Deccan succumbed to the Rāṣṭrakuṭas. The Colas of the far south who had persisted as feudatories of the Pallavas, revived in power, replaced their masters, captured the Tanjore region and dominated the Tamil country from around 900 till the early thirteenth century, giving Tamil culture its classical age. Soon after 1014 Rājendra Cola actually marched his army through Orissa to the Ganges, but otherwise the southern kingdoms tended to keep to the south. After 1150 Cola power began to give way to the harassment of local enemies – Hoysaḷas of the Mysore area and Yādavas of Deogiri (modern Daulatabad), but finally it was the long-lasting Pāṇḍyas of Madurai who became the dominant Hindu power in the south. All three kingdoms were prosperous and stable until the Muslim invasions in the early fourteenth century.

This period, 300 to 1300, saw major developments in the religious and philosophical life of India. New sects appeared, notably Tantricism – a mixture of early mother-goddess cults and magic which emerged about the fifth century and profoundly influenced Buddhism as well as Hinduism. The principal philosophical schools of Hinduism were evolved out of the debate between Buddhist and Brahman philosophers – the so-called six systems of which *Vedānta* eventually became the most widely accepted, later to be intensively preached by Śankarācārya in the ninth century as pure monism. Along with this rather arid doctrine ran a parallel stream of more personal, devotional religion known as *bhakti* which had its origin in the Tamil country in the seventh century and which later spread in a series of waves throughout India. On the other hand Buddhism, in the land of its origin at least, had become so inextricably mixed with Hinduism that it was practically extinct by the end of the pre-Muslim period.

Culturally this is the time when most of the modern languages of India first appear: Marathi, for example, in the territory ruled by the Yādavas of Deogiri, Gujarati in the lands of the Vāghela kings of Pāṭaṇ. The birth of classical Tamil in the Cola kingdom has already been mentioned and the other Dravidian languages – Kanarese, Malayalam and Telugu, took form in their respective regions from the ninth century onwards.

ISLAM IN INDIA

North India had experienced Arab raids before and thrown them back, but around AD 1000 began the attacks of Mahmud of Ghazna which conveniently mark the first major impact of an Islamic people upon India. The furthest that Mahmud got into India on his lightning raids was Somnāth in Saurāṣṭra where his sack of the temple in 1025 is burned into the minds of Hindus by many a ballad and story as one of the great disasters of their history (it also provided Wilkie Collins with the source of *The Moonstone*). Nevertheless the Rajput chieftains and the minor kingdoms of the north fought on amongst themselves oblivious of the threat of the Afghan Turks until 1192 when Pṛthvirāja, king of Delhi, was finally defeated by Muhammad Ghuri. This time the conquerors remained to found the Delhi Sultanate which survived rather than flourished until the time of Ala-ud-din Khalji, who conquered the Yādavas decisively in 1296. Under the succeeding dynasty, the Tughluqs, the boundaries of the Sultanate expanded and contracted once again till it covered little more than the Ganges Doab. In the South the Hindu kingdom of Vijayanagar took form in 1336, while Muslim generals began to carve out independent states for themselves in the rest of the north and central Deccan. In 1398 Delhi was sacked in the worst of the Mongol raids under Timur. Timur's man founded the Sayyid dynasty, succeeded by the Lodis from 1451 to 1526 when Babur, the descendant of Timur, defeated the last Lodi at Panipat and the rule of the Mughals began. For these two hundred odd years the Sultanate of Delhi was just another power in Northern India.

The south was dominated by Vijayanagar and the Muslim Bahmani kingdom, which strove against each other and their numerous minor neighbours with varying fortune. In 1538 the Bahmani kingdom fell apart to make five new Muslim states – Bijapur, Golconda, Ahmednagar, Bidar and Berar – while at the same time Vijayanagar was at the peak of its power under Kṛṣṇadev Rāya (1509–30), having conquered Orissa and being on friendly trading terms with the Portuguese newly established in Goa. Yet soon after, in 1564, four of these new Muslim kingdoms united to destroy Vijayanagar utterly.

At this point of time nearly the whole of India was controlled by rulers of Turkish or Afghan descent and of Muslim faith, and obviously the strength of Islam in India grew continuously through immigration and conversion. It should not be supposed however that the non-Muslim majority lived under continual oppression. At times there was of course slaughter, the burning of Hindu temples and forcible conversion, but in the main it seems that the motive for conversion was largely self-interest and that Muslim kings were happy to rule over Hindu subjects as long as they could collect their dues and taxes. The Muslim courts of India were great patrons of the arts, especially architecture and painting. Persian was the literary and diplomatic language of the invaders, but the regional language and literature was actively encouraged by many a Muslim prince: Telugu for instance by the Qutb Shāhi kings of Golconda; Bengali as far east as Chittagong.

In religion there was a new wave of *bhakti* devotionalism that seems to have arisen spontaneously in several parts of the north at the very end of the fifteenth century with Caitanya in Bengal, Kabir at Benares, and Guru Nānak in the Punjab who alone founded a movement – the Sikhs – which is still patently separate from the rest of Hinduism. Caitanya was pure Hindu, but Kabir's devotion was to God by whatever name, whether worshipped in mosque or temple. This strong revival of *bhakti* may well have been released by a parallel devotional movement within Islam – Sufism.

With the coming of the Mughal emperors we arrive at the threshold of modern times. Babur, who was fifth in line from Timur, in his second incursion into India in 1526 defeated and killed Ibrahim Lodi, the last Sultan of Delhi, and a year later fought off the more impressive army of the leader of the Rajputs, Rāna Sanga of Mewar. Babur's empire survived the vicissitudes of Humayun's reign (1530–56), until the great Akbar succeeded to the Mughal throne. First subduing the Rajputs once again, Akbar took Gujarat in 1572, Bengal by 1576, then Kashmir, Orissa and Sind, and started making inroads on the Muslim kingdoms of the Deccan before his death in 1605. Akbar not only conquered territory but established himself as a truly 'Indian' emperor by reconciling the Hindus, principally the Rajputs, and giving them real power. He also set up a system of bureaucratic government which lasted until the British era and in his later years tried to foster a cult centred upon himself which was intended to supersede both Hinduism and Islam.

EUROPEAN INFLUENCES

The seventeenth century saw the Mughal empire in full flower and expanding ever southwards at the expense of the Deccan kingdoms under Jehangir (1605–27), Shah Jahan, the builder of the Taj Mahal, and the great Aurangzeb (1658–1707). It was under Aurangzeb that the current leader of the Sikhs, Guru Gobind Singh, transformed his sect into a martial order. More significantly in the western Deccan, Śivāji, the Maratha chieftain, began to build himself an independent kingdom that was to culminate in the Maratha empire. At his death in 1680 the Marathi speakers of western India had begun to feel themselves to be a nation. The Europeans begin to arrive in India in force. The Portuguese had captured Goa in 1510 and for a century from there and other west coast strongholds kept a tight grip on India's overseas trade, acquiring in the process a reputation for bad faith and intolerance. At the end of the sixteenth century the Dutch seized the sources of the spice trade in the East Indies and established 'factories' or trading posts up and down India mainly as a subsidiary of the spice trade. England formed the East India Company in 1600 and had to concentrate on India only because the Dutch kept them out of the East Indies, for India was a much less profitable market. They had to beat the Portuguese before they could make much headway, but in 1612 they managed this, established themselves in Surat and through the mission of Sir Thomas Roe to the Mughal court obtained valuable trading privileges in 1618. From Surat they expanded to Madras (1640), to Bombay (1674) and Calcutta (1690). The French too had their factories, as well as the Danes. European adventurers, travellers and craftsmen were common enough at the Mughal court, but the merchants lived in their factories a life almost entirely cut off from the country around them.

This voluntary isolation was gradually worn away by the decline of central authority in India after the death of the last strong Mughal emperor Bahadur Shah in 1712. The Deccan was lost when Asaf Jah, the Nizam, set himself up in what was in practice the independent kingdom of Hyderabad which survived till 1948. The Marathas raided Delhi in 1738 and in the following year the Persians sacked it. Gujarat, Sind, Oudh: all became independent in the middle of the eighteenth century and no one could prevent them. In the Maratha kingdom the descendants of Śivāji had lost effective power to the Brahman Peśvā, the hereditary prime minister, and the Peśvā in turn rapidly lost control of his generals when successful raids in the north gave them little kingdoms of their own. In this way the Gaikwad family came to dominate most of Gujarat from Baroda, and the Bhosles ruled Berar and central India as far as Orissa from Nagpur. The Marathas might have inherited the old Moghul empire if a fresh wave of Afghans had not descended on Delhi and routed the Maratha army sent against them at Panipat in 1761. But Ahmad Shah, like so many previous invaders, went home again, and in the ensuing confusion the Maratha warlords rampaged over northern India more like leaders of mercenary bands than rulers of settled countries. In the Punjab the newly militant Sikhs, formerly repressed by the Mughals, began to re-emerge and under Ranjit Singh set up a new Sikh state at the end of the century.

Meanwhile in the south the English and the French were increasingly at loggerheads. The dash and leadership of Robert Clive was a major factor in the eventual English success and the French were decisively beaten at Wandiwash in 1760. The result was unchallenged English power, combined with overweening self-confidence. An admiration for disciplined European troops was instilled in the minds of Indian rulers and subsequently prompted them to call on European assistance on an increased scale and with fatal results.

Clive moved on to Bengal to recover Calcutta (or rather the fortified trading post called Fort William that was its nucleus) from Siraj-ud-daula of Bengal who had captured it in 1756. From this Clive went on to put a rival claimant on the throne of Bengal through bluff and the battle of Plassey (1757) and at one blow made the East India Company the only real power in north-east India.

The story of how the British gained and lost India is too well-known or too recent to be worth even summarising here, but a few points which bear directly on the modern languages and their literatures must be made.

As the East India Company gained more and more territory to govern, and as it exercised its control in more and more spheres within those territories it was led almost against its will to affect the social and cultural life of the Indian peoples. The first major impact of western culture came in Bengal which was the heart of British power and the seat of the Governor General – given authority over Bombay and Madras by the Regulating Act of 1773. The founding of Fort William College in 1800 and the establishment of a press at Serampore in the same year by the Baptist Missionary William Carey were twin growing points which eventually bore fruit in the form of the creation of text-books, which meant in effect the creation of expository prose itself, in Bengali, Hindi, Urdu and Marathi. The real impetus came later, however, when after the final defeat of the Marathas in 1818 and the clearing up of the ensuing mess, western educational institutions were imported wholesale from 1835 onwards. The year of the Mutiny was also the year of the foundation of the universities of Bombay and of Calcutta.

It was the Brahman caste, deprived of many of its traditional sources of livelihood, that took up the new opportunities of education with most enthusiasm. Throughout India the Brahmans turned themselves from a community of orthodox, highly traditionalist priests into the intellectual élite of India, providing the clerks and executives of government as well as most of the teachers in the new schools and universities. It was from the ranks of these same teachers, journalists and lawyers that came the first generation of writers of the western literary genres. Meanwhile the British concentrated on conciliating the old ruling classes – the princes and rich merchants who had almost without exception remained loyal to them during the Mutiny – and scarcely noticed that the new, westernised, city-dwelling Brahman élite was evolving within itself a fierce patriotism that would eventually make their rule untenable.

TOWARDS INDEPENDENCE

This opposition took shape within the framework of the Indian National Congress, founded in 1885 as a mildly reformist society professing loyalty to British rule and even having Englishmen as its first presidents, but by 1900 transformed into a forum for all kinds of criticism of the government. It was galvanised by the leadership of two Maharashtrian Brahmans, Gokhale and Ṭiḷak, each standing for a different way forward: the first liberal, admiring the west in many things, urging social reform of Hindu society to make it fit for independence; the second, Lokamānya Ṭiḷak, glorying in the romantic past of Hindu culture and the Maratha empire and demanding political independence first and reform, if at all, later. Though the moderates won the day in Congress in 1907, the troubled story of India until independence in 1947 is proof enough that the activists were not discouraged, especially when the charismatic leadership of Mahātmā Gāndhi brought popular backing to a demand which combined both social reform and hostility to British rule. There are few works of Indian literature written during this period which do not reflect in some degree these two themes.

Finally, independence brought on a whole series of changes which are proving crucial for the further development of Indian languages and literatures. First, Partition itself; this has made Urdu into the language of a separate and hostile nation – Pakistan, while Hindi, so closely allied to it, has been burdened with the additional responsibility of replacing English as the only viable interstate language of India. Secondly the central government of India has been increasingly and continuously subjected to demands to make the boundaries of the states of India correspond with the boundaries of the language areas, so that now Andhra includes all the Telugu speaking districts for instance, while Bombay has been split into Maharashtra and Gujarat. The linguistic nationalism that brought this about against the wishes of the central government may do much for the status and development of the individual languages, but is hardly a unifying force. The language problem, the attempt to create an acceptable national language for the whole of India, is among the most difficult that the Indian people have yet to settle.

INDIAN LITERATURE

THE VEDAS

Indian literature begins with the Vedas, or more strictly perhaps, with parts of the *Ṛg-veda*, that collection of hymns and ritual formulae of the first Aryan invaders of India which have already been referred to. Since the *Ṛg-veda* was preserved orally for many centuries before it became more or less fixed in the form in which we know it, it can only be given a very conjectural date of 1500 to 1000 BC. It is followed at later and still conjectural dates by the other Vedas – *Sāma-veda*, *Yajur-veda* and *Atharva-veda* – on the whole increasingly less poetic and more concerned with the proper technique of sacrifice and the exposition of ritual. Upon these was based a superstructure of works that are ostensibly commentaries, though many of them are works of philosophical speculation in their own right. These are listed traditionally under various names: *Brāhmaṇas*, *Āraṇyakas* and *Upaniṣadas* – these last well known in the west because in them the vein of mystical speculation predominates. All are collectively known as *śṛti*, literally 'heard', because they are deemed to have been dictated by a god and merely taken down by some sage or other mortal. Together with the *Vedāngas*, more prosaic works which elucidate the merely mechanical niceties of the *Vedas* (metre, grammar, etymology etc.), they constitute the Vedic period of Sanskrit literature, say 1500 to 200 BC, which is entirely devoted to these religious texts and their offshoots and is written in an archaic language which is patently more close to the Indo-Aryan parent language and to Old Iranian. This is an over-simplification of course and it should be remembered that many of the *Upaniṣadas* at least were produced well after this period.

The language of the later Vedic writings is that described by the grammarian Pāṇini in the fifth century BC in what is probably the most scientific and sophisticated account of any language to be given before the age of modern linguistics. Strictly speaking it is only from this time on that one can talk of Sanskrit, the purified and cultivated literary language that was bequeathed to future generations by Pāṇini and later grammarians such as Patanjali. By 500 BC the spoken tongues of Northern India had already developed to the stage called Prakrit. It is Prakrit that is used in the inscriptions of Aśoka in the third century BC and in the early writings of the Buddhists and Jains.

THE EPICS

There follow the Epics, the two great epic poems of the Indian tradition which are to India what Homer is to European culture and much more beside. The *Mahābhārata* tells the tale of the great battle that was waged for eighteen days at Kurukṣetra by the Ganges between the Pāṇḍava brothers (the heroes) and the hordes of Kauravas who were trying to dispossess them of their kingdom. It may well be that the story first arose from some real pitched battle between rival Aryan tribes in the shadowy years when they were establishing themselves in the north Indian plains, but in the course of time by constant accretions it has grown to mammoth size, absorbing subsidiary stories that are often retold in their own right, as well as long sections of religious speculation and propaganda. The *Bhagavadgītā* itself is no more than a late interpolation inserted into the *Mahābhārata* at a convenient point. Perhaps the basic story of the *Mahābhārata* was first evolved around the fifth century BC. Perhaps it attained the approximate form in which we know it today about the third century AD. Probably the *Gītā* was added in the eighth century. That is all we can say.

Similarly for the *Rāmāyaṇa* – the tale of king Rāma, the loss of his kingdom and later of his wife Sītā, and how he regained them both after conquering Rāvaṇa, the demon king of Ceylon, with the aid of the monkey king Hanumān. There is more unity to this epic, but again it has evolved over the centuries, been expanded, made into an exemplum of morality and loaded with moral exhortations. All we can say of it and of the sage Vālmīki who is supposed to have written it is that it is perhaps slightly more recent than the *Mahābhārata*. What one can say – and this is really more important than dates and attributions – is that the matter of these two epic poems, their characters, their main episodes, the doings of the gods and demigods into which their main protagonists have grown, form part of the mental furniture of every Hindu Indian, whether educated or illiterate, in a way that is unparalleled in Europe. To make a fair comparison as a source of reference and quotation you would need to combine the Bible with the Greek and Roman epics, then add *Pilgrim's Progress* and the better-known plays of Shakespeare.

SANSKRIT LITERATURE

The Epics provide a transition to the period of true Classical Sanskrit. From about the end of the first century AD with the fragmentary relics of the work of the Buddhist poet and dramatist Aśvaghoṣa, we find this polished, literary language used for an ever-growing flood of imaginative and didactic writing.

The branch of Sanskrit literature that has most status is called *kāvya* or *mahākāvya* and consists of long narrative poems usually based on stories from the Epics or other traditional material. The most celebrated Sanskrit poet Kālidāsa, who wrote at the Gupta court around AD 400, is credited with two of the best of these. Connected with this category are the prose romances – long rambling tales of love and separation – of which Bāṇa's *Kādambari* is the type and has given its name to the common noun for a novel in one of the modern Indian languages. There is also much lyric poetry; often short, one stanza poems which sometimes represent the sole known production of their authors and are only known from their inclusion in one of the anthologies of 'gems' or *subhāṣita* which were produced by later Sanskrit compilers. A great deal of later Sanskrit literature is marred for western tastes by rhetoric in the pejorative sense; by technical virtuosity of the sort that produces poems of which each couplet starts and finishes with the same letter of the alphabet, or a work such as one of Daṇḍin's which tells the story of the *Rāmāyaṇa* but can be read backwards to give an equally good version of the *Mahābhārata.* All the same there are many things in Sanskrit poetry which contain great beauty of description and evocation of subtle emotion. The *Meghaduta* of Kālidāsa, which was first introduced to the west by Tagore, is a great and beautiful poem by any standard.

Next one must mention the collections of fables and stories in a mixture of prose and verse whose themes are inextricably linked with the whole Indo-European stock of folk-tale themes. Most famous of these and most re-adapted in every modern language, are the *Pancatantra* and *Hitopadeśa,* dated vaguely to the eighth and ninth centuries respectively.

One of the great prides of Sanskrit literature is its drama with a string of famous plays from Kālidāsa's *Śakuntalā* to Śri Harṣa in the seventh century and including Śūdraka's *Mṛcchakaṭikā* – the one which with its strong plot and humour is most likely to appeal to a western audience. Sanskrit plays must have a happy ending and in general the resultant melodrama and the overworking of coincidence are a little hard to take. An interesting feature of Sanskrit drama is the convention that though kings and noblemen speak regular Sanskrit, women and lower class characters speak different brands of Prakrit. One should remember that during the classical Sanskrit period, say between AD 400 and 1000, works were also written in Prakrit languages which themselves were increasingly becoming dead languages conventionally associated with different literary forms or with the religious propaganda of specific sects (*eg* Maharashtri Prakrit used for love lyrics and also favoured by a sub-sect of Jain writers). The languages that men were actually speaking over these years are called Apabhraṃśas or 'corruptions' and a few of these made fleeting appearances as literary languages before giving way to the modern tongues which are their direct descendants. Apart from the dialogue in Sanskrit plays, the literature written in these Middle Indian Languages, as the Prakrits and Apabhraṃśas are collectively termed, is mainly sectarian and of small concern to the non-specialist.

Before leaving the imaginative half of Sanskrit literature one must mention the *Purāṇas*. These vast compendia of divine and earthly knowledge, of which there are eighteen major and eighteen minor ones, are undated and largely undatable. They evolved with the new, more personal worship of Śiva and Viṣṇu around the beginning of the millennium and were constantly re-worked and added to right up to the tenth century – indeed the bulk of some, such as the *Padma-purāṇa*, may date from as late as this. Many of them are Vaiṣṇavite – that is they deal with Viṣṇu and the tales of his different manifestations on earth or *avatārs*, with dynasties of kings who were connected with these stories, with prescription of the rites of Vaiṣṇavite worship, lists of holy places, directions for the siting and construction of temples and so on. Probably the most seminal is the *Bhāgavata Purāṇa* which has a tenth chapter (*Daśama skandha*) telling the story of Kṛṣṇa which has been used over and over again in every succeeding century and every single modern Indian language. Starting a little later and similar to the *Purāṇas* but connected with the worship of Śakti (the female principle) are the *Tantras*. These huge collections of legend and pseudo-history and ritual prescription provide an inexhaustible source of material to be added to the matter of the Epics.

Finally there is a whole class of works which are on the margins of literature. Beginning with the *Arthaśāstra* of Kauṭilya, Sanskrit proliferates with didactic works in prose and verse on government and politics (the *Arthaśāstras*), on law and ethics (the *Dharmaśāstras*), on medicine, astrology, music, grammar and lexicography, and, particularly important for later literatures, the *alankāraśāstras* or treatises on rhetoric and composition. Medieval Indian writers had a passion for categorisation and whatever subject they deal with, one can be sure to find a list, whether it concerns the *rāgas* of music, the permissible figures of speech in poetry or the ways in which a king may seek to undermine the government of a rival state.

Works of this type continued to be written in Sanskrit right up to the nineteenth century and beyond, for Sanskrit is still for many Indians the language of culture and traditional learning. However, one may say that major literary works in Sanskrit and Prakrit dry up to a thin trickle from about AD 1000 and it was then that the modern languages developed out of their various Apabhraṃśa predecessors. Their first flowering as carriers of literature appears roughly after the shock of the first Muslim invasions was over in the late twelfth century. This though was only in the North and one must not forget that in the Dravidian south of India Tamil had its own classical era that was contemporary with classical Sanskrit.

TAMIL LITERATURE

There is a tradition that writing was first introduced to the Tamil-speaking south by contact with the empire of Aśoka. Some of the more patriotic Tamils put the origins of their literature back to extravagantly early dates, motivated no doubt by the desire to equal the antiquity of the *Vedas*. There are supposed to have been two *sangams* or assemblies of bards of which the second lasted for 3,700 years at some vague time BC. The only work surviving from these mythical times is the *Tolkāppyam* which is partly a grammar and partly a work on rhetoric listing the various themes which are suitable for literary treatment. In fact this accords pretty well with the works of the third *sangam* era which is approximately coterminous with the first Cola dynasty, first to fourth century AD, so *Tolkāppyam* is probably of a similar date. The literature of this third *sangam* consists of verses by numerous poets of whom we know nothing but their names, collected into anthologies which are themselves grouped into three major collections known as *Eṭṭutokai* (the Eight Anthologies), *Paṭṭuppāṭṭu* (the Ten Songs) and *Padinenkiḷkkaṇakku* (the Eighteen Minor Works). The poems of these Tamil Anthologies are refreshingly secular by comparison with the contemporary Sanskrit literature of north India and are all concerned with the perennial themes of love and war. One of the latest (perhaps sixth century) and most famous of these anthologies is the *Tirukkural*, often referred to simply as the *Kural*, which is a collection of verse aphorisms.

Following on these earliest Tamil works come the so-called Epics, the *Cilappatikāram* with its Buddhist inspired sequel *Maṇimekalai*. They are romantic stories of love and death and retribution rather similar to the Sanskrit *kāvyas*. From now on (sixth to seventh century) the influence of Sanskrit becomes increasingly obvious and up to the twelfth century Tamil literature offers the spectacle of the accretion of two more vast anthologies of sectarian works which are much more in the main Indian tradition. The *Tirumurai* is a collection of religious verse in twelve books by the Śaiva saint poets or Nāyanmārs. The *Nālāyirapparipantam* is a comparable work by the Vaiṣṇava Ālvārs.

MEDIEVAL LITERATURE

It should be quite clear by now that all dates for all early periods of Indian literature are highly conjectural, and the dates of the earliest writings in the modern languages are no exception to this. Of course the languages which eventually attained literary status, such as Bengali, Kanarese and Malayalam, must have developed independently as spoken languages long before we find any trace of them, though inscriptions give us some clue in many cases. In general, though, they had to wait until some point after AD 1000 when the appearance of an appropriate minor kingdom could give them a territorial base and status. Thus in Kerala, the home ground of Malayalam, anything written before is in Classical Tamil which was the literary language of the whole Dravidian South. The Tamil epic *Ciloppatikāram* was written by one Ilankovaṭikaḷ, supposedly a younger brother of a Cera (Kerala) king and is claimed by Malayalam as well as Tamil. The Ceras were always peaceably dependent on the more powerful Cola kingdom in the East and it is not without significance that the end of the twelfth century, which saw the collapse of the late Cola empire, also gives us the first Malayalam literary work – the *Rāmacaritam* assigned vaguely to the early thirteenth century. Similarly the first Marathi works appear in the late thirteenth century towards the end of the short rule of the Yādavas of Deogiri. In the north-east Bengali is supposed to have developed under the Pāla kings of Bengal and Bihar in the tenth century, but the fact remains that the earliest example of Bengali literature, the Tantric hymns called *Caryāpadas,* cannot be shown to be earlier than the twelfth century and are claimed by all the north-eastern languages – Bengali, Oriya and even Assamese – as their earliest gem. In the north-west the earliest works in Gujarati, Rajasthani and western Hindi dialects such as Braj, are inextricably mixed at a comparable date and have to be lumped together under a heading devised by western scholars and called Old Western Rajasthani.

Kanarese, the Dravidian language most influenced by Sanskrit in vocabulary and poetic themes, claims its first work (the *Kavirājamārga* – another treatise on poetics) at the early date of *c* 850, which is then followed by a suspiciously large gap in well-attested, extant works until the twelfth century. It is to be doubted whether the language of these very early fragments is any closer to what is understood by Kanarese today than are, say, works in Jain Prakrit to modern Gujarati. All that the outsider can say is that their vocabulary appears to be so heavily Sanskritic that their status is at least questionable.

When one remembers the vast extent of the Indian sub-continent and the fact that literary effort has been pursued in a dozen or so major literary languages for an average of seven hundred years, it can be appreciated how difficult it is to generalise without distortion about the modern languages. Nevertheless one can broadly say that until *c* 1500 the main theme of Indian literature was the re-working of the Sanskrit classics (Epics, *Purāṇas* and *kāvyas*). Many of these often very free and localised re-workings have remained to this day as the most popular version of the relevant story. Such are the *Mahābhārata* of Sāraḷā Dāsa in Oriya, the *Rāmāyaṇa* of Kampan in Tamil and of Kṛttibas Ojhā in Bengali, Bhālaṇ's *Kādambari* in Gujarati, the *Rāmāyaṇa* and the *Bhagavadgītā* of the Paṇikkar brothers in Malayalam and the series of *sandeśa kāvya* (message poems) in the same language which take their inspiration from Kālidāsa's *Meghaduta.* In Telugu there is the *Āndhra Bhāgavatam* of Potana and the first major work of Marathi literature is Jnānadeva's great expansion of the *Gītā.*

There are other, lesser strands. In Old Western Rajasthani there is a bardic strain with poems celebrating kings and heroic battles. Such are the *Prithirāja Rāso* of Cand Bardāi and the *Kānhaḍade-prabandha* of Padmanābha – not unlike the *chansons de geste* of western Europe. Popular songs and sayings are recorded early in many literatures, though the modernised forms in which we have them prevent any exact dating. There are the early ballads of East Bengal, the *Ḍākar bachen* (Sayings of Dak) in Assamese, the *Brata kathā* of Orissa.

The strength of various religious sects in different parts of India produced more localised literary groupings. Thus the Mahānubhāva sect, which flourished in Berar from the late thirteenth century produced nearly all the early prose literature that exists in Marathi in accounts of their saints and founding fathers. In Kanarese, and to a lesser extent in Telugu, the Lingayat sect founded by Basava in the twelfth century produced many hymn-like Śaivite verses called *vacanas*. The residue of the once great Jain religion in the Gujarati and Kanarese regions has left these literatures with many long poems telling the life stories of the Jain saints or *tirthankaras*. In the north-east the greater influence of Tantric and Śākta sects gives a characteristic slant to early Bengali and Oriya. In Bengali especially the *Mangala kāvyas* in praise of the goddess Manasā have no counterpart in other literatures.

Undoubtedly, though, it is the emergence of the India-wide cult of Kṛṣṇa that is the most productive theme of this era. Developing from a walking-on part in the *Mahābhārata*, Kṛṣṇa has become God in the *Bhagavadgītā*. The stories and legends about his childhood and youth reached their fullest extent in the *Bhāgavata-purāṇa* and the trimmings were added in the Sanskrit poem *Gītā-Govinda* by the twelfth century Bengali court poet Jayadeva. It was here that a named partner, Rādhā, was introduced as heroine in place of the undifferentiated milkmaids of the *Bhāgavata*, giving rise to a great flood of Rādhā-Kṛṣṇa poetry, particularly in the North. Foremost amongst these are the love lyrics of Vidyāpati who wrote in Bihari in the fifteenth century, and Candidās in Bengali with his *Śri-Kṛṣṇa-kirtana*.

BHAKTI WRITING

It is in connection with Kṛṣṇa worship at the end of the fifteenth century that we meet the culmination of the first surge of *bhakti* writing which was to dominate Indian creative literature for the next couple of centuries – which is why 1500 makes a convenient watershed. *Bhakti* broadly means 'devotion' and expresses a personal feeling towards the deity – any deity – like that of a woman towards her lover. As a way of salvation it is discussed and even recommended in much earlier times. The attitude it entails is expressed in the Vaiṣṇavite hymns of Tamil Ālvārs, but it seems that to reach full fruition it needed the injection of enthusiasm from the fifteenth century Sufi poets of north India who wrote in a vein of mystical devotion to God – the Muslim God – that seems to have aroused an immediate response in their Hindu compatriots. The god of Kabir (1430–1518), born a Muslim and writing in Avadhi or Eastern Hindi, is a universal god neither Muslim nor Hindu and his 'hymns' have a place in the *Âdi Grantha* of the Sikhs, along with devotional works of the early Sikh gurus like Nānak and Arjun and of orthodox Hindu poets like the nebulous Marathi Nāmdev. One can think of this early *bhakti* as a kind of irrigation channel of pure water which flows into the fields of the various Indian literatures to nourish the local crops. In Bengal it merged with the Rādhā-Kṛṣṇa cult to give Caitanya (1486–1533), the great teacher whose followers believed him to be an incarnation of Rādhā and Kṛṣṇa combined: half the subsequent Kṛsṇa poetry of Bengal was produced by men from among their ranks. In the vague borderland between Hindi and Gujarati it inspired the poetess Mirābāi, claimed by both languages, whose poems of intense, almost sexual longing are addressed to Śri Kṛṣṇa in the great temple of Dvārkā in Saurāṣṭra. In Assam Śankaradev (1449–1568) who founded a Bhāgavata sect, is no doubt an offshoot of the Caitanya cult. In Western Hindi (Braj) Sur Dās and the group of poets known as the Aṣṭa Chāp wrote Kṛṣṇa verse in the sixteenth century. In Kanarese the Kṛṣṇa *bhakti* songs of Purandara Dās (1494–1564) are still among the most popular and deeply felt of southern devotional verse. In Marathi the *bhakti* stream was diverted towards Śri Viṭṭhal of Panḍharpur, a local god of disputed origins who had been brought within the Vaiṣṇavite fold by investing him with suitable legends. It was to Viṭṭhal that Tukārām in the early seventeenth century addressed his verse.

For other poets the god-hero of the *Rāmāyaṇa* became the chief object of devotion. Here the great name is the Hindi (Avadhi) poet Tulsi Dās (1532–1627) who, apart from lyric hymns to Rām, wrote what is the most important version of the *Rāmāyaṇa* for Hindi-speaking north India. This brings us back full circle to versions of classical Sanskrit works which continued in vogue in most languages of India right up to the modern period – the Tulsi *Rāmāyaṇa* in Hindi, the Bengali *Mahābhārata* by Kāśirām Das, the works of Baḷarām Dās and Jagannāth Dās in Oriya, the *Bhāgavata* and *Bhāvārtha Rāmāyaṇa* of Eknāth in Marathi, the Malayalam *Rāmāyaṇa* and *Mahābhārata* of Tuncattu Eruttacchan.

Allied to these, but less popular, are a host of works by learned and court poets who flourished under the patronage of Muslim rulers, or of the Hindu kingdom of Vijayanagar in the case of sixteenth century Telugu. These were poets using the main traditional material (originality of theme was never a virtue) but striving to emulate in their language the most intricate verbal conjuring of the Sanskrit rhetoricians. In general one can say that today most of these poets are admired but not loved.

MUSLIM LITERATURE

The literature of the Muslims of the sub-continent shows a somewhat parallel development. For them, Persian was the classical language of culture, as well as being a living language at the royal court and in the administration. Not until the early sixteenth century did Urdu, a language developed out of the impact of Persian upon the colloquial speeches of the Punjab-Delhi-UP region, become the vehicle of worthwhile literature. It first flourished in the Muslim kingdoms of the Deccan, where the language had been carried by migrants from the north, and reached its culmination in the lyric poetry of Wali (*d* 1707). His visit to Delhi, and the popularity his poetry won there, helped to stimulate the ousting of Persian as the language of poetry, and before long, the ousting of the Deccan as the centre of Urdu literature. From the mid-eighteenth to the mid-nineteenth century, first in Delhi, then in Lucknow, and then in both together, classical Urdu poetry reached its zenith. As in earlier Hindu poetry, lyric poetry (the *g͟hazal*) is dominated by the themes of passionate sexual love, which serve also as the vehicle for the mystic's expression of devotion to his God, with the difference, however, that here it is the male lover that is identified with the mystic worshipper. Strongly humanist values are also prominent in this context. Mīr (*c* 1723–1810) and G͟hālib (1797–1869) are the two great and still unsurpassed exponents of this form. Other major forms of this period are exemplified by the satires of Sauda, the love narratives (*maṣ̤navīs*) of Mīr Hasan, and the elegies (*marṣ̤iyas*) of Anīs on the martyrdom of Husain, grandson of the Prophet, and of his companions. And outside this range altogether is Nazīr of Agra, the one great poet of the period who in the main broke with the classical forms and wrote of the joys and preoccupations of the ordinary man in a style closer to folk idiom. This kinship with folk sentiment also characterises much of the Muslim writing in the regional languages such as Pushtu, Sindhi and Panjabi, which remain the major regional languages of present-day West Pakistan. In the east, the same is true of Muslim Bengali literature. The Muslims contributed largely to folk literature, while it has been the Hindus who, out of all proportion to their numbers, have produced the literature of sophisticated culture. Otherwise Urdu to a great extent inherited the place of Persian in that cultured Muslims (and a significant stratum of culturally assimilated Hindus) have throughout the sub-continent tended to regard it as the only language fit to be the vehicle of good quality literature.

These then were the main themes of Indian literature up to the nineteenth century. In the early period folk tales, bardic verse and versions of the Sanskrit classics; from the fifteenth century, and increasingly from 1500, *bhakti* devotional lyrics mainly addressed to Kṛṣṇa and Rām (but Śaivite too where the worship of Śiva was strong) and still more versions of the classics, both popular and learned. There are of course many other minor ingredients: satirists like Akhā of Gujarat; mystical philosophical poets like Lallā Devi of Kashmir in the fourteenth century; a few completely original works like the fourteenth-century Kanarese romance *Lilāvati* by Nemicandra or the eighteenth-century Oriya *Samara-taranga*, a war poem telling of the battles between the petty rulers of Orissa and the Marathas. One must recall too the Muslim poets, especially in Hindi, Panjabi and Bengali who frequently wrote romances and tales from Muslim history and legend in a style that is almost undistinguishable from their Hindu contemporaries: Manjhan, Qutban and Jāyasi in Hindi, Daulat Kāzi and Ālāol in Bengali. In the major Muslim language, Urdu, themes of human and divine love, and romantic tales also figure, often at a more sophisticated level and in a less fully syncretic form.

Nearly all literature is in verse, drawing either on the verse forms of Sanskrit (or, in the case of Urdu, of Persian) or on innumerable local metres suitable for singing which vary with each language. Of prose there was very little save that which occurs in *campu*, a style common in the Dravidian south where verse sequences are linked by short prose passages that carry the action forward. Still there was a little, and from the seventeenth century Assamese with its *buranjis* and Marathi with its *bakhars* both have a tradition of historical chronicles in prose. In the Deccan, there is some romantic prose narrative in Urdu.

True drama scarcely existed in spite of the strong dramatic tradition in Sanskrit, though most parts of India had a kind of folk theatre involving the enactment of puranic legends to the accompaniment of song, with seasonal variations at times of major festivals. In the south, and especially in Kerala, this developed into a kind of dance drama *Kathākali* – which is an art form in itself but has little to do with literature.

WESTERN INFLUENCES

This was the state of development which Indian literature had reached at the time when, with the arrival of the British, western cultural influence began to flood into India. From 1757 onwards the East India Company increasingly assumed political power in Bengal, which was followed by its unchallenged rule in Western India after the final collapse of the Maratha Empire in 1818. In this process of westernisation Bengal and Bengali were always slightly in the lead and Marathi a close second. After the founding of educational institutions and the sponsoring of school text-books and of modern prose in which to write them, it was some time before works of literature began to emerge from the welter of translations and adaptations of western models. Gradually, however, in each language at a date determined by its proximity to one of the new capital cities (Calcutta, Bombay, Madras) the various genres emerged and have since dominated the literary scene, bringing Indian literature fully into the world pattern.

At the earliest stage of western influence, when western ideas were being accepted wholesale, Bengali, in advance of the other languages had major representatives. Two of these were Rām Mohan Roy (1774–1833) who was the founder of the *Brahma Sabhā* and who attempted a synthesis of Hinduism with Christian ethics, and Michael Madhusudhan Datta, a great poet who was in fact converted to Christianity; these have no counterparts among the other languages of India. Later there came a partial reaction and between 1870 and 1900 each language seems to have produced its own 'grand old man': these men were usually a combination of journalist and essay writer, founders of literary magazines and patrons of younger writers; they were steeped in English literature, yet ardently patriotic and determined to use the best of western culture for the betterment of Indian and Hindu (or in the case of Urdu, of Muslim) society. One could single out Vidyāsāgar perhaps in Bengali (though Bengali has a galaxy of great men), Viṣṇuśāstri Cipaluṇkar for Marathi, Gauriśankar Rāy in Orissa, Vireśalingam for Telugu, Rājam Aiyar for Tamil and, pre-eminently the all-round litterateur, Bhāratendu Hariścandra in Hindi. Then come the first major novelists, some of them near professionals – Bankimcandra Chatterji in Bengali, Hari Nārāyaṇ Āpṭe in Marathi, Phakirmohan Senāpati in Oriya, G. M. Tripāthi in Gujarati, Matavaiyar in Tamil, O. Cantu Menon in Malayalam, and Nazīr Ahmad in Urdu. Kanarese and Telugu both had to wait for the twentieth century before they produced much in the way of novels and short stories.

Hand in hand with the creation of prose literature went drama, benefiting from the twin models of the western stage (mainly Shakespeare at first) and the rediscovered Sanskrit tradition. Bengali and Marathi especially produced a number of major dramatists around the turn of the century. Their plays, often using traditional stories to carry a social or political message, are thought of as 'classics' today and are still frequently performed. At the same time every language produced a rich vein of personal, lyric poetry, heavily influenced by the English Romantics. It would be impossible to list even the main artists who have practised these various forms in twelve languages over the last seventy years. It would be individious even to select a few typical writers from each language. Still, there are a handful of names who impose themselves. First, incontestably, is Rabindranāth Tagore, the Bengali poet, dramatist, novelist, short-story writer, painter; a master craftsman in almost every field of art and the only Indian writer to have made a serious impact on the outside world. Two other novelists: Śaratcandra Chatterji the Bengali and Prem Cand who turned from Urdu to Hindi half way through his career, though he continued to write in Urdu as well. The Urdu (and Persian) poet and thinker Iqbāl, the Marathi poet B. S. Marḍhekar whose experimental verse, admittedly influenced by Eliot and Pound, is still more exciting than anything written since his early death in 1956. And perhaps one should end with another world figure, Mahātmā Gāndhi, whose terse, vigorous prose style is arguably the best thing to have happened to Gujarati writing in the twentieth century.

INDIVIDUAL WRITERS AND WORKS

Āgarkar, Gopāl Ganeś (1856–95). Marathi essayist, journalist and social reformer. First colleague, then bitter opponent of Lokamānya Ṭiḷak.

Akbar of Allahabad (1846–1921). Urdu humorous and satirical poet. Mocked slavish imitation of British ways and dedication to material success, and inculcated pride in best Indian Muslim traditions.

Akhā (*c* 1615–74). Gujarati poet. Famous for his *chappās* – six-line satirical verse epigrams.

Ālāol (seventeenth century). Bengali Muslim poet of court of Arakan. Wrote *Padmāvati* a romance, and *Dārā Sikandar Nāmā*, an adaptation of Nizāmi's *Iskandarnāmah.*

Ālvārs. The twelve Vaiṣṇava religious poets of seventh-century (?) Tamil whose works appear in the collection called *Nālāyirappirapantam.*

Anīs (1801–74). Greatest exponent of the Urdu *marṣiya*, the elegy on the martyrdom of the Prophet's grandson Ḥusain and his companions, which is recited each year at the anniversary of their death.

Apṭe, Hari Nārāyaṇ (1864–1919). First major Marathi novelist. Wrote twenty-one novels of which *Mi* (1895) and *Uṣahkāl* (1897) are the most famous.

Arjun (1563–1606). Fifth *guru* of the Sikhs. Wrote verse in Panjabi Hindi and was the main compiler of the Sikh *Granth Sāhib.*

Arṇimāl (eighteenth century). Kashmiri poetess. Love lyrics addressed to her missing husband and nature poetry.

Aṣṭa Chāp. Collective name for a group of eight Hindi (Braj) Kṛṣṇa poets of the sixteenth century, of whom **Nand Dās** and **Sur Dās** are the most famous.

Āzād, Muḥammad Ḥusain (1827–1910). Urdu literary critic, essayist, poet and historical writer. Wrote the first account of the Urdu poets on modern lines. Encouraged, and wrote, new forms of Urdu verse on the model of English. A book on the reign of Akbar, Mughal emperor, 1556–1605.

Baḍajenā, Brajanāth (1730–95). Oriya. *Caturbinoda* – prose story cycle; *Samara-taranga* – martial poem.

Baḷarām Dās (early sixteenth century). Oriya poet. *Rāmāyaṇa* and *Lakṣmi Purāṇa Suānga*, a Vaiṣṇavite work.

Bāṇa (seventh century). Sanskrit. *Kādambarī*, a romance in ornate poetic prose; *Harṣa-carita*, a biography of his patron, king Harṣa.

Bandyopādhyāy: Bhabānī Caraṇ (1787–1848). Bengali reactionary writer. *Kalikātā Kamalālay* (1823) – a satire on Western influence on Bengal.

Bandyopādhyāy: Kṛṣṇamohan (1813–85). Bengali reformist writer and Christian convert. *Vidyā-kalpadruma* – an encyclopaedia in thirteen vols.; *Persecuted* (1831), a play in English.

Banerji (Bandyopādhyāy), Bibhuti Bhuṣaṇ (1894–1950). Bengali novelist. Author of *Pather Pāncāli*, *Aparājita* etc.

Bardaloi, Rajanikānt (1867–1939). Assamese novelist. *Mirijiyari* (1895) the first Assamese novel.

Baruā, Hemcandra (1837–96). Assamese author of plays, essays, grammar and a lexican, *Hemakośa*.

Bendre, Dattātray Rāmcandra (1896–). Leading modern Kanarese poet.

Beschi, Constantinus (1680–1746). Jesuit priest who became Tamil scholar and author. *Tempāvaṇi* (1724) – story of Joseph.

Bezbaruā, Lakṣmīnāth (1868–1938). Assamese essayist, playwright, short-story writer. Co-founder of the influential literary Journal *Jonaki*.

Bhagavadgītā. Philosophical work in the form of Kṛṣṇa's advice to Arjuna on the battlefield of Kurukṣetra, which forms a late eighth-century interpolation in the *Mahābhārata*.

Bhāgavata Purāṇa. The most popular of the Vaiṣṇavita *Purāṇas*. The tenth book or *skandha* is devoted to the story of Kṛṣṇa.

Bhālaṇ (*c* 1426–1500). The father of narrative verse in Gujarati. *Kādambarī* – from Bāṇa; *Nalākhyāna* – the Puranic story.

Bhanja, Upendra (1670–1720). Oriya poet to whom over fifty works are ascribed. Much influenced by Sanskrit rhetorical tricks.

Bhārati, C. Subrahmaṇya (1882–). Leading modern Tamil poet. *Kaṇṇan Pāṭṭu* – cycle of poems on Kṛṣṇa.

Bhartṛhari (seventh century). Sanskrit anthologist and poet.

Bhāsa (end of fourth century). Earliest Sanskrit dramatist. Thirteen plays attributed to him, esp. *Svapna-Vāsavadatta*.

Bhavabhuti (eighth century). Sanskrit dramatist, author of three plays, the best known being *Uttara-rāmacarita*.

Bihārī Lāl (*c* 1603–63). Hindi (Braj) court poet. *Sat-sai* – cycle of seven hundred short poems on the Rādhā-Kṛṣṇa theme.

Bulhey Shāh (1680–1758). Panjabi Muslim poet. *Kāfis* – short Sufi hymns.

Caitanya (1486–1533). Bengali religious reformer. See Kṛṣṇa Dās.

Cand Bardāi (twelfth century). Court poet of Pṛthvirāja, the last Hindu king of Delhi. *Prithirāja-rāso* – epic of the Muslim invasion in Old Western Rajasthani, known only in a seventeenth century version.

Candidās (fifteenth century). Bengali Vaiṣṇava poet. *Śri-Kṛṣṇa-kirtana*.

Caryāpadas (1050–1200). Obscure Buddhist and Śaivite Tantric hymns by various authors. The earliest texts of Bengali, also claimed by Assamese and Oriya.

Cavuṇḍarāya (tenth century). Kanarese Jain who erected the colossal statue at Srāvaṇ Belgol. First prose work in Kanarese ascribed to him: *Triṣaṣṭhi-lakṣaṇa-mahāpurāṇa* – a description of the twenty-four Jain *tirthankaras.*

Cayankoṇṭan (*c* 1100). Tamil poet. *Kalinkattupparam* – a bloodthirsty description of the Cola conquest of Kalinga.

Chātrik, Dhani Rām (1876–1954). Panjabi nature poet.

Chatterji (Caṭṭopādhyāy), Bankim Candra (1838–94). First great Bengali novelist. Fourteen novels on historical and nationalist themes, especially *Durgeśanandini* (1865), *Ānandamaṭha* (1882).

Chatterji, Śaratcandra (1876–1938). Most popular twentieth-century Bengali novelist who is widely known and translated throughout India.

Cipaluṇkar, Viṣṇuśāstri (1850–82). Marathi essayist. His periodical *Nibandhamālā* from 1874 marks the beginning of a truly indigenous Marathi prose style.

Ḍāk. A semi-mythical rustic wit, whose aphorisms under titles such as *Ḍāk-bhanita*, *Ḍāk-carita* appear in Assamese, Bengali, Oriya.

Dalpatrām Dahyābhāi (1820–98). Gujarati poet. Friend and collaborator of A. K. Forbes in founding Gujarat Vernacular Society in 1848.

Daṇḍin (seventh century). Highly artificial Sanskrit poet and prose writer. *Daśa-kumāra-carita* – a prose *kāvya.*

Datta, Michael Madhusudan (1824–73). Bengali poet, dramatist and Christian convert. Introduced sonnet into Bengali and wrote especially *Meghanāda* (1861), a European-style epic on a Puranic theme.

Dāud, Maulāna (fourteenth century). Earliest Hindi (Avadhi) Sufi poet. Wrote *Candāyan*, the Romance of Lorik and Candā, *c* 1370.

Daulat Kāzi (early seventeenth century). Bengali Muslim poet at Arakan court. *Sati-maynā* – romance on Lorik story – left incomplete and finished by **Ālāol.**

Dayārām (1767–1852). Last major Gujarati poet before impact of West. Erotic love lyrics (*garabo*) around Kṛṣṇa theme.

Dharma-Śāstra. Sanskrit manuals of law and ethics from various periods. About forty of them, of which *Mānava dharma-śāstra*, attributed to the legendary sage Bhṛgu, is most famous.

Diveṭiā, Narsiṃharāv (1859–1937). Gujarati romantic poet. *Smaraṇa-saṃhitā* (1915) – an elegy on the death of his son.

Duggal, Kartār Singh (1917–). Leading modern Panjabi short-story writer. Uses dialect of Rawalpindi.

Dvivedi, Mahāvir Prasād (1870–1938). Hindi essayist and man of letters. Editor of influential Allahabad journal *Sarasvati.*

Eknāth (1548–1600). Marathi Puranic poet and collator of *Jnāneśvari. Eknāthi Bhāgavata, Bhāvārtha Rāmāyaṇa etc.*

Eṭṭutokai – 'The eight anthologies' – one of the major collections of early Tamil verse, by many poets. Second to fourth centuries (?).
Gāḍgil, Gangādhar Gopāl (1923–). The most prolific living Marathi short-story writer. Also critic and humorist.
Gaḍkari, Ram Ganeśa (1885–1919). Marathi playwright (especially *Ekaca* Pyālā, 1917) and lyric poet – under the pen-name Govindāgraj.
Ghālib (1797–1869). Poet of Urdu and Persian. Perhaps the most popular of all Urdu *ghazal* poets. Classical themes with a strikingly modern ring. Ornate, but effective and moving Persian prose. Numerous Urdu letters; publication helped to establish cultured colloquial as a respectable literary medium. Many stories of his wit and humour.
Gobind Singh (1666–1708). The tenth Sikh *guru*. Composed religious and martial verse in Hindi and Panjabi.
Ḥālī (1837–1914). Urdu poet, biographer (including of Ghālib and of Sir Sayyid Aḥmad Khān), and critic. Good *ghazal* poet, but famous for his long poem *The Ebb and Flow of Islam*, which roused powerful support for the reforming movement of Sir Sayyid Aḥmad Khān. Wrote the first modern assessment of Urdu poetry, attempting to describe the essential features of poetry, and then surveying the major Urdu classical forms in this light.
Hariścandra, Bhāratendu (1846–84). Hindi dramatist, poet etc. Mainly famous as the patron and instigator of modern Hindi writing.
Harṣa. King of Kanauj (606–47) (See **Bāṇa**). Three Sanskrit plays: *Ratnāvali*, *Priyadarśikā* and *Nāgānanda* ascribed to him.
Hemacandra (1089–1173). Jain grammarian and polymath. His *Siddha-Hemacandra* and *Deśināmamālā* are unique sources of information on Prakrit and Apabhrāṃsa.
Hitopadeśa. Most celebrated expanded version of the Sanskrit story-cycle **Pancatantra,** by Nārāyaṇa in twelfth-century Bengal.
Ilankovaṭikaḷ. Reputed second-century royal author of the seventh-century Tamil epic: *Cilappatikāram* (The Ankle Bracelet).
Iqbāl, Sir Muḥammad (1873–1938). Incomparably the most popular Urdu poet of the present century. Much Persian verse also. Urges that God's will is that man must exert himself to make his own destiny. Pakistanis claim him as the prophet, and national poet, of Pakistan.
Jagannāth Dās (sixteenth century). Author of the Oriya *Bhāgavata*.
Jātaka. Early Buddhist tales illustrating verses from the Pali canon. Attributed to Buddhaghoṣa who collated the Theravada canon in Ceylon in the fifth century AD.
Jayadeva (twelfth century). Sanskrit court poet of the last Sena king of Bengal. Wrote *Gītā-Govinda*, a song-cycle on the life of Kṛṣṇa taken from the *Bhāgavata-purāṇa* and a major source of subsequent Kṛṣṇa poetry.
Jāyasi, Malik Muhammad (*fl* 1540). Hindi (Avadhi) Sufi poet. Wrote *Pad-*

māvati, an allegorical romance based on the sack of Chitor in 1303 and a seminal work throughout north India.

Jnānadeva (*fl* 1290). The first and greatest Marathi religious poet. His *Jnāneśvari* or *Bhāvārtha-dipikā* is an expansion and illustration of the *Bhagavadgītā*.

Jośi, Gauriśankar Govardhanrām (1892–). Prolific modern Gujarati short-story writer, under the name of 'Dhumaketu'.

Jośi, Umāśankar Jethālāl (1917–). Gujarati poet and critic.

Kabir (1430–1518 ?). Hindi (Avadhi) *bhakti* poet. *Bijak*, *Granthāvali* and hymns included in the Sikh *Grantha Sāhib*. A major figure who has inspired a living sect of Hinduism – the Kabir Panth.

Kālidāsa (376–454 ?). The unrivalled chief of Sanskrit poets: *Raghuvaṃśa*, *Kumārasambhava* (*kāvya*), *Meghaduta*, *Ṛtusaṃhāra*. Also plays: *Abhijnāna-Śakuntalā*, *Vikramorvaśiyā*.

Kampan (ninth–twelfth centuries ?). Author of the Tamil *Rāmāyaṇa*, one of the major works of classical Tamil.

Karanth, Kotā Śivarām (1902–). Popular Kanarese novelist, his best work being *Marali Mannige* (1940).

Kāśirām Dās (*c* 1600). Author of the best-known Bengali *Mahābhārata*.

Kaul, Zinda (1884–). Kashmiri poet, author of *Sumran* (1954).

Kauṭilya. Minister of Candragupta Maurya (*c* 322–298 BC) and supposed author of Sanskrit *Artha-śāstra*, a manual of statecraft which in its present form is definitely much later (AD 300 ?). Kautilya is also known as Cānākya and Viṣṇugupta.

Kavirāj Cakravarti. Court poet of Ahom king of Assam (1696–1714) and his successor. Translated *Śakuntalā* and *Gitā-Govinda*.

Kāvya. Sanskrit technical term for a long narrative poem (*cf* **Kalidāsa**) or even a rhetorical prose work such as **Daṇḍin's** *Daśa-kumāra-carita* or **Bāṇa's** *Kādambari*.

Keśav-Sut (1866–1905). Pen-name of the Marathi poet Kṛṣṇaji Keśav **Dāmle.** The first 'modern' Marathi poet with a strong element of social reformer in him.

Khāḍilkar, Kṛṣṇaji Prabhākar (1872–1948). Violently nationalist Marathi playwright (especially *Kicak-vadha*, 1910) and collaborator of **Ṭiḷak** on *Kesarī*.

Khān Khānā, Abdur Rahim (1556–1613). Hindi (Braj) poet at court of Akbar. *Sat-sai* – seven hundred couplets on Kṛṣṇa theme.

Kṛṣṇa Dās (Kavirāj) (*fl* 1581). Disciple of Caitanya and author of the most important work of Caitanya hagiography – *Caitanya-caritāmṛta.*

Kṛṣṇamurtti, R. ('Kalki') (1899–1954). Popular Tamil novelist of the inter-war years.

Kṛttibās Ojhā (fifteenth century). Bengali poet. Author of the first and most popular version of the *Rāmāyaṇa* in Bengali.

Kumāravyās (early fifteenth century). Produced an unfinished Kanarese version of the *Mahābhārata* in which Kṛṣṇa has the leading role.

Lakṣmiśa (eighteenth century). Kanarese poet. His main work is *Jaiminibhārata*, based on an episode of the *Mahābhārata*.

Lallādevi (*c* 1335–86). Kashmiri poetess. *Lallā-vākyāni* – mystical verse around themes of Śaivite philosophy.

Lallu Lāl (1763–1835). Wrote the first prose work that can be classified as Hindi (*Premasāgar*, 1803), as a textbook.

Mādaḷā Pānji. Perhaps the oldest Oriyan text – a chronicle of the kings of Orissa and the temple at Puri from 1042 – but some say that it is a late forgery.

Māḍgulkar, Vyankateś Digambar (1927–). Marathi short-story writer and novelist who specialises in village life.

Mādhav Kandali (fourteenth century). Early translator of the *Rāmāyaṇa* into Assamese.

Madhusudan Rāo (1853–1912). Oriya mystical poet who introduced the sonnet form into Oriya.

Mahabharata. The great Sanskrit epic attributed to **Vyāsa.** It grew with the ages but perhaps reached roughly its present form around AD 200.

Mahipati (1715–90). Marathi poet. All his works (*Bhaktavijaya*, *Santalilāmṛta*) are exhaustive accounts of the lives of the religious poets who preceded him.

Mahjur, Ghulām Ahmad (1885–1952). The 'father' of modern Kashmiri poetry.

Mānikyacandra (*fl* 1422). Author of Gujarati Jain prose romance – *Pṛthvicandra-caritra*.

Maṇimekalai. The second Tamil epic, a Buddhistic sequel to *Cilappatikāram*, attributed to Cāttanār. Seventh century (?).

Manjhan (early sixteenth century). Hindi (Avadhi) Sufi poet who wrote the romance *Madhu-mālati*.

Marḍhekar, Bāl Sitārām (1907–56). Marathi poet and critic. Instigator of the new trend towards personal, experimental, 'difficult' poetry.

Mātavaiyār, Appāvaiyā (1874–1926). Tamil novelist with tendency towards themes of social reform. *Muttumināk̦ṣi* (1903).

Menon, O. Cantu (1846–99). First Malayalam novel: *Indulekhā* (1889).

Menon, Vaḷḷattol Nārāyaṇ (1879–1958). Outstanding modern Malayalam poet.

Mīr (1722/3–1810). First great master of the Urdu g͟hazal, which he wrote prolifically. Also love narratives in *maṣ̤navi* form. An autobiography in Persian.

Mīr Ḥasan (1727?–1786). Urdu poet famous for his *maṣ̤navīs*, especially his longest, the love story of Prince Benaẕīr and his beloved Badr i Munīr.

Mirābāi (1498–1573?). Rajasthani poetess who wrote *bhakti* verse addressed to Kṛṣṇa in both Gujarati and Hindi.

Mitra, Piyāri Cand (1814–83). Author of first true novel in Bengali: *Ālāler Gharer Dulāl* – a social satire.

Mohan Singh (1905–). Modern Panjabi poet with strong Marxist leanings.

Moropant (1729–94). Marathi rhetorical poet. Especially *Kekāvali* ('The Cry of the Peacock') – an anguished invocation of God.

Mukherji, Prabhātkumār (1873–1932). Copious Bengali short-story writer.

Mukteśvar (seventeenth-century). Marathi learned poet. Used mainly Puranic themes especially *Mahābhārata: Ādiparva.*

Mukundarām Cakravarti (Kavikankana) (late sixteenth century). Author of most popular Bengali *mangala-kāvya* (poem celebrating a god, usually Devi): *Caṇḍi-mangala.*

Munśi, Kanaiyalāl Maneklāl (1887–). Prolific Gujarati novelist, short-story writer, literary historian *etc.*

Nabhā Dās (sixteenth century). Hindi (Braj) verse biographer of the saint poets in his *Bhaktamālā.* Cf. **Mahipati.**

Nāmdev (fourteenth–sixteenth centuries). Marathi *bhakti* poet, or a conflation of several.

Nāmputiri, Cerusśeri (fifteenth century). Malayalam poet: *Kṛṣṇa-gāthā.*

Nānak (1469–1538). Founder of the Sikhs. Author of verses in the *Grantha Sāhib* in Old Hindi.

Nannaya Bhaṭṭ (*fl* 1040). First notable poet in Telugu under the Cālukya kings. *Mahābhārata,* but only the first few sections.

Narmadśankar Lālśankar (1833–86). One of the creators of modern Gujarati. Poet, essayist, lexicographer and rebel.

Narsiṃha Mehta (*c* 1500–80). Gujarati *bhakti* poet.

Nāyanmārs. The Tamil Śaivite poets whose collected work is called *Tirumurai,* sixth to twelfth centuries.

Naẕīr Aḥmad (1831–1912). Urdu proto-novelist, educationist and reformer. Didactic tales, but with powerful realism, characterisation, and mastery of dialogue and description. Talented translator (*eg* of the Quran), scholar of Arabic and Islamic learning, and lecturer.

Naẕīr of Agra (1735–1830). Unconventional Urdu poet who wrote of the seasons, festivals (both Muslim and Hindu) and the joys and sorrows of the ordinary townsman.

Nemicandra (*fl* 1370). Author of *Lilāvati,* a uniquely original Kanarese verse romance.

Nur-ud-Din, Sheikh (*c* 1377–1440). Kashmiri Sufi mystic poet.

Ottakkutan (eleventh century?). Tamil poet, the completer of Kampan's unfinished *Rāmāyaṇa.*

Padinenkilkkaṇakku (fifth century?). The third and latest of the Tamil anthologies which includes the famous *Tirukkural.*

Padmanābha (fifteenth century). Author of the early Gujarati (or Old Western Rajasthani) epic *Kānhaḍade-prabandha.*

Pampa. Two Jain poets of this name wrote in Kanarese, one in the tenth century, and one called Abhinava Pampa, in the twelfth.
Pancatantra (eighth century). The earliest collection of stories in Sanskrit, in mixed prose and verse.
Paṇikkar (fourteenth–fifteenth centuries). Two brothers Rāma and Mādhava did versions of the *Rāmāyaṇa* and *Bhagavadgitā* respectively in Malayalam.
Paṇikkar, Kavalam Madhav (1895–1963). Internationally known statesman and historian, also wrote historical novels in Malayalam.
Pāṇini (fourth century BC). The first and greatest Sanskrit grammarian.
Paramānanda (1791–1879). Kashmiri poet who marks the change from Persian to Sanskritic influence in Kashmiri literature.
Paṭel, Pannālāl Nanalal (1912–). Modern Gujarati novelist, strong on the realistic depiction of village life. Especially *Mānavini bhavāi* (1947).
Pattuppāṭṭu. 'The 10 songs'. Second-fourth centuries. The second of the Tamil anthologies.
Peddana, Allasāni (*c* 1510–75). Telugu poet of the court of Kṛṣṇadevarāya of Vijayanagar. Composed the epic *Manucaritra.*
Penḍse, Śripād Nārāyaṇ (1913–). Leading Marathi novelist, renowned for his *Garambicā Bāpu*, *Rathacakra.*
Phaḍke, Nārāyaṇ Sitārām (1894–). Most prolific living Marathi novelist.
Piḷḷai, C. V. Rāman (1858–1922). Malayalam historical novelist.
Piḷḷai, Samuel Vetanāyakam (1826–89). Author of the first Tamil novel: *Piratāpa Mutaliyār Carittiram* (1879).
Piḷḷai, Takazi Śivaśankar (1914–). Malayalam novelist: *Camin.*
Pingali Suranna (seventeenth century). Telugu poet: *Kalāpurṇodaya.*
Ponna (ninth century). Very shadowy Kanarese Jain poet whose work only survives in fragments.
Potana, Bammera (*c* 1400–75). Author of Telugu *Bhāgavata.*
Prem Cand (1880–1936). The greatest Hindi short-story writer and novelist, who wrote also in Urdu. His most famous novel is *Godān* (1936).
Premānand (1649–1714). Most prolific Gujarati Puranic poet, especially *Okhāharaṇa* and *Kumvarabāinuṃ māmeruṃ.*
Pukaḷenti (eleventh century?). Tamil poet, contemporary of **Ottakkutan.** Especially *Nala-venpā.*
Purāṇa. Vast Sanskrit compendia of history and mythology. There are traditionally eighteen major and eighteen minor *Purāṇas*, of which the *Bhāgavata-purāṇa*, containing the story of Kṛṣṇa, has had the most influence on the modern literatures. Fifth-twelfth centuries.
Purandaradās (1494–1564). Kanarese singer and *bhakti* poet, whose devotional songs are still widely popular in South India.
Puttappa, K. Venkaṭappa (1904–). Kanarese poet and short-story writer.
Qutban (*c* 1500). Hindi (Avadhi) Sufi poet. *Mṛgāvati* – Muslim allegorical romance.

Rājam Aiyār, B. R. (1872–98). Author of an early picaresque Tamil novel *Kamalāmpāl*, published serially 1893–5, philosopher, essayist, *etc.*
Rāmāyaṇa (first century AD ?). Epic story of the adventures of King Rāma and his wife Sitā's abduction by the demon Rāvaṇa, king of Lankā (Ceylon). Attributed to **Vālmiki.**
Rāmdās (1608–81). Somewhat martial Marathi poet-saint, founder of the Rāmdāsi sect and author of *Dāsabodh* and *Manāce śloka.*
Rāmprasād Sen (*c* 1718–75). Bengali composer of Tantric lyrics addressed to Kāli.
Ranna (tenth century). Kanarese Jain poet, author of *Gadāyuddha.*
Rāy, Bhāratcandra (*c* 1712–60). Ornately Sanskritic Bengali court poet. Especially *Annadā-mangal* – a combination of hommage to Caṇḍi and flattery of his patron.
Rāy, Rādhānāth (1849–1908). Poet who switched from Bengali to Oriya, first to use Western sources in Oriya. *Mahāyātrā.*
Roy (Rāy) Rām Mohan (1774–1833). Bengali religious reformer and founder of the Brahma Sabhā (later B. Samāj). Translated five of the *Upaniṣads* into Bengali.
Rusvā, Muḥammad Hādī (1858–1931). Author of the first, and perhaps still the best, Urdu novel, *Umrāo Jān Adā.* Also wrote other novels and novelettes. Was an amateur scientist and inventor, translator, and religious theorist.
Ṣaḍākṣaradev (seventeenth century). Kanarese Lingāyat poet. Especially *Rājaśekharavilāsa* – a romance in *campu* (mixed prose and verse).
Sandeśa Kāvya – 'message poem'. Popular form of medieval Malayalam literature imitated from Sanskrit tradition of **Kālidāsa's** *Meghaduta.* Best is the anonymous fourteenth-century *Unnunili Sandeśam.*
Śankaradev (1449–1568). Assamese religious leader to whom are attributed numerous devotional songs and plays, as well as translations of parts of the *Bhāgavata* and the *Rāmāyaṇa.*
Sāraḷā Dās (fifteenth century). Oriyan poet, a devotee of Śakti, whose version of the *Mahābhārata* is still supreme in Orissa. Also *Bilankā Rāmāyaṇa.*
Sarshār, Ratan Nāth (1846–1902). Urdu journalist and novelist. His voluminous *Tale of Āzād* is a bridge between medieval romance and modern novel.
Saudā (1713 ?–81). Urdu verse satirist. Also master of the panegyric ode.
Sayyid Aḥmad Khān, Sir (1817–98). Educationist, and leader of the reformist movement in the Muslim, Urdu-speaking community, advocating re-vitalised Islam interpreted in harmony with Victorian British values. Voluminous essays in vigorous rough-hewn Urdu.
Senāpati, Phakir Mohan (1843–1918). The first major Oriyan novelist, especially *Cha māṇa āṭha gunṭha* (1897). He also wrote verse and an important autobiography.
Sharar, 'Abdul Ḥalim (1860–1926). Urdu journalist and prolific writer of

historical romances with a strong Muslim revivalist flavour. Social reformer, opposed to purdah.

Somadeva (eleventh century). Author of Kathā-sarit-sāgara ('ocean of stories') a Sanskrit story cycle in twenty-two thousand couplets drawn mainly from previous collections such as **Pancatantra.**

Śrīdhar (1678–1728). Marathi Puranic poet who told all the old stories in simple lively verse.

Śrinādha (1365–1440). Telugu poet. *Sṛngāra-naiṣadha* – a Puranic romance; *Palnāṭi-vira-caritra* and *Vidhi-nāṭaka* – a vivid picture of contemporary manners.

Śrīnivās Dās, Lāl (1851–87). Pioneer Hindi dramatist and novelist: *Parikṣā-guru* (1882).

Stephens, Thomas (1549–1619). English Jesuit who turned the main plot of the Bible into a Marathi epic: *Krista-purāṇa*, *c* 1600.

Subramaniyam, K. N. (1912–). Leading Tamil novelist and critic.

Śudraka (fifth–sixth centuries). Sanskrit dramatist, author of *Mṛcchakaṭikā* 'The little Clay Cart'.

Sur Dās (*c* 1483–1563). Hindi (Braj) poet. Especially *Sur-sāgar* – a long Kṛṣṇa poem based on the *Bhāgavata.*

Sutta Piṭaka. The only section of the Buddhist Pali canon that contains works of literary value, including **Jātaka** stories, and *Theragāthā* – 'the songs of the Elders'.

Tagore (Ṭhākur), Rabindranāth (1861–1941). Bengali all-round literary genius; author of novels (especially *Gorā*, 1910), short-stories, essays, plays, poetry, songs; painter and ballet impresario. In 1913 he received the Nobel prize for literature for his verse collection *Gitānjali* (1910).

Tantra. Sectarian work similar to a **Purāṇa,** but devoted mainly to the celebration and illustration of Śakti, the female element.

Tenāli Rāmakṛṣṇa (seventeenth century). Telugu court poet, especially *Pāṇḍurangamāhātmya.*

Tevāram. One of the best-known books of the Tamil *Tirumurai* (see **Nāyanmārs**). Seventh century (?).

Tikkana (thirteenth century). Telugu poet who completed the unfinished *Mahābhārata* of **Nannaya Bhaṭṭ.**

Ṭiḷak, Bāḷ Gangādhar (Lokamānya) (1856–1920). Marathi Nationalist leader and journalist. Editor of the influential newspaper *Kesarī* in between prison sentences. Also *Gītā-rahasya* – an interpretation of the *Bhagavadgītā.*

Tiruvaḷḷuvar (sixth–seventh centuries). Tamil author of the celebrated *Tirukkural* (or *Kural*) – verse aphorisms which form part of **Padinenkiḷkkaṇakku.**

Tolkāppyar (sixth–seventh centuries). Eponymous author of *Tolkáppyam*, the earliest Tamil grammar-cum-rhetoric.

Tripāṭhi, Govardhanrām Mādhavrām (1855–1907). Gujarati romantic novelist. *Sarasvaticandra*, 4 parts, 1887–1901.

Tripāṭhi. Four brothers of this name were Hindi (Braj) court poets in the seventeenth century. Of these Bhuṣan (1613–1712) attached himself to the Maratha kingdom of Śivāji.

Tukārām (1608–49). The greatest Marathi *bhakti* poet. His *abhangas* are still sung by devotees throughout Maharashtra and beyond.

Tulsi Dās (1532–1627). The greatest *Rām-bhakti* poet of Hindi (Avadhi). Especially *Gitāvali* (1571) and *Rāma-carit-mānas* (1575) – the most popular version of the *Rāmāyaṇa* in North India.

Tuncattu, Eruttacchan ('father of literature') (seventeenth century). Malayalam poet. Especially *Adhyātma Rāmāyaṇa* and *Mahābhārata.*

Tyāgarāj (1787–1848 ?). The greatest composer of the southern (Karnatak) style of music was also a Telugu poet.

Vacanas. Śaivite hymns of the Kanarese Lingayat sect in a kind of rhythmic prose. Some attributed to Basava, the founder, from the twelfth century.

Valī (1667–1707). Urdu *g͟hazal* poet, last and greatest of the Deccan school.

Vālmiki (first century AD ?). Traditionally the author of the original *Rāmāyaṇa,* of which Books 2–6 might well be the work of one hand.

Vāman Paṇḍit (1605–95). Marathi poet, very learned and rhetorical, but his erotic Kṛṣṇa poems, especially *Venusudhā etc,* are effective.

Varerkar, Bhārgavrām Viṭṭhal (Māmā) (1883–). Prolific and popular Marathi dramatist and novelist.

Vatsyāyana (fifth century ?). Sanskrit author of the world-famous but over-rated *Kāma-sutra.*

Vemaṇa (seventeenth century ?). Telugu author of short moral verses, rather like the Tamil *Tirukkural.*

Vidyāpati Ṭhākur (1352–1448 ?). Wrote Rādhā-Kṛṣṇa love lyrics in Maithili, a dialect of Bihari. Great influence on later Bengali poetry.

Vidyāsāgar, Iśvaracandra (1820–91). Bengali reformer, translator, essayist and writer of polemical prose.

Vir Singh (1872–1957). Panjabi poet and novelist, editor of the weekly *Khalsa Samācār.* The 'father' of modern Panjabi literature.

Vireśalingam (Kandukuri Viresalingam Pantulu) (1848–1919). Writer and social reformer, the creator of modern Telugu. Wrote the first Telugu novel – *Rājaśekhara-caritramu.*

Vyāsa. A legendary sage to whom is attributed the composition not only of the *Mahābhārata* but of all the *Purāṇas.*

Wāris Shāh (1735–98). Panjabi Muslim poet. Especially *Hira-Ranjhā* (1766) a romantic ballad on the Hero and Leander theme.

Yerrapragaḍa (*c* 1280–1350). Telugu poet. With **Nannaya Bhaṭṭ** and **Tikkana** one of the great trio of early Telugu.

BIBLIOGRAPHY

HISTORICAL BACKGROUND

ALLCHIN, Bridget and Raymond *The Birth of Indian Civilization* (India and Pakistan before 500 BC), London, 1968; New York, 1969.

BASHAM, A. L. *The Wonder that was India* 3rd edn., London, 1967; New York, 1968.

THAPAR, Romila *A History of India* vol. I, London, Penguin, 1966.

SPEAR, Percival *A History of India* vol. II, London, Penguin, 1965.

GRIFFITHS, Percival *Modern India* 4th edn., London and New York, 1965.

(All these books contain good bibliographies.)

LITERARY TRENDS

Both BASHAM and THAPAR (see Historical Background) have bibliographical material on the literary history of pre-Muslim India and on translations into English of Sanskrit and early Tamil works.

CHATTERJI, S. K. *Languages and Literatures of Modern India* Calcutta, 1963. (Has very full bibliography of works in English on the various literatures.)

CLARK, T. W., ed. *The Novel in India* London, 1970.

MANSINHA, Mayadhar *History of Oriya Literature* New Delhi, 1962.

PARAMESWARAN NAIR, P. K. *History of Malayalam Literature* New Delhi, Sahitya Akademi, 1967.

HARBANS SINGH *Aspects of Panjabi Literature* Ferozepore, 1961.

MUHAMMAD SADIQ *A History of Urdu Literature* Oxford U.P., 1964.

INDIVIDUAL AUTHORS

SAHITYA AKADEMI *Who's Who of Indian Writers* New Delhi, 1961.

For modern translations see UNESCO, *Index Translationum* Paris, annually. Some more recent translations of Indian works:

BANERJI, Bibhuti Bhusan *Pather Panchali*, trans. T. W. Clark and T. Mukherji, London, 1968.

CHATTERJI, Bankim Candra: *Krishnakanta's Will*, trans. J. C. Gosh, Norfolk, Connecticut, 1962.

JNĀNADEVA: *Jnāneśvari*, trans. V. G. Pradhan and H. M. Lambert, vol. I, London, 1967.

MĀDGULKAR, Vyankateś *The Village had no Walls* (Bangarvādi), trans. Ram Deshmukh, Bombay, 1958.

PILLAI, Takazi Śivaśankar *Chemmeen*, trans. Narayan Menon, New York, 1962.

PREM CAND *The Gift of a Cow* (Godān), trans. G. C. Roadarmel, 1968.

RUSSELL, R. and KHURSHIDUL ISLAM *Three Mughal Poets* London, 1968.

ŚUDRAKA *Mṛcchakaṭikā, Two Plays of Ancient India*, J. A. B. van Buitenen, 1968.

TULSI DĀS *Kavitāvali*, trans. R. Allchin, London, 1964.

The Petition to Rām, trans. Allchin, London, 1966.

VIDYĀPATI *Love Songs of Vidyāpati*, ed. by W. G. Archer, trans. Deben Bhattacharya, London, 1963; New York, 1970.

DILIP CHITRE, ed., *An Anthology of Marathi Poetry* 1945–65, Bombay, 1967.

HUMAYUN KABIR, ed., *Green and Gold – stories and poems from Bengal*, London, 1958.

RAESIDE, IAN trans. *The Rough and the Smooth* (Modern Marathi short-stories), Bombay, 1966.

SAHITYA AKADEMI *Contemporary Indian short-stories* vol. I, New Delhi, 1959; vol. II, 1967.

SINHALESE LITERATURE

C. H. B. Reynolds

HISTORICAL BACKGROUND

Ceylon was settled by Indo-Aryan invaders from north India about the fifth century BC – traditionally the invaders, under prince Vijaya, landed on the day of the Buddha's death. The Prakritic language which this people spoke developed in course of time into Sinhalese as we know it. The people adopted Buddhism in the third century BC and their capital city, Anurádhapura, grew to be a place of great importance at the time when the Chinese traveller Fa-Hsien lived there in AD 418–20. Between AD 850 and 1200, the capital was Polonnaruva. The civilisation which these cities represented was based on the cultivation of rice by artificial irrigation in the flat lands of the northern half of Ceylon, and of the south-east. The wet and hilly lands of the centre and south-west were then largely uninhabited jungle.

After 1200 this civilisation fell into decay and the reservoirs ('tanks') and channels were abandoned. The whole area of the dry-zone cities rapidly became malarial jungle, beneath which the ruins of Anurádhapura and Polonnaruva were buried for seven centuries. The centre of the Sinhalese kingdom then moved to the south-west, where artificial irrigation was unnecessary, and where foreign trade was more easily practised and foreign influences more easily absorbed. At the same time, permanent settlements of Tamil-speaking Dravidians from south India became established at the northern extremity of the island, under their own kings. These, however, had no effect on Sinhalese literature or culture, separated as they were from the Sinhalese centres by many miles of jungle.

After about 1200, Ceylon was no longer a political unit. There was a brief re-florescence of Sinhalese arts and culture in the fifteenth century, during the time of the Kóṭṭé kingdom; but after the Portuguese had occupied most of the coastline during the sixteenth century, the independent Sinhalese centre retreated to the hilly and forested interior, where the king of Kandy maintained control of a static society. The Roman Catholic religion became firmly established in the coastal region north of Colombo during this period.

The replacement of Portuguese control by Dutch about 1650 had little further effect on the situation. Some works of literature – mostly poetry of a less learned type than was previously current – were composed in the Kandyan kingdom during the eighteenth century. The assumption of control of the coastal areas by the British in 1796, and the final suppression of the Kandyan kingdom in 1815, eventually had the effect of bringing Sinhalese literary development to a halt for almost a century. Only in the present century has it been resumed, with new forms modelled on, or adapted from, European exemplars. Since Ceylon became independent in 1948, literary activity in the new genres has greatly increased.

MAIN TRENDS IN LITERATURE

The Sinhalese language, spoken only in Ceylon, is an Indo-Aryan language whose distinctive features emerged between AD 400 and 800. The earliest existing writings are found in inscriptions, and in the graffiti scratched on the 'Mirror Wall' at Sígiriya in the sixth–tenth centuries. Surviving written literature begins about AD 900. It is certain that works of literature existed before that date; the titles of some of them are known, and also the names of certain poets as early as the sixth century. This early literature, however, has all perished, probably chiefly because the language in which it was written differed considerably from the Sinhalese language as it developed later and as we know it today. The literary language had assumed a fixed form by about 1200, and has hardly altered since. The spoken language of today differs considerably from the written.

PROSE WRITING

In the surviving literature, there is a considerable amount of prose writing from the very beginning. This arises from a tradition of commentaries on the Buddhist scriptures. The commentaries written on various Pali texts grew into self-subsisting works in Sinhalese prose, and there is an unbroken line of such works in prose, from the twelfth century to the nineteenth.

Many of these prose works are substantial compilations of Buddhist stories, often with poetic and expressive titles. Such are the twelfth-century *Amávatura* (The Flood of Nectar), consisting of fifteen episodes from the life of the Buddha; the thirteenth-century *Saddharmaratnávaliya* (The Necklace of the Doctrine), a Sinhalese version of the *Dhammapadaṭṭhakathá*, a Pali classic; also the *Pújávaliya* (String of Praises), a life of the Buddha, and the *Butsarana* (Refuge in the Buddha); the fourteenth-century *Saddharmálamkáraya* (Adornment of the Doctrine), a Sinhalese version of the Pali book known as *Rasaváhiní*, and the *Játaka Pota* (547 Previous Births of the Buddha). During the eighteenth century, the *Vimánavastuprakaranaya* (Tales of Heavenly Mansions) was translated from the Pali.

The long list of works of Buddhist doctrine runs from the thirteenth-century *Dharmapradípikáva* (The Lamp of the Doctrine) to the eighteenth-century *Sárárthasangrahaya* (The Essential Compilation) and the *Milinda-prasnaya* (The Questions of Menander), translated from the Pali.

Medieval Sinhalese literature also contains a number of historical works, such as the *Thúpavamsaya* (Story of the Stupa), *Dhátuvamsaya* (Story of the Relic), *Daladásirita* (History of the Holy Tooth), *Attanagaluvamsaya* (Story of Attanagalla), *Bódhivamsaya* (Story of the Bo-Tree), *Nikáyasangrahaya* (The Buddhist Sects), and *Rájaratnákaraya* (The Mine of Kings).

POETRY

Verse inherited an older poetic tradition and tended therefore to be linguistically obscure. Hence most of the verse that was contemporary with the early prose has disappeared; what remains is difficult to understand without a commentary.

Then a new type of verse first emerged about 1300. This was the period when the old low-country dry-zone civilisation, which had flourished from the beginning of recorded Ceylonese history, had collapsed, when Anurádhapura and Polonnaruva had been finally abandoned as capital cities and the drift to the wet zones of the south-west had begun. This new verse was distinguished from the older type by a more regular metre and a regular rhyme. It has remained the normal type of Sinhalese verse up to the present century.

The two principal types of verse composition to be met with in Sinhalese are the *kávya* or heroic epic, and the *sandésa* or message poem. Both types are to a considerable extent derived from the Indian traditions of 'ornate poetry', and may strike the western reader at first as full of absurd exaggerations, highly strained similes and metaphors of a far-fetched nature. The *kávya*-type is represented firstly by three twelfth-century poems in unrhymed verse, difficult to understand at the present day. These are named *Sasadávata* (The Birth as a Hare), *Muvadevdávata* (The Birth as King Makhádéva), and *Kavsilumina* (The Crest-Jewel of Poesy). In the fifteenth century, two famous poems written in this genre were the *Kávyasékharaya* (The Garland of Poetry) and *Guttilaya* (Story of Guttila). During the eighteenth century, revivalist works in the same genre were composed, notably the *Sumugudákava* (The Casket Birth), *Kavminikoňḍola* (The Earring of Poetry), *Kavminimaldama* (The Garland of Poetic Gems), *Kavmutuhara* (The Garland of Poetic Pearls), *Asadisadákava* (The Incomparable Birth), and *Siyabasmaldama* (The Sinhalese Garland).

Of similar style and tradition, but much simplified in treatment, are the *Saňdakiňdurudákava* (The Birth as a Faun), *Budugunálamkaraya* (Adornment of the Buddha's Virtues), and *Kusajátakakávyaya* (The Birth as King Kusa).

This group of poems dates from the fifteenth to the seventeenth centuries.

As an example of this kind of poetry, a literal translation of *Kavsilumina* i. 45–46 is as follows (describing the glory of the king):

> 'When that best of beings overpowered the ends of the world with the range of his firelike majesty, the Celestial River caused the heavenly damsels who came to bathe to run back in disorder (thinking it was covered with flames). When that hero of men with the fire-ring of his majesty reduced to ashes the forest of his enemies, the red eyes of the wives of the enemies looked like sparks of the fire scattered about.'

Besides similes and metaphors, verbal felicities and assonances are sometimes carried to great lengths. The tradition of this kind of poetry remained unaltered up to the eighteenth century, except for the addition of rhyme; very similar lines could be quoted, for instance, from *Kavminikoňḍola*.

The subject matter of these *kávya* works is most frequently a játaka, or story of a previous birth of the Buddha.

The *sandésa* is an altogether different kind of work. This type of poem is based on Kálidása's *Méghadútam*, and consists essentially of a message – usually short and unimportant – which is sent through the agency of some bird or animal. This type of poetry took particular root in Ceylon and has survived into the present century as a literary form. The earliest surviving Sinhalese *sandésa* was written about 1390, namely the *Mayúra-sandésaya* (The Peacock's Message). This was followed in the fifteenth century by six others, entitled *Tisara* (The Swan's Message), *Hamsa* (The Goose's Message), *Parevi* (The Dove's Message), *Säla* (The Starling's Message), *Girá* (The Parrot's Message) and *Kókila* (The Cuckoo's Message). From the sixteenth century dates *Sävul* (The Cock's Message). Several more such compositions were produced in the eighteenth and nineteenth centuries.

The normal pattern of a *sandésa* poem is as follows: first, a few verses in praise of the chosen messenger; then an indication that a message is to be carried but that it will not be disclosed till the end of the poem. Then follows a lengthy description of the route to be followed, starting with a substantial description of the starting-point and finishing with a substantial description of the destination, with a number of briefer descriptions in between of other places *en route*. Finally there is a short message. Such poems differ in two notable ways from the *kávya* type; firstly, they are purely secular in inspiration and have no essential connection with Buddhism, and secondly, they describe and refer to scenes of contemporary Ceylon, and not to scenes of an imaginary Indian literary standard. These poems therefore – besides incidentally providing geographical and historical information – do also give scope for bringing factual touches into a poetic tradition hitherto dominated by an imported classical tradition. While it still remains true that all kings will be described as omnipotent, all cities as glorious as Álakamandá, all villages full of enticing maidens, all forests full of every conceivable type of tree, etc., we can also read descriptions such as the following:

> 'The cocks perch upon the tree-tops all around to watch the evening worship of the Muni; while at the glitter of the lighted lamps within the shrine of the Muni the black bats come flying out, like the darkness itself sweeping over the countryside' (*Hamsa-sandésaya* 98).

This is not a conventional description but a real one, large bats being a notable feature of the scene in Ceylon. Or again:

> 'Here is flourishing Kăragala, rich with fruits, mango, dang, banana, in the woods round about, sweetened by the waters of stream and torrent descending from the hills, an ever-pleasant sight to see. On every hill spring falls of cool water, by every stream are fields that bear at every season, in every corner are houses set about with coconut and palmyra, in every pool bloom waterlilies, the pink lotus and the white. The scented rice is ever ripe in every field around, the lowing of young calves is heard afar, and there is the village temple, like a heavenly palace: the breath of that place is as the breath of nectar. There are sweet mangoes, whose fruit hangs ever ripe; there are bunches of large bananas, ripe and scented, and innumerable clusters of wild bananas all around; and in the midst shines the temple, where we cast aside our worldly fears.' (*Hamsa-sandésaya* 155–8).

It is this kind of passage which makes it impossible to say, as some have done, that Sinhalese literature shows little real appreciation of the beauties of nature. This is a genuine appreciation of the beauties of the foothill country in the wet zone of Ceylon, but it is a practical appreciation, the appreciation of an agricultural society which finds beauty in utility, a classical rather than a romantic appreciation.

Other varieties of poetry also found in Sinhalese are the panegyric and the didactic poem; and there is, further, a large body of more 'popular' literature, belonging to the Kandyan period after 1500, which has not been accepted by educated literary tradition (which has been primarily ecclesiastic and learned) as being of comparable worth with the kinds already mentioned, and has therefore been less studied, published and edited; much of it, nevertheless, is of considerable poetic quality.

Very little of literary merit was written in Ceylon between 1850 and 1950. In the latter half of the present century, experiments have been made with various fresh kinds of verse and prose, based mostly on western models, and also with drama, which had been hitherto unknown as a literary form.

Much Pali literature was also composed in Ceylon, but this – as also the Tamil literature of Ceylon – is outside the scope of the present essay.

INDIVIDUAL WRITERS AND WORKS

Alagiyavanna (*fl* 1590–1620). He held the office of mukaväṭi or mohoṭṭála (clerk), which is sometimes referred to as if it were his name. During this period there was an independent Sinhalese king (Rájasimha I) at Sítávaka, thirty miles inland from Colombo, while the Portuguese controlled the nominal king in the coastal areas. Alagiyavanna served under Rájasimha, and possibly under the Portuguese also. (See introduction – in English – to *Kustantinu Haṭana*, ed. S. G. Perera and M. E. Fernando, Colombo, 1932.) His principal works are *Kusadákava* (or *Kusajátakakávyaya*), recounting the story of the Kusa játaka, one *sandésa* poem called *Sävul-sandésaya* (The Cock's Message), and a book of versified moral maxims entitled *Subhásitaya*. The best known of these is the first, which is written in an easy popular style with much action and comparatively little descriptive padding. It was translated by T. Steele (London, 1871) into Victorian-type verse. To him are usually also ascribed *Dahamsoňḍakava*, a versified játaka story, and *Kustantinu haṭana*, an historical ballad.

Dharmaséna. The monk who compiled *Saddharmaratnávaliya*, a large Sinhalese prose work (*c* 1250), which is a translation and adaptation of the stories in the Pali *Dhammapadaṭṭhakathá*. His style is particularly notable for his similes, many of them based on contemporary life in Ceylon.

Gajaman Nóná. A poetess who flourished in south Ceylon *c* 1800, and wrote love poetry as well as versified letters and petitions.

Gascon Adikáram. Of foreign descent, he served king Naréndrasimha of Kandy (1707–39). Various panegyric verses are attributed to him, and also a clandestine correspondence in verse with the Queen of the time, for which he is said to have been put to death.

Gurulugómi. A layman, the first real Sinhalese prose author, *c* 1200. His works are *Dharmapradípikáva* and *Amávatura*. *Dharmapradípikáva*, written in a highly Sanskritic style, is nominally a commentary on the Pali *Mahabódhivamsa*, though in fact it is a kind of compendium of Buddhist religious information. *Amávatura*, written in a pure Sinhalese style, is a series of stories from the life of the Buddha, told in an economical and charming way, in spite of being an almost word-for-word translation of various Pali texts.

Jayabáhu Dévaraksita (Dharmakírti). The most prominent member of the school of the Dharmakírtis. This monk was pupil to Sílavamsa Dharmakírti of Palábatgala, who led the convocation of 1369; he himself led the convocation of 1396, and, like his master, also became sangharája. In Sinhalese, he wrote *Saddharmálamkaraya* and *Nikáyasangrahaya*, and in Pali he wrote the *Gaḍaládeni sanne* (commentary) to the grammar *Bálávatára* (some authorities attribute *Bālāvatāra* itself to him), and a poem called *Jinabódhávalí*. *Saddharmálamkáraya* is a lengthy prose version of the 103 stories in Védéha's *Rasaváhiní* (based on the *Sahassavatthuppakaraṇa* of Raṭṭhapála), with two others as well. The *Nikáyasangrahaya* is an earlier work, a history of the Buddhist church in Ceylon up to AD 1386; subsequently it was continued up to the time of the convocation of 1396, by which time Jayabáhu had become 'sangharája' and adopted his teacher's name of *Dharmakírti*. This history is principally designed to illustrate the triumph of the orthodox Mahávihára school over the heretics of Maháyána leanings.

Mayúrapáda Théra. This *théra* (elder) presided over the Mayúra pirivena (college) at Vákirigala in the thirteenth century; he is sometimes known as Buddhaputra, although this is not a proper name. His principal work, the *Pújávaliya*, is a lengthy prose account of episodes from the life of the Buddha, designed to illustrate the title *araham* (Worthy). It was written for Déva Patirája, chief minister of king Parákramabáhu II of Dam̆badeniya, in AD 1266. The final chapters contain a history of Ceylon. It is still very popular as a text for temple recitations. He also wrote two medical texts called *Yógárnavaya* (dated 1284) and *Prayógaratnávaliya*. Popular legend speaks of him as a somewhat gay character.

Mihiripänne Dhammaratana (1768–1851). Was a monk from the Southern province who may be considered the first Sinhalese poet of whom 'collected works' can be published. He usually used Sanskritic metres, without rhyme – a style called in Sinhalese *elu siló* ('Sinhalese sloka'). The famous Savsatdam controversy arose shortly after his death from a criticism made by Mihiripänne of the opening words of Kaṭuváne Disánáyaka's poem *Gangáróhanavarnanáva*.

Parákramabáhu II, King of Ceylon (1236–70). His capital was Dam̆badeniya. His reign was a time of great literary activity, encouraged also by the king and his minister Déva Patirája. Mayúrapáda (*qv*) flourished at this time, and probably also Dharmaséna (*qv*), and works of literature in Pali were written by Védéha (*Samantakúṭavaṇṇaná*, *Rasaváhiní*) and others; the Pali *Mahávamsa* (history of Ceylon) was brought down to 1186. To the king himself are attributed the *sanne* or Sinhalese commentary to the Pali theological work *Visuddhimagga*, and the poem *Kavsilumina*. The latter is the most complete of the three surviving *kávyas* in *gí* style (unrhymed verse). It tells the story of the Kusa játaka in fifteen cantos, and is a *mahákávya* on the Sanskrit model.

Piyadása Siriséna (1875–1946). The first well-known Sinhalese novelist. His first and most famous novel, *Jayatissa and Roslin*, was published in 1906.

His style is a mixture of prose and drama. He was a follower of the Anagárika Dharmapála in attacking the Europeanised urban Christian society of Colombo of the time.

Ráhula, Srí, of Toṭagamuva (*fl* 1430–60). He was a Buddhist monk, and held the position of *sangharája* or head of the Buddhist Order in Ceylon. He was connected with the royal family of Ceylon, and was the principal court poet of the reign of king Parákramabáhu VI at Kóṭṭé, near Colombo. His principal works are *Kávyasékharaya*, recounting the story of the Sattubhasta játaka in fifteen cantos, and two *sandésa* poems, *Parevi-sandésaya* (the Dove's Message) and *Sälalihini-sandésaya* (the Starling's Message); the last-named was translated by W. C. Macready (Colombo, 1865) and by H. Jayasinghe and L. C. van Geyzel (in *Marg*, vol. V. 3, Bombay, 1951, and in *The New Lanka*, vol. VI. 3, Colombo, 1955). Ráhula's style is classical, in the Sanskrit tradition.

Silva, W. A. (1892–1957). Popular novelist. His best known works are costume novels. Some of them are based on English works. He also wrote numerous short stories.

Välivița Saranankara (1698–1778). A Buddhist monk who led a revival of learning in the Kandyan kingdom during the eighteenth century. He was born at Välivița in the Tumpane district. At this time Buddhism was at a low ebb in Ceylon, and the boy had some difficulty at first in even finding himself a teacher for ordination. He was eventually appointed *sangharája*, or chief of the Buddhist Order on Ceylon, by the king – a title which had been in abeyance since the fifteenth century. His chief literary composition in Sinhalese, called *Sárárthasangrahaya*, was written in 1726 and formed as a commentary in nine chapters on the word 'Buddha' (The Enlightened One). He quotes abundantly from Pali works, and writes in a learned and long-winded style. He wrote Sinhalese commentaries on the Pali *Bhésajjamanjúsá*, *Mahabódhivamsa*, and the *pirit* (*paritta*), and also wrote himself in Pali. According to Sásanávatírnaya, he headed a conspiracy of chieftains to murder king Kírti Srí, because of his alleged Hinduizing tendencies (the king was, in fact, a Hindu Tamil), and replace him by a Siamese prince. This conspiracy was unsuccessful, and Välivița Saranankara subsequently composed a *katikávata* or collection of instructions for Buddhist monks on behalf of king Kírti Srí. His life was written in prose by Áyittáliyadde lékama (without any mention of the above episode), and in verse form under the title *Saňgarajavata*, by Mumkoțuve.

Vättâve. An otherwise unknown monk from the village of Vättâva in the N.W. Province; the traditional author of the fifteenth-century *Guttilakávyaya*, perhaps the most admired of all classical Sinhalese poems. It tells the story of the Guttila játaka, the story of the ungrateful pupil who challenged his master to a musical competition, in a simple and delightful way, without overmuch ornamentation. The adjective used in Ceylon to describe this style is 'sweet'.

Vídágama Maitréya. Monk of the time of king Parákramabáhu VI of Kóṭṭé

(1412–67) who was principal leader of the 'puritan' outlook at the time, in contrast to Srí Ráhula (*qv*). His known works are *Budugunálamkáraya* (a poem about the Buddha's visit to Vésálí at the time of the plague), one version of *Elu Attanagaluvamsaya* (historical prose work about a third-century king of Ceylon), *Ló-väḍa-saňgaráva* (short didactic poem), *Kavlakunuminimaldama* (short poem on versification), and possibly *Hamsa-sandésaya* (the Goose Message).

Vilgammula. Srí Parákramabáhu Mahásámi of the Vilgam mula (school) was author of the Sinhalese *Bódhivamsaya*, or history of the Bo-Tree, based on the tenth-century Pali *Mahabódhivamsa* of Upatissa. His family name was Gaňgatalá Karaňbavalán, and he flourished in the reign of king Parákramabáhu IV of Kurunägala (*c* 1302–30), under whom he became sangharája. He also wrote *Anágatavamsaya*, and a Sinhalese *sanne* (commentary) to the Sanskrit *Súryasataka*.

Other members of the Vilgammula school also wrote literary works: *Vimuktisangrahaya* (*c* 1375) and *Saňdakiňdurudákava*. The latter is a poem of uncertain date, written in a 'popular' and unadorned style. The Pali poem *Vuttamálásandésa-sataka* and the Pali lexicon *Abhidhánappadípiká* also belong to this school.

BIBLIOGRAPHY

HISTORICAL BACKGROUND

CODRINGTON, H. W. *Short History of Ceylon.* Revised edn., London, 1939.

LUDOWYK, E. F. C. *The Modern History of Ceylon* New York and London, 1966.

NICHOLAS, C. W. and PARANAVITANA, S. *Concise History of Ceylon* (to 1505), Colombo, 1961.

LITERATURE

GODAKUMBURA, C. E. *Sinhalese Literature*, Colombo, 1955.

REYNOLDS, C. H. B. (ed.) *An Anthology of Sinhalese Literature up to 1815* London, 1970.

SARACHCHANDRA, E. R. *The Folk Drama of Ceylon* Revised edn., Colombo, 1966.

The Sinhalese Novel. Revised edn., Colombo, 1967.

WICKRAMASINGHE, Martin *Landmarks of Sinhalese Literature* (trans E. R. Sarachchandra). Revised edn., Colombo, 1963.

WIRZ, P. *Exorcism and the Art of Healing in Ceylon* (trans.) Leiden, 1954 (for 'popular' literature).

INDONESIAN AND MALAYSIAN LITERATURE

E. C. G. Barrett

HISTORICAL BACKGROUND

The young sovereign states of Indonesia and Malaysia together cover the bulk of what has traditionally been called in English the 'Malay Peninsula and Archipelago'. I shall use a shorter term for this, of local origin, 'the Malay World'. In this intentionally vague expression the word 'Malay' is used to describe the culture and ethnic type predominant in the area rather than the language.

The Malay World is an extensive and largely water-covered portion of the earth's surface where about two hundred and fifty indigenous mother tongues (mostly belonging to the closely inter-related 'Indonesian' group) are spoken and where one of their number, the Malay language, has for centuries been the inter-island *lingua franca.* Most of the two hundred and fifty languages are peculiar to small groups of people and therefore have no written literature; but this is far from true of some of them – Javanese (spoken by over forty-two million people), Sundanese (over eighteen million), Malay (spoken *as a mother tongue* by only about ten million), Achinese, Buginese, Madurese, Balinese and others. All these have their literatures – and the literatures of Old Javanese and Javanese are of particular importance – but the national, official and literary language now in general use throughout the Malay World is Malay (renamed *Bahasa Indonesia* – 'the Language of Indonesia' – in one of its nation states and *Bahasa Malaysia* in the other).

Malay in the course of centuries has inherited from, or influenced, nearly all the literary traditions of the Malay World, so, for the sake of simplicity, the present essay will have literature written in Malay as its main theme.

Certain parts of the Malay World, especially Java and the shores of the Straits of Malacca, came under Hindu influence early in the Christian era (or before) and there is reason to believe that there was a religious and court literature, in Old-Javanese and Old-Malay (both heavily sanskritised languages written in South-Indian-derived scripts) from a very early period. With the spread of Islam in the fourteenth and fifteenth centuries these languages gradually absorbed Arabic – and Persian – elements and thereby radically changed their nature. The Old-Malay language has survived only in inscriptions and its literature has disappeared. But much Old-Javanese literature has survived owing to the fact that the Balinese have remained Hindu to the present day with Old-Javanese as their religious language. Certain Old-Javanese works, such as the Old-Javanese *Rāmāyana*, the twelfth century *Bhārata Yuddha* and Prapañcha's *Nāgarakrĕtāgama* of 1365 – all epic poems – have been faithfully copied again and again by Balinese scribes. On the other hand, if any relics of Old-Malay literature ever passed into later Malay literature, they are now unrecognisable as such. Muslim Malay copyists throughout the centuries have had very little reverence for their texts, especially if they dealt with Hindu subjects.

ISLAM

The Malay World acquired the special character which its Malay literature reflects during the gradual spread of Islam in the fourteenth, fifteenth and sixteenth centuries. Indian Muslim and Arab merchants moved into the Straits of Malacca which had for centuries been part of the trade route from the Middle East and India to the Spice Islands and to China. There they came into contact with Malay-speaking ports which had once been fragments of the (by now) defunct trading empire called *Srivijaya*. The court of the little maritime state of Pasai in North Sumatra was first converted to Islam and then the influence of the new religion, with Malay as its medium, gradually moved south from port to port along the shores of the Straits of Malacca, the South China Sea and the Java Sea towards the Spice Islands. The Hindu kingdom of Majapahit, dominant both in Java and on the trade route throughout the fourteenth century, collapsed in the early fifteenth century under pressure from the newly islamicised ports on the north coast of Java. The Javanese as a whole were then gradually converted to Islam while retaining a culture (with a literature now to be expressed in 'Middle-Javanese') that remained strongly Hindu-influenced.

Throughout most of the fifteenth century the new Muslim kingdom of Malacca dominated the trade route and there became established there a new literary language now commonly called 'Classical Malay'. This, with very little change, remained the standard written form of Malay until the present century. In addition to its basic 'Indonesian' vocabulary it contained many Sanskrit and Arabic loan words. It was written in a modified form of the Arabic script. Its style was long-winded, rhythmical, dignified and particularly adapted to religion and romance.

THE PORTUGUESE

Malacca fell to the still-crusading Portuguese in the early sixteenth century. They disturbed the trade route for the next hundred years but paradoxically their coming helped to spread Islam and the Malay language more widely through the archipelago; for they caused a Malay 'diaspora' to take place from Malacca to outlying parts of the Malay world. Acheh in North Sumatra, where the mother tongue was Achinese and not Malay, became the most important of the centres of Classical Malay literature – a literature based on the life and needs of the many little Malay courts imbued with the half-Hindu half-Muslim traditions of the defunct kingdom of Malacca. These little courts, mostly situated at the mouths of jungly rivers or on small islands, where their grandiloquently-titled rulers could draw revenue from sea-borne trade, started on a period of decline in the late seventeenth or early eighteenth century as the Dutch, who by now had supplanted the Portuguese, built up an effective monopoly of trade in the products on which the Malay rulers had most depended for their income. From then on Malay court literature also declined but the folk literature of travelling story tellers, often drawn originally from court sources, continued to flourish in the kampongs. Even under Dutch auspices Malay continued to be the *lingua franca* of inter-island traders and Classical Malay continued to command respect as its literary form.

DUTCH AND BRITISH INFLUENCE

In the nineteenth century the Dutch and British intensified their economic and political penetration of the Malay World and the edges of their zones of influence gradually hardened into international frontiers. In the Dutch territories Christian missionaries established themselves in areas where the native people were still animists and spoke purely local languages. The medium they used for their activities was Malay written in a Dutch romanised, instead of the usual Malayo-Arabic, script. The result was that a new type of Malay literature developed, side by side with the old, throughout Netherlands India and especially amongst the Ambonese of the Moluccas, the Menadonese of North East Celebes and the Bataks of the interior of North Sumatra. This type of Malay was further disseminated when the government started its own vernacular schools and thus introduced the new romanised script and the europeanised style to Muslims as well as to pagans and Christian converts.

In the early twentieth century a teachers' training college was established in Minangkabau (West Sumatra) where the literary language had for centuries been Classical Malay but where the spoken language had strong characteristics of its own. The college gradually built up on a Classical Malay base a modern literary language strongly influenced by Dutch grammar and vocabulary and the local Minangkabau dialect. Even more important in the development of this new literary language was the foundation in Batavia of a 'Bureau for the People's Reading' later to be renamed the *Balai Pustaka* (Hall of Books), an institution which sponsored the publication in Malay (and Javanese and certain other languages) of a large number of translations from European works. With effect from roughly 1920 these influences together resulted in the gradual supplanting of centuries-old Classical Malay in Netherlands India by a new form of the language which for an interim period I shall call 'Netherlands India Written Malay'.

At about the same time another form of written Malay was coming into being in the British-influenced portion of the Malay World but the change there was much less far-reaching. The Sultan Idris Training College was opened in the Federated Malay States in 1922 and it was some time before the books published by its Malay Translation Bureau, with the help of the Malay newspapers and a handful of original writers, caused a modernised literary language to be generally accepted in Malaya. I shall call this 'Malayan Written Malay'. It was much more conservative than its Netherlands Indian counterpart and the new loan words required were taken from Arabic in preference to a European language. It remained written in the Malayo-Arabic script but an English-based romanised script was also used for certain purposes.

MODERN TRENDS

In 1928 delegates from all over Netherlands India attended a Youth Congress in Batavia (now Djakarta). They there resolved that they 'belonged to one fatherland, Indonesia; one nation, the Indonesian nation', and upheld as the language of unity the *Bahasa Indonesia* (the 'Language of Indonesia'). 'Netherlands India Written Malay' was thus for the first time given the name by which it is now generally called, but, as the world in general continued to call it 'Malay' until after the war, and as the war itself constituted an important break in the linguistic and literary history of the region, I shall use the name *Bahasa Indonesia* only with effect from 1945.

From 1920 to 1945 Netherlands India Written Malay went through a rapid process of modernisation at a pace set, for good or ill, by the journalist hurriedly wrestling with the midnight translation of foreign-language press reports; but the cruder aspects of modernisation were increasingly modified by a feeling for literature which built up, in the twenties, under the influence of the teacher-training college in Minangkabau and of the Balai Pustaka (now turned patron of literature); in the thirties, this continued under the influence of the cultural journal *Pudjangga Baru* and its talented writers and controversialists. During the Japanese occupation, from 1942 to 1945, the use of the new written language was greatly extended among the upper and middle classes of non-Malays because the Japanese suddenly forbade the use of Dutch in governmental and commercial offices. This process resulted in the further europeanisation of written Malay and the standardisation of a multitude of 'officialese' and technical terms. The sudden ending of the Japanese occupation and the accompanying wave of nationalism consolidated the position of the unifying language as the undisputed literary language of all the regional peoples of Indonesia. It was now fully time to call it by the name *Bahasa Indonesia* given to it by idealists seventeen years earlier.

As a result of circumstances described above, Netherlands India Written Malay and Malayan Written Malay had been drifting further and further apart from about 1920 until the end of World War II, but then the two branches of the language came together once again. Before the war the unpolitical Malayan Malays had felt little need for an indigenous written language that would express all aspects of modern thought; but, after the war, a newly aroused nationalism made them feel that this was essential and urgent. They found such a language ready-made across the Straits of Malacca and borrowed from it wholesale to form the vehicle for their own literary awakening (albeit retaining an English-based instead of a Dutch-based romanised spelling). With the coming of independence in 1957, the result was adopted as the Malayan (later to be renamed 'Malaysian') National Language. Today the *Bahasa Indonesia* and the *Bahasa Malaysia* have few essential differences except in spelling and even a common system of spelling has recently been agreed on by a commission composed of representatives from the two countries.

MAIN TRENDS IN LITERATURE

THE CLASSICAL MALAY PERIOD
(*approx. 1450 to 1920*)

This period has little literature that can be positively dated or attributed to any particular writer. It will be necessary therefore to classify its works under *genres*. What will be said about these *genres* will usually be capable of application also to the other literatures of the Malay World during the same period. It is only comparatively recently that the Malay World has made use of the printing press so that our sources of older Classical Malay literature must in most cases be manuscript copies many times removed from the version of the original writer.

Folk Literature

We can include the 'oral literature' of the wandering story-teller as coming within the title of this article, albeit story-telling was only part of his performance and the printed page of his modern recorder cannot do justice to his talents. As well as story-teller he could be actor, clown, mimic, viol-player, singer, puppeteer and wizard. He delighted the simple, closed communities of the kampongs for many centuries. His stock-in-trade of highly personalised stories was drawn from sources as diverse as the Buddhist *Jatakas*, the Hindu *Panchatantra* and *Katha Sarit Segara*, and Persian, Arabic and Javanese romances, as well as from Malay court literature and the humble life of the kampongs themselves. Typical of such a mixture of sources are the stories in which the clever mousedeer, like Brer Rabbit, outwits his fellow animals, and farcical tales about kampong simpletons, knaves and clowns. Then there are the folk romances, unsophisticated copies of court romances, aimed at capturing the hearts of the cloistered and bored maidens of the *kampong* in the same way as medieval European ladies were captivated by the Arthurian romances.

Under the head *Folk Literature* it would be fitting to mention what has been for centuries the most popular of the verse forms in the languages of the Malay World – the *pantun* – a quatrain adapted both to love-making and to singing in turn by *extempore* poets before a genial kampong audience. The first couplet of the quatrain has as its main object the establishment of the sound pattern that follows in the meaningful second couplet. This form can be illustrated by one of R. J. Wilkinson's translations:

The fate of a dove is to fly;
He flies to his nest on the knoll.
The gate of true love is the eye;
The prize of his quest is the soul.

Hindu-derived literature

There is a considerable quantity of Muslim-influenced but Hindu-derived literature written in Classical Malay. Most of it probably came into the language from Javanese. An exception seems to be the long Malay prose version of the *Rāmāyana* – the *Hikayat Sĕri Rama* – of which no Javanese version is known to exist. A manuscript of this has been in the Bodleian library at Oxford since 1633, but even this early manuscript is clearly the result of many previous copyings. The shorter *Hikayat Pandawa Jaya* contains many episodes from the *Mahābhārata* and may be descended from the Old-Javanese *Bhārata Yuddha*. A multitude of other romances contain Javanese (Wayang Purwa) shadow play plots based on the same two Indian epics. The Hindu society of Majapahit was the originator of a native cycle of romances which were translated not only into Malay but also into other languages of South East Asia. This was the *Panji* cycle about two lovers, a prince of Kuripan in East Java, and a princess of neighbouring Daha, who had fantastic adventures in a magical universe peopled by Hindu gods, goddesses, nymphs and spirits of all kinds. This cycle provides the plots for the *Wayang Gedog* shadow plays.

Early Islamic Literature

It is typical of the gradual and peaceful penetration of Islam into the Malay World through the medium of the Malay language that Hindu-derived literature such as the *Hikayat Sĕri Rama* was used to instruct in the new religion. But gradually Islamic or pre-Islamic romances – the *Hikayat Iskandar* (story of Alexander the Great) the *Hikayat Amir Hamza* (story of an uncle of the Prophet) and the *Hikayat Muhammad Hanafiah* (adventures of people about the Prophet) – took their place beside the Hindu ones, and new cycles of tales were introduced – the *Hikayat Bayan Budiman* (Tales of the Wise Parrot) the *Hikayat Kalila dan Damina* (The Fables of Bidpai) and the *Hikayat Bakhtiar* (a cycle of Persian stories told to postpone execution of a death sentence). Such comparative frivolities were of course accompanied by serious religious instruction, some of it translated word for word from the Arabic and some original. Hamzah Fansuri, who lived about 1600 in North Sumatra, wrote a systematic account of Sufi doctrines in Malay and, in doing so, gave the language a philosophical terminology. He also seems to have been the inventor of the Malay verse form called the *sha'er* which for the next three centuries was to be used for narrative poems. Other notable religious writers of the period in North Sumatra were Shamsu'ddin of Pasai and his enemy Nuru'ddin a'r-Raniri.

Histories

There are many anonymous histories belonging to different parts of the Malay World of the period, mostly a mythological blend of native, Hindu and Muslim elements. The earliest, the *Hikayat Raja-Raja Pasai*, deals with the coming of Islam to northern ports on the Straits of Malacca in the late thirteenth century and ends about 1350. This is followed chronologically by the *Sejarah Melayu* (Malay Annals), considered the finest work in Classical Malay literature. Predictably it starts with much mythical background to legitimate the Malacca dynasty but then it goes on to give the history of that kingdom from about 1450 to its fall in 1511 in a lively style coupled with many anecdotes and acute observation. The story of the *Sejarah Melayu* has been continued and imitated in a number of histories of Malacca's small successor states. The most notable of these are the *Silsilah Melayu dan Bugis* and the *Tuhfatal-Nafis*, written by Raja Ali Haji, a man with a modern outlook who was a member of the Buginese ascendancy in Riau in the nineteenth century.

'*A Picaresque Novel*'

The *Hikayat Hang Tuah* is in a *genre* all to itself. It is an anonymous quasi-historical work probably written in the seventeenth century and tells in a lively manner of the impossible adventures of a Malay warrior hero called 'Hang Tuah', a devoted servant of a fifteenth century Sultan of Malacca. Hang Tuah has shown signs of providing a 'national myth' for modern Malaysia but his unquestioning loyalty to a feudal lord has been attacked by left-wing nationalists.

The Early Beginnings of a Modern Literature

Up to the beginning of the nineteenth century Classical Malay Literature never dealt with everyday matters; but this tradition was then broken by Abdullah

Munshi, clerk to Sir Stamford Raffles, founder of Singapore. Abdullah, although his language was grounded on tradition, broke with traditional subject matter and wrote about current conditions, especially European contact with the Malays. His autobiography, the *Hikayat Abdullah*, can be said to be the first modern book published in Malay.

LITERARY TRENDS IN NETHERLANDS INDIA WRITTEN MALAY (1920–45)

The circumstances which led to the development of this form of Malay and of its literature have been described above. Its first literary expression was in the lyrical poetry of the youthful Minangkabau Muhammad Yamin (who many years later was to be President Sukarno's principal 'myth-worker'). He started to write in Malay in the Dutch-language journal *Jong Sumatra* in 1920. His first published collection of poems, *Tanah Air* (Fatherland) appeared in 1922. He made much use of the sonnet form, borrowed from Dutch literature, but was still tied to the clichés used in Classical Malay. Yamin and his successors, Rustam Effendi and Sanusi Pané, in following years gradually improved on the new poetry.

The first of many important modern novels, *Sitti Nurbaja*, by the Minangkabau Marah Rusli, was also published in 1922 and, although moralising and long-winded, had ten years of great popularity. *Sitti Nurbaja* was published by the Government Publishing House, Balai Pustaka, which now started to assume its new and important role as a patron of literature. It went on to publish Abdul Muis's novel *Salah Asuhan* (A Mistaken Education) in 1928 – the year of the Proclamation of *Bahasa Indonesia* – and Sanusi Pané's charming collection of largely mystical poems, *Madah Kelana*, in 1931. To this period also belong some nostalgic dramas about ancient Java – Rustam Effendi's *Bebasari* (1926?) Yamin's *Ken Angrok dan Ken Dedes* (1928) and *Kertadjaja* (1932) and *Sandhyakala ning Madjapahit* (Twilight in Majapahit, 1933), both by Sanusi Pané.

In 1933 there appeared in Batavia the first independent literary journal in Malay – *Pudjangga Baru* (The New Man of Letters). Its founders and first editors were Sutan Takdir Alisjahbana, essayist, poet, moralist, grammarian, novelist and sociologist; and Armijn Pané, brother of Sanusi Pané and himself a novelist, essayist, critic, dramatist and poet. *Pudjangga Baru* dominated prewar literature from then on and was dedicated to the concept that the new language had to be basically different from Classical Malay and that traditional literary forms had to be replaced by modern means of expression. From there controversy started on the relative merits of a dynamic modern outlook (favoured by Takdir) and a static traditional outlook (favoured by Sanusi Pané and others); and (as a corollary) of *l'art engagé* and *l'art pour l'art*. The latter controversy was on a theme which has permeated the literature of Indonesia to the present day.

The poets of the *Pudjangga Baru* period were apt to be unduly tied to nineteenth century Dutch models but one of their number, Amir Hamzah, writer of two collections – *Njanji Sunji* (Songs of Solitude, 1937) and *Buah Rindu* (Fruit of Longing, 1941) – is deservedly of international repute. He cannot be better described in brief than in the words of Professor Teeuw '... one is tempted to call Amir Hamzah the *penutup penjair Melaju*, the final Malay poet, who in his seventy-odd verses has set the seal on achievement in poetry; he was rooted in the Malay past, and completely tied to his traditional feudal society, to his paternal Moslem religion with its mystical overtones; to his Malay culture with its richness of subtle symbolism and its genius for naive joy in nature and life, but also to its innate melancholy about the transience of all things earthly; and his strongest ties of all were with his language, which has the power to inspire and convey beauty provided it is adequately explored and imaginatively handled.' Thus Amir Hamzah brought the Malay period to a glorious close.

This period was to be followed by a vacuum during the cataclysm of war, which was in turn to be followed by the dynamic new literature of the period of the Bahasa Indonesia. But before we leave the literature of Netherlands India Written Malay, we should turn briefly to an able novel which in a way bridges the gap between it and later literature in Bahasa Indonesia. This is *Belenggu* (Fetters) by Armijn Pané, the most discussed book of the pre-war period. It is a new departure – a psychological novel concerning a love triangle in a modern sophisticated milieu and is written in a very europeanised Malay. Balai Pustaka refused to publish it because it offended the accepted Indonesian morality of the time and in 1940 it was accordingly published in instalments in the pages of *Pudjangga Baru*.

LITERARY TRENDS IN MALAYAN WRITTEN MALAY (1920–45)

There were few signs of nationalism in the Malaya of this period and its Malay literature had little of the vigour shown in Netherlands India. The first modern novel was *Faridah Hanum* (a naive imitation of an Egyptian love-story) published by Sayyid Shaikh al-Hadi in 1928. Sayyid Shaikh also wrote detective stories – the *Rokambul* stories – which, like his novel, were copies from Egyptian models. More truly native were the short stories of the journalist Kajai who pioneered a *genre* which was to become very popular after the war.

LITERARY TRENDS IN BAHASA INDONESIA (1945–)

During the Japanese occupation of Netherlands India (1942–5) written

Malay came to be far more widely used there for governmental and business purposes but the publication in it of 'writings whose value lies in beauty of form or emotional effect' was confined almost entirely to Japanese propaganda. What true literature was written then was not to be published until after the war, *ie* within the period of the *Bahasa Indonesia* as defined above. This period was ushered in by a sudden national awakening during the sufferings of the Japanese collapse and the war of independence against the Dutch which followed it. A large number of journals containing controversial essays, poetry and short stories came to be published, albeit, for political reasons, most of them had a short life. The most important of these from the literary point of view was *Siasat* (Strategy) which appeared in 1947. The following year it started its own cultural column, called *Gelanggang* (Forum), which became the 'forum' for the many young writers now classified as the 'Generation of 1945'. The first members of the editorial board were Chairil Anwar, the 'vitalist' poet who has since become world-famous, and the essayists and critics, Asrul Sani and Rivai Apin. The *Gelanggang* 'testimonial of beliefs' was published in 1950, after Chairil Anwar's premature death. The latter's plea for vitality as a 'chaotic preliminary stage: having art as its cosmic final stage' is not there expressed but the other tenets of Chairil Anwar and his contemporaries are present: (a) they claim to be the heirs of 'all sorts of stimulating voices hurled from all corners of the world to be hurled back later in the form of our own voice'; (b) they reject an inclination to preserve and admire the Indonesian past for its own sake; (c) 'revolution is the substitution of new standards for the outmoded ones . . . the revolution in our own country is not yet finished'; (d) 'the most important thing for us to find is man'. Such was the 'universal humanists' ' doctrine which was later to be attacked as mere *l'art pour l'art* by the single-minded Marxist writers who in 1950 banded themselves together in *Lekra* (League for the People's Culture) and believed that the only function of the writer should be service to the masses. Between 1945 and 1958 the 'universal humanists' produced many writers of considerable distinction: Chairil Anwar himself; Idrus, a short-story writer who introduced a new, crudely realistic and defiant prose style; H. B. Jassin the literary critic; Mochtar Lubis, a courageous political journalist and the only Indonesian novelist whose work has been published in English; Achdiat Karta Mihardja, author of the very remarkable novel *Atheis* (The Atheist); and last but not least Pramudya Ananta Tur, a novelist described by Professor Teeuw as Indonesia's 'greatest modern prose-writer' in his earlier days. Pramudya later abandoned the humanists for the *art engagé* of *Lekra.* From 1958 to 1965 the humanists were under a cloud. 'Guided Democracy' and the rising cost of paper became less and less conducive to the publication of uninhibited literature; and *Lekra* was more and more successful in its insistence on recognition as the only true representative of young Indonesian ideas and ideals. In 1963 and 1965 it drove into intimidated inactivity twenty-two humanist signatories of a 'Cultural Manifesto' which had dared to state that they 'did not regard any one sector of culture as superior to other sectors of culture'. But with the failure of the Indonesian Communist Party's bid for supreme power in October 1965 *Lekra* suddenly lost its dominant position in literature. Now a 'generation of 1965' has gained intellectual freedom and started a new chapter in Indonesian literature, one which appears to be full of life and promise.

LITERARY TRENDS IN MALAYAN WRITTEN MALAY (1945–)

Malayan (and Malaysian) post-war literature, like the language in which it is written, has been imitated from Indonesia. The Indonesian 'Generation of 1945' has its later counterpart in the Malayan 'Generation of 1950' but the latter movement had less talent at its disposal. Those literate in Malay were far fewer in Malaya than in Indonesia and their emotions had been fired by fewer harrowing experiences. With the coming of independence in 1957 a semi-governmental corporation – the *Dewan Bahasa dan Pustaka* (Board for Language and Books) – was set up to promote the use of the national language and its literature, and it has done its work well through its journal, *Dewan Bahasa*, and other publications. Malaysian Malays are now intensely interested in their modern literature which consists mostly of very competent short stories and poems. Samad Said's able novel *Salina* should also be mentioned here.

BIBLIOGRAPHY

HISTORICAL BACKGROUND

HALL, D. G. E. *A History of South-East Asia.* 2nd edn., London, 1964.

SCHRIEKE, B. *Indonesian Sociological Studies* 2 vols., The Hague, 1955–59.

TEEUW, A. *A Critical Survey of Studies on Malay and Bahasa Malaysia* The Hague, 1961.

VLEKKE, B. H. M. *Nusantara, a History of Indonesia* The Hague, 1959.

WINSTEDT, Sir Richard *The Malay Magician* Revised edn., London, 1951.
Malaya and Its History 5th edn., London, 1958.

LITERATURE

BASTIN, J. and ROOLVINK, R. (ed.) *Malayan and Indonesian Studies* Oxford, 1964.

TEEUW, A. *Modern Indonesian Literature* The Hague, 1967.

WINSTEDT, Sir Richard 'A History of Classical Malay Literature'. Issued as vol. XXXI, Part 3 of *Journal of the Malayan Branch of the Royal Asiatic Society*, 1958. London agents, Luzac and Co.
The Malays – A Cultural History 6th edn., London, 1961.

CHINESE LITERATURE

Yin C. Liu and Tao Tao Sanders

HISTORICAL BACKGROUND

Along the course of the Yellow River farming communities living in villages had followed a neolithic way of life for many centuries. Archaeology tells us that in the eighteenth century BC a people called the Shang or Yin (1751–1112 BC) arose who possessed more advanced metallurgical techniques. They lived in a city at the site of modern Anyang, on the bank of one of the tributaries of the Yellow River and they gained control of the people in the central plain. The state of Shang was a kind of theocracy in which oracles controlled the king's political, military, religious and personal activities. The method of consulting the oracle consisted in piercing bones of animals and tortoise-shell, and applying heat on one side to form cracks. These cracks were interpreted as the oracle; sometimes the bone was further inscribed with the interpretation. Many such bones have been excavated at the site of Anyang and they have preserved the oldest form of Chinese writing, which in principle resembles the Chinese script still used today. The Shang people also cast bronze vessels with inscriptions, but these inscriptions on oracle bones or bronze vessels were either oracular or commemorative and they can hardly be said to mark the beginning of a literary tradition.

The Shang dynasty came to an end when it was overcome by a tribe from the north-west of China. The new dynasty of Chou (1111–256 BC) established feudal rule to the west of the Yellow River in the present Shensi province. The first king died when his son was still in his minority and the uncle the Duke of Chou was made regent. He laid the foundations of a dynasty that was to last for about eight hundred years. In the later stages the power of Chou was weakened by the expansion of subordinate states, some of which became more powerful than the central government. The time came when the vassal states struggled openly among themselves for supremacy, a period generally known as the Spring and Autumn (722–481 BC), while the power of the kings of Chou were gradually eroded and they themselves remained mere figureheads. This period gave way to even more internecine war between the states, a period known as the Warring States (500–246 BC) but it was at this time that the great Chinese philosophers flourished. Confucius, the first and perhaps the greatest of them, travelled from state to state trying to win the rulers to his ideas of loyalty and righteousness; Mo Tzu, a puritanical pacifist, opposed Confucian ritualism and advocated nonaggression; Lao Tzu and Chung Tzu, the Taoist philosophers, advocated a return to nature. None of the philosophers succeeded in convincing the rulers of their lifetime. Nevertheless, the influence of their teaching was felt throughout the subsequent history of China.

Towards the end of the third century BC, Ch'in, the most powerful state succeeded in conquering the other states and unified China. The first emperor of Ch'in (Ch'in Shih Huang Ti) imposed absolute control on the people: he standardised weights and measures, and the gauge of all vehicles throughout the land, he reformed the written script, and he divided the empire into thirty-six prefectures for administrative purposes. In an attempt to control the thought of the people, he ordered that all books with the exception of those on technology and medicine should be burnt and scholars buried alive. This book-burning caused great textual confusion to later generations in the study of the classics. The only works that escaped the conflagration were those hidden in walls or other places, or kept alive in the memory of the scholars who only committed them to writing after the fall of Ch'in. The emperor exhausted the country's resources in building the Great Wall which was intended to protect his empire from the barbarian tribes from the north. However, after his death, his son was overthrown by a peasant rebellion led by Liu Pang, a commoner who became the emperor and thus founded the Han dynasty (206 BC–AD 220).

THE HAN DYNASTY

Liu Pang ostensibly discarded laws established by the Ch'in emperor but in fact made good use of his machinery for central government. He revived the feudal system to some degree and ennobled members of his clan to strengthen the imperial family, but he kept them under strict control. During the first century BC Confucian teaching was adopted as the official philosophy and an imperial academy was set up to train civil servants, who formed the backbone of an effective central government. The curriculum in the academy consisted of the Confucian classics.

Although gradually the Han emperors succeeded in establishing internal stability, the empire was under constant threats from the tribe of Hsiung-Nu from the north-west of China, in present-day Mongolia; part of the same tribe travelled westwards and was identified as that of the Huns. Conscription was so ruthless in the Chinese frontier villages that they were often left with no able-bodied man: the misery of war was repeatedly depicted in poetry by Han writers. Eventually China was forced to make alliance with the foreigners. In the first century BC emissaries such as Chang Ch'ien went as far as India and Persia. At the same time there were merchants who made their way from the West to China and created a trade route. Through these channels came the Buddhist missionaries whose influence was to have a profound and lasting effect. Since many travellers took the desert and mountain road, the outpost town called Tunhuang provided them with shelter in Kansu on the north-west border of China, and this place became an important Buddhist settlement four centuries later. It was in the caves of Tunhuang that sculptures and important documents were preserved for posterity. During the Han dynasty China established diplomatic relations to the west even as far as Rome and to the east with Japan and Korea. The Han dynasty was not a creative period in literature, but important developments in poetic form took place which ensures it its place in the history of Chinese literature. It also initiated a tradition of classical studies which set a unique and long-perpetuated example.

When Buddhism spread through China, it was accepted first of all by the aristocracy. But at the same time the native Taoism had wide influence amongst the ordinary people who were burdened by high taxation, afflicted by drastic land reforms of the period, and suffered from the gradual decay of the government. Many sought refuge from reality in Taoist practice which at the highest level taught a spiritual way of life for attaining tranquillity but at worst was a superstitious comfort. More than one rebellion against the central government was led by Taoists, the largest of which was the Yellow Turban Revolt, its name deriving from the headgear of the rebels. In AD 220 the Han empire disintegrated and the period that followed was known as the Three Kingdoms (AD 220–80), the three kingdoms being Wei, Shu and Wu.

THE THREE KINGDOMS

By this time China extended economically and socially south towards the Yangtze River. Farming techniques developed in the north were now applied in the south where the soil and climate were more favourable. In the states of Wei and Shu taxes were readjusted to encourage large scale land-ownership. Thus, strong family clans were created who were able to protect their property and social privileges and whose family fortunes enabled them to educate their children to become members of the ruling class and eventually they dominated the political scene in China.

In the middle of the third century AD the Three Kingdoms fell one after another and were followed by the Tsin dynasty. The new dynasty was plunged into chaos at birth. Internally there was a struggle for power amongst the nobles and externally the nomadic tribes from the north-west penetrated Chinese territory on various occasions. The Tsin army was unable to stop these incursions and the tribes began to settle in the northern provinces of China and formed an empire of their own. After about two centuries these invaders were gradually assimilated culturally by the Chinese, who were still numerous in the north, and the resultant multi-racial society greatly stimulated arts and literature.

THE T'ANG DYNASTY

In the seventh century China was once more unified under the T'ang dynasty (618–907). The civil service examination system which had been initiated in the Han dynasty was re-introduced in a new form and those who attained the highest degree not only had to excel in administrative ability but also had to be competent in literary composition. Cultural relationship with Persia, India and Japan became closer. In the seventh century the Buddhist monk Hsüan Tsang went to India to study Buddhism and to bring back the Buddhist canon to be translated into Chinese. The prosperity of T'ang was reflected in the capital, Changan, on which all activities centred. Thousands of outstanding poets and essayists were produced in this period. In the field of trade the system of guilds was developed to a high degree and handicrafts of all kinds flourished, especially in Changan. The territory of the T'ang empire was also more extensive than any other previous dynasty and the power of the frontier armies, still needed to keep the ever marauding tribes at bay, increased dangerously. This led to the decline in the power of the central government of the T'ang empire. In 757 a rebel army led by a frontier general captured the capital and forced the emperor Hsüan Tsung to take refuge in the mountains. Apart from rebellions there were troubles with court eunuchs who started to meddle in politics and the dynasty came to an end.

THE SUNG PERIOD

After a period of continuous civil war, the Sung dynasty was established in 960 and for a time there was peace and prosperity in China reminiscent of the heyday of the T'ang. The manufacture of porcelain and silk flourished and printing was invented. New irrigation methods were introduced in the south-east which increased its agricultural production. During the rule of the Sung dynasty special privileges were granted to upper class landowners and monastic estates which led to great patronage of the arts. It was a culturally very civilised age and the leading families in the empire not only possessed great wealth but also good taste. New genres of literature were added to the literary repertoire and the art of living was developed to a high level of perfection.

THE MONGOLS

In spite of these improvements the government was increasingly harrassed by repeated invasions of the Kin Tartars who set up a kingdom in the north of China in 1125. Meanwhile the Mongols who rose from central Asia became a great and menacing power; having conquered part of Europe and Asia Minor they finally overran China. In 1280 the Sung dynasty fell and the Mongolians established the Yüan dynasty. The military prowess of the conquering Mongol rulers far surpassed their capability for civilised government: the Mongol troops ruined the irrigation system and turned farming land into hunting ground. Harsh restrictions were imposed on the Chinese who were treated as an inferior race. The intellectuals were most hard hit by the oppression and all branches of literature suffered. Drama, which had been only in an embryonic form previously, was almost the only form of literature which flourished for it was not only a means of popular entertainment but also the chief form of expression.

THE MING ERA

The Yüan dynasty lasted eighty-nine years and was succeeded by the Ming dynasty in 1368. At this time contact with the outside world prompted one of the emperors to send a powerful eunuch to sail with a fleet on a tour of the countries in south-east Asia where there were rumours of subversion. His journey opened up a sea route from China to the south and west. In the sixteenth century the Jesuit priests came to China, churches were built and many Chinese including distinguished politicians accepted the Christian faith.

Toward the end of the sixteenth century the court eunuchs had succeeded in appropriating great power. They were granted the authority to deal with intellectuals and others who spoke too freely in criticising the government in any way, and this resulted in a general massacre of scholars. In 1630 a rebellion swept the country, the imperial troops were defeated and the Forbidden City in Peking, which was the imperial palace, was besieged. The emperor committed suicide and the defending army, unable to stem the tide, called in the help of the Manchus who gladly took the opportunity to overrun China. After they had put down the rebellion they immediately seized power for themselves and set up the Ch'ing dynasty in 1644.

THE MANCHUS

Although the Manchus gradually adopted Chinese culture, politically they remained a race apart and debarred the Chinese from taking any high office. In the nineteenth century inefficiency and corruption demoralised the Ch'ing court and the losses in the Opium War and the Taiping Rebellion brought both political and financial ruin. When European thought was introduced into China via Japan in the middle of the nineteenth century, the younger generation looked to the West for new ideas and the French and American Revolutions had a considerable impact, though delayed. Reform was believed to be inevitable by those who hoped to avoid a revolution. During the eighteen-nineties even the Emperor Kuang Hsü was convinced by his tutor of the necessity of adopting some form of constitutional government, but as this met with the opposition of the Empress Dowager Tz'u Hsi, the emperor was forced to abdicate.

A few reforms were effected. For example, the old out-dated civil service examination was abolished at the beginning of this century and Peking University was founded to prepare young men for further study in Japan or the West in new disciplines apart from classical Chinese literature.

MODERN TIMES

Dr Sun Yat Sen and some followers of his were amongst those Chinese students in Japan, and they formed the revolutionary party the *T'ung Meng Hui*, the forerunner of the Chinese Nationalist Party. After their return to China, a revolution was launched in 1911 and in an almost bloodless war the revolutionary army seized Wuchang, a city in Hupei Province. The Manchu government surrendered to the revolutionaries and the first government of the Republic was established at Nanking. An effective democratic government could not function because the real power still lay in the hands of warlords, some of whom were bandits who had formed private armies and some were former soldiers. Dr Sun Yat Sen became the first president of the republic but he relinquished his powers to a former Ch'ing dynasty official and politician, Yüan Shih-kai, who subsequently proclaimed himself emperor. His reign, however, only lasted one hundred days and a republican government was once more formed in Peking. It was more of a success than the previous one. Demonstrations and demands for effective reform and modernisation which were led by students and intellectuals, such as the May 4th Movement, produced little effect upon the hardened warlords and politicians, instead they increased their suspicion of the intelligentsia.

Japanese aggression against China had existed on and off from the sixteenth century and after the Republic was set up, hardly a week passed without some incidents or disturbance instigated by the Japanese. The climax was reached in 1937 when the Sino-Japanese war broke out. This lasted for eight years with the Japanese army occupying large tracts of Chinese territory and only terminated with the end of the Second World War. When peace was declared in 1945 China was on the brink of a civil war between the Chinese Nationalists and the Communists. In spite of the efforts of the United States to make peace, civil war broke out with the Communists occupying all the rural areas in the south, west, and east and the Nationalists (or Kuomintang) occupying the cities. Both the intellectuals and the peasants were disillusioned with the Kuomintang so that the Communists marched with unexpected speed to Peking and Nanking. They instituted a new regime in Peking in 1948 which is still in power under the leadership of Mao Tse-tung. The Kuomintang government moved to the island of Taiwan (or Formosa) and Chiang Kai-shek continues to rule as the leader of the government in exile.

MAIN TRENDS IN LITERATURE

To anyone coming afresh to Chinese literature, the most striking thing must be its homogeneity and its enormous timespan, when compared with the literature of any other language. We find poems and fragments of prose from as early as the sixth century BC, which used essentially the same language, if not the same vocabulary, as the literature of the nineteenth century. The Chinese employ the ideogrammic form of writing which is not phonetic, and therefore surmounts all the difficulties produced by regional dialects and the changes of language caused by the passing of time. When we look at the geography of China and listen to the numerous dialects that are mutually incomprehensible, we realise what an amazing thing it is that China is one vast united country. Its greatest common bond is the written language in which any individual may acquire proficiency regardless of his region or his class. This unity of expression was fostered and promoted by the early unification of the country under a central government, which first successfully imposed itself on the people in the Ch'in dynasty, and consolidated itself in the Han dynasty (206 BC–AD 220). The mark of the Han dynasty was permanent on the entire social and economic structure of China. It also established the supremacy of the *literati*, which was practically never broken throughout the length of Chinese history. The prestige of the scholars ensured a profound respect for the written word, and China's early isolation and lack of contact with any other comparable civilisation fostered an aristocratic inbreeding of culture, which had all the dangers of stagnation. Only twice in the course of Chinese history did another culture of equal depth and advancement confront China, and on both occasions it provoked upheavals, not least in literature: they were, first, the coming of Buddhism from India about the second century AD to the sixth; and then the impact of the West during the nineteenth and twentieth centuries.

The literary inheritance safeguarded by the *literati* consisted predominantly of the Confucian classics. Broadly speaking, these included philosophical and historical writings, mainly of a didactic nature, and poetry in the metre of five or seven syllables to the line, which was called *shih*. A thorough knowledge of these classics, and an ability to compose poetry in the *shih* metre were the requirements of the civil service examinations, and upon these examinations depended a man's future, since society considered a career as a government official the only one worthy of esteem. The importance of these examinations exerted the greatest influence, or even stranglehold upon the school curricula, which could only teach the classics, but their predominance was not without virtue in the promotion of literature.

EARLY POETRY

The admiration for poetry grounded itself on the teachings of Confucius himself, who was supposed to have edited the anthology *The Book of Odes* (*c* 600 BC). The *shih* type of poetry with the five or seven syllables in the line began in the Later Han dynasty (AD 25–220), and, because of the educational system, produced the greatest bulk and lasted longer in time than almost any other genre of literature. This metre dominated poetry until the late nineteenth century, and even later. In spite of the apparent strictness of prosodic requirements, poets through the ages found little difficulty in producing greatly varied expressions. This was undoubtedly because the single syllable Chinese character could stand on its own without the trammels of grammatical inflexions, while the sense emerged from its position in the sentence. This afforded wide scope to the poet who could range his characters in such juxtapositions, so that he not only brought out the meaning, but added nuance to his words and images more concisely than is possible in any other language.

The subject matter was very much varied. Poetry was not considered to be the product of divine inspiration, but the expression of an individual's thoughts on any subject. Poems formed invitations; letters were exchanged in verse; and parties were organised at which the entertainment was poetry-making and wine-drinking; these were all fit subjects for writing verse as well as the expression of delight upon natural beauty, and the emotions of love and friendship. Romantic love, such as is known in the West, did not really exist in China, until the twentieth century, when it was introduced under the direct influence of western literature. Love between the sexes was regarded in a different light in Chinese society, an attitude reflected in its literature. The arranged match, and the almost total segregation of the sexes afforded less opportunity for an individual to choose his love. This is not to say that there were no stories of romantic elopements or lovelorn youths, which abounded in both history and fiction, but the pursuit of love was not seen to be an overwhelming passion that drove all before it, but rather as one aspect of a human need. In fact, there were just as many stories concerning the progress of married life. In Chinese literature, the pangs of romantic love are more than balanced by the sorrows of separation of married man and wife. Perhaps one of the most moving poems in Chinese is an anonymous ballad, probably of the Later Han dynasty, which tells of the enforced separation of a young married couple and their subsequent suicide (*A Peacock Flies to the South-east*), a tragedy that bears comparison with *Romeo and Juliet*.

Apart from the *shih* type of poetry, the Chinese produced other forms which were not found in the West. The *fu* was a form which started in the Han dynasty; it employed lines of irregular lengths, and was more like rhythmic prose. The subject matter tended to be restricted to descriptions of scenic beauty or eulogies on specific occasions. Its origins were wholly courtly, and its style was often stilted except in the hands of the most skilful.

Another genre of poetry which had no European counterpart was *tz'u*, which arose in the late T'ang dynasty (618–907). These were originally songs in irregular metre which were written with the aim of musical performance. Later other words were composed to fit the melodies which continued to bear the name of its original lyric. There were several hundred airs to which the *tz'u* was written. This genre of poetry emphasises the unique quality of the Chinese language which permitted itself to be easily accommodated in poetic metre. It also indicates the close relationship of Chinese poetry to music.

The Chinese poet appeared to have concentrated his energies on the lyric for there was no epic poetry and little narrative verse. Perhaps the myth-creating spirit that gave birth to the Greek and Teutonic epic was lacking in the Chinese cosmos. The Chinese tended to see their legendary heroes not as demi-gods but as great men. Life after death and the supernatural world were generally envisaged as counterparts to the earthly model. Chinese mythology has been preserved only in fragments, much of it pieced together by collecting allusions and fragments from early works, such as pre-Han classical texts on philosophy, and from early poetry. The loss can only be explained by the rejection of the supernatural by the Confucian scholars, following the example of Confucius himself, who preferred to ignore supernatural things. Another conspicuous lack is the theme of war in poetry; poems in praise of war and fighting are not found, while anti-militaristic poems abound. There were a few fragments, such as in the pre-Han *Ch'u Tz'u*, while historical writings and fictional prose did not omit the praises of famous generals and warriors. It is very hard to suggest any reasons for their general absence from poetry. Perhaps the influence of Buddhism meant that there was little glory in killing. The Chinese imagination delighted in the pleasures of being sociable, the joys of this life, and the infinite variations of nature, whose mortality, along with man's own, only served to intensify its present enjoyment, and the pathos of existence. And the expression of these feelings were most supremely embodied in the poetry.

These were the higher flights of the creative imagination in China. Concurrent with them was the vernacular literature, which belonged to the popular tradition. The classical literature was written in a language not in everyday use, but in the usage of the ancients. Naturally such usage altered with their period of composition but the aim released the language of literature from the idioms and grammar of everyday speech, and removed the subjects from the vulgarity of life. But the vernacular literature, written in the form of the novel and drama (both of which were late-comers to the literary scene) was written for immediate enjoyment, even that of the uneducated masses.

FICTION

It was not until the sixth century that fiction-writing began to appear, taking the shape of a story with a plot; it was first written in the classical language by learned men eager to display their skill. In spite of the rejection of the supernatural by Confucian ethics, many of them were ghost stories, or tales which dealt with the supernatural, written by scholars who treated them as a diversion from a serious mood. The long novel really took its shape from the public story-teller in temple grounds and fairs. There were men trained in the oral tradition of narrative, changing their style to suit their particular audience, and ending a session with a tantalising prophecy that ensured an audience for the next day's performance. Out of this art grew the long novel whose style evolved through the picaresque novel, such as the *Water Margin* and the *Monkey*, and culminated in the *Dream of the Red Chamber* which was written in the early Ch'ing dynasty (1644–1911). This was the only genre of literature in Chinese which finds a direct parallel with European literature and its highest achievement stands on a par with the great Russian novels. Yet, however much the novel was valued and enjoyed, it remained outside the stream of serious academic study in China until modern times.

DRAMA

The drama, such as the kind that came to be written down, came into existence even later than the novel. It rose at a time which coincided with a lack of other literary achievements, at the lowest ebb of scholarship under the Mongol government (Yüan dynasty 1280–1368), which made it a policy to suppress the literati. The Chinese drama was an interesting combination of poetry, singing, music, dancing and spectacle. It never left the structure and style of a popular entertainment, and remained at the level of melodrama with strong moral overtones. The plot consisted of romances and revenge stories which often retold familiar themes and legends, and cannot be compared with the heights of European drama. The most highly valued part of drama was the poetry which was sung and interspersed amongst the action by the leading actors. Although theatricals were enjoyed by all levels of society, the scholar-connoisseur picked out the poetry for special savour.

MODERN TIMES

The twentieth century presents some of the most interesting problems in literature, for the impact of the West broke down the isolation of China, demolished the supremacy of the intellectual élite by tearing down the huge Confucian edifice, and abolished the civil service examinations. Technology, which China was most behind in, became the vanguard of learning, and with it went the acquiring of foreign languages. Foreign literature in general, both in the original and in translation, was eagerly absorbed, and this naturally had great repercussions on Chinese literature itself. The narrow confines of traditional Chinese thought were regarded as worthless and backward by a young generation thirsty for scientific knowledge and liberal western philosophy. It was in this mould of thought that the new literature was created. It was a time of restless seekings, and wild expressions, all testifying to a state of mind searching for some identity in the new world, having rejected the old. It was joined with the stirrings of the theories of liberty and Marxism, in a land which, impoverished with mismanagement and wars, was fertile for such ideas. The writings of the twenties and thirties were inextricably intertwined with the political scene. The establishment of the vernacular as the accepted style of writing went hand in hand with the effort towards universal literacy and the whole revolutionary spirit was embodied in the *May 4th Movement*, which advocated among other things a 'literary re-birth' with literature in the colloquial language.

It marked a turning point in both the history and culture of China. The influence of foreign literature produced new forms. In drama, Ibsen and Chekhov were the greatest influence and plays of realism took the stage in complete contrast to the old Chinese opera. The subject and the style of the new plays often had a clear purpose in showing the grievances of the poor and the apathy or heartlessness of the rich. This was paralleled by a tremendous output of fiction-writing, especially of short stories, which became a powerful tool in the hands of young articulate writers. Fiction, which already had a firm basis in earlier Chinese literature, received new vigour from the examples of the West and was probably the most successful and skilful tool of the new generation.

In poetry the influence of foreign languages was perhaps the most obvious, but it was not the most easily assimilated. Turned away from the traditional means of versification, the poets virtually had to create a new poetic language. Pioneer efforts read uncomfortably, but it was a period of experimentation, which was followed by much that was worthwhile. Many literary societies were founded whose members debated in speech and print on literary as well as political theories with equally passionate conviction; one such group was known as *Crescent Society* including men like Wen I-to and Hsü Chih-mo who were well acquainted with western literature, especially with the Romantic Movement in England. They turned special attention to the refinement and beauty of language and their influence on the form and language of literature was lasting.

Much of the momentum for these literary activities came from political and social grievances and when the Chinese Communist Party took over the government, the energies devoted to bringing about a revolution were turned towards the encouragement of new cultural trends. The strength and seriousness applied to all aspects of social improvements coloured the entire literary output. There was no more room for abstruse thinking or tranquil contemplation. Although most of the propaganda literature produced, whether to praise the revolution or its leader Mao Tse-tung, provoked distaste in the majority of foreign readers, there were doubtless writings that were the genuine expressions of life and work. These were the work of authors who came from all walks of life and not just the intellectual élite, even though these new writers were restricted by ideology to certain specific subjects.

Literature had reached a clear turning-point at the beginning of this century. New life and ideas were forcibly injected into the blood stream of Chinese culture. This had less than fifty years of free growth before the restriction of ideology narrowed the general freedom of speech. The present day has not seen more than its initial growth, so that it is hard to be sufficiently detached to give a valid judgement, or compare the achievement with that of the past in China or the literature of other lands, which have had a less traumatic rebirth. If almost three thousand years was the life-span of classical Chinese literature, perhaps fifty years is too little time to judge the new literature.

INDIVIDUAL WRITERS AND WORKS

Chi Yün (1724–1805) was the chief editor of the collection of books known as the *Ssu-k'u-ch'üan-shu* which was made up from the imperial library in Ch'ien-lung's time and included almost all the important literary works in Chinese. Chi Yün held the post of the head of the Imperial Academy and was a trusted minister of the emperor, except for one brief period in exile in Urumchi for indiscretion with official secrets. He was recalled and began the task of editing the *Ssu-k'u-ch'üan-shu.* He supervised several hundred scholars at the task of editing old books. To each book he wrote a summary, and a brief critical introduction in which he assessed its value. He himself was also the author of several collections of short stories and essays, some of which were concerned with his stay in Urumchi.

Chou Tso-jen (1885–1958?) was an essayist and translator. He was the elder brother of Lu Hsün. He studied in Japan in his youth and came into contact with European literature through translations in Japanese, which he then re-translated into Chinese. On his return he became a lecturer at the University of Peking where he was highly thought of for his scholarship on Chinese literature. Although Chou's literary ability was comparable with Lu Hsün's yet he lacked his brother's vision and idealism. In character Chou was more like a traditional Chinese scholar.

Ch'ü Yüan (340?–278? BC), the author of *Ch'u Tz'u*, was a statesman and diplomat of the State of Ch'u in the period of the Warring States. He was nobly born and became a leading courtier when he was still a young man. His loyalty to his king was unquestionable but his fellow-courtiers, envious of his position, slandered him so that he lost his favour and was exiled. Soon afterwards, being recalled, he advised against the personal visit of the king to the neighbouring state of Ch'in which was very powerful, but the king went and was kept prisoner there until he died. The new king of Ch'u had no confidence in Ch'ü Yüan and again he was exiled. He was now an old man, disappointed with himself for not having prevented the death of his old master and disillusioned with his new master, so that when he heard that Ch'u had been annexed by Ch'in he drowned himself in the Milo River. He became a model of loyalty and steadfastness to whose image all later courtiers and statesmen aspired.

Of the poems in Ch'ü Yüan's work the *Ch'u Tz'u*, the most famous is the *Encountering Sorrow*, one of the longest poems in Chinese which is allegedly an allegory of his own life in terms of mythology. The poem is conceived in the form of a quest for a goddess from whom the poet received no help, and it ends in disappointment. There are many obscure passages in the poem but the beauty and scope of his imagination has made it a very important one. The language and use of symbolism has had great influence on all later literature and even gave rise to one particular genre called the *fu*, a kind of poetic prose which made use of his style and method of expression.

Ch'ü Yüan became a popular hero in legend after his death. The festival of the fifth day of the fifth month is held in his honour; during the festival food wrapped in bamboo leaves is thrown into the river as a sacrifice for his spirit whilst boats with dragon-shaped prows are rowed in races to scare away the other water spirits. This festival is also known as the Dragon Boat Festival.

Chuang Tzu (365–290? BC) was a contemporary of Mencius (*qv*), but Mencius made no mention of Chuang Tzu, probably because he despised Chuang Tzu's teaching. Chuang Tzu was a Taoist philosopher of the Warring States period. Some say that he lived before the time of Lao Tzu, but others say that he promoted the philosophy of Lao Tzu. Chuang Tzu's philosophy was atheistic; he believed that the many changes of nature were not ordered by a creator and that all things came about naturally. He also thought that all attributes, such as good and evil, beauty and ugliness, were relative and not positive. Chuang Tzu's most important tenet was the preservation of what is natural, and the purity of nature. He promoted a way of life which never interfered with nature, that of *wu wei*, 'doing nothing', which was completely opposed to that of Confucianism.

Chuang Tzu's writings were alleged to be numerous but what remains today cannot be proved to be authentic: they are famous for their passages of great beauty of language and breadth of imagination.

Confucius' name was **K'ung Ch'iu** (551–479 BC). Confucius was the Latinisation of the term Kung Fu Tzu, that is, Master Kung. He lived in the turbulent period when China was divided up into several city states which were constantly engaged in internecine warfare, a period known as that of the Warring States. Confucius travelled to the courts of different states to preach his philosophy of peace and contentment but none listened to him. He returned to his home in the State of Lu and turned his attention to teaching, and to research in ancient Chinese culture. He is alleged to have edited several ancient books, such as the *Spring and Autumn Annals* and the *Book of Odes* but he wrote nothing original himself. Although he cannot be counted as one of the writers of ancient China yet his philosophy has dictated much of Chinese thought; Chinese literature is permeated with Confucianism. The *Lung Yü* (*Conversations*) was compiled by Confucius' pupils to record his sayings and was the first and only book used by the early Confucianists. Confucius emphasised that good influence was of greater value in politics than force, and that in social relationships each man's position and responsibility should be governed by *li*, that is, the rules of natural ties and social expediency which everyone should be content to keep. *Li* therefore is one of the most important tenets of the Confucian school and by that means social harmony should be preserved. Since the Han dynasty the teaching of Confucius has been acknowledged and respected by the rulers of China and it has also formed the basis of Chinese education.

Han Yü (768–824) was an essayist of the T'ang dynasty. He came to hold very high office in the realm, including that of Imperial Academician. He was a dedicated Confucian scholar and held the view that literature should convey the way of righteous living to readers. One of the measures he advocated was the eschewing of an ornamented and flowery language much in vogue at the time and a return to the simplicity and directness of earlier times, such as the Han. This was known as the Movement for Ancient Style in which he was supported by Liu Tsung-yüan.

Han Yü's poetry was not rated as highly as his prose for the poems were more like prose with rhymes attached, rather than being intrinsically poetry.

Hsin Ch'i-chi (1140–1207) was a prolific writer of the *tz'u* style of poetry. He was born under the Sung dynasty, in the territory occupied by the Kin Tartars, the Chinese government having fled to the south of China to hold it against the invaders. Later, Hsin joined them to resist the Kin Tartars. Although the emperor was unwilling to wage a full scale war, Hsin was himself injured while taking part in a skirmish. His poetry was heroic in tone and was a product of his sense of patriotism combined with his personal emotions.

Hsü Chih-mo (1899?–1931) was a poet. After he graduated from the Peking University he went to study in the United States and later in England at Cambridge. When he returned he lectured for a time on English literature in various universities in China. He was one of the founders of the Crescent Society, a literary society, which consisted of a group of literary men who played an important part in the development of the form of new writing and poetry in the colloquial language. Hsü's poems are mostly lyrical. He was one of the poets who most successfully used the colloquial language in poetry. Hsü's attitude towards literature was thought by his contemporaries to be dilettante but he was a very popular person amongst his friends. He died in an air crash in 1931. Hsü dedicated many of his works to his second wife Lu Hsiao-man, a celebrated beauty of her time, to whom he claimed he owed the inspiration to write.

Hu Shih (1891–1962) was one of the literary reformers of the *May 4th Movement*. He received part of his education in the United States and belonged to that group of western-orientated authors. His greatest contribution was his promotion of early vernacular literature especially the novel and his advocacy of the use of the vernacular in all fields of communication to supersede the classical language. He was a professor at Peking University, where his lectures were enthusiastically attended, and he became its president after the Second World War. In 1948 he went to Taiwan and was the Chinese ambassador to Washington. In recent years he has been most severely criticised by the Marxist writers in China.

Kuan Han-ch'ing (1241?–1322?) was a dramatist of the Yüan dynasty. Of the Yüan dramatists he was perhaps the greatest but very little is known of his life. He was born in Peking and he was the actor-manager of a troupe of his own. He was also a song writer. About twenty of his plays are extant, the most famous being *The Injustice Done to Tou Ngo.*

Kuo Mo-jo (1893–) is a poet, essayist and playwright. He studied medicine in Japan. As a writer he has been prolific and his works include creative writing, learned treatises and translation on a wide range of subjects. His interpretation of history from a liberal point of view kindled the minds of many students but in his archaeological studies he is not always considered sound by other scholars. Kuo has been an impulsive and radical man all his life. He is one of the founders of the Creation Society, a society devoted to the propagation of new ideas in literature. He is one of the few literary men chosen by the Communist regime in China to be a representative of writers in the People's Congress.

Lao Shê (1898–1967), pseudonym of Shu Ch'ing-ch'un, was a novelist and satirist. He spent some years in England in his youth. His novels are situated in Peking and show a special concern for the ordinary people in this city, for whom he had a deep understanding, even whilst he satirised them. His books are full of the details of everyday life, including many comic scenes and characters. The *Rickshaw Boy* is his most famous novel. During the Sino-Japanese war he wrote the trilogy, *Four Generations under one roof*, in which his gaiety changed to a sadder note.

Li Ch'ing-chao (1081–?) was a poetess of the Sung dynasty. Her life is little known. Her only works are collected in the *Su-yü-tz'u.*

Li Ho (790–816) was a descendant of an aristocratic family in the Later T'ang dynasty. He was known as an infant prodigy. As a poet he was famous for his eccentricity. He was a thin man who used to ride an emaciated horse followed by a page boy carrying a bag. Whenever Li Ho felt inspired he would write down the lines which were then put into the page's bag and when he went home he would go over what he had written. He wrote ceaselessly and worked without stopping which contributed to his early death at twenty-six. Critics often praised his extraordinary genius which they pronounced as unearthly or ghostly because of his preoccupation with things of the twilight world.

Li Ju-chen (1763–1830) was a novelist of the Ch'ing dynasty. He was an excellent scholar but his dislike of artificialities such as the style of essay writing known as the 'eight-legged style' required for the civil service examinations caused him to be only moderately successful in examinations. He held a few minor posts, amongst them was the Supervisorship of Repairs of the Yellow River. His term of office coincided with a collapse of part of a dyke and it was only his speedy action carried out night and day that saved the area from flood disaster; but he was not acknowledged or rewarded. His family was not rich so he had to do many jobs to earn enough money, amongst them was that of a medical practitioner.

His novel *Flowers in the Mirror* set in the time of the Empress Wu of the T'ang dynasty is really a satire on contemporary society. In the novel the empress summons women to take the civil examinations and many talented and intelligent women arrived from strange countries. These imaginary countries are described as a means of satire, much like the different lands visited in Swift's *Gulliver's Travels.* Two hundred chapters were intended by Li, of which he only wrote one hundred.

Li Po (701–62) was a poet of the mid T'ang dynasty. His poetic output was enormous and he became a legendary character not only for his poetry but also for his colourful way of life. He never had any lasting employment for his nature could not put up with the restraints of a regular life. Instead he spent much of his life travelling to such places as south-west China, famous for its beautiful scenery, the effect of which can be seen in his poetry.

Li Po had great respect for the art of the samurai; his own skill with the sword was considerable and he frequently used the image of the sword in his poetry. But he loved drinking more and was said to be often drunk. One legend alleges that when he was summoned to the court by the emperor Ming Huang to compose poetry he was offered wine on which he quickly became drunk; thereupon he insisted that the emperor's favourite concubine, Yang Kuei-fei, should prepare his ink and brush and that the all-powerful eunuch Kao Li-shih should take his boots off for him. Both the requests were granted by the emperor but Yang Kuei-fei and Kao Li-shih, the proudest and the most powerful people in the empire at that time, became his enemies for the rest of his life.

His poetry gives the most vivid descriptions of natural scenes: for example:

A single sail, motionless, unturning,
Floating like breeze, falls beyond the edge of heaven.

He is unsurpassed in the scope of his fanciful imagination and he has been rightly dubbed by later critics as the 'immortal of poets'. The ease and natural flow of his verse show little signs of art but the unselfconsciousness of his poetry was also an expression of his character.

I am drunk, I wish to sleep; friend, you can go now,
If you are in the mood tomorrow morning, come with your lute.

He became very poor in his old age which also coincided with times of great hardship and civil war. He wandered from place to place and died on the road in the winter of 762. Characteristically, a legend grew up about his death which claimed that when drunk aboard a boat, he pursued the reflection of the moon in the water and so drowned.

Li Shang-yin (813–58) was a poet of the T'ang dynasty. His talents were recognised early in his youth but his political career was not a success because he was involved in a feud between two eminent politicians. Soon he resigned from his post. Li's poems make ingenious use of the colourful objects of everyday life as a background; a painted screen, an incense burner or a patterned lute all serve as symbols in his poetic imagery. This was especially apparent in his love-poems which were said to be inspired by three women. A thought of longing is reflected in the colourfulness and stillness of his chosen object:

> The lute like an embroidered needlework would have fifty strings,
> Each string and each nut is the memory of a wonderful year.

Li as a poet was not rated as highly as Li Po or Tu Fu in the history of Chinese literature but reading his poems one is spellbound by the nuances of simple sentences suggesting a profusion of feelings; in this sense he was unique. His love-affairs all ended sadly: after the death of his wife to whom he was deeply attached, he loved a nun who was beyond his reach; later he fell in love with two ladies of the imperial court, both of whom died in the palace when young. These experiences contributed to his poetry a sense of mystery and obscurity for he could not under such circumstances reveal the identities of the women who were to him 'forbidden fruit'. His poems and essays are collected in eleven volumes.

Li Yü (937–78). After the destruction of the T'ang dynasty the empire was split under five dynasties, and Li Yü was the emperor of the so-called Later T'ang. His nature, however, was ill suited to being an emperor; rather, he was an artist of great talent, skilled at poetry, painting and music. Li Yü's wife, the Lady Chou, to whom he was deeply attached, and for whom he wrote many poems, was also extremely gifted; she died, however while still young and Li Yü then married her younger sister and transferred to her the affection which he had had for his former queen. At that time the power of Sung, the next dynasty to reunite China, was growing and much of Li Yü's kingdom was already lost to the Sung; but although he was the emperor, he made no attempt to regain it and continued to lead a life of ease and leisure. Moreover he was a devout Buddhist and had no inclination to resist with military force, so that he was soon conquered and made a prisoner by the Sung emperor. In his despair he composed much of his best poetry; to his former ministers he wrote

> From midday to night here I wash only in tears.

At this time he wrote much poetry in the style of the 'little *tz'u*', in which he lamented his fate. When the Sung emperor read the poetry he realised that Li Yü had not resigned himself to his deposition, and that this might lead to open rebellion later; he therefore ordered Li Yü to commit suicide, which was a privileged means of execution for those of noble birth.

Liang Ch'i-ch'ao (1874–1929) was a writer who advocated reforms for China under a constitutional monarchy. He supported K'ang Yu-wei who brought about the Hundred Days' Reform under the emperor Kuang-hsü which ended disastrously when the empress dowager resumed power and had the emperor imprisoned. Liang had to flee from China and spent many years travelling abroad in Japan, the United States and Australia; he only returned home after the Revolution in 1911. When Yüan Shih-kai attempted to establish himself as emperor, Liang was strongly opposed to him and as a result had to leave the country again. Later after Yüan's fall he returned and devoted himself to his writings and lectured in various universities.

He was much influenced by European thought and introduced many European works of literature to China. His essays, collected under the title of *Essays from the Drink-Ice Studio*, covered a wide variety of subjects which included political theory, historical discussions and literary criticism. His writings had great influence amongst the young intellectuals, and students of that time.

Lin Shu (1852–1924) was a translator and novelist of the early era of the Republic. His best known works were translations, or rather paraphrases, of European novels such as those of Dumas fils, Dickens, Scott and others. Although he knew no other language than Chinese he made use of the services of friends who knew the original languages of these novels. They translated for him orally and he rendered them into classical Chinese. He was the first person whose translations received widespread acclaim. Because of his use of the classical language his position amongst modern novelists is anomalous, since the classical language at that time was being superseded as a literary medium.

Liu Hsiang (77–6 BC) was an essayist and *fu* writer of the Han dynasty. Of his surviving works the most famous are *Intrigues of the Warring States* which narrates historical events in chapters using the style of short-story writing, and *Lives of Virtuous Women* which show the exemplary lives of women of antiquity; the latter work was compulsory reading for women in former times. He also composed the *Catalogue of Books* for the *History of Han*, which consisted of all the books written before the Han dynasty and has proved an invaluable aid to our knowledge of Han dynasty bibliography, although most of the books included in his catalogue are now lost.

Liu Ngo (1857–1909) was a novelist of the Ch'ing dynasty. He had many occupations during his life; when a friend wrote a letter of recommendation for him, he stated that he had been trained in 'mathematics, water conservancy, engineering, electrical engineering and ship-building'. He was strongly in favour of the building of a network of railways all over China and advocated co-operation with foreign investors, for which he was criticised by many people, with the result that when the railways were built his name was omitted from the committee in charge. He lived in the decline of the Manchu administration when officials were corrupt and inefficient, particularly in the field of criminal law under which political prisoners suffered most. His novel *The Travels of Lao Ts'an* reflected the life that he saw around him.

Liu Ngo was also a collector of Shang dynasty oracle bones and made a great contribution to their study.

Liu Tsung-yüan (773–819) was an essayist of the T'ang dynasty whose name has often been linked with that of Han Yü. They were both involved in the literary movement which advocated a purging of the prose language from its ornamentions such as clichés and parallelisms and a return to the simplicity and directness of earlier times. Liu came very high in the civil service examination results and was given office in the imperial archives. Famous for his scholarship and for the excellence of his prose style, he always maintained that literary talents should be put to the service of the government. He insisted on clarity of expression and logic in argument and was against the flowery language so often employed by government officials. He wrote some poetry and also books on travel in which he expressed his own feelings by describing unusual natural scenery.

Lo Kuan-chung (1330?–1400?) was a dramatist and novelist of the Yüan dynasty. Very little is known of his life, and one of his friends recorded that he did not associate much with other people. His *Story of the Three Kingdoms* is the first great Chinese historical novel and remains as popular today as when it first came out in the middle of the fourteenth century.

Lu Hsün (1881–1936), the pen-name of Chou Shu-jen, a brother of Chou Tso-jen, was a novelist and essayist and one of the leading writers of the *May 4th Movement*. In his youth he went to Japan where he studied medicine which he soon abandoned. He became strongly aware of the weakness and decadence of China and realised that literature could be one of the means for a restoration of China. When he returned to China he devoted his time to writing and teaching at various schools and universities. Lu Hsün's dissatisfaction with Chinese society and government caused him much friction with the authorities and in 1925 he was obliged to leave Peking to teach in Amoy University, Fukien, and from there he went to the Chung Shan University at Canton. But in neither of these places was he happy: he left academic life to live in Shanghai in 1927, writing and editing various literary journals until his death in 1936.

His two selections of short stories *Na Han* and *P'ang Huang* which satirise Chinese life, contain some of the best of modern Chinese short stories. The most famous of his longer short stories are *The True Story of Ah Q* and *Diary of a Madman*, both of which express strong criticism of society.

He disapproved of traditional Chinese morals, and was opposed both to the government and its institutions. In his later years he devoted more time to the writing of polemics. Because of the amount of time he spent championing the causes of modern reform he was nicknamed Don Lu Hsün on the analogy of Don Quixote.

In addition to his creative writing and polemical essays he also devoted much time to the study of the history of Chinese literature, the translation of the works of western authors (especially Russian novels) and the introduction of western woodcuts. His *Brief History of Chinese Fiction* is one of the most important pioneering works in Chinese literary criticism. He can be rated as one of the most important Chinese writers of the twentieth century and once he was recommended as a candidate for the Nobel prize in literature.

Mao Tun (pseud. of Shen Yen-ping) (1896–   ) is a novelist. He was the editor of a Shanghai newspaper and joined the Kuomintang Northern Expedition as a press officer. Later he left the army and returned to Shanghai where he began to write novels. His first work was a trilogy consisting of *Disillusion*, *Vacillation* and *Pursuit*, published in 1927 which immediately gained a large readership amongst the young. The attitude of the novels reflected a deep pessimism about life which was felt by young people who were disillusioned with the decadence of society and the corruptness of politics. The best known of his novels *Midnight*, which was produced later, depicts the life of speculators in Shanghai in the thirties at the height of the speculation boom. It dealt with men who became rich overnight and who lived by oppression in a decadent Shanghai society. His novels are much admired for their ability to depict life realistically and for their sharp social satire.

After 1949 Mao Tun continued to write and was the representative for writers and artists to the People's Congress. Shortly before the Cultural Revolution he incurred disapproval and was severely criticised for his novel *Lin Family Shop*, in which he allegedly supported capitalist ownership of property.

Mencius (372–289 BC) was a philosopher of the time of the Warring States. A record of his conversations was preserved by his disciples under the title of *Meng Tzu*. Tradition has it that his mother moved house three times for his sake during his formative years. He was educated by a second generation disciple of Confucius. Finding the kings and princes of his time unscrupulous in their pursuit of riches and power, he followed in Confucius' footsteps as a travelling philosopher trying to spread his ideas of righteousness, love, justice and fairness. He cross-examined people with a penetrating thoroughness and argued vigorously with all and sundry. He failed in this, and retired to teach. All his life he advocated that human nature was fundamentally good, and that simple people were more important than kings and princes.

Pan Ku (AD 32–92) inherited the office of historian to the Han dynasty from his father Pan Piao but was dissatisfied with his father's work on the history of the Han. He decided on a different method of writing which was based on that of *Historical Records* (*qv* Ssu-ma Ch'ien). His book the *Han Shu*

(*The Book of Han*) is our major source for men and events of the Former Han dynasty. At his death the work was not complete and his sister Pan Chao continued and finished the writing.

Pien Chih-lin (1910–) is a poet of 'New Verse'. He studied European literature at Peking University and translated some of the works of Baudelaire and Mallarmé into Chinese as well as a large number of critical essays on poetry by various modern European scholars and poets. After World War II he spent a year at Oxford. The most famous collection of his poems is entitled *Leaves of Three Autumns.*

He felt that poetry was something that was firmly attached to life and he preferred a natural method of self-expression. As a person he is quiet and withdrawn and his modesty and love of solitude make him seem like an old poet of ancient China.

Ping Hsin (1903–), the pen-name of Hsieh Wan-ying, is a poetess and short-story writer. She was educated at Union College (afterwards renamed Yenching University), Peking and Wellesley College, US, and then joined the staff of Yenching University. Her writing is sensitive, gentle and limpid and she also writes for children and young people. She is one of the earliest women writers of the *May 4th Movement*.

Po Chü-i (772–846) also known as Po Lo-t'ien, was a poet of the T'ang dynasty. Through his early success in the civil service examinations he continued to hold office for the rest of his life, rising in rank until he became an academician and the tutor to the heir apparent. He was very successful because he was a loyal and responsible man but several times he incurred the enmity of higher officials through his outspokenness. On one such occasion he was demoted to the West Lake where an important dike, still remaining, was supposed to have been constructed by him. The outstanding virtues of Po's poetry were its readability and humanity. Amongst the most famous are his narrative poems and those such as the *Song of Everlasting Regret* and *Song of the P'i P'a* are known to every schoolboy. The former is the love story of the T'ang emperor Hsüan-tsung and Yang Kuei-fei and the latter is about a courtesan, aged and neglected in the provinces, to whom the poet extends his sympathy and kindness, which was unusual in the society of that time. He also wrote many long poems with the intention of showing the social abuse and unhappiness of the common people. One of the most famous is the *Old Man with the Broken Arm* which tells the story of an old man who in his youth was conscripted to fight in the far south in the empire-building campaigns of that time; very few men ever came back. In order to escape the misery of that campaign the old man had broken his arm with a large stone deliberately so that he could be sent home as being useless to the army; although the pain of the broken arm was great, yet it was preferable to being in the army on campaign. Po wrote many such poems which, although indictments of society in themselves, never lost their poetic beauty in the process.

P'u Sung-ling (1640–1715) was a novelist and essayist. In spite of many attempts at the civil service examinations he was never successful until the age of seventy-two, when he succeeded in gaining the honorary rank of *kung-sheng*. However he had long been famous for his literary abilities, especially in the ancient classical style. Of his works the most famous is *Strange Tales from Liao-chai* which consists of four hundred and thirty-one short stories. He was supposed to have gathered these stories by going round teahouses and listening to people's conversation. Some of them are popular traditional tales containing passages in local dialects. Some of them are his own invention, frequently on the subject of ghosts and the supernatural and they contain a large amount of satire. The tales for which he is most famous are written in the style of the T'ang dynasty classical short stories. He wrote a novel called *Hsing-shih Yin-yüan* which describes the life of several families in Shantung.

Shen T'sung-wên (1902–) is a novelist and short-story writer. He spent his youth in the army when he wrote under the pseudonym of the 'Little Soldier' but he left the army at the age of twenty-three and became a full time writer. He lectured at various universities.

His works are mainly concerned with provincial and country life. The most famous books are *Frontier Town* and *Portrait of Eight*; the former describes the life of a country girl and the effect of environment upon a person's character and the latter was a collection of short stories about the lives of people in the provinces.

Shih Nai-an (1296–1370) was a novelist in the Yüan dynasty and to him is attributed the authorship of the *Water Margin* also known as *All Men Are Brothers*. Details of his life are hardly known but he was thought to have taken part in an unsuccessful rebellion against the Mongol government for which he was obliged to flee and live in hiding until the Ming dynasty came to power. It is said that during this period of enforced leisure he found an old book describing certain men who became outlaws because of their refusal to live under an oppressive government. He then wrote a novel based on the adventures of these outlaws which is the *Water Margin*. This is one of the earliest Chinese novels in the colloquial language and the stories are linked together in a loose sequence of events without a central plot. Although the heroes in the book lived under the Sung dynasty much of it clearly attacked contemporary life and politics. It was condemned by many orthodox critics for presenting subversive thoughts but nevertheless it achieved fame amongst all classes of society, especially during periods of oppressive government when the ordinary citizen's only way of escape from injustice was to take to a mountain fastness or hide in the wastelands.

Ssu-ma Ch'ien (145–86 BC) inherited the office of Grand Historian of the Han dynasty from his father Ssu-ma Yen. Ssu-ma Ch'ien was a friend of a general who had surrendered to the enemy in a campaign against the tribesmen of the north. The surrender roused the anger of the Emperor Wu Ti who branded his name as that of a traitor and when Ssu-ma Ch'ien ventured to defend his friend the emperor turned on him and sentenced him to be castrated, which was a punishment of deep disgrace and was usually forestalled by the suicide of the man under sentence. However Ssu-ma Ch'ien lived through it, determined to complete his work which was the writing of the history of China from legendary times to his own day which was called *Historical Records*. His method of historiography was to devote chapters of the book to individual subjects such as law and astronomy and to individual people, starting with the emperors and going on to biographies of others, such as ministers, politicians, generals, empresses and even famous soldiers of fortune. He made good use of history books written earlier and gave a clear account not only of events but also of epochs and places. The dynastic histories of later times were modelled on the *Historical Records*.

Ssu-ma Hsiang-ju (200–118 BC) was writer of the *fu* in the Han dynasty. He was a native of Cheng-tu and as a young man was famous for his skill at playing the lute. Once he was asked to play at the banquet of a wealthy man where he was heard by the host's daughter, Cho Wên-chün, a talented young woman recently widowed. She fell in love with him and they eloped together. Her father angrily disowned her and the young couple had no means of livelihood so they opened a winehouse where Wên-chün herself served behind the counter. When her father heard of this, for the sake of the family's good name, he gave them enough money to live on so that they would not have to resort to such a trade.

Hsiang-ju's *fu* eventually attracted the attention of the emperor who was greatly pleased with them and rewarded him. One of the surviving *fu* is called the *Fu of the Tall Gate* which was allegedly written in sympathy with the empress who had offended the emperor. He neglected her and kept her out of sight in the palace of Tall Gate. The emperor was so moved by Hsiang-ju's ability to convey the loneliness of the deserted empress that he took pity on her and received her back into his favour.

Su Shih (1036–1101) who was often known as Tung-po (eastern slope of the mountain) was a poet and statesman of the Sung dynasty. He came from a famous literary family and after passing the civil service examinations at the age of twenty-two he took office. He disagreed with the minister Wang Anshih and criticised him before the emperor. Wang was greatly angered and had him exiled to Hangchou as the governor of the then unimportant town, which was near the West Lake in a beautiful region. He improved the amenities there and made it into a centre of attractions. Later in his life, because of conflict with another minister Chang Heng, he was exiled to the faraway area of the south-west which was hardly penetrated by Chinese culture. Here he set to work again to create a pocket of civilisation. Eventually he was recalled to the capital.

Amongst his numerous friends was a Buddhist monk and he was greatly influenced by Buddhism in his way of thinking. His literary output was enormous and he was particularly famous for his poems in the *tz'u* style; a large number of them were about the West Lake which he compared to a woman whose eyes were the water and whose eyebrows were the surrounding hills. He also wrote *Poetry Talks of Tung-po* which was a collection of essays on literature, painting and life. His achievement in prose writing has made him one of the 'Eight Great Men' of the T'ang and Sung dynasties.

T'ao Ch'ien (or **T'ao Yüan-ming**) (365–427) was a Taoist and a poet of the nature school whose philosophy of life was to refuse to seek fame or worldly success.

He was born into a family with a scholarly tradition and appointed to a minor government post when he was in his late twenties. Indignant at the servile attitude which petty officials adopted towards their superiors he relinquished his office after three months and went to live in the country. There he farmed and worked the land with the peasants and his close contact with natural scenery inspired his poetry.

> Rising before the dawn I make the land ready for the plough,
> I return in the evening with the moon hanging on my hoe.

In his poems he showed how his communion with nature attained a 'transcendant nothingness' which was in accord with Taoist ideas. T'ao enjoyed a simple life; he made his own wine and drank it in the company of his fellow farmers but poverty and starvation were never far away:

> My summer days are embraced by hunger,
> I sleep the long winter nights with no quilts.

In middle-age misfortune visited him time and again: he lost his son, and his house was destroyed by fire; the changing political world compelled him to remain in the country where he found the hardships of a peasant's life getting beyond his endurance. In spite of this T'ao's poems retained a spiritual peacefulness and are full of compassion and humanity. T'ao was disillusioned with society but not with man. His prose poem *The Source of the Peach Blossom River* was an allegory of a forgotten Utopia which a fisherman found by accident whilst letting his boat drift up the river for a long time. Both Tao's life and poetry were examples aspired to by poets of later times but his mode of life though constantly praised and sought by others was never quite attained again.

Ts'ao Chan (or **Ts'ao Hsüeh-ch'in**) (1716–63) was a novelist and poet. He wrote the *Dream of the Red Chamber* which is the most important novel in colloquial Chinese. We know very little about his life except that his grandfather Ts'ao Yin was a friend and trusted minister of the emperor K'ang-hsi. Ts'ao Yin was the Commissioner for Textiles in Nanking which was an important office carrying responsibility for the textile factories in the area;

at the same time he acted as the emperor's special agent keeping him secretly informed of local events. He was very wealthy and led a life of ease and refinement in whose atmosphere the young Ts'ao Chan grew up. After his grandfather's death the relationship between the new emperor and the family worsened and finally the family suffered the punishment of confiscation of all their property although the crime was obscure. At that time Ts'ao Chan was only ten years old and he moved to Peking with his father where they led a life of comparative poverty. He started the novel at the age of thirty and spent over ten years on it before he died, without completing it, although the events of the latter half of the book could be inferred.

The *Dream of the Red Chamber* is concerned with the love story of a young man called Pao-yü which is told against the background of a family like that of Ts'ao Chan's youth. Although it has been suspected that the novel is autobiographical, there is no real evidence to show that this is the case. All the events and characters in the book are described with great sensitivity and understanding. The complexities of personal relationships within a society are delicately explored and they form the basis of the tragedy. The greatness of the book and its breadth and scope have attracted many scholars so that there has been a whole school of scholarship based on the *Dream of the Red Chamber* alone, similar to the studies that have been made in the West on Shakespeare.

Ts'ao Chih (192–232) was a poet of the period of the Three Kingdoms, and his father was the famous General Ts'ao Ts'ao (155–220). Because Ts'ao Chih showed great literary talent even as a boy he was much loved by his father which gave rise to the rumour that he was to be made heir in place of his elder brother Ts'ao P'ei (186–226) for which his brother never forgave him. While his father was alive Ts'ao Chih led a life of great ease in the company of literary men. After his father's death Ts'ao Chih suffered from the jealousy and fear of his brother and nephew who became emperors.

Of his works the prose-poem on *The Goddess of River Lo* is thought to be about the Lady Chen, wife of Ts'ao P'ei. When she died Ts'ao Chih dreamt that he saw a goddess of the River Lo. This prose-poem is famous for its description of his brief encounter with the goddess.

His poetry derived much inspiration from the style of folk songs in its simplicity and directness. Many of his poems are gay and lyrical but some written later in his life express a self-awareness which raise the style far above the folk idiom. It was said of him that 'If the world's talents were reckoned as ten, eight parts belong to Ts'ao Chih'.

Ts'ao Yü (1910–   ) is a modern playwright. In the early days of the Republic colloquial drama in the western style was appreciated only by a few and never achieved any success on the stage but Ts'ao Yü changed this situation. His plays, written in a realistic manner, showed him to be a critic of the morality and society of his time, and they were received with acclaim. His most popular plays are *Thunderstorm*, *Sunrise*, *Wilderness* and *Peking Man*. He was greatly influenced by modern European drama, especially that of Ibsen and O'Neill.

Tu Fu (712–70) was a poet of the T'ang dynasty. He was a contemporary and friend of Li Po. He never succeeded in passing the civil service examinations and did not hold any high office in his life. When the rebel An Lu-shan took up arms and occupied the capital of Ch'angan, the emperor fled leaving it in the hands of the rebels. Tu Fu found himself stranded in a rebel area and unable to join his family. During the civil war the sight and suffering of the people made a deep impression on him and he expressed their hardship and agony in poems written in the style of old ballads, such as the *Recruiting Officer at Shih-hao* which described an incident of conscription during the war. Eventually he made his way in disguise from occupied territory and joined the legal government which he served as an official of a minor capacity and often depended on the charity of his friends to support himself and his family. Although he has been reckoned one of the greatest poets China ever produced, all his life he had a sense of failure because he never succeeded in becoming an official of any standing.

One of the outstanding qualities of his poetry is its compassion. The language is always simple and direct, dignified and self-effacing in tone and it was the model for many later poets. He has been called the greatest poet in China and has been the most popular and best loved of Chinese poets.

Wang Ch'ung (AD 27–*c* 97) was a philosopher and essayist of the Han dynasty. His best known collection of essays is entitled *Lun Hêng* which is distinguished not only for its philosophical argument but also its fine literary style. He brought a sceptical and critical attitude to bear upon contemporary values and beliefs which were being accepted by people without question. He also examined and revalued early philosophical works. In many respects he was well in advance of his own time.

Wang Shih-fu (*fl* thirteenth century) was a dramatist of the Yüan dynasty. He wrote many plays, but of his two surviving plays the more famous is the *Romance of the Western Chamber*. It is about the love between a young scholar and a young lady from a wealthy family. References to the play are often made in Chinese literature as the idealised love-story. Almost nothing is known of Wang except that he was a native of Peking.

Wang Wei (699–759) was a Buddhist poet of the T'ang dynasty. Thanks to his good performance in the civil service examinations he obtained a high office early in his career but in the rebellion of An Lu-shan he was taken prisoner by the rebel government which tried to force him to take office under it. When he refused he was imprisoned in a monastery until the rebellion was put down.

His best poetry was lyrical and descriptive. He was also a painter and his poetry was often expressed with a painter's awareness so that people have said of him, 'His poems paint a picture, his pictures write a poem'.

Wên I-to (1899–1946) was educated at Tsinghua College in Peking from where he went to the United States for further study. When he returned to China, he joined a group of western-educated young writers and poets known as the Crescent Society under whose auspices he published his well-known collection of poems entitled *Dead Water*. He wrote relatively little poetry but what he did write had a profound effect upon the course of modern poetry at that time when 'new verse' was in an embryo stage. His greatest achievement was his success in fashioning a highly disciplined and dramatic vehicle of poetic expression out of ordinary speech.

Soon afterwards he gave up creative writing and devoted himself to scholarship on classical Chinese literature to which he made a notable and lively contribution. At the start of Japanese aggression in 1937 he was evacuated to the interior of China where he soon began a period of intense political activity with the Democratic League, which was a third party which held a position between the Nationalists and the Communists. He was assassinated by Nationalist agents in 1946 for his political activities.

Wu Ch'êng-ên (1510?–1582) was a scholar and novelist of the Ming dynasty. He wrote some poetry and drama which are now lost but fortunately his most famous work *Journey to the West* or *Monkey* (tr. by Arthur Waley) has survived. This book is a combination of both Buddhist and Taoist fantasies. It is in the shape of a picaresque novel, its framework based on the journey of Tripitaka of the T'ang dynasty to fetch the true *sutra* from India. Tripitaka is accompanied by four disciples: a monkey, a pig, a horse and a novice monk; these are allegorical characters and the difficulties and dangers encounted on the journey symbolise the hardships and trials of a man striving for virtue. The gods and immortals who watch over Tripitaka come from both Buddhist and Taoist canons and are envisaged as being heavenly counterparts to earthly government officials. The novel is distinguished for its wit and humour, especially in the character of the monkey.

Wu Ching-tzu (1701–54) was a novelist of the Ch'ing dynasty. He refused to sit for the civil service examinations for he found the system and its products despicable and even comical. He came from a wealthy family which had produced many successful officials but he avoided such men and chose his company from amongst the poets, painters and writers of his time with whom he led a life of artistic indulgence. Soon he had exhausted the money and property that he had inherited and went to live in relative poverty in the suburbs where he died, but he always refused to seek help from wealthy friends and relatives.

His novel *The Unofficial History of Scholars* satirised the vulgarity and rapacity of the class of officials and expressed his own contempt for the inanity of Confucian ethics. It also contained stories of his contemporaries.

Yüan Mei (1716–97) was a writer of the Ch'ing dynasty. He was appointed to office at the early age of twenty-four through his success in the civil service examinations. He came from a wealthy family and when he was in office at

Chiangnan he bought a plot of land on which he constructed a villa with a garden which he called Sui-yüan which was a marvel of architecture and landscape gardening. He retired from office at the age of forty and spent the rest of his life in his Sui-yüan in pursuit of literary activities and artistic pleasures. One of his theories on poetry contended that the words should be beautiful and the sounds harmonious. In his scholarship he likewise avoided the severity of contemporary Confucians and was therefore often criticised by them. He wrote many essays and a collection of ghost stories which was called *What the Sage Did Not Discuss* which was an allusion to Confucius' reluctance to talk about the supernatural.

BIBLIOGRAPHY

CHINESE HISTORY

Ancient

CREEL, H. G. *The Birth of China: a Survey of the Formative Period of Chinese Civilization* New York, 1954; London, 1958.

CREEL, H. G. *Chinese Thought from Confucius to Mao Tse-tung* Chicago, 1953; London, 1954.

EBERHARD, W. *A History of China* London, 1950; rev. ed., Berkeley, 1969.

FAIRBANK, J. K. and REISCHAUER, E. O. *China: the Great Tradition* New York and London, 1960.

FITZGERALD, C. P. *A Short History of China* London, 1958.

GOODRICH, L. Carington *A Short History of the Chinese People* London, 1962.

GERNET, Jacques *La Chine Ancienne des Origines à l'Empire* Paris, 1964.

LOEWE, M. *Imperial China* New York; London, 1966.

NEEDHAM, J. *Science and Civilization in China* vols. 1, 2, 3 and 4, part one Cambridge, 1954 onwards.

PULLEYBLANK, E. G. *The Background of the Rebellion of An Lu-shan* London, 1955.

SCHAFER, Edward H. *Golden Peaches of Samarkand: a Study of T'ang Exotics* California UP, 1963.

SCHAFER, Edward H. *The Vermilion Bird: T'ang Images of the South* Los Angeles, 1967.

TSUI CHI *A Short History of Chinese Civilization* London, 1942.

WALEY, A. *The Real Tripitaka* New York; London, 1952.

WALEY, A. *Three Ways of Thought in Ancient China* New York; London, 1939.

WATSON, W. *Early Civilization in China* New York; London, 1966.

Modern

CHANG, Hsin-pao *Commissioner Lin* Harvard UP, 1964.

FAIRBANK, J. K. and TENG, Ssu-yu *China's Response to the West* Oxford for Harvard UP, 1954.

HAIL, W. J. *Tseng Kuo-fan and the Tai Ping Rebellion* Yale UP, 1927.
HOLT, E. *The Opium Wars in China* London, 1964.
LEVENSON, J. *Liang Ch'i-ch'ao* London, 1959; New York, 1969.
LEVENSON, J. *Confucian China and Its Modern Fate* 3 vols., Berkeley, Calif. and London, 1958–65.
MCALEAVY, H. *The Dream of Tartary: the Origin of Misfortunes of Henry Pu Yi* London, 1963.
MCALEAVY, H. *The Modern History of China* London, 1967.
MEADOW, T. T. *The Chinese and Their Rebellions* Stanford Academic Reprints, 1964; originally published in 1956.
MICHAEL, F. *The Tai Ping Rebellion* University of Washington, 1966.
MORSE, H. B. *International Relation of Chinese Empire* 3 vols., London, 1910–18.
PURCELL, V. *The Boxer Uprising* Cambridge, 1963.
SCHWARTZ, B. *In Search of Wealth and Power: Yen Fu and the West* Oxford UP for Harvard UP, 1964.
SPENCE, Jonathan D. *Ts'ao Yin and K'ang Hsi: Emperor, Bondservant and Master* Yale UP, 1966.
WALEY, A. *The Opium War through Chinese Eyes* London, 1958; New York, 1959.
WRIGHT, Mary *The Last Stand of Chinese Conservatism: T'ung Chih Restoration* 1862–74 Stanford UP, 1957.
WRIGHT, Mary *China in Revolution: the First Phase* A Symposium, New Haven and London, 1968.

CHINESE LITERATURE

1. *Introductory Works*

BISHOP, John L., ed. *Studies in Chinese Literature* Harvard UP, 1965.
BISHOP, John L. *The Colloquial Short Story of China: A Study of the San-yen Collection* Harvard UP, 1956.
BUCK, Pearl S. *The Chinese Novel* Nobel Lecture London, 1936.
CHÊN SHOU-YI *Chinese Literature, a Historical Introduction* New York, 1961.
DAWSON, Raymond, ed. *The Legacy of China* Oxford UP, 1964.
FÊNG YÜAN-CHÜN *A Short History of Classical Chinese Literature*, trans. Yang Hsien-yi and Gladys Yang, Peking, 1958.
FÊNG YU-LANG *A History of Chinese Philosophy*, trans. Derk Bodde, London, 1952–3.
GILES, Herbert A. *A History of Chinese Literature* New York, 1958.
HIGHTOWER, James R. *Topics in Chinese Literature* Harvard UP, 1953.
HSIA, C. T. *A History of Modern Chinese Fiction* Yale UP, 1961.
HU SHIH *The Chinese Renaissance* New York, 1963.

HUANG SUNG-KANG *Lu Hsün and the New Cultural Movement of Modern China* Amsterdam, 1957.
LAI MING *A History of Chinese Literature* New York, 1964.
LIN YUTANG *The Importance of Living* London, 1961.
LIU, James J. Y. *The Art of Chinese Poetry* Chicago, 1962.
LIU, James J. Y. *The Chinese Knight-Errant* London, 1967.
LIU TS'UN-YAN *Buddhist and Taoist Influence on Chinese Novel* Wiesbaden, 1962.
LIU WU-CHI *An Introduction to Chinese Literature* Indiana UP, 1966.
LU HSÜN *A Brief History of Chinese Fiction* trans. Yang Hsien-yi and Gladys Yang, Peking, 1959.
PRŮŠEK, Jaroslav, ed. *Studies in Modern Chinese Literature* Berlin, 1964.
SCOTT, A C. *Art and Literature in Twentieth Century China* New York, 1963.
SCOTT, A. C. *The Classical Theatre of China* London, 1957.
TING YI *A Short History of Modern Chinese Literature* Peking, 1959.
WATSON, Burton *Early Chinese Literature* Columbia UP, 1962.

2. *Anthologies in English Translation*

ACTON, Harold and Lee Yi-hsieh *Four Cautionary Tales* London, 1947.
ACTON, Harold and Chen Shih-hsiang *Modern Chinese Poetry* London, 1936.
ARLINGTON, L. C. and Harold Acton *Famous Chinese Plays* Peking, 1937.
BIRCH, Cyril, ed. *Anthology of Chinese Literature* New York, 1965.
BIRCH, Cyril, ed. *Chinese Communist Literature* London, 1963.
BIRCH, Cyril *Stories from a Ming Collection* London, 1958.
BYNNER, Witter and KIANG KANG-HU *The Jade Mountain* New York, 1964.
CANDLIN, Clara M. *The Herald Wind* London, 1933.
CHAI CH'U and WINBERG CHAI *A Treasury of Chinese Literature* New York, 1965.
CHENG HSI and FRODSHAM, J. D. *An Anthology of Chinese Verse* Oxford at the Clarendon Press, 1967.
DUBARRY, William Theodore, WING-TSIT CHAN and WATSON, Burton *Sources of Chinese Tradition* Columbia UP, 1960.
The Dragon King's Daughter (*Ten T'ang Dynasty Stories*) Peking, 1954.
GILES, Herbert A *Gems of Chinese Literature: Prose* New York, 1964
GRAHAM, A. C. *Poems of the Late T'ang* Penguin Books, 1965.
HART, Henry *A Garden of Peonies* Stanford UP, 1938.
HOWELL, E. BUTTS *The Inconstancy of Madame Chuang and Other Stories* London, 1924.
HOWELL, E. BUTTS *The Restitution of the Bride and Other Stories from the Chinese* London, 1926.
HSU KAI-YU *Twentieth Century Chinese Poetry* New York, 1963.

JENYNS, Soame *Selections from the 300 Poems of the T'ang Dynasty* London, 1940.

JENYNS, Soame *A Further Selection from the 300 Poems of the T'ang Dynasty* London, 1944.

KOTELWALL, Robert and SMITH, Norman L. *The Penguin Book of Chinese Verse* Penguin Books, 1962.

LEGGE, James *The Chinese Classics* New York, reprint, 1961.

LIN YUTANG *The Wisdom of China* London, 1944.

The Man Who Sold a Ghost (*Chinese Tales of the 3rd-6th Centuries*) Peking, 1958.

PAYNE, Robert *Contemporary Chinese Poetry* New York, 1947.

PAYNE, Robert *The White Pony* New York, 1947.

REXROTH, Kenneth *One Hundred Poems from the Chinese* New York, 1959.

SHIH CHING *The Books of Odes*, trans. Bernard Karlgren, Stockholm, 1950.

SHIH CHING *The Book of Songs*, trans. Arthur Waley, London, 1937.

SNOW, Edgar *Living China, Modern Chinese Short Stories* New York, 1937.

WALEY, Arthur *Ballads and Stories from Tun-huang* London, 1960.

WALEY, Arthur *Chinese Poems* London, 1946.

WANG CHI-CHEN *Contemporary Chinese Stories* Columbia UP, 1944.

WANG CHI-CHEN *Stories of China at War* Columbia UP, 1947.

WANG CHI-CHEN *Traditional Chinese Tales* New York, 1944.

WANG, Elizabeth Te-chen *Ladies of the Tang* (*22 Classical Chinese Stories*) Taipei, 1961.

YANG HSIEN-YI and YANG, Gladys *The Courtesan's Jewel Box* (*Chinese Stories of the 10th–17th Centuries*) Peking, 1957.

YANG, Richard F. F. and METZGER, Charles R. *Fifty Songs from the Yuan* London, 1967.

3. *Individual Works in English Translation and Studies*

CH'Ü YÜAN

Ch'u T'zu, the Songs of the South, trans. David Hawkes, Oxford UP, 1959.

Li Sao and Other Poems of Ch'ü Yüan, trans. Yang Hsien-yi and Gladys Yang, Peking, 1953.

The Nine Songs: a Study of Shamanism in Ancient China trans. Arthur Waley, London, 1955.

CHUANG TZU

Chuang Tzu: Basic Writing trans. by Burton Watson, Columbia UP, 1964.

Chuang Tzu: Mystic, Moralist and Social Reformer trans. Herbert A. Giles, London, 1961.

Chuang Tzu, a New Translation (*with an Exposition of the Philosophy of Kuo Hsiang*), trans Fêng Yu-lan, New York, 1964.

CONFUCIUS

The Analects of Confucius, trans. Arthur Waley, London, 1938.

The Great Learning and the Mean-in-Action trans. by E. R. Hughes, New York, 1943.

The Wisdom of Confucius trans. Lin Yutang, New York, 1938.

KUAN HAN-CH'ING

Selected Plays of Kuan Han-ch'ing trans. Yang Hsien-yi and Gladys Yang, Peking, 1958.

KUO MO-JO

Ch'ü Yüan trans. Yang Hsien-yi and Gladys Yang, Peking, 1953.

Selected Poems from the Goddesses Peking, 1959.

LAO SHÊ (LAU SHAW)

Rickshaw Boy trans. Evan King, New York, 1945.

LAO TZU

Lao Tzu: Tao Te Ching trans. D. C. Lau, Penguin Books, 1963.

WALEY, Arthur *The Way and Its Power: a Study of Tao Te Ching and Its Place in Chinese Thought* London, 1965.

LI JU-CHEN

Flower in the Mirror, trans. Lin Tai-yi, London, 1965.

LI PO

WALEY, Arthur *The Poetry and Career of Li Po* London, 1950.

The Works of Li Po, trans. Shigeyoshi Obata, New York, 1964.

LI YÜ

Poems of Lee Hou-chu, trans. Liu Yih-ling and Shahid Suhrawardy, Bombay, Orient Longman, 1948.

LIU NGO

Lao Ts'an Yu Chi: the Travels of Lao Ts'an, trans. Harold Shadick, New York, 1952.

LO KUAN-CHUNG

San Kuo Chih: Romance of the Three Kingdoms trans. C. H. Brewitt-Taylor, Charles E. Tuttle, Vermont, 1959.

LU HSÜN

Selected Works of Lu Hsün, trans. Yang Hsien-yi and Gladys Yang, Peking, 1960.

MAO TUN

Midnight, trans. Hsu Meng-hsiung, Peking, 1957.

Spring Silkworms and Other Stories Peking, 1956.

MENCIUS

Mencius trans. W. A. C. H. Dobson, Toronto UP, 1963.

The Book of Mencius, trans. Lionel Giles, London, 1942.

Mencius, trans. D. C. Lau, Penguin Books, 1970.

PA CHIN

The Family trans. Sidney Shapiro, Peking, 1958.

PAN KU

History of the Former Han Dynasty, trans. Homer H. Dubs, New York, 1959.

PO CHÜ-I

WALEY, Arthur *The Life and Times of Po Chü-i* London, 1949.

P'U SUNG-LING

Liao Chai Chih I trans. Herbert H. Giles, London, 1925.

SHEN T'SUNG-WÊN

The Chinese Earth and Other Stories, trans. Ching Ti and Robert Payne, London, 1947.

SHIH NAI-AN

Shui Hu Chuan: All Men Are Brothers, trans. Pearl S. Buck, New York, 1937.

Water Margin, trans. by J. H. Jackson, Hongkong, 1963.

IRWIN, Richard G. *The Evolution of The Chinese Novel: Shui Hu Chuan*, Harvard, 1953.

SSU-MA CH'IEN

Records of the Grand Historian of China trans. Burton Watson, New York, 1961.

WATSON, Burton *Ssu-ma Ch'ien, Grand Historian of China* Columbia UP, 1958.

SU SHIH

The Prose-Poetry of Su Tung-p'o, trans. Cyril D. Le Gros Clark, New York, 1964.

Su Tung-p'o. Selections from a Sung Dynasty Poet, trans. Burton Watson, New York, 1965.

T'AO CH'IEN

T'ao the Hermit, Sixty Poems by T'ao Ch'ien trans. William Acker, London, 1952.

The Poems of T'ao Ch'ien trans. Lily Pao-hu Chang and Marjorie Sinclair, University of Hawaii Press, 1953.

T'IEN HAN

Kuan Han-ch'ing Peking, 1961.

TS'AO CHAN (TS'AO HSÜEH-CH'IN)

Hung Lou Meng: Dream of the Red Chamber, trans. Wang Chi-chen, New York, 1958.

The Dream of the Red Chamber, trans. Florence and Isobel McHugh, New York, 1958.

WU SHIH-CHANG *On the Red Chamber Dream* Oxford UP, 1961.

TS'AO YÜ

Sunrise, trans. A. C. Barnes, Peking, 1960.

Thunderstorm, trans. A. C. Barnes and Wang Tso-liang, Peking, 1958.

TU FU

Tu Fu, Selected Poems, trans. Rewi Alley, Peking, 1962.

A Little Primer of Tu Fu, trans. David Hawkes, Oxford UP, 1967.

HUNG, William *Tu Fu, China's Greatest Poet* Harvard, 1952.

WANG CHUNG

Lun Heng trans. Alfred Forke, Leipzig, 1907–11.

WANG SHIH-CHEN

Chin P'ing Mei: The Golden Lotus trans. Clement Egerton, London, 1939

Chin P'ing Mei: The Adventurous History of Hsi-Men and His Six Wives, trans. B. Maill, New York, 1940.

WANG SHIH-FU

Hsi Hsiang Chi: The Western Chamber trans. Henry H. Hart, Stanford UP, 1936.

Hsi Hsiang Chi: The Romance of the Western Chamber, trans. S. I. Hsiung, London, 1935.

WANG WEI

Poems by Wang Wei, trans. Chang Yin-nan and Lewis C. Walmsley, Tuttle, Charles E., Vermont, 1958.

WU CH'ÊNG-ÊN

Hsi Yu Chi: Monkey, trans. Arthur Waley, London, 1942.

WU CHING-TZU

Ju Lin Wai Shih: The Scholars, trans. Yang-Hsien-yi and Gladys Yang, Peking, 1957.

YEH SHAO-CHÜN

Ni Huan-chih trans. A. C. Barnes, Peking, 1958.

YÜAN MEI

WALEY, Arthur *Yüan Mei* London, 1956.

TIBETAN LITERATURE

D. L. Snellgrove

HISTORICAL BACKGROUND

Tibet, a vast upland of much the same size as Scandinavia, is bounded on the south, west and north by massive mountain ranges, and on the east by uninhabited wastes and whole series of subsidiary mountain ranges. Thus until the mechanised Chinese invasion of the nineteen-fifties, the Tibetans have been generally free to pursue their own ways and develop their own kind of civilisation, receiving what they pleased from their neighbours and largely ignoring the rest. The small population, estimated at three millions, has been concentrated in the southern part of the country along the extensive valley system of the Tsangpo (Brahmaputra) and in the high upper valleys of the Salween, the Mekong and the Yangtse. Apart from a few small valleys in the far west, bordering on India, and some bordering on the Nepalese frontier, these represent the only favourable agricultural lands. Between the Tsangpo Valley and the wild uninhabited north (comprising about three-sevenths of the whole country) there are rolling plateaux, affording sometimes good grazing, interspersed with snow-capped mountains and great lakes. The basic economy of Tibet derives from the food-supplies (barley, wheat, buckwheat, root-crops etc.) of the valley-people combined with the products (meat, butter, cheese and wool) of the nomadic herdsmen. In intermediate areas there are those who are both farmers and herdsmen. Apart from tea, so beloved by Tibetans, which was imported from China, the Tibetan economy was self-supporting and their general living standard was one of the highest in Asia.

ANCIENT TIMES

The Tibetans began to enter recorded history in the early seventh century when certain powerful chieftains of the central Tsangpo Valley united to support the chief of Yarlung (a subsidiary valley of the Tsangpo about fifty miles south-east of Lhasa) as their overlord. We learn from an early Tibetan chronicle and from early stone inscriptions that a special kind of sanctity attached to the chiefs (known as *bTsan-po* 'Mighty Ones') of Yarlung. Forts and houses of solid stone and dried mud were built in this period, but the chiefs and their warriors seem to have preferred to live in large felt tents, more suited to their nomadic and fighting instincts. Under the Yarlung 'kings', especially from the time of Srong-brtsan-sgam-po (*d* 650) onwards, Tibet rapidly became a first-class military power in Central Asia. The Tibetans pressed hard on the Chinese border-lands and even captured Ch'ang-an (Sian) which was then the capital. Excavations made early this century in the Takla-makan basin by Professor Paul Pelliot and Sir Aurel Stein have now made available a lot of early Tibetan manuscript material bearing on this period of Tibetan military triumph (the early seventh to mid-ninth centuries). Ancient Tibetan forts have been excavated with their records of day-to-day living, and temples and caves (notably at Tun-huang) have been opened with their collections of the earliest surviving Tibetan Buddhist literature as well of royal annals and fragmented chronicles referring to the pre-Buddhist period.

The first small Buddhist temples were built in and around Lhasa during the reign of Srong-brtsan-sgam-po presumably to please the Chinese princess whom he had demanded as his queen from the vanquished Chinese. Thus Buddhism became a special court interest, seemingly depending for its existence on the Chinese connection. The Tibetans generally still practised their own indigenous cults through the medium of their priests, known as *Bon* (invokers) and *gShen* (sacrificers) whose function it was to ensure by means of invocations and sacrifice to their gods (often conceived of as mountain-gods and warrior-gods) the well-being of the land and success in war. They were also adepts at sortilege and astrological calculations, by which they discovered the causes of human ailments and failures, thus identifying the gods and demons, whose placation was required. Another important priestly function, mentioned in early literature, was the cult of the royal tombs. There are suggestions that even in the historical period close companions of the king accompanied him in death by immolation in his tomb, and animal sacrifices were certainly performed, even on behalf of those kings whom later Buddhist tradition treats as staunch supporters of Buddhism. King Khri-srong-lde-brtsan (who ruled in the second half of the eighth century) certainly sponsored invitations to Indian teachers (notably Śāntarakshita and his pupil Kamalaśīla), founded the first Tibetan monastery (*bSam-yas*) with its first seven Tibetan monks, and presided over a Buddhist council, at which the relative merits of Chinese Buddhism and Indian Buddhism were debated (*c* 792). The debate was decided, not without subsequent physical violence, in favour of the Indian party, and thereafter a serious court interest in Buddhism developed, based almost exclusively on the Indian connection, with Nepal operating as a kind of half-way house. Other important Buddhist kings were Khri-lde-srong-brtsan (*d* 815) and Ral-pa-can (assassinated 836), but even they seem to have respected the ancient cults. Ral-pa-can was succeeded by his brother Glang-dar-ma, who is treated as an apostate by later Buddhist historians. In 842 he was himself assassinated by a Buddhist monk, who is regarded as a religious hero. Unhappily for the Buddhist faction, which was already strong enough during Ral-pa-can's reign for Buddhist monks to be ministers, dispute over the rights of succession led to the break-up of the Tibetan kingdom followed not only by the collapse of Tibetan military power but also by the disappearance of organised Buddhism from Central Tibet for one hundred and thirty-six years. Descendents of the royal line migrated to western Tibet, where they established the small kingdoms of Mar-yul, Gu-ge and sPu-hrangs, and began to promote interest in Buddhism once again. These Western Tibetan kings were undoubtedly enthusiastic Buddhists, who sponsored visits by Indian teachers as well as cultural expeditions to neighbouring Indian lands, especially Kashmir, where Buddhism still flourished. Buddhism also established itself in eastern Tibet, but the process there is not so well documented. Meanwhile central Tibet remained fragmented under the rule of local chieftains, some of whom began to take an interest in Buddhism once more, especially in the founding of monasteries with which the chief's family might be powerfully connected. Thus *Sa-skya*, destined to be head of one of the great religious orders, was founded in 1073 by a member of the 'Khon family. Similarly the monastery of *gDan-sa-mthil*, founded by a saintly lama Phag-mo-gru (1110–70), gained the patronage of the aristocratic Rlangs family and thereafter this family provided the religious head of the monastery as well as the chief administrative officer. This close association of lay with religious interests, which has its beginning in the eleventh and twelfth centuries, developed into the kind of 'church' government which was typical of Tibet until 1959. At the same time certain other monasteries, notably *mTshur-phu*, chief seat of the *Karma-pa* order (*Karma-pa* was a kind of nickname given to their founder-lama) and *'Bri-khung*, which were not beholden to any one aristocratic family in particular, began to find their head-lamas in young children who were 'recognised' as reincarnations of departed lamas. The origin of this unusual practice is presumably Indian, for a series of Indian Buddhist yogins (from the eighth to tenth centuries) were supposedly linked in a series of successive reincarnations.

While wandering scholars, translators, monks and yogins were travelling to and fro from India and Nepal, importing new scriptures and religious traditions, and while other saintly lamas pursued religious studies and practised the arts of *yoga* at home in their own monasteries, other monks and prelates, ambitious for success in this world, were vying and often fighting with neighbouring establishments over property rights, thereby seeking to gain positions of power and influence for themselves and their following. Local chieftains with their traditional feuds still existed, but it was becoming increasingly difficult for them to operate except in conjunction with the monasteries. The prestige of the new religion with its ornate temples and its gilded and richly dressed images with its elaborate ceremonies and impressive body of literature, seems to have been enormous. The followers of the old pre-Buddhist religion, now known as *Bon*, were already busy adopting the ways of their powerful rivals, and the Buddhists, in order to win the hearts of simple people, adopted side by side with the Buddhist divinities many of the old local gods (conveniently regarded as protectors of Buddhism), as well as non-Buddhist practices. This was easily done, for late Indian Buddhism was already wide in its interests, embracing property rites, rain-making rituals and even destructive rites which could be turned against enemies. By 1200 when Buddhism disappeared from India, the new religion was firmly entrenched in Tibet and presumably accepted as the leading religion of the land. The monasteries could rely upon lay support, and the fortunes of the simplest Tibetans began to be bound up with the monasteries, to which their family-members would belong as ordinary monks, often needed as much as fighters as for regular domestic activities. Some small monasteries continued to remain quiet centres of religious life, but the great monasteries, on which the fortunes of Tibet were now beginning to depend, were developing as complex well-organised communities with political and commercial interests, where religion certainly remained a motivating force, but was practised single-mindedly only by a specially educated minority.

In 1207 envoys of Genghis Khan, whose Mongol hordes had just started upon their murderous course of world conquest, arrived demanding Tibetan submission. The Tibetans submitted unconcernedly and suffered nothing worse than a few raids into their country. Later Godan Khan summoned a Tibetan representative to his court and the grand-lama of *Sa-skya* went. Having won the confidence of the Khans, the *Sa-skya* grand-lamas were appointed 'vassal-rulers' of Tibet, and there developed between Mongol overlords, soon to be emperors of China, and the Tibetan grand-lamas the special relationship of 'Patron and Priest'. Nevertheless the *Sa-skya* privileges were resented, and with the weakening of Mongol power, *Sa-skya* rule was replaced in 1354, after much internal fighting and intriguing, by that of a forceful leader of the Phag-mo-gru family, named Byang-chub-rgyal-mtshan. He re-established good government and effective independence for Tibet, but his incompetent son lost his position to the princes of Rin-spung, and they in turn to the rulers of gTsang, who by the first half of the fifteenth century had made themselves the kings of almost the whole of Tibet. Struggles still continued between the great monastic orders, and the kings of gTsang ruled in close association with the *Karma-pa* order, which was the religious power of the day.

THE 'YELLOW HATS'

Meanwhile in the course of the fifteenth century a new religious order, subsequently known as the *dGe-lugs-pa* (Model of Virtue) (usually nicknamed 'Yellow Hats' by non-Tibetans), came into existence, deriving their improved standards of learning and monastic discipline from the great teacher and writer Tsong-kha-pa (1357–1419) and his two chief disciples rGyal-tshab and mKhas-grub-rje. A younger follower dGe-'dun-grub (1391–1475) subsequently became head of the whole order and grand-lama of the chief monastery of *'Bras-spung* (Drepung) founded in 1416. One of his successors, the third in the series, received the title of *Ta-le* (usually written *Dalai* in the West) meaning 'Ocean (of Wisdom)', and this has become attached as a nickname, never used in Tibet itself, to this whole line of hierarchs, who from the second in the series onwards have been identified as 'reincarnations' of the preceding grand-lama. The ambitions of this new religious order soon began to clash with the authority of the kings of gTsang and the interests of the *Karma-pa* order, which was the most politically powerful of the older schools. The 'Yellow Hats' called in the help of the Mongol supporters, and by 1640 they emerged victorious. By the time of the death of Gushri, the chief Mongol champion, in 1656, the regime of the fifth Dalai Lama, the first Dalai Lama to achieve political power, stretched from Mount Kailas in the west to the province of Khams in the east. Under his rule Tibet enjoyed a further half-century of national greatness, but despite the efforts of his powerful regent, Sangs-rgyas-rGya-mtsho, to hold the regime together after his death (1682) until his successor came of age, this sixth Dalai Lama was useless as a national leader and Tibet had no choice but to become involved in Mongol and Chinese rivalries. The Chinese Emperor K'ang Hsi played a skilful hand, and thus when the seventh Dalai Lama was installed in 1720, this came about under Chinese protection. Chinese representatives were established at Lhasa, and from this time dates the special relationship between the Manchu Emperors and the 'Yellow Hat' hierarchy which survived until the end of the Manchu dynasty in 1911. Succeeding Dalai Lamas, most of whom died young, had no substantial political power until we come to the thirteenth (*b* 1876), and Tibet was ruled by a kind of ecclesiastical bureaucracy of high 'Yellow Hat' prelates and specially trained monk clerics, supported by a lay aristocracy adhering to the 'Yellow Hat' order. The older orders survived, mainly in the outlying parts of the country, as separate religious groups, thus maintaining the continuity of their traditional teachings and producing their own scholars and writers, but they were never able to make a fresh bid for political power.

MODERN TIMES

From 1911 until 1950 Tibet enjoyed *de facto* independence. This was recognised by the British in India when it suited their convenience, and the Tibetan leaders, who continued to enjoy Chinese bounty even in the days of the Chinese Republic, hesitated to make too explicit a profession of Tibet's national independence. Since 1950 the country has been taken over by the Chinese Communists, and since 1959 the Dalai Lama (now the fourteenth) has lived in exile in India.

CULTURAL AND LITERARY TRENDS

EARLIEST RECORDS

The earliest literary records from the caves of Tun-huang (see above page 324) reveal a small world of rival chiefs living in forts and served by vassals and military retainers. Agriculture was practised and sheep and cattle were reared. Weapons and domestic articles were certainly produced locally and by the time of the Yarlung kings (who ruled from the seventh to ninth centuries) such luxury articles as wine-jars and bowls with decorative animal motifs are commonly referred to. Chinese influence began to be felt and it is likely that some court officials were beginning to become proficient in Chinese literature. At the same time Indian Buddhist influences were becoming effective and from the end of the eighth century onwards Indian influence became paramount, although political chaos in central Tibet after the assassination of Glang-dar-ma (*c* 842) delayed its effect for more than a century. Chinese influence seems to have disappeared altogether after small but perhaps promising beginnings. Thereafter the Tibetans never again took a deliberate interest in Chinese culture and literature.

A syllabary of thirty letters in which the vowel *a* was inherent, together with four extra vowel-signs for *i*, *u*, *e* and *o*, was devised on an Indian model, and promulgated once and for all during the reign of Srong-brtsan-sgam-po, probably about AD 640. Special rules of spelling were drawn up, regulating the use of prefixes and suffixes, many of which seem to have been silent in the seventh and eighth centuries, at least in some dialects, just as they are today. These rules have never been changed and thus there is a great difference between literary spellings and the common spoken language.

BUDDHIST WRITINGS

In Tibetan literature of the early royal period, especially as revealed to us in the *Chronicle*, retrieved from the Tun-huang caves, there is a freedom and spontaneity of expression, resulting in poems and songs of poetic value.

Mythical references, although often strange to later Tibetans as well as to present-day non-Tibetan readers, lend charm and interest to these early works. Strong traditions of spontaneous lay poetry have continued right up to the present day, but they have been relegated to a greatly inferior place by the ecclesiastical hierarchies which have controlled all formal education from the eleventh century onwards. Already under Khri-srong-lde-brtsan, Ral-pa-can and other early kings who took some interest in Buddhism, court interest seems to have concentrated on devising a new literary vocabulary adequate to the translation of Buddhist philosophical and doctrinal texts from the Sanskrit original. This in itself was a vast and complex task, which Tibetan Buddhist scholars completed so successfully, that it soon became possible to reproduce with remarkable verbal accuracy in their own language the great stocks of Buddhist literature which awaited their enthusiastic attention in India and Nepal. Indian scholars, who usually knew no Tibetan, would sit side by side with Tibetan translators, explaining the meanings of every phrase, and the Tibetan translators (known as *lo-tsa-ba*) would render it into Tibetan, using only the correct terminology as listed in the approved list of translations. Any works translated in the seventh or eighth centuries before the process was regularised, were methodically re-translated. When the kings of western Tibet continued the sponsorship of Indian Buddhism in the tenth and eleventh centuries, they followed exactly the same methods. Thus the whole surviving Buddhist literature of northern medieval India, as it existed up to the great destruction of Indian Buddhist centres of learning by the Moslems, was gradually translated into Tibetan and has since survived intact in the great Tibetan canon, known as the Kanjur (*bka'-'gyur* – translated [Buddha] word) and the Tanjur (*bsTan-'gyur* – translated treatises).

The first small Buddhist temples were build in and around Lhasa during the reign of Srong-brtsan-sgam-po. One or two of these have survived to the present day, more or less unaltered, simple and solid Tibetan buildings, constructed of stone and dried earth, and adorned over the main shrine with a simple pagoda-style roof of the kind typical of Indian and Nepalese temples of that period. Many more tenth and eleventh-century temples with their carved door-lintels and beautifully frescoed walls have survived in western Tibet as testimony of the far-reaching influence of Indian culture, mainly from Kashmir which was then still a Buddhist land. Images of Buddhist divinities were made of stucco, and later of metal under the direction of master-craftsmen from Nepal, who practised their craft for the Tibetan market both in Lhasa and Kathmandu right up to 1959. Even after the final destruction of Buddhist culture in India (*c* AD 1200), Nepal continued to serve Tibetan Buddhist interests until 1769 when the Gorkha conquest of the Nepal Valley began to have a restricting effect.

While the kings of western Tibet were sponsoring monastic Buddhism in their domains, scholar-travellers from central Tibet, such as 'Brog-mi (992–

1072) and Mar-pa (1012–96) were busily collecting in Nepal and Bihar initiations into tantric *yoga* and the relative treatises. While neither can be regarded as a great literary figure, both were 'fathers' of important religious orders. The great monastery of *Sa-skya* was founded in 1073 by one of 'Brog-mi's disciples, while Mar-pa was the master of the famous Mi-la Ras-pa, whose pupil sGam-po-pa inspired such religious enthusiasm in his direct followers that they were founders of no less than six schools, all known as *bKa'-rgyud-pa* and all looking back to Mar-pa as their first Tibetan teacher. These various religious orders and schools were based on famous monasteries, such as *gDan-sa-mthil*, *mTshur-phu*, *'Bri-khung*, *mTshal Gung-thang*, *sTag-lung* etc, which became the 'mother houses' of yet more religious foundations. Each school fostered its own interpretive literature, mainly received from Indian teachers of the tenth to twelfth centuries, but they all used and recognised the one basic canon consisting of all the Indian Buddhist works which might claim to be the actual teachings of the Buddhas as well as the commentaries of universally respected Indian teachers. These works must all have been in vogue at the great Indian Buddhist monasteries of Bihar, for example *Nālandā*, *Vikramashīla*, *Oddantapuri*, but credit for their overall arrangement should probably go to the Tibetans. The texts claiming to be Buddha's word were often of very late origin, for most of the *tantras* included in the Tibetan canon can scarcely be earlier than the fifth century AD. The important philosophical literature, known as the 'Perfection of Wisdom' texts, probably go back to the first and second centuries AD together with the great *Mahāyāna sūtras*. Only the texts on 'monastic discipline' (*Vinaya*) might have some claim, in part at least, to go back as early oral teachings to the time of Śākyamuni Buddha and the sixth century BC. The long task of translating, sorting, correcting and retranslating continued into the fourteenth century, when the great scholar Bu-ston (1290–1364) supervised the completion and issue of the approved Tibetan Buddhist canon. Its size and scope are enormous. Its later printed (xylograph) editions comprise a hundred or one hundred and eight volumes for the Kanjur and some two hundred and twenty-five for the Tanjur.

INDIAN INFLUENCES

Meanwhile great impetus was given to the practice of the religious life by the visits of renowned Indian teachers, especially Atīśa, who arrived in Tibet in 1042 and remained there until his death in 1056, and the great Kashmiri scholar, Śākya-śrī (1127–1225) who travelled around Tibet from 1204–13, visiting holy places, founding monasteries and bestowing teachings and initiations. The Tibetans seem to have shown from the start a marked preference for magic and mysticism, and the older schools all claimed to develop techniques of *yoga* which might guarantee the gaining of buddhahood in a single lifetime. Of special note in this respect are the 'Six Doctrines' of the famous Indian tantric yogin Nāropa, which were transmitted by Mar-pa to all the *bKa'-rgyud-pa* schools, and the teachings of 'The Way and its Fruits', received by 'Brog-mi from the Indian yogin Virūpa to the future benefit of the *Sa-skya* order. Other early schools, generally grouped together as *rNying-ma-pa*, the 'old' order, preserved sets of Indian *tantras* which were judged non-canonical and even heretical, and they developed a large anonymous mythical and liturgical literature centring on the Indian yogin Padmasambhava, who (according to later fourteenth century accounts) visited Tibet in the second half of the eighth century and won Tibet to Buddhism by the competent and resolute manner in which he quelled local Tibetan gods and demons. All the older orders accepted the texts included in the canon, including those concerned with monastic discipline, and thus side by side with their tantric and demonological interests they developed communities of reasonably well-behaved monks, a minority of whom were certainly great men of sanctity and learning. It was this aspect of Buddhism that the great Atīśa emphasised, and his work was continued by his chief disciple 'Brom-ston (1008–64) who founded a strict monastic order known as the *bKa'-gdams-pa* (bound by command).

There seems to have developed quite early, perhaps already in the eleventh century, an indigenous tradition of story-telling relating to the great Buddhist sages and teachers. Its finished form is the 'religious biography' (*rnam-thar* meaning 'works of salvation') of which two well known ones in the west are those of Mar-pa and Mi-la Ras-pa. This form of literature seems to have been cultivated particularly by the *bKa'-rgyud-pas* and many of their lamas are credited with collections of religious verses and songs, usually coupled with the biography. Atīśa referred to the lack of independent works on Buddhist doctrinal themes in Tibet despite the great learning of many Tibetan prelates. In the early twelfth century sGam-po-pa produced an important doctrinal work (see biographical section, p. 335), and during the following century the grand-lamas of *Sa-skya* came to the fore as great doctrinal writers. An added incentive was the developing interest in Buddhism in Mongolia which was thus becoming an important mission field for Tibetan lamas. This connection with the Mongols, who became from 1263 rulers of China under the Mongol Emperor Kublai Khan, brought the Tibetans into contact with Chinese culture again after four centuries of almost complete separation. With the end of the Mongol (Yüan) dynasty in 1368 the political connection came to an end for another three hundred and fifty years, but cultural contacts, slight as they were, continued uninterrupted until the twentieth century. Such items as brocade and rich robes, incense-burners and gilded bronze and copper images of Chinese workmanship, entered the monasteries as gifts or the results of trading ventures, and adorned the houses of aristocrats and wealthy traders. Tibetan weaving designs began to show Chinese influence, and styles of Tibetan religious painting were affected. However, it is remarkable that the Tibetans should have learned so little from the advanced culture of their great neighbours, despite the many centuries of association between the two countries. Tibetan monks and lay scholars seldom, if ever, learned Chinese, thus remaining to this day generally ignorant of Chinese literature and religion. Because of the barrier of language there was no contact between Tibetan and Chinese Buddhists except in the frontier areas, and this small personal contact never affected Buddhist doctrine or forms of religious practice in Tibet. Indian Buddhism, although no longer active in the land of its origin, continued to serve as the one inspiration to the Tibetans.

THE 'YELLOW HAT' ERA

The new religious order of the 'Yellow Hats' which came into existence in the fifteenth century claimed to return to the philosophical teachings of great Indian teachers of the past, Nāgārjuna, Asaṅga, Diṅnāga etc, and their stricter monastic discipline was based upon earlier Indian models and codes. With their emphasis upon philosophical and logical studies and detailed works of exegesis, they tended to reject writings of a more magical and mystical flavour, so beloved by the older orders. While they by no means neglected the canonical *tantras*, they studied them more as external rituals, the correct performance of which might benefit the community as a whole, rather than as techniques of *yoga* directed towards the personal reintegration of a solitary practiser. But it seems that they soon began to affect the older orders of Tibetan religion with their stricter forms of monastic life, while they themselves began to get laxer in their religious life, when political and bureaucratic power made it so easy for them to enjoy all the pleasures of lay life under cover of religious garments. Nevertheless a firm distinction can be made between the 'Yellow Hats' and the older orders, in that the highest religious type of the former is the scholar and religious writer, while of the latter it is the revered lama, whether celibate or married, who is the enlightened repository of secret doctrines into which he may, at his pleasure, initiate a few chosen disciples.

From 1721 onwards when the country was ruled by a 'Yellow Hat' bureaucracy in political and religious concord with the Manchu court at Peking, there was a steady increase in Chinese influence in art, architecture and artifacts. The great new monasteries, housing thousands of monks, were often recipients of lavish gifts from the emperor, who even financed the construction of whole monasteries. With their solid inward-sloping walls and narrow windows Tibetan buildings have remained fundamentally unchanged during fourteen hundred years, but the external decorations, the gilded pagoda roofs and pillared balconies with their superbly carved and painted woodwork, have owed much to the Chinese connection during the last two centuries. Also the internal decorations, the silk hangings, the carpets and low tables of delicately carved painted wood, are Chinese in origin or in inspiration. Yet the Tibetans never took to Chinese paintings and drawings, always prefering their traditional Tibetan religious motifs, whether with or without slight Chinese nuances, and they never adopted Chinese literature and philosophy. Thus the effects of the Chinese connection have remained remarkably superficial, when all aspects are considered.

The one craft the Tibetans learned from the Chinese was that of printing from carved wooden blocks (xylographs). The Tibetan canon was first printed by this method in Peking in 1411. In the fifteenth century this method of printing was a great advance, for up till then manuscripts had always to be laboriously copied by hand; the Tibetans adopted it with zeal, so that there was scarcely a work of literary importance in the whole of Tibet, for which the master printing blocks did not repose in some monastery or other. The canon itself was reprinted several times at sNar-thang, sDe-ge, Co-ne, and in this century in Lhasa itself, always by the time-honoured method of wood-carving, despite the great advances in printing methods made in China and elsewhere in the world. Likewise the Tibetans have persisted in retaining elongated books with loose folios, copied originally from the shape of Indian palm-leaf manuscripts to which they were accustomed a thousand years ago.

Apart from such specifically religious subjects as Buddhist doctrine, philosophy and logic, liturgy and pietistic biography and legend, Tibetan literature embraces history (seldom anything but religious history), medicine (based again upon Indian and – by implication – Buddhist physio-philosophical conceptions), craft-manuals (concerned with the production of Buddhist works of art) and drama which always develops traditional Buddhist themes. The great Tibetan epic of *Ge-sar of Gling*, although doubtless non-Buddhist in its original core, is now so overlaid with Buddhist myths and doctrines, as to render it a religious book in its own right. Similarly *Bon-po* literature is no less religious in a strictly Buddhist sense, for during the last thousand years the *Bon-pos*, while claiming to represent pre-Buddhist traditions, have incorporated into their teachings and practices everything Buddhist which was usable, from philosophical theories to monastic organisation. The life of their supposed founder gShen-rab, extant as a complete work since the fourteenth century at least, is filled with Indian and Buddhist teachings in transparent *Bon-po* guise, and they revere their literature, just as other Tibetan communities revere theirs. The only lay literature consists of popular songs and ditties, but it is seldom that anyone judges them worth recording. Such 'geography' as exists, takes the form of guides to holy places.

INDIVIDUAL WRITERS

Blo-ldan sNying-po (approximate pronunciation: Lo-den Nying-po) (fourteenth century). A famous literary figure of the *bon-pos*, he was born at Khyung-po in Khams (eastern Tibet) *c* 1360, and is said to have died in his twenty-fifth year. He is the compiler, if not the author, of a large work in twelve volumes, entitled 'The Precious Compendium, the Blazing *Sūtra*, Immaculate and Glorious', known briefly as *gZi-brjid* (The Glorious). It tells the legendary story of gShen-rabs, founder of *Bon*, and also gives detailed accounts of the various ways in which *Bon* may be practised. For some doctrinal extracts, see D. L. Snellgrove, *Nine Ways of Bon*, Oxford UP, London, 1967.

Blo-bzang Chos-kyi Nyi-ma (Losang Chö-kyi Nyi-ma) (1737–1802). He was one of the great prelates of the 'Yellow Hat' order during the period of close political and religious co-operation between the Manchu dynasty and the 'Yellow Hat' hierarchy. He spent most of his life in Peking, where he belonged to the line of hierarchs known as the Thu-kuang Incarnation, supposedly manifestations of the fierce Indian divinity Hayagrīva. He is chiefly known for his treatises on the origins and beliefs of all the various schools and for his history of his own order.

Bo-dong Phyogs-las rNam-rgyal (Bo-dong Chog-lai Nam-gyel) (1306–86). A famous disciple of Shes-rab rGyal-mtshan (*qv*), he was born in far west Tibet and went as a youth to study in the central provinces (dBus and gTsang) where he met his chosen master. He played a leading part in the foundation of Ngams-rings Monastery, of which he later became abbot and was surrounded by many disciples. He was an adept in the interpretation of the *Kālacakra Tantra*, and produced many works on the 'Perfection of Wisdom' doctrines and on logic. Tsong-kha-pa (*qv*) as a young man may be counted among his students.

Bu-ston (Bu-tön) (1290–1364). A great scholar and encyclopaedic writer, he brought to completion the monumental task of compiling the Tibetan Buddhist canon, as well as producing an enormous collection of works of about two hundred titles, treating of every aspect of Tibetan Buddhism. He lived a quiet life of study, meditation and literary production at the monastery of *Zhva-lu* (about twenty miles south of Tashilhunpo). His history of Buddhism in India and Tibet is well known thanks to its English translation (see E.

Obermiller, *History of Buddhism by Bu-ston*, 2 parts, Heidelberg, 1931 and 1932). *The Life of Bu-ston*, ed. and trans. D. S. Ruegg, Rome Oriental Series, vol. xxxiv, Rome, 1966.

sGam-po-pa (Gam-po-pa) (1079–1153). An important philosophical and mystical writer, who was educated in accordance with *bKa'-gdams-pa* teachings and having later become one of the chief disciples of the *yogin* poet Mi-la Ras-pa, mastered the tantric doctrines transmitted from India by Mar-pa. The founders of the six schools which made up the whole *bKa'-rgyud-pa* order were all disciples of his. Thus his influence was considerable. An important work of his is available in English translation: 'The Jewel Ornament of Liberation' (*Thar-pa rin-po-che'i rgyan*) trans. H. V. Guenther, Rider & Co., London, 1956.

Grags-pa rGyal-mtshan (Drag-pa Gyel-tsen) (1147–1216). A great *Sa-skya-pa* lama, he was born as the third son of Kun-dga' sNying-po (*qv*) and became abbot of *Sa-skya* from 1172. He produced detailed studies on tantric literature, especially on *Hevajra* and *Samvara*, showing a vast grasp of his subject by copious quotations. He wrote also on medicine, on the career of a 'would-be buddha', and is especially noteworthy for his history (from the *Sa-skya* standpoint) of the beginnings of Tibetan Buddhism.

Gro-lung-pa Blo-gros byung-gnas (Dro-lung-pa Lo-trö Chung-nai). The chief disciple of the famous translator of *rNgog*, Blo-ldan shes-rab (1059–1109), he composed many commentaries dealing with *tantras* and *sūtras* as well as an important dissertation on Buddhist doctrine (*bsTan-rim*) which foreshadowed Tsong-kha-pa's great work (*qv*).

rGyal-tshab-rje (Gyel-tsab-je) (1364–1432). One of Tsong kha-pa's (*qv*) two chief disciples, he continued his master's literary activities as a great interpreter of *Mahāyāna* philosophical works, notably on the *Abhisamayālaṃkara* and the *Uttarantantra*. He wrote on *Abhidharma* (basic philosophical notions), on the 'career of the would-be buddha', and especially on logic.

mKhas-grub-rje (Khai-drub-je) (1385–1438). The second of Tsong-kha-pa's (*qv*) two chief disciples, he wrote mainly on *tantras*, especially the *Kālacakra* and its important Indian commentary, the *Vimalaprabhā*. He also wrote important works on logic, *Mahāyāna* philosophy and monastic discipline, as well as two biographies of his master Tsong-kha-pa.

Klong-chen rab-'byams-pa (Long-chen Rab-jam-pa) (1308–63). A great mystic and hermit, he practised and taught the 'Heart-Drop' (*snying-thig*) doctrine of the *sNying-ma-pa* (old) order of Tibetan Buddhism. As a writer he is famous as the codifier and commentator of these so-called 'Great Perfection' (*rDzogs-chen*) teachings, thus providing them with a respectable scholarly basis so that they have since held their own against the more orthodox types of Buddhist practice.

Klong-rdol Bla-ma (Long-döl La-ma (*b* 1729). An important 'Yellow Hat' lama whose complete works (*gSung-'bum*) represent a kind of encyclopaedia of Tibetan learning. It contains an important summary of the history of Tibetan Buddhism.

bKra-shis rGyal-mtshan (Ta-shi Gyel-tsen) (nineteenth to twentieth centuries). A famous *bon-po* lama scholar who died about 1925 in Khams (eastern Tibet). He produced fifteen volumes of works including a history of *Bon.* A great ascetic and mystic, he is supposed to have dissolved into nothingness at death.

Kun-dga' rGyal-mtshan (Kün-ga Gyel-tsen), known as the Great *Sa-skya* Pundit (1182–1251). One of the greatest of *Sa-skya* scholars, he wrote extensively and authoritively on philosophy and logic. He initiated missionary activities amongst the Mongols, continued by his famous successor 'Phags-pa (*qv*).

Kun-dga' sNying-po (Kün-ga Nying-po) (1092–1158). The son of dKon-mchog rgyal-po (1034–1102) who founded *Sa-skya* in 1073), he was thus the second great *Sa-skya* lama and a noted scholar for works of exegesis on the *tantras*, especially *Hevajra* and *Samvara.*

Kun-dga' bZang-po (Kün-ga Sang-po) (1382–1444). A renowned *Sa-skya* lama and a prolific writer, he founded the great monastery of Ngor Evam Chos-ldan which became the centre of a *Sa-skya* sub-order, the *Ngor-pa* school.

Mi-la Ras-pa (Mi-la Re-pa) (1040–1123). Chosen disciple of Mar-pa and in turn master of sGam-po-pa, he comes near the top of the *bKa'-rgud-ypa* hierarchy and is especially revered as a great hermit and mystic. He is famed as the author of a large number of religious and didactic songs which have been worked by his followers into cycles of biographical anecdotes. For a complete translation see *The Hundred Thousand Songs of Milarepa* translated by Garma C. C. Chang (New York, 1962). His biography (by his pupil Ras-chung) has been translated by a Sikkimese lama, Kazi Dawasamdup and edited by W. Y. Evans-Wentz as *Tibet's Great Yogi Milarepa*, Oxford UP, London, 1928.

Mi-pham rGya-mtsho of sDe-dge (De-ge Mi-pham Gyamtso) (1846–1912). A famous nineteenth-century *rNying-ma-pa* lama who raised philosophical studies within his own order onto a par with those of the 'Yellow Hat' scholars at a time when they were enjoying all the advantages that wealthy (Manchu) patronage could bring. He is chiefly famous for his exegeses on the important (philosophical) ninth chapter of the *Bodhicāryāvatāra* (Embarking on the Career of a Would-be Buddha), concerning which he was involved in long-term disputes with a 'Yellow Hat' lama (Blo-bzang rab-rgyal) of *Bla-brang*. In keeping with the general *rNying-ma-pa* antipathy to book-learning for its own sake, his followers like to believe that he gained his vast knowledge intuitively and effortlessly through a vision of *Mañjuśri*, the 'Lord of Wisdom', who was his favourite divinity.

Ngag-dbang Blo-bzang rGya-mtsho (Nga-wang Lo-sang Gyamtso) (1617–82). The fifth Dalai Lama, who with Mongol aid united the whole of Tibet under his government from 1640 onwards, is one of the greatest figures of Tibetan history. He wrote authoritatively on basic philosophical notions (*Abhidharma*) on monastic discipline (*Vinaya*), on *Mahāyāna* philosophy, on protecting divinities (*chos-skyong*), on the previous reincarnations of his line of hierarchs and produced a history. He also wrote treatises on liturgy and methods of invocation and commentaries of *tantras*. He was a great statesman and a great builder and patron of the religious arts.

dPa'-bo gTsug-lag 'Phreng-ba (Pa-wo Tsug-la Trheng-wa) (1503–66). An incarnate lama of the *Karma-pa* sect of the *bKa'-rgyud-pa* order, he is known chiefly for a great history of Tibet in seventeen volumes completed just before his death. It is important for the materials it contains for the early royal period, and throughout he seems to have drawn on old records which are now quite unobtainable.

Pad-ma dKar-po (Pe-ma Kar-po) (1526–92). Recognised as an incarnation of the *'Brug-pa* sect of the *bKa'-rgyud-pa* order, he is now chiefly remembered in Bhutan which, since the seventeenth century, has become the main home of this sect. His complete works are in ten volumes, including an important history of Tibet.

'Phags-pa Blo-gros rGyal-mtshan (P'ag-pa Lo-trö Gyel-tsen) (1235–80). The nephew of Kun-dga' rgyal-mtshan (*qv*) he continued his missionary activity amongst the Mongols (1252–65 and 1268–76), becoming the religious preceptor of Kublai Khan. He invented a script for the Mongolian language, named *'Phags-pa* after him. He wrote extensively on tantric literature and produced a large number of 'epistles' for his chief patron as well as for other disciples.

Red-mda'-pa gZhon-nu Blo-gros (Re-da-pa Shön-nu Lo-trö) (1349–1412). One of the last of the really great *Sa-skya-pa* scholars, he wrote extensively on 'Perfection of Wisdom' (*prajñāpāramitā*) literature.

Rin-chen bZang-po (Rin-chen Sang-po) (954–1054). Encouraged by the religious kings of Gu-ge (western Tibet), he was the leading scholar in their great work of reintroducing sound Buddhist doctrine to Tibet. He was a great translator, as well as being trainer and guide to his many assistants. He was also a builder of temples and encouraged Buddhist arts and crafts in western Tibet.

Rong-ston sMra-ba'i Seng-ge (Rong-tön Ma-wai Senge) (1367–1449). A saintly and learned *Sa-skya-pa* lama, he was the author of many works of exegesis, especially on *Mahāyāna* philosophy, and was famed as a great religious teacher. In 1435 he founded the monastery of Nālandā (in 'Phan-yul) named after the famous Indian Buddhist monastery of that name.

Sangs-rgyas rGya-mtsho (Sangye Gyamtso) (1653–1705). As a young man he attracted the attention of the fifth Dalai Lama, Nga-dbang Blo-bzang rGya-mtsho (*qv*) who appointed him as Regent in 1679. For justifiable political reasons he concealed the death of the Dalai Lama (1682), pretending he was in strict meditation, and continued to rule in his name. In 1696 he confessed the matter, enthroning the sixth Dalai Lama whom he had kept concealed. He was put to death in 1705 by lHa-bzang Khan, the Mongol 'king' of Tibet with Chinese connivance. He was a great statesman and builder, as well as a literary figure. He wrote on astrology, medicine and the history of the 'Yellow Hat' order. He is also the author of a lengthy biography of the fifth Dalai Lama.

Shes-rab rGyal-mtshan of Dolpo (Dolpopa She-rab Gyel-tsen) (1292–1361). A great scholar and writer, who developed theories about self-nature which were later branded by the 'Yellow Hats' as heretical in that they implied the real existence of a 'self'. He founded the monastery of Jo-mo-nang, after which his school, a sect of the *bKa'-rgyud-pa* order, was named. His sect was wiped out by order of the fifth Dalai Lama.

Sum-pa mKhan-po Ye-shes dPal-'byor (Sum-pa Khempo Ye-shei Pal-jor) (1704–88). Born in Amdo (eastern Tibet), he travelled to the central provinces when his home monastery of dGon-lung was involved in local wars. He studied at 'Bras-spung (Drepung) Monastery near Lhasa, and later became abbot of one of its colleges. He returned to Amdo in 1731 and became head of the rebuilt monastery of dGon-lung in 1731. He produced eight volumes of exegetical writings, but is chiefly known by western scholars for his historical works. Like other great 'Yellow Hat' lamas of the period, he was honoured by the Manchu court at Peking.

Tsong-kha-pa (1357–1419). Born in eastern Tibet, he came for higher studies to the central provinces where he studied under most of the great teachers of his time. Following the tradition of Atīśa and 'Brom-ston, he concentrated upon philosophical and tantric studies, combined with an enthusiasm for strict monastic discipline. In 1409 he founded his own monastery of dGa'-ldan (Ganden), destined to become one of the three great monasteries of the *dGe-lugs-pa* (Yellow Hat) order, to which his teachings and inspiration gave birth through his immediate disciples. By his own order, which became politically supreme in Tibet from the time of the fifth Dalai Lama onwards, he is honoured as a Buddha and as the greatest Tibetan teacher.

gZhon-nu-dpal (Shön-nu-päl) of 'Gos (1392–1481). A famous historian, well known for his detailed history of Tibetan Buddhism, translated into English as *The Blue Annals* by G. N. Roerich, Calcutta, 1949 and 1953.

BIBLIOGRAPHY

BACOT, J. *Trois Mystères Tibétains* Paris, 1921.

EVANS-WENTZ, W. Y., ed. *Tibet's Great Yogi Milarepa* London, 1928.

The Tibetan Book of the Dead, trans. W. Y. Evans-Wentz, new edn., London, 1957.

SGAM-PO-PA *Jewel Ornament of Liberation*, trans. H. V. Guenther London, 1956.

OBERMILLER, E., trans. *History of Buddhism by Bu-ston.* 2 parts, Heidelberg, 1931–2.

ROERICH, G. N. *The Blue Annals of gZhon-nu-dpal*, 2 vols., Calcutta, 1949–53.

SNELLGROVE, D. L. ed. and trans. *The Hevajra Tantra*, 2 vols., London, 1959.

For detailed information and other references see:

HOFFMANN, H. *The Religions of Tibet*, London, 1961.

SNELLGROVE, D. L. *Buddhist Himâlaya*, London, 1957.

SNELLGROVE, D. L. and RICHARDSON, H. E. *A Cultural History of Tibet* London, 1968.

STEIN, R. A. *Recherches sur L'Épopée et le Barde au Tibet* Presses Universitaires de France, 1959.

TUCCI, G. *Tibetan Painted Scrolls* 3 vols., Rome, 1949.

MONGOLIAN LITERATURE

C. R. Bawden

HISTORICAL BACKGROUND

With the exception of the Manchus, the Mongols were the last of those aggressive peoples, usually nomadic, who emerged from time to time in east-central Asia to establish continental empires. The great Mongol empire was rapidly built up by Genghis Khan (?1162–1227) out of what had hitherto been a scattering of unimportant tribes. The Mongols as such appear in history at a relatively late date, being of no significance before the thirteenth century. However, the earliest work in the Mongol language, the Secret History of the Mongols, written down probably in 1240, shows by its artistic form and by references to old traditions, that the language and culture must have passed through a longer period of development than just the years of the meteoric rise to military pre-eminence of the parvenu Mongols. As unified by Genghis Khan, Mongol society displayed certain characteristics of feudalism. The emperor ruled his people, who fell into definite social classes, through a steppe aristocracy who acted in their, and his, special interests.

The Mongols were a nomad people, though like other nomads who had preceded them they did build an imperial capital, the short-lived city of Karakorum where for a while the civilisations of Asia and Europe met. On their early foreign campaigns the Mongols had spared only craftsmen from the general massacres, but later, when occupying China, they had progressed beyond the negative policy of securing their conquests by the obliteration of the city cultures. Yet there is comparatively little record of their literature at this time; apart from the Secret History, there are a number of stone inscriptions, a little poetry, including fragments of a version of the Alexander romance, and some translations of Buddhist books. The Mongols adapted the Uighur script to their language and in spite of experiments with other modes of writing, this script was to be used till very recently in the Mongol People's Republic and still is in Inner Mongolia.

That little literature of the imperial period has survived in contemporary written form is due to at least two factors. Literature must have been then, as later, to a great extent oral. Moreover, the collapse of the empire in the late fourteenth century heralded a period of civil war during which most documents were lost. For two centuries Mongolia was the scene of bitter and fruitless fighting as the imperial family, once again dwelling on the steppes, tried to maintain itself against upstarts, especially the Oirats or West Mongols, who once even usurped the throne. By the late sixteenth century the imperial power was a nullity. What power there was lay in the hands of individual princes who built up khanates, some of which managed to survive, as in Khalkha or Outer Mongolia, while others quickly collapsed. The most important of these princes was perhaps Altan Khan of the Tümet, in Inner Mongolia, who not only built at Huhehot the first Mongol city since Karakorum, but was responsible for initiating the conversion of the Mongols to Tibetan Buddhism or Lamaism, a process which profoundly affected society and culture. Other centres of culture and book learning grew up at this time, inspired by the new religion which the Mongols took to avidly. Lamaseries were founded and much systematic translation of Tibetan scriptures undertaken.

The decline of the idea of Mongol unity coincided with the rise to power of the Manchus, who in 1636 obtained the allegiance of the princes of Inner Mongolia after the death of Ligdan Khan, the last emperor. At the end of the century the Khalkha khans, squeezed between Russians, Oirats and Manchus, submitted to the latter, so that Mongolia proper became part of the Chinese empire. In the mid-eighteenth century the Manchus exterminated the powerful Jungar state of West-Mongols. Other West-Mongols, known as Kalmucks, were to be found in south Russia where they were cut off from the main stream of Mongol life. Mongolia for long remained a sort of reservation, a source of fighting men for the Manchu army, cut off as far as possible from foreign, and even Chinese, contacts. In these circumstances it was the lamaist church, and especially its head, the Jebtsundamba Khutuktu, or Living Buddha of Urga, which became the centre of attraction of Mongol loyalties, rather than the fragmented secular nobility.

From the eighteenth century onwards Mongolia stagnated and declined economically as a semi-colony of China. The nomadic way of life persisted, though the country was organised into a large number of territorial units run by a Mongol bureaucracy. The four khans of Khalkha were reduced to the level of importance of the other eighty-odd banner princes and no longer controlled their khanates which were renamed leagues and were subjected to Manchu-appointed Mongol governors. The learned language was Tibetan, but Mongol was the language of the administration, so that a tradition of literacy was kept up.

In 1911 the Mongol nobility seized the opportunity offered by the collapse of the Manchu empire to proclaim an independent Mongolia with the Living Buddha as king. Their efforts to incorporate the Mongols of Inner Mongolia and Sinkiang in the new kingdom failed, and from 1915 onwards Mongolia was recognised only as an autonomous state, within borders similar to those of today. Yet even autonomous Mongolia was an unstable creation, and when its protector, Tsarist Russia, collapsed, it was annexed by China in 1919. A complicated chain of events culminating in 'liberation' in 1921 by Mongol partisans and the Soviet army brought about Mongolia's *de facto* independence. A People's Government, set up within Russia, was established in Urga by the invading force, and when in 1924 the Living Buddha died, Mongolia became the first People's Democracy. Her subsequent history has paralleled that of the USSR. For many years after 1929 she was totally cut off from the world at large. The native nobility and then the church were destroyed, and the old generation of revolutionaries ruthlessly purged in 1937 and the succeeding years.

Russian influence has entirely displaced that of Tibet and China in all spheres of life, not least in education and literature. Since the mid-fifties in particular Mongolia has made great material and social progress, and the establishment of a system of universal education and the introduction of modern means of communication have made possible the emergence of a new mass 'socialist' culture.

MAIN TRENDS IN LITERATURE

European scholars long held the opinion that Mongolian literature consisted almost entirely of translations, principally of Buddhist works. Research and publication during this century have fortunately provided evidence showing that the Mongols have possessed, since the thirteenth century, a rich written and oral literature. The earliest work extant is the Secret History of the Mongols, dating from the early thirteenth century, and preserved only in a transcription in Chinese characters used phonetically and a summary Chinese translation. This history, devoted principally to the life of Genghis Khan, depicts the tribal-feudal atmosphere of Mongol life on the eve of the great empire. As well as narrative, it contains much alliterative verse, and is an important source for the early culture of the Mongols. Historical writing revived in the early seventeenth century, from which time onwards a large number of chronicles were written, much influenced by Lamaism.

Many legends and tales concerning Genghis Khan have survived, either embedded in chronicles or in oral form. There is also a body of didactic literature in which Genghis appears either as the originator or the chief protagonist. A strong didactic strain has always characterised Mongol literature, and the prestige of the great Khan seems to have been used to reinforce the lessons taught in such a work, for example, as *Oyun Tülkigür* (The Key of Understanding) apocryphally ascribed to him.

ETHICAL LITERATURE

The popularity of moralising literature was enhanced with the appearance of Buddhism in Mongolia in imperial times. The Tibetan manual *Subhāṣitaratnanidhi* was one of the first books to be translated into Mongol. From the time of its first appearance in the early fourteenth century, different translations have been reprinted many times, most recently in 1958. Of native Mongol didactic genres we may notice, after the second conversion to Buddhism in the sixteenth century, the *surgaal* or admonition, in which rules of conduct are presented together with a condemnation of bad behaviour. These admonitions were widely known. Academician Damdinsüren mentions that of twenty-eight kept in the State Library, all but three were familiar to him as a child. The artificial conversation and the *üg* or 'word', as composed by such men as Nagwangkhaidub and Sandag, were also powerful vehicles of social criticism.

EPICS AND STORIES

There was a purely Mongol tradition of entertainment literature. The heroic, or fantastic epic was particularly popular with the West-Mongols among whom it enjoyed noble patronage. Traditional epics, whose theme was usually the subjugation of a demon by a hero, would be passed down from bard to pupil, while competent bards would also create new epics. One or two, especially the Geser Khan epic, which was printed in Peking in 1716, are known of in book form. At the same time, the contacts with Tibeto-Indian and Chinese culture, made possible by the introduction of Buddhism and by the Manchu conquest, introduced the Mongols to a wider range of literary forms and themes. Collections of stories with an Indian background were brought to Mongolia and achieved immense popularity, while the great Chinese romances were translated into Mongol and also furnished themes for the *bengsen-ü üliger* or book-opera.

Mongolia has a rich stock of folk tales. In the fairy tales world-wide motifs and themes can be recognised. There are historical tales, of which an excellent example is the *Ubasi Qungtaiji-yin tuguji* (Tale of Ubashi Khungtaiji) dating probably from the end of the sixteenth century. Important historical figures are also remembered in verse of an elegiac sort, for example the unsuccessful aristocratic rebel Chingunjab who was executed in 1757, or in the form of the 'conversation song' (see below) as with the famous nineteenth century robber Toroi Bandi. Strangely, they do not seem to be the heroes of epic. There is also a repertory of satirical stories centring on the two figures of the Badarchin (mendicant lama) and the Eulenspiegel-like Baldansengge, also known as Dalan Qudalchi. These two minor genres are whimsical and picaresque and do not display the forceful social criticism appearing, for example, in those tales attached to the early twentieth-century renegade lama Mad Shagdar.

Lyric poetry abounds in Mongolia, usually in the form of the folk song.

DRAMA

The theatre was never a widely popular form of entertainment in pre-revolutionary Mongolia, through there were some Chinese theatres and at certain lamaseries mystery-type religious plays, of which the most celebrated is the

Saran Köküge (Moon Cuckoo) of Rabjai, might be put on. A characteristic form of drama was the *Qarilchaga Dagu* (conversation song) in which a simple tale would be enacted, from a sitting position, by one or more singers, telling the story to musical accompaniment without benefit of stage or even of movement.

MODERN TRENDS

The revolution of 1921, and more especially the political swing to the left of 1929, mark a complete break in Mongol literary tradition. The old forms were suppressed, and literature became an instrument of political persuasion, which it still is, at least ideally. However, epic, for example, has still not entirely disappeared as a living art form, and older Mongol literature, after having been ignored for over twenty years, is once again being studied and taught. Contemporary writers practise modern forms of literature, and these, the novel and short story for example, are post-1921 innovations. In the twenties and thirties there was a certain amount of literary experimentation, but with the execution in 1937 on false charges, of men like Buyannemekh, Yadamsüren and Ayush all this came to an abrupt end, and from then on literature became subjugated to political policies. The main influence on modern Mongolian writers is of course the Soviet example, especially as in their formative years most writers were cut off from any but Russian contacts. It is only now that a new generation of really professional writers is emerging: previously the acute shortage of educated men meant that writing was only one of the tasks an intellectual had to turn his hand to.

The aim of Mongol writers as presented at their Third Congress in 1962 is 'to permeate the masses with communist ideals and, under the leadership of the Mongolian People's Revolutionary Party, to help actively in the education of the people of the new socialist era'. Not all writers attain this goal, however, and Mongolian literature is not as uniform as might be expected.

INDIVIDUAL WRITERS

B. Baast (*b* 1921) is perhaps typical of the younger generation of professional writers. He was born into a poor family in western Mongolia and educated at a local primary school and then at a secondary school in Ulan Bator. He began to write in 1936 and his work was first published in 1940. Since then he has produced numerous poems, songs, stories, a travel book and some novels. His work is concerned mainly with the description of the ordinary life of the people, and is meant to appeal to a broad, relatively unsophisticated, public. Of his many stories one, *Hornless White Goat*, a rather naive tale with some slight love interest, has appeared in English translation.
(See: *Mongolia Today*, vol. V, no. 2, New Delhi, February, 1963.)

S. Buyannemekh (1902–37) might have become one of the formative influences upon modern Mongolian literature, but his career was cut short by political assassination in 1937 and his work suppressed. Together with his other contemporaries, whose work was, as is now admitted, 'for a time illegally suppressed' he was rehabilitated in 1962.

He was the son of an impoverished nobleman, obtained an education in Urga and in 1920 was in Irkutsk where he worked on the revolutionary newspaper *Mongolyn Ünen* (Mongol Truth). In 1921 he met Lenin in Moscow. He was active in the organisation of the League of Revolutionary Youth, and in 1924 was imprisoned for a time as a result of a coup d'état. In 1929 he participated in the formation of the first Writers' Circle in Mongolia, together with Damdinsüren, Rintchen and others. This Circle collapsed in 1937 when Buyannemekh and others were executed, and other members suffered imprisonment. He is known to have written theoretical works. These are not available but extracts from their not very daring suggestions have been published to illustrate Buyannemekh's ideological errors. He stated, for example, that there should be both an obvious and a hidden meaning to poetry, the latter addressed to those capable of appreciating it. This idea clashed with the official conception of literature as a means of training the masses in socialism, and its expression is still held against him.

Ts. Dambadorj (1899–1934) was primarily a politician and revolutionary, but is known also for his one realistic novel *Tolbo Nuur* (Lake Tolbo), the first modern Mongolian novel. Dambadorj was born into a family of *shabi* or retainers of the Living Buddha. He attended primary school at Urga and

Russian Khiakta and worked as a telegraph operator. He knew Manchu, Chinese, Russian and English. He was a delegate to the first Congress of the Mongolian People's Party in 1921 and after the campaign against Mongol Khiakta he went to the west with the lama and General Khasbator to deal with invading White Russian bands. Here he was involved in a prolonged siege at a lamasery near Lake Tolbo, which forms the climax of his novel. He recounts the events leading up to the siege in a realistic and factual manner, avoiding all literary artifice and display of emotion. He wrote in classical Mongol, which his younger contemporaries were to abandon in favour of something closer to colloquial speech. *Tolbo Nuur* was written in 1924 and published in 1927. In 1928 Dambadorj fell from political favour as a 'rightist' and died in Russia in 1934. His book was not republished until 1964.

Ts. Damdinsüren (*b* 1908) is typical of the 'universal intellectual'. His active life covers the whole period of the revolution in Mongolia. As a boy he received his first experience of life in a local administrative office, and in 1924 joined the Mongol Revolutionary Army. In 1926 he became a member of the Central Committee of the League of Revolutionary Youth, since when he has had a many-sided career as a political worker, a scholar, university professor and academician, and as an imaginative writer. His scholarly works include a monograph on the Geser Khan epic, and a translation into modern Mongol of the Secret History. He helped to adapt the Cyrillic script to the Mongol language, but has also shown himself deeply concerned for the preservation of old Mongol cultural traditions. He has published a number of articles critical of national policy towards the old culture and has also edited and printed old and rare Mongol texts, for which he has been exposed to public criticism. His work ranges from learned articles on such subjects as Tibetan loan-words in Mongol to short stories and a film-script for his own short novel *Gologdson Khüükhen* (The Forsaken Girl). Some of his work, for example a poem entitled *We all wish for Peace* is on the level of political pamphleteering, and in all his work there is a strong moralising strain, sometimes implicit, but sometimes directly expressed, as in the story *Lamyn Rashaan* (The Lama's Elixir). Like all his contemporaries, his work is closely linked with contemporary developments and is constructive in the sense of illustrating principles of 'socialist' behaviour more often than it is concerned with merely human emotions.

M. Gaadamba (*b* 1924) is a graduate of the University of Ulan Bator and a specialist in literature who has written a book on literary theory. He has composed many poems and short stories which are of interest in depicting contemporary Mongol life and attitudes. As does Baast, he shows due deference to the principle of socialist realism.

(See: *Mongolia Today*, vol. V, no. 4–5, April–May 1963 for a translation of *Elbeg Deel* (An oversized gown).)

Gelegbalsang (1846–1923) was the son of a herdsman who was a *khamjilga* or retainer of a nobleman in the Ongin river area. At the age of about ten he was put as a novice into a lamasery, but finding the life uncongenial he ran back home. Here he became interested in Mongol literature and learned to read Mongol. He had already studied Tibetan in the lamasery. From the age of twenty he began to earn his living as a carrier for Chinese merchants on the Kalgan and Peking route, and learned Chinese. At the age of about thirty he began to compose extemporary poems of circumstance, *irügel* or benedictions, which were in much demand at the customary festivals and celebrations of Mongol life. On the invitation of the abbot who was impressed by his skill as an impromptu poet, he returned to his lamasery as a business manager, in which capacity he travelled a great deal. His fame as a poet spread, and he became known as far away as Urga. It was his habit to note down some of his poems in the Tibetan script. Amongst these, perhaps the most famous is his *Plea for Rain* composed and recited during a great drought in the year 1905.

Injanashi (1837–91), the son of an Inner Mongolian nobleman, is an isolated and exceptional figure in Mongolian literature. His family was descended directly from Genghis Khan, and prided itself on never having intermarried with non-noble families. Injanashi's father, a civil and military official, died in 1847 leaving completed only eight chapters of a history of the Mongols which he had planned and which his son was to continue. Injanashi led a scholarly life, devoting himself to study, writing and painting. He knew Chinese, Tibetan and Manchu as well as Mongol. In early middle-age troubles overcame him. His trade ventures were unsuccessful, and he lost his wife and son. After a near breakdown he applied himself to literature, adding sixty-one chapters to his father's history and producing several imaginative works.

Apart from some essays and poems, Injanashi's fame rests on three large works, his history, *Köke Sudur* (Blue Chronicle), a novel *Nigen Dabqur Asar* (The One-storied Tower), written in close imitation of the Chinese romance *Hung Lou Meng*, and a sequel, *Ulagan-a Ukilaqui Tingkim* (The Pavilion of Red Weeping). His literary work displays a fundamental contradiction. He was nothing if not a Mongol patriot, bitterly regretting the denationalisation of his people which was taking place under the pressure of Chinese culture, yet his modes of thought and expression were typically Chinese. His arguments were frequently reinforced by parallels from ancient Chinese history. His novels are Chinese in all but language, and even so he made such constant use of neologisms built up in imitation of Chinese expressions that a knowledge of Chinese is essential in order to appreciate them properly.

Injanashi never envisaged any change in the social order, his ambitions being limited to the revival of Mongol self-awareness. He shows himself not insensitive to suffering, but he never equated material want with unhappiness and his novels are fundamentally idyllic in tone, lacking the sense of doom which pervades *Hung Lou Meng*. Recent attempts to characterise him as a 'progressive' writer, squarely opposed to the oppression of the masses, are unacceptable. Injanashi is far from being the forerunner of socialist realism which Inner Mongol Marxist critics seek to make of him, his novels giving, rather, an impression of escapism and flight from reality.

Ishidanzangwangjil (1854–?) was born in Chahar in Inner Mongolia as the son of an official. At the age of seven he entered a lamasery in the Ordos region with the rank of *shabrong*, that is, a minor incarnation. His lamasery was destroyed in the Moslem uprising of 1868 and he went back to Chahar for some time. After residing again in the restored lamasery he went to study philosophy and medicine at the famous Kumbum lamasery in Amdo. For some years he lived as an itinerant doctor and wrote some medical treatises. His rank lends more power to the criticism he levelled against injustice, neglect of social duty, and insensitiveness at all levels of society, and which was expressed in his long and famous satirical poem *Güng-ün Juu-yin Gegegen-ü Altan Surgal* (The Golden Admonition of the Incarnation of the Güng-ün Juu Temple) which not only circulated in manuscript but was printed in Ulan Bator in 1928 and also in Inner Mongolia.

(For partial translations see W. HEISSIG: 'Ein Beitrag zur mongolischen Literaturgeschichte, *Central Asiatic Journal*, II, 1, and W. HEISSIG: *A Lost Civilisation, The Mongols Rediscovered*, London, Thames and Hudson, 1966.)

Ishisangbo (1848–?) was a lama of Urga who considered himself a reincarnation of Nagwangkhaidub. His *üg* are similar to those of Sandag, though perhaps closer to Buddhist ideas than those of his predecessor who drew his themes from popular life. Ishisangbo's social criticism was also more keenly engaged, and he wrote sharply of the decay of morality within the lamaist church, and especially of the misuse of women by lamas who 'look on their lamaseries as prison and the villages as their pleasure-gardens'. His work circulated in both Tibetan and Mongol, but nothing has appeared in any European language.

Nagwangkhaidub (1779–1838) entered religious life at an early age, and reached the rank of *khanpo* or abbot at Urga. He wrote in Tibetan but Mongolian versions of his work exist. He wrote in a satirical and highly critical fashion of abuses within the lamaist church and of misbehaviour on the part of lamas. In the only one of his writings to have been translated into English, the *Qoni Imaga Üker Gurba-yin Yariya* (Conversation between a Sheep, a Goat and an Ox) he develops an argument between these three animals, who are lying bound in the courtyard of a lamasery, waiting to be killed for the lamas' dinner, and one of the lamas. Much of the irony of the piece lies in the animals' mastery of Buddhist theology and morality and their ability to express their philosophical arguments elegantly, and the blunt refusal of the lama to admit that anything can be done to relieve their situation. Nagwangkhaidub's writings had considerable influence among the lamas of Urga and were elaborated upon by his disciple Dandar in a commentary dated about 1860.

(See: *New Orient*, Prague, I, 1966.)

D. Natsagdorj (1906–1937) was born the son of an impoverished nobleman. In 1921 he became a clerk in the Army Department and for a few years was a member of an amateur literary and dramatic group in Ulan Bator which devised and staged dramas on traditional themes. Between 1925 and 1929 he studied abroad, in the USSR and in Germany. Little of his writing from these years survives. His most important work was done in the last six or seven years of his life, when he was working in the Committee of Sciences and in the National Theatre. As well as writing lyrics, short stories and librettos he produced a number of translations from European languages. His first marriage was unhappy, but his second one, to a Russian lady, brought him brief happiness. However, his wife and small daughter were deported to Russia in 1936 and Natsagdorj, who had already been wrongfully imprisoned for some months during the leftist terror of 1932, was overwhelmed by his misfortune and began drinking heavily. He died of a stroke at the age of thirty-one.

Natsagdorj has been built up posthumously to fill the role of founder of modern Mongolian literature. His actual talent, as visible in his works which altogether fill only one volume, would seem too insubstantial to support this part, but he had the good fortune to be an early exponent of the socialist realist school which alone survived the purges of the late thirties. He himself died early, so that his work is not marred by the adulation of the party leadership which marks the work of men who lived through the period of the cult of personality. His lyrics, when not personal, are devoted to the praise of the changes and progress he saw taking shape in his then backward homeland. Of his librettos the best known is *Uchirtai Gurvan Tolgoi* (usually referred to in English as 'Among the Sad Mountains'). This has been set to music as an opera and still holds the stage. In its original form it was a version of an old folk theme of jealousy between two girls who love the same man. After Natsagdorj's death the libretto was thoroughly revised by Damdinsüren who introduced a completely new element of class struggle and changed what had been a simple human tragedy into a political manifesto. It is this version which is now popular.

Ch. Oidov (1917–63) is perhaps the most important of modern Mongolian dramatists. As a boy he was interested in Mongolian folklore and his most successful play, *Dalan Khudalch*, is based on stories attached to the figure of Baldansengge. He also wrote realistic drama, such as *Törsön Ödör* (Birthday), a play set in the Mongol army at the time of the 1945 campaign against the Japanese, and social comedy, such as *Tsolmon*, a play set on a building site and presenting various character types such as the efficient woman worker, the dishonest Lothario, and the eager girl-newcomer from the countryside.

Parchen (1855–1926) was the best known of West-Mongol singers of epics. He learned his first epic before entering a lamasery at the age of ten, and learned further epics both in the lamasery and at the court of a local prince who patronised him. He achieved much fame by encouraging the Mongol soldiers at the siege of Khobdo in 1912 by his singing, but it was his meeting with the Russian orientalist Vladimirtsov which assured him celebrity beyond Mongolia. In the thirties he even figured in a semi-fictional sketch by the English writer Ralph Fox. Vladimirtsov published Parchen's repertory in Russian translation, together with the information that Parchen composed a new epic about the siege of Khobdo.

Rabjai (1803–56) was born into a very poor family in the Gobi. His parents managed chiefly by begging. At the age of eight he was 'recognised' as the fifth incarnation of a series known as the *Noyon Khutuktu*. He was active as a founder of lamaseries and travelled widely, to China, Tibet and Alashan. He never seems to have lost the common touch, and gained among his colleagues the reputation of being a drunkard and womaniser. Apart from his play *Moon Cuckoo* and a number of admonitions, including a didactic work known as *Chagasun Sibagu* (The Kite), he wrote numerous lyrics, some expressive of his piety, some critical of clerical misbehaviour, and some of them down to earth love-poems. Some of the latter are so widely familiar as to have achieved the status of folk poetry. He also made use of the conventional form of the conversation for didactic purposes.

B. Rintchen (*b* 1905) has, like Damdinsüren, enjoyed a many-sided career as scholar, newspaper editor, film-script writer and novelist. He was born in north Mongolia and showed scholarly leanings at an early age. By the time he was nine he could read Russian as well as Mongol, and has since learned other European languages, including French and Czech. He has travelled widely, to China, India, the USSR and Europe, and studied for and obtained the doctorate of the University of Budapest.

As a pupil and friend of the great Buriat scholar Jamtsarano (*d* 1939), Rintchen has devoted himself above all to the care and protection of traditional Mongol culture, and has thereby earned official disapproval more than once. His film-script for the historical film *Tsogtu Taiji* was awarded a Choibalsang prize after its publication in 1944, but was later temporarily suppressed and then rehabilitated. His volume of poems *Ber Tsetseg* (Larkspur) in which he reflected in his individual fashion upon the achievements of socialism was especially criticised for glorifying the past and 'playing into the hands of the imperialists'. Rintchen's language is often deliberately archaic and obscure.

His main work of fiction is the three-volume novel *Üüriin Tuyaa* (Dawn on the Steppe) in which he depicts life around the year of the revolution, 1921. He uses this novel, as also some later writings such as *Zaan Zaluudai*, a novel about prehistoric times, partly as a vehicle for publicising Mongol folklore.

Sandag. It is not known precisely when Sandag lived, but he was probably active at the beginning of the nineteenth century. He was a master of improvisation, and is best known for his *üg*, epigrammatic poems in which he commented, half sentimentally, half seriously, on themes suggested by circumstance or put to him by his companions. Beneath their suave polish there lay a deeper strain of sympathy with suffering and of rejection of insensitivity, which in later writers in this genre was to develop into a more direct and cutting social satire.

(See: *Mongolia Today*, III, 5 and 6, May and June 1961.)

BIBLIOGRAPHY

HISTORICAL BACKGROUND

BAWDEN, C. R. *The Modern History of Mongolia* London, 1967; New York, 1968.

de FRANCIS, J. *Chinese Agent in Mongolia* Baltimore, 1949.

HASLUND, Henning *Mongolian Journey* Routledge and Kegan Paul, London, 1949.

HEISSIG, Walther *A Lost Civilisation: The Mongols Rediscovered* New York; London, 1966. (The German original: *Ein Volk sucht seine Geschichte, Econ Verlag, Düsseldorf-Wien*, contains a large number of plates not found in the English/American version.)

HEISSIG, Walther *Ostmongolische Reise* Leske Verlag, Darmstadt, 1955.

LATTIMORE, Owen *Nationalism and Revolution in Mongolia* Oxford UP, New York, 1955.

LATTIMORE, Owen and NACHUKDORJI, S. *Nomads and Commissars* Oxford UP, New York, 1962.

OLSCHKI, Leonardo *Marco Polo's Asia* California UP, Berkeley and Los Angeles, 1960.

VLADIMIRTSOV, B. *Le régime social des Mongols* Adrien-Maisonneuve, Paris, 1948.

SLATKIN, I. J. *Die Mongolische Volksrepublik* Dietz Verlag, Berlin, 1954.

GENERAL ACCOUNTS

The best sketch of traditional literature, with a full bibliography is:

HEISSIG, Walther 'Mongolische Literatur', *Handbuch der Orientalistik*, Erste Abteilung: Fünfter Band, Altaistik: Zweiter Abschnitt, Mongolistik. E. J. Brill, Leiden/Köln, 1964, pp. 227–74.

Also:

HEISSIG, Walther 'Ein moderner mongolischer Beitrag zur mongolischen Literaturgeschichte', *Central Asiatic Journal*, II, 1.

LAUFER, Berthold 'Skizze der mongolischen Literatur', *Keleti Szemle*, VIII, Budapest, 1907.

POPPE, N. 'Stand und Aufgabe der Mongolistik', *Zeitschrift der Deutschen Morgenländischen Gesellschaft*, 100, 1950

FOR MODERN LITERATURE SEE:

GERASIMOVICH, L. K. *Literatura Mongol'skoi Narodnoi Respubliki 1921–64 godov* Leningrad, 1965.

MIKHAILOV, G. I. *Ocherk Istorii Sovremennoi Mongol'skoi Literatury* Moscow, 1955.

COLLECTIONS OF LITERATURE IN TRANSLATION:

HEISSIG, Walther *Helden-, Höllenfahrts- und Schelmengeschichten der Mongolen* Manesse Verlag, Zurich, 1962.

HEISSIG, Walther *Mongolische Märchen* Diedrichs Verlag, Düsseldorf-Köln, 1963.

MOSTAERT, Antoine *Folklore Ordos* Peking, 1947.

POPPE, N. *Mongolische Volksdichtung* Franz Steiner Verlag, Wiesbaden, 1955.

ON THE SECRET HISTORY OF THE MONGOLS:

HAENISCH, Erich *Die Geheime Geschichte der Mongolen* Otto Harrassowitz, Leipzig, 1948.

PELLIOT, Paul *Histoire secrète des Mongols* Adrien-Maisonneuve, Paris, 1949.

WALEY, Arthur *The Secret History of the Mongols and other Pieces* London, 1963; New York, 1964.

ON EPIC:

DAMDINSÜREN, TS. *Istoricheskie Korni Geseriady* Moscow, 1957.

POPPE, N. *Khalkha-mongol'skii geroicheskii epos* Moscow-Leningrad, 1937.

VLADIMIRTSOV, B. Y. *Mongolo-oriatskii geroicheskii epos* Petrograd-Moscow, 1923.

SCHMIDT, I. J. *Die Taten Bogda Gesser Chan's* Berlin, 1925.

See also:

BAWDEN, Charles 'The Mongol "Conversation Song",' in *Uralic and Altaic Series*, vol. 23, Indiana University, Bloomington and Mouton and Co., The Hague, 1963.

BAWDEN, Charles 'The Tale of Ubashi Khungtaiji of the Mongols', *New Orient*, Prague, 2, 1967.

KOREAN LITERATURE

W. E. Skillend

HISTORICAL BACKGROUND

Korea as a country has its origins in the middle of the seventh century, with the conquest by the kingdom of Silla of two other kingdoms, Paekche and Koguryŏ. Silla was aided in its conquests by T'ang China, and subsequently acknowledged the suzerainty of T'ang. It also remodelled its government on the pattern of that of T'ang. The United Kingdom of Silla disintegrated towards the end of the ninth century as a result of attacks from the tribes to the north-east, and in 935 the king of one of the kingdoms which had arisen in Korea established himself as king of the whole country. He named his dynasty Koryŏ, an abbreviation of Koguryŏ and the origin of our name for the country, and re-established with the new Sung Dynasty in China the relationship which Silla had had with T'ang. The system of government was also aligned with that of Sung. After some two hundred years this dynasty was weakened internally by the acquisition of excessive wealth and power by the Buddhist church and externally by attacks of increasing magnitude by raiders from Japan. The conquest of Korea by the Mongols in the late thirteenth century was followed by a century of occupation by Mongol forces accompanied by a policy of holding members of the royal family hostage in China and marrying them to Mongols.

When the Mongol empire collapsed, there was little effective power in the hands of the Koryŏ government, and in 1392 a general, Yi Sŏn'gye, proclaimed himself king. His dynasty is now usually known as the Yi Dynasty, though it called itself Chosŏn, taking the name of what was reported to be the dynasty ruling Korea before the Chinese first reached the country in the third century BC. It is this name which is popularly translated as 'The Land of the Morning Calm'. Yi Sŏn'gye not only set up a system of government which paralleled that of the new Ming Dynasty in China exactly, but he also based his kingship on his recognition by Ming and on the philosophy of neo-confucianism which had been developed in China in the twelfth century.

Through the fifteenth century Korea enjoyed a period of peace and stability in which considerable advances were made in the techniques of astronomy, meteorology, printing, and so on, and in which colleges and academies were established. However, the ruling class continued to be a small and largely inter-related group, as it had always been whatever system of government was in operation. As differences of opinion arose within this group, they were perpetuated through the sixteenth century as personal, inter-family and inter-school disputes which could not be resolved by reason. The result was bitter factional strife in the court, and frequent persecutions by the party in power of all against whom they held any grudge. On top of this came first the invasions by Hideyoshi from Japan between 1592 and 1598, which were devastating in their effects upon the country and have since been remembered with particular bitterness, and then, forty years later, the invasions by the Manchu, which were not only equally terrible physically, but also struck at the very basis of Korea's existence, the powei of the Ming Dynasty. The king's decision to accept the Ch'ing Dynasty which the Manchu established in China was desperately opposed by many, but was by and large accepted as inevitable.

From the end of the seventeenth century, a new school of thought came to prevail, that of the *sirhakp'a* or 'Real Learning School', a group of neo-confucianists who stressed that all theory should not only be based upon realities, but should also have practical purposes. Under the rule of the Yi Dynasty's longest reigning king, Yŏngjo (1724–76), and his successor, Chŏngjo (1776–1800), the country enjoyed a period of peace and of steady, though unremarkable development. Contact was maintained with Peking through the annual exchange of embassies and prolonged private visits of Koreans to Peking, and through westerners in Peking something was glimpsed of the rest of the world. In the comparatively liberal atmosphere of the eighteenth century, many of the practical ideas and the theories of the west were discussed, but Christianity was consistently outlawed and persecuted as subversive.

Society remained rigid and illiberal in structure, and the nineteenth century produced many expressions of discontent. In the early part of the century there was, for instance, a revolt in P'yŏngan Province in 1812, and later in the century provincial discontent merged into the general confusion caused by the impact of the outside world on the country. Russia's expansion to the Far East was followed by Japan's entering on its period of expansion onto the mainland, and the interests of these two countries clashed in Korea. The Korean court was divided on the question of how best to meet the threats presented by them, the queen advocating reliance on China and the regent advocating abandonment of this traditional relationship in favour of more general alliances with other countries. The queen's party was in control when a serious revolt broke out in the south in 1894, in the name of a religion, Tonghak, which had arisen some thirty years earlier, and quickly spread through all the provinces. Chinese troops were called in to help suppress it, and the Japanese took this as their pretext for sending troops to Korea, where they decisively defeated the Chinese. In 1896 the involvement of the Japanese in the murder of the queen led to a complete loss of Japanese influence in the country, and for a few years something like a truly independent Korean government operated with western advisers. However, the only western country with any vital interest in Korea was Russia, and after the Japanese defeat of Russia in 1905, no other power opposed the Japanese appointment of a Resident General to supervise the government of Korea. In 1910 the Resident General was replaced by a Governor General, the king was deposed, and for the next thirty-five years Korea was administered as Chōsen – Japanese for Chosŏn – a territory of Japan in which Koreans had no political rights or administrative power.

During this period the modernisation of Korea's communications, industry and society was accelerated, though it was geared entirely to the needs of Japan and the territory which she later acquired in China and named Manchukuo. Within Korea every expression of Korean nationalism, even, for the last four years, the use of the Korean language, was severely repressed. In 1919 there was the remarkable demonstration of naive belief in the justice of Korea's claims to independence known as the 'March 1st Movement', but the presentation of the Declaration of Independence and the demonstrations of support for it throughout the country were not backed by any organisation and lacked any practical, attainable aims. During the nineteen-twenties and nineteen-thirties various attempts to organise a communist party were thwarted by the alert and efficient 'thought police', and other programmes for Korean participation in public life foundered because such programmes had to be approved by the Governor General if they were to be practicable, and nothing approved by the Governor General could win wide support among Koreans.

After the defeat of Japan in August 1945, the northern half of Korea was occupied by Russian armies and the southern half by American. With the Russians came a Korean communist ex-guerrilla from Manchuria known as Kim Ilsŏng, who swiftly gained control of the machinery of communications, education and trade. Behind the Americans came the titular head of the defunct Korean government in exile, Syngman Rhee (Yi Sŭngman), who established himself as the only possible choice for the people in the south. Elections were called for by the United Nations in 1948, but were possible in the south only. A National Assembly was elected, which declared the Republic of Korea – taking the name Taehan, which had been used from 1897 to 1905 – and named Syngman Rhee its President. Elections subsequently held in the north resulted in a congress of the communist and allied parties which elected Kim Ilsŏng premier of the Democratic People's Republic of Korea – retaining the name Chosŏn by which their country was still generally known.

War broke out between north and south in June 1950. The south was saved from defeat by the rapid dispatch of first American and later other forces in the name of the United Nations, and within a few months the north had to be saved from defeat by the dispatch of Chinese forces with a volunteer status.

All outside powers were careful to limit the war to Korea, and acquiesced, by the 1953 armistice, in the division of the country more or less as it had been since 1945, along the 38th parallel. Since that time the division has been broken only by a handful of deserters and agents and a barrage of radio propaganda both ways. News from North Korea is scarce and unreliable, but it would appear that Kim Ilsŏng is more firmly in power now than he has ever been, and that North Korea has successfully demonstrated its independence of both Russia and China. In the south, a revolution started in the universities after the blatantly fraudulent elections of March 1960 ousted Syngman Rhee. This was followed by a year of government which was if anything even more corrupt and so inefficient that the country was almost in a state of collapse when a military revolution took place in May 1961. The military government, continuing still as an elected government, has been ruthless in its suppression of anything that might lead to a communist takeover, and has used the full power of its massive bureaucracy to limit the abuse of privilege and corruption in general. Both north and south appear to be reasonably prosperous by Asian standards, the north by operating and developing under state control the heavy industry placed there by the Japanese, the south by attracting heavy investment from America, other western countries and Japan for its private and state enterprises.

MAIN TRENDS IN LITERATURE

Any general description of Korean literature must be prefaced by several admissions: that barely a beginning has yet been made on investigating the subject, that it is not at all clear how much Korean literature from the past has been lost, and that it is impossible to say how representative of the works of the past is the material which has survived.

Nevertheless, we must face the fact that, of what has survived from before about 1850, very little, some fraction of one per cent, is in Korean. In pre-modern Korean society there was virtually no culture, in the sense of literature, art and music, among the masses of the people, and the ruling classes wholeheartedly accepted the culture of China. Although a native culture has persisted even into the heart of modern cities in the forms of folk songs and the totems and practices of shamanism, it has never been more than a substratum, which very seldom showed through the cultural surface of writing. The writing of the ruling classes, in Chinese, on the other hand, was intended to form a part of Chinese culture, and only a very hazy notion of it percolated down to the masses through the teaching of Chinese to young hopefuls aiming at the civil service examinations. While it seems certain that no competent history of literature in Korean can be written without reference to Korea's literature in Chinese, such a history cannot be written while almost all Korea's literature in Chinese remains unread. We shall therefore restrict ourselves here to bare descriptions of certain well-defined groups of works in Korean.

POEMS

First we may take the forty-one poems which have survived from the Silla and Koryŏ periods. Fourteen poems or songs from late Silla are recorded in a history, *Samguk Yusa* (Traditions from the Three Kingdoms), written in the thirteenth century. These are written down with Chinese characters, but are clearly in Korean. Although it is widely believed that this idea of using the writing of China to record one's own language was taught by Koreans to Japanese, there is no evidence now of any wide use of the method in Korea, nor does the material we have suggest that the method was ever as well developed for the writing of Korean as it was for the writing of Japanese. In fact the total quantity of such material is so small that we shall probably never now be sure of the exact Korean forms which were recorded in this way. This is a pity, since, in spite of all the difficulties, we can glimpse in some of the poems striking uses of poetic imagery, such as two leaves falling from the same branch in a poem to a dead sister. Some of the songs are thought to be ritualistic, with a shamanist content, and the preponderance of buddhist thought in the fourteen pieces as a whole may be simply due to the fact that the work in which they are preserved was written by a Buddhist priest. The eleven other poems which are written in the same way, and are usually classified with these fourteen as *hyangga* (literally 'local songs', that is, poems by Koreans) are, however, purely Buddhist, religious works by a priest, Kyunyŏ (923–73). Apart from these, there are sixteen other poems and songs of the Koryŏ period which were either preserved orally or in Chinese translation until they were written down in Korean in the fifteenth century. Among these again it is thought that some are ritualistic, but, as more research is done on them, it is becoming apparent that some of them at least are true poetic compositions. One may cite in particular one in the form of a song by a prostitute which pillories the society of about 1300 apparently deliberately, one stanza for the occupying army, another for the priesthood, the third for the king, and the last for the common people. Another poem, apparently modelled on a Chinese original, uses impressions of the twelve months of the year to sketch a story of love consummated in marriage and ended by the death of the writer's husband. Thus there are indications that Korea has always had its share of poetic genius, but the scarcity of material makes it difficult to be sure what was the particular Korean genius for poetry until a much later age.

The Korean alphabet was devised by a group of scholars under royal patronage in the fourteen-forties and although it is rather cumbersome in use because of the heavy influence of Chinese philology on those who devised it, there is no denying its ingenuity, especially as it was first used by and at the command of King Sejong (1418–50). The first work published in the new alphabet was in 1445, *Yong Pi Ŏ Ch'ŏn Ka* (The Song of the Dragons Flying to Heaven), a long poem in praise of the founders of the Yi Dynasty, and in 1447 there was a life of the Buddha, *Sŏkpo Sangjŏl*, by the crown prince, to which the king added in 1449 his own poem *Wŏl In Ch'ŏn'gang chi Kok* (The Song of the Moon Reflected in a Thousand Rivers). The last two works survive only partially, and none of the three has yet been investigated as literature. They share certain philological difficulties with a mass of interpreters' manuals and translations of Chinese classics, poems, medical works and Buddhist scriptures, which form the bulk of writing in Korean from the first century or so following the promulgation of the Korean alphabet.

Korean Literature

The greater part of the literature in Korean which has been described at all critically consists of poems from the late sixteenth to the early nineteenth centuries, and even among these, far more attention has been given to the short poems than to the longer ones. In particular it is now generally felt that the poetic form which is most typically Korean is that known as *sijo*, or more specifically *p'yŏng sijo*, 'ordinary *sijo*'. The word *sijo* itself was originally a musical term, an abbreviation of the phrase *sijŏl kajo*, meaning something like 'tunes for amateurs', but since most amateur singing in the eighteenth and nineteenth centuries was of songs with a particular form of lyric, when the literary historians turned their attention to literature in Korean in the twentieth century and began naming the forms of poems in Korean, this term was taken for those poems which were similar in form to those lyrics. Whether there is any closer connection than this between *sijo* poems and music is one of the many questions which still awaits investigation. The *sijo* is constructed of the same basic units as are found in almost all Korean poetry, the three and four syllable phrases which give a rhythm of phrase length. Stress, which is infinitely variable in Korean, appears to play no part at all in poetic rhythm. Also, as in almost all poetry in Korean, the phrases are arranged in groups of four, forming a couplet of two lines, each of two phrases, and the couplets generally match the syntax of the words. The couplet typically consists of a complete sentence or a major subordinate clause, with its verb, as is the rule in Korean, at the end. It can be divided into a clause in the first line with the sentence finished in the second line, or the two lines can even be two linked sentences, each ending with a verb. The first line again can be broken by the syntax into two fairly independent phrases, but the second line of the couplet usually forms a tighter unit. Neither the phrase-length rhythm nor the syntactic structure are applied with consistent accuracy, but a typical couplet in a poem in Korean may be represented as '3, 4; 4–4'. What is distinctive about 'ordinary' *sijo* is that they consist of three couplets and that the second phrase of the last couplet is always at least five syllables long. The following famous poem may serve as an example:

i momi	chugŏ chugŏ	this body	dies dies
ilbaekpŏn kŏch'yŏ chugŏ		hundred times through dies	
paekkori	chint'oe toeyŏ	white bones	dust become
nŏksirado ikko ŏpko		spirit even is is not	
nim hyanghan	ilp'yŏntansimiya	lord facing	devoted heart
kasuil churi isirya		will change can it	

My body is mortal, commonly mortal.
My bones end in dust, soul or no soul.
My lord owns my heart, though, and that cannot change.

Sijo are seldom clever, witty or cruel, and normally rather understated, and assonance of any sort is the exception rather than the rule, but the significance of such qualities is currently being debated. The debate is inconclusive perhaps partly because not so much attention has been given to the strictly factual history of *sijo*. There is a body of *sijo* of known authorship composed between about 1550 and 1650, which is well known and well liked in Korea, very little of certain authorship from before about 1550, and a great mass of *sijo* from later than 1650. The later poems are generally regarded as over-conventional and lacking in originality, but, quite apart from the question of whether originality was ever a quality valued by Koreans of the Yi Dynasty, there is a marked tendency for literary historians to telescope the two hundred years which these poems span, and to disregard the signs of the passing of these years.

One exception is, however, made, for the *sijo* which are hardly *sijo*, but which are called *sasŏl sijo*, literally 'narrative *sijo*'. Under this category come poems which anyone who was not instructed otherwise would regard as free verse. Such poems appear from the beginning of the eighteenth century, and since this coincides with the rise of the *sirhakp'a*, the factual content of these poems and the realism of their descriptions is attributed to the influence of the *sirhakp'a*. We may take the following poem as typical of the early seventeenth century:

Blue stream in the green hills, do not revel in your swiftness,
For your path to the broad sea is one which is hard to retrace.
While the bright moon fills the bowl of the hills, why not rest on your way?

This may be a perfectly harmless comment on nature, or it may be, as is generally supposed, 'Bright Moon', the courtesan Hwang Chini, inviting a gentleman whose pen-name was 'Blue Stream' to patronise her. Either way, it contrasts markedly with this anonymous poem from the early eighteenth century:

Little maid, buy all the heats: that of too early summer; that of too late summer; that of the summer for which the heat has been stored up for years;
The heat in which, in the dog days of summer, you meet your lover and lie curled up on a flat wooden bed in the bright moonlight, and then for some reason feel feverish and suffocated, sweat beads of perspiration, and pant; the heat in which, in the long, long nights of midwinter, you are with your dear one, and, on the hottest part of the floor under a warm quilt, your two bodies become one body in your activity, hands and feet tense, and when your throat is on fire, you gulp down cold rice-tea from the iciest part of the room. If you will buy them, little maid, buy what pleases you best.
Merchant, among all your heats, your two heats of meeting my lord would please anyone. Do not sell them to another, but please sell them to me.

Almost every poem from the Yi Dynasty which is not called a *sijo* is usually now called a *kasa*, but the word *kasa* itself only means 'the words of a song', and such poems consist simply of an indefinite repetition of couplets. This form was used for such mundane purposes as teaching household duties to daughters-in-law, but also in it one finds long diaries of journeys, descriptions of nature, elegies, and other expressions of deep personal emotion. The *kasa* far outweigh the *sijo* in quantity. Some thousand *kasa* of the Yi Dynasty are known, averaging several hundred couplets each, as opposed to some two thousand five hundred *sijo* of three couplets each. In addition, good *kasa* are both known to have been written as early as any *sijo* and continued to be produced with a high degree of poetic feeling long after the *sijo* is supposed to have become a mere formality. Yet the *sijo* continue to monopolise the critics' attention, and our appreciation of Korean poetry is the duller for it.

PROSE

Korean prose before the twentieth century consists almost entirely of *sosŏl*. *Sosŏl* is the Korean pronunciation of the Chinese word *hsiao-shuo*, and the history of this cannot be detailed here, but in Korean it is used now as the equivalent of 'novel'. About half of the *sosŏl* of the Yi Dynasty are translations of Chinese 'novels', from the famous *Romance of the Three Kingdoms*, which, in translation, is probably still the best-seller in Korea, to tedious accounts of loyal subjects of the Ming which were translated once and have been ignored ever since. Among the Korean compositions one finds also many imitations of these Chinese works, and a great number of stories from Korean history. Indeed, Korean histories are often so spiced with fiction and Korean *sosŏl* often so tediously factual that one wonders how the two can be distinguished by content or theme. However, such an overwhelming number of the *sosŏl* are written in Korean, in marked contrast to every other kind of literature, that one might almost say that *sosŏl* are in Korean by definition, that is to say that they form the body of popular Korean literature as opposed to the literature of the ruling class. Furthermore, among the most popular of the *sosŏl* are those which have been told since the eighteenth century at least, by *kwangdae*, groups of entertainers who travel around with the markets. The *kwangdae* recite their stories in a chant which is called *p'ansori*, and their versions of *sosŏl* bear a remarkable resemblance in form to the poems known as *kasa*.

More than five hundred *sosŏl* in the style of the Yi Dynasty are now known, and more are uncovered every time a private collection is made public, but many of these have not even been read, and practically nothing is known about the history of their composition. A start might perhaps be made by investigating the history of their publication. Although this would be of only limited use, since most *sosŏl* exist in single manuscript copies made for private reading, it does at least give us some firm information on the history of all the most popular of the *sosŏl*.

Sosŏl are known to have been printed in three places: in Seoul, at Ansŏng (about forty miles south of Seoul) and at Chŏnju (further south again, in Chŏlla Province). Those printed at Ansŏng seem to have little importance, since they are few, very late, and virtually identical with Seoul printings. The Seoul printings are the most numerous today, with about fifty *sosŏl* known in a total of about one hundred editions. The earliest dated publication is a collection of nine short stories in three volumes entitled *Samsŏlgi*, which appears to mean 'Three Tales', printed in 1848. The stories form an interesting commentary on the society of the time, with frank, though not bitter criticism of bribery in the law courts, social climbing, fawning and flattery as a means to promotion, and so on, and also very mildly critical descriptions of the pattern of life in general at the time. The style is artless, and may well have been very close to the spoken language of the time. The latest date on any text printed in Seoul is actually 1887, on two texts, but all other texts are dated between 1851 and 1864, and most of the texts are undated. Little is now known that was not known in the west at the end of the nineteenth century, and we therefore have to assume that all the texts we have are from the second half of the nineteenth century. From these we may select a few *sosŏl* which Korean literary historians consider important.

Sa-ssi Namjong ki (The Lady Hsieh's Journey to the South), published in 1851, is a nicely told tale of a concubine displacing a wife and bringing the husband to ruin. This appears to be a translation of a story written in Chinese by Kim Ch'unt'aek (1670–1717), but he himself wrote that his work was a translation of one in Korean by his great uncle, Kim Manjung (1637–92). Furthermore, at about the time of this publication, it was suggested that the story was an allegorical criticism of King Sukchong's treatment of his second wife, Queen Inhyŏn, between 1689 and 1694, and the earliest dated copy of the *sosŏl Queen Inhyŏn* is a manuscript dated 1852.

Kuun mong (The Cloud Dream of the Nine), is dated 1887 in one edition, but other editions appear to be earlier, and this is also a translation of a work in Chinese by Kim Ch'unt'aek. Although the translations are not particularly remarkable in themselves, the work itself is regarded by Koreans as technically the best of the *sosŏl*. It gives us, in the form of a highly readable story of a successful man who had eight wives, a picture of Korea's three main religions, Buddhism, Confucianism and Taoism, as they actually operated in Korean life.

Hong Kiltong chŏn is a story of a Korean Robin Hood, which may be based on the life of one or other of the historical persons called Hong Kiltong. The *sosŏl* is not very well told, either in plot or style, but it has assumed some importance in Korean literary histories because a reference has been found stating that Hŏ Kyun (1569–1618) wrote a story of this title.

Sugyŏng Nangja chŏn (The Maiden Sugyŏng), published in 1860, tells of a marriage which survives all difficulties, even the death of the wife, thanks to her powers in magic. In spite of the supernatural elements in it, the story is well told and convincing in detail, and although it is a translation of a work in Chinese by a Korean, the translation is so effective that the story was even incorporated into the repertoire of some *kwangdae* at one time in fairly recent years.

Sukhyang chŏn (Shu-hsiang), published in 1858, is among the best of the Korean imitations of Chinese novels. The heroine begins life abandoned during a war in Sung China, and survives a whole series of similar misfortunes during the course of a highly successful career.

Sim Ch'ŏng chŏn (Shen Ch'ing), is probably the best, stylistically, of all purely Korean works of fiction published in Seoul in the nineteenth century, and it also seems to have been the most popular *sosŏl* until very recently. The heroine's mother dies soon after giving birth to her, and her father goes blind. The girl supports her father meagrely for some years, and then sells herself for the money which the father has been told he must offer to the Buddha to regain his sight. The merchant who buys her offers her as a sacrifice to a monster who is wrecking his ships, but the sea-king is so impressed by her filial piety that he returns her to the surface wrapped in a flower of wondrous beauty and fragrance. This is taken to the king, and when she steps out of the flower one night, Shen Ch'ing becomes his queen. Her advice on affairs of state produces a Utopia, and at the end of the story a banquet is given for all the blind of the kingdom, at which father and daughter are reunited and the scales fall from Shen's eyes. The story is not so popular today, but it is clear that a close study of it would be very rewarding.

Ch'unhyang chŏn, the story of a faithful wife, is the most popular today of all the *sosŏl* of the Yi Dynasty, partly because of its credibility, and partly because a version of it, published in Chŏnju, derived from a *kwangdae* version, was in an excellent style itself and has been adapted into many well written versions in modern Korean. The outline of the story is as follows: Ch'unhyang, the daughter of a *kisaeng* or professional hostess, attracts by her beauty and learning Master Yi, son of the governor of her town, Namwŏn. The two are married in secret, and when the Yi family move to Seoul, Ch'unhyang is left behind. Yi is replaced as governor by one Pyŏn, the epitome of all that is worst in officials, unjust, corrupt and sybaritic. When he calls the roll of the *kisaeng* of Namwŏn, Ch'unhyang claims that her marriage excuses her from attendance, and she is imprisoned. Meanwhile her husband has passed his examinations in Seoul and been appointed Secret Roving Envoy of the King. When his duties take him to Namwŏn, he uncovers all Pyŏn's wickedness and frees Ch'unhyang to live happily with him ever after.

Shen Ch'ing, as well as *Ch'unhyang*, was also published in Chŏnju towards the end of the nineteenth century, and also shows the influence of the *kwangdae* version. In fact all of the fourteen *sosŏl* known to have been published in Chŏnju are stylistically interesting. The outstanding ones among them are the two just mentioned, *Hwayongdo* (Hua-yung-tao), derived from *The Romance of the Three Kingdoms*, *Ch'ohan chŏn* (Ch'u and Han), derived from *The Romance of Western Han*, and two other war tales set in China, but of unknown origin, *Yu Ch'ungnyŏl chŏn* (Liu Chung-lieh), and *Yi Taebong chŏn* (Li Ta-feng). The printing of these works in Chŏnju continued well into the twentieth century, the last known blocks being lost in the Korean War, but few of them can be found today, and all we can say is that it is by no means certain that printing in Chŏnju began later than in Seoul. The date 1862 for one volume of a two volume translation of *The Cloud Dream of the Nine* seems to be absolutely incontestable, and one edition of *Cho Ung chon* (Chao Hsiung), another tale set in China, bears a date which may be 1906, but which some take as 1846.

THE 'NEW LITERATURE'

The search for links between Korea's traditional literature and her modern literature has not yet been very rewarding. For a start there is a period between 1887, the date of the last dated Seoul wood block print, and 1906, when Korea's first modern novel was serialised in a newspaper, when we have not one single dated event in Korean literature. However, the newspapers of the period are now coming to light again in various private collections and yielding some information, particularly so far on the early days of the theatre in Korea. Most theatrical performances in Seoul in the first decade of this century were given by *kwangdae* and other folk entertainers. Through such events we may link, for instance, Yi Haejo (1869–1927), whose earliest works include several modern novel versions of the stories told by *kwangdae*, with Sin Chaehyo (1812–84), whose texts of these stories as he rewrote them and taught them to *kisaeng*, and perhaps also to *kwangdae*, still exist in manuscript.

However, the writers of the 'New Literature' by and large set out deliberately to break with the traditions of the past. In poetry, this was done by experimenting with different metres, that is to say with different combinations of the basic unit of three or four syllables, and by introducing western words and references where the older poets had embellished their works with Chinese phrases and references to Chinese literature. In prose, the novels abandoned the old opening formulas, the settings in Ming and Sung China, and also the miraculous coincidences and deeds of magic, together with much of the old language. Both in the earliest modern poetry and the earliest modern novels, one can read consistent criticism of society as it was in the first decade of this century, which is extremely interesting for what it is. Though little of it is now counted as of great literary value, in some cases at least it is coming to be realised that there has been some bias in the criticism of these works. At the time when a beginning was made on Korean literary history in the 1930s,

Korean writers were hardly able to think of anything to express in their novels and poems other than their patriotism and the injustices of the Japanese rule. The writers of the first decade of this century, however, were as a rule bitterly critical of their fellow-countrymen, and if they mentioned Japan at all, it was usually as models of how Korea and Koreans should adapt to the twentieth century. Yi Injik (1862–1916), author of what is generally held to be the first modern novel in Korean, *Hyŏl ŭi Nu* (Tears of Blood), has suffered particularly in this respect, and also because the only text of this novel which was available from the nineteen-thirties to the late nineteen-fifties was a version put out under Japanese censorship, from which had been expurgated every one of the passages urging the need for patriotism upon what Yi Injik believed were his essentially selfish fellow-countrymen. If he is being rehabilitated now, this is due largely to the recognition of his services to the theatre.

MODERN LITERATURE

Korean literary historians distinguish usually between 'New Literature' taking the term from the expressions 'New Novel' and 'New Poetry' which were used by the first writers of the twentieth century, and 'Modern Literature', a term which critics devised for the works which come a little later. One distinguishing feature of 'Modern Literature' is that the writers engaged in it have been prolific in their comments on their own writings. While little in the way of literary criticism has yet been produced, largely perhaps because the writing élite in Korea still forms a fairly small group, all the members of which are well known to each other personally, a great deal of work has now been done on modern literature in the universities. Questions of style, influence and purpose, as well as questions of authorship and date, have now been fairly well answered in the academic journals of South Korea. Indeed, with the current boom in magazines, much of this is now widely available, the only difficulty being to keep abreast of the output of information. (The situation in North Korea is more difficult to assess, not only because it is difficult to obtain publications from there, but also because the terminology of the north's very closed society is fairly meaningless to anyone who has not grown up with it. What follows will therefore refer primarily to the situation in South Korea.)

Two figures stand out as the founders of Korea's 'modern' literature, Yi Kwangsu (1892–about 1950?) and Kim Tongin (1900–51), both prodigious producers of novels and short stories and regular contributors to literary magazines. Kim Tongin's *Study of Yi Kwangsu* is a model of literary criticism. These two, with four more of the most significant 'modern' writers, are given in the biographies which follow, but perhaps one should mention here also the gifted, but short-lived, romantic poet Kim Sowŏl (1902–34), author of what is without any doubt the most popular modern poem, *The Azaleas*. Most of the writers who brought the 'modern' touch of quality to Korean literature are still living and writing today, though some have lost their lives in the recent political turmoil, including one of Korea's best essayists, Yi T'aejun. (On the other hand, one of the most promising short-story writers of the 1930s, Yu Chino, abandoned writing for the law, and is at present leader of the opposition in the National Assembly.) It is invidious to choose a few names from the current list of hundreds of devoted writers, but amongst those who are most highly respected are novelists and short-story writers Sŏnu Hwi and Hwang Sunwŏn, as well as the perennially successful Pak Chonghwa and the consistently competent An Sugil, poets Sŏ Chŏngju, Cho Chihun and Pak Tujin, not forgetting poetess Kim Namjo, and Korea's only established dramatist, Yu Ch'ijin.

Much has been written about the influence of various western writers, schools and movements on Korean authors, but one may beg to question the significance of this. There can be little doubt that what attracted Korea's first modern writers was that writers of contemporary literature in the West could be counted important in their societies. Also some of the ideas of the West which percolated through to Korea – social justice and sympathy for the underprivileged, especially women – and various literary notions – realism, art-for-art's sake, vorticism, stream of consciousness and the rest – had their effects. However, among the first rank writers in Korea, there has probably not been one who has been able to appreciate any western works for himself. Conversely, a number of promising writers who have spent enough time in the West to become competent have given up writing in their own language. Those who have not, have in most cases devoted themselves to the literatures in which they have become competent, and it has been from among these experts in foreign cultures that most of Korea's essayists have come, Yi Yangha and Kwŏn Chunghŭi being two prime examples. A sort of exception to this rule may be found among the writers who spent a considerable time in Japan, including almost all those who began writing in the nineteen-twenties or earlier. None of these seems to have been influenced by Japanese literature as such, though what they learned of western literature was learned mainly through Japanese and the effect of the West on Korean writers followed fairly closely the effect that it had already had on Japanese writers. Also, although many Koreans became extremely competent in Japanese, none of them has become famous as a writer in Japanese. For some twenty years after 1945, Koreans were cut off from contact with Japan by deliberate government policy, and such contacts as were made, in writers' congresses and so on, tended to result in discussions of world literature rather than Japanese or Korean literature.

'Modern' literature continued the trend, started with the 'New' literature, to treat current questions more often than not. There have been many historical novels, and Sŏ Chŏngju seeks in his poetry for the spirit of Korea in the Silla period, but the typical novels of the thirties deal with questions of education, land-ownership and freedom of expression, and the poems tend to be soul-searching: the novels and poems of 1945–50 throb with the 'after-the-bomb' uncertainty of the world, and recent works depict the tragedies of the Korean War and the division of the country. (In North Korea, as one might expect, the current favourite subjects appear to be the guerrilla fight against the Japanese, the economic and social changes after 1945, and the fight against American imperialism – in that order.)

For the future, there is no doubting the sincerity of the wish of many writers in Korea to create a truly Korean literature, and there is a growing confidence that it is being created. The comparative helplessness of Korea throughout this century is felt keenly, and while this has spurred many writers to great efforts in their work, it has discouraged others severely, and has caused many readers to look rather to other literatures for guidance and hope. It is still a fact of Korean literary life that 'literature' means 'English literature' to a great number of Koreans, and another fact that publishers prefer translations to originals while Korea does not subscribe to the international copyright agreements. No one who gives any thought to Korean literature can feel anything but sympathy for Korean writers, or wish them anything but success.

INDIVIDUAL WRITERS

Chŏng Ch'ŏl (1536–93). With two of his elder sisters married into the royal family, Chŏng Ch'ŏl spent much of his childhood in the royal palace and was particularly friendly with Prince Kyŏngwŏn. There was a dispute over the succession to King Chungjong (1506–44), and one of Ch'ŏl's brothers-in-law was associated with the faction which supported the crown prince, who succeeded to the throne, but reigned for only eight months. When Prince Kyŏngwŏn became King Myŏngjong at the age of eleven, the faction which had supported him persecuted the opposition, and Chŏng Ch'ŏl's family was banished. In 1551 they were allowed to go to their own land at Ch'angp'yŏng, in Chŏlla Province, and for ten years Ch'ŏl studied in a retreat on the banks of a small river, the Songgang, from which he took the pen-name by which he is usually known. He also attended classes given by some of the best neo-confucianist scholars of the time, in the company of others who became the leading teachers of the next generation. He passed the civil service examinations in 1561 and 1562, and led a successful career for some sixteen or seventeen years, and also later served as a provincial defence administrator during the Japanese invasions and went on one embassy to Peking in the last year of his life, but from 1580 to 1592 his faction was usually in opposition, and he spent most of these years either in provincial posts or in retirement writing his famous *kasa* and *sijo*. His poems in Korean were published several times by his descendants, both along with his works in Chinese in *Songgang chip*, his collected works, and also separately as *Songgang Kasa*. He is the first major writer of *kasa*, though a few earlier examples of the form from up to a century earlier are also famous, and he is also the undisputed master of the form. His five *kasa* express primarily his philosophy as a loyal subject of the king in the form of descriptions of the beauty of the provinces and love-poems. His ninety-three known *sijo* also place him among the leading exponents of this form, but they are more explicitly didactic, and remembered for their moral tone rather than their literary qualities.

Han Yongun (1879–1944). Han Pongwan was still at his local school when the Tonghak rebellion broke out in 1894, but he participated in it, and on its failure entered a Buddhist monastery, becoming a priest with the name of Yongun in 1905. Within three years he was playing a leading role in the church. From the very first he was concerned at Korean Buddhism's failure to meet any of the needs of modern man, and visited Japan in 1908 to examine the situation there. He also seems to have realised the danger to Korea from Japan, since, immediately upon the annexation in 1910, he went on a three-year tour of Korean independence groups in China and Russia. On his return, he worked to make Buddhism effective in Korea by teaching in Buddhist schools and publishing Buddhist magazines. As one of the signatories of the Declaration of Independence in 1919, he was imprisoned for three years, but continued his work of encouraging Korean nationalism in Buddhist organisations, and was arrested again in 1937. His importance in Korean literary history lies in his poetry. This is dense with allusions, and this, together with the beauty of his language, mark him as probably the first Korean poet whose works will repay deep and prolonged study.

Hyŏn Chin'gŏn (1900–41). A student of German in Tokyo and Shanghai, Hyŏn Chin'gŏn provides an exception to the rule that writers who show promise in appreciating foreign cultures abandon Korean literature. Although his very first work, a short story *The Sacrifice* in 1920, neither impressed his contemporaries greatly nor is highly regarded today, he persisted in his efforts. In these he was much encouraged by his friend Yŏm Sangsŏp (*qv*), and like him he is primarily looked upon as a realist. There is also a dream-like or exotic quality in his works, which may betray some German influence. He earned his living as a journalist, and is famous in Korea for having obliterated the Japanese flag from the picture published in the *Tonga Ilbo* of the Korean winner of the marathon in the Berlin Olympics of 1936, Son Kijŏng. He was imprisoned for one year for this offence, and was unable to support himself afterwards. Although his works are not numerous, they show that his untimely death was a great loss to Korean literature.

Kim Ch'ŏnt'aek. A commoner who is known to have been deputy director of a criminal investigation department during the reign of King Sukchong (1674–1720), Kim Ch'ŏnt'aek was also a talented singer. He established a club for the appreciation of *sijo* which is thought to have been largely responsible for the vogue for *sijo* during the eighteenth century. The anthology *Ch'ŏnggu Yŏngŏn* (Eternal Words of the Green Hills), which he compiled in 1728, exists now only in several markedly different manuscript versions, but the six hundred to one thousand poems which the various versions contain are the most important material which we have for studying the history of Yi Dynasty poetry. Fifty-seven of his own *sijo* are also recorded in the anthology compiled by his friend Kim Sujang (*qv*).

Kim Sakkat (1807–63). Born as Kim Pyŏngyŏn into one of the noblest families, when he was five years old, his grandfather was put to death for his part in the revolt of 1812, and his descendants were barred from holding office for ever. He soon left home, and under the name Sakkat (Bamboo Hat), by which he is now usually known, he spent the rest of his life wandering the country and composing poems in outrageously Korean Chinese. He is

perhaps the only complete individualist in all Korea's literary history.
Kim Sujang (born 1691). A commoner who worked as a government clerk in his youth, Kim Sujang, together with his friend Kim Ch'ŏnt'aek (*qv*), devoted most of his life to the writing, collecting and teaching of *sijo*. Two manuscript copies of an anthology *Haedong Kayo* (Songs from the East of the Sea), survived into the twentieth century and have been re-published, and research has shown that these represent some thirty years of Kim Sujang's work, up to about 1770. One hundred and seventeen of his own poems are included in this anthology, and a few more are found elsewhere. Not only does this place him first in the list of known writers of *sijo* in the Yi Dynasty, but his works also show a remarkably consistent style which is usually described as realistic.
Kim Tongin (1900–51). A native of P'yŏngan Province, Kim Tongin, like other writers from the same area, was very close to Yi Kwangsu (*qv*). He was a student in Japan at the same time as Yi Kwangsu, but unlike him saw himself only as a writer and avoided all involvement in politics after being imprisoned for four months in 1920 for violation of the censorship law. From about 1925 to 1935 he concentrated his efforts mainly on literary magazines, in which he advocated the 'purity' of literature, that it should have its own standards and purposes; subsequently he turned to one of Korea's favourite traditional forms of literature, the *yadam* or 'stories from history'. In spite of a series of failures in business ventures, and a drug addiction which makes the hardness of his life even more pitiable, he never paused in his output of short stories, and occasional novels. Korea's premier literary award is named in his honour.
Pak Hyogwan. A commoner and a singer, Pak Hyogwan, with one of his pupils, An Minyŏng, compiled in 1876 an anthology of *sijo* which is well organised and includes critical essays. This anthology is generally known by the title on one copy of it, *Kagok Wŏllyu* (A Source Book of Songs), but another copy of it is entitled *Kasa chip* (Collected Lyrics) and the third *Ch'ŏnggu Akchang* (Verses from the Green Hills). His work caught the attention of the regent, and his club for poets, modelled perhaps on that of Kim Ch'ŏnt'aek (*qv*), attracted many of the leading figures of society. Thirteen of his own *sijo* are preserved.
Pak Illo (1561–1642). An established poet in Chinese in his youth, Pak Illo distinguished himself in active service against the Japanese, and in 1599 passed the military service examinations. His services to the localities in which he served are recorded with gratitude, and at the age of seventy-one he was given high honorary office. *Nogye chip* (The Collected Works of Nogye [Pak Illo]), published several times during the nineteenth century by his descendants, contain eight *kasa* and more than seventy *sijo*. His *kasa T'aep'yŏng sa* (Peace), commemorating the defeat of the Japanese, is the most famous of his works, and his poems are enjoyed chiefly for their expressions of patriotism, though they also show both his learning and his love of nature.
Sim Hun (1901–36). Between his imprisonment for his activity in the demon-

strations of 1919 and his deathbed poem, *Oh Korean Boys!*, in a pirate newspaper edition reporting Son Kijong's victory in the Olympic marathon of 1936, Sim Hun (born Sim Taesŏp) was an enthusiastic writer of short stories and novels aimed at encouraging all that is best in the Korean character. Outstanding is his novel *Sangnoksu* (The Evergreen Tree), written during a period spent in the countryside, the story of a teacher who transformed the spirit of a rural community by her devotion to her duties. Sim Hun was also a pioneer writer for the cinema from 1925, and a lively newspaper reporter.

Yi Haejo (1869–1927). Although he was the most prolific of the first modern novelists, and may be said to have established the modern novel in Korean, virtually nothing is known of Yi Haejo's private life, and even the dates of many of his works are uncertain. Some thirty novels are known to have been written by him from 1908 on, and it is also believed that many of the anonymous pieces of literature, including essays, which appeared in newspapers were by him. He is known to have used eight pen-names. His versions of traditional *sosŏl* were based on the *p'ansori* versions, and have been the inspiration for all later rewritings. These form about one-third of his known works, and were all published under new titles, *Ch'unhyang chŏn*, for instance, as *Okchunghwa* (The Flower in Prison). The remainder of his novels deal with contemporary life, generally very much from the point of view of the individuals living that life. His humanity and his pleasant style contrast sharply with the works of his only predecessor in the field, Yi Injik (*qv*), and in so far as these qualities can be seen to mark the works of the writers who followed him in date, one may assume that his influence on all modern writing has been profound.

Yi Injik (1862–1916). The first known fact in Yi Injik's life is that he received a Korean government scholarship in 1900 to study at the College of Politics in Tokyo, graduating in 1903. He returned to Korea as an interpreter with the Japanese army during the Russo-Japanese War and later became editor first of one newspaper, *Kungmin Sinbo*, of which little is known, and then, in 1906, of another newspaper, *Mansebo*. *Mansebo* was owned by O Sech'ang, a leading figure then in the Ch'ŏndo (previously known as Tonghak) religion, and later also in the March 1st Independence Movement. The newspaper was a semi-official organ of the Ch'ŏndo religion and progressive, but was specifically opposed to the policy of unity with Japan. Yi Injik, however, serialised in this paper his work *Hyŏl ŭi Nu* (Tears of Blood), Korea's first modern novel, which advocates at one point unity with Japan. This paper failed in little over a year, and Yi Injik was set up as publisher of a new paper, *Taehan Sinmun*. While holding this position, he took up the cause of the theatre, being encouraged at a vital stage by the Japanese Resident General. Korea's first theatre, the Hyŏmnyul-sa, founded in 1902, had not been a great success, and Yi Injik founded the second, the Wŏn'gak-sa, in 1908. This put on a dramatised version of one of his novels, *Ŭn Segye* (The Silver World), but otherwise seems to have featured only *p'ansori* and other traditional forms of entertainment. Yi Injik frequently sponsored conferences to propagandise for the development of the theatre over the next few years, and when his connections with pro-Japanese politicians finally gained him a secure post in the confucian academy, he seems to have regarded such activities as his first duty. His novels show that he was an enthusiastic propagandist rather than a capable writer. All his works start with force and deteriorate after a few episodes. Indeed one was finished by another writer (Kim Kyoje) and another was never finished at all. Nor is his total output great – only five or six short novels, but he may be said to have changed the course of Korean literature more than any other single writer.

Yi Kwangsu (1892–about 1950?). A native of P'yŏngan Province, Yi Kwangsu spent the years 1910 to 1919 in Japan, at college, teaching, and finally as a student at Waseda University. He was the author of the Declaration of Independence by Korean students in Japan in February 1919, and after this incident fled to Shanghai, where he was active in the abortive Independent Government for a while. Soon after his return to Korea in 1922, he took up journalism, and was imprisoned in 1937 for his nationalist associations. However, he fell ill in prison and was released within six months. Within a year he was advocating that Koreans should accept their position under Japanese rule, and he took the lead in the movement for Koreans to adopt Japanese names. It is perhaps worth noting that he was associated in his pro-Japanese activities with Ch'oe Namsŏn, author of the March 1st (1919) Declaration of Independence. After 1945 he, as all who had engaged in such activities, led a life of seclusion, and Yi Kwangsu was one of those who were imprisoned under the retrospective 'Anti-People's Law' of 1949, though only for a short while because of his ill-health. He disappeared completely during the Korean War. In spite of the sad ending to his life story, Yi Kwangsu towers above all other writers of the twentieth century and is highly respected still. He is known first and foremost as a novelist, and he certainly added one new dimension to the novel in Korean, that of length, a point on which Tolstoy was his model. Most of his novels were serialised, beginning with *Mujŏng* (Heartlessness), in 1917. They tend to flag a little in the course of their length, and even his short stories, which are as long as most of the earlier New Novels, show a lack of discipline, but when all criticisms have been made, there is no denying his natural talent as a writer, whether of novels, short stories, essays, letters or poems, and his zeal on behalf of Korean literature matches his talent. There is also a very marked thread of Buddhist transcendentalism running through his works, and while these works reflect very strongly the Korean situation under Japanese occupation, he himself saw them, at least by the mid nineteen-thirties, as describing the whole human situation.

Yŏm Sangsŏp (1897–1963). Seoul born and bred, Yŏm Sangsŏp is probably the first major writer to have had a proper Korean education in the sense that it was neither in the old Chinese style nor at one of the colleges established by Christian missionaries, but at the Posŏng High School, later Posŏng College and now Korea University. Further, although he did have some education in Japan, it was in the literature department of the highly independent Keiō University, which showed a remarkable corporate sympathy for Posŏng College. Yŏm Sangsŏp was the leading light of various groups which tended to go to extremes in literary experiment in the 1920s. His first short story, *The Green Frog in the Specimen Room*, was a necessary shock, perhaps, for Korean writing in 1921, and for the rest of his life, while he worked as a journalist (in Manchukuo from 1936 to 1945), he kept up a steady, though not very voluminous production of realistic short stories and novels. He was much honoured in his last ten years with appointments to academies and cultural prizes, and it has been under his aegis that most of the encouragement of the arts has taken place.

Yun Sŏndo (1587–1671). Yun Sŏndo passed the civil service examinations in 1612, but held office for only a few years between 1628 and 1635, and again for a few years during the reign of King Hyojong (1649–60), whom he had tutored as prince. He suffered for his complaints against an academician during the reign of the 'unjust' king Kwanghae-gun (1568–1623), for his failure to stand by the king during the Manchu invasions, and for belonging to the faction which lost a vital argument over the proper period of mourning for a queen. His seventy-seven *sijo* depict country life, reflecting his long years in exile. His series of forty *sijo*, *Ŏbu Sasisa* (The Fisherman's Calendar), are counted the acme of perfection in the *sijo* form, particularly for their lively use of the Korean language.

BIBLIOGRAPHY

GENERAL

COURANT, Maurice *Bibliographie Coréenne*. École des Langues Orientales Vivantes, 3 vols. and supplement, Paris, 1894–1901.

HAKWONSA *Korea, Its Land, People and Culture of All Ages* Hakwonsa, Seoul, 1960.

LEE, Peter H. *Korean Literature, Topics and Themes* Arizona UP, Tucson, 1965.

CLASSICAL LITERATURE

The two following articles are useful contributions to the study of their subjects:

RUTT, C. R. (Bishop Richard Rutt) 'An Introduction to the Sijo', *Transactions of the Korea Branch of the Royal Asiatic Society*, vol. XXXIV, 1958.
'Kim Sakkat, Vagabond Poet', ibid., vol. XLI, 1964.

The following are two translations of *sosŏl*, both difficult to find:

YI HAEJO 'Choon Yang', trans. James S. Gale, from *Okchunghwa*, serialised in *Korea Magazine* vol. I, 9, September 1917, vol. II, 7, July 1918.

GALE, James S. *Cloud Dream of the Nine* Daniel O'Connor, London, 1922. (This is a translation of a modern Korean explanation of the novel by Kim Ch'unt'aek in Chinese.)

There are several paraphrases of summaries of *sosŏl*:

CHAI HONG SIM (Sim Chaehong) *The Waiting Wife* (A paraphrase in English of *Ch'unhyang Chŏn* published several times in recent years.)

ALLEN, H. N. *Korean Tales* G. P. Putnam, New York and London, 1889. (Contains various stories.)

ZONG IN-SOB (Chong Insop) *Folk Tales from Korea* Routledge and Kegan Paul, London, 1952. (Contains various legends.)

MODERN LITERATURE

There are two volumes of translations of modern short stories:

INTERNATIONAL P.E.N. CLUB, KOREAN CENTER: *Collected Short Stories from Korea* Eomun Kak Publishing Company, Seoul, 1961.

ZONG IN-SOB *Modern Short Stories from Korea* Munhosa, Seoul, 1958.

In addition the English language monthly *Korea Journal*, published by the KOREAN NATIONAL COMMISSION FOR UNESCO, contains translations of contemporary poems and short stories in almost every issue.

Anthologies of translations of poems, mainly short poems, include:

HYUN, Peter *Voices of the Dawn* John Murray, London; Paragon, New York, 1959.

KIM DONG-SUNG *Selected Poems of Kim Sowol* Sung Moon Kak, Seoul, not dated.

KOREAN POETS ASSOCIATION *Korean Verses* Mun Won Publishing Company, Seoul, 1961.

LEE, Peter H. *Anthology of Korean Poetry* John Day, New York, 1964.

INEZ KONG PAI *The Ever White Mountain* John Weatherhill, Tokyo, 1965.

ZONG IN-SOB *Pageant of Korean Poetry* Eomun, Seoul, 1963.

BURMESE LITERATURE

Anna Allott

HISTORICAL BACKGROUND

THE SETTING – GEOGRAPHICAL AND CULTURAL

Burma, a small agricultural country rich in natural wealth and relatively underpopulated, lies between two large and populous neighbours, India and China. Her land frontiers, however, are mountainous, and it has been her long western seaboard which has left her open to successive waves of outside influence. Ethnically she is linked with China, as her people are of Mongoloid stock and must have come originally from Central Asia, migrating slowly southwards down the great river valleys of the Chindwin and the Irrawaddy. Linguistically too she belongs with China, as Burmese is a tonal, basically monosyllabic language belonging to the Sino-Tibetan family, with syntax and grammar quite different from the languages of India and Europe. Culturally, however, she has been dominated throughout her known history by influences from the West, and above all from India, even though some of these actually reached her through her Eastern neighbour and former rival, Siam.

By the eleventh century many Indian cults had found their way to Burma, but the only one which took firm root was Buddhism. At this time King Anorahta established the first powerful Burmese kingdom with its capital at Pa-gan in Upper Burma. In 1057 he captured the city of Thaton, the capital of a non-Burmese people, the Mon of Lower Burma. Here he found, so the legend goes, a complete set of the Pali Tripitaka, the sacred writings of Buddhism, which he took back with him to Pagan. From this time onwards the kings of Burma gave their official patronage to pure Hīnayāna Buddhism, which remained the dominant cultural influence in the life of Burma until it was challenged by western ideas in the middle of the nineteenth century. The Burmese language was extended and enriched by numerous Pali loans which were necessary to express the religious and philosophical concepts of Buddhism.

It must be remembered that Buddhism was concerned only with life hereafter; for the ordinary Burman, the sky and earth were peopled with a multitude of spirits (*nat*), witches, ghosts and other good and evil supernatural beings. They were ever-present in his imagination, obliging him to arrange his life so as to come to terms with them. This element of Burmese culture, barely present in her written literature, is reflected in a rich heritage of legend, folklore and popular tales.

PA-GAN – WRITING ON STONE, FOR FUTURE GENERATIONS

Our first written records in Burmese date from after 1057 AD. The captive Mon scholars, who had been taken back to Pa-gan by King Anorahta, taught the Burmans how to adapt the South-Indian script they themselves used, and in this way Burmese was first reduced to writing. The main legacy that we have from the Pa-gan period is an incredible number of pagodas; this tradition of glorifying the Buddha in brick, initiated by Anorahta, flourished until Pa-gan fell to the Mongols in 1287. All that survives of the literature are the stone inscriptions; amongst their historical details and passages of Buddhist piety there are occasional lines of verse which allow us to guess at the state of the literary language of the time.

AVA – RELIGIOUS VERSE FOR KING AND BUDDHA

The Tartars did not stay long; by defeating Pa-gan they disturbed the balance of power in central Burma so that for a time the Shans, a Tai people from the east ('Shan' is the same word as 'Siam'), became dominant. The Shans founded a dynasty which had its capital at Ava (near modern Mandalay) from 1364 until 1555; here, in spite of the Shan origin of the rulers, the influence of Buddhism and of Burmese prevailed, and it was during the last hundred years of the Ava period (*c* 1450–1550) that the first great flowering of Burmese imaginative literature took place.

As the period is characterised by protracted warfare between the Burmese, the Shan and the Mon it is perhaps not surprising that nearly all the outstanding works that have come down to us are by monks, as only they could find the necessary peace and quiet to compose and copy poems. We must assume that by this time writing was no longer being done only on stone, but also on strips of processed palm-leaf; these were scratched with a metal stylus and wiped over with oil to make the letters more distinct. For storing, the strips were piled on top of one another and tied up with a strong piece of wood on the top and bottom. This was called *pei-sa*, palm-leaf writing.

We must also assume that the literature that we have would not have survived unless the monks (of the day and later) had considered it suitable to be copied and preserved. At this period a suitable work was one which glorified Buddha or expounded his teachings, which marvelled at the beauties of nature or praised the reigning monarch, and which was written in an elegant and learned style intelligible only to a restricted circle. Literature at this time, and indeed up to the nineteenth century, is marked by an overwhelming preponderance of verse. It is only in verse that the imagination is called into play and the author's skill is displayed. Prose is not considered an artistic medium but is reserved for works of a practical or technical nature such as texts dealing with law, astrology, medicine, grammar, and particularly those concerned with the interpretation of the Pali scriptures (the latter are known as *nissaya*).

BURMESE CLASSICAL VERSE

At this point a brief mention should be made of the structure of Burmese classical verse and of its major genres, as this style dominated the literary scene until the eighteenth century. As Burmese is a tonal language in which each syllable, broadly speaking, has its own 'meaning' and can be used as a 'word', what counts in verse is the rhyme (including a tonal 'rhyme') and the number of syllables in a line; rhythm, that is, vowel length and stress, play almost no part. Classical verse is composed of lines of four syllables, grouped into long stanzas of thirty or forty lines, each stanza being terminated by an irregular line of five, seven or nine syllables. The rhyme 'climbs' from the fourth syllable in the first line to the third syllable in the second line to the second syllable in the next line, where a new rhyme appears in the fourth syllable. This 'climbing' principle, with variations, runs through all classical and modern poetry and seems to have originated in Burma.

The Ava period was the great age of the *pyo*, a long religious poem which narrates an episode from Buddha's life or re-tells one of the *jatakas*, together with a great expansion and embellishment of the philosophic and religious precepts embodied in the chosen story. These long sermons in verse (about two hundred to three hundred of the stanzas mentioned above) are the Burmese equivalent of the epic; they were written mainly by monks (see Thi-lawun-tha and Rat-hta-tha-ra, pp. 398–99), and usually addressed to the reigning monarch. Two other important genres had also developed by the fifteenth and sixteenth centuries: the *ei-gyin* (cradle song), extolling the achievements and lineage of the king, and the *maw-gun*, commemorating notable public events. These were composed in the same classical stanzas, and were written, with the main aim of glorifying the king, by courtiers and ministers as well as by monks.

TAUNGOO – ROMANTIC POETRY FOR KING AND COURT

The indecisive wars of the Ava period were suddenly terminated in about 1540 by the rise of the independent Burmese kingdom of Taungoo, a city situated between Ava in central Burma and the Mon capital of Pegu towards the sea coast. Within a few years the rulers of the Taungoo dynasty overcame first the Mon, then the Shan rulers of Ava and the neighbouring princedoms. Having formed these into a united kingdom, they proceeded to extend their empire to the east into Thailand and to the west into Arakan. The courtiers and soldiers who served these successful monarchs (see Nawadei and Nat-shin-naung, p. 397) wrote not only about the glories of the king but also, for the first time, of their own personal emotions. They still used the classical four-syllable verse but in a short poem of just three stanzas, known as a *yadu*. Rather like an ode, these works were inspired by a mood of joy or sorrow, or by a place or an incident, and were often addressed to a wife or lover. Poetry was no longer only religious: it could now be romantic too.

The final hundred years of the Taungoo dynasty (1650–1752) were a time of weakness and insecurity; various parts of the empire revolted, the capital was moved back to Ava for greater safety, and fell before a Mon attack from the South in 1751. The uncertainty and the pressures from outside were accompanied by a decline in literary activity; at the same time a more secular note was beginning to make itself heard. The first serious history of Burma was written (see Kala, U, p. 396). Successful *pyo* were written on non-religious subjects such as the fairy Manohara, or the arrival of Thai envoys at the Burmese court, by the remarkable ministeı Padei-tha-ya-za (see p. 398). Evidently there was opposition to this use of the sacred *pyo* form for such secular subjects, as it is on record that the minister's 'abuse' of the *pyo* was believed to have caused the downfall of Ava. Probably under Thai influence, Padei-tha-ya-za introduced new forms as well. He wrote the first Burmese drama, the first classical songs and, most unorthodox of all, gave us the first short poems (*tya-bwe*) about the joys of simple village life.

THE KON-BAUNG PERIOD (1752–1886) – DRAMA FOR COURT AND MARKET PLACE

The Burmese did not remain long under Mon rule. By 1754 a rebel leader from a small town just north of the capital had rallied sufficient support to drive the Mons out of Ava. Under the name Alaung-paya he founded the Kon-baung dynasty, which lasted until the end of the Burmese kingdom in 1886. During the early part of the period, the Burmese empire once again expanded eastwards into Thailand, and westwards into Manipur and Arakan. (Ayuthia, the Siamese capital which finally fell in 1767, gave the Burmans their word for Thailand, *yo-daya*.) But the British empire was also expanding and slowly, in three stages, Burma was annexed: the two coastal strips in 1826; Lower Burma, including Rangoon in 1852; and Upper Burma in 1886. Not until the monarchy was ended, and the British administration established over the whole country, did a purely popular literature emerge, bringing with it (after the turn of the century) magazines, short stories and novels.

Why was Burmese literature so slow to change? Why were new genres so slow to take hold? Between the years 1750–1885, several new types of work began to be written and on increasingly secular themes, but the nature of the literature did not really change. Basically it remained of the court and for the court, didactic or eulogistic; and its dissemination was in the hands of monks. The court was despotic and (with the exception of Mindon 1853–78) inward-looking; it demanded a servile and largely sycophantic literature. Moves to broaden the range of subjects forming part of a monastic education were resisted by King Bodaw-paya (1782–1819). The main new liberalising factor was the appearance of humour and satire, first in a kind of long narrative poem called *yagan*, which was very popular at court, and, from the eighteen-forties, in dramas called *pya-zat* (shown-story). In the *yagan* it was most usual to take a jataka or a well-known story or Hindu legend (for example, of Rama or Manohara) and to retell it in verse, together with comic asides and satirical attacks on fellow writers and ladies of the court. The best known of these is U To's *Yagan about Rama* (*c* 1780).

Seinda-kyaw-thu (U Aw) wrote mostly *yadu*, *ei-gyin* and *pyo* for his great King Alaung-paya (1752–60), though he introduces a new note of realism in the *yadu*, in his account of mud and mosquitos on the battlefield. Nawadei the Younger chronicled the triumphant conquests of Bodawpaya's reign in a series of vivid *mawgun*, as tradition required. A literary form of a more personal kind which gained popularity in this period is the epistle or *myit-taza*; these are letters giving advice, practical or moral, written from or on behalf of a great variety of people. The authors (among them Kyigan Shin-gyi (*c* 1757–1807), and U Pon-nya, see p. 398) adopted a 'mixed style', which varies, from line to line, between prose, rhyming prose and classical verse, thus enabling them to show their skill and be learned, witty and lyrical by turns.

Prose however, which one might have expected to emerge as a new force in the literary field, remains at the service of court and cloister. One of the major reasons for this was that printing did not become widespread until the eighteen-seventies. Nevertheless the foundations of a prose style were being laid in the pages of the great Glass Palace Chronicle (see p. 396), and in the translations of all the five hundred and fifty Buddha's birth stories, ten by U Obhasa at the end of the eighteenth century (see p. 397), and the rest by another monk, the Nyaung-gan Saya-daw. These stories were copied on palm leaf and began to be more and more widely read during the mid nineteenth century. It is worth noting that efforts by western missionaries to translate the Bible, (A. Judson's version was published by the American Baptist Mission Press in 1840), and to spread a knowledge of Christianity aroused no interest among Burmans. Missionary presses had been established in Rangoon since 1817, but they printed only evangelising material, none of which appears to have had any appreciable effect on the language or literature of Burma at this stage.

It was necessary first to have a large reading public, and this began to be formed in Burma partly as a result of the tremendous growth in the popularity of drama during the nineteenth century. The captive Siamese had brought with them the captivating idea that literature could be simply for pleasure and for entertainment. The Burmese began to compose songs and plays; first 'literary' plays (those by the Princess of Hlaing, see p. 396), then stage plays of a rather literary nature (those by U Kyin U and U Pon-nya, see p. 398); and by 1875 we have the first printed version, complete with additional songs, of a new type of stage-play (still in verse), clearly intended for a popular audience.

We may gather from accounts of visiting English envoys that drama, presented by human actors or puppets, was a very popular entertainment throughout the nineteenth century. The owners of the new printing presses (after 1870) soon realised that there was a good market for printed playlets: and a reading public, which could recognise itself in the partly real, partly fantasy-world of these plays, was born. By this time the downfall of the monarchy was imminent; the ensuing disorder in Upper Burma was not a time for literature to flourish there. In Lower Burma prose translations of the jataka and other Pali works were reprinted again and again; they were used as government school text books.

COLONIAL PERIOD (1886–1948) AND AFTER – BOOKS FOR ALL

In Lower Burma a new form of literature was needed for the rapidly changing society, but it required one or two generations of English rule and English education to produce Burmans capable of creating this new form. They needed to have a sufficient knowledge of both English and Burmese to choose the right western works to be represented in a natural Burmese setting for their fellow-countrymen. Thus it was not until 1904 that the first widely-read Burmese novel appeared. James Hla Gyaw, a Government Translator and District Officer aged forty, found the inspiration in Dumas', *The Count of Monte Cristo* to create for his fellow Burmans a new genre, a story in prose to entertain and divert them, entitled *Maung Yin Maung Ma Me Ma*. The idea caught on, newspaper editors asked their staff for other people who could produce stories like this (at the time it was not known to be based on a foreign work) and more came forward including U Kyi, who wrote a series of quite original stories about *Maung Hmaing, the Roselle Seller*, an incorrigible philanderer with a wife in every town. These were enormously popular, widely read and not in the least improving.

As in other countries it was the establishment of newspapers and periodicals which contributed most to the rise of the novel, and by 1920 large numbers of adapted and original works had appeared. Foreign works chosen were mostly adventure stories such as those of Conan Doyle and Rider Haggard, whilst the best of the Burmese authors tended to remain aware of the writer's duty to inform and instruct as well as entertain. Thus in 1910 and 1914 U Lat (see pp. 396–97) defended the traditional way of life in Mandalay against the new anglicised habits of cosmopolitan Rangoon in two outstanding novels; in structure and style however they are still closely linked with classical verse, and the dramas of the preceding decades.

At about this time two activities initiated by the colonial government helped in a small way to foster and sustain the Burman's pride in his own literary and cultural heritage; for under the colonial regime it was an English education which brought much the greatest social advantages. In 1910 the Burma Research Society was founded to promote 'the arts, science and literature in relation to Burma'. In 1921 a four-volume anthology of Burmese literature from the earliest times was published; it had been compiled (in 1916–17) by an advisory board set up by Government resolution, 'as a means for imparting instruction on the lines of the Imperial Idea'. In the event, it served to strengthen the awakening national idea, as also did the historical novels of U Maung Gyi, and the brilliant satire of Thakhin Ko-daw Hmaing (see p. 398).

Two writers who had considerable influence in the twenties and thirties were P. Monin and Maha Swei. The former (1883–1940) was a practical person with a modern outlook who wrote novels (*Nei-yi-yi* is the best known) and short stories set in the society of the moment. He adapted western books on sociology and psychology also, and his writings did a great deal to help the 'Burmese mind adjust to the modern world'. Maha Swei (1900–53), who wrote some sixty novels and six hundred short stories as well as newspaper articles, had a more direct, less sophisticated appeal, sometimes sensational (*The Bazaar Woman*), often nationalistic and revolutionary (*Our Mother* 1934, *Rebel* 1935).

National consciousness was growing fast. The first signs of an awareness of the need to create a new style of prose-writing, more fitted to the tempo and outlook of the developing society, appeared among students of Burmese at Rangoon University. The University, which at first provided a purely English education, had been founded in 1920; the first course in Burmese literature was started by Pe Maung Tin in 1923–4. It was he who, in 1934, collected some of his students' writings together and published them in a little book called *Khit-san pon-byin* (Experimental Tales). The word *Khitsan* (experiment), was used to describe the new short sentences, and clear unelaborate prose-style adopted by these young writers, especially Theip-pan Maung Wa (see p. 399), Zaw-gyi and Min-thuwun. In a similar way they attempted to free poetry from its restricted forms and themes.

In 1936, a novel called *Tet Hpon-gyi* (Modern Monk) gained a certain amount of notoriety for its young author, Thein Pe Myint (1914–). His attack on certain itinerant preachers of doubtful morals outraged the Sangha, and he had to apologise, but the work remains a fascinating description of the attitudes and motives of certain of his contemporaries. In fact, this author has continued to chronicle the major events in Burma from that time until today in a series of extremely readable short stories, novels and memoirs.

Between 1942 and 1946 the rigorous conditions of the Japanese occupation discouraged literary activity, but it was resumed with renewed vigour afterwards, and especially after 1948, when Burma regained her independence from the British. In reviewing the contemporary literary scene the foreign student comes up against two difficulties: the first is the almost total absence of book-lists and reviews of works as they appear, which might help to distinguish the significant from the trivial; the second is the fact that writing is so badly paid that some authors try to produce too much, or resort to indiscriminate translation of second-rate western works (often unacknowledged).

Nevertheless, there are many names which deserve mention, though here it can only be a very brief one. Min-thu-wun (U Wun, 1909–) is a sensitive lyric poet as well as an outstanding scholar of his own language. Zaw-gyi (U Thein Han, 1907–), a philosopher-poet and essayist, is admired for his critical biography of Thakin Kodaw Hmaing (*qv*). Several of the works of U Nu (1907–), Prime Minister from 1948 till 1961, have been translated into English: notably *Man, the Wolf of Man*, a pre-war novel about life in prison under the British, and *Burma under the Japanese*, a personal account of World War II. Maung Htin (U Htin Fatt, 1909–), a journalist and critic, wrote a short novel called *Nga Ba*, which gives a moving account of the trials of a Burmese peasant during the Japanese occupation. Among women authors two should be noted: Khin Khin Lei is a prolific writer of popular novels and short stories; one of her pre-war novels, *Mein-ma bawa* (A Women's Life), gives a realistic picture of the life of an ordinary wife and mother. Ma Ma Lei (1917–) does not hesitate to tackle problems and even abuses of the moment in her writings; her novel, *Moun-ywei mahu* (Not that I hate Him), about a young girl of Burmese upbringing married to a very westernised man, rightly won for her the Burma Translation Society prize in 1955. Another significant prize-winner was *Min-hmu-dan* (The Civil Servant) by Tet Toe (U On Pe, 1913–) in 1950. This novel, which draws largely on the author's own life, helps us to see some aspects of the pre-war British administration as they appeared to Burmans involved in it. He tried, he said, 'to give a true picture of the overbearing attitudes of certain British officials and of the corruption that was rampant in some parts of the civil service'.

One writer who has done much to raise the standard of serious literary and critical writing is Dagon Ta-ya (1919–); as well as poetry and short stories, he has written a lively book of 'Profiles' (*yok-pon-hlwa*, 1955) of his contemporaries. His controversial theories led to his imprisonment from 1964–7. Another writer who has suffered for his revolutionary views, contained in many novels concerned with Burma's recent history, is Bhamo Tin Aung (1920–). The accounts of life in prison given in several of the novels of Ludu U Hla are absorbing reading. The young authoress, Khin Hnin Yu, has won many admirers with her highly personal stories, which are full of vivid imagery and poignant sadness. There are many other names which should be mentioned, such as Min Shin, Min Aung, Yan Aung, Zawana, Zey-ya, Man Tin, Tha-du, Thaw-ta Swei and Thu-hka. Finally there is one, Shwei U Daung (1888–), who will be remembered by many Burmans for his skilful and understanding adaptations of numerous great classics of western literature, from Sherlock Holmes (in the twenties) to M. Sholokhov's *Quiet Flows the Don.*

In the last five or six years there has been evidence of a new interest in the nature and function of literature. Earlier writings are being reprinted, works collected and edited, and the recently formed Mandalay Writers' Association has produced several books of critical essays; modern Burmese literature has become a serious subject of study.

INDIVIDUAL WRITERS AND WORKS

Glass Palace Chronicle. A history of Burma (in prose) written at the command of King Ba-gyi-daw (1819–37) by a committee of scholars working in a chamber of the palace – hence its name. It is largely based on the previous chronicle of U Kala, but brings the history of Burma down to 1831. Under Mindon (1853–78) it was continued up to 1854 (renamed *kon-baung-zet*), and in 1905, U Tin, a civil servant, brought it up to 1886, the year in which the British annexed Upper Burma.

Hlaing, Princess of (1833–75). Daughter of King Tharrawaddy and the poetess Ma Mya-galei, she was the wife of the Crown Prince Kanaung, son of Mindon. A gifted poetess and a sensitive woman, she had to endure the execution of her mother and later of her son, as well as the unfaithfulness of her husband. She wrote mostly *baw-le* (a literary song in a freer style closer to everyday language). The sad dignity with which she begs the Prince not to stay out late and assures him of her fidelity is very moving and marks a new attitude towards the individual in Burmese literature.

Kala, U or **Maung** (1678?–1738?). The author of the *Ya-zawin-gyi* chronicle, the first important history of Burma. Little is known about the author; his work is based on various sources (poems, legends and inscriptions) but is written in straightforward prose, which has been put forward as a model by some twentieth-century writers. Although he begins in the same way as the Pali *Mahāvamsa* chronicle, the major part of the work deals with the history of Burma up to 1728. It was being compiled at a time when the Taungoo empire was in decline and little court poetry was being produced; the glories of the past were needed to serve the rulers of the present.

Kin-wun Min-gyi (1821–1908). A remarkable man who served as a minister under the last two kings of Burma and later headed a consultative body of ministers under the British. He was sent as an envoy from the Burmese king (Mindon) in 1871 and 1873 to Italy, France and Great Britain, and wrote two journals of these missions known as *The London Diary* and *The Paris Diary*. His intelligent interest in what he saw and his serious and informative accounts of negotiations are a model of official reporting.

Lat, U (1866–1921). First important Burmese novelist. Son of a Rangoon jeweller, he had an English education together with a true Burmese upbringing; became a senior police officer and travelled widely; retired from the service in 1911 and took a job as translator with the Burma Oil Company. He knew his country well and felt great love and respect for the traditional Burmese Buddhist way of life and its moral values, and was concerned that these should not be swept aside by the advancing tide of westernisation and English education. His two major novels were *Sabe-bin* (Jasmine) 1911, and *Shwe-pyi-zo* 1914. In both, the main, rather idealised, love-story, with a happy ending brought about by unlikely, almost magical coincidences, is accompanied by a realistic sub-plot rich in satire, humour and accurate observation of the contemporary social scene. In style, his works are a mixture of old and new; songs as in the drama, quotations from the classics with comment and exhortation, proverbs galore together with exciting narrative and natural, often very comic, dialogue. His novels deserve more detailed study; only the second has so far been translated into a western language (Russian).

Let-we Thon-dara (1723?–1799?). A poet whose fame illustrates a common phenomenon in Burmese literature: namely that a work becomes famous because of how it came to be written. From a penal settlement at Me-za in the North, whither he had been exiled, this royal minister and court poet sent back to his king a pair of *yadu* poems describing the misery of his life at Me-za and his longing for the capital and his family. The story goes that the king was so moved that he recalled the exile. The opening lines are as well known as 'To be, or not to be'.

Nat-shin-naung, Prince (1578–1613). Son of the Lord of Taungoo; at the age of nine he accompanied his father on a campaign against Siam. An accomplished soldier and brave fighter whose love-poems, inspired by his long unrequited passion for the Princess Raza-datu-kalya, have captured the imagination of posterity. He was the first poet to make the *yadu* poems throb with his own real heartache and longing; with great poetic skill he sings of his sadness that fate had made his beloved the wife of another. He was executed as a traitor by King Anaukpetlun, as he had allied himself with the Portuguese mercenary, Felipe de Brito; his was a tragic career whose details are as well-remembered by Burmans as the lines the poet wrote.

Nawadei the Elder (1520?–1600?). Soldier-poet, son of a prince's tutor, greatly sought after as a courtier and poet-laureate by the successive monarchs of the Prome, Ava and Taungoo kingdoms. As he moved from court to court, or accompanied princes on their campaigns, he recorded royal prowess, important places and things, events and emotions of the moment in more than three hundred *yadu* poems. He perfected this short classical lyric form with its new emphasis on personal feelings and longing for the far off loved one, and also wrote several long *egyin*, official 'songs in praise' of the ruling dynasty and its new empire.

Obhāsa, U (1758?–1798?). A scholarly monk of the early Konbaung period whose life's work was the translation from Pali of eight of the ten greater Jataka (Buddha's Birth) stories into Burmese prose. His ornate, elegant style, often including rhymed passages, has long remained a model for Burmese prose writers and could be found in school readers even after 1948.

Padei-tha-ya-za (1683?–1754). A minister and poet, a brilliant innovator in genre and subject matter. He wrote a court drama about a magic horse (*Mani-ket*), an entirely new form for Burmese literature; his best known *pyo* (Thu-za) is not religious, but based on the Hindu legend of the fairy Manohara, well known in Thailand at the time. Most important, he left us four short songs, *tya-bwe,* which for the first time tell about the joys of simple village life and describe ordinary peasants, farmers and boatmen at work. It is tempting to see in his innovations the influence of the not so strictly Buddhist-oriented Thai court.

Pon-nya, U (1812?–1866?). Born in Sale, much-travelled poet, dramatist, essayist and letter-writer. Today we could call him a 'man-about-town'; in his day he was a 'monk-about-court', learned and devout, brilliant and witty, eloquent and charming. Women flocked to his monastery to hear his sermons, he was in constant demand as composer of *myit-taza* (epistles) for other people, and he was one of the first writers of stage-plays (*pya-zat*, literally 'shown-story'). We are not surprised to learn that he laid aside his monk's robes more than once, only to resume them to escape the king's wrath. Later when Mindon came to the throne (1853), Pon-nya became the court poet of the Crown Prince Kanaung, and was not afraid in his dramas to satirise various aspects of life at court, by apt choice of subjects from the Jataka. He excelled in writing flowing and brilliant dialogue, which although rhymed, came nearer to the spoken language than the literary prose of his day; at the same time he wrote numerous classical style works: some call him Burma's Shakespeare. Never good at keeping out of trouble, he met his death at the hands of his 'gaoler', while detained under suspicion of conspiracy; the latter was jealous of U Pon-nya's intrigue with his wife.

Rat-hta-tha-ra, Shin (1468–1530). A monk-poet, the greatest writer of the Ava period, famous for five long religious poems, the first written during his teens, as well as numerous lyrics and a detailed and lively *mawgun* on the building of a pagoda at Tada-u. His masterpiece, the *Ko-gan Pyo* (1526) based on the *Haṭṭhipāla* birth story, concerns the conflicting claims of the ascetic and worldly life. His understanding of human emotions and his poetic skill have made him one of Burma's most cherished and admired poets. There is a directly personal quality in his writing which appeals to Western reader and Burman alike.

Thahkin Ko-daw Hmaing (U Lun) (1876–1964). Poet, playwright, political commentator and satirist, historian, staunch nationalist, the single most important literary personality in modern Burma. Born in the village of Wa-le, Lower Burma; he was sent to Mandalay for monastic education, and returned to Lower Burma to work on Burmese newspapers as compositor, proof-reader and Burmese language editor from 1895. He was a great scholar in his own tongue and never knew English well. Under the name Maung Lun, by about 1910, he had reached a wide popular audience through his eighty or more stage plays on themes drawn from Burmese history and legend. Only four or five survive as he preferred not to attach his name to such 'frivolous' works. He wrote one novel, *Hma-daw-boun* (1915), with a poor plot but good characterisation. In 1920 he was appointed professor of Burmese and History at Burmese national college. Around 1911 his interest in politics was aroused through working with U Ba Pe etc. on *Thuriya* (Sun) newspaper; from then on he contributed regular articles on current political events, brilliantly presented as literary poems with accompanying learned commentary (*tika*).

An acknowledged master of his chosen poetic form (*lei-jou-gyi*), he was also an inspiration to the growing generation of nationalists, urging them to decisive action (student strikes in the nineteen-thirties) whilst at the same time satirising them for futile squabbling and political opportunism. The allusive and very literary style of his writings made them most popular with his fellow countrymen but at the same time preserved them from government censorship; they have only just begun to be studied by western scholars.

Theip-pan Maung Wa (U Sein Tin) (1899–1942). Essayist, literary critic, short-story writer. He was the first student of Burmese literature at Rangoon University (1924–27); he spent one year at Oxford; served as a civil servant in many parts of Burma, till he was shot by bandits during the Japanese occupation. He was the chief exponent of the *Khit-san* style (Experiment for a new age), together with Zaw-gyi and Min-thu-wun. He is best known for his short sketches, part fiction, part documentary, of Burmese provincial and village life, whose hero, Maung Lu Aye, is largely a self-portrait. He gives a realistic and sympathetically critical picture of Burmese life, between 1929–36, pointing out its backwardness and inadequacies with dry, unsentimental humour. A prolific contributor to literary journals under other names; much of this work has just been republished in Burma.

Thi-lawun-tha, Shin (1453–1520?). A monk from Taung-dwin-gyi who came to the royal city of Ava soon after writing his first work at age thirty-eight, a *pyo* on the ten essential perfections of the Buddha, called *Parami-daw-gan.* His erudition and profound exposition of the tenets of Buddhism brought him great fame, but also the rivalry of the younger Rat-hta-tha-ra (*qv*). He wrote many religious *pyo* which are felt by Burmese to be among the greatest in the language; they are also the most difficult to understand. Later on he turned to prose as a teaching medium; his *Pārayanavatthu* (1511?), based on the *Dhammapada,* was the first of the many collections of stories to be translated from the Pali Scriptures; his 'Celebrated Chronicle' (1520) could be considered the first attempt at writing history, though it is largely an adaptation of the Pali historical chronicle, *Mahāvaṁsa,* with notes added on some Burmese kings.

BIBLIOGRAPHY

BACKGROUND

MINN LATT 'Mainstreams in Burmese Literature', *New Orient Bimonthly*, Prague. No. 1, 3, 6, 1960; 6, 1961; 6, 1962. Series of 5 articles – best published survey in English.

HLA PE (with ALLOTT and OKELL) – long article 'Burmese Literature' published in Italian in *Letterature d'Oriente*, Milan, 1969. English version available from the School of Oriental and African Studies, London, 1964.

STEWART, J. A. *Buddhism in Burma* (pamphlet), 1939. (Effect of Buddhism on literature.) Available SOAS as above.

HARVEY, G. E. *History of Burma* London, 1925 (see index under 'literature').

ON PE 'Modern Burmese Literature; its background in the independence movement', (article), *Perspective of Burma, Atlantic Monthly*, 1958.

LITERATURE

Drama

HTIN AUNG *Burmese Drama* Oxford UP, London, 1937. (A good general survey; lively translations of *The Water Carrier* by U Pon-nya, and of extracts of several other plays.)

HLA PE *Konmara Pya-zat* Luzac, London, 1952. (Translation of a popular nineteenth-century play, including songs, with introduction.)

Classical verse, Jātaka

Numerous articles and translations in the journal of the *Burma Research Society*, Rangoon 1910–41, especially

BA HAN 'Shin Uttama-gyaw and his Taw-la, a nature poem', *JBRS* vol. 7, 8, 9 and 10. (Translation and notes.)

BA HAN 'Letwe-thon-dara and his *yadu*', *JBRS* vol. 7. (Translation and notes.)

WHITE, O. 'A Translation of Wethandaya (Vessantara jātaka) from Burmese of U Obhāsa', *A.B.M.P.* Rangoon, 1906.

OKELL, J. 'Translation and embellishment in an early Burmese *jātaka* poem', *Journal of the Royal Asiatic Society*, October, 1967. (Article giving a good general account of the genre with translated excerpts.)

Modern Works

NU, (U) *Burma Under the Japanese* (*nga-hnit ya-thi*) Ed. and trans. J. S. Furnivall, New York, St Martin's Press, 1954.

ZAW-GYI *Selections. Poems and Four short stories.* Rangoon, 1960. (Burmese with English translation.)

MINTHUWUN *Selection. Poems and one short story* Rangoon, 1960. (Burmese with English translation.)

From 1954 onwards, *The Guardian Magazine*, an English language monthly published in Rangoon has included translations of many short stories by contemporary writers, especially Theip-pan Maung Wa, Dagon Taya, Ma Ma Lei; also, in 8 parts:

NU, (U) 'Man, the Wolf of Man (yet-set-pa-bei kwe)' vol. 1 and 2, 1954–5.

Tales, Epistles

HTIN AUNG *Burmese Folk Tales* Oxford UP, 1948.

HTIN AUNG *Burmese Monk's Tales* Columbia UP, New York and London, 1966.

HTIN AUNG *Burmese Law Tales* Oxford UP, 1962.

HTIN AUNG, trans. and edit. *Epistles Written on the Eve of the Anglo-Burmese War*, by Kyi-gan Shin-gyi, Nijhoff, The Hague, 1968.

JAPANESE LITERATURE

C. J. Dunn and K. L. C. Strong

HISTORICAL BACKGROUND

EARLY TIMES

The earliest surviving Japanese chronicle, *Kojiki* (Records of ancient matters) was completed in 712. It records the oral traditions of the Japanese, and may also incorporate material from slightly earlier but now lost written sources. From it and other, later, works, as well as from archaeological investigation, there arises a picture of early Japan suggesting a stone-age culture related to those of the northern circumpolar region, which was replaced some two thousand five hundred years ago by metal-using agricultural communities. By a process of conquest and amalgamation, the political power came into the hands of a ruling clan whose headquarters were in the Yamato plain, round the present city of Nara. In these early times, relations with Korea were close, and, through Korean intermediaries, Chinese culture came to exert increasing influence upon Japan. Thus the Japanese borrowed the Chinese writing system, and also introduced the religious and philosophical ideas prevalent in China at the time, especially those of Buddhism, which came to join the animistic nature religion (to be known later as *Shintō*, 'Way of the gods'), at the head of which, on earth, was the Yamato emperor, claiming descent from the Sun Goddess. In the early seventh century the Prince-Regent Shōtoku had erected some Buddhist temples in the contemporary Chinese style, and also started the process of introducing Chinese administrative systems into Japan. There ensued a period of some three centuries in which Japan maintained close links with China by means of embassies and the despatch of students.

THE NARA AND HEIAN PERIODS

Power became firmly established in the hands of the emperor when the old clans, with their hereditary duties, lost their dominance toward the end of the seventh century. In 710 the capital, which had hitherto been transferred to a new site for each new emperor, was established as a permanent town on the

Chinese model at Nara, and this inaugurated the period of history known usually as the Nara period. This was characterised by much building, by continued contact with China, and by the first mature products of native Japanese art and literature. The great Buddhist monasteries became very powerful and in 794 the imperial capital was again moved, this time to the present Kyoto, where it was to remain for over a thousand years. One of the motives for the move is said to have been an attempt by the emperor to free himself from excessive influence from the Buddhist priesthood; in this he may have been successful, but as an attempt to keep the power in his own hands it was to prove of little avail. The administration of the court and government became the monopoly of the powerful Fujiwara family, who provided almost all the officials of the government and, by having their daughters become imperial consorts, came to dominate the emperor himself. The latter spent more and more of his time in ceremonial and amusements, and the court became an inward-looking centre of intrigue and high culture. It derived its resources from country estates and high taxation, but failed to maintain an efficient organisation outside of the capital. This situation developed into a near-anarchy which threw up powerful local groups of warriors, and by the middle of the twelfth century the Fujiwaras were being replaced as the dominant family by that of the Taira, whose support came from forces mainly in the west of Japan. They in their turn were overthrown by the Minamoto clan, whose strength lay in the east and north. This was in 1185, and thus was brought to an end the Heian period, in which the government had been centred in Kyoto, known as the capital of Heian (Peace and security).

MEDIEVAL JAPAN

To the rule of pleasure-loving aristocrats in Kyoto now succeeded a military government, headed by the commander-in-chief, Minamoto Yoritomo. To protect his men from the demoralising influences of the imperial capital, he moved his centre of administration to Kamakura, in the east of Japan, in an area where his family was powerful. Rules of conduct based upon aesthetic principles and the performance of ritual were replaced by those deriving from the military virtues of loyalty and obedience. The hero of society became the warrior rather than the poet. The mysteries of the esoteric Buddhist sects of Shingon and Tendai yielded pride of place to the non-intellectual Zen and easily understood Pure Land sects.

However, the efficient rule of the Kamakura generals was to last only some seventy years, and was brought to an end by a resurgence of Kyoto as a political force, with the country plunged into civil war by fighting between two rival imperial lines, lasting from 1336 to 1392. From 1400 to 1600 ensued two centuries of gradually increasing prosperity and progressively more settled conditions, not, however, without some serious setbacks and relapses into disorder. Trade and agriculture made some progress, and relations with China, which had greatly declined in the intervening period, were once again encouraged, but now on the basis of commerce rather than culture-exchange. In the mid sixteenth century Portuguese sailors and missionaries arrived in Japan, and Christianity started to spread through the western island of Kyūshū and eventually into the other islands. To the influences from China were added those from Europe, and they were to prove very powerful, if temporary. Nagasaki, in Kyūshū, became virtually a Christian city; western art and culture, and even western dress, began to have their effect on their native counterparts. Two powerful leaders, Oda Nobunaga, whose dominance lasted from 1573 to 1582, and his successor, Toyotomi Hideyoshi, who died in 1598, brought a more peaceful period to the land, and encouraged the Japanese to develop new skills and techniques in agriculture, industry and commerce. Contacts with the outside world increased when the Japanese themselves traded with China and South-east Asia and even established overseas trading colonies.

THE GREAT ISOLATION

Between the death of Hideyoshi and 1615 (when his family was finally defeated in Osaka), a new ruler, Tokugawa Ieyasu, established himself. He was appointed by the emperor as *shōgun* (commander in chief) in 1603. For the next two hundred and fifty years, which make up the Tokugawa period, his family was to rule unchallenged. He moved the centre of government once more from Kyoto, this time to Edo, on the site of the present Tokyo, again with the object of removing his warrior retainers from the temptations of the old culture. After an initial period of tolerance for Christianity and Europeans, in 1639 all ports were closed to foreigners, with the exception of the Dutch and Chinese, who were allowed to have access only to Nagasaki, where they maintained small factories or trading centres. All overseas voyages by Japanese were prohibited. This was the beginning of the great isolation of Japan, when, apart from a small, sometimes clandestine, interest in Dutch medicine and technology, there was no new influence from abroad. The whole country was kept under tight control, with the object of preserving order and maintaining the Tokugawa position, in accordance with the Confucian concepts that dominated official thought. Lords were allotted domains, but their freedom of activity was restricted by constant inspection and a system of enforced periodical residence at the capital, where the lords' wives had to live permanently. This served the purpose of maintaining hostages under the immediate control of the Tokugawa rulers, and also of requiring the lords to spend a considerable part of their resources in keeping up establishments in Edo as well as on their domains, and on travelling in great progresses from one place to another. Farmers, who provided the rice-incomes by which the lords were paid, had restricted liberty and often suffered repression. The merchants, although theoretically forming a lower class than the farmers, had considerably more freedom than they, and various new factors, including their participation in the conversion of the warrior class's rice-incomes into cash, as well as greatly increased trade in consumer goods in the absence of expensive civil wars, made them prosperous and able to indulge their taste for entertainment and extravagance.

WESTERN PRESSURES

The isolation of Japan came under pressure in the nineteenth century from various sides – from the Russians in the north, and from America and Europe – and in 1853 Commodore Perry of the US Navy came and demanded that trade relations should be opened up with America. From 1854 this was done, and similar arrangements were swiftly made with other countries. The Tokugawa regime was unable to outlast these new conditions. Already weakened by increasing inefficiency at the centre and growing power in the provinces, it was finally replaced in 1868 by a return to rule by an emperor. The imperial capital, up to now still in Kyoto, where an impoverished court had barely managed to survive, was transferred to Edo, now named the Eastern Capital, Tōkyō, and with the removal there of the Emperor Meiji, the modern period began.

MODERN JAPAN

By the end of the nineteenth century Japan had become a modern state. Government, transport, commerce, industry and the armed forces were all transformed. The old culture did not die out, but alongside it grew up a complete set of western-style arts. Japan acquired great international prestige by her victories in wars against China in 1895 and Russia in 1905. She was one of the Allies in the 1914–18 war, and the nineteen-twenties and early thirties formed a period when democracy appeared to flourish. However, with the deterioration of economic conditions throughout the world, Japan embarked in the mid-thirties on a course of nationalistic militarism which led her to increase her area of dominance in Asia, but also led to her defeat in 1945.

She has, however, always shown great recuperative powers. She has been made accustomed by her position in the earthquake and typhoon belts of the

West Pacific, and by great conflagrations, to calamity, and she has recovered from the greatest disaster in her history with characteristic energy.

Her industriousness and technical skill have placed her high among the great nations of the post-war world, and it can be argued that she has achieved by peaceful means most of the objectives which she sought unsuccessfully by military power.

MAIN TRENDS IN LITERATURE

One can accept with very few provisos a statement that Japanese literature has always had the tendency to follow closely changes in the system of government. Culturally, what is new has always been widely received, and although conservative influences have always been at work to ensure that old art forms and old literary genres have very rarely entirely disappeared, those who have continued to work in the old styles have more often than not been deficient in genius, so that their work tends not to be highly valued. With changes in the political and social conditions in the country, changes in the field of literature have always arisen, and the history of Japanese literature is the history of these changes. It follows too that the same divisions which separate the periods of the political history of Japan can be transferred with no change to the domain of literary history.

The first writing system that the Japanese came into contact with was that of China, and the first literary efforts they made were in the Chinese language. The earliest extant attempt at writing Japanese is in the chronicle mentioned above, *Kojiki* (712), which is of great interest not only linguistically, but also anthropologically, for the myths recorded in it, and as a piece of literature; it contains, for instance, many poems and songs from earlier times, and although some elements, such as the singing of military conquest, were to disappear, these poems already clearly contain the elements which were to remain characteristic of Japanese poetry throughout the ages until the twentieth century.

THE NARA PERIOD

After *Kojiki*, and certain other works of official or ritual nature, the Nara period produced a great anthology of poetry, *Man-yōshū* (Collection for a myriad ages), which includes works up to 759. It contains some four thousand five hundred poems, with about four hundred and fifty named poets, although many of the poems are anonymous. The earliest poems probably date from the fifth century, and one can see reflected in the changing themes and styles the increasing sophistication of the Nara court. The native Japanese element in this poetry is predominant, but there was a considerable influence from China, which some of the poets had visited. After the collection had reached its present form, little attention seems to have been paid to it for many years because of the preoccupation of the contemporary public with Chinese poetry. It was also difficult to read because of the still incomplete adaptation of the Chinese script to the writing of Japanese. With the coming of the Heian period, however, and the development of a syllabic phonetic script to supplement the ideographic Chinese characters, many of the difficulties of writing easily identifiable Japanese also disappeared.

THE HEIAN AND MEDIEVAL PERIODS

Tales began to appear in Japanese and the writing of Japanese verse became once more a desirable activity. Under the Fujiwara rule, the court devoted a great deal of its time and energy to ritual and to formalised love-making. Most activities were accompanied by the writing of poetry, and in addition the practice arose of holding poetry competitions, so that much verse was occasional and expressed fictional sentiments. The emperor began the sponsoring of anthologies of Japanese poetry, the first of which, *Kokinwakashū* (Collection of Japanese poems old and new) appeared in 905. Among much that is obviously artificial, there are many love and nature poems of great skill and depth of sentiment. In prose, the early tales had paved the way for what is probably the masterpiece of Japanese literature, *Genji-monogatari* (The tale of Genji) by Murasaki Shikibu, a novel written to be read aloud to the empress in whose court she served; it is a triumph of subtle description of character, revealing the mentalities and motives of the Heian aristocracy. Another work of the same period and giving a slightly different point of view is *Makura-no-sōshi* (Pillow book) by Sei Shōnagon. The literature of the period is generally intended for court readers, and is written in an allusive language that would be fully comprehensible only to members of a tightly-knit group. There is, however, one exception, *Konjaku-monogatari* (Tales of long ago), a collection of religious and other anecdotes, written in a much more popular, not to say practical, language.

Linguistically, this work looks toward the future, for the mixture of Chinese and Japanese in which it was written was to become the language of modern Japan. The next stage in the development was brought in by the civil wars of the twelfth century, which gave birth to a series of warlike tales; of these *Heike-monogatari* (Tales of the Heike) in the early thirteenth century and *Taiheiki* (Record of the great peace) (*c* 1340) are the best known. The themes are battle and loyalty, and preoccupation with the transience of this world, the Buddhist influence being strong. In poetry, a tendency to melancholy was reflected in the works of poets like Saigyō, who abandoned the world to become a wandering priest, and similar themes are found in *Hōjōki* (Records of a six-foot-square hut) by Kamō Chōmei and *Tsurezure-gusa* (Essays in Idleness) by Yoshida Kenkō. The most important innovation of the years between the Heian and Tokugawa periods, and one of considerably more importance than the war-romances, was the *nō* play. In the hands of Kannami, and his more illustrious son, Zeami, a crude popular performance was turned into a subtle dramatic form of great depth, with an aesthetic vocabulary and critical apparatus that have been significant in the formation of Japanese thought.

THE TOKUGAWA PERIOD

In these years, too, arose the practice of group-composition of chains of thirty-one syllable poems (*renga*) in which the half-poems of seventeen and fourteen syllables were composed by different writers in turn. Often a mere game, this form also produced its masterpieces, but is mainly important because the first seventeen-syllable half-verse came, in the Tokugawa period, to have an independent existence, in the hands of Bashō, a poet, who, like Saigyō, wrote much of his poetry while travelling. Bashō's *haiku*, as the new form was later called, show a strong influence of Zen Buddhism, and are often verbal pictures of a small scene which can be taken as typical or symbolic of a whole landscape or a whole season. His fellow human beings, and time other than the present, have little place in his work, but later *haiku* poets, though of less stature than Bashō, have a wider range of subject.

He is one of the three great writers of the early Tokugawa period, along with Ihara Saikaku and Chikamatsu Monzaemon. These authors demonstrate most clearly the new values that had come in with the rise to importance of the merchants. Saikaku took over a moralising religious genre of prose and initiated novels of contemporary life, written in a racy style, and preoccupied with the merchant virtues of industry and thrift, and with the delectable ways in which hard-won fortunes could be dissipated in far shorter time than it took to amass them. Successors to Saikaku were to appear throughout the period, their subject being contemporary life, especially with the brothel-culture as its background. On the other hand Kyokutei Bakin developed a fantastic novel with themes often taken from Chinese literature, heavily Chinese in style, and of great length. In the late eighteenth century appeared novelists like Jippensha Ikku whose object was to arouse laughter. This they did in comic satirical stories, often at the expense of countryfolk and provincials. Novel production in the whole period was immense, and the reading public avid.

DRAMA

Chikamatsu Monzaemon was a playwright who wrote for both the live stage and the puppet theatre. At the beginning of the period, the *nō* play having become fixed in style, there arose a new popular entertainment, the *kabuki*. After a good deal of official opposition, it developed by the end of the seventeenth century into a complete drama form, but it had considerable competition from the puppet plays. Chikamatsu's best work was for the latter, and alongside a fantastic and complicated type of historical drama, which leaned heavily on earlier puppet plays, he developed a counterpart to Saikaku's tales of the follies of love, in plays with a contemporary theme. These were often taken from actual events, and in them unfortunate lovers, perhaps a respectable shopkeeper and a courtesan, are driven to commit suicide. These plays show a depth of characterisation and pathetic realism which make them masterpieces. As *kabuki* established itself, it took over the puppet repertory, and Chikamatsu's plays, unfortunately usually in an adapted form, can now be seen on both the live and puppet stage. After the seventeenth century, plays often included both historical and contemporary ingredients, and the great theme of conflicting loyalties became dominant. The literary value of the drama diminished, but its technical excellence increased.

MODERN TIMES

When Japan allowed in foreigners in the mid nineteenth century she also let in a flood of literary influences. Novel-writing had reached a low ebb and although one or two comic writers managed to show some skill in satirising the West, the native novel soon disappeared before translations of those from abroad. Inspired by the political themes of some European novels, and reassured by the obvious respectability of such writers as Lord Lytton and Disraeli, the Japanese recognised the novel as a legitimate genre. Political subjects were common at first, but there was also a movement towards realistic writing. After a period of English, Russian and German influence, shown respectively in the work of Tsubouchi Shōyō, Futabatei Shimei and Mori Ōgai, the inspiration became predominantly French. The Naturalist school, taking over only part of the ideas of Zola and Maupassant, began writing a type of novel describing the deterioration of human character when dominated by animal impulses, usually those of obsessive sex. There was a tendency for such novels to be autobiographical and their influence is still very powerful. Modern Japanese novelists have been very involved with theory, and the Naturalist novel had many enemies, especially Ōgai and Natsume Sōseki, who were in favour of a more detached attitude and an artistic approach. Both were concerned with ethical problems, and Sōseki's realistic, objective writings are of great value. Among other writers taking a more or less independent line were Sōseki's pupil, Akutagawa Ryūnosuke, with his original and cynical interpretations of old stories, and Tanizaki Jun'ichirō, who had a long career as a writer, and whose most interesting novels are concerned with the conflict of East and West in Japan.

In the early thirties, there was a so-called 'Proletarian School' of communist writers, which soon disappeared, however, under government control of thought as the military took more power to themselves. Writers turned more and more inwards as they sought for material that would not offend, and original production languished until after Japan's defeat in 1945. Then there was a great outpouring of novels of all sorts, and schools came and went. One product of this time, Dazai Osamu's *Shayō* (Setting sun, 1947) is a sensitive description of the effect of the defeat upon a well-to-do family. Some proletarian writers started work again; one such was Noma Hiroshi, with his vivid novel on army life, *Shinkūjitai* (Empty zone).

Novel-writing seems now to present a diversified picture, with a tendency to concentrate upon unusual psychological states, with Mishima Yukio as a representative novelist. Poetry has virtually abandoned the old styles and uses free forms. Drama seems to be moving towards the amalgamation of extant forms, including the modern, western-type drama, but leaving out *nō*, though the most original writers, such as Kinoshita Junji, are trying to use traditional materials within the framework of western forms.

The best modern Japanese literature is becoming known to the West by means of translation, and is proving that its writers merit world-wide recognition.

SPECIAL COLLECTIONS AND WORKS

ANONYMOUS WORKS

The earlier periods of Japanese literature have left many works the authorship of which is either unknown, or is attributed to some semi-mythical personage about whom nothing else is known, or to some great figure of the time who clearly could not have produced all that he is credited with. Almost the whole of the prose literature of the Heian period (794–1185) is in this category, as are the historical romances of later times.

In this first alphabetic section, therefore, are listed the most important of these works of unknown authorship.

Gikeiki (The story of Yoshitsune). Yoshitsune (1159–89), the young general who was mainly responsible for the defeat of the Heike, became a popular figure when his brother, Yoritomo, had him hounded to death. His short life, much embellished with supernatural and martial material, is recounted in this work, which dates from the early fifteenth century.
Translation: *Yoshitsune*, trans. Helen Craig McCullough, Tokyo, 1966.

Heike-monogatari (Tales of the Heike). The version of this fictionalised history which is recognised today is of the early thirteenth century. It is a long account of the struggles between the great clans of Taira (otherwise known as Heike) and Minamoto (Genji), which transferred the power from the Fujiwara ministers at the imperial court to the series of military families who were to rule Japan until the nineteenth century. To the descriptions of amorous intrigue and ceremonial by the court novelists, succeed accounts of military achievement and of the rise to glory and subsequent utter defeat of the great Taira line. Buddhism had increased its influence, and at the same time events had underlined the Buddhist insistence on the transitory nature of this earthly existence, only one insignificant step in the great series of stages towards final peace.

This work was not intended so much for individual reading as for recitation by members of a guild of blind priests, to the accompaniment of the lute (*biwa*). Its influence on later times was immense. The style of recitation developed into that of the puppet plays; the vivid accounts of battle and individual action furnished plots for *nō* plays and many other forms; the language, with its admixture of Chinese into the almost exclusively Japanese vocabulary of earlier novels (except *Konjaku-monogatari*), and its generous inclusions of technical and colloquial elements, was a stage in the development towards modern Japanese.

A modern reader can read it with enjoyment for its vivid original treatment of episodes that have since become commonplaces of Japanese literature, and to catch a hint of the glamour of these old warriors.

Translation: Keene's anthology includes a short sample of this work. Much more is to be found in A. L. Sadler, *Tales of the Heike and the Four Square Hut*, Sydney, 1928; Sadler has a complete translation in *Transactions of the Asiatic Society of Japan*, XLVI, 1, 1921.

Ise-monogatari (Tales of Ise). This work probably dates from the first half of the tenth century. It is a mixture of prose and poetry, being a collection of short stories or even shorter anecdotes, usually on the theme of love, with accompanying poems. Alternatively it might be said to be a collection of mainly love-poems with accompanying explanatory prose. Many of the poems are connected with Ariwara Narihira (825–80), and the various events have traditionally been assigned to his biography, almost certainly without justification. Its authorship is unknown.

The language is generally straightforward, even though some of the poems are now difficult of interpretation. *Ise-monogatari* gives an interesting account of certain aspects of the court, and the sentiments of its denizens, one or two generations before Murasaki Shikibu's description in *The tale of Genji*.

Translation: *Tales of Ise*, trans. Helen Craig McCullough, Stanford, 1968.

Kagerō-nikki (The Gossamer Diary). This was written in the seventies and eighties of the tenth century, and is not really anonymous, being the diary of a woman whose own name has not been preserved even though those of her son and his father are known. It is largely an account of her relations with the boy's father, in a typical marriage of the times, when the wife stayed in her home, and the husband visited her with a frequency that was apt to vary with his feelings for her. The emotions of the woman, whom different people might describe as either tragically suffering from a system that had little consideration for feminine feelings, or as a possessive, peevish person worthy of little sympathy, as expressed in the diary, give a fascinating and rarely offered glimpse into the heart of an ancient Japanese.

Translation: *The Gossamer Years*, trans. Edward Seidensticker, Tokyo, 1964.

Konjaku-monogatari (Tales of Long Ago). This collection of tales was compiled in the middle of the eleventh century. It was the first of its kind to be written in Japanese, but was preceded by several similar collections written in Chinese by Japanese compilers. *Uji-shūi-monogatari* (Tales from the Uji collection), of the fourteenth century, is the best-known of many later compilations.

There are more than a thousand stories in *Konjaku-monogatari*, of which about one hundred and eighty each are ascribed to Indian and Chinese sources, the rest being said to be Japanese in origin. There are Buddhist themes in all the sections, with some material taken from the *jātaka*, Indian tales relating to the birth of the Buddha; there are also some typically Chinese stories of filial piety. The Japanese component has many earthily comical incidents taken from the popular store, and gives an impression of the sort of thing that occupied the mind of the ordinary Japanese at the time. The language and the tone throughout are practical and explicit; the vocabulary is a mixture of Chinese and Japanese that gives an indication of how the language was to develop into the form that it possesses today.

To appreciate the full range of literature during the Heian period one must not only read the prose (such as Murasaki's *Genji-monogatari*) and poetry (as found in *Kokinwakashū*) of the introspective imperial court, with its allusive language amounting almost to a system of secret communication among adepts, and its almost purely Japanese vocabulary, but also this collection of tales. It represents not only the interests of a far wider section of the Japanese people but also shows the use of the contemporary language as an efficient and unaffected tool for straightforward communication. Those who appreciate commonsense applied to magical or supernatural situations, and other uncomplicated popular stories, accompanied with circumstantial details about the society of the time, will enjoy these tales.

Translations: A complete translation of *Uji-shūimonogatari* by D. E. Mills appeared in 1970 from the University of Cambridge Press. Of *Konjaku-monogatari*, thirty-seven tales have been translated by S. W. Jones in *Ages ago*, Cambridge, Mass., 1959.

Ochikubo-monogatari (*The Tale of the Lower Room*). The date of composition is usually placed in the last years of the tenth century. The 'lower room' of the title is the apartment in which lives a beautiful girl, in the house of her father and stepmother. The plot is concerned with the wooing of this girl, against her stepmother's wishes, and her subsequent marriage. It is said to be the first 'mother-in-law' story in Japanese literature.

The procedures of arranged marriage, and the system of values among the courtiers which inhabit this book make it of absorbing interest to those who wish to know more of the life of the time. There is a considerable degree of humour and realistic characterisation in the narrative.

Translation: William Whitehouse, *Ochikubo-monogatari*, London, 1934.

Taiheiki (Record of the Great Peace). This enigmatically titled romance probably assumed its present form in the third quarter of the fourteenth century. It deals with events between 1319 and 1368, when the supporters of the imperial court were endeavouring to rid the country of military dictatorship. The Buddhistic themes characteristic of *Heike-monogatari* are partly replaced by a Confucianist morality of loyalty, and the language indulges in

more ornamentation. In particular it introduces rhythmical prose in highly elaborate passages descriptive of emotion-wrought journeys. Many of its episodes join those from *Heike-monogatari* as constantly-recurring elements in later literature of all forms.
Translation: Helen Craig McCullough, *The Taiheiki*, New York and London, 1959, has translated a large section of this work.

Taketori-monogatari (The Tale of the Bamboo-cutter). This tale probably dates from the first quarter of the tenth century. A moon-princess is exiled to earth, and is found by the bamboo-cutter as a beautiful child in the hollow stem of a bamboo. She quickly grows to lovely womanhood, and is courted, in traditional Japanese fashion with poems, by ardent aristocrats. To keep them at a distance, she sets them tasks, which they pretend to fulfil. Their trickery is exposed but she is faced with a more serious situation when the emperor himself comes to woo. However, her exile is brought to an end in the nick of time, and she is transported back to the moon.

Although the setting is Japanese, the story, with its elements that can be found in the folklore of many parts of Eurasia, has a continental flavour. It is told with a freshness and humour that makes it very readable.
Translation: 'The tale of the bamboo cutter' trans. Donald Keene, *Monumenta Nipponica*, II, iv, Tokyo, 1955–6.

Tsutsumi-chūnagon-monogatari (Tales by the Middle Commander who lived by the Dike). This collection of ten stories, probably completed in the second half of the eleventh century, was formerly attributed to Fujiwara Kanesuke (877–933), nicknamed 'Middle Commander of the dike', but this is no longer thought possible. The stories were perhaps offered at some story-composing competition at court. They all have a certain whimsicality, or decadent humour, such as that of the 'Lady who loved insects', a girl who flouted convention by refusing to blacken her teeth or pluck her eyebrows, and preferred caterpillars to butterflies. Needless to say, suitors were soon frightened away.
Translations: Arthur Waley's version of 'The lady who loved insects' appears in Keene's *Anthology of Japanese literature*, Penguin, 1968. There is a complete translation of *Tsutsumi-chūnagon-monogatari* in Reischauer and Yamagiwa, *Translations From Early Japanese Literature*, Cambridge, Mass., 1951.

Uji-shūi-monogatari. *See* **Konjaku-monogatari.**

POETRY COLLECTIONS

The treasures of Japanese traditional verse, other than the seventeen syllable *haiku*, are to be found in great collections, the result of imperial command or private enterprise. These collections very often have a character of their own, over and above that of the individual authors' works that compose them, and anonymous poems always make up a considerable proportion of the total.

Four collections are taken as representative of the whole phenomenon, and are presented in chronological order.

Translations and further reading

Brower and Miner, *Japanese court poetry*, London, 1962, is a superb piece of critical writing, for those familiar with the vocabulary of modern literary studies. Miner, *An introduction to Japanese court poetry*, Stanford and London, 1968, is an excellent introductory work. Bownas and Thwaite, *The Penguin book of Japanese verse*, 1964, is wider in scope, since it covers the whole range of poetry from earliest times to the present. *The Manyōshū*, New York and London, 1965, is a fine translation and study of a thousand poems from the first collection.

Man-yōshū (Collection for ten thousand generations). This is the earliest surviving collection of Japanese poetry, and reached its present form some time in the second half of the eighth century, when the capital was still in Nara. It contains over four thousand poems, the majority from the seventh and eighth centuries, but some possibly earlier. The range of authorship is wide, from the emperor and his family at one extreme, to frontier guards at the other, and the language, while usually that of the court, sometimes is of local dialects. Prosody, although fundamentally (as ever in Japanese verse in the traditional forms) of a combination of lines of seven and five syllables, includes a considerable number of long poems, in which the poets have scope to develop more involved themes than in the shorter forms. The subject matter is of considerable variety. There are simple love and nature-poems, ballads and beggars' songs, expressions of grief at separation from dear ones while on official missions, and regret at being distant from the capital and the beloved presence of the emperor; sorrow at the death of one's wife, of the emperor, and on coming across a dead stranger on the sea-shore or mountain pass. Chinese influence is often apparent (several of the poets had been to China), and there is an astonishing sequence of poems in praise of drunkenness.

Many Western readers find the poems of *Man-yōshū* more satisfying than those of later collections. This is probably because they are often of a simple lyricism that makes them easily accessible, and because they often give an impression of sincerity, of being written because the poet was expressing the emotion he was experiencing at the time, whereas later poetry is often overtly fictional. This impression may not however be entirely justified, for many of the later *Man-yōshū* poems were probably occasional.

There may have been a succession of compilers over the years, but the last editor was probably Ōtomo Yakamochi, who died in 785. When he died, his family was in disgrace, and maybe partly through this, but mainly because Chinese poetry for the next hundred and fifty years became dominant in

Japan, *Man-yōshū* sank for some time into obscurity. When it reappeared into public light, the antique methods used in its writing, with Chinese characters used sometimes for their ideographic content, sometimes phonetically, sometimes in a mixture of both in the same word, made its interpretation difficult. And this difficulty has not entirely gone even today, although most has been deciphered. (See also **Kakinomoto Hitomaro.**)

Kokinwakashū (Collection of Japanese poems ancient and modern). The title of this collection is often abbreviated to *Kokinshū*. It was the first collection of Japanese poetry to be made at the command of the emperor, and was completed in 905. The principal compiler was Ki Tsurayuki (*qv*). There are two prefaces, one in Japanese, by Tsurayuki himself, and one in Chinese. The poems number 1,111 and are almost all *tanka* (short poems) of thirty-one syllables. *Kokinshū* is divided into volumes, some for each of the seasons, and others for various categories, of which love-poetry is outstanding.

In all these respects, except for a number of poems, *Kokinshū* was to furnish the model for collections to come. It set a fashion that was not to be seriously departed from in subsequent imperially ordered collections, and its influence extended into *haiku* (*see* Matsuo Bashō) and, in so far as traditional verse forms are still in use, survives until the present day.

The tenth century marks the great flowering of the court literature of the Heian period. By then the twofold role of poetry in everyday life at the court had become established. For a hundred years there had been poetry competitions of various kinds, participants in which had to compose on set themes, or even to employ acrostics and other devices; a subsidiary activity was the writing of poetry on request, on some chance theme, without there necessarily being an element of competition. The second purpose of poetry was to communicate with other persons, especially in the course of a love affair, wherein the correct choice of words, the aptness of phrase, and the careful matching to sentiment of the calligraphy, the paper used and the accompanying decoration of leaf and flower, were almost of greater importance for success than the physical or other charms of the wooer.

It follows that a great deal of the poetry of the Heian period was fictional, and that the sentiments expressed in it were not those actually being experienced by the poet at the time. The poetry of the earlier collection, *Man-yōshū* was probably far more often written in response to an emotion really felt.

Nevertheless, in *Kokinshū*, there are great poets whose work has all the appearance of truth. As befits its title, some of its poetry dates from ancient times, being ascribed either to poets of *Man-yōshū* or listed as anonymous. The next element chronologically is that of the poems by the poets mentioned in Tsurayuki's *Preface*, of whom Ariwara Narihira (825–80) and Ono Komachi (*fl* 900) are outstanding.

Narihira has the reputation of being a great lover, partly derived from his legendary biography given in *Ise-monogatari* (*qv*), and partly from his poetry, in which passion is combined with a delicate humour and a philosophical preoccupation with change. Ono Komachi is one of an extraordinary number of female writers of the period. There seems to have been little or no social censure of expressions of passion by women, and Komachi writes poetry in which great technical skill in extracting the utmost meaning from the small *tanka* form is combined with profound feeling. Her themes are the pangs of love and sorrow at the passing of beauty with the years. Virtually nothing is known of her life, but legend has it that after the age for passion had passed, she left the court and became a beggar.

Later female poets include Izumi Shikibu (*c* 970–1030), even more prone than Komachi to love-affairs, and reputedly author of a poem-studded diary *Izumi Shikibu nikki* (The diary of Izumi Shikibu), which tells of them. Tsurayuki himself composed many poems, some distinguished, but his greatest contribution was his preface, the first piece of literary criticism in Japanese, in which he sketches an aesthetic and assesses the work of individual poets.

Shinkokinwakashū (New collection of Japanese poetry ancient and modern); abbreviated title, *Shinkokinshū*; compilation completed in 1206. This was eighth in the series of imperial collections, and is usually considered the most important after its model, *Kokinwakashū* (*qv*). It comprises 1,981 poems, in the same general arrangement as its predecessor. The chief compiler was Fujiwara Teika (1162–1241), Japan's greatest poetry critic, but, unusually, the emperor himself, Toba II, participated actively in the selection. Since *Kokinshū* the power in the country had shifted to a military government in Kamakura, and the imperial court was busying itself more and more with the pursuits of leisure, such as poetry contests, and was also prey to a certain nostalgia for the good old times. Buddhism at the Heian court had been a matter of ritual carried out by an initiated priesthood; this had to some extent been replaced by the Zen sect which believed that enlightenment could come to the individual by meditation. This, and a more general involvement in Buddhistic thinking, brought about by the civil strife which saw the end of the power of the old court, and which more and more made men's minds turn to consider this life as transitory, were partly responsible for a new element in poetry. In particular, the poet Saigyō (1118–90) is representative of the age. A warrior who had renounced arms and abandoned his wife and family, he divided his time between attendance at court and wandering about the country composing poetry inspired by the sights he saw. His best poetry has a typical melancholy, it is all dew on autumn leaves, and autumn evenings, their sad monotony made more poignant by the sudden flight of snipe.

In terms of Japanese aesthetic theory, *Shinkokinshū* marks the boundary between *mono no aware* and *yūgen*. The first may crudely be said to be the spirit of empathy; the artist views the world, both of nature and human, with an eye that causes him to suffer the same emotion that the world seems to feel. The ruinous exterior of a house causes the wooer to feel pity for the lonely female residing therein, and, thence, love. The relation of nature and man is similar to that of the European Romantic, except that in Japan emotion was inspired by nature, whereas in Europe the poet sought a landscape which fitted his emotion. *Yūgen* changed in content over the centuries, but always tended to require that a work of art should have depths of meaning beyond that of the simple expression. A very obvious example might be found in Saigyō's poem on the snipe, mentioned above, in which the gloom of the autumn scene is riven by the sudden flight of the bird, as enlightenment comes suddenly to the Zen practitioner in the midst of protracted meditation.

Fūgashū (Collection of elegance), compiled between 1344 and 1346, and generally considered the last of the great imperial collections. It is remarkable also because the chief anthologist, and writer of the Japanese and Chinese prefaces, was the emperor, Hanazono II. Poetry had made some advances in the way of enlarging its vocabulary and of using deeper symbolism, and even mysticism, than in earlier collections. Perhaps, however, the true greatness of *Fūgashū* – and also of *Gyokuyōshū* (Collection of jewelled leaves), of 1314 – is the subtle unity of the whole, in which poems from the past and present are welded into a succession in which virtually every one has a connection, either near or remote, direct or through the intermediary of a poem not included in the anthology, with its neighbours. This is not a complete innovation, for *Kokinshū* and *Shinkokinshū* had already gone some way towards forming sequences. In these two collections, however, the process is carried as far as it will go.

This was not an isolated phenomenon, for it was closely connected with *renga* (linked poems), the basic rules for which were formulated shortly after the compilation of *Fūgashū.* Starting in the distant past with the composition of a *tanka* in two parts of seventeen and fourteen syllables by different authors, this form had developed by the fourteenth century into series of up to a hundred half-poems, composed by three or four poets, in which each is connected to the preceding half-poem by some near or close connection of season, sentiment or subject, the whole progressing in a non-rational way to the final stage. Rules related to such things as the frequency with which certain words could be used, the maximum and minimum number of a series of half-poems in which a certain topic could be introduced, and so on. Composition was extemporary, and the poems were recorded by an amanuensis, in a fixed order of portions of the sheet of paper. Those on the front of the sheet had to be more serious than those on the back, and so a succession of different tones and emotions was pre-established. This, and the sequential structure of *Fūgashū*, afford an indication of how the very abbreviated *tanka* form could be the basis of a far lengthier poetic whole.

INDIVIDUAL WRITERS

Abe Kōbō (1924–). Novelist. The son of a doctor who till the end of the war practised in Manchuria, Abe himself was trained as a doctor. From an early age, however, he had shown an astonishingly deep and catholic interest in both western and Japanese literature, and the shock of defeat stimulated his desire to write. On his graduation from the medical school of Tokyo University in 1948, he decided not to practice medicine but to devote himself wholly to literature. Since 1950, when he won a leading literary prize, Abe has been acclaimed as one of the most serious and original of the avant-garde novelists – the forerunner, perhaps, of a new generation of Japanese writers who while remaining unmistakably Japanese will belong equally to 'international' culture, and whom it will therefore no longer be possible to discuss in a purely Japanese context.

Surrealism, the poetry of Rilke, the existentialism of Heidegger and Jaspers, and to a lesser extent, communism, have been influential in Abe's development. The problem of alienation and loss of identity is central to his novels. In *The Crime of Mr S. Karuma* (1951) the hero loses his name, and with it his relationship to other human beings, but is drawn into a sense of intimacy with animals and window-dummies. *The Intruders* (1952) is a satire on democracy: the intruders of the title invade a private room in an apartment building and enslave its solitary occupant by 'majority vote'. The central figure of *Woman of the Dunes* (1962) (trans. Saunders, London, 1964) is an insect-collector who is held captive by seaside villagers at the bottom of a dune, together with a young woman, to shovel away the sand that is for ever threatening to engulf their homes. Desperate at first to escape and rejoin society, after years of struggle with himself and the woman, he attains a kind of inner self-sufficiency, till when the villagers at last free him he no longer desires to go. (It is interesting to note that the book has been popular in Russia – perhaps because of its powerful claustrophobic atmosphere.) In *The Face of Another* (1964), (trans. Saunders, London, 1969) a scientist in a research institute has had his face mauled in an explosion. To conceal the disfigurement he makes a mask so perfect as to be undetectable. But gradually the mask takes over, subtly altering his very personality, and he never succeeds in regaining control – or so it would seem, for the ending is deliberately ambiguous. Though his themes can be said to be universal, Abe's treatment of them is peculiarly Japanese. His characters, who are always few in number, show an extraordinary subtlety of introspective thought, and more particularly of feeling; there is much tension, but little dramatic action.

Stick and *Red Cocoon*, both trans. Nathan, in *Japan Quarterly*, XIII–2, 1966.

Akutagawa Ryūnosuke (1892–1927). Short-story writer. A shadow hung over Akutagawa's life from the beginning. Seven months after he was born his mother went mad, and he was adopted by the Akutagawas (his mother's brother and sister-in-law), an old priestly family of considerable literary and artistic culture. His academic career was brilliant, culminating in graduation with high honours from the English Literature Department of Tokyo University (William Morris being the subject of his graduation essay); throughout his school and college years and subsequently he read extensively in French, Scandinavian, Russian and Chinese literature as well as English and Japanese. His first story, *The Nose* (trans. Shaw in his Akutagawa anthology, *Tales Grotesque and Curious*, Tokyo, 1930), which appeared in the opening number of a coterie magazine he started with some friends in 1914, was favourably noticed by the great novelist Natsume Sōseki, whose weekly 'Thursday meeting' of scholars, writers and artists he was at once invited to join. From then on his reputation grew rapidly; and after a year of teaching English at the Naval Engineering School, he devoted himself entirely to writing. Like the humanism of Mushakōji Saneatsu, Akutagawa's so-called 'neo-realism' was conceived in revolt against the naturalists; in place of their unadorned first-person confessions, he went to great lengths to avoid intruding his own experience, basing many of his stories on obscure classical tales, but presenting his characters with modern psychological realism and in a highly-wrought, original style. An exceedingly sensitive, almost morbid temperament, combined with a restless critical intelligence, led him early to a pessimistic view of human nature, an abnormally keen awareness of the disparity between appearance and reality. *In a Grove* (1913) (trans. Kojima in *Rashōmon and Other Stories*, Tokyo and New York, 1952) – the story from which the film *Rashōmon* was in the main derived – is a famous example. His is a gloomy world, in which only the palest light flickers (*cf Rashōmon* in Kojima, *op cit*). Sometimes his scepticism is relieved by a mordant wit, as in *The Nose*, a tale of a long-nosed priest who thinks a shorter nose essential to his happiness, or *Kappa* (trans. Bownas, London, 1970), a mini-Swiftian satire on Japanese society, art and morals. Yet in spite of, or perhaps because of, his disillusionment with humanity, Akutagawa believed passionately in art and the aesthetic attitude. 'All life is not worth a line of Baudelaire' he says in a posthumously-published autobiographical piece; and for Akutagawa this was no very great exaggeration, as the student of his work soon comes to realise. The Chinese sages in *An Autumn Mountain* (trans. Morris in *MJS*), sharing an intuition of the elusive secret of beauty, clap their hands in delight. A story such as *The Spider's Thread* (1918) (trans. Shaw, *op cit*) is in itself, on its own small scale, a perfect work of art.

In the end, however, art succumbed to a more tragic reality. As Yoshihide, the artist in *Hell Screen* (1918) (trans. Norman in *MJL*), who has had his daughter burnt in a carriage to provide him with a model for his painting of Hell, hangs himself the night the painting is finished, so, after some twelve prolific years, Akutagawa drank poison, ending his life in a carefully planned suicide as dramatic as any of his macabre stories. A Bible was found at his pillow. The sudden death at the age of thirty-five of the most brilliant writer of the day, attributed in letters he left behind to nothing more specific than 'a vague uneasiness', shocked the literary world, and argument has continued ever since as to whether his suicide is to be seen as the victory of art over life, in the purest, most selfless 'artistic' act known to Japanese tradition, or the reverse – the final surrender of a man whose sensibility belonged essentially to a past age, and who therefore could not bring himself to face the realities of the modern Japan. Over-sensitive as he was from childhood, the real reasons for his suicide were probably more personal – gradual loss of confidence in himself as an artist, practical worries, and frequent illness.

With their terse, dramatic style, rare in Japanese fiction, Akutagawa's stories are easily appreciated by the western reader. His work has been more often translated than that of any other pre-war writer.

Japanese Short Stories by Ryūnosuke Akutagawa, trans. Kojima, New York, 1961.

Tu Tze-chun, trans. Britton, Tokyo and London, 1965.

A Clod of Earth, trans. McKinnon in *HIA*.

Arishima Takeo (1878–1923). Novelist. The son of an official in the Finance Ministry, Arishima was brought up during much of his boyhood in Yokohama, where at that time more foreigners lived than in any other part of Japan. Here he experienced in his most impressionable years the clash of two cultures – the peculiarly western combination of materialism and idealism, represented by the foreign merchants and missionaries, and the strict discipline of the traditional samurai code in which his parents insisted in training him. In 1896 he entered Sapporo Agricultural College in Hokkaido, then a famous centre both for its scholarship and its Christian atmosphere, and lodged for a time with Dr Nitobe, the Japanese Quaker, scientist and philosopher. Before long he became an active Christian. After graduation, and a year's military service, Arishima went to America, where he studied economics and political science at Haverford College and Harvard University. Several factors combined to weaken his Christian faith – his studies, disillusion with the 'lack of sincerity' in American life, and in particular some searing experiences he underwent while doing vacation work at a callously-run mental hospital. He read the works of many western writers, such as Whitman, Ibsen, Gorky, and Tolstoy, and became interested too in socialism and anarchism. Not till 1911, however, did he formally abandon Christianity.

Returning to Japan in 1907, Arishima taught English for six years at his old college in Hokkaido, contributing stories and articles from time to time to Mushakōji Saneatsu's humanistic journal *Shirakaba*. The death in 1911 of both his wife and his father seemed to unlock his energies: released from the constraints they symbolised, he poured out a stream of novels, stories, essays and plays, all preaching a creed of dynamic self-realisation based on the rejection both of the hierarchic conventions of Japanese society and of the Christian dichotomy of flesh and spirit. Yet Arishima was not a shallow thinker, and inevitably his confidence in his new-found idealism did not last long. His political radicalism too began to ring hollow; even when he presented the family lands in Hokkaido to the peasants who lived on them – an incident that caused a considerable stir at the time – he could see himself only as a 'bourgeois dreamer' who could play no part in the new order that was coming. Finally he committed 'double suicide' with a Mrs Hatano at his summer villa in the mountains.

The best of his work reflects the tragic conflict of these later years. *Descendants of Cain* (1917–18) (trans. Morrison in *Modern Japanese Fiction*, Salt Lake City, 1955) describes the struggle of a Hokkaido peasant to survive; he is too independent to kowtow to the landlord like his fellows, and as a result he is hated by both the landlord and his fellow peasants. The subject is treated with a dramatic realism and power rare in Japanese literature. In *The Agony of Coming into the World* (1918) (trans. Fujita, Tokyo, 1955) the intense desire of a poor fisherman's son to paint is almost, but not quite, destroyed by poverty and his family's mockery. The story is told with less naivete than such a summary might suggest, but is spoilt here and there by sentimentality. Arishima's masterpiece is undoubtedly *A Certain Woman* (begun in 1911, but not completed till 1918). Satsuki Yōko – the literary successor to Tokutomi Roka's (*qv*) *Namiko* – has had a thoroughly modern education, and is filled with notions of a life in which her individuality will find free expression. After the rapid breakdown of her love-marriage, she sets sail for America to marry a Japanese living there, but becomes involved with the ship's purser, and returns to Japan without setting foot in America. As a result the purser is disgraced and loses his job. For a while they live in great happiness. In time, however, he is driven by money worries to sell himself as a spy, and leaves her. After much suffering she dies, alone and in misery, crying 'The way I loved was wrong, but whose fault was it? I cannot tell.' Because of its taut plot-structure and mature characterisation *A Certain Woman* is regarded by many Japanese as the most 'western' of all the novels of the modern period, at least until 1945.

Ariwara Narihira (825–80). See *Ise-monogatari*, *Kokinwakashū*.

Ariyoshi Sawako (1931–). Novelist. A Catholic who was educated at one of the country's leading Protestant women's colleges, Miss Ariyoshi has emerged as a leading woman writer of the post-war years. Her work, principally novels, although she has also written plays, already covers a remarkably wide range. *The Ki River* (1960), set in her native prefecture of Wakayama, in central Japan, describes the vicissitudes of Japan's modern century as they are experienced by a sensitive provincial woman. *Incense and Flowers* (1960–2) is a sympathetic study of the world of the geisha and its relationships. Tomoko, the central figure, is sold by her mother to the gay quarters while still a child. With the help of aristocratic patronage she prospers as a business-woman, buying and successfully running a hotel – and rescuing, in the process, the mother who had sold her into geishadom. She survives the destruction of her hotel in an air-raid in the Pacific War, and before long is back in business as the proprietress of a high-class business-men's restaurant.

In *Not Because of Colour* (1964) Miss Ariyoshi achieves something new in Japanese fiction – a convincing picture of life abroad, marred neither by hints of a supposed superior spirituality in Japanese culture nor by any uncomfortable feeling of Japanese political or material inferiority. Written after a session at Sarah Lawrence College (ostensibly studying drama), the novel tells of the experiences of a Japanese girl who married an American negro soldier in Tokyo. She finds him a perfect husband. Life changes, however, when he is demobilised and they return to America to live in Haarlem. He can rarely find work; she has to slave in restaurants and domestic service to keep him and their children alive. The point is made that it is not colour that is at the root of white prejudice against negroes, but poverty: the proof being that negroes, too, are prejudiced – against Puerto Ricans, who are even poorer than themselves. But there is no overt moralising to the tale, which is told with humour and compassion. *Hanaoka Seishū* (1967) is also unusual, this time for the deliberate and subtle ambivalence – a sign, perhaps, of the maturity the novel has now reached in Japan – of its attitude to Japanese culture and history. On one level the novel is a panegyric of a historical figure, a pioneer doctor named Hanaoka (*d* 1836) who successfully used a general anaesthetic some forty years before the same feat was achieved in the West. At the same time, by emphasising the debasement of human relationships within the doctor's family – unknown to him, his mother and wife, famous in the district as paragons of womanly loyalty and sweetness, serve as guinea-pigs for his experiments out of no other motive than the crudest jealousy of each other – it questions whether the cost in human terms of this Japanese 'first' may not have been too high.

Miss Ariyoshi's latest novel, *A Time of Distrust* (1968) is an exposure of the continuing arrogance of men in a society where since the war, the sexes have been officially equal.

Prayer (short story), trans. Bester in *Japan Quarterly*, Vol. VII, No. 4, 1960.

Chikamatsu Monzaemon (1653–1725), playwright. The first half of the seventeenth century saw a considerable reduction in the number of warriors who were actually in the service of some lord. Many became masterless, and had children who never followed the warrior life. Although still technically of the warrior class, they had to earn a living outside it and often brought a strong ingredient of intelligence and ability into professions which began to flourish at the time. Chikamatsu seems to have been one of these. He had apparently received a broad education, with some experience of life in a Buddhist temple.

In 1676 he is known to have been in Kyoto, and to have already embarked upon his career. He was writing for the *kabuki*, the live popular theatre that had come into being in the first years of the seventeenth century, when the *nō* plays (see Zeami) were becoming fossilised as an upper class entertainment and polite attainment, and the rising merchant class were seeking ways to enjoy themselves and spend some of the money that they devoted their lives to amassing. *Kabuki*, and the puppet theatre, which was at the time of equal, if not greater, importance, developed from various popular and folk performances into formally staged professional dramatic forms. Chikamatsu Monzaemon played a great part in their growth into great theatre. In the *kabuki* in Kyoto he formed part of a team, including actors and managers, which specialised in the writing and production of plays centred on idealised courtesans. This was also the period of the great *onnagata* (men who took female roles) and of the mystique that surrounded them. These plays have now almost completely disappeared from the repertory.

The puppet theatre had from the start put on full-length plays, at first demonstrating in their structure their origin in narrative forms such as *Heike-monogatari* (*qv*) and taking as their subjects either Buddhist themes or fantastic feats of military skill. Chikamatsu Monzaemon, in his first puppet plays, followed the same pattern, but in the 1680s there came in a strong influence from the *nō*, which gave the puppet plays a true dramatic unity. There also appeared on the scene in Osaka a great chanter (in the Japanese puppet drama, all the words are spoken or chanted by a separate performer), Takemoto Gidayū, who combined the styles of all preceding schools, and established the school of chanting still used with the puppets in Japan. In collaboration with him Chikamatsu Monzaemon wrote improved plays, but did not strike his greatest vein until 1703, when he wrote *Sonezaki Shinjū* (Love suicides at Sonezaki). This was his first 'domestic' play, in which he followed a trend set up previously by Ihara Saikaku (*qv*) in his stories of merchant life, in which actual tragedies were turned into plays within weeks. These plays often have to do with the love of some shopkeeper or other tradesman for a girl from the brothel district, a love normally doomed to failure, and often ending in the suicide of the lovers.

The best of these 'domestic' dramas, which also include tragedies of love in which the women are wives and not prostitutes, and one murder for money, have been translated by Keene in *Major Plays of Chikamatsu*. The reader will discover in them that the author was skilled in depicting real characters, with some of the complex make-up of real human beings, as distinct from the stereotypes of virtue or vice which had been usual in much of preceding and, indeed, subsequent Japanese literature. He was also master of the pathetic, shown particularly in the poetic passages describing lovers' last journeys to their death.

Although the text of *kabuki* plays were from the start presented in the form of speeches from actors, that of the puppet plays was a continuous narrative with descriptive passages alternating with and interpenetrating pieces of conversation. For several reasons, including the use of a very subtle style in the descriptions, few of Chikamatsu Monzaemon's plays survived unrevised, although there are occasional attempts today to play them with the original text.

Translation: Donald Keene, *Major Plays of Chikamatsu*, New York and London, 1961.

Futabatei Shimei (1864–1909). Pioneer of the modern novel. He was born in Tokyo, or Edo as it was then, of samurai stock. After three times failing the preliminary examination for the Military Academy, he entered the Department of Russian at the Tokyo School of Foreign Studies, in the hope of a diplomatic career; but this ambition did not survive his reading of the great Russian novelists, Belinsky's criticism, and Herzen's writings on socialism. Encouraged by Tsubouchi Shōyō, the leading interpreter of western literary theory and translator of Shakespeare, he began his own translations from the Russian. Later, indeed, his skill in this field was to become famous. His first published work, however, was the novel *Drifting Clouds* (trans. Ryan, *Japan's First Modern Novel – The Ukigumo of Futabatei Shimei*, New York and London, 1967), which appeared in three parts (1887–9) over the name of Tsubouchi Shōyō – such was the low esteem accorded to prose fiction at the time that work by an unknown author had little chance of selling. *Drifting Clouds* broke new ground in two respects: its critical realism, with none of the whimsical, fantastic elements of earlier fiction, and the simplicity of its colloquial style – an early and powerful shot in the long battle to release literature from the straightjacket of the stiff 'literary' language. The hero is Utsumi Bunzō, the son of a samurai who has come down in the world after the Meiji Restoration. Studious, idealistic, and sincere, he enters a government office after graduation; but his refusal to toady to his corrupt superiors costs him both his job and the love of the 'modern' girl he had hoped to marry. The clash between Bunzō's independent spirit and the hierarchical structure of society, and between his old-fashioned principles and the shallow westernising around him, reduces him finally to a state of nervous inaction. Technically, the novel is flawed: dissatisfied with the later chapters, and doubting his literary ability, Futabatei found himself unable to finish it. Yet it is still readable today, a penetrating analysis both of the society of his day and of certain continuing aspects of Japanese life.

It was seventeen years before Futabatei wrote his two other novels, *An Adopted Husband* (trans. Mitsui and Sinclair, New York, 1919) and *Mediocrity* (trans. Shaw, Tokyo, 1927), both of which lack the impact of *Drifting Clouds*. During these years Futabatei was in turn government translator, teacher in various institutions, and journalist. He contracted tuberculosis while serving as correspondent in Russia for the Asahi newspaper, and died on the way home to Japan.

Hagiwara Sakutaro (1887–1942). Poet. He began by writing *tanka* (traditional thirty-one syllable poems) and by the time he was twenty his name was linked with that of Ishikawa Takuboku (*qv*) as one of the most promising young poets in this form. Under the influence of the symbolist poet Kitahara Hakushū, however, he discarded the classical form in favour of *shintaishi*, 'new-style' poetry in the freer western manner. Earlier new-style poets had rarely been successful; centuries of the *tanka* and *haiku* tradition, of a strictly regulated literary grammar and diction, and the peculiarities of the Japanese language, made their task exceptionally difficult. Hagiwara made the breakthrough. The themes of his poetry – the isolation of the individual, the search for stability in a too rapidly changing world, contempt for fashion and formalism in art – were modern enough; but his fame is due equally to his skill in moulding the natural speech of the Japanese into genuine poetic rhythms, 'free' yet imposing their own kind of structure, in a way for which there was no precedent in Japanese poetics. *Baying at the Moon* (1917), his first collection, has been called a Japanese *Waste Land*, such has been its influence on subsequent new-style poets. Part of the secret of his success lay in his interest in the musical quality of words (in his native town of Maebashi, where he directed a thriving mandolin club, he was for a long time better-known as a musician than as a poet), and in his insistence, derived no doubt from his experience with the *tanka*, that 'all true poetry must be lyrical'.

In later years Hagiwara's poetry grew increasingly gloomy, reverting at the same time to the old literary style. Towards the end of his life, like many of the Japanese romantics, he sought consolation in his own brand of nationalism. *Face at the Bottom of the World, and Other Poems*, trans. Wilson, Tokyo, 1969.

Higuchi Ichiyō (1872–96). Novelist. Her life was short and tragic. She was the daughter of a farmer who came to Edo shortly before the Restoration of 1868, managed to acquire samurai status as a constable, and finally became a minor official in the service of the new government. Her wish to continue her education beyond primary school was frustrated by her mother, who did not believe in girls learning too much: even to read her favourite heroic romances she often had to hide in the shed. Fortunately, though, the ladylike pursuits she was allowed to follow at the age of twelve did include poetry. Four years later her father resigned his official post to set up in business. The venture was a complete failure, and within a year he was dead. For a while the women of the family stayed with Ichiyo's brother; but mother and son quarrelled, and

Ichiyō, aged seventeen, was left to support her mother and sister by taking in sewing and washing. Other troubles followed. Jealousy and scandal-mongering forced a break between her and her poetry teacher, to whom she was deeply attached; attempts to earn a living by fiction-writing, to which she was inspired by the success of a novel published by a woman friend in her poetry class, failed miserably. For ten months, on borrowed money, she ran a small shop, but this too failed. While eking out a living by teaching poetry and calligraphy she made the acquaintance of the lively young writers of the *Bungakkai* group (Kitamura Tōkoku, *qv*) who encouraged her to continue writing. Her *Dark Night*, a novel attacking the corruption of politics and business, appeared in *Bungakkai* in 1894. There followed in 1895 and 1896 her four short masterpieces, *Muddy Bay* (trans. Tanaka in *MN*, XIV, 1–2, 1958), *Thirteenth Night* (trans. Tanaka in *MN*, XVI, 3–4, 1960), *The Parting of the Ways* (trans. Bickerton, *TASJ*, VII, 1930), and *Growing Up* (trans. Seidensticker in *MJL*). Their success was immediate and brilliant. But Ichiyō, exhausted by overwork and worry, had already contracted tuberculosis, and in a few months she was dead. Mori Ōgai (*qv*) whose public praise had established her reputation – by now he was Commandant of the Army Medical College, and a respected literary figure as well – asked permission of her sister to ride beside her coffin, but was refused, on the ground that the honour would have been too great.

Inevitably, Ichiyō's output was small. The pathos of her life has played its part in securing her place in literary history. Her language and style are premodern (though this is not apparent in translation). Yet her stories, brief poetic evocations for the most part, of the loneliness of young people deprived like herself of the chance of loving, can still move the reader deeply by virtue of their restrained lyricism and the compassion which, as much as Ichiyo's own suffering, is their inspiration.

Ibuse Masuji (1898–   ). Novelist, short-story writer and essayist. A native of Hiroshima, Ibuse studied French literature and painting in Tokyo. He decided on a literary career while at Waseda University, but failed to achieve recognition till the publication in 1929 of *Salamander*, a reworked version of a story he had written eleven years earlier as a student. *Salamander*, a gentle satire on his own lack of confidence – he himself is the mountain salamander, mocked by fishes and frogs because he has thrown away the chance of leaving his comfortable hole and joining them in the wide world – displays two of the qualities that have pervaded much of Ibuse's work right up to the present: humour (in pleasant contrast to the sombre colouring of a high proportion of modern Japanese writing), and an unobtrusive lyricism. From 1930 he was a prominent member of the so-called 'neo-artistic' school, a group of writers and critics who attempted to preserve literature from subservience to either Marxism or militant nationalism. Typical of many novels of this period is *Tajinko Village* (1939), a day-to-day record of the life of a simple, warm-hearted country policeman. During the war Ibuse continued to write desultorily, even when he was conscripted and sent to south-east Asia. Defeat, however, liberated his energies, and since 1946 his output has been immense. In the best of his post-war writing, compassion for the common man, bearing the burden of events he cannot control – a Buddhist compassion, rooted in acceptance of suffering rather than in revolt against it – blends harmoniously with the Ibuse humour and lyricism. Especially notable are *The Far-Worshipping Commander* (1950) (trans. Shaw in *The Shadow of Sunrise, Selected Stories of Japan and the War*, ed. Saeki, Tokyo and Palo Alto, 1966), a delightful account of the commotion caused in a village when a patriotic soldier, much given to bowing in the direction of the Imperial House and to reciting the Five Articles of the Charter Oath, comes home after the surrender still suffering periodically from the delusion that the war is still on; *The Charcoal Bus* (1950) (trans. Morris in *MJS*), a short but pungently satirical allegory of wartime Japan; and *No Consultations Today* (1949) (trans. Seidensticker in *Japan Quarterly*, VIII–1, 1961), a picture of a town built up through the stories told by patients to an understanding doctor. But most readers will probably regard *Black Rain* (1965) (trans. Bester, Tokyo and Palo Alto, 1969), Ibuse's long novel of the Hiroshima atom bomb, as his masterpiece. Though closely based on diaries and eye-witness accounts and covering in great detail the horrors of the bomb and its aftermath, *Black Rain* is neither sensational nor tedious; the tragedy is recalled and relived, if not in tranquillity, at least with an amazing objectivity, devoid of either self-pity or bitterness, and an obstinate undercurrent of hope. It would be hard to imagine a finer response of the Japanese spirit, in terms of literature, to the events of August 1945.

An admirer of Mori Ōgai (*qv*), like his contemporary Inoue Yasushi (*qv*), Ibuse has also written historical fiction, notably *John Manjiro, the Castaway, His Life and Adventures* (1938) (adapted and trans. Kaneko as *Manjiro, The Man Who Discovered America*, Tokyo, 1954).

Ihara Saikaku (1642–93), novelist and poet. He was born into a rich merchant family in Osaka, but appears to have left the running of his business to a manager, and to have lived a life free from financial cares. However, the death of his wife in about 1675, and the blindness of his daughter, and her death in 1692, seem to have hit him hard. Unusually for the period, he did not remarry.

He devoted his early productive years to the composition and study of *haiku*, in which he cultivated a facetious style. None of these are now considered worth reading, and his main claim to fame in this field is his reputed composition, in 1684, of 23,500 verses in one period of twenty-four hours. In 1682 he more or less took over a genre of prose, known as *kana-zōshi* (books written in *kana* – the phonetic syllabary), which had existed since early in the century, and which had included Buddhistic tales, a translation of Aesop's fables and other items of a fictional or didactic nature. His new genre was called *ukiyo-zōshi* (tales of the floating world) and comprised realistic descriptions of the current social scene, often, but not always, with an erotic theme. Ihara Saikaku was the pacemaker in this genre, and although he had many imitators, only a few had any merit.

His *ukiyo-zōshi* included some interesting collections of anecdotes collected from all over Japan, but the purely fictional ones have more importance. The first of these, *Kōshoku ichidai-otoko* (The life of an amorous man) (1682) is an account of the amorous adventures of Yonosuke, son of a prosperous merchant and a courtesan, during fifty-four years of his life from the age of seven to sixty. The number fifty-four is derived from the number of chapters of Murasaki Shikibu's *Tale of Genji*, which is also a description of a man's total sex life. We hear of Yonosuke's first experiences, with members of both sexes, and then of vicissitudes of fortune and encounter which finally bring him to his rebirth age of sixty, when, with six companions, he embarks on a ship full of souvenirs of his adventures, in search of an island in the Pacific, inhabited entirely by eager women.

In 1686 appeared two works in which Saikaku turns his attention to women in love or, at least, driven by sexual appetite. The first of these, *Kōshoku gonin-onna* (Five women who loved love) consists of five separate stories, each based on actual scandals that had aroused public interest, in which women not of the courtesan class had fallen prey to love. Later in the same year was published *Kōshoku ichidai-onna* (Life of an amorous woman), the heroine of which Morris likens to Moll Flanders. It is the life of a woman who constantly ruins her chances of success in various occupations by yielding to her lusts, but who is prevented from establishing herself in the profession to which she might seem ideally qualified by the wilfulness which makes her disobey the rules of the house. The book incidentally gives a glimpse of the whole range of occupations available to a female making her own living, and, in that the plot is somewhat more convincing than that of the amorous man, gives a greater impression of reality.

Saikaku left the further development of this style to his imitators, and went on to write a series of accounts of homosexual love and revenge among the *samurai*. These, which have no universal value, were followed by a period in which he returned to a description of merchant-life, mainly in *Nippon eitai-gura* (The Japanese Family storehouse) (1688), a collection of thirty anecdotes of success or failure in business, in which merchant morality is explored in detail. In this collection there are many references to actual people to increase the reality, and it forms a series of lively pictures of contemporary life that makes attractive reading.

Saikaku's training in *haiku* writing has a strong influence on his style in his prose works, which progress on the pattern of linked verse, by a process of association of ideas. This makes for great liveliness, flexibility and complexity, but does not help translation.

Translations:

Five women who loved love, trans. T. de Bary, New York, 1956.
The Japanese family storehouse, trans. G. W. Sargent, Cambridge, 1959.
The life of an amorous man, trans. K. Hamada, Tokyo, 1964.
The life of an amorous woman, trans. Ivan Morris, London, 1963.

Inoue Yasushi (1907-). Novelist. In his youth, in consequence of his father's frequent moves – he was an army surgeon – Inoue was for long periods separated from his parents, and attended schools in various parts of the country, where he was distinguished more for his expertise in judo than for any literary aspirations. Poetry became his chief avocation during some years of rather desultory study at the Universities of Kyushu and Kyoto. In 1936, however, the year of his graduation, his first novel won him a literary prize and a job with the Mainichi newspaper, with which he was to stay, except for six months of military service, till 1951. The years of militarism silenced him, apart from day-to-day journalism. But not permanently; as soon as the clouds cleared, he made a fresh start with the two short novels *Bullfight* and *The Hunting Gun* (trans. Yokoo and Goldstein, Rutland, Vermont, and Tokyo, 1961; also trans. Saito, as *The Shotgun*, in *MJS*), both published in 1949, which established his post-war reputation. Since then he has maintained a steady output (mostly of fiction although he has written some poetry) interrupted only by the frequent wanderings up and down the land to which Inoue, like so many other Japanese writers, is addicted. He has travelled too in China and the West, serving as Mainichi correspondent at the Rome Olympic Games in 1963. Among many literary awards he has won are the 1953 Art Academy Prize for *Ice Cliff* and the 1954 Minister of Education's Prize for *Temple Tiles of the Tempyō Era*. Inoue's studies of the nuances behind the appearances of human relationships, with the suggestion of an inevitable loneliness that is at once a cause of suffering and a source of inspiration, are in the authentic Japanese mode. *The Hunting Gun* is an example. Consisting of four letters from a middle-aged man, his lover, his wife, and his lover's daughter, it has been compared to Akutagawa's (*qv*) *In a Grove* (trans. Kojima in *Rashōmon and Other Stories*, New York, 1952), on which the internationally famous film *Rashomon* was based, but surpasses it in complexity and insight. *Temple Tiles of the Tempyō Era*, an account of the long years of study and travel in China by four Japanese priests sent to study Buddhism in the eighth century AD, is typical of another genre to which Inoue (like Mori Ōgai (*qv*), whom he much admires) has been attracted – historical fiction, based on extensive and thorough research. Like most of his work, it is written in a style of extreme economy, so extreme, in fact, that he is one of the most difficult Japanese authors to translate without losing the concise suggestiveness of his language.

Inoue has lectured at the University of Hawai as a Visiting Scholar. He is now working on *Wadatsumi* (Sea), an epic historical novel dealing with Japanese migration to the USA.

The Azaleas of Hira, trans. Seidensticker in *Japan Quarterly*, II–3, 1955.
Lou-lan, trans. Seidensticker in *Japan Quarterly*, VI–4, 1959.
A translation of *Temple Tiles of the Tempyō Era* is in preparation in the UNESCO Collection of Contemporary Works.

Ishikawa Takuboku (1886–1912). Poet. He was born in a village in north-eastern Japan, the son of a Zen priest. While still at school he wrote many poems in the classical *tanka* form, but none were published till 1902, when one was accepted in the journal *Myōjō* (Morning Star). On the advice of Yosano Tekkan, editor of *Myōjō*, Ishikawa switched to European-style 'free' verse, and his collection *Akogare* (Longings) (1905) made a considerable impression, though he soon reverted to the *tanka*, preferring the discipline its brevity imposed. He was married the same year, but after a few settled months the rest of his life was dogged by poverty and illness; he worked as a teacher, a clerk, and a newspaper reporter, but never succeeded in earning an adequate living. His mother and one of his children died of tuberculosis, his wife caught the same disease, and after several operations he himself died of a combination of tuberculosis and peritonitis.

Two years before his death Ishikawa published *A Handful of Sand* (trans. Sakanishi, Boston, 1934), a volume of five hundred and fifty-one *tanka*. A further collection, *Sad Toys*, was published posthumously. The material of his poems is not the elegant sentiment of which for centuries the *tanka* had been the vehicle, but everyday experience, expressed with directness and in the simplest of language. Although sadness pervades them all, Ishikawa's courage and fine sensibility, together with the strictness of the form, prevent it from degenerating into self-pity. Ishikawa also wrote novels, although it is on his poetry that his reputation has always rested; and in spite of the fact that his poetry is so personal a remarkable breadth of literary vision is evident in a posthumously-published essay, *The Cul-de-sac of Our Times*, in which he analyses the irrelevance of naturalism as a literary response to the social and political realities of Japanese life in the first decade of the twentieth century. His *Romaji Diary* (trans. Keene in *MJL*) gives a glimpse of the complexity and modernity of his preoccupations.
Poems to Eat, trans. Sesar, Tokyo, 1966.

Jippensha Ikku (1765–1831), a comic novelist. At all periods Japanese literature has had a humorous ingredient, sometimes separate from and acting as a foil to the serious form, as comic *kyōgen* interludes set off and act as a relaxant for audiences of the tense *Nō* plays; sometimes they are incorporated in the same work as the serious elements, as in some humorous touches in *Ochikubo-monogatari* (*qv*). During the Tokugawa period (1600–1868) more and more writers devoted themselves to comic and satirical themes, from composers of seventeen-syllable verse, to those who wrote biographies of eccentrics or made fun of country bumpkins astray in the world of brothels.

The townsfolk and country people of the time often travelled great distances to visit famous places of pilgrimage of which the Imperial Shrines at Ise were the most frequented. To help travellers on their journeys along the great roads, guide-books were prepared, giving indications of the scenic beauties along the route, and setting out accommodation available and the entertainment offered. Jippensha Ikku took the guide-book form, and rewrote it as a comic novel. Although he was to cover most of the main roads of Japan, and a successor was even to extend the series to the west after the Meiji Restoration, in fact the first, *Tōkaidō-chū Hiza-kurige* (On Shanks's Mare along the Tōkaidō) is the most deserving of survival. It takes two picaresque heroes along the road from Edo to Osaka, with a diversion to the great pilgrimage centre at Ise. They possess the normal Edo dwellers' attitude of contempt for countryfolk, and seek to take advantage of them, not always with success. Their adventures involve them and those they meet in practical jokes, petty trickery and thwarted lasciviousness. The humour, although vulgar and repetitive, at least serves to show the common humanity of the western reader and the Japanese merchants of the time, and can also raise more than an occasional laugh.

The author produced many other works, including plays and verse, which are no longer read. He travelled widely, and lived at various times both in Edo and Osaka. People who eagerly made his acquaintance in anticipation of a lively companion, are said to have been bitterly disappointed, for he had no conversation and was constantly taking notes of what went on around him. He is said to have been the first Japanese writer to live entirely on his literary work. One of the best stories related of him is that he arranged to have fireworks placed in his shroud when he was cremated, but this is thought to be an invention.

Translation: *Shank's Mare*, trans. T. Satchell, Tokyo, 1960.

Kakinomoto Hitomaro, early eighth-century poet. His work is to be found in *Man-yōshū* (*qv*). He seems to have been a minor official, but virtually nothing is known of his life outside of his poetry. He is one of the greatest poets of the collection, and is representative of a middle period, between that of the primitive work of the early writers, and the relatively sophisticated, already mannered, members of the later Nara court. He shows no particular Chinese influence, unlike some others whose work is in the anthology, and, as would be expected from the period in which he was writing, displays adherence to the old *shintō* religion, and to his emperor.

He wrote both short and long poems, but he is more renowned for the latter, which he can be said to have developed into an important vehicle, even though the form was to prove to be short-lived. As is often the case with poets of the *Man-yōshū*, he is very concerned with his fellow human beings, and the subject of death – that of a stranger whose body he finds on a journey, as well as those near to him – seems particularly to have concerned him. There is much that can still move us in his work, which has a true humanity.

Kamo Chōmei (1153–1216), poet and essayist. He was born in Kyoto, where his father was a priest at the great Kamo shrine. He spent his life at court, and lived through fire, typhoon, famine and earthquake, which were particularly severe when he was a young man. He became a celebrated performer on musical instruments, and was sufficiently esteemed for his verse-writing to receive an appointment to the imperial poetry department. Some of his short poems are in *Shinkokinwakashū* and other collections. A little after reaching the age of fifty, he withdrew from court and went off to live in seclusion in the mountains that enclose the capital. From these retreats he made excursions into Kyoto, and even to Kamakura, which was by now the seat of government.

In 1212 he wrote the work which was to prove his masterpiece. It includes a description of the harrowing scenes he had witnessed when he was younger, which he quotes as examples of the impermanence of human life. He relates his own search for peace and enlightenment, and describes his idyllic existence in his 'six foot square hut', from which the title *Hōjōki* (Records of a six foot square hut) is derived. A critical work *Mumeishō* (Nameless notes) is one of standard authorities of the poetics of the end of the twelfth century, and carries an account of *yūgen* (the mysterious or allusive element in artistic writing) which is as important as it is obscure. The style of *Hōjōki*, however, is a model of classical prose writing, which owes something to Ki Tsurayuki's Preface to *Kokinwakashū*.
Translation: *An account of my hut*, trans. Keene, Penguin Books, 1968 (*Anthology of Japanese Literature*).

Kawabata Yasunari (1899–). Novelist. All Kawabata's work is touched with a sense of deprivation, the result of an unusually sad childhood. He lost both his parents, his sister, and his grandmother when he was very small, and his grandfather, the only close relative left to bring him up, died when he was sixteen. *Diary of a Sixteen-year Old*, written at the time, tells with a calm sadness how he nursed the old man, by now almost totally blind, till his death.

His mother's family helped him to finish his education. After graduating from Tokyo University, where he studied first English then Japanese literature, Kawabata shared in the launching of a new journal, *Bungei Jidai* (Age of the Arts), in company with a group of young writers who became known as the 'Neo-Sensualists'. The group thus unhappily labelled (the Japanese term, it should be said, is far less precise) rejected both the naturalism that had persisted since early in the century despite the popularity of such writers as Natsume Sōseki and Mushakōji Saneatsu, and aimed at a new style based on startling images and *haiku*-like suggestiveness, though it also owed something to European influences, including Surrealism (*cf* Kawabata's *One Arm*, trans. Seidensticker in *Japan Quarterly*, XIV–1, 1967). *The Izu Dancer* was one of Kawabata's first stories to appear in *Bungei Jidai*. It is a simple but exquisite piece, based on a brief encounter with a young girl member of a troupe of travelling entertainers Kawabata had met on a trip to the Izu Peninsula seven years before, while still a high-school student. With *Snow Country* (serialised between 1935 and 1937, but not published in book form till 1947) (trans. Seidensticker, Tokyo and New York, 1957), Kawabata's art reached its maturity. In this beautiful story of a country geisha's love for a Tokyo dilettante, set among the cold purity of snow-covered mountains, the girl Komako is at once simple geisha and a modern re-creation of Kannon, the Buddhist Goddess of Mercy, presiding over a remote, tranquil world – it is not surprising, indeed, that though there is nothing overtly religious (in the western sense of the term) about Kawabata, the word often recurs in Japanese discussion of his work. 'His novels emit a certain smell. The smell of the man himself. The smell of a Buddhist consciousness' is one comment. It is a consciousness much concerned with tranquillity, with certain kinds of beauty, with the narrow dividing-line between life and death. Kawabata has described the Buddhist scriptures as being for him the greatest *literature* in the world.

Militarism and the war hardly touched him. Defeat, however, was a profound shock. 'I felt myself to be no longer living, a corpse buried under autumn leaves,' he wrote in 1948. 'I had no life left in the "real" world. . . . Sadness had always been present in my life; the defeat merely drove this sadness deeper into my being, but strangely this brought me a new freedom and security. Such years as I have left to me I feel, quite naturally, not to be "mine"; they have been lent to me as a means to the re-expression of the Japanese tradition of beauty.' In these words lies the clue to all Kawabata's writing. Some idea of the nature of the sadness and beauty of which he speaks can be gained from such post-war novels as *Thousand Cranes* (1949–51) (trans. Seidensticker, London, 1959) and *The Sound of the Mountain* (1949–53) (extracts trans. Seidensticker in *Japan Quarterly*, XI–4, 1964). *The Sound of the Mountain*, Kawabata's own favourite, consists, in the typical Kawabata manner, of a series of short scenes ('dumplings on a skewer', the technique has been called) in the domestic life of an elderly Tokyo business-man and his family – wholly contemporary material, yet suffused with the feeling for nature and the unsentimental awareness of the 'pity of things' that is the ground of so much of classical Japanese culture. Kawabata is a profound admirer not merely of the sutras, but of Japanese classical and medieval literature. In 1968 he became the first Japanese writer (and the second Asian, after Tagore) to win the Nobel Prize. Characteristically, the lecture, 'Japan, the Beautiful, and Myself', which he delivered in Stockholm on receiving the award is more concerned with centuries-old Zen poetry and painting than with any of the burning issues of 'modern' literature. In his work he has achieved the remarkable feat of expressing, in a style and with characters that are strictly of the present, a classical sensibility. The effect of reading him is suggested by a younger Japanese contemporary, who compares his reactions after reading Sartre and Kawabata: 'One feels tension and excitement in both cases, but with Sartre it is the excitement of being drawn inexorably, struggling, into a vortex – with

Kawabata, the strange, penetrating tension that comes from slowly steeping one's face in ice-cold water. . . .'

The Mole, trans. Seidensticker in *MJL.*

The Moon on the Water, trans. Saito in *MJS.*

The House of the Sleeping Beauties, and other stories (includes, besides the title piece, *One Arm* and *Of Birds and Beasts*), trans. Seidensticker, London, 1969.

Ki Tsurayuki (*c* 870–946), poet, anthologist and diarist. Details are lacking of his private life. He was deeply involved in the compilation of *Kokinwakashū* (*qv*), which appeared in 905. He wrote for this collection its Japanese preface, the first piece of critical writing in this language, which established the aesthetic standards and accepted subjects and techniques which were to be valid for centuries to come. A considerable number of poems by Ki Tsurayuki have been preserved, and in these he shows considerable competence, but no outstanding genius.

As with most men at the court Ki Tsurayuki had to put in a period of service in the provinces. In the early years of the decade 930–40, he was in Tosa (in Shikoku) as governor, and in 936 he returned to the capital after his spell of duty. He has left an account of his journey home in *Tosa Nikki* (The Tosa diary). This was a period when men tended to write in Chinese, and in order to justify his choice of Japanese as a medium, he pretended that it was written by a serving-woman in his establishment. The hazards of the sea journey included storms, inability to navigate by night, and pirates, and the direct narrative reveals the terrors of the delicately-nurtured court-folk. It thus gives some account of conditions and ways of feeling at the time, and demonstrates a humanity which appeals to the modern western reader.

Translation: *The Tosa Diary* (extract) trans. Keene, Penguin Books, 1968 (*Anthology of Japanese Literature*).

Kinoshita Junji (1914–). Dramatist. He had originally intended to become a historian of drama, but turned to writing plays himself as an outlet for his keen social conscience. Since the war, while teaching English literature in a number of universities in Tokyo, he has established himself as one of the most influential figures in the Japanese theatre-world.

Two main motifs run through his work, both of them traceable, it seems, to his school years in the island of Kyushu – the most conservative region of Japan, where both feudal attitudes and the old folk-culture have survived longer than elsewhere. One is a left-wing political commitment: some of his plays deal overtly with political issues such as Japanese resistance to the US-Japan Security Treaty or the campaign for the return to Japan of Okinawa. *Winds and Waves*, the first play he wrote (it was completed in 1939, the day before he joined the army as a conscript, but was not published till 1947) is of this kind. Concerned with the post-Restoration upheavals in Kyushu, it shows Kinoshita's deep interest in the social and psychological, as well as the political effects of modernisation. The second motif is the use of folk-lore as material for drama. Of Kinoshita's numerous experiments in this field, *Twilight Crane* (1949) (trans. Scott in *Playbook*, New York, 1956) is the best-known. Like the classical Nō and Kabuki, it suffers in translation; but like them also, it conveys something of the essential quality of the Japanese poetic imagination, yet in a modern dramatic form, using modern speech and characters no larger than life.

But Kinoshita's leading position in the development of drama since the war has resulted above all from his concern with the theory and techniques of drama. His determination, in fact, to take drama seriously, both as an art form and as a criticism of life. The lack of this respect for the form has hindered the emergence of an effective 'modern' drama in Japan since its introduction into the country in the early years of the present century.

Kinoshita Naoe (1869–1937). One of the first, and in potential, at least, the best, of Japan's many politically committed novelists. For ten years from about 1897 he was intensely active as one of a small group of idealists campaigning against the growing authoritarianism and chauvinism of the Meiji bureaucracy; but in the end the severity with which the government stamped on every manifestation of socialism or pacifism, however small-scale, broke his faith in both politics and literature, and for the last thirty years of his life his principal interest was the Seiza-kai (Society for Sitting in Silent Meditation), which at one time had seventy-seven groups throughout the country. This pattern of early and passionate commitment to ideology followed in later life by a retreat into silence, or at most, into the writing of contemplative, semi-religious novels, is common to a number of modern Japanese authors, who have often – particularly before 1945 – felt themselves to be impotent to comment on a society so many of whose assumptions they rejected. In this respect their lives have repeated in a modern context the 'withdrawal from the world' of the medieval Buddhist poets and essayists.

Kinoshita's first and best-known novel, *Pillar of Fire* (English translation in progress for the UNESCO *Collection of Contemporary Works*), appeared first in 1904, but for many years every edition was heavily censored; a complete version did not become available till 1950. Written in the midst of the popular clamour for war with Russia, it has for its hero a non-violent Christian socialist and newspaper-editor, whose exposure of the corruption of Meiji capitalism and the stupidity of war isolates him in turn from his church and from the workers he has championed, and in the end leads inevitably to his arrest. It is more tightly constructed than most Japanese novels, while the author's sincerity and courage make themselves felt with sufficient power to offset the excessive simplicity – by more modern standards – of the characterisation and the dialogue.

Kitamura Tōkoku (1868–94). Poet and essayist. Japanese literary historians now speak of Kitamura as one of the founding fathers of the country's modern literature, though for two generations after his death he was either ignored or despised as 'unpatriotic'. The epoch-making journal *Bungakkai* (Literary World), which was started by a group of young writers in 1893 as the organ of the short-lived Japanese Romantic Movement, owed much to his inspiration. Combining a passionate temperament with mystical leanings, together with a sharp sense of social injustice and of the superficiality of much of the headlong westernisation of the time, he strove to reconcile with the ugly world he saw about him the visions of beauty, freedom and justice he found in such writers as Byron, Wordsworth, Shelley, Emerson, and in the life of Ninomiya Sontoku, the Japanese saint and practical reformer of the early nineteenth century, whom he revered as a 'Japanese George Fox'. The lofty ethical ideal of Christianity fascinated him (Zen, it may be noted, he dismissed with Zennish brevity: 'Zen is no good – it blocks the imagination'), as did the concept of romantic love. Yet he remained very Japanese in his eclecticism, in the intensity of his attempt to live out the ideals of two radically different cultures. In the end the strain proved too great. At the age of twenty-five, after an unsuccessful attempt some months earlier to cut his throat, he hanged himself in the garden of his Tokyo home.

For Kitamura there were no models in the earlier literature of his own country, as there were for the English Romantics, to which he could turn for example and refreshment. Partly for this reason, his poems, stories and essays lack artistic maturity. They are nevertheless a most vivid record of the white-heat impact of western romanticism on the Japanese spirit, and the mirror of an impressive personality.

The Magic Mirror, trans. Strong, *MN*, XXI, 3–4, 1966.

MATHY, F. *Kitamura Tōkoku, the early years, MN*, XVIII, 1–4, 1963.
MATHY, F. *Kitamura Tōkoku, Essays on the inner life, MN*, XIX, 1–2, 1964.
MATHY, F. *Kitamura Tōkoku, final essays, MN*, XX, 1–2, 1965.

Kobayashi Takiji (1903–33). His family, once prosperous farmers, had fallen on bad times before Takiji was born. When he was five they moved from Akita Prefecture, in the north of the main island of Honshu, to the still bleaker shores of Hokkaido, and opened a small bread-shop in Otaru. After working his way through the local Commercial College Takiji joined the staff of the Development Bank; but writing was his main preoccupation. Though he admired Shiga Naoya, Dostoevsky and Gorky were a stronger influence, and from the beginning he concerned himself with the plight of the underdogs in Japanese society – first women, and then the workers – acquiring in the process a Marxist outlook which came before long to dominate both his life and his writing. In 1929 he was dismissed from the bank for his political activities. Later the same year he published *The Cannery Boat* (extract trans. anonymously in *MJL*), which led to his arrest and imprisonment on charges of communism and lèse-majesté. After his release, though driven underground by the intensifying persecution of all left-wing activities, Kobayashi continued to work indefatigably to organise resistance to totalitarianism. Before long, though, he was again arrested, and tortured to death in a Tokyo police station. His final novel, *Men Who Lead the Party Life*, was published posthumously. Kobayashi has been revered ever since as a martyr of the resistance – few writers during the rise of Japanese fascism dared to defy authority so openly – and as a central figure in the movement of the late twenties and early thirties, abortive but pursued with great tenacity till it was crushed along with all other manifestations of dissidence, to create a 'proletarian' literature. *The Cannery Boat*, a story of the exploitation of students and farm boys tricked into manning a floating cannery during their summer holidays, and of their revolt, on hearing of communism from some Russians in Kamchatka, exemplifies the uneasy marriage in the 'proletarian' writers of passionate feeling with a naively political view of the function of literature.

Kyokutei Bakin (1767–1848), novelist. He was a professional intellectual. Of warrior rank, he earned his living, precariously at times, in many ways, but is best remembered now for his *yomi-hon* 'reading books' (see Ueda Akinari), although his collections of antiquarian materials are still of use. Of his *yomi-hon*, the best known is *Nansō Satomi Hakkenden* (The biographies of eight dogs), a story of loyalty and military prowess involving eight heroes, in each of whose name the word for dog is included, and who are figuratively descended from a noble hound. All his *yomi-hon* involved immensely complicated plots, often derived from Chinese originals, and the language he uses is extremely intricate, with much interconnection of strands of meaning, and an immense vocabulary. He is the typical author of works demonstrating the defeat of evil and the triumph of virtue. Once considered a novelist second only to Murasaki Shikubu (*qv*), he is now thought of as much less interesting than Ihara Saikaku (*qv*). Zolbrod (*Takizawa Bakin*, New York, 1967) has written an English biography.

Masaoka Shiki (1867–1902). Poet. His father having died when he was six, Masaoka was brought up by his grandfather, a Confucian scholar formerly in the service of the Lord of Matsuyama in the island of Shikoku. His early education followed strictly classical lines, and much of his early poetry is in Chinese. Political ambitions, fired by the 'popular rights' movement (which was at its height during his school years, and particularly strong in Shikoku) quickly faded, and apart from two unsuccessful excursions into novel-writing poetry filled the rest of his short but feverishly active life. Active service in the Sino-Japanese War of 1894–5 aggravated a previous tendency to tuberculosis. From then on till the final stage of the disease, when he was nursed round the clock by his many disciples, he was rarely out of bed, though his creative energy never flagged.

While Shimazaki Tōson (*qv*) and Kitamura Tōkoku (*qv*) were experimenting with 'new-style' verse under western influence, it was Masaoka's achievement to revitalise traditional poetic forms that had long been in decline – the seventeen-syllable *haiku* by the freshness of his language and poetic outlook, and his refusal to worship uncritically at the shrine of Matsuo Bashō (*qv*), and the thirty-one-syllable *tanka* by his advocacy of a return to the style of the *Man-yōshū* (*qv*), less contrived and 'more purely Japanese' than that of the hitherto authoritative *Kokinshū* (*qv*). In keeping with this preference for the 'Man-yō spirit', towards the end of his life Masaoka preached *shasei*, literally 'direct copying from life' (which, though never clearly defined, is closer to the 'contemplation of things in order to see into their true nature' practised in Japanese and Chinese art and religion, than to what the West understands by 'realism') and started a vogue for *shaseibun*, short prose sketches in a detached, contemplative style. Many poets and novelists were influenced by his ideas and example, in particular his friend Natsume Sōseki (*qv*).

The Verse Record of My Illness, trans. Miner in *Japan Quarterly*, XII–2, 1965. Some of Masaoka's *haiku*, trans. Henderson, appear in *MJL*.

Matsuo Bashō (1644–94), writer of *haiku* and travel diaries. *Haiku* had originated in the first half-verse of *renga* (see *Fūgashū*); this was called *hokku* ('starting verse'), and was normally composed by the senior poet taking part. It had, by rule, to include a reference to a season, either direct or indirect (*eg* the mention of cherry blossom indicated spring); it gradually became established as an independent form. Until the middle of the seventeenth century it tended to be comic in sentiment, although some attempt was made from time to time to write serious poetry in the form.

The town of Ueno in the province of Iga had a small castle, and Bashō, born in the town, was assigned to the lord's son as a companion. They learned together all the things that a young lord had to learn, including the composition of *haiku*. In 1666 his young master died, and Bashō left the castle, becoming a masterless warrior. After a short period of drifting, he travelled to Edo (the Tokugawa capital, now Tokyo), and settled down to a mainly literary life. The dominant school of *haiku* was that of Danrin, with a tendency to the comic, and Bashō applied himself to studying its style. For a time a sinecure found for him by a fellow disciple of his old poetry teacher provided him with an income. By 1680 his reputation as a poet was increasing, and his pupils were collecting his poems and publishing them. About this time he took up his abode in what is now a crowded Tokyo suburb, at Fukagawa, then in the country. There a patron allowed him to live in a hut, which come to be known as Bashō-an (Banana-tree retreat) from a decorative banana-tree that he was given to plant beside his door. From this he took the name by which he is most commonly known.

From then his life took on the pattern it was to keep until his death. Periods of residence at Fukagawa, where he taught his pupils, maintained contact with other poets, and had lessons in other arts, were interspersed with journeys to distant parts of Japan. The travel diaries that he wrote for these trips form some of the most appealing of his literary productions. He comments in a deceptively simple way on the various places he passes through, mentions the poets and friends he meets, and whenever he espies a scene or situation that inspires him, he writes a *haiku.* Many of his most enduring poems derive from such diaries, and often acquire a far deeper significance when removed from their context. The account of his journey to northern Japan, *Oku no hosomichi* (The narrow road of Oku) is the best known of these, and has been translated by Keene in his Anthology.

Bashō transformed *haiku* from a rather whimsical, frivolous genre into a vehicle for a poet of genius which could summon up a whole scene by the mention of a salient detail, and add to it the flavour of astringency and the feel of patina characteristic of the Zen sect of Buddhism, whose teachers he followed. His subjects are almost always the non-human components of nature under his observation. Later writers were to extend these to other periods of time, and to human relationships, but there is no doubt that the *haiku* form reached its zenith with him.

Translations: All anthologies of Japanese verse in translation contain examples by Bashō. Two more specialist works are Henderson, *An Introduction to haiku,* New York 1958, and Hisamatsu, *Haiku and haibun*, Tokyo.

Mishima Yukio (1925–70). Novelist and playwright. Mishima wrote his first novel at the age of thirteen, and published his first collection of short stories in 1944, the year he entered Tokyo University. After taking a degree in law he went into government service, but resigned after eight months to write full-time. His output was enormous, hardly a year passing without his producing at least one best-seller.

Though he did not see active service in the Pacific War (he was called up in 1945, but sent home the same day), Mishima's youth was conditioned by it, and for several years after the defeat his writing reflected the sense of betrayal and isolation of his generation. Examples are the semi-autobiographical *Confessions of a Mask* (1949) (trans. Weatherby, London, 1960), the record of awakening sexuality in a lonely, introspective youth during and after a war, *Thirst for Love* (1950) (trans. Marks, published in London, 1969), about a love-deprived woman who is driven to commit murder, and *Forbidden Colours* (1951) (trans. Marks, London, 1968), a long – and, one is tempted to say, loving – exploration of the world of homosexuality; though in the light of some of his more recent work, mentioned below, the homosexuality of *Forbidden Colours* may seem to stand for more than the probing into hitherto off-limits areas of a generation morally disinherited by war. Mishima's characteristic qualities – aestheticism, a fascination with unusual psychological states, an ornate style, rich in imagery and at times almost wearisomely paradoxical – abound in these earlier novels.

The restrained lyrical beauty of *The Sound of Waves* (1954) (trans. Weatherby, Tokyo, 1956), the love-story of a young Japanese fisherman, is less typical. Mishima describes it as a 'Japanese Daphnis and Chloe', the fruit of a round-the-world journey in 1951, when he fell in love, temporarily at least, with the mythology and humanism of classical Greece. *The Temple of the Golden Pavilion* (1956) (trans. Morris, Tokyo, 1956) is a dramatic display of Mishima's skill in taking an actual incident (in this case the burning to the ground in 1950, by a neurotic young acolyte, of the five-hundred year old Kinkakuji Temple, one of the most perfect artworks in Japan) and making it the basis of a complex, many-layered fiction. Told with incomparable power, the story can be read as implying a total rejection of Japan's pre-modern culture, as a study in the pathology of a frustrated individual, as an allegory of the tragic relationship between art and life, or even as a case-study of the origins of violence. There is some evidence that Mishima has become increasingly attracted by the 'pure beauty' of violent action performed by men of total dedication, whether neurotic or not. The trilogy *Voices of Dead Heroes* (1966) is concerned with the patriotic young officers who assassinated several of the country's leaders in the February 26 Incident of 1936. In one of the three parts, which is modelled on a Nō play, the spirits of the young officers of 1936 and of the suicide-pilots of 1945 speak through a medium of their bitterness that the purity of their sacrifice had been betrayed on both occasions by the emperor, who thereby showed himself unworthy of his divinity. The second, which may revolt the western reader even while he is compelled to admire the controlled power of the writing (trans. in *Death in Midsummer and Other Stories*, London, 1967), is a detailed description of the ceremonial suicide of an army officer (and of his young wife after him) who prefers death to the prospect of being ordered to attack his 'patriotic' colleagues who have taken part in the February 26 assassinations.

The same affirmation of the beauty and value of 'pure' action is evident in *The Sailor Who Fell from Grace with the Sea* (1963) (trans. Nathan, London, 1966), whose hero betrays the sea, with its challenge of 'glory and death', by fancying he could find fulfilment with a woman. It is easy to see a homosexual implication here, particularly since Mishima had already dealt specifically with this theme in *Forbidden Colours*, and in one other novel also. One may well feel, however, that more light was shed on this novel (and on *Voices of Dead Heroes*) by Mishima's dramatic death in November 1970, when he committed ritual *harakiri* after breaking into a Tokyo barracks and haranguing the soldiers on the moral corruption and materialism of postwar Japan, and the need to return to a pure, Emperor-centred patriotism. From his youthful nihilism, Mishima appears to have moved to a whole-hearted acceptance of pre-modern, samurai values. His death stunned the Japanese, but as yet there has been little serious attempt to assess its significance.

For his talent is certainly extraordinary and wide-ranging. Other themes too numerous to list appear in his novels besides those mentioned. *After the Banquet* (1960) (trans. Keene, London, 1963), for example, presents the conflict between nature and principle, in the shape of a middle-aged woman restaurant-owner and the elderly politician who marries and tries, unsuccessfully, to educate her. Mishima has also written a large number of plays, which show his usual brilliance of language and a tauter dramatic construction than most Japanese playwrights can command (*eg Tropical Tree*, trans. Strong in *Japan Quarterly*, XI–2, 1964). Finally there are his highly original 'modern Nō' plays, which are not simply the classical Nō in modern dress, but experimental combinations of freely adapted Nō plots with contemporary characters and situations.

Five Modern Noh Plays, trans. Keene, New York, 1957.

The Marquise de Sade (play), trans. Keene, London, 1968.

Miyazawa Kenji (1896–1933). Poet and story-teller. Unknown in his life-time, Miyazawa's name is now universally honoured, as much for the quality of his life as for his writings. The eldest son of a prosperous pawnbroker in Iwate Prefecture in north-east Japan, he showed no desire to enter his father's business. After graduating top of his class from the Agricultural Chemistry Department of the Morioka Agricultural High School (or as we would say, College), he stayed on to teach and carry out research in soil science. At home, however, there was friction. From his primary school years Miyazawa had been reading with growing fascination the Buddhist scriptures, in particular the Lotus Sutra, the sacred book of the Nichiren Sect. For generations the family had been adherents of the Pure Land Sect. When Kenji insisted the time had come for them all to change to Nichiren, his father not only refused, but forbade him to recite the Nichiren scriptures in the house. Rather than compromise, early in 1921 Kenji left home for Tokyo. There too much of his time was spent studying Buddhism, but soon he began to write, stimulated by the desire to give artistic expression to his understanding of Buddhism, by the idealism of the *Shirakaba* group (see under Mushakōji Saneatsu), and by the appearance of a number of magazines devoted to literature for young people, to which he felt particularly drawn. On hearing of his sister's serious illness, however, he returned home after less than a year in the capital; and for the next six years taught at Hienuki Agricultural High School, where he is remembered as a brilliant and beloved educator. In 1924 he brought out at his own expense the only two books he published in his life-time, one volume of verse and another of children's stories. Two years later, Miyazawa gave up formal teaching to work on the land himself. For the rest of his life this poet-agriculturalist devoted himself to sharing the lives of the poor farmers among whom he had grown up – with a harsh climate, poor soil, and no capital, the north-east region of Japan has for centuries been one of the country's depressed areas – acting as universal, and often unpaid, technical adviser, organising community self-help, writing and producing plays of peasant life to give the peasants self-respect, teaching their young men music, and continuing all the while to record them and their lives and the wild beauty of their land in poem and story. Twice he broke down from exhaustion: the most famous, though not the best, of his poems, *Not Yielding to the Rain* (trans. Bownas and Thwaite in *Penguin Book of Japanese Verse*, London, 1964), describing 'the man I should like to be', was written during his second illness, which eventually proved fatal. After his death, in accordance with instructions in his will, a thousand copies of the Lotus Sutra were distributed among his friends.

Miyazawa's many-sided personality – he was at once religious mystic, scientist, teacher and philanthropist, poet, practical farmer, and a man of quiet happiness throughout a hard and frugal life – is reflected in all he wrote. His stories, though described as 'children's literature' by his category-loving countrymen, are as universal in their appeal as Andersen's; his poetry, admittedly less translatable, distils with clarity, humility and humour the essence of his Buddhist faith and of the beauty and suffering around him.

Winds and Wildcat Places (Stories), trans. Bester, Tokyo, 1967.

Some of Miyazawa's poems have been translated by Ninomiya and Enright in *The Poetry of Living Japan*, London, 1967, and by Gary Snyder in *A Range of Poems*, London, 1966.

Mori Ōgai (1862–1922). Novelist, poet (in both Japanese and Chinese), translator, army doctor and administrator, polymath; one of the most outstanding personalities of the modern period. Scion of a family of hereditary physicians serving a feudal lord in western Japan, Mori graduated from the medical school of Tokyo University at the age of nineteen, and decided to become a surgeon in the new Imperial Army. Before long he was sent to Germany, where he studied not only medicine but German literature, aesthetics and philosophy for nearly four years at the universities of Leipzig, Munich and Berlin. After his return to Japan promotion was rapid and continuous, till he had served successively as Commandant of the Army Medical College, Director of the Medical Bureau of the War Ministry, and Surgeon-General. Following his voluntary retirement from the army in 1916, he was appointed Director of the Imperial Museum and Library and Head of the Imperial Institute of Fine Arts.

Paralleling his brilliant military career, Mori's numerous critical and philosophical articles, and his translations from German and English prose, poetry and drama, played a leading part in fostering Japanese knowledge and understanding of western culture. His creative writings, too, were exceedingly influential, providing, together with the work of his younger contemporary, Natsume Sōseki (*qv*) a counterbalance to the somewhat crude, half-digested naturalism that swept literary circles soon after the turn of the century. Yet a question-mark seems to hang over this life of such apparently great achievement. A clue is provided by his moving short story, *The Dancing Girl* (1890), published soon after his return from Germany, and based on his own experiences abroad. Ōta Toyotarō, studying in Berlin on a Japanese Government scholarship, falls in love with an unfortunate German dancer, and goes to live with her and her mother – as a result of which he is deprived of his scholarship and ostracised by the Japanese community. Later he reluctantly accepts an offer, made through the good offices of an old friend, of reinstatement and an official career in Japan, provided he gives up the girl, who by now is pregnant. She goes mad from the shock of his betrayal. Ota leaves her, bound by his duty to his family and country to do so, but hating the friend who has made it possible. The story is thus a *Madame Butterfly* in reverse, but with a deeper, symbolic meaning. There is no doubt that Mori was deeply impressed with western culture, and excited by its theories of freedom and democracy: yet in contrast to Natsume Sōseki (*qv*) he was by upbringing, temperament and profession too much a part of the ruling autocracy to be able to give unfettered expression to his thought. Hence the note of resignation, the classical poise with a hint of melancholy, that is to be found in much of his fiction. Examples are *The Wild Geese* (1911–13) (trans. Ochiai and Goldstein, Tokyo and Rutland, Vermont, 1959), about a young girl whose happiness is frustrated by the inexplicable workings of chance, and *Takasebune* (1916) (trans. Paschall in *HIA*), a short story in which a warder marvels at the peace of mind of a prisoner on his way to exile. Once at least the conflict found overt expression. The suicide of Mori's friend General Nogi, 'following his lord in loyalty' when the Emperor Meiji died in 1912, inspired him to write in rapid succession two novels from opposite points of view – *The Testament of Okitsu Yagoemon* (1912), lauding the custom of a retainer committing suicide when his lord dies, and *The House of Abe* (1913), bitterly attacking it for the suffering it brings to the retainer's family. Some such inner frustration may help to explain why Mori turned in later life to the safer waters of scholarly historical biography, in which his *Shibue Chūsai* (1916) set a new standard of scientific accuracy and literary elegance. But though he never expressed it in so many words, one may wonder whether to the end of his life Mori did not retain a certain scepticism in relation to the public, authoritarian world in which he lived. His last instructions before dying were that he should be given no military or other honours at his funeral, and that nothing should be carved on his tombstone but his name and the province of his birth.

Sanshō-dayū, trans. Fukuda, Tokyo, 1952.
Under Reconstruction, trans. Morris in *MJS*.
The House of Abe has been trans. into German as 'Der Untergang des Hauses Abe' in Donat, *Die fünfstockige Pagode: japanische Erzählungen des 20 Jahrhunderts*, 1960.

Murasaki Shikibu (978 ?–*c* 1020) novelist and diarist. She lived at the imperial court in Kyoto, and was a member of the great Fujiwara family which at the time wielded the actual power. Her name itself is something of a mystery. *Shikibu* was an office in the court hierarchy, and in her case probably refers to an appointment held by her father. *Murasaki* is the colour purple, and is in the nature of a nickname, derived possibly from the colour of wisteria, the Japanese for which, *fuji*, forms part of the name Fujiwara, or possibly taken from an important character of the same name in her novel. This was written, probably over a period of years early in the eleventh century, to be read to the Empress Akiko and her ladies. Its title *Genji-monogatari* (The tale of Genji), refers to the handsome 'shining prince', Hikaru Genji, who is the hero of the first forty-four chapters of this the most remarkable work in Japanese literature. Its last ten chapters tell the story of Kaoru, whom Genji thought to be his son, though he was in fact the Emperor's. That, in an earlier part of the book, an Emperor had believed his own a son begotten by Genji gives a nice touch of dramatic irony.

The novel gives a feminine view of life at the court, where women played moreover a very important part (at a time too when women writers were predominant). There was clearly a constant sexual tension between the large number of ladies in waiting, attendants, and, indeed consorts, and the many male officials, and aristocrats, whose duties often left them much leisure to pursue the traditional rituals and entertainments in the fields of religion, dance, poetry, music and excursions, and also to carry on love affairs at many levels, ranging from mere flirtation to nearly permanent cohabitation. All these were conducted with due regard to the intricate etiquette of the court, and used the sending and receipt of specially composed verse, written on paper of appropriate design and accompanied by appropriate flowers or leaves. Through these barely fictionalised surroundings moves the hero, preoccupied with love, indulging in short affairs, having a succession of titular wives, even bringing up a girl in an attempt to form his ideal of womanhood. A less happy aspect was the early age at which his wives died, often saddened by the spiteful treatment they had from the women around them, and harried on their deathbeds by the jealous ghosts of their predecessors. The general tone of melancholy which pervades the book, and in which nature and humanity reflect each other, demonstrates one aspect of *mono no aware*, the contemporary prevalent aesthetic theme of empathy between author and subject.

The subtle descriptions of character, background and motive which characterise this novel are greatly assisted by its language, which reflects the speech of the time. This has a great number of degrees of politeness and other indications of the class and social relations of the speakers, which make it difficult of full comprehension today. Waley's translation (*The Tale of Genji*, London, 1965) is well on the way to being as great a work as the original, and is highly recommended to those ready to undertake the reading of a work of considerable length.

The author was descended from a literary family, and her ability was demonstrated at an early age when she sat in on her brother's Chinese lessons, and learned, it is said, faster than he. This was an unusual feat at a time when Chinese studies were a male prerogative. In 999 she married a man who was older than she; this marriage was brought to an end in two years by his death. Their one child, a daughter, was to have some literary fame on her own account. In 1007 Murasaki entered the service of the Empress Akiko. We can read an account of this stage of her life, with revealing but sometimes caustic comments on her contemporaries, in her diary; it is a valuable document for the study of the sentiments and inter-relationships of the 'World of the Shining Prince', so well described in Morris's book of this title (London, 1964).

Mushakōji Saneatsu (1885–). Novelist and playwright. The son of a viscount, Mushakoji attended Tokyo University and the Peers College. While a student at the latter, he founded the journal *Shirakaba* (White Birch), which rapidly became a focus for the idealism of a group of young writers who were tired of the gloomy naturalism to which most of the novelists of the day (with the exception of Mori Ōgai (*qv*) and Natsume Sōseki (*qv*)) still subscribed. The journal continued to appear till the great earthquake of 1923. Though Arishima Takeo (*qv*) and Shiga Naoya (*qv*), who had been his enthusiastic helpers in the launching of *Shirakaba*, grew dissatisfied before long and left the journal to go their own ways, Mushakōji has never abandoned his early faith – a simple optimistic humanism, owing a good deal to Christianity and to such western writers as Tolstoy and Maeterlinck. For several reasons this principal quality of his has never seemed foreign to his Japanese readers, and even now he is widely read. The philosophy of the *Shirakaba* group coincided with the mood of confidence to which the nation as a whole had attained after the first hectic decades of modernisation, and with the first serious gropings towards bourgeois democracy. It also reflects the attitude to life of countless ordinary Japanese, which contrary to much western supposition is resilient and positive. Mushakōji's style matched his matter perfectly: he wrote with a simplicity that verges on the naive. Unfortunately, owing to the difference between the Japanese and English languages, this impression of naivete is even stronger in translation that in the original. *Friendship* (1919), (trans. Matsumoto, Tokyo, 1958), a typical Mushakōji novel, in which the hero is disappointed in love but quickly overcomes his disappointment, illustrates this tendency to naivete both in style and thought. Occasionally the dramatic form serves Mushakōji better: *Three Cheers for Man* (trans. Strong in *Japan Quarterly*, X–1, 1963), a comic fantasy about God, Man and the Angels, is one of his most successful pieces.

At the end of the Pacific War Mushakoji was appointed to the House of Peers as an 'Imperial nominee', but was purged soon after for his support of the war effort. Undeterred, he continued to write in the same vein as before, founding a new journal with some friends in 1948. *Dr Truth*, one of his major works and a summing-up of his lifelong philosophy, appeared the following year. He has also written voluminously on western painting.

Some of Mushakōji's Japanese critics have charged him with shallowness and an upper-class dilettantism, out of touch with real life. This is hardly fair. In 1918 he put his ideas to the test by founding in a remote corner of south-west Japan a Tolstoyan agricultural community, which proved more successful than many similar western ventures, and lived in it himself for eight years, contributing all his literary earnings to its upkeep. Twenty-one years later he started a second such community near Tokyo.

'Judas' Explanation' and *'John, on hearing Judas' Explanation'*, trans. McKinnon in *HIA*.

Bodhidharma, I don't know either and *Monk Ikkyu*, trans. Hirano in *Buddhist Plays from Japanese Literature*, Tokyo, 1962.

Nagai Kafū (1879–1959). Novelist. He was a native of Tokyo. After some academic study of Chinese at the Tokyo University of Foreign Languages, he attached himself as a disciple to the novelist Hirotsu Ryūrō, and took training with other private teachers in several of the traditional arts of the Edo period, including balladry, flute-playing, classical dance, and oral story-telling. Before long, French literature attracted his interest; his translations from Zola, and several of his earlier, French-influenced novels were responsible in part for the vogue of naturalism in Japan. In 1903 his father, hoping to make a business-man of him, sent Nagai to America, where he spent five and a half years, ostensibly as an employee of the Yokohama Specie Bank, but dividing most of his time between writing and women. There being evidently no hope of his taking up an orthodox career, he was allowed to visit his beloved France for a few months before returning to Japan in 1908. A flood of novels and stories followed, almost uninterrupted till shortly before his death.

Despite his worship of French literature, Nagai's work is more Japanese in essence that of any other modern writer except Kawabata Yasunari (*qv*). From *The River Sumida* (1909) (trans. Keene in *MJL*) onwards it is characterised by a profound nostalgia for the old Edo culture that was disappearing before his eyes – its teahouses, its courtesans, its diverse arts, its street life, its love of beauty, its response to the changing seasons; a nostalgia that is redeemed from sentimentality by the concreteness with which he embodies the essence of the old culture in his writing, and by the genuineness and depth of his own love of it. No other Japanese writer has so captured the flavour of a city, of a civilisation, that has now vanished. Yet in his very lack of compromise with the modern there is a flaw. Nagai was most at home in the gay quarters. Many of the characters in his novels (which are often semi-autobiographical prose-poems rather than novels of the western type) are prostitutes or geishas, and there is in his attitude to them a self-indulgence, a readiness to use them unthinkingly for his own entertainment or pleasure, that jars today. Which is only another way of saying, perhaps, that Nagai's picture of Edo culture is remarkably true to reality.

Outstanding examples of his work are *Quiet Rain* (1921) and *A Strange Tale from East of the River* (1937). Translations of these and other stories are available in E. Seidensticker's *Kafū the Scribbler: The Life and Writings of Nagai Kafū* (Stanford, 1965), the only full-length study of a modern Japanese writer to appear in English so far.

Natsume Sōseki (1867–1916). Novelist, possibly the greatest of the modern period. The fifth – and unwanted – son of a family of merchants whose fortunes were in decline, his father sent him out to be adopted at the age of two, but took him back again, reluctantly, when his adoptive parents separated seven years later. After an early education centred on Chinese, he turned to the study of English, as the best preparation for a writer's career (against the advice of his father and elder brother, who took the still common view that writers were 'frivolous'), and graduated in 1893 from the English Literature Department of Tokyo University. Some years of teaching in Tokyo and the provinces followed. In 1900 the Japanese government sent him to England on a scholarship. Outwardly, the trip was not a success. Fifteen years older than the average English student, and too shy and poor to mix easily with the English 'gentlemen' the Japanese of the day held in such exaggerated admiration, he could find little to like about England, and spent most of his time shut up in his lodgings reading. These years of concentrated study abroad convinced Sōseki of the futility of slavishly imitating western cultural forms, as many of his countrymen were doing, but they also taught him the full significance of the novel as an artistic instrument for the analysis of man and society; a lesson which decided him to attempt within the conditions of his own culture what western novelists had achieved within theirs. On his return to Japan he taught again for four years, succeeding to the lectureship at Tokyo University that had been held immediately before him by Lafcadio Hearn. His resignation from the University in 1907 caused a minor sensation, such was the prestige of the scholar's life he was abandoning; but dissatisfaction with the hierarchical atmosphere of the University led him to accept an offer from the Asahi newspaper that would assure his independence, the only condition being that his novels should be serialised in its pages.

For by now he was already a well-known author in a variety of styles. *I Am a Cat* (trans. Shibata and Kai, Tokyo, 1961) an over-long but revealing satire, from a feline point of view, of Japanese life and attitudes, had appeared in Masaoka Shiki's *haiku* journal *Cuckoo* in 1905–6. *Botchan* (1906) (trans. Sasaki, Rutland, Vermont and Tokyo, 1968; extract, trans. Watson, in *MJL*) followed, the tragi-comic record of a naive young Tokyo teacher's experiences in a provincial school. *Kusamakura* (trans. Turney as *The Three-Cornered World*, London, 1965), published in the same year, is of quite another kind: a 'novel in the manner of the *haiku*', Natsume called it (though it is hardly a novel in the western sense), in which plot and characters are deliberately subordinated to the atmosphere of beauty and calm created around them. It is a remarkable work, close to the long Japanese tradition of what has been called the 'discursive lyric'.

But Sōseki was not content with lyricism. It is on the eight novels, the last of them unfinished, which he wrote between 1908 and his death in 1916 that his fame principally rests. The theme of all of them, particularly *The Gate*

(1910), *The Wayfarer* (1912–13) (trans. Yu, Detroit, 1967), *Kokoro* (trans. McClellan, Chicago, 1956), and *Light and Dark* (published posthumously), is loneliness – the loneliness of a morally sensitive Japanese, freed at last from centuries of living by rule and convention, only to find himself imprisoned in his own egoism. *Kokoro* (literally – 'Heart'; a better translation is the title of the French version, *Le Pauvre Coeur des Hommes*, trans. Horiguchi and Bonneau, Paris, 1957), the most famous of the series, describes the tragic failure of a man who in his youth had betrayed his best friend to find a moral basis for living. Fully realised individuals though they are, Natsume's suffering characters are also symbols of the strain imposed by 'modernisation' on a country which, as he said, had had to absorb in forty years what western countries had needed three centuries to assimilate. And because the spiritual crisis through which Natsume felt himself to be living has more recently afflicted western culture too, his novels, though sometimes of too unrelieved a seriousness for western taste, have at their best a reference far beyond Japan. The hero of *The Wayfarer* can see no way out of the modern dilemma but death, madness, or religion. From *The Gate*, whose hero, seeking enlightenment, knocks on the gate of a Zen temple, only to be refused admission, to *Light and Dark*, there is a discernible progress towards a religious solution of an oriental kind, in the sense of the complete negation of the ego; though critics dispute whether any of Natsume's characters can be said to have attained to the state of *sokuten kyoshi* (conformity to heaven and absence of self) which was Natsume's own avowed aim. Whether he himself attained it has also been a matter of much argument.

La Porte, trans. Martinie, Paris, 1927.

McClellan, 'An Introduction to Soseki', in *HJAS*, XXII, 1959.

Light and Dark (trans. Viglielmo, London, Peter Owen, 1971).

Niwa Fumio (1904–). One of Japan's most prolific and popular contemporary novelists. Born into a family of hereditary priests of the Pure Land sect of Buddhism in the provincial town of Yokkaichi, he himself was ordained as a novice priest at the age of eight, and was expected to take charge in his turn of the ancient temple his forbears had served for more than two centuries. At Waseda University, however, where he specialised in Japanese literature, he conceived an ambition to write; and though on graduating in 1929 he did return home to serve under his father as deputy priest, two years later he walked out of the temple – abruptly and in the middle of the night, to dramatise his break with the family tradition. Since then, except for a quiet period during the war years, when he was drafted as a naval reporter (two of his wartime books were banned) Niwa has produced novels and short stories in rapid succession, most of them enhancing his reputation. Niwa's dominant theme for much of his career has been woman's sensuality. Two special influences seem to have been at work here: the traumatic effect of his abandonment by his mother, who absconded with a lover when he was six, and the traditional Buddhist attitude to sex. In almost every case, however, underlying his exposure of the sensuality of his heroines is a quiet, Buddhist compassion for the suffering to which it so often leads. The religious tone has become more explicit in his later work, as for example in *The Buddha Tree* (1955) (trans. Strong, London, 1966), a long novel about a Buddhist priest's inner struggle to free himself from bondage to the woman who had adopted him as her son twenty years before, and had been his mistress ever since. An earlier work, with the compassion less in evidence, is *The Hateful Age* (1947) (trans. Morris in *MJS*), a study of the nasty habits of an old woman of eighty-six and the trouble they cause her family. By implication it is a plea for greater honesty in the relations between young and old, and less lip-service to filial piety. Written in the first flush of post-war reaction against traditional values, it reflected a change in attitudes which has now established itself in Japanese society.

A Touch of Shyness, trans. Seidensticker, in *Japan Quarterly*, II–1, 1955.

Ōe Kenzaburō (1935–). Leading novelist of the post-war generation. Oe graduated from the French Literature Department of Tokyo University in 1959. While still a student he attracted attention with his short stories, one of which, *The Catch* (trans. Bester in *The Shadow of Sunrise*, ed. Saeki, Tokyo and Palo Alto, 1966) – a horrific account of the encounter of a Japanese boy of ten (Oe's age when the war ended) with an American negro pilot who is shot down over his village and taken prisoner – was awarded the thirty-ninth Akutagawa Prize. Depicting youth in a closed world of frustration, disease, imprisonment and death, his novels have spoken for a generation feeling itself to be cut off from the past more completely than its western counterpart, and driven, in its search for identity, to desperate experiments with sex and violence. At times the rather woolly leftism for which he is well known in Japan seems to vie with serious concern for deeper human issues. In *Seventeen* (1951), a novel based on the assassination by a right-wing youth of the Socialist leader Asanuma Inejirō, it is not clear whether the lonely, masturbating young assassin or the grim truth about the fascist group he joins is the focus of interest. There is no more certainty in *A Personal Matter* (1964) (trans. Nathan, London, 1969). In this novel reality confronts the protagonist, a teacher in a cramming-school, in the shape of his first child, who is born deformed: he dreams of having it killed, of escaping to Africa to fulfil his manhood in a life of freedom and adventurous action (here, and elsewhere in modern fiction, there are hints of nostalgia for the martial world of the samurai and his cult of freedom through action-cum-Zen) but eventually, in a tame if true-to-life ending to a striking book, he accepts domestic responsibilities, and is content to watch a freighter carry his mistress off to Zanzibar without him. (There is a curious parallel here with the ending of a novel that seems at first glance to belong to a totally different world – Mushakōji Saneatsu's (*qv*) *Friendship*.) He even dreams of becoming a guide for foreign tourists. So, in this strictly contemporary novel, traditional imperatives reassert their hold. Despite its title, some critics have seen *A Personal Matter* as an allegory of the emergence of Japan as a stable, mature member of the world community.

Other novels of Ōe include *Screams* (1962) and *Perverts* (1963). More directly than that of any other writer, his work conveys a sense of the tensions behind the facade of economic success, and the intensity of the search by the youth of Japan for identity and significance.

Lavish are the Dead (1957), trans. Nathan in *Japan Quarterly*, XII–2, 1965.

Sei Shōnagon (*fl* 1000). This contemporary of Murasaki Shikibu has one claim to fame; she wrote *Makura no sōshi* (The Pillow-book), being a collection of pieces of various lengths, none very extensive, on all sorts of themes, including collections of names of mountains, *etc*, of pleasing things, unpleasant things, and so on, the length of the items varying from a word or two to several pages. It is particularly attractive for its vignettes of little incidents in the life of a courtier, minute descriptions of nature, and its tart comments on human beings. Whereas Murasaki firmly prevented would-be lovers from passing her screens, Sei Shōnagon is particularly cutting about the deficiencies of lovers who make an inelegant exit or otherwise behave awkwardly. A beautiful young priest fills her with thoughts that make her wonder if it would not have been better for her in the next world if she had not had him read the scriptures in her presence.

The charm of the *Pillow-book* is enhanced by the contrast which it makes with the sensibility of Murasaki's *Tale of Genji*. Sei Shōnagon served a different consort, Sadako, when Murasaki was with Akiko. Sadako (who died in 1000) was allegedly more frivolous and more elegant than Akiko, and the works of their respective ladies reflect this difference.

Sei Shōnagon's father was Kiyohara Motosuke, who was known for his poetry criticism and his wit, and among her more distant ancestors were several whose literary works have survived. Nothing much else is known of her life than what can be inferred from the *Pillow-book*; a few mediocre poems have survived, and she is known to have still been alive in 1011. Her name Sei is the Sino-Japanese reading of the first two syllables of Kiyohara, and Shōnagon is the name of a court rank, held presumably by one of her male relatives.

Translation: *The Pillow-book of Sei Shōnagon*, trans. Ivan Morris, London, 1968.

Shiga Naoya (1883–). Novelist, short-story writer. The second son of a Tokyo bank official and successful business-man, descended from a long line of feudal retainers, he was largely brought up by his grandfather, a samurai of the old school. In maturity he named as the three greatest influences on his life this grandfather, the Christian leader Uchimura Kanzō, and Mushakōji Saneatsu (*qv*), whose acquaintance he made while a student at the Peers

College. Shiga's academic career was undistinguished in the extreme. Though for a while he attended classes in English, and subsequently in Japanese literature at Tokyo University, he was already more interested in writing than in study, and left the University in 1908 without graduating. A succession of his stories appeared in the journal *Shirakaba*, founded by Mushakōji Saneatsu, from its first issue in March 1910. They share the anti-naturalistic idealism of the other members of the *Shirakaba* group.

For several years before this literary debut, relations between Shiga and his father had been deteriorating. The two had quarrelled violently in 1901 over Shiga's sympathy with the peasants whose livelihood was endangered, in a notorious industrial scandal, by poisonous effluent from a copper refinery; and again in 1910 over Shiga's proposal to marry the family maid. Nor did his father approve of his literary aspirations. The breach between them widened with Shiga's success, which was rapid. In 1912 he ran away from home – the authority of father over son in the traditional family system was still so strong that no other phrase is appropriate, though Shiga was twenty-nine at the time. He did not return permanently to Tokyo for twenty-six years, despite a rapprochement with his father in 1917, described in great detail in the autobiographical 'novel' *Reconciliation* (1917). With this decisive assertion of his personal and artistic independence (neatly symbolised in *Seibei's Gourds*, trans. Morris in *MJL*), Shiga diverged from the *Shirakaba* coterie. The long quarrel is reflected in the famous (and in Japan several times filmed) *Dark Road* (1937) which took him sixteen years to complete, and is his only full-length novel. It depicts the long progress of a man of sensitive and fastidious temperament through conflict with his family and himself to a type of oriental serenity, but is marred, for some, by the hero's unattractive egoism. Shiga's immense reputation rests principally, however, on his short stories. The *Shirakaba* humanism and psychological subtlety (for the latter, see *eg Han's Crime*, trans. Morris in *MJL*) of his early period give way to short contemplative sketches of human beings, animals and insects (*eg At Kinosaki*, trans. Seidensticker in *MJL*). The sensibility at work here is very Japanese, seeing significance in the small rather than the great, and moved by the aesthetic rather than the moral aspects of experience; for as Shiga himself has said, 'My feelings of like and dislike have invariably been my criteria for judging whether things are "good" or "bad" – and I have rarely been mistaken in these judgements.' Such considerations go far to explain the esteem in which he is held in Japan, despite the small scale and volume of his work, most of which was completed by the late nineteen-twenties; he wrote little after the rise of Japanese fascism, and devoted himself to the study of classical Japanese sculpture and painting. He is also noted for his terse and delicate style, contrasting with the vagueness and prolixity of many authors.

The Patron Saint, trans. Matsudaira in *HIA*.

Shimazaki Tōson (1872–1943). Poet and novelist. With Mori Ōgai (*qv*) and

Natsume Sōseki (*qv*), one of the towering literary figures of the modern period. Tōson was the fourth son of a hereditary village headman in the mountainous Nagano Prefecture, whose home was also a *honjin* or inn used by feudal lords and government officials travelling to and from the capital on the Nakasendo, one of the five great national highways of the Edo period. The Shimazakis were thus prominent in the locality – modest country gentlemen, though without the prestige of a samurai past. Most of Tōson's school years were spent in Tokyo, away from his family. In 1887 he entered Meiji Gakuin, a Christian college, to experience to the full the atmosphere of intellectual emancipation that was the great attraction of the early mission schools. Another formative influence was his close friendship with Kitamura Tōkoku (*qv*), whom he came to know while teaching at a Christian Women's College in 1893, and whose suicide the following year moved him deeply. The influence both of Christianity and of Kitamura and the *Bungakkai* group is evident in *Seedlings* (1897) (extracts trans. Ninomiya and Enright in *The Poetry of Living Japan*, London, 1957), the collection of romantic if naive and stylistically not very revolutionary poems which established his reputation. (Looking back seven years later, Tōson wrote: 'At last the age of the new poetry arrived. It was like a beautiful dawn. Some cried out as the prophets of old, others gave voice like the poets of the West. All seemed intoxicated with new light, with new tongues, with new imaginings . . .'.) But although *Seedlings* was something of a landmark in the development of modern poetry in Japan, Tōson's romantic phase did not last long. During a six-year 'retreat' into the mountains of Nagano, where he taught in a small school, he switched to prose writing. *Sketches of the River Chikuma* (written at this time, but not published till 1911), a series of studies of country life and landscape, was followed by the novel *Broken Commandment* (1906) (extract trans. Seidensticker in *MJL*), which has figured in literary histories ever since (together with Tayama Katai's (*qv*) *Quilt*) as one of the milestones of Japanese naturalism, though neither now nor later did Toson's style or outlook have much in common with the avowed prophets of the naturalist creed. The hero, Segawa Ushimatsu, is an *eta* (a member of the despised pariah community) who by concealing his *eta* origin in obedience to his father's dying command achieves a position as a teacher, but is forced at last to reveal the truth and surrender to prejudice, like his ancestors before him (or nearly so – the book is spoilt by a fairy-tale ending, with Ushimatsu setting up happily in America). To the western reader, *Broken Commandment* has a more immediate appeal than many Japanese novels, for it can be read as a work of social protest, all the finer for the splendidly evoked backdrop of mountain landscape against which the action takes place. It is doubtful, though, whether protest was uppermost in the author's mind: he never wrote in the same vein again. If it impresses, it is largely because it embodies so well the author's own deep loneliness, deriving from a solitary childhood, from the shock of the death of his three young daughters while he was writing, and from his sense of the isolation of the artist in an unsympathetic society.

Tōson followed *Broken Commandment* with four autobiographical novels of varying quality, dealing mostly with his family and his relationships with the romantic poets of the nineties. The fourth is an unpleasantly complacent attempt to justify his own part in an illicit relationship he had with a niece after his wife had died. His masterpiece, however, is the last novel he completed – *Before the Dawn* (written between 1927 and 1935), the only serious attempt to portray in fiction the vast national upheaval that resulted in the Meiji Restoration, by one who was close enough in time to the period to be able to feel what the impact on ordinary people of those great events must have been. Unfortunately it has not yet been translated. Hanzō, the protagonist, is modelled on Tōson's father. A village headman of culture and high ideals, in common with many reformers of his day he looks beyond the overthrow of feudalism to a new golden age when Japan will rid herself of Buddhist superstition and the shackles of Confucian ethics and return to the supposedly juster, more humane society of the remote past. But in the new Japan there is no place for such anachronistic simplicities. Unable to understand the society that is being born around him, Hanzō fails to win the sympathy of the peasants he loves, and in addition incurs the hostility of Meiji officialdom; eventually he is dismissed as village headman, to end his days in the total isolation of madness. Though it suffers from a somewhat heavy, humourless style and lack of precise characterisation, *Before the Dawn* is that most rare phenomenon in Japanese literature, a tragic novel on the grand scale, matching the grandeur of its subject.

ROGGENDORF, 'Shimazaki Tōson', in *MN*, VII, 1951.
McCLELLAN, 'The Novels of Shimazaki Tōson' in *HJAS*, XXIV, 1962–3.

Takeda Izumo (1690–1756), playwright. The Takeda family were responsible for the staging and properties at the Takemoto theatre in Osaka, where Takemoto Gidayū (see Chikamatsu Monzaemon) was the principal attraction. After Chikamatsu Monzaemon had given up writing, his work at the theatre was taken over by a group of authors of whom Takeda Izumo was the most important. From this collaboration emerged a series of long plays which combined the two types – historical and domestic – of Chikamatsu pieces. The two most famous are *Sugawara denju tenarai kagami* (Sugawara's secrets of penmanship) (*c* 1746), and *Kanadehon Chūshingura* (The loyal league) (1748). The former (trans. in Ernst, *Three Japanese plays*, London, 1959) took its theme from an episode from early Japanese history, the disgrace and exile of Sugawara Michizane, and combined with this the novelty of triplets, of which there had been an actual occurrence recently, the heroes being three brothers. The latter took up the story of a vendetta involving the retainers of a provincial lord who had been provoked into drawing his sword by an insulting senior official, and for this offence was condemned to self-execution. They formed a secret conspiracy and finally sought out and killed the official, before killing themselves in their turn. Into this story were inserted various sub-plots concerning the personal affairs and relationships of the plotters.

By this time the live *kabuki* theatre had become more important than the puppets, and was fast taking over their repertory. These two plays became typical *kabuki* pieces, and were those in which were clearly set out the conflicts between loyalty and human affection that were the characteristics of plays derived from the puppet theatre. The loyal retainer sacrificed his son to save his lord's child, a son would kill himself to save his father, a crying baby was put out in the snow so that a querulous grandmother could sleep. Although this was in accordance with approved morality, the playwrights and the chanters exercised their skill in stressing the pathetic straits of the human hearts that suffered in these feudal situations.

The plays of Takeda Izumo and his colleagues have survived to the present, although their great length (contemporary audiences were used to watching performances from dawn to dusk) has meant that for a long time now it has been customary to give only a selection of famous scenes.

Takeyama Michio (1903–). Novelist, critic, essayist, and translator of Goethe, Schopenhauer and Nietzsche; he has also been Professor of German Literature at Tokyo University. Takeyama's reputation as a novelist rests on one work, *Harp of Burma* (1948) (trans. Hibbett, Tokyo and Rutland, Vermont, 1966). Though appearing first in serial form in a magazine of children's literature, *Harp of Burma* won immediate recognition, and was awarded two major literary prizes. It has since been dramatised and acted on innumerable occasions throughout the country and on television, and is used as a text for discussion in High Schools. Written in a simpler style than most Japanese novels, it tells the story of a Japanese army unit in Burma at the end of the war. In defeat, it is music that holds the men together – from the beginning of the campaign their commander, a trained musician, had taught them to sing as a choir. When the time comes for repatriation, one of their number, the most resourceful soldier of them all, who had taught himself to accompany their singing on a home-made Burmese harp, refuses to return to Japan with the rest. The bodies of Japanese soldiers lie scattered without a grave all over Burma, and he vows to walk the length and breadth of the country burying their remains, that the spirits of the dead may rest in peace. To those who find it difficult to sympathise with the Japanese outlook, the book may appear sentimental in places. *Harp of Burma* is well worth reading, though, for its absence of all bitterness, its simple but genuine humanism, and its vivid portrayal of many characteristic Japanese attitudes – not least the unaffected love of art and of doing things 'art-fully', conveyed here in the delight of the soldiers in choral singing.

Tanizaki Junichirō (1886–1965). Novelist. His ancestors were successful and cultured Edo merchants, but under the headship of his father the family did not prosper, and had it not been for the help of a teacher and some relatives, Junichirō would probably have had to leave school at fourteen. At Tokyo University he entered the Department of Japanese Literature – on the ground, he says, that he would thus have plenty of time for writing, since lectures in that subject could be more easily missed than in any other. In 1910 the University expelled him for not paying his fees. The same year he published a short story, *Tattoo* (trans. Morris in *MJS*), about the tattooing of an enormous spider on a girl's back. *Tattoo* shows something of the influences at work on the young Tanizaki – Oscar Wilde, Poe, Baudelaire, and Nagai Kafū (*qv*). It also expresses in concentrated form two of Tanizaki's lifelong preoccupations: an aestheticism uncompromisingly opposed to the naturalism which was then in its heyday, and a sensuous reverence for woman, that is at times almost religious in its intensity. There is a streak of cruelty in this and some subsequent stories – 'flowers of evil', as Akutagawa Ryūnosuke (*qv*) called them, 'as beautiful as the iridescent sheen of a blister-beetle'. But Tanizaki's 'diabolism' as it came to be called, did not last very long. After the publication of *The Sorrows of a Heretic* (1917) came a period of experimentation, not often successful, with long novels and plays. The turning-point in his career came when he moved from Tokyo to western Japan after the great earthquake of 1923. Osaka, whose merchant families still preserved something of the distinctive townsmen's culture of the pre-modern period, and the more refined world of Kyoto, with its aura of classical beauty, awakened in him a profound response. Nostalgia for the past, expressed in a less exuberant but still elegant language, is the keynote of the rest of his work. Sometimes old and modern ways are contrasted, as in *Some Prefer Nettles* (1929) (trans. Seidensticker, Tokyo, 1955), a subtle study of the effect on a middle-aged man's marriage of a Eurasian prostitute, an old-style geisha, and a renewed acquaintance with the traditional puppet theatre. *A Blind Man's Tale* (1931) and *A Portrait of Shunkin* (1933) (both trans. Hibbett in *Seven Japanese Tales*, London, 1964) tell of the loyalty of servants to two beautiful women. *A Portrait of Shunkin*, which was inspired by Thomas Hardy's *Barbara of the House of Grebe*, and is in fact an attempt to recreate Hardy's theme in the terms at once of traditional Japanese morality and of Tanizaki's brand of aestheticism, was and is enormously popular in Japan; it has frequently been dramatised on film, radio and television. There is a masochistic quality about the devotion to the blind woman musician Shunkin of her servant and lover Sasuke, who never reproaches her for her harsh treatment of him, and who even blinds himself so that he may share with her her world of darkness. But there is much that is beautiful in this short novel, even apart from the fascinating glimpses it provides of Osaka life in the mid-nineteenth century: Sasuke's self-negating worship of his mistress, matched by her extraordinary loyalty to her art, rises in the end to a note of religious exaltation. The essay *In Praise of Shadows* (extracts trans. Seidensticker in *Japan Quarterly*, I–1, 1954), written at about the same time as *A Portrait*, evokes in loving detail the beauty of many common things – lacquer table-ware, Japanese paper, and the like – that were beginning to fall out of use at the time in the name of 'modernisation'.

Tanizaki spent most of the war years working on his masterly translation into modern Japanese of the eleventh-century classic by Murasaki (*qv*), *The Tale of Genji*, and finishing *The Makioka Sisters* (trans. Seidensticker, Tokyo, 1957), publication of which had been begun in 1938 but was stopped by government order as 'prejudicial to national discipline' (it did not appear in final form till after the war). This long and impressive work describes in detail the encroachment of a harsher age on the peaceful rhythms of middle-class life in pre-war Osaka. But there is more to it than that. Yukiko, the third of the four sisters around whom the novel revolves, is the central figure: beautiful, withdrawn, mysterious, she is Tanizaki's archetypal woman, lineal descendant of his earlier loyalty-demanding ladies, but refined this time into a symbol of classical Japanese beauty.

The Mother of Captain Shigemoto (1950) (trans. Seidensticker in *MJL*) is another variation on the theme of elusive beauty. *The Key* (1956) (trans. Hibbett, London, 1962), however, a study of the impact of the fear of impotence on a middle-aged married man, is reminiscent of Tanizaki's early 'satanic' period. The same may be said of *Diary of a Mad Old Man* (1961) (trans. Hibbett, London, 1966).

Tayama Katai (1871–1930). Novelist. His father, a low-ranking samurai retainer in a small provincial clan, was killed in the Civil War of 1877, and Katai grew up in extreme poverty. In his twenties he was associated for a time with the *Bungakkai* group (together with Kitamura Tōkoku, *qv*), though his aspirations were decidedly more mundane than theirs. A quantity of sentimental romances and verse was the result. Subsequently, however, wide reading of European literature, in particular of Nietszche, Maupassant, Zola, and the brothers Goncourt, altered his outlook completely; and with his critical articles and a series of novels, notably *The Quilt* (1907) ('A bold confession of a man of the flesh . . . almost unbearable in its frank treatment' according to one contemporary comment), *Life* (1908), *Wife* (1908–9), and *Bondage* (1910), he became the acknowledged leader of the naturalist school. All these novels were avowedly autobiographical records, revolutionary in frankness but limited in range. As such they helped to determine the peculiar quality of the whole spectrum of Japanese naturalism – its concentration upon the details, usually sordid, of an author's personal life, without any readily discernible purpose other than defiant self-exposure. In extenuation one may say that some such outburst of confessional literature was doubtless inevitable sooner or later, as the restraints of traditional society began to weaken. Also, the Japanese mind turns more readily inward than outward – hence, at least in part, the comparative lack of the dramatic in modern Japanese literature, either in drama itself or the novel, and the popularity of the 'I-novel', the slice-of-personal-life genre, among many other writers besides the naturalists. One piece of Katai's which transcends this limitation is the powerful *One Soldier* (1907) (trans. Sargent in *MJL*), written out of his experience as a reporter in the Russo-Japanese war.

Apart from some historical fiction, Katai continued to write in much the same vein all his life, though in his final work, *A Hundred Nights* (1927), there is an almost religious tone to the earnest quest of the hero (Katai himself, of course) for harmony between himself, his wife, and his mistress.

Tokutomi Roka (1868–1927). Novelist. He was the younger son of a prosperous country family in Kyushu, whose people have long had the reputation of being at once the most conservative and the most spirited and stubborn of all the Japanese. Shy and introspective as a young man, much of his life was conditioned by his struggle to free himself from dependence on the dominating personality of his elder brother, Tokutomi Sohō, the head of the family and an influential political journalist and editor in Tokyo. After some years of hack-work in his brother's office (including translations of biographies of General Gordon, Gladstone, Cobden, John Bright, and Tolstoy), the extraordinary success of his first novel *Hototogisu* (1898) (literally – 'The Cuckoo': trans. Edgett as *Namiko*, Boston, 1904) launched him on a career which resulted in a dramatic breach with his famous brother – a revolt against the tightly-knit family system which caused a sensation at the time. *Hototogisu* is crude and melodramatic by modern standards; but the pathos of the subject, the suffering and final death of a young bride who is divorced at her mother-in-law's command when she contracts tuberculosis (the story was inspired by an actual case, the original of the heroine being the daughter of an army general) appealed strongly to a public which besides having a taste for the sentimental in fiction was beginning to realise the cost in human terms of the rigidity of the traditional family system.

Nature and Life (1900), a collection of lyrical and meditative sketches (prefaced somewhat incongruously by the short story *Ashes*, a thinly-veiled attack on the author's brother), proved almost as popular. But it is Tokutomi's second novel, *Omoide no ki* (1900–1) (literally – 'Memoirs': trans. Strong as *Footsteps in the Snow*, London, 1969) which has the most interest for a western reader. A fictional autobiography of a young provincial Japanese of samurai stock who runs away to Tokyo from his country home in the eighteen-eighties, fired with a passion to make his way in the world, not in material terms, but as a writer and pioneer of the glamorous new ideas of liberty, democracy and progress, it conveys vividly the mood of excitement among the youth of the time, the fascination of Christianity and the narrowness of many of its missionaries, and the sense of disillusion generated by the harsher realities of Meiji society. Tokutomi himself had become a Christian while a student, and talked of himself as a socialist; but he proved unable to develop, as a writer or thinker, beyond the relative simplicities of *Footsteps in the Snow* – the rest of his work is little but tedious autobiography and the outpourings of a confused mixture of unorthodox Christianity and sexual libertarianism.

Ueda Akinari (1734–1809). Though known today as a novelist, Akinari was a typical intellectual of the eighteenth century, turning his hand to literary production of many sorts – poetry, satirical novels, *yomi-hon* (fantastic or moralistic tales in a heavy Chinese style), and studies of old literature. His parentage is unknown, but his adoptive father, a prosperous Osaka oil-merchant, allowed him to live a life devoted to pleasure and aesthetic pursuits. In his thirty-eighth year his family business was destroyed in a fire, and he had to earn a living from medicine – a study which required a knowledge of Chinese rather than anatomy. At the age of sixty (when, with the sexagenary cycle of years coming to an end, one looks forward to a renewed birth) he retired to Kyoto and spent the rest of his life in temples, teaching his disciples the literary arts.

His best known work is *Ugetsu-monogatari* (Tales of the rainy moon) (completed 1768, published 1776). This is a collection of nine fantastic tales of ghosts, a priest who dreams that he is a carp swimming in Lake Biwa, only to be hooked and nearly a prey to the cook's knife, a man who turns into a snake, *etc*. The sources are in Chinese and Japanese legend and story. The style is typical of *yomi-hon*, elaborate, serious, and full of weighty Chinese vocabulary, but not so turgid as that of the later author, Kyokutei Bakin (*qv*).
Translation: 'Ugetsu-monogatari' trans. W. Whitehouse, *Monumenta nipponica*, I, 1, 2 and IV, 1, Tokyo, 1938 and 1941.

Yoshida Kenkō (1282–1350), poet and essayist. His family were hereditary holders of the priesthood of the Yoshida shrine, an important centre of the *shintō* religion in Kyoto. He himself held various offices close to the Emperor Uda II, and when the latter died in 1324, Yoshida Kenkō retired from Kyoto, taking Buddhist vows. The rest of his life was spent in periods of retreat from the world, interspersed with renewed visits to the court. In his lifetime he had a considerable reputation as a poet but he is best remembered now for *Tsurezure-gusa* (Essays in Idleness), a collection of pieces of varying length whose subject-matter includes descriptions of his hermitage and of his companions' thoughts upon good taste and aesthetics. He wrote in a language which is typical of the pure literary style, and his nostalgia for the life of the Heian court and his formulation of the principles of literary and artistic taste have been at the basis of much later appreciation and have set the traditional pattern for critical thought.
Translation: *Essays in Idleness*, trans. Donald Keene, New York, 1967.

Zeami (1363–1443). Actor, playwright and dramatic theorist. He was the son of another important figure in the development of the *Nō* play, Kannami. Their family formed one of the groups giving performances at the Kasuga shrine in Nara, and when he was twelve, he and his father came under the protection of the current ruler of the country, Yoshimitsu. He pursued a career of acting and composition, in the course of which, by incorporating the best elements of various entertainments and dramatic forms, he made *Nō* into the great art that it is today. Many of his pieces are still played, and form the core of the modern repertory. Interesting though his plays are, even more important to the modern student of drama is his collection of notebooks and other critical material, in which many aspects of the actor's craft are discussed. Along with the influence of Zen Buddhism, which urges towards simplicity and symbolism, there is much consideration given to realism and the concentration required of the performer.

Translations, *etc.* P. G. O'NEILL, *Early Nō drama*, London, 1958; M. SHIDEHARA and W. WHITEHOUSE, 'Seami's sixteen treatises', *Monumenta nipponica*, iv,2 and v,2, Tokyo, 1941, 1942; ARTHUR WALEY, *The nō plays of Japan*, London, 1921.

BIBLIOGRAPHY

(a) HISTORY AND GENERAL

ALLEN, G. C. *A Short Economic History of Modern Japan* London, 1962.
ALLEN, G. C. *Japan's Economic Expansion* London, 1965.
BEASLEY, W. G. *The Modern History of Japan* New York and London, 1963.
BENEDICT, R. *The Chrysanthemum and the Sword* New York and London, 1947.
BURKS, W. A. *The Government of Japan* New York and London, 1966.
DORE, R. P. *City Life in Japan* New York and London, 1958.
DORE, R. P. *Land Reform in Japan* New York and London, 1959.
DUNN, C. J. *Everyday Life in Traditional Japan* New York and London, 1969.
HALL, J. W. and BEARDSLEY, R. K. *Twelve Doors to Japan* New York, 1956.
Harvard Journal of Asiatic Studies, Cambridge, Mass. (*HJAS*).
KIDDER, J. E. *Japan Before Buddhism* New York and London, 1959.
KOJIKI, trans. D. L. Philipi, Tokyo, 1968.
MORRIS, I. *The World of the Shining Prince* New York and London, 1964.
PAINE, R. T. and SOPER, A. *The Art and Architecture of Japan* New York and London, 1955.
SANSOM, G. B. *Japan: A Short Cultural History* New York and London, 1946.
SANSOM, G. B. *The Western World and Japan* New York and London, 1950.
STORRY, G. R. *A History of Modern Japan* New York and London, 1960.
STORRY, G. R. *The Double Patriots* London, 1957.
TREWARTHA, G. T. *Japan: A Physical, Cultural and Regional Geography* London, 1965.
TSUNODA, R., ed. *Sources of Japanese Tradition* New York, 1958.

(b) LITERATURE AND DRAMA

ARAKI, J. T. *The Ballad-drama of Medieval Japan* Berkeley, 1964.
BOWERS, F. *Japanese theatre* New York, 1952.
BOWNAS, G. and THWAITE, A. *The Penguin Book of Japanese Verse* New York and London, 1964.
BROWER, R. and MINER, E. *Japanese Court Poetry* New York and London, 1962.
DUNN, C. J. *The Early Japanese Puppet Drama* New York and London, 1966.

DUNN, C. J. and TORIGOE, B., eds. *The Actors' Analects* New York and Tokyo, 1969.
ERNST, E. *The Kabuki Theatre* New York, 1956.
HALFORD, A. S. and G. M. *The Kabuki Handbook* New York and Tokyo, 1959.
KEENE, D. *Anthology of Japanese Literature* New York and London, 1968.
KEENE, D. *Bunraku: the Art of the Japanese Puppet Theatre* New York and Tokyo, 1965.
KEENE, D. *Modern Japanese Literature* New York and London, 1957 (*MJL*).
KEENE, D. *Nō: the Classical Theatre of Japan* New York and Tokyo, 1966.
MCKINNON, R. N., ed. *The Heart is Alone*, Tokyo, 1957 (*HIA*).
MINER, E. *An introduction to Japanese court poetry* New York and London, 1968.
Monumenta Nipponica, published by Sophia University, Tokyo (*MN*).
MORRIS, I., ed. *Modern Japanese stories* New York and London, 1961 (*MJS*).
NIPPON GAKUJUTSU SHINKŌKAI. *Japanese Noh drama* Tokyo, 1955, 1959 and 1960.
O'NEILL, P. G. *Early Nō drama* London 1958.
SCOTT, A. C. *The Kabuki Theatre of Japan* New York and London, 1955.
Transactions of the Asiatic Society of Japan, Tokyo (*TASJ*).
WALEY, A. *The Nō plays of Japan* New York and London, 1921.

INDEX

INDEX

NOTE: A simplified transliteration has been adopted for the index.

Index

Index

Index

Index

Index

Index

Index

Index

Index

Liu Ngo, 302–3
Liu Pang, 284
Liu Tsung-yüan, 298, 303
Lives of Virtuous Women (Liu Hsiang), 302
Living Buddha of Urga (Head of Mongolian lamaist church), 344, 349
Lo Kuan-chung, 303
Lodi dynasty (in India), 220
London Diary (Kin-wun Min-gyi), 396
Lotus Sutra, 446, 447
Love of King David and Michal (Gordon), 71, 84
Lu Hsun (Chou-jen), 296, 303–4
Ludu U Hla, 395
Lun Héng (Wang Ch'ung), 310
Lung Yü (*Convervations*) (Confucius' sayings), 297
al-Luzūmiyyat (Poems of Necessity: al-Ma'arri), 17–18, 30
Luzzatto, Moses Hayim, 63, 66, 69, 85–6
Luzzatto, Shmuel David (Shadal), 86
Ma Ma Lei, 394
Ma Mya-galei, 396
Ma'arra, 30
Machberoth Ithiel (Al-Hariri), 78
Mad Shagdar, 347
Madā'en (Khāqānī), 137
Madah Kelana (Pané), 275
Madā'ini, 41
Mādalā Pānji, 242
Mādgulkar, Vyankateś Digambar, 242
Mādhav Kandali, 242
Madhusudan Rāo, 242
madīh (Arabic panegyric passage in ode), 14
madrasa (Turkish: *medrese*) (Islamic religious school), 110, 134, 155, 160
Māgadha, kingdom of (Bihar), 216, 217, 218
Magamas (Harīrī), 78
maghāzi (accounts of Prophet's life), 20
Maha Swei, 393
Mahābhārata (Indian epic), 216, 226, 227, 230, 231, 232, 242, 243, 245, 247, 273
Mahabódhivamsa (Pali prose work), 259, 261, 262
mahākāvya see kāvya
Mahānubhāva sect (in India), 231
Mahāvamsa (The Great Chronicle of Celyon), 396, 399
Mahavihára school (in Ceylon), 260
Mahāvir, 216
Mahāyāna (Buddhist philosophy), 330, 335, 337
Mahfūz, Najib, 27
Mahipati, 242
mahjar (Syro-American poetry, poets), 28–9
Mahjur, Ghulam Ahmad, 242
mahla see ghazal
Mahmūd, Sultan of Ghazna, 33, 115, 116, 134, 219–20
Maḥmūd II, Ottoman Sultan, 149
Maḥmūd Abdülbakî (Efendi) *see* Bakî
Maḥmūd b. Sebuktakin, Sultan of Ghazna, 110, 134
Maimonides (Moses Ben Maimon), 61–2, 69, 70, 77, 86
Majapahit, Hindu kingdom of, 268, 273
majāzī (Islamic profane love), 120
Majma'al-Baḥayn (Confluence of the Two Seas: Yāziji), 24
Makber (The Tomb: Hâmit), 167
The Makioka Sisters (Tanizaki Junichiro), 461
Makkī, Aḥmad, 28
Makura-no-sōshi (Pillow Book: Sei Shōnagon), 411, 455
Malacca, Malacca Straits, 267, 268–9, 271, 274
al-Malā'ika, Nāzik, 29
Malay language, Old-, 267–8; modern division into Netherlands-India Written and Malaya Written, 269–71
Malay Translation Bureau, 270
Malay World (Indonesia and Malaysia), Dutch and British influences in, 269–70; Islam in, 268; languages of, 267–8, 269–71; modern trends in, 270–1; Portuguese in, 268–9; *see also* Malaysian and Indonesian literature
Malayalam language (India), 219, 229, 230
Malaysian and Indonesian literature, *267–78*; in Bahasa Indonesia, 276–8; Classical Malay period, 269, 272–5; early beginning of modern period, 274–5; early Islamic, 273–4; folk, 272–3; Hindu-derived, 273; historical background to, 267–71; histories, 274; 'A Picaresque Novel', 274; in Malaya (1920–45), 276; and Malay (1945–), 278; modern (written), Malaya, 275–8; in Netherlands India (1920–45), 275–6
Malek Shah (Saljuk ruler), 137
Malkam Khan, Mīrzā, 127, 137
malke' (Ethiopic type of religious poetry), 203, 209
Mamlūks, Mamlūk Sultanate (White Slave), 11, 24, 183
Ma'mūn, Caliph, 9–10, 39
Man, the Wolf of Man (U Nu), 394

Index

Index

Peking, 287, 288, 289
Pelliot, Prof. Paul, 324
Penḍse, Sripād Nārāyaṇ, 244
Pentateuch (1st 5 books of Old Testament), 53, 56, 62
Perelman *see* Ben Yehuda
Peretz, Isaac Leib, 72, 73, 74, 88, 89
'Perfection of Wisdom' (Buddhist texts in Tibet), 330, 334, 337
Persia, Persian Empire, Arab conquest of, 6, 98, 100, 101, 109, 112, 123; Armenia and Georgia under rule of, 182, 187; Armenians in, 186; cultural role in Arab empire of, 8, 10–11, 30, 110; early history of, 97–9, 109–10; India and, 122, 216, 286; Jews in, 54, 57; Mongol invasions of, 109–10, 118; Qajar dynasty in, 111, 126–7; Shi'ite movement in, 7, 110; Twentieth century, 111; Zoroastrianism in, 97, 98
'Persian is as sweet as sugar' (short story by Jamāl Zādeh), 128
Persian lanauage, 11, 23, 98, 112, 220, 225, 233, 267
Persian literature, *109–41*; belles-lettres, 124; bibliography, 141; biographical, 125; classical prose, 122–6; epic, 100–1, 114–16; emergence of new language in, 112; geographical, 126; *Ghazal*, 118–21; historical background to, 109–11; historical works, 125; Indian school of, 122; individual writers, 132–40; influence on Turkish literature of, 112, 153–4; journalism, 127–8; *Maṣnavi*, 121–2, 153; modern prose, 128–31; modern trends in, 126–7; philosophy, 126; poetry, 113–14; *Qaṣida*, 116–18; *Ruba'ī*, 118; theological works, 125; *see also* Old Iranian literature
A Personal Matter (Oe Kenzaburo), 454–5
Phaḍke, Nārāyam Sitārām, 244
Phag-mo-gru (Tibetan family), 325, 326
'Phags-pa Blo-gros rGyal-mtshan, 336, 337
'*Phags-pa* Mongolian script, 337
Philosophus Autodidactus see Ḥayy b. Yaqẓān
Philoxenus of Mabug, 203
Pien Chih-lin, 305
Piḷḷai, C. V. Rāman, 244
Piḷḷai, Samuel Vetanāyakam, 244
Piḷḷai, Takazi Śivaśankar, 244
Pillar of Fire (Kinoshita Naoe), 440
Pillow Book see Makura-no-soshi
Pingali Suranna, 244
Ping Hsin, 305
Piyadása Siriséna, 260–1
Plea for Rain (Gelegbalsang), 351
Po Chü-i (Po Lo-t 'ien), 305
Po Lo-t'ien see Po Chü-i
Poetry Talks of Tung Po (Su Shih), 308
Polonnaruva (medieval capital of Ceylon), 253, 258
Ponna, 244
Pon-nya, U, 391, 392, 398
Portrait of Eight (Shen T'sung-wên), 306
A Portrait of Shunkin (Tanizaki Junichiro), 460, 461
Portuguese in Ceylon, 253, 259; in Ethiopia, 199; in Goa, 220, 221; in Japan, 407; in Malay World, 268–9
Potana, Bammera, 230, 244
Prakrit languages (India), 217, 226, 227–8, 230, 253
Pramudya Ananta Tur, 277
Premānand, 244
Prem Cand, 235, 244
Prithirāja Rāso (Cand Bardāi), 231, 238
'Profiles' (*Yok-pon-hlwa*), 394–5
'Proletarian School' (of Japanese communist writers), 414
Prophetic Tradition (*ḥadith*), 7, 9, 33
P'u Sung-ling, 306
Pudjangga Baru (New Man of Letters: Malay journal), 270, 275–6
Pújávaliya (String of Praises), 255, 260
Pukalenti, 244
puppet theatre in Japan *see* drama, Japanese
Purāṇa(s) (Sanskrit collections of history and mythology), 228, 230, 244, 246, 247
Purandaradās, 232, 244
Pure Land sect (Japanese Buddhists), 406, 453
Pursuit (Mao Tun), 304
Puttappa, K. Venkaṭappa, 244
pya-zat (Burmese 'shown story'), 391, 398
pyo (Burmese religious poem), 389, 390, 391, 398, 399
p'yŏng sijo see sijo

Qā'ānī, 116, 130
Qabus-name (Kay Kavus), 124
Qa'em Maqam, 127, 138
Qajar dynasty, 111, 126, 127
Qanun (Persian newspaper), 127, 137
Qarilchaga Dagu (Mongolian Conversation song), 347, 348
Qarya Zalima (Sinful City: Ṭāhā Husayn), 27
qaṣida (Turkish: *kaside*) (Islamic formal ode), 16, 17, 28, 29, 32, 33; Persian, 113, 116–18, 121; Seven Odes, collection of, 14–15; structure and themes of, 13–14; Turkish, 155, 170

Index

Index

Index

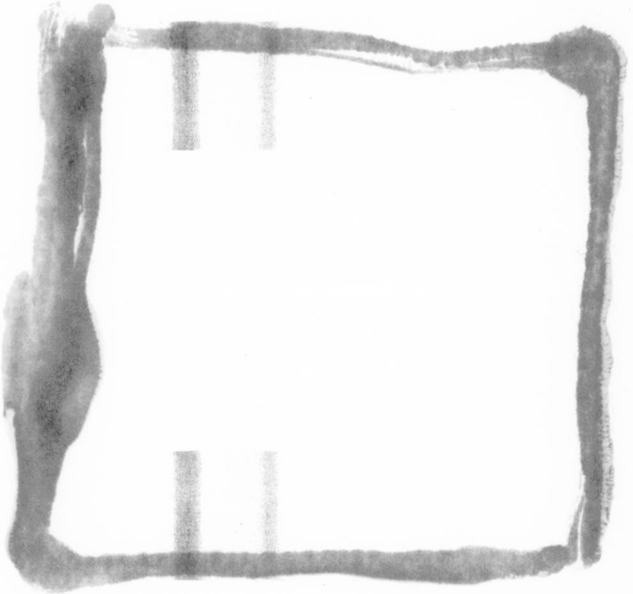